SQL Anywhere Studio 9 Developer's Guide

Breck Carter

Wordware Publishing, Inc.

Library of Congress Cataloging-in-Publication Data

Carter, Breck.
    SQL anywhere Studio 9 developer's guide / by Breck Carter.
        p. cm.
    ISBN 1-55622-506-7
    1. SQL (Computer program language)   2. Relational databases.   I. Title.
    QA76.73.S67C36 2004
    005.13'3—dc22   2004011573

ISBN 1-55622-506-7

10 9 8 7 6 5 4 3 2 1
0406

All inquiries for volume purchases of this book should be addressed to Wordware
Publishing, Inc., at the above address. Telephone inquiries may be made by calling:

(972) 423-0090

Contents

Preface

There's a good reason that SQL Anywhere has over 70% of the mobile database market. In fact, there are several good reasons: It's easy to use, easy to administer, and it doesn't take up much space. Those are all good things if you're trying to deploy hundreds or thousands of databases. And they're good things to have if you're trying to embed relational databases inside tens of thousands of routers or switches or other hardware devices.

But SQL Anywhere isn't just for mobile and embedded databases; it's got the features and the flexibility to work as a network server with hundreds of active users pounding away on a single database. And it's got a solid foundation and a long history, from its roots with Watcom in the 1980s through to Powersoft and Sybase in the 1990s and now with iAnywhere Solutions in the new millennium.

Through all those years, the SQL Anywhere development team has never strayed from one central virtue; as Richard Williams of VMI Communication and Learning Systems said it, "Watcom does things the way they should be done."

Here's an overview of the history behind SQL Anywhere Studio Version 9:

- **1965** The WATFOR FORTRAN compiler was initially developed for the IBM 7040 at the University of Waterloo.
- **1981** The company Watcom was founded.
- **1988** The PACEBase SQL Database System was released as part of the Watcom Information Workbench. It ran on PCs using DOS, and included ISQL, transaction processing, declarative referential integrity, CREATE TABLE and ALTER TABLE statements, inner joins, subqueries in SELECT lists, multiple user IDs, and a separate rollback file for recovery. This was "Version 1"; no Version 2 was ever released.
- **1992** Watcom SQL 3 became commercially available. It was a multi-user server with row-level locking, a separate transaction log, and multi-table updates. Later versions added Windows 3 support, an ODBC driver, outer joins, DEFAULT values, CHECK constraints, TIME, DATE, and LONG data types, and online backup.
- **1993** Powersoft included Watcom SQL 3.2 in the box with PowerBuilder 3.
- **1994** Powersoft bought Watcom.
- **1994** Watcom SQL 4 was released. It included stored procedures and triggers, cascading updates and deletes, temporary tables, multiple databases in one server, a self-tuning query optimizer, and TCP/IP support.
- **1995** Sybase bought Powersoft.
- **1995** SQL Anywhere 5 was released. It included SQL Remote, SQL Central (now Sybase Central), Transact SQL syntax, and support for the Sybase Replication Server.
- **1996** SQL Anywhere 5.5 was released as a bundled product that included InfoMaker, NetImpact Dynamo (later PowerDynamo), and a plug-in architecture for Sybase Central.

■ **1998** SQL Anywhere 6 was released, with the new names "Adaptive Server Anywhere" applied to the engine itself and "SQL Anywhere Studio" applied to the product bundle, which now included SQL Modeler (later called PowerDesigner). SQL Anywhere 6 was the version that introduced Java in the database; later releases added proxy tables, the UltraLite deployment option, MobiLink synchronization, and an interactive debugger.

■ **2000** SQL Anywhere 7 was released. It supported ASA databases as MobiLink remote databases, and included UltraLite improvements, an OLEDB driver, and dynamic cache resizing. Version 7 also introduced the Java versions of ISQL and Sybase Central.

■ **2000** iAnywhere Solutions, Inc. was founded as a subsidiary of Sybase.

■ **2001** SQL Anywhere 8 was released. This version included hundreds of enhancements but the big news was all about the query engine, which was completely rewritten to improve performance and support future enhancements.

■ **2003** SQL Anywhere 9 was released. It included hundreds more enhancements including more performance improvements, the Index Consultant, support for OLAP, XML, and 64-bit processors, and many new SQL features including recursive union and stored procedure calls in the FROM clause.

In the years to come, as the prices of computers and hard drives continue to fall and the performance and capabilities of SQL Anywhere continue to improve, SQL Anywhere will be used for larger and more sophisticated applications. This book is dedicated to that prospect, and the belief that you, the database designer and application developer, will want to explore the capabilities of SQL Anywhere and exploit its features to the fullest.

This book is divided into 10 chapters, each with a single verb as its title, arranged in a rough approximation of the tasks performed during the life cycle of a typical database:

1. Creating
2. Inserting
3. Selecting
4. Updating
5. Deleting
6. Fetching
7. Synchronizing
8. Packaging
9. Protecting
10. Tuning

Chapter 1, "Creating," starts with Codd's 12 rules that define what a relational database management system like SQL Anywhere really is. It then proceeds to describe the five different kinds of tables SQL Anywhere uses: global permanent, global temporary, local temporary, remote, and proxy. Chapter 1 also covers data types, column properties like DEFAULT, and column and table constraints like CHECK and FOREIGN KEY, and ends with a discussion of normalized design.

Chapter 2, "Inserting," talks about putting data into the database, and it covers five different flavors of INSERT as well as the LOAD TABLE statement and ISQL's client-side alternative, the INPUT statement.

Chapter 3, "Selecting," talks about the inverse of Chapter 2, getting data out of the database with SELECT, UNLOAD, and the ISQL OUTPUT statement. This is the longest chapter in the book, which should come as no surprise; the SQL SELECT statement may be the most powerful, most complex single syntactic construction available in any programming language.

Chapter 3 starts with an explanation of the SELECT statement, the logical execution of a SELECT, which shows how all the various clauses fit together and contribute to the final result set without concern for how SQL Anywhere actually executes a SELECT. Most of the rest of Chapter 3 follows the steps laid out and explained in the beginning of the chapter. If you've ever had trouble with the GROUP BY clause, or had a SELECT that returned 10,000 rows instead of the three you wanted, or wondered why you can't call NUMBER(*) in a WHERE clause, this is the chapter for you.

Chapter 4, "Updating," covers the UPDATE statement and how it can be used to update a single row in one table, or multiple rows, or even multiple rows in multiple tables. This chapter also includes a section on the logical execution of a set UPDATE and a discussion of cursor UPDATE statements using the WHERE CURRENT OF clause.

Chapter 5, "Deleting," is the evil twin of Chapter 4; it talks about deleting single and multiple rows, and includes a section on the logical execution of a set DELETE as well as information about cursor DELETE statements using WHERE CURRENT OF. Chapter 5 also includes a section on TRUNCATE TABLE and how it compares with DELETE: sometimes faster, sometimes not, and why.

Chapter 6, "Fetching," talks about the DECLARE, OPEN, FETCH, and CLOSE statements as they apply to cursors using SELECT queries and procedure calls. It also describes the cursor FOR loop, which vastly simplifies the cursor loops in SQL by eliminating the need to DECLARE all those local variables or code those endless FETCH lists.

Chapter 7, "Synchronizing," is the MobiLink chapter; it discusses how the MobiLink server works together with the MobiLink client for ASA to synchronize data back and forth between a consolidated database and dozens or thousands of remote databases. MobiLink scripts are classified by level (connection, session, table, and row) and by direction (upload versus download), and error handling on the server and client sides is described.

Chapter 8, "Packaging," talks about moving application logic into the database using BEGIN blocks and SQL modules based on BEGIN blocks: procedures, functions, triggers, and events. The SET assignment statement is described, as well as the flow-of-control structures IF, CASE, and WHILE, the EXECUTE IMMEDIATE statement, and the connection-level CREATE VARIABLE statement. This chapter also introduces the basics of exception handling, a topic that is expanded on in Chapter 9.

Chapter 9, "Protecting," is the second-longest chapter, and it explores the widest variety of topics including options, transactions, exceptions, errors, subtransactions, locks, blocks, isolation levels, deadlocks, mutexes, user IDs, privileges, user groups, logging, recovery, backup, restore, and (gasp!) database validation. Many of these topics are only loosely connected to one another, but they all fall under the general heading "Crashing, Bashing, Thrashing, and the Protection Therefrom."

Chapter 10, "Tuning," might be the one with the biggest audience: Everyone's interested in speed, speed, speed. This is also the chapter that should be read last, because the first rule of optimization is "Don't do it." If you're an expert, Rule 2 also applies: "Don't do it yet."

Chapter 10 starts by explaining the four big performance tuning tools that SQL Anywhere provides: request-level logging, the Index Consultant, the Execution Profiler, and the Graphical Plan. It then moves on to more arcane topics such as file, table, and index fragmentation, and table, index, and database reorganization. Sections on the syntax of CREATE INDEX and database performance counters are included, and the book ends with a performance tuning "Tips and Techniques" section that lists 36 do's and don'ts that didn't find a home as a tip somewhere earlier in the book.

This book includes working code examples of just about every single point made in the text. Except for some references to SQL Anywhere's own demonstration database, ASADEMO.DB, and a cute organization chart in Chapter 3 on the recursive UNION feature, there are no extended case studies or attempts to mimic the detail and complexity of real-world applications. Instead, most of the examples use simple tables with artificial names like "t1" and "t2". The examples focus on the syntax and semantics of SQL Anywhere: They're short, they stick to the current topic, and there's lots of them.

The companion CD includes the full BNF from the book in HTML format for easy browsing. It also includes all of the examples from the book, plus a full copy of SQL Anywhere Studio 9 Developer Edition for Windows.

Acknowledgments

I am grateful to Chris Kleisath, Dave Neudoerffer, Michael Paola, Glenn Paulley, and Tom Slee at iAnywhere Solutions for the years of encouragement, and to Steven McDowell for bringing me together with Wordware Publishing to get the project finally started. I also want to thank Wes Beckwith and Beth Kohler at Wordware, for their enthusiasm and their patience.

I am also grateful to Ruth Haworth for coordinating the official iAnywhere Solutions "tech check" process, and to the following people who performed that duty: Peter Bumbulis, Russ Chamberlain, Reg Domaratzki, Bruce Hay, and Glenn Paulley; especially Glenn, who provided the starting point for the BNF and also put up with daily phone calls over weeks and months to ask about this detail and that. And yes, some folks are getting mentioned here more than once.

Several people reviewed material and provided valuable feedback: Hartmut Branz, Kerry Ferguson, Jonathan P. Groves, Ruth Haworth, Margaret Kammermayer, Tom Slee, and Carol Stone.

Tom Slee pushed me past a stumbling block, the organization of the book as a whole, by pointing out that when you're trying to explain a relational database system "you need to introduce everything before everything else." In other words, there's no way to get the order perfect, and it's okay to put SELECT INTO #table_name in Chapter 1 because it creates a table and that's what Chapter 1 is all about, even though the syntax for SELECT doesn't appear until Chapter 3.

In a way, Tom Slee and his colleagues at iAnywhere Solutions made this book more difficult to write by making the SQL Anywhere Help so good. Many of the differences between this book and the Help are simply intended to be just that: different, not necessarily better or worse, but different. One example is the Backus-Naur Form (BNF) notation used for the syntax in this book (which, by the way, is explained in the introduction to Chapter 1); the Help uses a different notation for the syntax. For this and other differences, the hope is that they will be useful and that if you find something is confusing in one place, you'll be able to turn to the other, this book or the Help, and find the answer.

Many folks provided ideas and answered questions, among them Richard Biffl, Ivan Bowman, Mark Culp, Mahesh Dixit, Nick Elson, Dan Farrar, Greg Fenton, David Fishburn, Anil Goel, Jason Hinsperger, Graham Hurst, Chris Irie, Ian McHardy, Martin Neumann, Graeme Perrow, John Smirnios, Dave Wellstood, and Matthew Young-Lai (yes, these lists are alphabetic).

I also want to thank Ken Schrader, NASCAR Nextel Cup competitor, from whom I copied the phrase "best loser" as a synonym for second place; you can find it used in a stored procedure name in the section titled "SELECT FROM Procedure Call" in Chapter 3.

And finally, seriously, I want to thank my wife, Bonnie, for her support and encouragement over all the years, including but not limited to the year it took to write this book.

About the Author

 Breck Carter first worked with a relational database in 1973, even before there were any practical commercial implementations. Over the years he has worked as an independent consultant to develop enterprise databases and applications using IMS DB/DC, DB2, Oracle, SQL Server, ASE, and, beginning in 1995, SQL Anywhere. Breck has been a member of Team Sybase since 1993, which means you can find him answering questions on the SQL Anywhere newsgroups on behalf of Sybase and iAnywhere Solutions. Breck is also a member of the iAnywhere Solutions Customer Advisory Board, where he is helping to shape future product direction.

You can reach Breck at bcarter@risingroad.com.

Chapter 1

Creating

1.1 Introduction

This chapter discusses the first step in the life cycle of a SQL Anywhere 9 relational database: the creation of tables and columns.

Relational databases are popular because they are easy to understand. They're powerful too — as are other kinds of databases and file systems — but it is the simplicity of relational databases that make them more popular than other technologies.

Relational databases are easy to understand because they are constructed from a very simple building block: the table. A table consists of zero or more rows, with each row consisting of one or more data elements or columns. All the rows look the same — they have the same number of columns in the same order, with the same column names and data types.

Note: The question "Is column order important?" is subject to debate. The point here is that whatever the column order happens to be, in whatever context (e.g., SELECT * FROM t), it's the same for all the rows in a table.

This chapter begins with 12 rules to answer the question "What is a relational database?" It ends with a discussion of normalization to answer the question "What is a good relational database?" In between, the seven different formats of the CREATE TABLE statement and the five different types of tables are described in detail. Column data types are also covered, as well as various table and column properties and constraints.

This book uses Backus-Naur Form (BNF) notation for the SQL syntax. This notation takes the form of concise and precise rules for forming more complex objects from simpler ones. Each rule is called a production and consists of a single item on the left, the special operator "::=" meaning "is defined as," and an expanded definition of the item on the right.

For example, the following production means "the <in_dbspace_clause> item is defined as one of the IN or ON keywords, followed by either the DEFAULT keyword or a <dbspace_name> item":

```
<in_dbspace_clause> ::= ( IN | ON ) ( DEFAULT | <dbspace_name> )
<dbspace_name>      ::= <identifier>
```

The <dbspace_name> item is then defined in a second production as being the same as an <identifier>, and somewhere else there will be a production that explains <identifier>.

Table 1-1 describes the symbols used in BNF notation.

Table 1-1. BNF notation

Symbol	Description
::=	This means "is defined as."
<name>	An item that is defined by a "::=" production.
|	A vertical bar means "or" as in <color> ::= RED | ORANGE | YELLOW.
{ items }	Curly braces mean "zero or more repetitions of items."
(items)	Parentheses means "pick one of the alternative items."
[items]	Square brackets means "these items are optional."
WORD	A keyword that appears as is.
","	A punctuation mark or special character that appears as is, without double quotes.
words	A free-form description, bending the rules of BNF to make it even more concise.
-- words	A comment.

The BNF in this book is different from the notation in the Help. This is done on purpose: If you don't understand the Help for some particular command, perhaps you will find the BNF easier. And vice versa — if some piece of BNF confuses you, then maybe the Help will be helpful. Be careful of the little differences, though; for example, curly braces in this book mean "zero or more repetitions" whereas curly braces in the Help mean "pick one of these items."

BNF can be awkward to read at first. Here is an example of a very common construction in SQL, a comma-separated list:

```
<user_name_list> ::= <identifier> { "," <identifier> }
```

A strict interpretation of this production is "a <user_name_list> is defined as an <identifier> followed by zero or more commas each followed by an <identifier>." With practice you will see it simply as "a comma-separated list of identifiers."

The full BNF used in this book also appears in HTML format on the companion CD, with hypertext links between all the <items> and their definitions.

1.2 Codd's 12 Rules for Relational Databases

"Table" is another word for "relation," from the Relational Model of Data first proposed by E. F. Codd in the 1970s. The word *relation* is used when speaking of the theoretical basis for relational databases, and the word *table* is used when speaking of actual implementations, such as SQL Anywhere 9.

Codd laid down strict rules for what is, and what isn't, a true relational database:

Rule Zero. A relational database manages all of its data through the capabilities defined by Rules 1 through 12.

It must not be necessary to break these rules for any reason, such as achieving better performance. This means you can trust the rules without worrying about special exceptions.

Rule 1. Tables must be used to logically represent all the data in a database.

That's it — everything's in tables. You don't have to learn about different layouts or arrangements. No variable-format records, arrays, pointers, heaps, stacks, or lists.

Rule 2. The table name, column name, and primary key value may be used to uniquely identify every data element.

This means every table must have a primary key: one or more non-null columns whose composite value is unique for each row in the table. SQL Anywhere 9 lets you create a table without a primary key, but that's a really bad idea for many reasons including performance. It's up to you to obey Rule 2, and SQL Anywhere 9 provides facilities for defining an artificial primary key if you can't or don't want to specify one that is based on business-related data.

Rule 3. Null values must be available to systematically represent missing or inapplicable data. Null values must be independent of the data type, and they must be distinct from all other values such as the empty string, blank string, or zero. It must be possible to specify "nulls not allowed" for primary key and other columns.

Rule 4. Tables must be used to logically represent the database description or system catalog. Authorized users must be able to query the system catalog in the same manner as ordinary tables.

In other words, the system catalog is stored as data in the database, and Rule 1 applies.

Rule 5. There must be at least one single programming language that supports all of the data definition, data manipulation, integrity constraints, user authorization, and transaction control operations.

Today that language is SQL, and it contains all the different kinds of commands such as CREATE, UPDATE, GRANT, and COMMIT.

Rule 6. Every view must be updatable if it is theoretically updatable.

This rule applies to inserts and deletes as well as updates. A view is a query involving one or more tables. It is theoretically updatable if it is possible to determine which rows in which base tables must be updated to achieve the requested effect on the view. For example, a view defined as SELECT * FROM t1 is updatable because everything about the base table t1 is known from the view, but a view defined as SELECT 1 is not updatable because it doesn't even refer to a table.

Rule 7. Set-oriented insert, update, and delete operations must be available.

Set-oriented operations are often more efficient to write and execute than row-by-row operations.

Rule 8. Application programs must not be affected by changes in the physical data representation.

Application programs must only deal with the logical view of data offered by SQL, not the underlying physical layout or access methods. In particular, application programs should not care about the physical order of rows in a table, or the order of columns in a row. This was a big advance over other technologies, which often required program changes when file names, locations, record layouts, or sort orders were changed.

Rule 9. Application programs must not necessarily be affected by logical data design changes that preserve information.

For example, if tables are split or combined in a way that preserves the original data, it should be possible do this without changing the application program logic. This means it is often possible to enhance or repair the database design without rewriting applications.

Rule 10. Integrity constraint definitions must be stored in the system catalog tables rather than application programs. Entity integrity must be satisfied for every table: No component of the primary key may be null. Referential integrity must be satisfied for every foreign key relationship: There must be a matching primary key value for each non-null foreign key value.

Integrity constraints ensure data consistency in the long term because they are built in to the database and cannot be avoided. They also help in the short term by catching application programming errors that violate data integrity.

Rule 11. If distributed data is supported, application programs must not be affected when data is distributed.

For example, it must be possible to write a program involving multiple tables in the same way whether the tables reside in the same or different locations. SQL Anywhere 9 uses proxy tables to support distributed data in a way that satisfies this rule.

Rule 12. It must not be possible to bypass the integrity rules or constraints when manipulating the data.

The same rules apply whether set-oriented or row-by-row operations are performed, and there must be no low-level access method that breaks these rules. In practice, however, some rule checking may be deferred on a temporary basis to solve some application design problems.

1.3 Five Types of Tables

The CREATE TABLE statement comes in seven different formats to create five different types of tables. The different statement formats have the same basic purpose: to define the name and layout of a new table, the names and data types of the columns in each row, and the constraints which apply to the table and columns. The table types differ as to whether a table is available to different connections (global versus local), whether the schema and data are permanent or temporary, and where the data resides (remote versus proxy).

```
<create_table> ::= <create_global_permanent_table>
                 | <create_remote_and_proxy_table>
                 | <create_proxy_table>
                 | <create_global_temporary_table>
```

```
| <create_local_temporary_table>
| <declare_local_temporary_table>
| <select_into_local_temporary_table>
```

Global permanent tables are the most common type. They exist in the current database and both the schema and data are available globally to all connections that have the appropriate permissions. The schema is permanent until the table is explicitly dropped, and the data is permanent until it is explicitly deleted.

Note: The term "global permanent table" is unique to this book. The Help and other sources just call them "tables" or sometimes "base tables."

Remote tables exist in some other database or file, different from the current database, and they are only visible in the current database via proxy tables. Remote tables don't actually have to be tables in the strictest sense; they simply have to look and feel like tables as far as the proxy table interface is concerned. Remote tables can be spreadsheets, text files, or even views involving other tables and views. Otherwise, remote tables are similar to global permanent tables in that their schema and the underlying data are permanent.

Proxy tables exist in two places at once. The schema exists in the current database but the actual data sits somewhere else, in a remote table in a different database or file. The term *proxy* means "surrogate" or "substitute"; each proxy table is a mapping between the data in a remote table and the schema in the current database.

Proxy tables are a mechanism for treating remote tables as if they were global permanent tables: They are available to all connections, and the schema and data are permanent. Proxy tables are often used to gather data from other sources, including legacy databases, distributed databases, spreadsheets, and flat files. It is possible to update proxy tables as well as query them, and the changes are reflected in the other data source.

Global temporary tables exist in the current database. The schema is permanent and available to all connections, but the data is temporary: Each connection inserts its own data, that data is visible only to that connection, and it is automatically deleted when the connection is dropped. The data may also be deleted each time a COMMIT or ROLLBACK is executed.

Local temporary tables exist in the current database. Both the schema and data are temporary: Each connection must create the table and insert its own data, and the table and data are both visible only to that connection. The table is automatically dropped when the connection is dropped or when the table name falls out of scope. The data may be automatically deleted when a COMMIT or ROLLBACK is executed; otherwise, it lasts until the table is dropped. There are three different statements that create temporary tables, one of which inserts data at the same time.

1.4 Global Permanent Table

The CREATE TABLE statement for a global permanent table specifies the table name, an optional owner name if it is different from the current connected user, a list of table elements, and the optional name of the physical DBSPACE or file where the data will reside.

```
<create_global_permanent_table> ::= CREATE TABLE
                             [ <owner_name> "." ] <permanent_table_name>
                             <table_element_list>
                             [ <in_dbspace_clause> ]
<owner_name>                ::= <identifier>
<identifier>                ::= <alphabetic> { ( <alphabetic> | <numeric> ) }
                             | reserved word in double quotes or square brackets
                             | any string in double quotes or square brackets
<alphabetic>                ::= letter, underscore (_), at sign (@), dollar sign ($)
                                 or number sign (#)
<numeric>                   ::= digit 0 to 9
<permanent_table_name>      ::= <non_temporary_identifier>
<non_temporary_identifier>  ::= <non_temporary_alphabetic>
                                 { ( <alphabetic> | <numeric> ) }
                             | reserved word in double quotes or square brackets
                             | any string in double quotes or square brackets
<non_temporary_alphabetic>  ::= letter, underscore (_), at sign (@) or
                                 dollar sign ($)
<table_element_list>        ::= "(" <table_element> { "," <table_element> } ")"
<in_dbspace_clause>         ::= ( IN | ON ) ( DEFAULT | <dbspace_name> )
<dbspace_name>              ::= <identifier>
```

Global permanent tables have two-part names consisting of the owner name and the table name. In most SQL Anywhere databases there is only one set of table names and they all have DBA as the owner. However, it is possible to have different tables with the same table name but different owners. Other statements may refer to these tables by explicitly specifying the respective owner names. This makes it possible for different people to "own" their own set of tables, and for different versions of the same table to exist at the same time.

By default, CREATE TABLE takes the current user as the owner. It is rare, but possible, to explicitly provide a different owner name. Table ownership is discussed further in Sections 9.10.1, "Table Privileges," and 9.10.5, "GRANT GROUP."

Here is an example of a simple CREATE TABLE statement that creates a global permanent table t1 with three columns:

```
CREATE TABLE t1 (
   key_1       INTEGER NOT NULL PRIMARY KEY,
   non_key_1   VARCHAR ( 100 ) NOT NULL,
   non_key_2   VARCHAR ( 100 ) NOT NULL );
```

Owner, table, and DBSPACE names are all standard SQL Anywhere identifiers. An *identifier* is a string of up to 128 characters optionally surrounded by double quotes (" ") or square brackets ([ ]). The quotes or brackets are necessary if the string is an SQL Anywhere reserved word. They are also necessary if the string is something other than one alphabetic character followed by alphabetic and numeric characters, where alphabetic includes the special characters underscore (_), at sign (@), dollar sign ($), and number sign (#).

Table names beginning with a number sign (#) are a special case, described in Section 1.15.2, "Local Temporary Tables." A global permanent table name must not start with a number sign unless it's surrounded with double quotes or square brackets in the CREATE TABLE statement.

The dbspace clause specifies which one of the up to 13 physical files is to hold the data for this table. When a database is first created it has one dbspace file, with the file name you gave it and the dbspace name of SYSTEM, and that's the one used by default for new tables. The CREATE DBSPACE statement may be used to create the other 12 files and give them dbspace names. Separate files are used to increase storage capacity on some operating systems, and to increase performance by placing different sets of data on different physical disk drives. Dbspaces are discussed in Chapter 10, "Tuning," and the CREATE DBSPACE statement is documented in the SQL Anywhere Help file.

The comma-separated list of table elements consists of one or more column definitions plus zero or more table properties and constraints. Each column definition consists of a column name, data type, and optional column properties. The column name is a SQL Anywhere identifier, and the data type may be a built-in data type or a reference to a user-defined data type.

```
<table_element>      ::= <column_definition>
                       | <table_property>
                       | <table_constraint>
<column_definition> ::= <column_name> <data_type> [ <column_definition_list> ]
<column_definition_list> ::= <column_definition_term> { <column_definition_term> }
<column_definition_term> ::= <column_property>
                       | <column_constraint>
<column_name>        ::= <identifier>
<data_type>          ::= <builtin_data_type>
                       | <user_defined_data_type>
                       | <builtin_user_defined_data_type>
```

1.5 Data Types

SQL Anywhere provides a wide variety of built-in string, date-time, and numeric data types. A data type has four important properties:
- How it is physically stored in the database
- How it is manipulated by SQL operations executed by the database server
- How values are received as input from client applications
- How values are presented for output to client applications

This section concentrates on the first two properties: physical storage and rules for manipulation. Input and output are discussed in later chapters.

```
<builtin_data_type> ::= <string_type>
                      | <date_time_type>
                      | <exact_numeric_type>
                      | <float_numeric_type>
                      | <integer_type>
```

The rules for relational databases imply that the details of physical data type storage are not as important to application programmers as the other three properties: the rules for manipulation, input, and output. In particular, rules 0 and 12 apply here: A relational database manages all of its data, and it not possible to bypass the integrity rules or constraints when manipulating the data.

1.5.1 A String Is a String: BINARY, CHARACTER, LONG

All character and binary columns are stored as varying length character strings regardless of how they are declared. The maximum length specifies a limit on the byte size of the data portion of the string, with a default of 1 byte. The LONG VARCHAR and LONG BINARY types have an implied maximum length of 2GB.

```
<string_type>    ::= <char_type> [ "(" <maximum_length> ")" ]
                   | LONG BINARY
                   | LONG VARCHAR
<char_type>      ::= BINARY
                   | CHAR [ VARYING ]
                   | CHARACTER [ VARYING ]
                   | VARBINARY
                   | VARCHAR
<maximum_length> ::= integer literal in the range 1 to 32767
```

Tip: All these data types, including LONG VARCHAR and LONG BINARY, may be used for local and global variables in stored procedures and other SQL scripts, as well as for columns in tables.

Storage requirements depend on the current length of each column value rather than the maximum length. Long strings are split and require more overhead than short strings, whereas short strings are stored efficiently even if they are declared as LONG VARCHAR. Here's how it works: String values up to 254 bytes in length are always stored together with the other columns in the row. When the length grows to 255 bytes or larger the value is partitioned into two pieces; the first piece is 254 bytes long and remains where it was, while the remainder is called a blob continuation and is placed on one or more separate pages called extension pages. These extension pages are kept separate so that a query or sequential scan that doesn't need to look at the long values won't have to retrieve all these pages. This arrangement is described in more detail in Section 10.6.2, "Table Fragmentation."

From a SQL programming point of view, a string is a string in SQL Anywhere 9 and you don't have to worry about the declared data type. For example, if you think all company names will fit into 30 characters but you are concerned about exceptions, there is no performance penalty for using CHARACTER (100) or even 1000. Similarly, a description column that will usually require only a few hundred characters can be declared as LONG VARCHAR to handle those special cases; your database won't grow in size until you actually store very long values.

Exactly the same data may be stored in either CHARACTER or BINARY columns. In particular, the zero byte (hexadecimal 00) may be stored in a CHARACTER column and it is treated as data, not a string terminator.

Tip: In some programming environments the zero byte string terminator is called "null." This is not the same as the database NULL value implemented by SQL Anywhere 9; database NULLs require special handling when they are used in applications.

There are a few exceptions to the assumption "a string is a string." First, sorting and comparisons involving BINARY columns always use the actual binary values, whereas CHARACTER columns are sorted and compared according to the database collation sequence and case sensitivity. For example, in a case-insensitive database (the default) the CHARACTER values 'a' and 'A' are treated as being equal, whereas the BINARY 'a' is treated as being less than the BINARY 'A' when they are compared or sorted.

Tip: Use the CAST function when you need to perform case-sensitive comparisons in a case-insensitive database; e.g., IF CAST (char1 AS BINARY) = CAST (char2 AS BINARY). This also works in the WHERE and ORDER BY clauses, and can be used when you need to ignore the database collation sequence.

Note: This book doesn't discuss multi-byte character sets, except to note that some techniques, like the Tip above, are only intended for single-byte character sets.

Second, a few functions only work on the first 255 bytes of the character string arguments: SOUNDEX, SIMILAR, and all the date and time functions ignore anything past 255 bytes.

Third, a conversion from string to numeric will also ignore any data past 255 bytes.

Fourth, an attempt to assign a long string value to a column declared with a shorter maximum length will result in right truncation. This truncation will happen silently when only spaces are being truncated by an INSERT or UPDATE command, or when non-spaces are truncated but the STRING_RTRUNCATION option is still set to the default 'OFF'. To generate an error message when non-spaces are truncated you must set STRING_RTRUNCATION to 'ON'. Note that trailing spaces are significant, and are never truncated unless they won't fit in the declared maximum length.

Tip: The LTRIM, RTRIM, and TRIM functions can be used to get rid of leading and trailing spaces.

Fifth, some application development tools generate different code and user interface elements depending on how a string is declared. In some cases a column declared as CHAR may be treated as a fixed-length string even though SQL Anywhere 9 does not implement it that way.

Note: Other database products may implement CHAR columns as fixed-length strings, and that might affect you if you're sending data back and forth via proxy tables or MobiLink synchronization.

Finally, there are some performance implications to declaring a string column with a maximum length far larger than you need. The declared width of columns in an index is used to determine if a compressed B-tree index can be used instead of a hash B-tree index. Subquery and function caching may be turned off in cases where the total declared maximum length of the columns and arguments is very large. Also, the query optimizer may be able to get better information from the column statistics for columns with a declared maximum size less than 8 bytes. Some of these topics are discussed in Chapter 10, "Tuning."

Otherwise, a string is still a string, and you can happily store and copy and assign values with different declared string types without any problems.

1.5.2 Dates and Times

Date and time values can be input and displayed in many different external formats, but they are always stored in one of three fixed physical formats. The DATE data type requires 4 bytes to store the numeric year, month and day. The TIME data type requires 8 bytes to store the numeric hour, minute, second, and fraction of a second up to six decimal places. The TIMESTAMP data type also requires 8 bytes to store numeric year, month, day, hour, minute, second, and fraction of a second.

```
<date_time_type> ::= DATE
                   | TIME
                   | TIMESTAMP
```

The TIME data type supports the range 00:00:00.000000 to 23:59:59.999999, and DATE supports 0001-01-01 to 9999-12-31. The TIMESTAMP data type fully supports the range 1600-02-28 23:59:59 to 7911-01-01 00:00:00. Outside this range, the date portion supports years from 1 to 9999 but the time portion may not be complete.

On some platforms CURRENT TIME and CURRENT TIMESTAMP will only return two or three significant digits to the right of the decimal point in the seconds portion. However, TIME and TIMESTAMP columns are always capable of storing all six digits.

Tip: Use SET OPTION PUBLIC.TIME_FORMAT = 'HH:NN:SS.SSSSSS' and SET OPTION PUBLIC.TIMESTAMP_FORMAT = 'YYYY MM DD HH:NN:SS.SSSSSS' to retrieve all six digits from the database, even if they are zero. The default is three digits, which means even if you store more you can't retrieve them into your application.

1.5.3 Exact Decimals

Exact decimals give exact results when they are combined in arithmetic expressions, making them ideal for financial calculations.

The DECIMAL and NUMERIC data types are one and the same: an exact decimal number up to 127 digits in length (the precision). The number of digits to the right of the decimal point (the scale) can range from zero to all of the digits.

```
<exact_numeric_type> ::= <exact_keyword>
                       [ "(" <exact_precision> [ "," <exact_scale> ] ")" ]

<exact_keyword>     ::= DEC
                      | DECIMAL
                      | NUMERIC
<exact_precision> ::= integer literal in the range 1 to 127
<exact_scale>     ::= integer literal in the range 1 to <exact_precision>
```

If both the precision and scale are omitted, the default is (30, 6). If the precision is specified but the scale is omitted, the scale defaults to zero. If both the precision and scale are specified, the scale must be in the range 0 <= scale <= precision. In other words, the decimal point cannot be shifted away from the actual digits of precision.

The storage requirements depend on the precision and scale of the actual values stored, not the declared precision and scale. For example, 123456789 will take more storage than 123, and 1.123456789 will take more disk space than 1.1. The formula for the bytes required is:

```
2 + TRUNCNUM ( ( p - s + 1 ) / 2, 0 ) + TRUNCNUM ( ( s + 1 ) / 2, 0 )
```

where p and s are the actual precision and scale after any leading and trailing zeroes are ignored.

1.5.4 Floating-Point Numbers

Floating-point numbers have far larger ranges than exact decimals so they are useful in scientific calculations where a minimum precision is required regardless of how large or small the values are. However, they are not suitable for exact calculations because they are subject to rounding errors. In particular, two different calculations that are supposed to yield the same result may in fact give slightly different answers when floating-point numbers are used.

The REAL, DOUBLE, and FLOAT data types are implemented as single- and double-precision approximate floating-point binary numbers.

```
<float_numeric_type> ::= REAL
                       | DOUBLE [ PRECISION ]
                       | FLOAT "(" <single_precision> ")"
                       | FLOAT "(" <double_precision> ")"
                       | FLOAT
<single_precision>   ::= integer literal in the range 1 to 24
<double_precision>   ::= integer literal in the range 25 to 53
```

REAL is stored in exactly the same manner as FLOAT (24), and so are all the declarations from FLOAT (1) through FLOAT (23): a single-precision number with 24 binary digits of precision, which is roughly equivalent to six decimal digits. REAL values always require 4 bytes of storage and can have positive and negative values with absolute values ranging from 1.175495e–38 to 3.402823e+38. Values may appear to have more than six decimal digits of precision but they are subject to round-off error after the sixth digit.

DOUBLE is the same as FLOAT (53), and so are FLOAT (25) through FLOAT (52): a double-precision number holding 53 bits of precision or 15 decimal digits. DOUBLE values always need 8 bytes and can have positive and negative values with absolute values ranging from 2.22507385850721e–308 to 1.79769313486231e+308. Values are subject to round-off error after the 15th digit.

If FLOAT is specified without a precision, REAL is assumed. You can set the FLOAT_AS_DOUBLE option to 'ON' to change this assumption to be DOUBLE.

1.5.5 **Binary Integers**

Binary integers are very popular when computational efficiency is a primary concern. Binary computers can often perform calculations involving 2- and 4-byte binary integers much faster than other data types.

SQL Anywhere provides unsigned binary integers containing 1, 8, 16, 32, and 64 binary digits, and signed values with 15, 31, and 63 digits plus a sign bit. These are exact data types, similar in usefulness to DECIMAL (p, 0) values.

```
<integer_type> ::= BIT
                 | [ UNSIGNED ] TINYINT
                 | [ UNSIGNED ] SMALLINT
                 | [ UNSIGNED ] ( INT | INTEGER )
                 | [ UNSIGNED ] BIGINT
```

The BIT data type is useful for boolean data where 0 represents FALSE and 1 is TRUE. A full byte of physical storage is used for each value but only the values 0 and 1 are allowed.

By default, BIT columns are created as NOT NULL but can be explicitly created as NULL. This differs from other data types where NULL is the CREATE TABLE default and NOT NULL must be explicitly specified.

The TINYINT and UNSIGNED TINYINT data types are the same: an unsigned binary integer in the range 0 to 255 requiring 1 byte of storage. This data type is useful for very small positive numbers including primary keys for tiny "code" tables.

The SMALLINT data type requires 2 bytes of storage and holds values in the range –32,768 to 32,767.

UNSIGNED SMALLINT numbers also require 2 bytes but hold values in the range 0 to 65,535. This doubles the range of positive values as compared with SMALLINT.

The INTEGER data type requires 4 bytes of storage and holds values in the range –2,147,483,648 to 2,147,483,647. This data type is commonly used for DEFAULT AUTOINCREMENT primary keys for large tables.

UNSIGNED INTEGER numbers also require 4 bytes but hold values in the range 0 to 4,294,967,295. This is an even better choice for large positive primary keys.

The BIGINT data type is the largest binary integer, requiring 8 bytes of storage and holding values in the range –9,223,372,036,854,775,808 to 9,223,372,036,854,775,807. This is often the data type of choice for DEFAULT GLOBAL AUTOINCREMENT primary keys because there is plenty of room for many large partitions.

UNSIGNED BIGINT numbers also require 8 bytes but hold values in the range 0 to 18,446,744,073,709,551,615. Like the other UNSIGNED integer types this one doubles the range of positive values.

Tip: Some programming languages use different names for these data types. SQL Anywhere 9's SMALLINT may be called "short integer" or just "integer." INTEGER may be called "long integer," "long," or even "integer." BIGINT may not be available, so you must use some variation of an exact decimal type.

1.5.6 **Literals**

Character string literals are coded inside single quotes (' '), as opposed to double quotes (" "), which are used for identifiers. You can represent an embedded single quote as two single quotes, as in 'Fred''s Not Here'. Be careful with the backslash character because it may be interpreted as an escape character, which changes the meaning of one or more characters that follow.

\xnn and \Xnn represent the single character with the hexadecimal value nn from 00 to FF. For example, '\x31\x32\x33' is the same as '123', and 'Fred\X27s Not Here' is the same as 'Fred''s Not Here'.

\n represents the new-line character, the same as \x0A, which makes 'c:\new' a dangerous thing to write. But 'c:\New' is okay because there is nothing significant about '\N'.

\\ represents a single backslash, which you can use to fix things: 'c:\\new'.

Tip: The backslash isn't always interpreted as an escape character, but it's always safe to use '\\' when you want a single backslash. For example, '\abc' and '\\abc' have the same value.

Binary string literals may be written just like character string literals, but they may also be written without quotes as 0xnn... where nn... is one or more hexadecimal values in the range 00 to FF. For example, 0x48656C6C6F2C20776F726C6421 is the same as 'Hello, world!'. Note that this isn't the same as the '\xnn' format for string literals, which require quotes and must repeat the \x in front of every character.

Tip: If you want to force a binary value to be treated as character data by an application program, use the CAST function to change the type. For example, ISQL will display SELECT CAST (0x48656C6C6F2C20776F726C6421 AS VARCHAR) as 'Hello, world!' instead of the incomprehensible hex value. Don't forget, there is no difference in the way binary and character strings are stored; the differences only appear in the way they are interpreted.

Dates may be written as string literals with a variety of formats, with the year-month-day format being the safest. For example, the following values will always be interpreted as July 6, 2003 when converted to a DATE: '2003-07-06', '2003 07 06', '2003/07/06', '2003 07/06', '2003/7-6', '2003 7 6', '20030706', '2003/007-6', and '2003 July 6'.

Other formats, such as '7-6-2003', are ambiguous and are interpreted according to the database option DATE_ORDER. If DATE_ORDER is set to 'MDY' then '7-6-2003' is interpreted as July 6. However, if DATE_ORDER is set to 'DMY' then '7-6-2003' is interpreted as June 7 instead.

Times may be written as string literals in the format 'h:m:s.ssssss', with or without leading zeroes in the hours, minutes, and seconds positions. You can omit the seconds, but hours and minutes are required. You can also add a trailing AM or PM if you want to write the literal in the 12-hour-clock format. For example, one minute past noon may be written as '12:1', '0:1:0.000000PM', '12:01:00.000000', and '0012:0001:0000.00000000'.

Timestamp literals are written as the concatenation of date and time literals; e.g., '20030706 14:30' is one way of representing 2:30PM on July 6, 2003.

> **Tip:**   It's important to remember that dates and times are always stored in the same, safe formats. It is only the input and output formats that cause confusion, and the layout of a string literal is just another example of input formatting.

Numeric literals may be written as integer literals such as 123, exact decimals such as 1.23, and in scientific notation where 123E–2 represents 1.23.

1.6 Column Properties

Columns can have useful properties in addition to the data type. They can have formulas like cells in a spreadsheet, they can be given default values, and they can be updated automatically without writing triggers.

```
<column_definition>        ::= <column_name> [ AS ] <data_type>
                               [ <column_definition_list> ]
<column_definition_list> ::= <column_definition_term> { <column_definition_term> }
<column_definition_term> ::= <column_property>
                           | <column_constraint>
<column_property>          ::= COMPUTE "(" <expression> ")"
                           | DEFAULT <default_value>
                           | IDENTITY
                           | NULL
```

> **Note:**   The IDENTITY property is discussed together with DEFAULT AUTOINCREMENT in Section 1.8.1 because they are implemented in exactly the same way.

1.7 Computed Columns

The COMPUTE clause turns a column into a read-only computed column whose value is based on an expression. Computed columns cannot be given explicit values in INSERT or UPDATE statements, but they can be used to create indexes, and they are useful for performing calculations that would otherwise require triggers.

Here is an example of a query that runs up against the limitation that only one index per table will be used when optimizing a query; this WHERE clause involves two columns that could benefit from separate indexes:

```
CREATE TABLE street (
    pkey          INTEGER NOT NULL DEFAULT AUTOINCREMENT,
    street_name   VARCHAR ( 100 ) NOT NULL,
    range_part_1  INTEGER NOT NULL,
    range_part_2  VARCHAR ( 100 ) NOT NULL,
    postal_code   VARCHAR ( 6 ) NOT NULL,
    PRIMARY KEY ( pkey ) );

SELECT *
  FROM street
 WHERE street_name LIKE 'GRAND%'
   AND postal_code LIKE 'L6H5%';
```

> **Note:**   In an application program, host variables would probably be used to hold values like 'GRAND%' but once they reach SQL Anywhere 9 they are treated just like string literals.

In this example, the user can be expected to enter at least the first three characters of the desired postal code and the first two from street name before asking for a list to be displayed, so a computed column called fast_search can be added:

```
CREATE TABLE street (
    pkey          INTEGER NOT NULL DEFAULT AUTOINCREMENT,
    fast_search   VARCHAR ( 5 ) NOT NULL
                  COMPUTE ( STRING ( LEFT ( postal_code, 3 ),
                                     LEFT ( street_name, 2 ) ) ),
    street_name   VARCHAR ( 100 ) NOT NULL,
    range_part_1  INTEGER NOT NULL,
    range_part_2  VARCHAR ( 100 ) NOT NULL,
    postal_code   VARCHAR ( 6 ) NOT NULL,
    PRIMARY KEY ( pkey ) );
```

Now a beneficial index can be created and the new column added to the WHERE clause; the optimizer will use the new index to speed things up.

```
CREATE CLUSTERED INDEX xfast ON street ( fast_search );

SELECT *
  FROM street
 WHERE fast_search = 'L6HGR'
   AND street_name LIKE 'GRAND%'
   AND postal_code LIKE 'L6H5%';
```

All the computed columns in a single row are automatically calculated whenever a row is inserted and they are recalculated when the row is updated. All the computed columns in all the rows are recalculated whenever the table schema is altered to change any column data type or COMPUTE clause, to add, delete, or rename any column, or to rename the table. Computed columns are not recalculated when rows are retrieved; this makes them efficient for queries and indexes but they may be unsuitable for time-dependent expressions.

Tip: A computed column with an index can be used to optimize existing queries. For example, suppose many queries containing WHERE (x + y + z) would benefit from an index on (x + y + z), where x, y, and z are columns in the same table. You can have the query optimizer automatically replace the expression with a reference to the computed column if you follow two rules. First, code the COMPUTE expression in the same order of arguments and operators as it appears in the WHERE clause. Second, make the data type of the computed column the same as that of the expression; use the EXPRTYPE function to figure out what that is.

Here is a table that could benefit from a computed column because the SELECT does a full-table scan:

```
CREATE TABLE t (
    pkey INTEGER NOT NULL DEFAULT AUTOINCREMENT,
    x    INTEGER,
    y    INTEGER,
    z    INTEGER,
    PRIMARY KEY ( pkey ) );

SELECT * FROM t WHERE ( x + y + z ) BETWEEN 1501 AND 1510;
```

Run the following command in ISQL to determine that (x + y + z) returns an 'int':

```
SELECT EXPRTYPE ( 'SELECT ( x + y + z ) FROM t', 1 );
```

Now the computed column can be added, together with a clustered index to improve the BETWEEN range query:

```
CREATE TABLE t (
    pkey INTEGER NOT NULL DEFAULT AUTOINCREMENT,
    x    INTEGER,
    y    INTEGER,
    z    INTEGER,
    xyz  INTEGER COMPUTE ( x + y + z ),
    PRIMARY KEY ( pkey ) );

CREATE CLUSTERED INDEX xyz ON t ( xyz );

SELECT * FROM t WHERE ( x + y + z ) BETWEEN 1501 AND 1510;
```

The SELECT may now use the new index even though the column xyz doesn't appear in the WHERE clause.

> **Note:** The index may be used, or it may not, depending on conditions in the data and choices made by the query optimizer. It is difficult, if not impossible, to predict exactly what the query optimizer will actually do in any given situation, but the point of this example is that the computed column makes it possible for the index to be used.

For more information about clustered indexes, see Section 10.7, "CREATE INDEX."

1.8 DEFAULT Values

DEFAULT values are assigned whenever an explicit value is not provided when a row is inserted. Some special default values are also applied when the row is updated.

```
<default_value> ::= NULL
                  | AUTOINCREMENT
                  | GLOBAL AUTOINCREMENT
                  | GLOBAL AUTOINCREMENT "(" <partition_size> ")"
                  | <string_literal>
                  | [ "-" ] <number_literal>
                  | <special_literal>
                  | <special_update_default>
                  | <constant_function_call>
                  | "(" <constant_expression> ")"
<partition_size> ::= integer literal in the range 1 to 4611686018427387903
<string_literal> ::= a sequence of characters enclosed in single quotes
<number_literal> ::= integer, exact numeric or float numeric literal
```

DEFAULT NULL is the default DEFAULT, so to speak. It means this column will be set to NULL if no value is given.

1.8.1 DEFAULT AUTOINCREMENT

DEFAULT AUTOINCREMENT assigns the values 1, 2, 3, … to each successive row. This property is very useful for creating efficient single-column artificial primary keys. This is often done when a business-related primary key would have to contain several columns, when the business-related columns are very large, when they may change in value over time, or when there is simply no obvious primary key. They are also useful when the original INSERT or LOAD TABLE input order must be preserved, as with text data stored line by line.

More than one DEFAULT AUTOINCREMENT column may appear in the same table. The starting point for each column is stored in the SYSCOLUMN catalog table, so there is no performance requirement for indexes on DEFAULT AUTOINCREMENT columns, even though indexes are often used for other reasons. The DEFAULT AUTOINCREMENT property does not cause any concurrency problems; i.e., different users may insert rows in the same table without the calculation of new values causing any locking or blocking.

You can override DEFAULT AUTOINCREMENT by providing an explicit value when inserting. If that value is larger than any existing values, then it is used as the new starting point and a gap is created. For example, if the largest value is 3 and you explicitly insert 7, then the next DEFAULT AUTOINCREMENT value will be 8. Gaps may also appear when rows are deleted. You can fill the gaps yourself by explicitly inserting the missing values without affecting the next default value.

Another way to fill in gaps is to call the sa_reset_identity system procedure to reset the last-value-used for a particular table so a different default value will be used on the next INSERT. Be careful, however, because this procedure does exactly what you tell it to do and doesn't check to see what values are actually being used. Here is an example that can be safely used after inserting and deleting high values in a column; it removes the gap above the highest value in t1.key_1 by using a SELECT to calculate the actual highest-value-used and then passing that value to sa_reset_identity:

```
BEGIN
    DECLARE @max_key_1 INTEGER;
    SELECT MAX ( key_1 ) INTO @max_key_1 FROM t1;
    CALL sa_reset_identity ( 't1', 'DBA', @max_key_1 );
END;
```

For more information about BEGIN blocks, DECLARE statements, and CALL statements, see Chapter 8, "Packaging."

Note: The sa_reset_identity system procedure asks for the table name and owner name, but not the column name. If a table has more than one DEFAULT AUTOINCREMENT column, the same last-value-used will get set for all of them.

The IDENTITY property is implemented by DEFAULT AUTOINCREMENT. Unlike the IDENTITY property in Sybase Adaptive Server Enterprise, however, there is no requirement for the column to be NOT NULL, and there are no gaps created when the server is shut down abnormally.

1.8.2 DEFAULT GLOBAL AUTOINCREMENT

The DEFAULT GLOBAL AUTOINCREMENT property adds partitioning to DEFAULT AUTOINCREMENT. This is very useful for primary keys in a distributed database environment using MobiLink; by giving each database a different starting point, all the rows across all the databases can have unique values. In this environment each remote database is assigned a unique global database identifier 1, 2, 3, ... via the GLOBAL_DATABASE_ID option, with the value 0 often used to identify the central consolidated database.

The starting point for each DEFAULT GLOBAL AUTOINCREMENT column in each database is then calculated by multiplying the GLOBAL_DATABASE_ID option value g by the column's partition size p, and adding 1: (g * p) + 1.

In the following example, the starting point is (5 * 1000) + 1, so the first two rows are inserted with 5001 and 5002.

```
SET OPTION PUBLIC.GLOBAL_DATABASE_ID = '5';
CREATE TABLE t (
   auto UNSIGNED BIGINT DEFAULT GLOBAL AUTOINCREMENT ( 1000 ) );
INSERT t VALUES ( DEFAULT );
INSERT t VALUES ( DEFAULT );
COMMIT;
SELECT * FROM t ORDER BY t.auto;
```

Explicit values outside the partition are allowed and do not affect the next default value. However, explicit values inside the partition behave like they do with DEFAULT AUTOINCREMENT: They can create gaps, and they can be used to fill gaps.

For example, the following code inserts the values 9999 (outside the partition), 5003 (next default inside the partition), 5100 (to create a gap), 5004 (to start filling the gap), and 5101 (next default).

```
INSERT t VALUES ( 9999 );
INSERT t VALUES ( DEFAULT );
INSERT t VALUES ( 5100 );
INSERT t VALUES ( 5004 );
INSERT t VALUES ( DEFAULT );
COMMIT;
SELECT * FROM t ORDER BY t.auto;
-- Displays 5001, 5002, 5003, 5004, 5100, 5101, 9999
```

The end of the partition comes at (g + 1) * p, which is (5 + 1) * 1000 = 6000 in the example above. After that, the next default value will be NULL, which is usually unacceptable (a primary key cannot be NULL). If overflow is a possibility, an EVENT of type GlobalAutoincrement can be written to assign a new value to GLOBAL_DATABASE_ID.

In most applications, however, the partition is much larger than 1000 so overflow is virtually impossible. For example, with UNSIGNED BIGINT the partition size can be as large as 4,294,967,298 with a GLOBAL_DATABASE_ID up to 2,147,483,646. That means you can have over four billion different default values in each of two billion databases and they are all unique. With a smaller number of databases the partition size can grow even larger; with a GLOBAL_DATABASE_ID limited to 1000 you can create one quadrillion unique values in each database.

```
SET OPTION PUBLIC.GLOBAL_DATABASE_ID = '1000';
CREATE TABLE t (
    auto UNSIGNED BIGINT DEFAULT GLOBAL AUTOINCREMENT ( 1000000000000000 ) );
INSERT t VALUES ( DEFAULT );              -- 1000000000000001
INSERT t VALUES ( DEFAULT );              -- 1000000000000002
INSERT t VALUES ( 1001 * 1000000000000000 ); -- 1001000000000000
INSERT t VALUES ( DEFAULT );              -- NULL
```

1.8.3 Literal Defaults

Simple literal DEFAULT values can be specified for string, numeric, and date/time columns. Here are some examples:

```
CREATE TABLE t (
    c1  INTEGER,
    c2  VARCHAR ( 1 )    DEFAULT 'Y',                  -- Y
    c3  BINARY ( 20 )    DEFAULT 0x48656C6C6F,         -- Hello
    c4  VARCHAR ( 1 )    DEFAULT '\n',                 -- new line
    c5  VARCHAR ( 100 )  DEFAULT 'c:\\new',            -- c:\new
    c6  LONG VARCHAR     DEFAULT '\x61\x62\x63',       -- abc
    c7  INTEGER          DEFAULT 0,                    -- 0
    c8  DECIMAL ( 9, 2 ) DEFAULT 27.95,               -- 27.95
    c9  DOUBLE           DEFAULT -123.456E-2,         -- -1.23456
    c10 DATE             DEFAULT '2003 07 06',        -- July 6, 2003
    c11 TIME             DEFAULT '00:01',             -- 1 minute past midnight
    c12 TIMESTAMP        DEFAULT '20030706 14:30' ); -- 2:30 PM, July 6, 2003
```

SQL Anywhere offers several special literals for use in expressions and DEFAULT specifications. These literals are sometimes called "special constants" but they aren't really constant; some of them change over time, others change to reflect the state of program execution. When used as DEFAULT values, however, their values are frozen at the time they are copied to a row being inserted.

```
<special_literal> ::= CURRENT DATABASE
                    | CURRENT DATE
                    | CURRENT TIME
                    | CURRENT TIMESTAMP
                    | CURRENT USER
                    | CURRENT UTC TIMESTAMP
                    | SQLCODE
                    | SQLSTATE
                    | USER
```

The CURRENT DATABASE special literal returns the VARCHAR (128) run-time name of the database (e.g., 'test').

CURRENT DATE returns a DATE value containing today's date (e.g., 2003 06 11).

CURRENT TIME returns a TIME value containing the current time (e.g., 10:16:40.940000). On some platforms the seconds may only contain two or three significant digits to the right of the decimal point.

CURRENT TIMESTAMP returns a TIMESTAMP value containing the current date and time (e.g., 2003 06 11 10:16:40.940000). This DEFAULT can be used to answer the question "When was this row inserted?" On some platforms the seconds may only contain two or three significant digits to the right of the decimal point.

CURRENT USER returns the VARCHAR (128) user ID of the current connection (e.g., 'DBA'). A column with this DEFAULT can be used to answer the question "Who inserted this row?"

CURRENT UTC TIMESTAMP returns the CURRENT TIMESTAMP value adjusted by the server's time zone adjustment value, to form a Coordinated Universal Time (UTC) value. For example, if the TIME_ZONE_ADJUSTMENT option is '-240' and the CURRENT TIMESTAMP is 2003 06 11 10:16:40.940000, then CURRENT UTC TIMESTAMP is 2003 06 11 14:16:40.940000.

SQLCODE returns an INTEGER containing the numeric warning or error code from the previous statement (e.g., 100 for "row not found" and -306 for "deadlock detected").

SQLSTATE returns a VARCHAR (5) value containing an alphanumeric warning or error code from the previous statement (e.g., '02000' for "row not found" and '40001' for "deadlock detected").

The USER special literal is exactly the same as CURRENT USER: the currently connected user ID.

Tip: These special literals aren't restricted to DEFAULT values. They can be used anywhere in SQL that a literal is allowed; for example, your application can find out the date and time on the server by issuing SELECT CURRENT TIMESTAMP.

1.8.4 Special Update Defaults

SQL Anywhere offers three special DEFAULT values that apply to update operations as well as insert, when explicit column values are not provided. Unlike the special literals described earlier, these special values can only be used as DEFAULT values.

```
<special_update_default> ::= LAST USER
                           | TIMESTAMP
                           | UTC TIMESTAMP
```

DEFAULT LAST USER returns the VARCHAR (128) user ID of the current connection. A column with this default answers the question "Who was the person who inserted or updated this row?"

DEFAULT TIMESTAMP returns a TIMESTAMP value containing the current date and time, to answer the question "When was this row inserted or updated?"

DEFAULT UTC TIMESTAMP works the same way as DEFAULT TIMESTAMP, with an adjustment for Coordinated Universal Time.

These special update defaults can be used to implement simple audit trails without writing any special trigger logic. DEFAULT TIMESTAMP is especially valuable in a MobiLink distributed environment to answer the question "Does this row need to be downloaded because it was inserted or updated since the last synchronization?"

1.8.5 Expressions as Defaults

Some limited forms of function calls and expressions are allowed as DEFAULT values. Unlike computed columns, these expressions are evaluated only once when the row is inserted. Also, they cannot refer to any database objects — no columns or user-defined functions — just literal values and built-in functions with literal values as parameters.

```
<constant_function_call> ::= a built-in function call that does not reference
                             database objects
<constant_expression>    ::= an expression that does not reference database objects
```

Here are some examples:

```
CREATE TABLE t (
   c1 INTEGER,
   server   VARCHAR ( 100 ) DEFAULT PROPERTY ( 'MachineName' ),
   today    VARCHAR ( 100 ) DEFAULT DAYNAME ( CURRENT DATE ),
   tomorrow DATE            DEFAULT ( CURRENT DATE + 1 ),
   guid     BINARY ( 16 )   DEFAULT NEWID() );
```

The t.server column will be initialized to the machine name or IP address of the computer running the server. The t.today column defaults to the day name of the current date (e.g., 'Thursday'). The t.tomorrow column is initialized by adding 1 (day) to the CURRENT DATE.

The initial value for t.guid is a globally unique identifier, which looks like '28c47c41-9cb8-11d7-88d6-0000863a7c57' when formatted via the UUIDTOSTR() function.

Tip: The NEWID() default can be used instead of DEFAULT GLOBAL AUTOINCREMENT when you can't assign a unique value to the GLOBAL_DATABASE_ID option. The resulting values might not make the most efficient primary key index but they are guaranteed to be globally unique with no additional programming effort.

1.9 NULL Property

The NULL property is a declaration that this column may contain NULL values. This is true by default for all columns unless the NOT NULL constraint is used, with one exception: BIT columns are NOT NULL by default so you must use the NULL property if you want a BIT column to be nullable.

NULL and DEFAULT NULL are two different things. NULL says you may explicitly assign a NULL value to this column when the row is inserted or updated, whereas DEFAULT NULL says this column will be assigned a NULL value when the row is inserted unless you explicitly provide a different value.

1.10 Column Constraints

A column constraint is a rule about which values may be stored in a column. They are coded as assertions about validity and they are evaluated at run time as rows are inserted, updated, and deleted. Whenever a constraint fails (evaluates as FALSE) one of two things happens: In most cases an error message is produced and the offending operation is cancelled, and in some cases the data is silently and automatically repaired. When a constraint succeeds, the operation is allowed to proceed.

Column constraints are the programmer's friend. They provide an early warning about mistakes involving data. The more constraints there are in a database, the more likely it is that programming errors will be found very early in the development process, and that's a good thing.

Constraints are also the database administrator's friend because they make it very hard to store invalid data. You can use a column constraint to store a business-related validation rule in a single central location (the database) and have it apply to all applications and ad hoc updates. No program or power user can escape or bypass a column constraint.

```
<column_constraint>  ::= NOT NULL
                       | [ <constraint_prefix> ]
                           CHECK "(" <boolean_expression> ")"
                       | [ <constraint_prefix> ]
                           PRIMARY KEY [ <clustering> ]
                       | [ <constraint_prefix> ]
                           REFERENCES
                           [ <owner_name> "." ]
                           <table_name>
                           [ "(" <column_name> ")" ]
                           [ <on_action> ]
                           [ <clustering> ]
                       | [ <constraint_prefix> ]
                           UNIQUE [ <clustering> ]
<constraint_prefix>  ::= CONSTRAINT [ <constraint_name> ]
<constraint_name>    ::= <identifier>
<boolean_expression> ::= see <boolean_expression> in Chapter 3, "Selecting"
<clustering>         ::= CLUSTERED
                       | NONCLUSTERED
<table_name>         ::= <identifier>
<on_action>          ::= ON UPDATE <action>
                       | ON UPDATE <action> ON DELETE <action>
                       | ON DELETE <action>
                       | ON DELETE <action> ON UPDATE <action>
<action>             ::= CASCADE | SET NULL | SET DEFAULT | RESTRICT
```

1.10.1 **NOT NULL Constraint**

The NOT NULL constraint prevents NULL values from being stored in the column. This constraint is recommended for all columns whenever possible, to simplify expressions, queries, and other SQL statements. For a discussion of NULL and its relationship to the special three-value logic system using TRUE, FALSE, and UNKNOWN values, see Section 3.12, "Boolean Expressions and the WHERE Clause."

1.10.2 **Column CHECK Constraint**

The column CHECK constraint allows a search condition to be tested every time a column is changed. A search condition can range from a simple comparison like CHECK (salary >= 0) to much more complex expressions involving all of the features available in a query WHERE clause. Search conditions are described in more detail in Chapter 3, "Selecting."

Here is an example of a table used to record when the schema for a data-base was first created; the CHECK constraint ensures that only one row can ever exist in this table:

```
CREATE TABLE schema_created (
    pkey    INTEGER NOT NULL DEFAULT 1 CHECK ( pkey = 1 ),
    created TIMESTAMP NOT NULL DEFAULT CURRENT TIMESTAMP,
    PRIMARY KEY ( pkey ) );

INSERT schema_created VALUES ( DEFAULT, DEFAULT );
```

Here is an example of a CHECK constraint that makes sure new values are always increasing:

```
CREATE TABLE t (
    c1 INTEGER CHECK ( c1 > ( SELECT MAX ( c1 ) FROM t ) ) );

INSERT t VALUES ( 3 ); -- OK
INSERT t VALUES ( 4 ); -- OK
INSERT t VALUES ( 1 ); -- Fails
```

CHECK constraints only fail when they return FALSE. Both TRUE and UNKNOWN values are treated as success. That's why the first INSERT works in the example above — the table t is empty, SELECT MAX (c1) FROM t returns NULL, and the CHECK constraint returns UNKNOWN.

The second INSERT works because 4 is greater than 3 so the CHECK constraint is TRUE.

The third INSERT fails because 1 is less than 4, the new maximum value. An error message is produced: "Constraint 'ASA92' violated: Invalid value for column 'c1' in table 't'." The 'ASA92' is the automatically generated name assigned to this CHECK constraint because no constraint name was specified in the CREATE TABLE.

You can make these error messages more meaningful by assigning your own constraint names:

```
CREATE TABLE t (
    c1 INTEGER CONSTRAINT "c1 must increase in value"
            CHECK ( c1 > ( SELECT MAX ( c1 ) FROM t ) ) );
```

Now the error message will look like "Constraint 'c1 must increase in value' violated: Invalid value for column 'c1' in table 't'."

Tip: Every name and identifier in SQL Anywhere can be up to 128 characters in length, and you can use long phrases with spaces and special characters if you surround the name in double quotes or square brackets.

1.10.3 PRIMARY KEY Column Constraint

A PRIMARY KEY column constraint specifies that this column may contain only non-NULL values that are all different from one another. A unique index is automatically created for every PRIMARY KEY constraint so you don't have to define one yourself. This index may be defined as CLUSTERED or NONCLUSTERED, with NONCLUSTERED being the default. For more information about clustered indexes, see Section 10.7, "CREATE INDEX."

Every table should have a primary key. They are invaluable for defining hierarchical and other relationships among different tables, and they are very important for performance.

A PRIMARY KEY constraint is different from a unique index because an index allows NULL values and a PRIMARY KEY does not.

1.10.4 Foreign Key Column Constraint

A foreign key column constraint uses the REFERENCES clause to define a relationship between this table (called the "child" or "foreign" table) and another table (called the "parent" or "primary" table). Foreign key constraints are used to represent one-to-many relationships between parent and child tables, as in this example where one country may contain multiple offices:

```
CREATE TABLE country (
   country_code  VARCHAR ( 2 ) PRIMARY KEY,
   name          VARCHAR ( 100 ) NOT NULL );

CREATE TABLE office (
   office_code   VARCHAR ( 10 ) PRIMARY KEY,
   country_code  VARCHAR ( 2 ) NULL
                 CONSTRAINT "office.country_code must be valid or NULL"
                 REFERENCES country ( country_code )
                 ON UPDATE CASCADE ON DELETE SET NULL );
```

In this example the country_code column in office may be NULL. If it is not NULL, then it must contain a value that matches the country_code column in the country table. That's what the REFERENCES clause is for; it points to the parent table and its PRIMARY KEY column by name.

The REFERENCES clause is used to identify a single row in the parent table that matches this row in the child table. It can point to the PRIMARY KEY column or to a parent column with a UNIQUE constraint. Either one will do, but PRIMARY KEY columns are almost always used, and they are the default if the parent column name is omitted from the REFERENCES clause.

The example above includes a name for the foreign key constraint. This name will appear in the error message if the constraint fails; for example, the fourth INSERT below will fail with the error message "No primary key value for foreign key 'office.country_code must be valid or NULL' in table 'office'."

```
INSERT country VALUES ( 'CA', 'Canada' );
INSERT office VALUES ( '001', 'CA' ); -- OK
INSERT office VALUES ( '002', NULL ); -- OK
INSERT office VALUES ( '003', 'XX' ); -- fails
```

Foreign key constraints can fail for two main reasons: An attempt was made to INSERT or UPDATE a child row with a value that doesn't satisfy the constraint, or an attempt was made to UPDATE or DELETE a parent row in a way that causes one or more child rows to suddenly violate the constraint. There's nothing you can do to bypass errors caused by changes to the child table, but violations caused by changes in the parent table can be repaired on-the-fly with the ON UPDATE and ON DELETE clauses.

The ON UPDATE clause says that when the parent column changes in value, one of three different actions will be taken in all the corresponding child rows that would now violate the foreign key constraint. ON UPDATE CASCADE makes the same change to the child column so it matches the new parent column. ON UPDATE SET NULL changes the child column to NULL so at least it doesn't violate the constraint. ON UPDATE SET DEFAULT changes the child column to its DEFAULT value, one which presumably matches some other row in the parent table.

The ON DELETE clause says that when a parent row is deleted, one of three actions will be taken with all the corresponding child rows. ON DELETE CASCADE eliminates the violation in a brute-force fashion by deleting all the corresponding child rows. ON DELETE SET NULL changes the child column to NULL so it no longer violates the constraint. ON DELETE SET DEFAULT changes the child column to its DEFAULT value, one which matches some other row in the parent table that hasn't been deleted yet.

All these repairs are made silently, with no error messages. There is a fourth choice in each case: ON UPDATE RESTRICT and ON DELETE RESTRICT are the default actions, which produce an error message and prevent the operation on the parent table.

For performance reasons an index is created for every foreign key constraint, so you don't have to define the index yourself. This index may be defined as CLUSTERED or NONCLUSTERED, with NONCLUSTERED being the default. For more information about clustered indexes, see Section 10.7, "CREATE INDEX."

1.10.5 **UNIQUE Column Constraint**

The UNIQUE column constraint specifies that all values must be non-NULL and they must all be different from one another. A unique index is used to implement this constraint, but a UNIQUE constraint is different because a unique index allows NULL values. Also, a UNIQUE constraint can be treated just like a PRIMARY KEY when a foreign key constraint is defined in another table. A table may have more than one "candidate key," only one of which can be defined as the PRIMARY KEY; the others must be UNIQUE constraints.

The index corresponding to a UNIQUE constraint may be defined as CLUSTERED or NONCLUSTERED, with NONCLUSTERED being the default. For more information about clustered indexes, see Section 10.7, "CREATE INDEX."

1.11 **User-Defined Data Types**

SQL Anywhere provides a facility to combine built-in data types with DEFAULT values, CHECK conditions, and NULL properties into user-defined data types. These user-defined data types can then be used just like built-in data types.

```
<create_domain>            ::= CREATE DOMAIN <domain_definition>
                             | CREATE DATATYPE <domain_definition>
<domain_definition>        ::= <user_defined_data_type> [ AS ] <data_type>
                               [ <domain_property_list> ]
<user_defined_data_type> ::= <identifier>
<domain_property_list>     ::= <domain_property> { "," <domain_property> }
<domain_property>          ::= DEFAULT <default_value>
                             | IDENTITY
                             | NULL
                             | NOT NULL
                             | CHECK "(" <boolean_expression> ")"
```

User-defined data types are simply a shorthand notation for the full column definition. Ease of coding is the only real advantage, and there are several disadvantages. First of all, a user-defined data type cannot be dropped or changed without dropping all the references to it first. Second, a user-defined data type hides the true column definition from the application programmer, and that information is often important when writing applications. Third, constraint names cannot be used so it's hard to make the error messages meaningful.

Finally, except for the built-in base data type, all the properties of a user-defined data type can be overridden in the CREATE TABLE. Here is an example where the INSERT puts an empty string into address_2 and NULL into address_3 even though those values deviate from the CREATE DOMAIN definition:

```
CREATE DOMAIN address AS VARCHAR ( 100 )
                       NOT NULL
                       DEFAULT ''
                       CHECK ( LENGTH ( TRIM ( @col ) ) > 0 );

CREATE TABLE office (
   office_code INTEGER PRIMARY KEY,
   address_1   address,
   address_2   address CHECK ( address_2 IS NOT NULL ),
   address_3   address NULL DEFAULT ( NULL ) );

INSERT office ( office_code, address_1 ) VALUES ( 1, '123 Main Street' );
```

To refer to the current column name in a CREATE DOMAIN CHECK condition, use any identifier beginning with @. In the example above, @col is replaced with address_1, address_2, and address_3 when the CREATE TABLE is processed.

SQL Anywhere 9 provides several simple user-defined data types for compatibility with Microsoft SQL Server and Sybase Adaptive Server Enterprise. For example, DATETIME corresponds to the built-in type TIMESTAMP, and TEXT is defined as LONG VARCHAR.

```
<builtin_user_defined_data_type> ::= DATETIME
                                   | IMAGE
                                   | MONEY
                                   | OLDBIT
                                   | SMALLDATETIME
                                   | SMALLMONEY
                                   | SYSNAME
                                   | TEXT
                                   | UNIQUEIDENTIFIER
                                   | UNIQUEIDENTIFIERSTR
                                   | XML
```

Table 1-2 describes the built-in user-defined data types.

Table 1-2. Built-in user-defined data types

Data Type	Definition
DATETIME	TIMESTAMP
IMAGE	LONG BINARY
MONEY	NUMERIC (19, 4)

Data Type	Definition
OLDBIT	TINYINT
SMALLDATETIME	TIMESTAMP
SMALLMONEY	NUMERIC (10, 4)
SYSNAME	VARCHAR (30) NOT NULL
TEXT	LONG VARCHAR
UNIQUEIDENTIFIER	BINARY (16)
UNIQUEIDENTIFIERSTR	CHAR (36)
XML	LONG VARCHAR

1.12 Free Space

Currently there is only one CREATE TABLE element that classifies as a "table property": the PCTFREE free space percentage.

```
<table_element>  ::= <column_definition>
                  | <table_property>
                  | <table_constraint>
<table_property> ::= PCTFREE <free_percent>
<free_percent>   ::= integer literal in the range 0 to 100
```

By default SQL Anywhere will attempt to leave 100 bytes of free space in every page when inserting new rows into a database using a page size of 1K, and 200 bytes if the page size is larger than that. Free space allows rows to grow in size without being split into pieces stored on separate pages. Rows grow in size when columns become longer, and the internal fragmentation caused by too many row splits causes database I/O to slow down.

You can override the default free space amount by specifying a PCTFREE percentage in the range 0 to 100. Zero means you're not worried about fragmentation and it's okay for the server to fill up each page when inserting data. Use 100 if you want to force the server to insert each new row in a separate page; 100% free space is an impossible goal, as one row per page is as close as the server's going to get.

Large strings won't necessarily fill up a page, regardless of the free space setting. That's because the portion of a string past byte 254 is stored in one or more separate extension pages; see Section 10.6.2, "Table Fragmentation," for more information about long columns and extension pages.

Also, when a new row is inserted it will not be split if it would fit entirely on a single page, regardless of the free space setting.

1.13 Table Constraints

Table constraints can be used instead of column constraints to define the same things. Table constraints are exactly like column constraints with one major exception: A table constraint can apply to more than one column at the same time.

```
<table_constraint> ::= <table_check_constraint>
                     | <primary_key_table_constraint>
                     | <foreign_key_table_constraint>
                     | <unique_table_constraint>
```

1.13.1 Table CHECK Constraint

```
<table_check_constraint> ::= [ <constraint_prefix> ] CHECK
                             "(" <boolean_expression> ")"
```

Unlike a column CHECK constraint, a table CHECK constraint can refer to more than one column in the current row. Here is an example where all the columns must have ascending values:

```
CREATE TABLE t (
    c1 INTEGER,
    c2 INTEGER,
    c3 INTEGER,
    CONSTRAINT "0 < c1 < c2 < c3"
    CHECK ( 0 < c1 AND c1 < c2 AND c2 < c3 ) );

INSERT t VALUES ( 1, 2, 3 ); -- OK
INSERT t VALUES ( 2, 2, 2 ); -- fails
```

The second INSERT fails with this message: "Constraint '0 < c1 < c2 < c3' violated: Invalid value for column 'c2' in table 't'."

1.13.2 PRIMARY KEY Table Constraint

A PRIMARY KEY table constraint must include a list of one or more column names that make up the primary key. None of these columns can hold a NULL value, and their combined values must be unique for every row.

```
<primary_key_table_constraint> ::= [ <constraint_prefix> ] PRIMARY KEY
                                   [ <clustering> ]
                                   "(" <column_name_list> ")"
<column_name_list>             ::= <column_name> { "," <column_name> }
```

Primary keys consisting of more than one column are often called "composite primary keys." Here is an example of an audit trail table that can contain multiple copies of the same row from another table, with a date/time column ensuring that each copy has a unique primary key:

```
CREATE TABLE audit_office (
    copied        TIMESTAMP DEFAULT TIMESTAMP,
    office_code   VARCHAR ( 10 ),
    country_code  VARCHAR ( 2 ),
    PRIMARY KEY ( copied, office_code ) );
```

Tip: Use DEFAULT TIMESTAMP instead of DEFAULT CURRENT TIMESTAMP if you want different values assigned no matter how fast rows are inserted. The DEFAULT_TIMESTAMP_INCREMENT option ensures each value is at least 1 microsecond apart, but it applies only to DEFAULT TIMESTAMP, not DEFAULT CURRENT TIMESTAMP.

The unique index automatically created on the primary key columns may be defined as CLUSTERED or NONCLUSTERED, with NONCLUSTERED being the default. For more information about clustered indexes, see Section 10.7, "CREATE INDEX."

Tip: Always specify a PRIMARY KEY, or at least a UNIQUE constraint or non-NULL unique index. This keeps the transaction log small because the row can be uniquely identified by the key or index entry. Without this identification the entire row must be written to the transaction log for every change. This inflates the log file and slows down the server.

1.13.3 FOREIGN KEY Table Constraint

FOREIGN KEY table constraints have more options than the corresponding column constraint, but they also require more work because you must specify the list of column names that comprise the foreign key.

```
<foreign_key_table_constraint> ::= [ <constraint_or_prefix> ]
                                   [ NOT NULL ]
                                   FOREIGN KEY [ <role_name> ]
                                   "(" <column_name_list> ")"
                                   REFERENCES [ <owner_name> "." ] <table_name>
                                   [ "(" <column_name_list> ")" ]
                                   [ <on_action> ]
                                   [ CHECK ON COMMIT ]
                                   [ <clustering> ]

<constraint_or_prefix>      ::= CONSTRAINT
                              | CONSTRAINT <constraint_name>
                              | <constraint_name>
<role_name>                 ::= <identifier>
```

Here is an example of a three-level hierarchy where the primary and foreign keys grow in size with each level:

```
CREATE TABLE country (
   country_code  VARCHAR ( 2 ),
   name          VARCHAR ( 100 ),
   PRIMARY KEY ( country_code ) );

CREATE TABLE office (
   country_code VARCHAR ( 2 ),
   office_code   VARCHAR ( 10 ),
   address       VARCHAR ( 1000 ),
   PRIMARY KEY ( country_code, office_code ),
   FOREIGN KEY ( country_code ) REFERENCES country );

CREATE TABLE representative (
   country_code       VARCHAR ( 2 ),
   office_code        VARCHAR ( 10 ),
   representative_id INTEGER,
   name               VARCHAR ( 100 ),
   PRIMARY KEY ( country_code, office_code, representative_id ),
   FOREIGN KEY ( country_code, office_code ) REFERENCES office );
```

You can specify a constraint name in one of two places: as a leading name (with or without the CONSTRAINT keyword), or as a role name following the FOREIGN KEY keywords. Either way, this name will appear in any error messages so it's an opportunity for you to make the messages more meaningful.

The NOT NULL clause is a way of specifying that all the foreign key columns must be NOT NULL regardless of whether the individual columns are defined as NULL or NOT NULL.

The REFERENCES clause must specify the parent table name. The list of column names is optional; the default is the parent table primary key columns. If you want to reference a parent table UNIQUE constraint instead of the primary key, you must specify the column names from the UNIQUE constraint in the REFERENCES clause.

The ON UPDATE and ON DELETE clauses work as they do in a foreign key column constraint: They specify what action, if any, will be taken to silently repair constraint violations caused by update and delete operations performed on the corresponding parent row. RESTRICT is the default; it produces an error message and prevents the operation.

The CHECK ON COMMIT clause defers checking of this constraint until a COMMIT is executed. This feature bends Rule 12 of relational databases, which states "it must not be possible to bypass the integrity rules or constraints when manipulating the data." The FOREIGN KEY constraint isn't being bypassed altogether; its application is simply being postponed.

CHECK ON COMMIT can help when it is inconvenient to make changes in "the correct order," (i.e., insert parents first, delete parents last, and so on). An application can insert, delete, and update rows in any order it wants as long as the FOREIGN KEY constraint is not violated when the changes are complete and a COMMIT is issued.

The index automatically created on the foreign key columns may be defined as CLUSTERED or NONCLUSTERED, with NONCLUSTERED being the default. For more information about clustered indexes, see Section 10.7, "CREATE INDEX."

1.13.4 **UNIQUE Table Constraint**

```
<unique_table_constraint> ::= [ <constraint_prefix> ] UNIQUE
                              [ <clustering> ]
                              "(" <column_name_list> ")"
```

The UNIQUE table constraint is exactly the same as the UNIQUE column constraint, except that a list of one or more column names is required. If you specify two or more column names, it is the combination of column values that must be unique, not each separate column. Here is an example of three inserts that work and one that violates a UNIQUE constraint:

```
CREATE TABLE t (
  c1 INTEGER PRIMARY KEY,
  c2 INTEGER,
  c3 INTEGER,
  UNIQUE ( c2, c3 ) );

INSERT t VALUES ( 1, 1, 1 ); -- OK
INSERT t VALUES ( 2, 1, 2 ); -- OK
INSERT t VALUES ( 3, 2, 1 ); -- OK
INSERT t VALUES ( 4, 1, 1 ); -- fails
```

The unique index automatically created on the UNIQUE constraint columns may be defined as CLUSTERED or NONCLUSTERED, with NONCLUSTERED being the default. For more information about clustered indexes, see Section 10.7, "CREATE INDEX."

1.14 **Remote Data Access**

Remote tables exist in some location outside the current database. Examples include Oracle tables, text files, Excel spreadsheets, and tables in a different SQL Anywhere database. The schema and data are permanent.

Proxy tables provide indirect access to the data in remote tables. The schema for a proxy table resides in the local database but the data resides in the remote location. Each proxy table represents a single remote table, and schema for the proxy table is either identical to or closely resembles the schema for the remote table.

Tip: Proxy tables can also be defined on remote views. That's because the term "remote table" applies to anything that looks and feels like a table as far as the proxy table interface is concerned. Views fall into that category, and can be used to improve performance (by pushing query processing back to the remote server where the indexes live) and flexibility (by making use of syntax only supported on the remote server).

Note: Proxy tables are wonderful things but sometimes they don't perform very well. In fact, sometimes it might feel like they're running on a geological time scale, with the continents drifting apart faster than your query is running. And that's why improving the performance of a proxy table can be very important.

Proxy tables allow cross-database joins and updates because they can be referenced in SQL statements just like any other table. For example, this query joins employee and sales projection tables from two different remote databases to produce a result set in SQL Anywhere:

```
SELECT *
  FROM Oracle_employee
  JOIN DB2_sales_projection
    ON Oracle_employee.employee_id
     = DB2_sales_projection.employee_id;
```

Another popular use for proxy tables is to copy data to and from outside locations. Here is an example where the sales projection data is copied from a remote table, via the DB2_sales_projection proxy table, to the sales_projection permanent table:

```
INSERT sales_projection
SELECT *
  FROM DB2_sales_projection;
```

Access to remote tables via proxy tables is provided by special "middleware" software. This software used to be a separate product called OmniConnect but is now built into the SQL Anywhere database engine. When an application queries or updates a proxy table, this middleware takes care of passing the operation over to the remote location and returning the results as if the proxy table held the data itself.

It is possible to create a new remote table and its corresponding proxy table in one operation via the CREATE TABLE statement with the AT clause. It is also possible to define a proxy table that corresponds to a remote table that already exists. In both cases, however, it is necessary to tell the middleware how to find the remote table. That is the purpose of the CREATE SERVER and CREATE EXTERNLOGIN commands.

1.14.1 **CREATE SERVER**

The CREATE SERVER command defines a local name for the remote data server.

```
<create_server>        ::= CREATE SERVER <server_local_name>
                           CLASS <server_access_class>
                           USING <connection_string>
                           [ READ ONLY ]
<server_local_name>   ::= <identifier>
<server_access_class> ::= 'ASAJDBC'
                        | 'ASEJDBC'
                        | 'ASAODBC'
                        | 'ASEODBC'
                        | 'DB2ODBC'
                        | 'MSSODBC'
                        | 'ORAODBC'
                        | 'ODBC'
<connection_string>   ::= ODBC string literal containing Data Source Name
                        | UNIX ODBC string literal 'driver=file_spec;dsn=dsn_name'
                        | JDBC string literal 'machinename:portnumber[/dbname]'
```

The server access class specifies the access mechanism (ODBC versus JDBC) and in some cases the server type; currently the list includes ASA, ASE, DB2, Oracle, and Microsoft SQL Server. Use 'ODBC' for a server type that isn't explicitly named in the list (e.g., use 'ODBC' for Excel and text files).

The connection string specifies the exact location of the remote server, either via an ODBC Data Source Name or a JDBC machine, port, and database name string.

The READ ONLY clause prevents you from making any changes to the data on this server.

Tip: The CREATE SERVER and CREATE EXTERNLOGIN commands don't actually connect to the remote database. You won't find out if the connection works until you try to create or use a proxy table.

1.14.2 **CREATE EXTERNLOGIN**

The CREATE EXTERNLOGIN statement is optional for some remote data, such as text files, but it is required for remote servers that control access such as SQL Anywhere and Oracle.

CREATE EXTERNLOGIN names a local user ID that will be used to manipulate remote and proxy tables via a server named in the CREATE SERVER command. A remote user ID can be provided, together with a remote password, so that the middleware can make a connection to the remote server.

```
<create_external_login>  ::= CREATE EXTERNLOGIN <local_user_id>
                             TO <server_local_name>
                             [ REMOTE LOGIN <remote_user_id>
                               [ IDENTIFIED BY <remote_password> ] ]
<local_user_id>         ::= <identifier>
<remote_user_id>        ::= <identifier>
<remote_password>       ::= <identifier> -- to be used as a password
                          | non-empty string literal containing a password
```

1.14.3 **CREATE Remote and Proxy Tables**

The CREATE TABLE ... AT command creates both the remote and proxy tables at the same time. You must specify a list of column definitions and other properties just like with a global permanent table, with the exception that this list will also be sent to the remote server to create a table there. You must also provide a string literal pointing to the remote server and specifying the table name on that server.

```
<create_remote_and_proxy_table> ::= CREATE TABLE [ <owner_name> "." ] <table_name>
                                    <table_element_list>
                                    AT <remote_location>
<remote_location>    ::= literal 'server_local_name;[db_name];[owner];object_name'
```

The remote location string consists of four components separated by semicolons or periods, with semicolons necessary when the components themselves contain periods. The first component is always the local name for the remote server as defined by the CREATE SERVER command, and the last component is always the table, view, or object name on that server. The other two components depend on the remote server. For example, with Excel the second component is the file specification, the third component is omitted, and the last component is the sheet name. With DB2, SQL Anywhere, and most other relational databases, the second, third, and fourth components are database name, owner name, and table or view name respectively. Oracle is an exception where the database name is omitted.

Here is an example that creates a new Excel spreadsheet called test1 inside a workbook asaexcel.xls. A row is inserted and retrieved through a proxy table called etest. Note that CREATE EXTERNLOGIN is not required.

```
CREATE SERVER ASAEXCEL CLASS 'ODBC' USING 'EXCEL SAMPLE';

CREATE TABLE etest
  ( pkey INTEGER NOT NULL,
    fld1 VARCHAR ( 20 ) NOT NULL,
    fld2 INTEGER NOT NULL )
  AT 'ASAEXCEL;c:\\temp\\asaexcel.xls;;test1';

INSERT INTO etest VALUES ( 1, 'Hello, World', 9 );

SELECT * FROM etest;
```

Tip: When creating an Excel ODBC DSN to use with proxy tables, you must specify a dummy workbook file specification with the ODBC Administrator "Select Workbook..." button. This file specification is ignored by CREATE TABLE, and the one specified in the remote location string is used instead.

Tip: Most remote servers have to be running before you can create a proxy table, but that's not true of Excel.

1.14.4 **CREATE EXISTING TABLE**

The CREATE EXISTING TABLE command retrieves the definition of an existing table on the remote database and uses that definition to create a proxy table.

```
<create_proxy_table> ::= CREATE EXISTING TABLE [ <owner_name> "." ] <table_name>
                         [ <proxy_column_list> ]
```

```
                                AT <remote_location>
<proxy_column_list>  ::= "(" <proxy_column> { "," <proxy_column> } ")"
<proxy_column>       ::= <column_name> <data_type> [ [ NOT ] NULL ]
```

In most cases CREATE EXISTING TABLE is used without a column list to create a proxy table with exactly the same layout as the remote table. Here is an example where an Oracle table, SCOTT.DEPT, is made available through a proxy table called ora_dept:

```
CREATE SERVER ORASAMPLE CLASS 'ORAODBC' USING 'ORA SAMPLE';

CREATE EXTERNLOGIN DBA TO ORASAMPLE
  REMOTE LOGIN system IDENTIFIED BY 'manager';

CREATE EXISTING TABLE ora_dept AT 'ORASAMPLE..SCOTT.DEPT';

SELECT * FROM ora_dept;
```

Here's a DB2 example where the remote table, ADMINISTRATOR.DEPARTMENT, is queried through the proxy table, db2_department:

```
CREATE SERVER DB2DELL180 CLASS 'DB2ODBC' USING 'DB2 SAMPLE';

CREATE EXTERNLOGIN DBA TO DB2DELL180
  REMOTE LOGIN db2admin IDENTIFIED BY 'secret';

CREATE EXISTING TABLE db2_department
  AT 'DB2DELL180.SAMPLE.ADMINISTRATOR.DEPARTMENT';

SELECT * FROM db2_department;
```

It is possible to provide an explicit list of column names, data types, and NULL/NOT NULL properties. You can use this list of column names to omit columns, rearrange the order of the columns, and fiddle with the data types. These changes do not affect the remote table, just the layout of the corresponding proxy table. You cannot change the column names because that's how columns are matched up between the remote and proxy tables. Here is an example that creates another proxy table called etest2 based on the same Excel spreadsheet created earlier; note that etest2 has a different layout than etest but the INSERT still works:

```
CREATE EXISTING TABLE etest2
  ( pkey NUMERIC ( 10 ) NOT NULL,
    fld1 VARCHAR ( 100 ) NOT NULL )
  AT 'ASAEXCEL;c:\\temp\\asaexcel.xls;;test1';

INSERT INTO etest2 VALUES ( 2, 'A value that is longer than 20 characters.' );

SELECT * FROM etest2;
```

Here is a full, end-to-end example using two SQL Anywhere 9 databases. The first database is the remote database and the second database contains the proxy tables. On the first database a global permanent table t1 is created:

```
CREATE TABLE t1 (
  pkey INTEGER NOT NULL,
  c1   VARCHAR ( 20 ) NOT NULL,
```

```
    PRIMARY KEY ( pkey ) );

INSERT INTO t1 VALUES ( 1, 'Hello, World' );
COMMIT;
```

On the second database the following commands create the server, external
login, and two proxy tables. The first proxy table t1proxy points to the existing
table t1, and the second proxy table t2proxy causes a new table t2 to be created
on the remote database:

```
CREATE SERVER other CLASS 'ASAODBC' USING 'otherdsn';

CREATE EXTERNLOGIN DBA TO other
  REMOTE LOGIN DBA IDENTIFIED BY "SQL";

CREATE EXISTING TABLE t1proxy AT 'other;otherdb;dba;t1';

SELECT * FROM t1proxy; -- displays 'Hello, World'

CREATE TABLE t2proxy (
   pkey INTEGER NOT NULL,
   c1   VARCHAR ( 20 ) NOT NULL,
   PRIMARY KEY ( pkey ) )
   AT 'other;otherdb;dba;t2';

INSERT INTO t2proxy VALUES ( 1, 'Goodbye' );

SELECT * FROM t2proxy; -- displays 'Goodbye'
```

1.15 Temporary Tables

Temporary tables are different from permanent tables in terms of the location
and life span of the data. A permanent table's data is stored in the database file
and it lasts until it is explicitly deleted. The data in a temporary table is never
stored in the actual database file, and it never lasts longer than the connection
that inserted it in the first place. The server keeps temporary table data in memory, and if there isn't room in memory the server will use a special "temporary
file" that is separate from the database file. The server only creates one temporary file per database, and it gets deleted when the server is shut down.

Temporary tables are very useful in complex applications. They allow programs to load and process raw input data before storing it in permanent tables.
They also permit a "divide and conquer" approach to writing huge queries; temporary tables can be loaded with parts of an original query and then combined in
a final, simpler query. Sometimes the optimizer can do a better job with several
smaller queries, with the overall execution being much faster.

A temporary table is often used in a stored procedure that returns a result
set. The procedure can use a cursor loop or whatever other complex techniques
are required to load the temporary table, then it executes SELECT * FROM on
that table to return a simple result set. This approach can be used to transform
non-relational data from external sources into relational data for further
processing.

Tip: In SQL Anywhere 9 you can call a procedure in the SELECT FROM clause. This means you can treat a procedure call just like a table, and join it to other tables.

1.15.1 Global Temporary Tables

The global temporary table is the only kind of temporary table where the schema is permanently recorded in the system catalog tables. The schema persists until the table is explicitly dropped, and the table is available to all connections. The data, however, is partitioned separately for each connection, as if each connection owned its own copy of the table.

Like global permanent tables, global temporary tables are created ahead of time and then used by whatever connections need them. Like local temporary tables, the data inserted by one connection is invisible to all other connections.

```
<create_global_temporary_table> ::= CREATE GLOBAL TEMPORARY TABLE
                                     [ <owner_name> "." ] <table_name>
                                     <table_element_list>
                                     [ <commit_action> ]
<table_name>                     ::= <identifier>
<commit_action>                  ::= ON COMMIT DELETE ROWS
                                   | ON COMMIT PRESERVE ROWS
                                   | NOT TRANSACTIONAL
```

It doesn't matter if the table name begins with a number sign or not; a global temporary table is created either way.

A global temporary table can have the same list of table elements as a global permanent table: one or more column definitions plus any table constraints and properties that might apply.

The commit action controls what happens to the data when a COMMIT or ROLLBACK is executed. ON COMMIT DELETE ROWS means that all the data will be deleted when a COMMIT is executed, that changes will be rolled back when a ROLLBACK is executed, and that otherwise the data persists until explicitly deleted or the connection is dropped. This is the default behavior, and often comes as a surprise during testing: "Where did all my data go? All I did was commit!"

ON COMMIT PRESERVE ROWS means that a COMMIT will commit the changes instead of deleting all the data. This is useful during long processes where commits are frequently done to free locks. Here is an example that shows that COMMIT and ROLLBACK behave normally with ON COMMIT PRESERVE ROWS; only the second row shows up in the SELECT:

```
CREATE GLOBAL TEMPORARY TABLE t (
   c1 INTEGER )
   ON COMMIT PRESERVE ROWS;

INSERT t VALUES ( 1 ); -- gets rolled back
ROLLBACK;
INSERT t VALUES ( 2 ); -- gets committed
COMMIT;
INSERT t VALUES ( 3 ); -- gets rolled back
ROLLBACK;
SELECT * FROM t;       -- only shows row # 2
```

Tip: Use ON COMMIT PRESERVE ROWS when using a global temporary table
to pass data between MobiLink scripts executing on the upload and download
sides of a synchronization. That's because MobiLink issues a COMMIT between
upload and download. But don't forget to delete the old data when a new synchronization begins because MobiLink can reuse the same connection for
different synchronizations.

NOT TRANSACTIONAL means that COMMIT and ROLLBACK commands
will have no effect on the data. There is no automatic deletion on COMMIT; in
fact, there is no concept of commit or rollback, and the data persists until explicitly deleted or the connection is dropped. This example shows how rows are
unaffected by ROLLBACK and COMMIT; both inserted rows show up in the
SELECT:

```
CREATE GLOBAL TEMPORARY TABLE t (
   c1 INTEGER )
   NOT TRANSACTIONAL;

INSERT t VALUES ( 1 );
ROLLBACK;            -- has no effect
INSERT t VALUES ( 2 );
COMMIT;              -- has no effect
SELECT * FROM t;     -- shows both rows
```

Tip: When using a temporary table in a long-running cursor loop, use both
ON COMMIT PRESERVE ROWS on the CREATE and WITH HOLD on the cursor
OPEN. That way, you can execute a COMMIT during the loop without losing the
rows or having the cursor close. The NOT TRANSACTIONAL clause is even better
if you're not planning to restart the loop after a failure but just run it again from
the beginning.

1.15.2 Local Temporary Tables

Local temporary tables don't show up in the system catalog; both the schema
and data are visible only to the connection that created the table and inserted the
data. Neither the schema nor the data lasts longer than the current connection,
and sometimes they disappear even sooner.

Local temporary tables are created three ways: by CREATE TABLE specifying a table name beginning with #, by DECLARE LOCAL TEMPORARY
TABLE, and by a SELECT statement with an INTO clause specifying a # table
name.

1.15.2.1 CREATE TABLE #table_name

```
<create_local_temporary_table> ::= CREATE TABLE <temporary_table_name>
                                       <table_element_list>
<temporary_table_name>         ::= "#" { ( <alphabetic> | <numeric> ) }
```

With this format the table name must begin with a number sign (#) to inform
SQL Anywhere that this is a local temporary table rather than a global permanent table.

Unlike CREATE GLOBAL TEMPORARY TABLE, there is no commit
action clause. The default behavior is the same as ON COMMIT PRESERVE
ROWS; i.e., COMMIT and ROLLBACK behave as expected, to commit and

roll back changes, and there is no automatic deletion of rows on commit. Here is an example:

```
CREATE TABLE #t ( c1 INTEGER );

INSERT #t VALUES ( 1 ); -- gets rolled back
ROLLBACK;
INSERT #t VALUES ( 2 ); -- gets committed
COMMIT;
INSERT #t VALUES ( 3 ); -- gets rolled back
ROLLBACK;
SELECT * FROM #t;        -- only shows row 2
```

If a CREATE TABLE #table_name is executed inside a stored procedure or other compound statement using a BEGIN block, it will get automatically dropped when that compound statement ends. If it is executed all by itself, outside any compound statement, the table and its data will persist until it is explicitly deleted or dropped or the connection ends.

Temporary table names have nested scope. That means once you CREATE a table with the same #table_name inside a compound statement, then only that nested table will be visible until the compound statement ends. After that, the nested table is dropped and the outer table becomes visible again.

Here is an example that shows how the same SELECT can produce different results inside and outside the scope of a nested table; note that the CREATE TABLE can appear anywhere inside the compound statement, but once it has been executed the outer table is no longer visible.

```
CREATE TABLE #t ( c1 INTEGER );
INSERT #t VALUES ( 1 );
SELECT * FROM #t; -- displays 1

BEGIN
   SELECT * FROM #t; -- still displays 1
   CREATE TABLE #t ( c1 INTEGER );
   INSERT #t VALUES ( 2 );
   SELECT * FROM #t; -- now displays 2
END;

SELECT * FROM #t; -- displays 1 again
```

This form of CREATE TABLE doesn't cause an automatic COMMIT as a side effect. That means it's safe to create this kind of table inside a transaction and it won't disrupt the commit-versus-rollback logic.

Tip: Local temporary tables aren't just for stored procedures. You can create and use them from client-side application code; for example, PowerBuilder's EXECUTE IMMEDIATE can be used to create a temporary table that you can then reference in a DataWindow SELECT.

1.15.2.2 DECLARE LOCAL TEMPORARY TABLE

```
<declare_local_temporary_table> ::= DECLARE LOCAL TEMPORARY TABLE <table_name>
                                    <table_element_list>
                                    [ <commit_action> ]
<table_name>                     ::= <identifier>
```

With this format it doesn't matter if the table name begins with a number sign or not; a local temporary table is created either way.

You can use DECLARE LOCAL TEMPORARY TABLE inside a proce-
dure or other compound statement, but if you do it has to go at the top with the
other DECLARE statements. The table name has nested scope: Only the inner
table will be visible until the compound statement ends, even if it has the same
name as a global permanent, global temporary, or another local temporary table
created outside the compound statement.

Here is an example showing how a local temporary table name overrides a
permanent table inside a BEGIN/END block:

```
CREATE TABLE t ( c1 INTEGER ); -- permanent table
INSERT t VALUES ( 1 );
SELECT * FROM t;    -- displays 1


BEGIN
   DECLARE LOCAL TEMPORARY TABLE t ( c1 INTEGER );
   INSERT t VALUES ( 2 );
   SELECT * FROM t; -- displays 2
END;

SELECT * FROM t;    -- displays 1 again
```

The commit action clause works like it does for CREATE GLOBAL
TEMPORARY TABLE. ON COMMIT DELETE ROWS is the default, ON
COMMIT PRESERVE ROWS turns off the automatic deletion when a commit
is executed, and NOT TRANSACTIONAL causes commit and rollback commands to ignore rows in this table.

Tip: Use NOT TRANSACTIONAL whenever you can, if you're interested in
performance. Temporary table changes are never recorded in the transaction
log, but they are recorded in the rollback log unless you specify NOT
TRANSACTIONAL. Performance may improve if you can eliminate the use of the
rollback log for temporary tables.

You can use DECLARE LOCAL TEMPORARY TABLE just like an executable
statement outside a compound statement. When you do that, the new table overrides any global permanent or global temporary table with the same name. Here
is an example that shows how DECLARE LOCAL TEMPORARY TABLE
overrides a global temporary table until the new table is explicitly dropped:

```
CREATE GLOBAL TEMPORARY TABLE t ( c1 INTEGER );
INSERT t VALUES ( 1 );
SELECT * FROM t; -- displays 1

DECLARE LOCAL TEMPORARY TABLE t ( c1 INTEGER );
INSERT t VALUES ( 2 );
SELECT * FROM t; -- displays 2

DROP TABLE t;    -- drops the temporary table
SELECT * FROM t; -- displays 1 again
```

The same thing happens with a global permanent table of the same name, which
means you can temporarily redefine an existing table as a temporary one.

DECLARE LOCAL TEMPORARY TABLE doesn't cause an automatic
COMMIT as a side effect, so it's safe to use inside a transaction.

1.15.2.3 **SELECT INTO #table_name**

```
<select_into_local_temporary_table> ::= SELECT              -- also see <select>
                                         [ <summarizer> ] --   in Chapter 3
                                         [ <row_range> ]
                                         <select_list>
                                         INTO <temporary_table_name>
                                         [ <from_clause> ]
                                         [ <where_clause> ]
                                         [ <group_by_clause> ]
                                         [ <having_clause> ]
<temporary_table_name>                ::= "#" { ( <alphabetic> | <numeric> ) }
```

With this format the table name must begin with a number sign (#) to inform SQL Anywhere that it is a table name rather than a variable name appearing in the INTO clause.

The SELECT INTO #table_name method is very powerful — not only does it create the table but it loads it with data at the same time. Here's how it works: The temporary table column names and data types are taken from the select list, and the rows are filled by executing the SELECT. This means the columns in the select list must actually have names; in the case of an expression you can use "AS identifier" to give it a name. For more information about the SELECT statement, see Chapter 3, "Selecting."

Here is an example where an exact copy of table t is made in the temporary table #t; it has the same column names, same data types, and same rows of data:

```
CREATE TABLE t ( -- permanent table
   c1 INTEGER,
   c2 VARCHAR ( 10 ),
   c3 TIMESTAMP );

INSERT t VALUES ( 1, 'AAA', CURRENT TIMESTAMP );
INSERT t VALUES ( 2, 'BBB', CURRENT TIMESTAMP );

SELECT * INTO #t FROM t; -- temporary copy
```

Tip: If you want to know what the data type of a column actually is, code it in a SELECT and call the EXPRTYPE function. For example, SELECT EXPRTYPE ('SELECT * FROM #t', 2) shows that the second column of #t is 'varchar(10)'.

Tables created with SELECT INTO #table_name have nested scope just like the ones created with CREATE TABLE #table_name. They are also safe to use inside a transaction because SELECT INTO #table_name doesn't cause an automatic COMMIT as a side effect.

Tip: The INSERT #t SELECT * FROM t command can be used to add more rows to a table that was created with SELECT INTO #t, without having to list the column names in either command. For more information about the INSERT statement, see Chapter 2, "Inserting."

1.16 **Normalized Design**

Normalization is the refinement of a database design to eliminate useless redundancy in order to reduce effort and the chances of error. Redundant data increases effort by making it necessary to change the same data in multiple locations. Errors occur and inconsistencies creep into the data when that extra effort is not taken.

Redundancy can be useful if it increases safety and reliability. For example, a check digit is redundant because it can be derived from other data, but it is useful because it catches input errors. Most redundant data, however, gets that way by accident, and it serves no useful purpose.

Each step in normalization changes one table into two or more tables with foreign key relationships among them. The process is defined in terms of "normal forms," which are guidelines for achieving higher and higher levels of refinement. There are six normal forms, numbered one through five, plus an intermediate level called Boyce-Codd Normal Form, which falls between numbers three and four.

It's not important to identify each normal form as the normalization progresses; it's just important to remove redundancies and prevent inconsistencies in the data. The normal forms are presented here because they identify different problems that are commonly encountered and the changes they require.

Here is a table that violates the first three normal forms; it represents a simple paper-based order form with a unique order number plus information about the client, salesperson, and products ordered:

```
CREATE TABLE order_form (
    order_number              INTEGER NOT NULL PRIMARY KEY,
    client_name               VARCHAR ( 100 ) NOT NULL,
    shipping_address          VARCHAR ( 1000 ) NOT NULL,
    salesperson_name          VARCHAR ( 100 ) NOT NULL,
    salesperson_phone         VARCHAR ( 100 ) NOT NULL,
    salesperson_commission    NUMERIC ( 6, 3 ) NOT NULL,
    product_number_1          INTEGER NOT NULL,
    product_description_1     VARCHAR ( 100 ) NOT NULL,
    requested_quantity_1      INTEGER NOT NULL,
    estimated_shipping_date_1 DATE NOT NULL,
    product_number_2          INTEGER NULL,
    product_description_2     VARCHAR ( 100 ) NULL,
    requested_quantity_2      INTEGER NULL,
    estimated_shipping_date_2 DATE NULL,
    product_number_3          INTEGER NULL,
    product_description_3     VARCHAR ( 100 ) NULL,
    requested_quantity_3      INTEGER NULL,
    estimated_shipping_date_3 DATE NULL );
```

1.16.1 First Normal Form

First Normal Form (1NF) eliminates rows with a variable number of columns, and all repeating columns and groups of columns. Relational databases don't allow variable numbers of columns, but it is possible to have different columns holding the same kind of data. The order_form table has three such groups of data, each containing product number and description, order quantity, and shipping date. This violates First Normal Form.

Repeating columns cause several problems: First, it is difficult to increase the maximum number of entries without changing the schema. Second, it is difficult to write application code to process multiple entries because they all have different column names. Finally, it is difficult to determine how many entries are actually filled in without defining a separate counter column or storing a special value; in this example NULL is used to indicate missing data.

The solution is to split order_form into order_header and order_detail with the repeating columns moved down into order_detail. The order_number column in order_detail is a foreign key pointing to the order_header table; this makes order_detail a repeating child of order_header. The product_number column is part of the primary key to identify different detail rows that are part of the same order.

```
CREATE TABLE order_header (
    order_number            INTEGER NOT NULL PRIMARY KEY,
    client_name             VARCHAR ( 100 ) NOT NULL,
    shipping_address        VARCHAR ( 1000 ) NOT NULL,
    salesperson_name        VARCHAR ( 100 ) NOT NULL,
    salesperson_phone       VARCHAR ( 100 ) NOT NULL,
    salesperson_commission  NUMERIC ( 6, 3 ) NOT NULL );

CREATE TABLE order_detail (
    order_number            INTEGER NOT NULL REFERENCES order_header,
    product_number          INTEGER NOT NULL,
    product_description     VARCHAR ( 100 ) NOT NULL,
    requested_quantity      INTEGER NOT NULL,
    estimated_shipping_date DATE NOT NULL,
    PRIMARY KEY ( order_number, product_number ) );
```

The number of order_detail rows in a single order is now truly variable with no artificial maximum. Each order_detail row can be processed like any other in an application program loop, and the number of rows can be easily counted.

1.16.2 Second Normal Form

Second Normal Form (2NF) eliminates any non-key column that only depends on part of the primary key instead of the whole key. The order_detail table has a two-column primary key (order_number and product_number), but the product_description column only depends on product_number. This violates Second Normal Form.

One problem here is redundancy: If a product description changes, it must be changed in every order_detail row containing that value. Another problem is there's no place to store a new product number and description until that product is ordered.

The solution is to move product_description up into a new table, product_catalog, which holds information about products separate from orders. The order_detail table becomes product_order, and the product_number column becomes a foreign key pointing to the new product_catalog table.

```
CREATE TABLE order_header (
    order_number            INTEGER NOT NULL PRIMARY KEY,
    client_name             VARCHAR ( 100 ) NOT NULL,
    shipping_address        VARCHAR ( 1000 ) NOT NULL,
    salesperson_name        VARCHAR ( 100 ) NOT NULL,
    salesperson_phone       VARCHAR ( 100 ) NOT NULL,
    salesperson_commission  NUMERIC ( 6, 3 ) NOT NULL );

CREATE TABLE product_catalog (
    product_number          INTEGER NOT NULL PRIMARY KEY,
    product_description     VARCHAR ( 100 ) NOT NULL );

CREATE TABLE product_order (
    order_number            INTEGER NOT NULL REFERENCES order_header,
```

```
    product_number          INTEGER NOT NULL REFERENCES product_catalog,
    requested_quantity      INTEGER NOT NULL,
    estimated_shipping_date DATE NOT NULL,
    PRIMARY KEY ( order_number, product_number ) );
```

Redundancy is eliminated because the product_description for each different product is stored exactly once. Plus, there is now a place to store product information before the first order is received and after the last order has been deleted.

1.16.3 Third Normal Form

Third Normal Form (3NF) eliminates any non-key column that does not depend on the primary key. In the order table the salesperson_phone column depends on salesperson_name, which is not part of the primary key. This violates Third Normal Form.

The problems are the same as with Second Normal Form. First, there is redundancy: If a salesperson's phone number changes, it must be changed in every order row containing that value. Second, there is no place to store information about a new salesperson until that person gets an order.

The solution is to move the salesperson columns up into a new table, salesperson, with the new salesperson_id column as the primary key. The order table becomes sales_order, with a salesperson_id column added as a foreign key pointing to the new salesperson table.

```
CREATE TABLE salesperson (
    salesperson_id          INTEGER NOT NULL PRIMARY KEY,
    name                    VARCHAR ( 100 ) NOT NULL,
    phone                   VARCHAR ( 100 ) NOT NULL );

CREATE TABLE sales_order (
    order_number            INTEGER NOT NULL PRIMARY KEY,
    client_name             VARCHAR ( 100 ) NOT NULL,
    shipping_address        VARCHAR ( 1000 ) NOT NULL,
    salesperson_id          INTEGER NOT NULL REFERENCES salesperson,
    salesperson_commission  NUMERIC ( 6, 3 ) NOT NULL );

CREATE TABLE product_catalog (
    product_number          INTEGER NOT NULL PRIMARY KEY,
    product_description     VARCHAR ( 100 ) NOT NULL );

CREATE TABLE product_order (
    order_number            INTEGER NOT NULL REFERENCES sales_order,
    product_number          INTEGER NOT NULL REFERENCES product_catalog,
    requested_quantity      INTEGER NOT NULL,
    estimated_shipping_date DATE NOT NULL,
    PRIMARY KEY ( order_number, product_number ) );
```

Redundancy is eliminated because information about each salesperson is stored exactly once. Also, there is now a place to store salesperson information before the first order is received and after the last order has been deleted.

Normalization depends on the business rules governing the data. It is not always possible to normalize a design by simply looking at the schema. For example, if each salesperson receives a fixed commission for all sales, the salesperson_commission column should also be moved to the salesperson table. In this example, however, salesperson_commission remains in the sales_order table because the commission can change from order to order.

Normalization isn't always obvious or clear-cut; mistakes are possible, and it's important not to get carried away. For example, the client_name column may also be a candidate for its own table, especially if other client-related columns are added, such as phone number, billing address, and so on. The shipping_address column may not be one of those columns, however. It may be more closely related to the order than the client, especially if one client has more than one shipping address, or if an order can be shipped to a third party.

1.16.4 Boyce-Codd Normal Form

Boyce-Codd Normal Form (BCNF) eliminates any dependent column that does not depend on a candidate key. A candidate key is one or more columns that uniquely identify rows in the table. A table may have more than one candidate key, only one of which may be chosen as the primary key.

BCNF is slightly stronger than 3NF. BCNF refers to "any dependent column" whereas 3NF talks about "any non-key column." Another difference is that BCNF refers to candidate keys, not just primary keys.

In the following example, salesperson_skill identifies which skills are possessed by which salespersons. Both salesperson_id and salesperson_name are unique for all salespersons. That means salesperson_name, together with sales_skill_id, forms a candidate key for salesperson_skill; this is shown as a UNIQUE constraint separate from the PRIMARY KEY.

```
CREATE TABLE sales_skill (
   sales_skill_id          INTEGER NOT NULL PRIMARY KEY,
   description             LONG VARCHAR );

CREATE TABLE salesperson_skill (
   salesperson_id          INTEGER NOT NULL,
   salesperson_name        VARCHAR ( 100 ) NOT NULL,
   sales_skill_id          INTEGER NULL REFERENCES sales_skill,
   PRIMARY KEY ( salesperson_id, sales_skill_id ),
   UNIQUE ( salesperson_name, sales_skill_id ) );
```

The salesperson_skill table is in Third Normal Form because there are no columns that violate the rule that non-key columns must depend on the primary key, simply because there are no non-key columns at all; every column in salesperson_skill is part of one or the other candidate keys.

However, salesperson_skill is not in Boyce-Codd Normal Form because salesperson_name depends on salesperson_id, and vice versa, and neither one of those columns forms a candidate key all by itself. The solution is to move one of the offending columns, either salesperson_id or salesperson_name, to the salesperson table.

```
CREATE TABLE salesperson (
   salesperson_id          INTEGER NOT NULL PRIMARY KEY,
   salesperson_name        VARCHAR ( 100 ) NOT NULL UNIQUE );

CREATE TABLE sales_skill (
   sales_skill_id          INTEGER NOT NULL PRIMARY KEY,
   description             LONG VARCHAR );
```

```
CREATE TABLE salesperson_skill (
    salesperson_id          INTEGER NOT NULL REFERENCES salesperson,
    sales_skill_id          INTEGER NULL REFERENCES sales_skill,
    PRIMARY KEY ( salesperson_id, sales_skill_id ) );
```

In practice it's hard to tell the difference between Third Normal Form and Boyce-Codd Normal Form. If you transform a table into Third Normal Form, the chances are good that it will also be in Boyce-Codd Normal Form because you removed all the redundancies, regardless of the subtle differences in the definitions.

In fact, chances are your Third Normal Form database design will also be in Fourth and Fifth Normal Form. The next two sections discuss the rare situations where Fourth and Fifth Normal Forms differ from Third.

1.16.5 Fourth Normal Form

Fourth Normal Form (4NF) eliminates multiple independent many-to-many relationships in the same table. In the following example the salesperson_skill table represents two many-to-many relationships. First, there is a relationship where one salesperson may have many sales skills, and conversely, one sales skill can be shared by multiple salespersons. Second, there is a many-to-many relationship between salesperson and technical skill. These two relationships are independent; a salesperson's technical and sales skills do not depend on one another, at least as far as this design is concerned.

```
CREATE TABLE salesperson (
    salesperson_id          INTEGER NOT NULL PRIMARY KEY,
    salesperson_name        VARCHAR ( 100 ) NOT NULL );

CREATE TABLE sales_skill (
    sales_skill_id          INTEGER NOT NULL PRIMARY KEY,
    description             LONG VARCHAR );

CREATE TABLE technical_skill (
    technical_skill_id      INTEGER NOT NULL PRIMARY KEY,
    description             LONG VARCHAR );

CREATE TABLE salesperson_skill (
    salesperson_id          INTEGER NOT NULL REFERENCES salesperson,
    sales_skill_id          INTEGER NOT NULL REFERENCES sales_skill,
    technical_skill_id      INTEGER NOT NULL REFERENCES technical_skill,
    PRIMARY KEY ( salesperson_id, sales_skill_id, technical_skill_id ) );
```

It is not clear how the rows in salesperson_skill should be filled when a salesperson has different numbers of sales and technical skills. Should special "blank" values be used for the missing skills, should disjointed rows be filled with either sales or technical skills but not both, or should a cross product of all combinations of sales and technical skills be constructed? All these alternatives have problems with redundancy or complex rules for updating, or both.

The solution is to replace salesperson_skill with two separate tables, as follows:

```
CREATE TABLE salesperson_sales_skill (
    salesperson_id          INTEGER NOT NULL REFERENCES salesperson,
    sales_skill_id          INTEGER NOT NULL REFERENCES sales_skill,
    PRIMARY KEY ( salesperson_id, sales_skill_id ) );
```

```
CREATE TABLE salesperson_technical_skill (
   salesperson_id              INTEGER NOT NULL REFERENCES salesperson,
   technical_skill_id          INTEGER NOT NULL REFERENCES technical_skill,
   PRIMARY KEY ( salesperson_id, technical_skill_id ) );
```

These tables are in Fourth Normal Form because different many-to-many relationships are represented by different tables.

1.16.6 Fifth Normal Form

Fifth Normal Form (5NF) splits one table into three or more if the new tables have smaller primary keys, less redundancy, and can be joined to reconstruct the original. This differs from the other normal forms, which divide one table into two.

Here is an example where salesperson_company_line contains information about which company's product lines are handled by which salesperson. The following special business rule applies: If a salesperson handles a product line, and a company makes that product line, then that salesperson handles that product line made by that company. This is a three-way relationship where the individual many-to-many relationships are not independent, so salesperson_company_line is in Fourth Normal Form.

```
CREATE TABLE salesperson (
   salesperson_id              INTEGER NOT NULL PRIMARY KEY,
   salesperson_name            VARCHAR ( 100 ) NOT NULL );

CREATE TABLE company (
   company_id                  VARCHAR ( 10 ) NOT NULL PRIMARY KEY,
   company_name                VARCHAR ( 100 ) NOT NULL );

CREATE TABLE product_line (
   product_line_id             VARCHAR ( 10 ) NOT NULL PRIMARY KEY,
   product_line_description    VARCHAR ( 100 ) NOT NULL );

CREATE TABLE salesperson_company_line (
   salesperson_id              INTEGER NOT NULL REFERENCES salesperson,
   company_id                  VARCHAR ( 10 ) NOT NULL REFERENCES company,
   product_line_id             VARCHAR ( 10 ) NOT NULL REFERENCES product_line,
   PRIMARY KEY ( salesperson_id, company_id, product_line_id ) );
```

Not only does salesperson_company_line require redundant values to be stored, it is possible to violate the special business rule with these rows:

```
INSERT salesperson_company_line VALUES ( 1, 'Acme', 'cars' );
INSERT salesperson_company_line VALUES ( 2, 'Acme', 'trucks' );
INSERT salesperson_company_line VALUES ( 2, 'Best', 'cars' );
```

The first row, for salesperson 1, proves that Acme makes cars. The second row indicates that salesperson 2 also handles Acme, albeit for trucks. The third row shows salesperson 2 does handle cars, this time for Best. Where is the row that shows salesperson 2 handles cars for Acme?

The salesperson_company_line table is not in Fifth Normal Form because it can (and probably should) be split into the following three tables:

```
CREATE TABLE salesperson_company (
   salesperson_id              INTEGER NOT NULL REFERENCES salesperson,
   company_id                  VARCHAR ( 10 ) NOT NULL REFERENCES company,
   PRIMARY KEY ( salesperson_id, company_id ) );
```

```
CREATE TABLE company_line (
    company_id              VARCHAR ( 10 ) NOT NULL REFERENCES company,
    product_line_id         VARCHAR ( 10 ) NOT NULL REFERENCES product_line,
    PRIMARY KEY ( company_id, product_line_id ) );

CREATE TABLE salesperson_line (
    salesperson_id          INTEGER NOT NULL REFERENCES salesperson,
    product_line_id         VARCHAR ( 10 ) NOT NULL REFERENCES product_line,
    PRIMARY KEY ( salesperson_id, product_line_id ) );
```

Here is how the three new tables can be filled, with a SELECT to rebuild the original table including the row showing that yes, salesperson 2 does in fact handle cars for Acme:

```
INSERT salesperson_company VALUES ( 1, 'Acme' );
INSERT salesperson_company VALUES ( 2, 'Acme' );
INSERT salesperson_company VALUES ( 2, 'Best' );
INSERT company_line VALUES ( 'Acme', 'cars' );
INSERT company_line VALUES ( 'Acme', 'trucks' );
INSERT company_line VALUES ( 'Best', 'cars' );
INSERT salesperson_line VALUES ( 1, 'cars' );
INSERT salesperson_line VALUES ( 2, 'cars' );
INSERT salesperson_line VALUES ( 2, 'trucks' );

SELECT DISTINCT
       salesperson_company.salesperson_id,
       company_line.company_id,
       salesperson_line.product_line_id
  FROM salesperson_company
  JOIN company_line
    ON salesperson_company.company_id = company_line.company_id
  JOIN salesperson_line
    ON salesperson_company.salesperson_id = salesperson_line.salesperson_id
   AND company_line.product_line_id = salesperson_line.product_line_id;
```

Tables requiring a separate effort to reach Fifth Normal Form are extremely rare. In this example, if the special business rule was not in effect the original salesperson_company_line table would be the correct choice because it implements a three-way many-to-many relationship among salesperson, company, and product line... and it would already be in Fifth Normal Form. In most cases, once you've reached Third Normal Form, you've reached Boyce-Codd, Fourth, and Fifth Normal Forms as well.

1.17 Chapter Summary

This chapter described how to create the five different types of tables in SQL Anywhere 9: global permanent, remote, proxy, global temporary, and local temporary. Also discussed were the basic column data types; column properties like COMPUTE and DEFAULT; and column and table constraints such as CHECK, PRIMARY KEY, foreign key, and UNIQUE. The 12 rules for relational databases and the six normal forms of good database design were explained.

The next chapter moves on to the second step in the life cycle of a database: inserting rows.

Inserting

2.1 Introduction

The second step in the life cycle of a relational database, after creating the tables, is to populate those tables with data. SQL Anywhere offers three distinct techniques: the INSERT, LOAD TABLE, and ISQL INPUT statements.

The INSERT statement comes in two flavors, depending on whether you want to explicitly provide VALUES for each column, one row per INSERT, or to copy an entire set of rows into a table from some other source with a single INSERT, where the "other source" is anything a SELECT can produce.

Those two flavors of INSERT are broken down further in this chapter, into five separate formats depending on whether values are provided for some or all of the target table's columns and whether the AUTO NAME feature is used.

LOAD TABLE and ISQL INPUT provide two different ways to insert data into a table from an external file.

Each of these techniques offer interesting features discussed in this chapter. For example, the ON EXISTING UPDATE clause lets you turn an INSERT into an UPDATE when primary keys collide, LOAD TABLE takes dramatic short-cuts to offer better performance, and the ISQL INPUT statement can be used to load fixed-layout records and other file formats from legacy sources.

2.2 INSERT

The INSERT statement comes in five different formats, discussed in the next five sections:

- INSERT a single row using a VALUES list for all the columns.
- INSERT a single row using a column name list and matching VALUES list.
- INSERT multiple rows using a SELECT to retrieve values for all the columns.
- INSERT multiple rows using a column name list and a matching SELECT.
- INSERT multiple rows using the WITH AUTO NAME clause instead of a column name list.

2.2.1 INSERT All Values

The simplest form of the INSERT statement is the one where you specify values for each and every column in a single row.

```
<insert_all_values> ::= INSERT [ INTO ]
                        [ <owner_name> "." ] <target_table_name>
                        [ <on_existing> ]
                        VALUES "(" <all_values_list> ")"
<owner_name>        ::= <identifier>
<target_table_name> ::= <identifier>
<identifier>        ::= see <identifier> in Chapter 1, "Creating"
<on_existing>       ::= ON EXISTING ERROR  -- default
                      | ON EXISTING UPDATE
                      | ON EXISTING SKIP
<all_values_list>   ::= <value_list> -- for all the columns in the table
<value_list>        ::= <value> { "," <value> }
<value>             ::= <expression>
                      | DEFAULT
<expression>        ::= see <expression> in Chapter 3, "Selecting"
```

Note: You can insert rows into a view if that view qualifies as an updatable view and it involves only one table. For more information about updatable views, see Section 3.23, "CREATE VIEW."

The expressions in the VALUES list must appear in the same order as the columns to which they apply appear in the CREATE TABLE. Also, you must specify a value for every single column in the table.

Note: The ALTER TABLE command can be used to append columns to an existing table. These new columns are placed after all the columns that were originally defined in the CREATE TABLE, and any other columns that were appended by previous ALTER TABLE commands. When you see a mention of "the order of columns in the CREATE TABLE" it should be interpreted as shorthand for "the order of columns as listed in the original CREATE TABLE and appended by subsequent ALTER TABLE commands." The various ALTER commands are very powerful and useful but for reasons of space they aren't discussed in this book.

In the following example the value 1 is placed in key_1, 'first row' goes in non_key_1, and '2003 09 29 13:21' is placed in last_updated:

```
CREATE TABLE t1 (
   key_1        INTEGER NOT NULL DEFAULT AUTOINCREMENT,
   non_key_1    VARCHAR ( 100 ) NOT NULL,
   last_updated TIMESTAMP NOT NULL DEFAULT TIMESTAMP,
   PRIMARY KEY ( key_1 ) );

INSERT t1 VALUES ( 1, 'first row', '2003 09 29 13:21' );
```

Tip: To see the order of columns in a table called t1, run this command in ISQL: SELECT * FROM t1 WHERE 1 = 0. It will display the column names without retrieving any data. Don't worry about performance — this query will always run quickly no matter how big the table is because the database engine knows that WHERE 1 = 0 means no rows will ever be returned.

The VALUES list supports a special keyword, DEFAULT, which can be used in place of an explicit value when you want the DEFAULT value to be used. In the following example the DEFAULT AUTOINCREMENT value 2 is generated for key_1, 'second row' goes into non_key_1, and the DEFAULT TIMESTAMP current date and time is placed in last_updated:

```
INSERT t1 VALUES ( DEFAULT, 'second row', DEFAULT );
```

The DEFAULT keyword cannot be used for the second column in this particular table because it has been declared as NOT NULL without an explicit DEFAULT value in the CREATE TABLE. The default DEFAULT is NULL, and that won't work because this column can't contain a NULL. And that means INSERT t1 VALUES (DEFAULT, DEFAULT, DEFAULT) will fail with the error "Integrity constraint violation: Column 'non_key_1' in table 't1' cannot be NULL."

Tip: Special literals such as CURRENT TIMESTAMP and CURRENT TIME may be used in the INSERT VALUES list, even in an INSERT coming from a client application; the SQL Anywhere database engine will fill in the actual values when the row is inserted. For more information about special literals, see Section 1.8.3, "Literal Defaults."

The three ON EXISTING clauses allow you to specify what happens when a row with the same primary key value already exists in the table. This implies the table must have an explicit PRIMARY KEY; otherwise you can't use the ON EXISTING clause at all, not even if a UNIQUE constraint has been substituted for a PRIMARY KEY.

The default is ON EXISTING ERROR, which will produce the familiar "Primary key for table 't1' is not unique" error and reject the insert.

The ON EXISTING SKIP clause will cause the INSERT to be ignored rather than raise an error; that is useful if you are inserting rows that overlap and you simply wish to ignore duplicates. The ON EXISTING UPDATE clause will turn the INSERT into an UPDATE rather than raise an error; that is handy if you are inserting overlapping rows and you want to overwrite old values with new ones.

In the following example all three INSERT statements work without error even though they all specify the same primary key value; only one row exists when they finish, the row with 'replaced' in the non_key_1 column.

```
CREATE TABLE t1 (
   key_1         INTEGER NOT NULL DEFAULT AUTOINCREMENT,
   non_key_1     VARCHAR ( 100 ) NOT NULL,
   last_updated  TIMESTAMP NOT NULL DEFAULT TIMESTAMP,
   PRIMARY KEY ( key_1 ) );

INSERT t1 VALUES ( 1, 'first row', DEFAULT );
INSERT t1 ON EXISTING UPDATE VALUES ( 1, 'replaced', DEFAULT );
INSERT t1 ON EXISTING SKIP  VALUES ( 1, 'ignored', DEFAULT );
```

The ON EXISTING clauses can be used in all the forms of the INSERT statement described in this chapter. They are also mentioned in Section 7.6.4.5, "Handling Upload Errors," as one way to avoid primary key collisions in uploaded data.

2.2.2 INSERT Named Values

If you want to use a VALUES list but don't want to list every single value, or you want to rearrange the order of the values, you can add a column name list to the INSERT.

```
<insert_named_values> ::= INSERT [ INTO ]
                   [ <owner_name> "." ] <target_table_name>
                   "(" <column_name_list> ")"
                   [ <on_existing> ]
                   VALUES "(" <named_values_list> ")"
<column_name_list>   ::= <column_name> { "," <column_name> }
<column_name>        ::= <identifier>
<named_values_list>  ::= <value_list> -- for the named columns
```

When you use this kind of INSERT, the expressions in the VALUES list are applied to the columns in the order they are specified in the column name list, and the number of values must match the number of column names. Missing columns are assigned their default values.

Note: All columns have default values whether or not you code explicit DEFAULT clauses when creating the tables; the default DEFAULT is NULL.

Here is an example where 'A' is placed in col_2 and 'B' in col_3, out of order, and all the other columns are assigned their default values:

```
CREATE TABLE t1 (
  key_1        INTEGER NOT NULL DEFAULT AUTOINCREMENT,
  col_2        VARCHAR ( 100 ) NOT NULL DEFAULT 'X',
  col_3        VARCHAR ( 100 ) NOT NULL DEFAULT 'Y',
  updated_by   VARCHAR ( 128 ) NOT NULL DEFAULT LAST USER,
  last_updated TIMESTAMP NOT NULL DEFAULT TIMESTAMP,
  PRIMARY KEY ( key_1 ) );

INSERT t1 ( col_3, col_2 ) VALUES ( 'B', 'A' );
```

In the CREATE TABLE above, every single column has a DEFAULT value. That means the following insert will work just fine, and you can execute it over and over again without error:

```
INSERT t1 ( key_1 ) VALUES ( DEFAULT );
```

However, that's as easy as it gets; you cannot write INSERT t1() VALUES().

Tip: If you have a feature you'd like to see in SQL Anywhere, don't be afraid to make the suggestion. That's how ON EXISTING got added to the INSERT statement — a request was posted in the public newsgroup called sybase.public.sqlanywhere.product_futures_discussion, which is located on the NNTP server at forums.sybase.com. You can post to this newsgroup with NNTP client software like Forte Agent, or use your web browser to go to www.ianywhere.com/developer and click on Newsgroups. Not every suggestion is implemented, but every suggestion is taken seriously by the folks responsible for product development.

2.2.3 INSERT Select All Columns

If you want to insert data into a table by copying data that already exists somewhere else, you can use a select instead of a VALUES list. The simplest form uses a select that provides values for every column in the table.

```
<insert_select_all_columns> ::= INSERT [ INTO ]
                                   [ <owner_name> "." ] <target_table_name>
                                   [ <on_existing> ]
                                   <select_all_columns>
<select_all_columns> ::= <select> -- values for all the columns in the target table
<select>             ::= see <select> in Chapter 3, "Selecting"
```

INSERT statements using a select have two main advantages over ones that use a VALUES list. First, you can insert more than one row with a single INSERT. Second, you can insert data without specifying explicit values.

Here is an example where all the rows and columns in t1 are copied into t2:

```
CREATE TABLE t1 (
    key_1        INTEGER NOT NULL DEFAULT AUTOINCREMENT,
    non_key_1    VARCHAR ( 100 ) NOT NULL DEFAULT 'xxx',
    last_updated TIMESTAMP NOT NULL DEFAULT TIMESTAMP,
    PRIMARY KEY ( key_1 ) );

CREATE TABLE t2 (
    key_1        INTEGER NOT NULL DEFAULT AUTOINCREMENT,
    non_key_1    VARCHAR ( 100 ) NOT NULL DEFAULT 'xxx',
    last_updated TIMESTAMP NOT NULL DEFAULT TIMESTAMP,
    PRIMARY KEY ( key_1 ) );

INSERT t2
SELECT key_1, non_key_1, last_updated
  FROM t1;
```

Since the two tables above have exactly the same number of columns in the same order, the INSERT could be even simpler:

```
INSERT t2 SELECT * FROM t1;
```

Tip: This form of INSERT is very popular for loading data from external sources via proxy tables (e.g., INSERT local_table SELECT * FROM proxy_table). For more information about proxy tables, see Section 1.14, "Remote Data Access."

Here's the rule you must follow: The select must return the same number of columns as exist in the target table, with the same or compatible data types in the same order as they exist in the CREATE TABLE for the target table. In other words, if the result set fits, it will be inserted.

As long as you follow that rule you can use all of the sophisticated features described in Chapter 3, "Selecting," when coding an INSERT. Here's an example that uses a UNION to add two more rows to the ones selected from t1:

```
INSERT t2
SELECT 0, 'first', '2001-01-01'
UNION
SELECT * FROM t1
  WHERE key_1 BETWEEN 1 AND 9998
UNION
SELECT 9999, 'last', CURRENT TIMESTAMP;
```

Note: A select can be more than just a SELECT. What that means is the word "select" in lowercase is used in this book to refer to a query that returns a result set. Every query or select involves at least one "SELECT" keyword, written in uppercase in this book. However, a select may involve more than one SELECT, as shown in the example above. For more information about queries, see Chapter 3, "Selecting."

The result set from the SELECT in an INSERT statement is completely materialized before any rows are inserted. If the target table itself is named in any clauses of the SELECT, only those rows that already exist in the table will affect the result set produced by the SELECT. The example below illustrates the point. The final INSERT statement copies values from t2.non_key_1 into t1.key_1, and the WHERE clause specifies that only values that don't already exist are to be selected. This is an attempt to prevent any duplicate values from being inserted into t1.key_1. It works okay for the value 1 because it already exists in t1.key_1, but not for the value 2 because it doesn't exist in t1.key_1 before the INSERT is started, and the statement fails with the error "Primary key for table 't1' is not unique" because there are two rows in t2 with the value 2.

```
CREATE TABLE t1 (
   key_1    INTEGER NOT NULL PRIMARY KEY );

INSERT t1 VALUES ( 1 );

CREATE TABLE t2 (
   key_1    VARCHAR ( 10 ) NOT NULL PRIMARY KEY,
   non_key_1 INTEGER NOT NULL );

INSERT t2 VALUES ( 'A', 1 );
INSERT t2 VALUES ( 'B', 2 );
INSERT t2 VALUES ( 'C', 2 );

INSERT t1
SELECT t2.non_key_1
   FROM t2
 WHERE NOT EXISTS ( SELECT *
                      FROM t1
                     WHERE t1.key_1 = t2.non_key_1 );
```

2.2.4 **INSERT Select Column List**

If you want to use a select but don't want to list every single column, or you want to rearrange the order of the columns, you can specify a column name list in the INSERT.

```
<insert_select_column_list> ::= INSERT [ INTO ]
                                  [ <owner_name> "." ] <target_table_name>
                                  "(" <column_name_list> ")"
                                  [ <on_existing> ]
                                  <select_column_list>
<select_column_list>        ::= <select> -- values for the specified columns
```

When you use this kind of INSERT, the values returned by the select are applied to the columns in the order they are specified in the column name list. The select must return the same number of columns, with the same or compatible data types, in the same order as they appear in the column name list.

Data may be copied between tables even if they have different schema.
Here is an example where t1.key_1 is converted to VARCHAR and placed in
t2.col_3, t1.non_key_1 is copied into t2.col_2, and all the other columns of t2
are assigned their default values:

```
CREATE TABLE t1 (
   key_1        INTEGER NOT NULL,
   non_key_1    VARCHAR ( 100 ) NOT NULL,
   PRIMARY KEY ( key_1 ) );

CREATE TABLE t2 (
   key_col      INTEGER NOT NULL DEFAULT AUTOINCREMENT,
   col_2        VARCHAR ( 100 ) NOT NULL,
   col_3        VARCHAR ( 100 ) NOT NULL,
   updated_by   VARCHAR ( 128 ) NOT NULL DEFAULT LAST USER,
   last_updated TIMESTAMP NOT NULL DEFAULT TIMESTAMP,
   PRIMARY KEY ( key_col ) );

INSERT t2 ( col_3, col_2 )
SELECT key_1, non_key_1
   FROM t1;
```

Tip: Watch out for problems caused by implicit data conversions when values
are inserted into columns with different data types. Long strings may be silently
truncated when inserted into columns with short maximum lengths. Also, there
are problems with precision when converting between NUMERIC and FLOAT
data types, and with data types when expressions involving values of different
types are computed and the results inserted. For example, the expression 1 +
32767 will be stored as –32768 when inserted into a SMALLINT column.

2.2.5 INSERT Select With Auto Name

The WITH AUTO NAME clause lets you omit the column name list from the
INSERT while still using a select that omits some columns or specifies columns
in a different order. Columns in the target table are automatically matched up,
by name, with the values returned by the select. This means each value returned
by the select must have a name, either a column name or an alias name, and that
name must match a column name in the target table.

```
<insert_select_auto_name> ::= INSERT [ INTO ]
                              [ <owner_name> "." ] <target_table_name>
                              [ <on_existing> ]
                              WITH AUTO NAME
                              <select_auto_name>
<select_auto_name> ::= <select> -- with names or aliases to match target columns
```

The following example shows how values are specified for col_2, col_3, and
col_4 in t2 by using alias names in the SELECT:

```
CREATE TABLE t1 (
   key_1        INTEGER NOT NULL,
   non_key_1    VARCHAR ( 100 ) NOT NULL,
   PRIMARY KEY ( key_1 ) );

CREATE TABLE t2 (
   key_col      INTEGER NOT NULL DEFAULT AUTOINCREMENT,
   col_2        VARCHAR ( 100 ) NOT NULL,
   col_3        VARCHAR ( 100 ) NOT NULL,
   col_4        VARCHAR ( 100 ) NOT NULL,
```

```
                  PRIMARY KEY ( key_col ) );

INSERT t2 WITH AUTO NAME
SELECT key_1           AS col_3,
       non_key_1       AS col_2,
       CURRENT TIMESTAMP AS col_4
  FROM t1
 WHERE key_1 > 1;
```

The WITH AUTO NAME clause isn't just for copying data between tables; it can also be used as a self-documenting substitute for the VALUES list. For example, some people don't like to use the following form of INSERT because it's hard to tell which value is going into which column, and you are forced to specify all the column values:

```
INSERT t1 VALUES ( DEFAULT, 'aaa', 1, 'bbb', 2 );
```

This next alternative solves one of the problems by letting you omit columns where the default should be used, but for very large tables it's still hard to tell which value is going where:

```
INSERT t1 ( non_key_1,
            non_key_2,
            non_key_3,
            non_key_4 )
   VALUES ( 'aaa',
            1,
            'bbb',
            2 );
```

The WITH AUTO NAME clause solves the remaining problem by letting you code the target column names side by side with the corresponding values:

```
INSERT t1 WITH AUTO NAME
SELECT 'aaa' AS non_key_1,
       1     AS non_key_2,
       'bbb' AS non_key_3,
       2     AS non_key_4;
```

2.3 LOAD TABLE

The LOAD TABLE statement is a highly efficient way to copy data from a flat file into a database table.

```
<load_table>      ::= LOAD [ INTO ] TABLE
                         [ <owner_name> "." ] <target_table_name>
                         [ "(" <input_name_list> ")" ]
                         FROM <load_filespec>
                         [ <load_option_list> ]
<input_name_list> ::= <input_name> { "," <input_name> }
<input_name>      ::= <column_name> -- in the target table
                    | "filler()"    -- to ignore an input field
<load_filespec>   ::= string literal file specification relative to the server
<load_option_list> ::= <load_option> { <load_option> }
<load_option>     ::= CHECK CONSTRAINTS ( ON | OFF )   -- default ON
                    | COMPUTES ( ON | OFF )            -- default ON
                    | DEFAULTS ( ON | OFF )            -- default OFF
                    | DELIMITED BY <load_delimiter>    -- default ','
                    | ESCAPE CHARACTER <escape_character> -- default '\'
                    | ESCAPES ( ON | OFF )             -- default ON
                    | FORMAT ( ASCII | BCP )           -- default ASCII
                    | HEXADECIMAL ( ON | OFF )         -- default ON
```

```
                  | ORDER ( ON | OFF )              -- default ON
                  | PCTFREE <free_percent>
                  | QUOTES ( ON | OFF )             -- default ON
                  | STRIP ( ON | OFF )              -- default ON
                  | WITH CHECKPOINT ( ON | OFF )    -- default OFF
<load_delimiter>    ::= string literal 1 to 255 characters in length
<escape_character> ::= string literal exactly 1 character in length
<free_percent>      ::= integer literal in the range 0 to 100
```

The target table name is required but the input name list is optional. If the input name list is omitted, the layout of the input file is assumed to match the layout of the table (i.e., there are the same number of input fields as there are columns in the table, and they are arranged left to right in each input record in the same order as the columns appear in the CREATE TABLE).

The default input file format is comma-delimited ASCII text with each line representing a separate row. Here is an example of a simple LOAD TABLE statement; note that the file specification uses a pair of backslashes to represent each single backslash so there won't be any problems with how the escape character (\) is interpreted:

```
CREATE TABLE t1 (
    key_1       INTEGER NOT NULL,
    col_2       VARCHAR ( 100 ) NULL,
    col_3       DECIMAL ( 11, 2 ) NULL,
    col_4       TIMESTAMP NULL,
    col_5       INTEGER NOT NULL,
    PRIMARY KEY ( key_1 ) );

LOAD TABLE t1 FROM 'c:\\temp\\t1_a.txt';
```

Here are the four lines of data contained in the t1_a.txt file:

```
1,'Hello, World',67.89,2003-09-30 02:15PM,999
2,   stripped string without quotes    , 0 , , 0
3,,,,
4,"   double quoted padded string   ",0,2003 9 30,-111
```

Here's what the four rows in t1 look like after the LOAD TABLE has run:

key_1	col_2	col_3	col_4	col_5
1	'Hello, World'	67.89	2003-09-30 14:15:00.000	999
2	'stripped string without quotes'	0.00	NULL	0
3	NULL	NULL	NULL	0
4	' double quoted padded string '	0.00	2003-09-30 00:00:00.000	-111

The input name list can be used for three purposes: to change the order in which input fields are applied to table columns, to skip columns for which there is no corresponding input field, and to skip input fields that are not to be copied into any column.

- To change the order, code the column names in the order in which the corresponding input fields actually appear in the file.
- To skip a column in the table, leave its name out of the list.
- To skip an input field, use "filler()" in its position in the input name list.

Here is an example of a LOAD TABLE using an explicit input name list; the second input field is ignored, the third, fourth, and fifth input fields are applied to col_4, col_3, and col_2 respectively, and no input field is provided for col_5:

```
CREATE TABLE t1 (
  key_1       INTEGER NOT NULL,
  col_2       INTEGER NOT NULL,
  col_3       TIMESTAMP NULL,
  col_4       DECIMAL ( 11, 2 ) NULL,
  col_5       VARCHAR ( 100 ) NULL,
  PRIMARY KEY ( key_1 ) );
```

```
LOAD TABLE t1 ( key_1, filler(), col_4, col_3, col_2 ) FROM 'c:\\temp\\t1_b.txt';
```

If the input file contains this record:

```
1, 'Hello, World', 67.89, 2003-09-30 02:15PM, 999
```

then the row inserted into t1 will look like this:

```
key_1 col_2 col_3                         col_4 col_5
===== ===== ========================= ===== =====
1     999   '2003-09-30 14:15:00.000'  67.89 NULL
```

The LOAD TABLE input file specification is relative to the server, not the client. More specifically, the drive and path is relative to the current folder when the SQL Anywhere database engine was started. This becomes a challenge when you're running LOAD TABLE from ISQL on a desktop but the database server is located somewhere else on the network. Even though you might enter the LOAD TABLE statement on the same computer that holds the input file, it is executed on the server, and it is the database server that goes looking for the file, not ISQL.

The Universal Naming Convention (UNC) for network files can be used with LOAD TABLE. Here is the layout of a UNC file specification:

```
\\<server-name>\<share-name>\<directory/filename>
```

For example, if the file C:\temp\t1_c.txt is sitting on a machine called TECRA, and the C: drive is shared as "TecraC," then the following LOAD TABLE can be used to reach out across the network and read the file as \\TECRA\TecraC\temp\t1_c.txt. Once again, each single backslash (\) is represented as two backslashes in the file specification:

```
LOAD TABLE t1 FROM '\\\\TECRA\\TecraC\\temp\\t1_c.txt';
```

If that's where the file resides, relative to the computer running the database engine, that's how you have to code the file specification; it doesn't matter on which machine ISQL is running.

Tip: Watch out for operating system permissions when specifying a file specification in LOAD TABLE. For example, if the database engine is run as a Windows service it may or may not have sufficient privileges to read the file.

The LOAD TABLE input file specification must be a string literal, not a variable. If you want to use a variable, run LOAD TABLE via EXECUTE IMMEDIATE. The following example puts the file specification in a variable called @filespec and then builds the LOAD TABLE command in another variable called @sql before running it via EXECUTE IMMEDIATE. This time, sadly, each single backslash in \\TECRA\TecraC\temp\t1_c.txt must be represented as four backslashes.

```
BEGIN
DECLARE @filespec VARCHAR ( 1000 );
```

```
DECLARE @sql      VARCHAR ( 1000 );
SET @filespec = '\\\\\\\\TECRA\\\\TecraC\\\\temp\\\\t1_c.txt';
SET @sql = STRING ( 'LOAD TABLE t1 FROM ''', @filespec, '''' );
EXECUTE IMMEDIATE @sql;
END;
```

The escape character (\) is processed each time a string is parsed. In the example above, each pair of backslashes (\\) is reduced to a single \ as part of that processing, and it happens twice — once when the SET @filespec parses the string literal, and once when EXECUTE IMMEDIATE parses the command in @sql. That means each \ you want to survive until the LOAD TABLE actually runs must be represented by four backslashes in the original string literal, and for a pair of backslashes to survive, you must code them as eight.

The way LOAD TABLE works is controlled by an extensive list of options, as follows:

- **CHECK CONSTRAINTS OFF** disables CHECK constraints while LOAD TABLE inserts new rows. The default is ON, to check the CHECK constraints.

- **COMPUTES OFF** disables the calculation of computed column values and accepts the input values. The default is ON, to ignore the input values and calculate the values instead.

- **DEFAULTS ON** enables the setting of DEFAULT values for columns that are not being filled from the input file. The default is OFF, to disable column DEFAULT values; the effect of this is described later in this section.

- **DELIMITED BY** can be used to change the field delimiter; for example, DELIMITED BY '\x09' specifies that the input file is tab-delimited. The default is the comma (,).

- **ESCAPE CHARACTER** can be used to specify which single character will be interpreted as the escape character in string literals in the input file (e.g., ESCAPE CHARACTER '!'). The default is the backslash (\). Note that this option affects how the input data is processed; it doesn't have anything to do with the way escape characters in the input file specification are handled.

- **ESCAPES OFF** can be used to turn off escape character processing altogether so that all characters will be treated as data. The default is ON, to process escape characters. Once again, this option refers to the data in the file, not the file specification in the LOAD TABLE statement.

- **FORMAT BCP** specifies that the special Adaptive Server Enterprise Bulk Copy Program (bcp.exe) file format is being used by the input file. The default is FORMAT ASCII for ordinary text files. This book doesn't discuss the details of FORMAT BCP.

- **HEXADECIMAL OFF** turns off the interpretation of 0xnnn-style input values as unquoted binary string literals; the input characters will be stored as they appear. The default is ON, to interpret 0xnnn-style values as strings of hexadecimal characters to be converted into strings. For example, 0x414243 will be stored as "0x414243" if HEXADECIMAL is OFF and as "ABC" if HEXADECIMAL is ON. This affects both binary and character columns.

- **ORDER OFF** suppresses the sorting of the input file when a table with a clustered index is being loaded. This will speed up LOAD TABLE if the input is already sorted by the clustered index column values. The default is ON, to sort the input if there is a clustered index defined.

- **PCTFREE** specifies the amount of free space to be left in each page as LOAD TABLE inserts rows. The amount is expressed as a percentage in the range 0 to 100; it overrides the PCTFREE value specified in the CREATE TABLE, if any, but only for the duration of the LOAD TABLE statement. For more information about PCTFREE, see Section 1.12, "Free Space."

- **QUOTES OFF** specifies that all string input values are to be treated as unquoted, regardless of whether or not they are actually surrounded by quotes; in other words, quotes are stored as part of the data no matter where they appear. It also specifies that leading spaces will not be removed from unquoted input strings, except for blank input fields, which are always treated as empty strings. The default behavior, QUOTES ON, is to remove the quotes surrounding quoted input values; the details are described later in this section.

- **STRIP OFF** specifies that trailing spaces in unquoted string input values will not be removed. The default is ON, to strip trailing quotes from unquoted string values. Quoted string values are not affected by either setting. Note that leading spaces are affected by the QUOTES option, not STRIP.

- **WITH CHECKPOINT ON** specifies that a checkpoint operation will be automatically carried out when the LOAD TABLE finishes. This guarantees that all the new rows are written to the physical database file; that may be important to you because LOAD TABLE doesn't write the new rows to the transaction log. The default is OFF, don't bother taking a checkpoint.

Tip: Be careful coding the DELIMITED BY option. Pretty much any string value will be accepted, including 'x09' which is an x followed by a zero and a nine. If you want the tab character, don't forget the escape character: DELIMITED BY '\x09'.

The rules for handling missing input values are fairly complex, and difficult to explain clearly in plain English, so here's a bit of pseudocode to describe how a single value for a single column is handled:

```
IF this column has been omitted from an explicit LOAD TABLE input name list
OR the field on this input record corresponding to this column is empty
THEN
   IF this column has no DEFAULT value in the CREATE TABLE
   OR the LOAD TABLE DEFAULTS option is OFF
   THEN
      IF this column accepts NULL values
      THEN
         The NULL value will be used.
      ELSE
         An attempt will be made to convert the empty string '' to the column's
         data type and use that value; this process will assign zero to numeric and
         BIT columns, and the empty string to character and binary columns, but it
         will fail with an error message for DATE, TIME, and TIMESTAMP columns.
```

```
ELSE
    The column's DEFAULT value will be used.
ELSE
    The input field value corresponding to this column will be used.
```

The rules for handling quoted input strings are also complex. Here are some points to consider when preparing a LOAD TABLE input file for use with QUOTES ON; these comments apply to each line of input:

- Quotes, and QUOTES ON, are necessary if the delimiter character appears as part of an input string value.

- Leading spaces before a leading quote are discarded. If there is no leading quote, leading spaces before the first non-blank character are discarded.

- The first non-blank character determines whether the input value is treated as quoted or unquoted.

- If the first non-blank character is not a quote, the value is treated as unquoted, and all the remaining characters up to but not including the next delimiter are stored as they appear. Note that it doesn't matter that QUOTES is ON, you can still use unquoted input values.

- If the first non-blank character is a single or double quote, the value is treated as quoted. The remaining rules only apply to quoted values.

- The type of the opening quote, single or double, determines the type of closing quote.

- Embedded quotes of the other type are treated as part of the data (e.g., "Fred's not here" is a valid input value).

- Pairs of embedded quotes of the same type are reduced to one quote and treated as part of the data (e.g., 'Fred''s not here' is stored as Fred's not here).

- A quote of the same type that follows the opening quote, but isn't part of a pair, is treated as the closing quote.

- Characters following the closing quote, up to but not including the next delimiter, are discarded. That's what happens when you forget to double an embedded quote of the same type (e.g., 'Fred's not here' is stored as 'Fred' because the embedded quote is treated as the closing quote).

- If no closing quote is found, all the data up to the end of the record is treated as part of the data in this input field.

Here is an example of how LOAD TABLE options may be used for a special purpose: to load free-form text into a table. The raw_text table consists of a line_number column used to preserve the original ordering of the input file and a line_text column to receive each line of input, as is, without any reformatting or processing:

```
CREATE TABLE raw_text (
    line_number        BIGINT NOT NULL DEFAULT AUTOINCREMENT,
    line_text          LONG VARCHAR NOT NULL DEFAULT '',
    PRIMARY KEY ( line_number ) );

LOAD TABLE raw_text ( line_text )
    FROM 'c:\\temp\\test.txt'
    DEFAULTS ON
    DELIMITED BY ''
    ESCAPES OFF
```

```
QUOTES OFF
STRIP OFF;
```

The LOAD TABLE statement above uses the input value list (line_text) to specify that the input file only contains data for the line_text column, not the line_number column. The DEFAULTS ON option is used so the DEFAULT AUTOINCREMENT feature will work to generate line_number values; by default, the LOAD TABLE command does not fill in DEFAULT values. The DELIMITED BY " option specifies nothing should be treated as a field delimiter, and ESCAPES OFF says there's no need to look for escape characters either. QUOTES OFF tells LOAD TABLE to treat leading quotes as part of the data and to preserve leading spaces. STRIP OFF tells LOAD TABLE to preserve trailing spaces.

Here is a sample input file designed to demonstrate some of the challenges involved in getting LOAD TABLE to store the text without reformatting it:

```
This is a flat text file, containing free-form text with embedded
commas, 'single quotes', and "double quotes". Even lines with
'leading and trailing quotes will be stored as is.'
It will be stored in the line_text column as is, line-by-line, with
one line per row. Empty lines

will be ignored, but blank lines consisting of at least one space

will be stored. Trailing blanks will be stored,
    and so will leading blanks.
Backslash characters \, \\, \\\, \\\\, etc., will be stored as is.
```

Here is what the raw_text table looks like when you run SELECT * FROM raw_text ORDER BY line_number in ISQL. It shows that the empty line after line 5 was ignored, but the line consisting of one space was stored as row 7. Also, it shows that the trailing spaces were stored in row 8 as well as the leading spaces in row 9.

```
#  line_text
=  =========
1  'This is a flat text file, containing free-form text with embedded'
2  'commas, ''single quotes'', and "double quotes". Even lines with'
3  '''leading and trailing quotes will be stored as is.'''
4  'It will be stored in the line_text column as is, line-by-line, with '
5  'one line per row. Empty lines'
6  'will be ignored, but blank lines consisting of at least one space '
7  ' '
8  'will be stored. Trailing blanks will be stored,                    '
9  '     and so will leading blanks.'
10 'Backslash characters \\, \\\\, \\\\\\, \\\\\\\\, etc., will be stored as is.'
```

LOAD TABLE is fast because it takes three shortcuts. First of all, it does not fire any insert triggers. This doesn't mean that LOAD TABLE bypasses foreign key checking; on the contrary, if you attempt to load a row that violates a referential integrity constraint, the LOAD TABLE statement will fail. But if you have critical application logic in an insert trigger, it won't get executed, and you may want to use another method to load data.

The second shortcut is that LOAD TABLE does not acquire locks on the individual inserted rows but instead places an exclusive lock on the entire table. This has implications for concurrency; if you run LOAD TABLE on a table that's frequently updated by other users, two bad things might happen: The

LOAD TABLE statement might sit and wait before starting to run because it can't get the exclusive lock, and once it starts running other users might be blocked until LOAD TABLE finishes. LOAD TABLE doesn't do commits along the way, just one commit if it works or a rollback if it fails.

The third shortcut is that LOAD TABLE does not write the individual inserted rows to the transaction log file, just a record of the LOAD TABLE command itself. This means that LOAD TABLE should not be used on a table that is being uploaded via MobiLink if you want the inserted rows to be included in the upload stream. MobiLink determines which rows to upload by examining the transaction log, and rows inserted via LOAD TABLE will be missed. (For more information about MobiLink, see Chapter 7, "Synchronizing.")

The third shortcut also has implications for recovery using the transaction log if WITH CHECKPOINT isn't specified to force a checkpoint when the LOAD TABLE is finished. Since the transaction log only contains the LOAD TABLE command itself, not the individual rows, the original file must still be available for a recovery process to work.

Here is an example to show what LOAD TABLE actually writes to the transaction log:

```
CREATE TABLE t1 (
   key_1        INTEGER NOT NULL,
   col_2        INTEGER NOT NULL,
   PRIMARY KEY ( key_1 ) );

LOAD TABLE t1 FROM 't1_d.txt';
```

The dbtran.exe utility can be used to reformat the operations recorded in the transaction log file into SQL statements in a text file. The following example shows what it produces for the LOAD TABLE above. Note that there is no information about the individual rows, just the original LOAD TABLE statement itself plus a CHECKPOINT.

```
--CHECKPOINT-0000-0000507397-2003/oct/27 14:57
...
--SQL-1001-0000466662
load into table t1 from 't1_d.txt'
go
```

Note: LOAD TABLE automatically performs a checkpoint before the load operation is started, as shown in the dbtran output above. This is different from the optional checkpoint that is performed after the LOAD TABLE is completed if you specify the WITH CHECKPOINT option.

LOAD TABLE has another advantage besides speed: It is a mechanism whereby a statement inside a stored procedure can load data from a text file into a table; no client application or interface is required.

If you are willing to give up some speed to avoid the disadvantages of all three shortcuts described above, while still taking advantage of the fact that LOAD TABLE can be used from inside a stored procedure, you can use a temporary table in the LOAD TABLE and then copy the data via INSERT. Here is how the LOAD TABLE from the previous example can be changed to use a temporary table:

```
BEGIN
   DECLARE LOCAL TEMPORARY TABLE temp_t1 (
      key_1          INTEGER NOT NULL,
      col_2          INTEGER NOT NULL,
      PRIMARY KEY ( key_1 ) )
      NOT TRANSACTIONAL;
   LOAD TABLE temp_t1 FROM 't1_d.txt';
   INSERT t1 SELECT * FROM temp_t1;
END;
```

Now the individual inserted rows are recorded in the transaction log. Here is what the output from dbtran.exe looks like:

```
--INSERT-1001-0000475402
INSERT INTO DBA.t1(key_1,col_2)
VALUES (1,1)
go
--INSERT-1001-0000475411
INSERT INTO DBA.t1(key_1,col_2)
VALUES (2,2)
go
```

Note that operations involving temporary tables are not recorded in the transaction log, and with the NOT TRANSACTIONAL clause they aren't recorded in the rollback log either. That means the LOAD TABLE statement isn't written to the transaction log, the rows it inserts aren't written to the rollback log, and it doesn't cause a commit or a checkpoint; the speed disadvantage of this technique might not be so bad after all. For more information about temporary tables, see Section 1.15 in Chapter 1, "Creating."

2.4 ISQL INPUT

The Interactive SQL utility (dbisql.exe, or ISQL) supports a statement that looks similar to LOAD TABLE but is profoundly different in many respects — the ISQL INPUT statement.

The ISQL INPUT statement comes in three formats. The first format uses the FROM option to read data from a file. The second format uses the PROMPT option to initiate an interactive dialog for manual entry of individual column values, one row at a time. The third format uses neither FROM nor PROMPT but reads lines of text that appear inline immediately following the INPUT statement, either in the ISQL SQL Statements pane or in the command file containing the INPUT statement. Processing of inline data is terminated by the keyword END all by itself on one line, with no semicolon, or by the physical end of input.

The syntax for all three formats is presented here, but only the first format, using the FROM clause, will be discussed further. The other two formats are handy for small amounts of data but are not appropriate for loading large tables.

```
<isql_input>                ::= <isql_input_from_file>
                              | <isql_input_with_prompt>
                              | <isql_inline_input>
<isql_input_from_file>      ::= INPUT <file_input_option_list>
<isql_input_with_prompt>    ::= INPUT <prompt_input_option_list>
<isql_inline_input>         ::= INPUT <inline_input_option_list>
                                  <inline_data>
                                  <end_of_input_marker>
<file_input_option_list>    ::= <input_option_list> including FROM option
```

```
<prompt_input_option_list> ::= <input_option_list> including PROMPT option
<inline_input_option_list> ::= <input_option_list> not including FROM or PROMPT
<input_option_list>        ::= { <input_option> }
<input_option>  ::= INTO [ <owner_name> "." ] <target_table_name> -- required
                  | "(" <column_name_list> ")" -- default all columns
                  | FROM <input_file>
                  | PROMPT
                  | BY NAME        -- for self-describing file formats
                  | BY ORDER       -- default
                  | COLUMN WIDTHS "(" <column_width_list> ")" -- for FORMAT FIXED
                  | DELIMITED BY <input_delimiter>          -- default ','
                  | ESCAPE CHARACTER <input_escape_character> -- default '\'
                  | FORMAT <input_format>                   -- default ASCII
                  | NOSTRIP        -- default strip unquoted trailing blanks
<input_file>    ::= string literal file specification relative to the client
                  | double quoted file specification relative to the client
                  | unquoted file specification relative to the client
<column_width_list>  ::= <column_width> { "," <column_width> }
<column_width>       ::= integer literal column width for FORMAT FIXED
<input_delimiter>    ::= string literal containing column delimiter string
<input_escape_character> ::= string literal exactly 1 character in length
<input_format>       ::= string literal containing <input_format_name>
                       | double quoted <input_format_name>
                       | unquoted <input_format_name>
<input_format_name>  ::= ASCII   -- default
                       | DBASE   -- input is in DBASEII or DBASEIII format
                       | DBASEII -- a self-describing file format
                       | DBASEIII -- a self-describing file format
                       | EXCEL   -- a self-describing file format
                       | FIXED
                       | FOXPRO  -- a self-describing file format
                       | LOTUS   -- a self-describing file format
<inline_data>        ::= lines of data immediately following the INPUT statement
<end_of_input_marker> ::= END -- all by itself on a separate line
                       | end of the executed lines in the SQL Statements pane
                       | end of file in the ISQL command file
```

The default input file format is comma-delimited ASCII text, with each line representing a separate row. Here is the table from the first example from the previous section, together with an INPUT statement instead of LOAD TABLE:

```
CREATE TABLE t1 (
   key_1        INTEGER NOT NULL,
   col_2        VARCHAR ( 100 ) NULL,
   col_3        DECIMAL ( 11, 2 ) NULL,
   col_4        TIMESTAMP NULL,
   col_5        INTEGER NOT NULL,
   PRIMARY KEY ( key_1 ) );

INPUT INTO t1 FROM 'c:\\temp\\t1_a.txt';
```

Here is the contents of t1_a.txt, same as before:

```
1,'Hello, World',67.89,2003-09-30 02:15PM,999
2,   stripped string without quotes    , 0 , , 0
3,,,,
4,"   double quoted padded string   ",0,2003 9 30,-111
```

In this case, the INPUT statement performs exactly the same function as the corresponding LOAD TABLE; the contents of t1 are the same:

```
key_1 col_2                                  col_3 col_4                    col_5
===== ==================================== ===== ====================== =====
1     'Hello, World'                        67.89 2003-09-30 14:15:00.000 999
```

```
2    'stripped string without quotes'      0.00  NULL                         0
3    NULL                                  NULL  NULL                         0
4    '    double quoted padded string '    0.00  2003-09-30 00:00:00.000   -111
```

One advantage the INPUT statement has over LOAD TABLE is the ability to read input from several different sources. INPUT doesn't support FORMAT BCP, but it does support FORMAT ASCII, FORMAT FIXED for fixed-length input fields, and several self-describing file formats: DBASEII, DBASEIII, EXCEL, FOXPRO, and LOTUS, as well as FORMAT DBASE, which means "I don't know whether the file is in dBaseII or dBaseIII format, so let the INPUT statement figure it out."

The INPUT statement will actually create the target table if it doesn't exist, if you use a FORMAT DBASE, DBASEII, DBASEIII, EXCEL, FOXPRO, or LOTUS input file. This is certainly a quick and easy way to get data into your database, but it does have drawbacks: The supported file formats are limited (Excel version 2.1, for example), you don't have control over target data types or constraints, and some input data types aren't supported at all. For these reasons, it's better to explicitly create your tables before executing the INPUT statement, or to use the proxy table facility described in Section 1.14.4, "CREATE EXISTING TABLE." The INPUT statement's ability to create tables won't be discussed any further.

The column name list can be used with FORMAT ASCII and FORMAT FIXED input for two purposes: to change the order in which input fields are applied to columns in the table and to skip columns for which there is no corresponding input field.

- To change the order, code the column names in the order in which the corresponding input fields actually appear in the file.
- To skip a column in the table, leave its name out of the list.

Unlike the LOAD TABLE input name list, the INPUT column name list cannot be used to skip input fields that are not to be copied into any column; there is no equivalent to the "filler()" notation available with LOAD TABLE.

If the column name list is omitted, the layout of the input file is assumed to match the layout of the table (i.e., there are the same number of input fields as there are columns in the table, and they are arranged left to right in each input record in the same order as the columns appear in the CREATE TABLE).

Here is an example of an INPUT command using an explicit column name list; the second, third, fourth, and fifth input fields are applied to col_5, col_4, col_3, and col_2, respectively. Note that the keyword INPUT must come first but the rest of the options can appear in any order.

```
CREATE TABLE t1 (
   key_1        INTEGER NOT NULL,
   col_2        INTEGER NOT NULL,
   col_3        TIMESTAMP NULL,
   col_4        DECIMAL ( 11, 2 ) NULL,
   col_5        VARCHAR ( 100 ) NULL,
   PRIMARY KEY ( key_1 ) );

INPUT ( key_1, col_5, col_4, col_3, col_2 ) FROM 'c:\\temp\\t1_e.txt' INTO t1 ;
```

If the input file contains this record:

```
1, 'Hello, World', 67.89, 2003-09-30 02:15PM, 999
```

then the row inserted into t1 will look like this:

```
key_1 col_2 col_3                     col_4 col_5
===== ===== ======================== ===== =============
1     999   '2003-09-30 14:15:00.000' 67.89 'Hello, World'
```

The INPUT FROM file specification is relative to the client computer running ISQL, not the computer running the database server. This makes it more convenient for ad hoc usage than LOAD TABLE because you don't have to mess around with UNC file specifications.

The bad news is, you are stuck using a string literal for the file specification. You cannot use EXECUTE IMMEDIATE to run an INPUT statement, nor can you embed an INPUT statement inside a stored procedure or even a simple BEGIN block. That's because the INPUT statement is parsed and executed by ISQL, not the server, whereas other statements like EXECUTE IMMEDIATE and BEGIN blocks are passed on to the database engine to be parsed and executed. If you try to get the database engine to process an INPUT statement, it will give you a syntax error.

The way INPUT works is controlled by several options:

- **BY NAME** specifies that the field names defined inside the file are to be matched with the column names in the table to determine which fields are to be used for which columns. This option can only be used with the self-describing file formats DBASE, DBASEII, DBASEIII, EXCEL, FOXPRO, and LOTUS.

- **BY ORDER** (the default) specifies that the layout of the input file matches the layout of the table. Note that BY NAME and BY ORDER are the only choices you have for the self-describing file formats; the column name list is ignored. For FORMAT ASCII and FORMAT BCP, you can choose between the default BY ORDER or an explicit column name list.

- **COLUMN WIDTHS** is used with FORMAT FIXED input to list the input file field widths from left to right. In theory, COLUMN WIDTHS is optional, but for all practical purposes it is a requirement for FORMAT FIXED input; no attempt will be made here to describe how the INPUT statement calculates column widths if this option is omitted.

- **DELIMITED BY** can be used with FORMAT ASCII to change the field delimiter; for example, DELIMITED BY '\x09' specifies that the input file is tab-delimited. The default is DELIMITED BY ','.

- **ESCAPE CHARACTER** can be used with FORMAT ASCII to specify which single character will be interpreted as the escape character in string literals in the input file; e.g., ESCAPE CHARACTER '!'. The default is the ESCAPE CHARACTER '\'. Note that input fields in FORMAT FIXED files are processed as is; there is no notion of delimiters or escape characters.

- **NOSTRIP** can be used with FORMAT ASCII to specify that trailing blanks will be preserved when processing unquoted strings. The default is to remove trailing spaces from unquoted strings. Note that leading spaces are always removed from unquoted strings, but leading and trailing spaces are never removed from quoted strings, regardless of whether or not NOSTRIP is specified.

The INPUT statement doesn't take any of the shortcuts used by LOAD TABLE, so it isn't nearly as fast. What INPUT actually does is pass each row to the database engine, one at a time, to be inserted. You can see this by turning on the Request-Level Logging feature to see what the engine sees. Here is an example that compares LOAD TABLE with INPUT when a two-line input file is loaded into a two-column table:

```
CREATE TABLE t1 (
   col_1        INTEGER NOT NULL,
   col_2        INTEGER NOT NULL );

CALL sa_server_option ( 'Request_level_log_file', 'r.txt' );
CALL sa_server_option ( 'Request_level_logging', 'SQL+hostvars' );

LOAD TABLE t1 FROM 't1_f.txt';
INPUT INTO t1 FROM 't1_f.txt';

CALL sa_server_option ( 'Request_level_logging', 'NONE' );
```

Here is the contents of t1_f.txt:

```
1, 1
2, 2
```

The Request-Level Logging file r.txt shows that the engine received the LOAD TABLE command as it was coded:

```
STMT_PREPARE  "LOAD TABLE t1 FROM 't1_f.txt'"
STMT_EXECUTE  Stmt=66327
```

However, the INPUT statement got changed into an INSERT that was executed twice, once for each record in the input file, with two host variables used, one for each field:

```
STMT_PREPARE  "INSERT INTO "t1" ("col_1","col_2") VALUES (?,?)"
STMT_EXECUTE  Stmt=66339
HOSTVAR       0 varchar '1'
HOSTVAR       1 varchar '1'
STMT_EXECUTE  Stmt=66339
HOSTVAR       0 varchar '2'
HOSTVAR       1 varchar '2'
```

This explains why INPUT is slower than LOAD TABLE, but also why the disadvantages of the LOAD TABLE shortcuts are avoided: The INPUT statement does cause insert triggers to be fired, it does acquire individual row locks, and it does write the inserts to the transaction log.

The Request-Level Logging feature is explained further in Section 10.2 of Chapter 10, "Tuning."

2.5 Chapter Summary

This chapter described the five different formats of the INSERT statement: INSERT with a VALUES list for all columns or a list of named columns, INSERT with a SELECT for all column values or a list of named columns, and INSERT using the AUTO NAME facility. Also described were the LOAD TABLE and ISQL INPUT statements for inserting data from an external file.

The next chapter moves on to the third step in the life cycle of a database: selecting rows.

Chapter 3

Selecting

3.1 Introduction

This chapter talks about three different ways to select data from the database: the SQL select and the UNLOAD and ISQL OUTPUT statements. Of the 40 sections and subsections in this chapter, 36 are devoted to the SQL select, a testament to its importance. Even section 3.23, "CREATE VIEW," is really about the SQL select.

Simply put, a SQL select is a mechanism that returns a result set, where a result set is zero or more rows consisting of one or more columns of data. In this book, the lowercase word "select" refers to this general mechanism for returning a result set, and the uppercase "SELECT" refers to the keyword that appears at least once in each select.

Section 3.2 presents a list of imaginary or logical steps that could be used to execute a SQL select. This list is presented to help explain what each clause can do for you. This is important, because the order in which the clauses are coded gives few clues about what they do and how they interact, and more importantly, how they interfere with one another. If you've ever had trouble with the GROUP BY clause, or had a SELECT that returned 10,000 rows instead of the three you wanted, or wondered why you can't call NUMBER(*) in a WHERE clause, this chapter has the answers. With examples.

Sections 3.3 through 3.24.1 explain the syntax and semantics of the various clauses and components, in roughly the same order as the logical steps presented in Section 3.2. That's the reason the FROM clause comes first, for example, long before the SELECT list.

This is also the chapter that discusses the syntax of expressions, including boolean expressions. Expressions may appear in many other SQL statements, but it's in the SELECT where they get their heaviest workout, and that's why they're explained here.

Sections 3.25 and 3.26, about UNLOAD and ISQL OUTPUT, close this chapter with discussions of two methods where result sets can be written directly to files.

3.2 Logical Execution of a SELECT

A SQL select consists of a query expression with some optional clauses: WITH, ORDER BY, and FOR. The simplest query expression is a single query specification; the simplest query specification is defined as the SELECT keyword followed by a select list; and the simplest select list is a single literal like 1.

That means the simplest SQL select is SELECT 1, which returns a single row consisting of a single column. That's one extreme; at the other end of the spectrum are giant selects spanning hundreds of lines of code, involving dozens of tables in complex relationships, and returning thousands of rows.

```
<select>                ::= [ <with_clause> ]          -- WITH...
                            <query_expression>        -- at least one SELECT...
                            [ <order_by_clause> ] -- ORDER BY...
                            [ <for_clause> ]          -- FOR...
<query_expression>      ::= <query_expression> <query_operator> <query_expression>
                          | <subquery>
                          | <query_specification>
<query_operator>        ::= EXCEPT    [ DISTINCT | ALL ]
                          | INTERSECT [ DISTINCT | ALL ]
                          | UNION     [ DISTINCT | ALL ]
<subquery>              ::= "(" <query_expression>
                            [ <order_by_clause> ]
                            [ <for_xml_clause> ] ")"
<query_specification> ::= SELECT
                            [ DISTINCT ]
                            [ <row_range> ]
                            <select_list>
                            [ <select_into> ]
                            [ <from_clause> ] -- default is FROM SYS.DUMMY
                            [ <where_clause> ]
                            [ <group_by_clause> ]
                            [ <having_clause> ]
<for_clause>            ::= <for_intent_clause>
                          | <for_xml_clause>
<for_intent_clause>    ::= FOR READ ONLY
                          | FOR UPDATE
                          | FOR UPDATE BY <concurrency_setting>
<concurrency_setting> ::= VALUES
                          | TIMESTAMP
                          | LOCK
<for_xml_clause>       ::= FOR XML RAW [ "," ELEMENTS ] [ "," ROOT ]
                          | FOR XML AUTO [ "," ELEMENTS ] [ "," ROOT ]
                          | FOR XML EXPLICIT [ "," ELEMENTS ] [ "," ROOT ]
```

Note: This section begins a long discussion of the <query_specification> shown above. Other clauses are described much later, or not at all. In particular, the <with_clause> is discussed in Section 3.24, the <order_by_clause> is discussed in Section 3.17, and the EXCEPT, INTERSECT, and UNION operators are discussed in Section 3.22. For more information about the <for_intent_clause> and <for_xml_clause>, see the SQL Anywhere Help.

The SQL select is the most important, most powerful, and most difficult construction in all of SQL. One of the main reasons for the difficulty is the fact that the order in which the various clauses are coded bears little relationship to what they actually do or the way the SQL select is executed. This section addresses the question, "What does the SQL select do?" The answer to the question, "How is the SQL select executed?" is a mystery as far as this book is concerned; some aspects of how a query is actually executed are discussed in Chapter 10, "Tuning," but for the most part this book concentrates on the end result.

One way to explain what a SQL select does is to describe a simple series of steps that could be used to perform the required functions. The key word is "simple" in terms of human understanding, not "fast" in terms of computer execution. These are logical or imaginary steps, steps that "could be used"; they most definitely are not the steps that are actually used.

Here's an overview of how a select is processed, step by step, from a logical point of view:

1. The FROM clause is evaluated to produce a candidate result set consisting of virtual columns.
2. All select list items, except for those including aggregate function and NUMBER(*) calls, are evaluated and appended to each row.
3. The WHERE clause is applied to eliminate rows.
4. The GROUP BY clause is applied to partition the rows into groups.
5. All aggregate function calls, except for GROUPING, are evaluated for each group and appended to each row in each group.
6. GROUP BY ROLLUP summary rows are computed and added to the candidate result set as separate groups.
7. All GROUPING calls are evaluated for each group and appended to each row in each group.
8. The HAVING clause is applied to eliminate entire groups.
9. The ORDER BY clause is applied to sort the groups; the order within each group doesn't matter.
10. Each row is reduced to only the select list items, and each group is reduced to a single row.
11. The DISTINCT keyword is applied to eliminate duplicate rows.
12. The row range (FIRST, TOP, etc.) is applied to eliminate rows.
13. Each NUMBER(*) call in the select list is computed for each row and appended to the row.
14. The FOR XML clause is applied to transform the result set into a single column.
15. The INTO clause is executed to fill host variables or a temporary table.

The rest of this section will expand each step in terms of a running example. Sections 3.3-3.24.1 explain the various clauses and components of the SQL select in more detail, more or less in the order of these steps.

Note: Most of these steps are optional, and they are only performed if the corresponding element is actually present. Some steps are mutually exclusive; for example, a NUMBER(*) call can't appear together with DISTINCT so steps 11 and 13 will not both be performed for the same select. Also note that the UNION, EXCEPT, and INTERSECT operators don't appear in this list; those operators come later, and they work on result sets that have already been through these steps.

Here is an example to illustrate the steps in the overview; data is inserted into three simple tables and then retrieved by a select that includes most of the major clauses:

```
CREATE TABLE t1 (
    key_1       INTEGER NOT NULL,
    non_key_1   INTEGER NOT NULL,
    PRIMARY KEY ( key_1 ) );

CREATE TABLE t2 (
    key_1       INTEGER NOT NULL,
    key_2       INTEGER NOT NULL,
    PRIMARY KEY ( key_1, key_2 ),
    FOREIGN KEY fk_t1 ( key_1 ) REFERENCES t1 ( key_1 ) );

CREATE TABLE t3 (
    key_1       INTEGER NOT NULL,
    non_key_1   INTEGER NOT NULL,
    PRIMARY KEY ( key_1 ) );

INSERT t1 VALUES ( 1, 1 );
INSERT t1 VALUES ( 2, 2 );

INSERT t2 VALUES ( 2, 21 );
INSERT t2 VALUES ( 2, 22 );
INSERT t2 VALUES ( 2, 23 );

INSERT t3 VALUES ( 3, 333 );
INSERT t3 VALUES ( 4, 333 );
INSERT t3 VALUES ( 5, 0 );
INSERT t3 VALUES ( 6, 333 );

SELECT DISTINCT
    TOP 4 START AT 2
    t1.key_1 * 100     AS a,
    t3.key_1 * 1000    AS b,
    COUNT(*)           AS c,
    SUM ( t3.non_key_1 ) AS d
  FROM ( t1 LEFT OUTER JOIN t2 ON t1.key_1 = t2.key_1 )
    CROSS JOIN t3
 WHERE b <= 5000
   AND t3.non_key_1 = 333
 GROUP BY ROLLUP ( t1.key_1, t3.key_1 )
HAVING COUNT(*) > 1
 ORDER BY 1, 2;
```

The result set produced by the above SELECT looks like this:

a	b	c	d
100	NULL	2	666
200	NULL	6	1998
200	3000	3	999
200	4000	3	999

Here's how that SELECT is processed, with each logical step presented in more detail:

Step 1: The FROM clause is evaluated to produce the candidate result set consisting of all the columns returned by the FROM clause. These are called virtual columns because they may or may not be the same as any select list items. These virtual columns are required at this point because other clauses (WHERE, ORDER BY, etc.) may refer to them even if they don't appear in the select list. Each virtual column is named t.c, where t is a table, view, or correlation name, and c is a column or alias name.

Here's what the equivalent SELECT looks like at this point:

```
SELECT t1.key_1,
       t1.non_key_1,
       t2.key_1,
       t2.key_2,
       t3.key_1,
       t3.non_key_1
  FROM ( t1 LEFT OUTER JOIN t2 ON t1.key_1 = t2.key_1 )
       CROSS JOIN t3;
```

The full details of LEFT OUTER JOIN, CROSS JOIN, and other components of the FROM clause will be explained in later sections. For the purposes of this discussion, the FROM clause is processed first, separately from all the other clauses, and simply returns a single result set for further processing by the rest of the select.

Here is what the result set returned by the FROM clause looks like; each row has been given a letter A, B, C, ... to identify it for the purposes of discussion:

	t1. key_1	t1. non_key_1	t2. key_1	t2. key_2	t3. key_1	t3. non_key_1
A	1	1	NULL	NULL	3	333
B	1	1	NULL	NULL	4	333
C	1	1	NULL	NULL	5	0
D	1	1	NULL	NULL	6	333
E	2	2	2	21	3	333
F	2	2	2	22	3	333
G	2	2	2	23	3	333
H	2	2	2	21	4	333
I	2	2	2	22	4	333
J	2	2	2	23	4	333
K	2	2	2	21	5	0
L	2	2	2	22	5	0
M	2	2	2	23	5	0
N	2	2	2	21	6	333
O	2	2	2	22	6	333
P	2	2	2	23	6	333

Note: Don't think for one second that the SQL Anywhere query processor actually builds a result set like this for every select. If it did that, some queries would take years to execute and would consume all the RAM and disk space that's ever been manufactured. In reality, the query processor takes many short-cuts, and does as little unnecessary work as possible in order to speed things up. This step-by-step list is only a conceptual list, to explain how all the clauses fit together and contribute to the final result.

Step 2: With the exception of aggregate function calls and NUMBER(*) calls, the items in the select list are evaluated and appended to each row in the candidate result set. This may lead to some duplication between virtual columns and select list items but that will only be temporary. Eventually all the virtual columns will be eliminated, but they are still needed for a while.

Here's what the equivalent SELECT looks like now:

```
SELECT t1.key_1,
       t1.non_key_1,
       t2.key_1,
       t2.key_2,
       t3.key_1,
       t3.non_key_1,
       t1.key_1 * 100  AS a,
       t3.key_1 * 1000 AS b
  FROM ( t1 LEFT OUTER JOIN t2 ON t1.key_1 = t2.key_1 )
       CROSS JOIN t3;
```

Here is what the candidate result set looks like at this point:

	t1. key_1	t1. non_key_1	t2. key_1	t2. key_2	t3. key_1	t3. non_key_1	a	b
A	1	1	NULL	NULL	3	333	100	3000
B	1	1	NULL	NULL	4	333	100	4000
C	1	1	NULL	NULL	5	0	100	5000
D	1	1	NULL	NULL	6	333	100	6000
E	2	2	2	21	3	333	200	3000
F	2	2	2	22	3	333	200	3000
G	2	2	2	23	3	333	200	3000
H	2	2	2	21	4	333	200	4000
I	2	2	2	22	4	333	200	4000
J	2	2	2	23	4	333	200	4000
K	2	2	2	21	5	0	200	5000
L	2	2	2	22	5	0	200	5000
M	2	2	2	23	5	0	200	5000
N	2	2	2	21	6	333	200	6000
O	2	2	2	22	6	333	200	6000
P	2	2	2	23	6	333	200	6000

Note: The rows are shown in a sorted order so it's easier to see what's going on. In reality, no particular order can be assumed until the ORDER BY clause is applied, and that doesn't happen until much later.

Step 3: The WHERE clause is applied to eliminate rows.

The WHERE clause may refer to both virtual columns and select list items, but not to aggregate function calls or NUMBER(*) calls. Here's what the equivalent SELECT looks like now:

```
SELECT t1.key_1,
       t1.non_key_1,
       t2.key_1,
       t2.key_2,
       t3.key_1,
       t3.non_key_1,
       t1.key_1 * 100      AS a,
       t3.key_1 * 1000     AS b
  FROM ( t1 LEFT OUTER JOIN t2 ON t1.key_1 = t2.key_1 )
       CROSS JOIN t3
 WHERE b <= 5000
   AND t3.non_key_1 = 333;
```

Now the candidate result set is much smaller:

	t1. key_1	t1. non_key_1	t2. key_1	t2. key_2	t3. key_1	t3. non_key_1	a	b
A	1	1	NULL	NULL	3	333	100	3000
B	1	1	NULL	NULL	4	333	100	4000
E	2	2	2	21	3	333	200	3000
F	2	2	2	22	3	333	200	3000
G	2	2	2	23	3	333	200	3000
H	2	2	2	21	4	333	200	4000
I	2	2	2	22	4	333	200	4000
J	2	2	2	23	4	333	200	4000

Step 4: The GROUP BY clause is applied to partition the rows into groups. At this point each group consists of one or more rows; the reduction to one-row-per-group happens much later. Also note that only grouping takes place at this point; the actual "GROUP BY ROLLUP (t1.key_1, t3.key_1)" clause is interpreted as "GROUP BY t1.key_1, t3.key_1" and the ROLLUP process happens later.

The GROUP BY clause may refer to both virtual columns and select list items, but not to aggregate function calls or NUMBER(*) calls. However, if there is a GROUP BY clause, the select list may only consist of aggregate function calls, NUMBER(*) calls, and items that appear in the GROUP BY clause.

Note: If a column appears in the select list, it must also appear in the GROUP BY clause. However, the opposite is not necessarily true; if a column appears in the GROUP BY clause it does not necessarily have to appear in the select list. A GROUP BY clause often guarantees that the final result set will contain no duplicate rows, but this is not necessarily the case if a column named in the GROUP BY clause is omitted from the select list.

If there is no GROUP BY clause, each row in the candidate result set is treated as a separate group.

In the end, each group will be reduced to a single row, but that can't happen until later. Here's what the groups look like at this point, after the "GROUP BY t1.key_1, t3.key_1" process has finished:

	t1. key_1	t1. non_key_1	t2. key_1	t2. key_2	t3. key_1	t3. non_key_1	a	b	
A	1	1	NULL	NULL	3	**333**	100	3000	-- **Group 1**
B	1	1	NULL	NULL	4	**333**	100	4000	-- **Group 2**
E	2	2	2	21	3	**333**	200	3000	-- **Group 3**
F	2	2	2	22	3	**333**	200	3000	
G	2	2	2	23	3	**333**	200	3000	
H	2	2	2	21	4	**333**	200	4000	-- **Group 4**
I	2	2	2	22	4	**333**	200	4000	
J	2	2	2	23	4	**333**	200	4000	

Note: In this logical view of query processing, the multiple rows in each group are going to hang around until much later in the process. One of the reasons for this, looking ahead, is the fact that GROUP BY ROLLUP summarization of statistical function calls like AVG is based on the underlying rows. Because the GROUP BY ROLLUP process doesn't happen for a long time, the underlying rows must be preserved for a long time.

Step 5: Except for calls to GROUPING, each aggregate function call in the select list, GROUP BY clause, and HAVING clause is computed for each group as a whole. The resulting values are then appended to each row in each group; this results in duplicate aggregate values in different rows in the same group, but that duplication will be eliminated eventually.

In the example, one of the aggregate function calls, SUM (t3.non_key_1), refers to a virtual column that is not one of the select list items. That's one of the reasons virtual columns are still required up to this point, and why each group hasn't been reduced to a single row yet.

Here's what the groups look like after COUNT(*) and SUM (t3.non_key_1) have been added:

	t1. key_1	t1. non_key_1	t2. key_1	t2. key_2	t3. key_1	t3. non_key_1	a	b	COUNT AS c	SUM AS d
A	1	1	NULL	NULL	3	333	100	3000	1	333
B	1	1	NULL	NULL	4	333	100	4000	1	333
E	2	2	2	21	3	333	200	3000	3	999
F	2	2	2	22	3	333	200	3000	3	999
G	2	2	2	23	3	333	200	3000	3	999
H	2	2	2	21	4	333	200	4000	3	999
I	2	2	2	22	4	333	200	4000	3	999
J	2	2	2	23	4	333	200	4000	3	999

Step 6: ROLLUP summary rows are computed and added to the candidate result set as separate groups.

In this example, the GROUP BY ROLLUP (t1.key_1, t3.key_1) clause creates one subtotal row for each different t1.key_1 value; this row summarizes all the groups with different t3.key_1 values within that value of t1.key_1. The ROLLUP process also creates one single grand total row. For the purposes of this step-by-step explanation, each ROLLUP row forms its own single-row group.

Here's what the result set looks like after the three new single-row ROLLUP groups have been added. R1 is the ROLLUP grand total group, and the two subtotal ROLLUP groups are marked R2 and R3. Note that the COUNT and SUM values have been summarized in the ROLLUP groups:

	t1. key_1	t1. non_key_1	t2. key_1	t2. key_2	t3. key_1	t3. non_key_1	a	b	COUNT AS c	SUM AS d
R1	NULL	NULL	NULL	NULL	NULL	NULL	NULL	NULL	8	2664
R2	NULL	NULL	NULL	NULL	NULL	NULL	100	NULL	2	666
A	1	1	NULL	NULL	3	333	100	3000	1	333

	t1.key_1	t1.non_key_1	t2.key_1	t2.key_2	t3.key_1	t3.non_key_1	a	b	COUNT AS c	SUM AS d
B	1	1	NULL	NULL	4	333	100	4000	1	333
R3	NULL	NULL	NULL	NULL	NULL	NULL	200	NULL	6	**1998**
E	2	2	2	21	3	333	200	3000	3	999
F	2	2	2	22	3	333	200	3000	3	999
G	2	2	2	23	3	333	200	3000	3	999
H	2	2	2	21	4	333	200	4000	3	999
I	2	2	2	22	4	333	200	4000	3	999
J	2	2	2	23	4	333	200	4000	3	999

Note:　The ROLLUP summarization of statistical functions like AVG work on the individual rows rather than the groups. This does make a difference, and it's one of the reasons the groups still contain the separate rows in this explanation. For example, if the SELECT list had contained AVG (t1.key_1) the ROLLUP grand total row would contain 1.75, which is the average of t1.key_1 across all eight rows. That's the right answer; wrong answers include 1.5, which is the average of t1.key_1 for the four groups, and 4, which is the average of t1.key_1 for the two ROLLUP subtotal rows.

Step 7: All GROUPING calls are evaluated for each group and appended to each row in each group. This example doesn't have any GROUPING calls, but if it did, each call would result in yet another item appended to each row containing a 1 or a 0. The GROUPING function is described in Section 3.15, "GROUP BY ROLLUP Clause."

Step 8: The HAVING clause is applied to eliminate entire groups.

In this case, the HAVING COUNT(*) > 1 clause eliminates the two single-row groups where a = 100, and that means the candidate result set no longer "adds up" to the subtotal R2 or the grand total R1:

	t1. key_1	t1. non_key_1	t2. key_1	t2. key_2	t3. key_1	t3. non_key_1	a	b	COUNT AS c	SUM AS d
R1	NULL	NULL	NULL	NULL	NULL	NULL	NULL	NULL	8	2664
R2	NULL	NULL	NULL	NULL	NULL	NULL	100	NULL	2	666
R3	NULL	NULL	NULL	NULL	NULL	NULL	200	NULL	6	1998
E	2	2	2	21	3	333	200	3000	3	999
F	2	2	2	22	3	333	200	3000	3	999
G	2	2	2	23	3	333	200	3000	3	999
H	2	2	2	21	4	333	200	4000	3	999
I	2	2	2	22	4	333	200	4000	3	999
J	2	2	2	23	4	333	200	4000	3	999

The HAVING COUNT(*) > 1 clause doesn't affect any of the ROLLUP summary rows in this example even though they appear as single-row groups; that's because COUNT(*) returns 8, 2, and 6 for each of the ROLLUP rows labeled R1, R2, and R3, respectively. In other words, COUNT(*) for a ROLLUP row counts the number of rows that the ROLLUP row represents. If the HAVING clause had specified COUNT(*) > 2 instead, the ROLLUP row labeled R2 would have been eliminated at this point.

Step 9: The ORDER BY clause is applied to sort the groups. The order within a group doesn't matter because only one row is going to survive; it's just the relative order of the groups that is determined at this point.

In all the previous steps the groups and rows have been shown in sorted order for convenience, but it's important to note that the actual ordering does not occur until this point. And that's why certain features like FIRST and NUMBER(*) haven't been evaluated yet, because they depend on row ordering.

Note: ORDER BY places NULL values ahead of non-NULL values when ASC (the default) is used.

Step 10: Each row is reduced to only the select list items, and each group is reduced to a single row. This step is performed after the ORDER BY because virtual columns can appear in the ORDER BY clause, so they have to survive until this point.

Here's what the five groups look like after being reduced to five rows; the original row labels are shown on the left so you can see which groups the final rows came from:

```
         a      b     c  d
         ====   ====  =  ====
R1       NULL   NULL  8  2664
R2       100    NULL  2  666
R3       200    NULL  6  1998
E/F/G    200    3000  3  999
H/I/J    200    4000  3  999
```

Note: This step-by-step explanation assumes that select list items are evaluated as soon as they can be. For example, at this point it is possible for a select list expression involving a call to GROUPING to have been evaluated because Step 7 took care of GROUPING calls. However, a select list expression involving NUMBER(*) still can't be calculated, not until Step 13 at least.

Step 11: The summarizer (DISTINCT versus ALL) is applied to eliminate duplicate rows; only DISTINCT has any effect. In this example, DISTINCT has no effect because this particular GROUP BY clause guarantees that each row will be distinct in the final result.

It is possible, however, for duplicate rows to remain after a GROUP BY clause has been processed; this can happen if one or more columns named in the GROUP BY clause are omitted from the select list. In that case the DISTINCT summarizer would remove those remaining duplicate rows.

Step 12: The row range (FIRST, TOP, etc.) is applied to eliminate rows.

At this point the SELECT has reached its final form, at least as far as this example is concerned:

```
SELECT DISTINCT
       TOP 4 START AT 2
       t1.key_1 * 100      AS a,
       t3.key_1 * 1000     AS b,
       COUNT(*)            AS c,
       SUM ( t3.non_key_1 ) AS d
  FROM ( t1 LEFT OUTER JOIN t2 ON t1.key_1 = t2.key_1 )
       CROSS JOIN t3
```

```
WHERE b <= 5000
   AND t3.non_key_1 = 333
GROUP BY ROLLUP ( t1.key_1, t3.key_1 )
HAVING COUNT(*) > 1
ORDER BY 1, 2;
```

The START AT 2 clause eliminates the grand total row to produce the final result set in this example:

```
a     b      c   d
===   ====   =   ====
100   NULL   2   666
200   NULL   6   1998
200   3000   3   999
200   4000   3   999
```

Step 13: Each NUMBER(*) call in the select list is computed for each row and appended to the row. Note that NUMBER(*) can't be evaluated until all the other clauses have had their turn; the rows can't be numbered until all the rows have been sorted and all unwanted rows have been eliminated. And that's why there are so many restrictions on where you can call NUMBER(*); for example, you can't use it in a WHERE clause because that's much too early to calculate NUMBER(*).

Here is what the example SELECT looks like with a NUMBER(*) call added; the DISTINCT clause has been commented out because it conflicts with NUMBER(*):

```
SELECT --DISTINCT
       TOP 4 START AT 2
       t1.key_1 * 100        AS a,
       t3.key_1 * 1000       AS b,
       COUNT(*)              AS c,
       SUM ( t3.non_key_1 )  AS d,
       NUMBER(*)             AS e
  FROM ( t1 LEFT OUTER JOIN t2 ON t1.key_1 = t2.key_1 )
       CROSS JOIN t3
 WHERE b <= 5000
   AND t3.non_key_1 = 333
 GROUP BY ROLLUP ( t1.key_1, t3.key_1 )
HAVING COUNT(*) > 1
ORDER BY 1, 2;
```

The resulting output shows the row number as column e:

```
a     b      c   d      e
===   ====   =   ====   =
100   NULL   2   666    1
200   NULL   6   1998   2
200   3000   3   999    3
200   4000   3   999    4
```

Step 14: The FOR XML clause is applied to transform the result set into a single row consisting of a single XML document column.

Step 15: The INTO clause is executed to fill host variables or a temporary table. A temporary table can accept multiple rows, while host variables can only be used if the result set is a single row.

Here's what the example SELECT looks like with INTO and FOR XML clauses added; the NUMBER(*) call has been removed because it conflicts with FOR XML:

```
SELECT DISTINCT
       TOP 4 START AT 2
       t1.key_1 * 100       AS a,
       t3.key_1 * 1000      AS b,
       COUNT(*)             AS c,
       SUM ( t3.non_key_1 ) AS d
  INTO #t
  FROM ( t1 LEFT OUTER JOIN t2 ON t1.key_1 = t2.key_1 )
       CROSS JOIN t3
 WHERE b <= 5000
   AND t3.non_key_1 = 333
 GROUP BY ROLLUP ( t1.key_1, t3.key_1 )
HAVING COUNT(*) > 1
 ORDER BY 1, 2
   FOR XML AUTO;
```

This book doesn't go into the details of XML processing. However, here is what the single column in the single row in the temporary #t looks like, wrapped to fit the page:

```
<t1 a="100"><t3 c="2" d="666"/></t1><t1 a="200"><t3 c="6" d="1998"/><t3 b="3000"
c="3" d="999"/><t3 b="4000" c="3" d="999"/></t1>'
```

For more information about the SELECT INTO method of creating a temporary table, see Section 1.15.2.3, "SELECT INTO #table_name."

3.3 FROM Clause

Logically speaking, the FROM clause specifies a "virtual table" or candidate result set on which all the other clauses operate. Once upon a time the FROM clause was just a simple list of table names, but no more; modern advances have added complex table expressions with nested operations and boolean expressions that once were found only in the WHERE clause.

Here is the basic syntax for the FROM clause:

```
<from_clause>            ::= FROM <table_specification>
<table_specification>    ::= <table_expression_list>
<table_expression_list>  ::= <table_expression>
                             { "," <table_expression> } -- avoid the comma
```

The FROM clause consists of a comma-separated list of table expressions, which in turn may consist of nested table expressions, subqueries, and even lists of table expressions inside brackets:

```
<table_expression>       ::= <table_term>
                           | <table_expression>
                             CROSS JOIN
                             <table_term>
                           | <table_expression>
                             [ <on_condition_shorthand> ] -- do not use
                             <join_operator>
                             <table_term>
                             [ <on_condition> ]            -- use this instead
<table_term>             ::= <table_reference>
                           | <view_reference>
                           | <derived_table>
                           | <procedure_reference>
                           | "(" <table_expression_list> ")"
                           | <lateral_derived_table>
<on_condition_shorthand> ::= KEY     -- foreign key columns; do not use
                           | NATURAL -- like-named columns; do not use
```

```
<join_operator>          ::= <inner_join>
                          | <left_outer_join>
                          | <right_outer_join>
                          | <full_outer_join>
<inner_join>             ::= INNER JOIN
                          | JOIN
<left_outer_join>       ::= LEFT OUTER JOIN
                          | LEFT JOIN
<right_outer_join>      ::= RIGHT OUTER JOIN
                          | RIGHT JOIN
<full_outer_join>       ::= FULL OUTER JOIN
                          | FULL JOIN
<on_condition>          ::= ON <boolean_expression> -- highly recommended
<table_reference>       ::= [ <owner_name> "." ] <table_name>
                              [ [ AS ] <correlation_name> ]
                              [ <hints> ]
<view_reference>        ::= [ <owner_name> "." ] <view_name>
                              [ [ AS ] <correlation_name> ]
                              [ <hints> ]
<owner_name>            ::= <identifier>
<table_name>            ::= <identifier>
<correlation_name>      ::= <identifier>
<view_name>             ::= <identifier>
<identifier>            ::= see <identifier> in Chapter 1, "Creating"
```

This book concentrates on FROM clauses that use modern join operators like INNER JOIN and LEFT OUTER JOIN, and it avoids discussions of comma-separated lists of table expressions. The comma in a list of table expressions is actually a kind of "comma join" operator, often equivalent to CROSS JOIN, but not always; sometimes it works like an INNER JOIN, and when it is combined with other join operators it can become very confusing. One exception comes in Section 3.8, "LATERAL Procedure Call," where the comma is required to take advantage of a useful feature: a join involving a stored procedure call that receives a column from another table as an argument. Throughout the rest of this book, however, there aren't many commas in the FROM clause.

Tip: Don't use defaults or the shorthand notation when specifying join operators. In particular, don't just code the JOIN operator without one of the qualifiers INNER or OUTER, don't use the shorthand keywords KEY and NATURAL, and don't forget to code an ON condition for every join except CROSS JOIN. Be clear and explicit with the join operators and the result will be easier to understand and debug. The defaults and shorthand notation don't save much coding, and the results can be confusing, especially with multi-table joins.

Table and view references in the FROM clause may contain hints that influence how SQL Anywhere handles this particular table or view, for this particular query:

```
<hints>     ::= HOLDLOCK       -- ISOLATION_LEVEL = 3
              | WITH "(" [ <hint_list> ] ")"
<hint_list> ::= <hint> { <hint> }
<hint>      ::= FASTFIRSTROW   -- OPTIMIZATION_GOAL = 'first-row'
              | NOLOCK         -- ISOLATION_LEVEL = 0
              | READUNCOMMITTED -- ISOLATION_LEVEL = 0
              | READCOMMITTED  -- ISOLATION_LEVEL = 1
              | REPEATABLEREAD -- ISOLATION_LEVEL = 2
              | HOLDLOCK       -- ISOLATION_LEVEL = 3
              | SERIALIZABLE   -- ISOLATION_LEVEL = 3
```

These hints may temporarily override the OPTIMIZATION_GOAL and ISOLATION_LEVEL option settings. For more information about ISOLATION_LEVEL, see Section 9.7, "Blocks and Isolation Levels" in Chapter 9, "Protecting."

The following sections describe the FROM clause in terms of the different join operators and special table terms such as derived tables and stored procedure calls. Full details of the <boolean_expression> syntax is left until Section 3.12, "Boolean Expressions and the WHERE Clause."

3.4 JOIN

There are five different operators involving the JOIN keyword, discussed in the next five sections:

- CROSS JOIN to create a Cartesian product of two tables.
- INNER JOIN to select matching combinations of rows from two tables.
- LEFT OUTER JOIN to include all the rows from the left-hand table in addition to the matching combinations of rows from both tables.
- RIGHT OUTER JOIN to include all the rows from the right-hand table.
- FULL OUTER JOIN to include all the rows from both tables.

3.4.1 CROSS JOIN

The simplest table expression is a table term, the simplest table term is a table reference, and the simplest join operator is CROSS JOIN. Here is an example of a CROSS JOIN between two tables:

```
CREATE TABLE t1 (
    c1  INTEGER NOT NULL );

CREATE TABLE t2 (
    c1  INTEGER NOT NULL,
    c2  INTEGER NOT NULL );

INSERT t1 VALUES ( 1 );
INSERT t1 VALUES ( 2 );

INSERT t2 VALUES ( 1, 7 );
INSERT t2 VALUES ( 1, 8 );
INSERT t2 VALUES ( 1, 9 );

SELECT t1.c1,
       t2.c1,
       t2.c2
  FROM t1 CROSS JOIN t2
 ORDER BY t1.c1,
       t2.c1,
       t2.c2;
```

A join is a operation on two tables, to combine or join rows from each table to create rows in a single result set. This result set is sometimes called a virtual table, and it contains (logically speaking) all the columns from both tables.

Different join operators combine rows in different ways. In particular, the CROSS JOIN operator combines every row in one table with every row in the other table; in other words, it produces every combination of rows in the two tables, and it is also called a Cartesian product. In the example above, one table has two rows and the other one has three, so there are six rows in the result set:

```
c1  c2  c3
==  ==  ==
1   1   7
1   1   8
1   1   9
2   1   7
2   1   8
2   1   9
```

The CROSS JOIN operator is the only one that doesn't allow unwanted rows to be eliminated with the ON clause. That's why it's the simplest join operator, and also why it's the least useful: It usually returns too many rows. For example, a CROSS JOIN of two ten-thousand-row tables would return one hundred million rows.

3.4.2 INNER JOIN

The INNER JOIN operator together with an ON condition is far more useful and far more common than CROSS JOIN. The INNER JOIN is often used to join two tables using a foreign key relationship. Here is an example that joins rows from a parent and child table using an ON condition to restrict the result set; each child row is combined with only a single row in the parent table:

```
CREATE TABLE parent (
   parent_key    INTEGER NOT NULL,
   data_1        VARCHAR ( 1 ) NOT NULL,
   PRIMARY KEY ( parent_key ) );

CREATE TABLE child (
   child_key     INTEGER NOT NULL PRIMARY KEY,
   parent_key    INTEGER NULL REFERENCES parent ( parent_key ) );

INSERT parent VALUES ( 1, 'x' ); -- parent with three children
INSERT parent VALUES ( 2, 'x' ); -- parent with no children
INSERT parent VALUES ( 3, 'y' ); -- parent with no children

INSERT child VALUES ( 4, 1 );    -- child with parent
INSERT child VALUES ( 5, 1 );    -- child with parent
INSERT child VALUES ( 6, 1 );    -- child with parent
INSERT child VALUES ( 7, NULL ); -- orphan

SELECT parent.parent_key,
       parent.data_1,
       child.child_key,
       child.parent_key
  FROM parent INNER JOIN child ON parent.parent_key = child.parent_key
 ORDER BY parent.parent_key,
       child.child_key;
```

Note: The detailed syntax for the <boolean_expression> is discussed later, in Section 3.12, "Boolean Expressions and the WHERE Clause." Even though both ON and WHERE use the same <boolean_expression> syntax, ON conditions don't often take advantage of all the features available. A typical ON condition takes the form of "ON a = b AND c = d" to join tables using simple equality relationships plus the AND operator. WHERE clauses, on the other hand, tend to be more complex and that's why a full discussion of <boolean_expression> is deferred until Section 3.12.

The INNER JOIN operator combines every row in one table with every row in the other table where the data in the two rows satisfies the ON condition. In this example, the first parent row is combined with the first three child rows to produce a result set consisting of three rows.

```
parent.      parent.  child.     child.
parent_key   data_1   child_key  parent_key
==========   =======  =========  ==========
    1          x         4           1        -- parent and child
    1          x         5           1        -- parent and child
    1          x         6           1        -- parent and child
```

The second and third parent rows don't appear in the final result set because they can't be combined with any child rows and still satisfy the ON condition; more specifically, parent.parent_key = 2 and 3 don't match any child.parent_key values. The same is true of the fourth child row: It can't be matched with any parent row because child.parent_key = NULL doesn't match any parent.parent_key value. In other words, childless parent rows and orphaned child rows aren't included in the INNER JOIN using a foreign key relationship in the ON condition.

3.4.3 LEFT OUTER JOIN

If you want to include all the rows in one or the other or both tables, even if they don't satisfy the ON condition, you can use one of the OUTER JOIN operators. In the example from the previous section, the second and third rows from the parent table could be included in the result set by using the LEFT OUTER JOIN operator instead of INNER JOIN:

```
SELECT parent.parent_key,
       parent.data_1,
       child.child_key,
       child.parent_key
  FROM parent LEFT OUTER JOIN child ON parent.parent_key = child.parent_key
ORDER BY parent.parent_key,
       child.child_key;
```

Here's how LEFT OUTER JOIN works: First, the INNER JOIN operation is performed, as described earlier, to construct a result set. Then, any row in the left-hand table that didn't participate in the INNER JOIN is appended to the result set, with NULL values being used for the columns that would otherwise come from the right-hand table. Note that the ON condition is only applied in the first step, and is ignored in the second step.

In the example above, the LEFT OUTER JOIN appends two more rows to the result set from the INNER JOIN, and these rows correspond to the second and third rows from the parent table:

```
parent.    parent.  child.    child.
parent_key data_1   child_key parent_key
========== =======  ========= ==========
     1        x        4          1        -- parent and child
     1        x        5          1        -- parent and child
     1        x        6          1        -- parent and child
     2        x       NULL       NULL      -- parent with no children
     3        y       NULL       NULL      -- parent with no children
```

In a LEFT OUTER JOIN operation, the left-hand table is called the "preserved table" because every row is represented at least once in the result set. The right-hand table is called the "null-supplying table" because NULL may be used for its column values in some of the rows in the result of the join. The word "LEFT" in LEFT OUTER JOIN means that the left-hand table is the preserved table. In the example above, only two new rows were added, corresponding to the parent rows with no corresponding child rows. The orphan child row, the one with no corresponding parent row, still doesn't appear in the final result because only one table can be the preserved table in a LEFT OUTER JOIN.

The LEFT OUTER JOIN operator is very commonly used to gather required and optional data from different tables when you want to make sure all the required data is included, even when no corresponding optional data exists. Or to put it another way, "show me all the parent and child data, including all the childless parents."

3.4.4 RIGHT OUTER JOIN

The RIGHT OUTER JOIN operator exactly reverses the roles of the two tables in a LEFT OUTER JOIN. For example, the following statement defines the child table as the preserved table because it is on the right side of the RIGHT OUTER JOIN, and the parent table is the null-supplying table because it is on the other side:

```
SELECT parent.parent_key,
       parent.data_1,
       child.child_key,
       child.parent_key
  FROM parent RIGHT OUTER JOIN child ON parent.parent_key = child.parent_key
 ORDER BY parent.parent_key,
          child.child_key;
```

Now the orphan child row is included in the final result set, with parent.parent_key and data_1 set to NULL, but the parent rows with no corresponding children are missing:

```
parent.    parent.  child.    child.
parent_key data_1   child_key parent_key
========== =======  ========= ==========
    NULL     NULL      7         NULL      -- orphan
     1        x        4          1        -- parent and child
     1        x        5          1        -- parent and child
     1        x        6          1        -- parent and child
```

Note that every RIGHT OUTER JOIN can be transformed into a LEFT OUTER JOIN, which performs exactly the same function, by simply switching the table names. For example, the following LEFT OUTER JOIN returns the same rows as the RIGHT OUTER JOIN above:

```
SELECT parent.parent_key,
       parent.data_1,
       child.child_key,
       child.parent_key
  FROM child LEFT OUTER JOIN parent ON parent.parent_key = child.parent_key
 ORDER BY parent.parent_key,
          child.child_key;
```

Tip: Outer joins are confusing at the best of times, so don't make the situation worse by using both LEFT OUTER JOIN and RIGHT OUTER JOIN operators. Stick with LEFT OUTER JOIN and your code will be easier to understand because the preserved table will always be on the same side.

3.4.5 FULL OUTER JOIN

The FULL OUTER JOIN operator is an extension that combines both LEFT OUTER JOIN and RIGHT OUTER JOIN functionality. In other words, all the rows in both tables are preserved, and both tables are null-supplying when they have to be. Here's how it works: First, the INNER JOIN is computed using the ON condition. Second, any rows from the left-hand table that weren't included by the INNER JOIN process are now appended to the result set, with NULL values used for the columns that would normally come from the right-hand table. And finally, any rows from the right-hand table that weren't included by the INNER JOIN process are now appended to the result set, with NULL values used for the columns that would normally come from the left-hand table.

Here's what the FULL OUTER JOIN looks like, using the parent and child tables:

```
SELECT parent.parent_key,
       parent.data_1,
       child.child_key,
       child.parent_key
  FROM parent FULL OUTER JOIN child ON parent.parent_key = child.parent_key
 ORDER BY parent.parent_key,
          child.child_key;
```

Now the result set contains all the columns from all the rows in both tables. It includes parent-and-child combinations from the INNER JOIN, plus the orphan child row from the RIGHT OUTER JOIN, plus the childless parent rows from the LEFT OUTER JOIN.

```
parent.      parent.   child.      child.
parent_key   data_1    child_key   parent_key
==========   =======   =========   ==========
   NULL       NULL        7          NULL      -- orphan
    1          x          4           1        -- parent and child
    1          x          5           1        -- parent and child
    1          x          6           1        -- parent and child
    2          x         NULL        NULL      -- parent with no children
    3          y         NULL        NULL      -- parent with no children
```

It's important to understand that the ON condition only applies to the first step in any OUTER JOIN process. All the rows in the preserved table(s) are included in the final result set no matter what the ON condition says. Here's an example where the restriction parent.data_1 = 'x' has been added to the ON condition of the LEFT OUTER JOIN presented earlier:

```
SELECT parent.parent_key,
       parent.data_1,
       child.child_key,
       child.parent_key
  FROM parent LEFT OUTER JOIN child ON  parent.parent_key = child.parent_key
                                   AND parent.data_1    = 'x'
 ORDER BY parent.parent_key,
          child.child_key;
```

In this case the result set is exactly the same as it was before:

```
parent.    parent.  child.     child.
parent_key data_1   child_key  parent_key
========== =======  =========  ==========
        1      x         4          1     -- parent and child
        1      x         5          1     -- parent and child
        1      x         6          1     -- parent and child
        2      x       NULL       NULL    -- parent with no children
        3      y       NULL       NULL    -- parent with no children
```

The fact that a row with parent.data_1 = 'y' is included even though the ON condition specified only rows with 'x' were to be included often comes as a surprise. It's the way an OUTER JOIN works, and it's the way it's supposed to work, but it is often not exactly what you want.

Tip: Be very careful what you code in the ON condition of an OUTER JOIN. A good rule of thumb is to only code conditions that affect how rows from both tables are joined, not conditions affecting only one or the other table. If you want to eliminate rows in one or the other table before the OUTER JOIN is applied, use a derived table or a view.

3.5 Derived Tables

A *derived table* is a mechanism where you can code an entire subquery inside a FROM clause, and have the result set from that subquery treated like any other table term in the FROM clause.

```
<derived_table>           ::= <subquery>
                              [ AS ] <correlation_name>
                              [ <derived_column_name_list> ]
<derived_column_name_list> ::= "(" <alias_name_list> ")"
<alias_name_list>         ::= <alias_name> { "," <alias_name> }
<alias_name>              ::= <identifier>
```

In the previous example, a LEFT OUTER JOIN was written using an ON condition that didn't satisfy the requirements, (only parent rows with parent.data_1 = 'x' were to be included in the result set). The problem was that a row with parent.data_1 = 'y' was included because of the way OUTER JOIN operators work. Here's how a derived table can be used to solve that problem by eliminating the unwanted rows before the LEFT OUTER JOIN is applied:

```
SELECT parent.parent_key,
       parent.data_1,
       child.child_key,
       child.parent_key
  FROM ( SELECT *
           FROM parent
          WHERE parent.data_1 = 'x' ) AS parent
```

```
        LEFT OUTER JOIN child ON parent.parent_key = child.parent_key
ORDER BY parent.parent_key,
        child.child_key;
```

Tip: The minimum coding requirements for a derived table are a subquery inside brackets, followed by a correlation name by which the subquery's result set will be known in the rest of the FROM clause. If all you want from a derived table is to apply a WHERE clause to a table, there's no reason not to use SELECT * in the subquery. You can also use the table name as the correlation name if you want, and you don't have to specify alias names for any of the columns; in other words, the derived table can look exactly like the original table, as far as the table and column names are concerned. Also, you don't necessarily have to worry about performance; the query optimizer does a pretty good job of turning subqueries into joins and eliminating columns that aren't actually needed.

In the LEFT OUTER JOIN example above, the derived table is called "parent" and it looks like this:

```
( SELECT *
    FROM parent
    WHERE parent.data_1 = 'x' ) AS parent
```

Now only rows with parent.data_1 = 'x' are considered for the LEFT OUTER JOIN with the child table, and the final result set looks like this:

```
parent.     parent.  child.     child.
parent_key  data_1   child_key  parent_key
==========  =======  =========  ==========
    1          x         4          1         -- parent and child
    1          x         5          1         -- parent and child
    1          x         6          1         -- parent and child
    2          x        NULL       NULL       -- parent with no children
```

It is sometimes tempting to use a WHERE clause in the outer SELECT, instead of an ON condition inside a FROM clause, especially if the ON condition doesn't work and you don't want to bother with a derived table. With an OUTER JOIN, however, a WHERE clause is like an ON condition — sometimes it does what you want, and sometimes it doesn't. In particular, a WHERE clause is applied long after the FROM clause is completely evaluated, and it can accidentally eliminate rows where columns were filled with NULL values from the null-supplying table.

Here is an example using the FULL OUTER JOIN from earlier; an attempt is being made to restrict the parent rows to ones where parent.data_1 = 'x' by adding that restriction in a WHERE clause:

```
SELECT parent.parent_key,
       parent.data_1,
       child.child_key,
       child.parent_key
  FROM parent FULL OUTER JOIN child ON parent.parent_key = child.parent_key
 WHERE parent.data_1 = 'x'
 ORDER BY parent.parent_key,
          child.child_key;
```

According to the explanation in Section 3.2, "Logical Execution of a SELECT," the FROM clause is evaluated first and the WHERE clause is applied later. That means the initial result of the FROM clause looks exactly as it did earlier, in

Section 3.4.5, "FULL OUTER JOIN," because the WHERE clause hasn't been applied yet:

```
parent.    parent.  child.     child.
parent_key data_1   child_key  parent_key
========== =======  =========  ==========
   NULL      NULL      7         NULL      -- this row is going to disappear: not OK
    1         x        4          1
    1         x        5          1
    1         x        6          1
    2         x       NULL       NULL
    3         y       NULL       NULL      -- this row is going to disappear: OK
```

When the WHERE clause is applied to produce the final result set, two rows are eliminated, not just one. The first row above is eliminated because parent.data_1 is NULL and the last row is eliminated because parent.data_1 is 'y'; neither match the WHERE condition parent.data_1 = 'x'.

In other words, the FULL OUTER JOIN isn't a FULL OUTER JOIN anymore because the orphan child row is no longer represented in the final result set; adding the WHERE clause effectively turned it into a LEFT OUTER JOIN.

```
parent.    parent.  child.     child.
parent_key data_1   child_key  parent_key
========== =======  =========  ==========
    1         x        4          1
    1         x        5          1
    1         x        6          1
    2         x       NULL       NULL
```

In fact, if there were a thousand orphan rows in the child table, they would all be eliminated by that WHERE clause, when all we wanted to do is eliminate one parent row, the one with parent.data_1 different from 'x'.

The solution once again is a derived table that eliminates the unwanted parent row before the FULL OUTER JOIN is computed:

```
SELECT parent.parent_key,
       parent.data_1,
       child.child_key,
       child.parent_key
 FROM ( SELECT *
          FROM parent
         WHERE parent.data_1 = 'x' ) AS parent
       FULL OUTER JOIN child ON parent.parent_key = child.parent_key
ORDER BY parent.parent_key,
         child.child_key;
```

Now the result set makes more sense — the orphan child row is included, and the unwanted parent row is eliminated:

```
parent.    parent.  child.     child.
parent_key data_1   child_key  parent_key
========== =======  =========  ==========
   NULL      NULL      7         NULL      -- orphan
    1         x        4          1        -- parent and child
    1         x        5          1        -- parent and child
    1         x        6          1        -- parent and child
    2         x       NULL       NULL      -- parent with no children
```

Note: It is very common for a WHERE clause to accidentally eliminate rows in an OUTER JOIN. Typically, a LEFT OUTER JOIN or RIGHT OUTER JOIN becomes an INNER JOIN, or a FULL OUTER JOIN becomes a LEFT or RIGHT OUTER JOIN. Here's the technical explanation for this symptom: Any null-intolerant predicate that refers to attributes from a null-supplying table will eliminate NULL-supplied rows from the result. A null-intolerant predicate is a predicate that cannot evaluate to true if any of its inputs are NULL. Most SQL predicates, such as comparisons, LIKE, or IN predicates, are null-intolerant. Examples of null-tolerant predicates are IS NULL and any predicate p qualified by a null-tolerant truth value test, such as p IS NOT TRUE. (from "Semantics and Compatibility of Transact-SQL Outer Joins" by G. N. Paulley, 15 February 2002, iAnywhere Solutions Technical White Paper, Document Number 1017447.)

3.6 Multi-Table Joins

The syntax of the FROM clause allows for joins among endless numbers of tables, with or without parentheses to create nested table expressions, and with or without ON conditions on each join. In most cases, parentheses are not required, but it is a very good idea to provide an ON condition for every join operator whenever possible.

```
<table_expression>      ::= <table_term>
                        | <table_expression>
                           CROSS JOIN
                           <table_term>
                        | <table_expression>
                           [ <on_condition_shorthand> ] -- do not use
                           <join_operator>
                           <table_term>
                           [ <on_condition> ]          -- use this instead
<table_term>            ::= <table_reference>
                        | <view_reference>
                        | <derived_table>
                        | <procedure_reference>
                        | "(" <table_expression_list> ")"
                        | <lateral_derived_table>
<on_condition_shorthand> ::= KEY     -- foreign key columns; do not use
                        | NATURAL -- like-named columns; do not use
<join_operator>        ::= <inner_join>
                        | <left_outer_join>
                        | <right_outer_join>
                        | <full_outer_join>
```

In the absence of parentheses, join operators are evaluated from left to right. That means the first pair of table terms are joined to create a virtual table, then that virtual table is joined to the third table term to produce another virtual table, and so on.

The following example shows a four-way join among tables that exist in the ASADEMO database that ships with SQL Anywhere Studio 9. Here is the schema for the four tables (customer, product, sales_order, and sales_order_items) plus two other tables that will appear in later examples (employee and fin_code):

```
CREATE TABLE customer (
    id          INTEGER NOT NULL DEFAULT AUTOINCREMENT,
    fname       CHAR ( 15 ) NOT NULL,
    lname       CHAR ( 20 ) NOT NULL,
```

```
   address        CHAR ( 35 ) NOT NULL,
   city           CHAR ( 20 ) NOT NULL,
   state          CHAR ( 16 ) NULL,
   zip            CHAR ( 10 ) NULL,
   phone          CHAR ( 12 ) NOT NULL,
   company_name   CHAR ( 35 ) NULL,
   PRIMARY KEY ( id ) );

CREATE TABLE employee (
   emp_id            INTEGER NOT NULL PRIMARY KEY,
   manager_id        INTEGER NULL,
   emp_fname         CHAR ( 20 ) NOT NULL,
   emp_lname         CHAR ( 20 ) NOT NULL,
   dept_id           INTEGER NOT NULL,
   street            CHAR ( 40 ) NOT NULL,
   city              CHAR ( 20 ) NOT NULL,
   state             CHAR ( 16 ) NULL,
   zip_code          CHAR ( 10 ) NULL,
   phone             CHAR ( 10 ) NULL,
   status            CHAR ( 2 ) NULL,
   ss_number         CHAR ( 11 ) NULL,
   salary            NUMERIC ( 20, 3 ) NOT NULL,
   start_date        DATE NOT NULL,
   termination_date  DATE NULL,
   birth_date        DATE NULL,
   bene_health_ins   CHAR ( 2 ) NULL,
   bene_life_ins     CHAR ( 2 ) NULL,
   bene_day_care     CHAR ( 2 ) NULL,
   sex               CHAR ( 2 ) NULL );

CREATE TABLE fin_code (
   code        CHAR ( 2 ) NOT NULL PRIMARY KEY,
   type        CHAR ( 10 ) NOT NULL,
   description CHAR ( 50 ) NULL );

CREATE TABLE product (
   id          INTEGER NOT NULL,
   name        CHAR ( 15 ) NOT NULL,
   description CHAR ( 30 ) NOT NULL,
   size        CHAR ( 18 ) NOT NULL,
   color       CHAR ( 6 ) NOT NULL,
   quantity    INTEGER NOT NULL,
   unit_price  NUMERIC ( 15, 2 ) NOT NULL,
   PRIMARY KEY ( id ) );

CREATE TABLE sales_order (
   id          INTEGER NOT NULL DEFAULT AUTOINCREMENT,
   cust_id     INTEGER NOT NULL REFERENCES customer ( id ),
   order_date  DATE NOT NULL,
   fin_code_id CHAR ( 2 ) NULL REFERENCES fin_code ( code ),
   region      CHAR ( 7 ) NULL,
   sales_rep   INTEGER NOT NULL REFERENCES employee ( emp_id ),
   PRIMARY KEY ( id ) );

CREATE TABLE sales_order_items (
   id         INTEGER NOT NULL REFERENCES sales_order ( id ),
   line_id    SMALLINT NOT NULL,
   prod_id    INTEGER NOT NULL REFERENCES product ( id ),
   quantity   INTEGER NOT NULL,
   ship_date  DATE NOT NULL,
   PRIMARY KEY ( id, line_id ) );
```

The customer table holds information about companies that may buy products, the product table defines each product for sale, sales_order records each sale to a customer, and the sales_order_items table is a many-to-many relationship between product and sales_order to record which products were included in which orders. There are foreign key relationships among these tables to define the relationships, and these foreign key relationships are used in the ON conditions of the four INNER JOIN operations, which gather all the information about which products were sold to which customers as part of which order:

```
SELECT customer.company_name,
       sales_order.order_date,
       product.name,
       product.description,
       sales_order_items.quantity,
       product.unit_price * sales_order_items.quantity AS amount
  FROM customer
       INNER JOIN sales_order
              ON sales_order.cust_id = customer.id
       INNER JOIN sales_order_items
              ON sales_order_items.id = sales_order.id
       INNER JOIN product
              ON product.id = sales_order_items.prod_id
 ORDER BY customer.company_name,
       sales_order.order_date,
       product.name;
```

Here's how this FROM clause works from a logical point of view:

- First, rows in customer are joined with rows in sales_order where the customer id columns match. The virtual table resulting from the first INNER JOIN contains all the columns from the customer and sales_order tables.

- In the second INNER JOIN, the rows from the first virtual table are joined with rows in sales_order_item where the sales order id columns match. Note that the columns in the first virtual table may be referred to using their base table name; e.g., sales_order.order_id in the second ON condition. The result of the second INNER JOIN is a new virtual table consisting of all the columns in customer, sales_order, and sales_order_item.

- In the final INNER JOIN, the rows from the second virtual table are joined with rows in product where product id columns match. The result of the final INNER JOIN is a virtual table consisting of columns in all four tables. Even though this is (conceptually speaking) a single virtual table, individual columns may still be referred to using their original table names; e.g., customer.company_name in the ORDER BY clause.

The final result set consists of 1,097 rows. Here are the first six rows, showing the detail of the first three orders placed by Able Inc.:

company_name	order_date	name	description	quantity	amount
Able Inc.	2000-01-16	Sweatshirt	Hooded Sweatshirt	36	864.00
Able Inc.	2000-01-16	Sweatshirt	Zipped Sweatshirt	36	864.00
Able Inc.	2000-03-20	Baseball Cap	Wool cap	24	240.00
Able Inc.	2000-04-08	Baseball Cap	Cotton Cap	24	216.00
Able Inc.	2000-04-08	Baseball Cap	Wool cap	24	240.00
Able Inc.	2000-04-08	Visor	Cloth Visor	24	168.00

Each ON condition applies to the preceding join operator. The following FROM clause uses parentheses to explicitly show which ON goes with which INNER

JOIN in the preceding example; note that this particular FROM clause performs exactly the same function with or without the parentheses:

```
FROM ( ( ( customer
          INNER JOIN sales_order
               ON sales_order.cust_id = customer.id )
          INNER JOIN sales_order_items
               ON sales_order_items.id = sales_order.id )
          INNER JOIN product
               ON product.id = sales_order_items.prod_id )
```

Parentheses are useful in arithmetic expressions when you have to override the natural order of execution of the different operators (e.g., if you want addition to come before multiplication). Even if they're not required, parentheses in arithmetic expressions help the reader understand the order of evaluation. Those arguments do not apply as strongly to parentheses in the FROM clause. First of all, there is no difference in precedence among the different join operators like INNER JOIN and LEFT OUTER JOIN; without parentheses they're simply evaluated from left to right. Also, FROM clauses tend to be long, drawn-out affairs where matching parentheses appear far apart, so they're not much help to the reader. Even in the simple example above, it's hard to see what the parentheses are doing; an argument can be made that the version without parentheses is easier to read.

Having said that, parentheses in the FROM clause are sometimes necessary and helpful. The following example illustrates that point using the four tables in the ASADEMO database discussed above: customer, product, sales_order, and sales_order_items. The requirement is to show how many of each kind of shirt were sold to each customer in Washington, D.C., including combinations of product and customer that had no sales. In other words, show all the combinations of Washington customers and shirt products, whether or not any actual sales were made.

At first glance it appears four joins are required: a CROSS JOIN between customer and product to generate all possible combinations, a LEFT OUTER JOIN between customer and sales_order to include customers whether or not they bought anything, a LEFT OUTER JOIN between product and sales_order_items to include products whether or not any were sold, and an INNER JOIN between sales_order and sales_order_items to match up the orders with their order items.

Perhaps it is possible to write these four joins, in the right order, with or without parentheses, but a simpler solution uses a divide-and-conquer approach:

- First, separately and independently compute two different virtual tables: the CROSS JOIN between customer and product, and the INNER JOIN between sales_order and sales_order_items.
- Second, perform a LEFT OUTER JOIN between the first and second virtual tables. Parentheses are used to separate the first step from the second.

Here is the pseudocode for the FROM clause using this approach:

```
SELECT ...
  FROM ( all the combinations of customer and product )
     LEFT OUTER JOIN
       ( all the matching combinations of sales_order and sales_order_items )
  WHERE ...
```

The full SELECT is shown below; the FROM clause has only three joins, two of them nested inside parentheses to create two simple virtual tables. The final LEFT OUTER JOIN combines these two virtual tables using an ON clause that refers to all four base tables inside the two virtual tables. The parentheses make it easy to understand: The CROSS JOIN is the simplest kind of join there is, and the INNER join is a simple combination of sales_order rows with their associated sales_order_items row.

```
SELECT customer.company_name         AS company_name,
       product.name                  AS product_name,
       product.description           AS product_description,
       SUM ( sales_order_items.quantity ) AS quantity,
       SUM ( product.unit_price
           * sales_order_items.quantity ) AS amount
  FROM ( customer
         CROSS JOIN product )
       LEFT OUTER JOIN
       ( sales_order
         INNER JOIN sales_order_items
              ON sales_order_items.id = sales_order.id )
       ON  customer.id = sales_order.cust_id
       AND product.id  = sales_order_items.prod_id
 WHERE customer.state = 'DC'
   AND product.name LIKE '%shirt%'
 GROUP BY customer.company_name,
       product.name,
       product.description
 ORDER BY customer.company_name,
       product.name,
       product.description;
```

The final result is shown below. There are two customers in Washington, D.C., and five different kinds of shirts for sale, making for 10 combinations of customer and product. Five combinations had no sales as shown by the NULL values in quantity and amount, and five combinations did have actual sales.

company_name	product_name	product_description	quantity	amount
Hometown Tee's	Sweatshirt	Hooded Sweatshirt	24	576.00
Hometown Tee's	Sweatshirt	Zipped Sweatshirt	NULL	NULL
Hometown Tee's	Tee Shirt	Crew Neck	NULL	NULL
Hometown Tee's	Tee Shirt	Tank Top	24	216.00
Hometown Tee's	Tee Shirt	V-neck	NULL	NULL
State House Active Wear	Sweatshirt	Hooded Sweatshirt	48	1152.00
State House Active Wear	Sweatshirt	Zipped Sweatshirt	48	1152.00
State House Active Wear	Tee Shirt	Crew Neck	NULL	NULL
State House Active Wear	Tee Shirt	Tank Top	NULL	NULL
State House Active Wear	Tee Shirt	V-neck	60	840.00

A *star join* is a multi-table join between one single "fact table" and several "dimension tables." Pictorially, the fact table is at the center of a star, and the dimension tables are the points of the star, arranged around the central fact table.

The fact table stores a large number of rows, each containing a single fact; for example, in the ASADEMO database the sales_order table contains over 600 rows, each containing the record of a single sale. The dimension tables store information about attributes of those facts; for example, the customer table contains the name and address of the customer who made the purchase.

Each dimension table is related to the fact table by a foreign key relation-ship, with the fact table as the child and the dimension table as the parent. For example, the sales_order table has foreign key relationships with three dimen-sion tables: customer, employee, and fin_code. The employee table contains more information about the salesperson who took the order, and the fin_code table has more information about the financial accounting code for the order.

Dimension tables are usually much smaller than the fact table; in the ASADEMO database there are three times as many rows in the sales_order fact table than there are in all three dimension tables put together. Dimension tables also tend to be highly normalized; for example, each customer's name and address is stored in one row in the customer table rather than being repeated in multiple sales_order rows. Star joins are used to denormalize the tables in the star by gathering data from all of them and presenting it as a single result set. For more information about normalization, see Section 1.16, "Normalized Design."

A star join may be represented as a FROM clause where the fact table appears first, followed by a series of INNER JOIN operators involving the dimension tables. The ON clauses on all the joins refer back to the first table, the fact table. Following is an example that selects all the sales orders in a date range, together with information from the customer, employee, and fin_code tables; the sales_order table is the central fact table in this star join.

```
SELECT sales_order.order_date      AS order_date,
         sales_order.id            AS order_id,
         customer.company_name     AS customer_name,
         STRING ( employee.emp_fname,
                  ' ',
                  employee.emp_lname ) AS rep_name,
         fin_code.description      AS fin_code
  FROM sales_order
         INNER JOIN customer
             ON sales_order.cust_id = customer.id
         INNER JOIN employee
             ON sales_order.sales_rep = employee.emp_id
         INNER JOIN fin_code
             ON sales_order.fin_code_id = fin_code.code
 WHERE sales_order.order_date BETWEEN '2000-01-02' AND '2000-01-06'
 ORDER BY order_date,
         order_id;
```

Here is the result of the star join, which effectively "denormalizes" four tables into a single result set:

order_date	order_id	customer_name	rep_name	fin_code
2000-01-02	2131	BoSox Club	Samuel Singer	Fees
2000-01-03	2065	Bloomfields	Samuel Singer	Fees
2000-01-03	2126	Leisure Time	Rollin Overbey	Fees
2000-01-06	2127	Creative Customs Inc.	James Klobucher	Fees
2000-01-06	2135	East Coast Traders	Alison Clark	Fees

3.7 SELECT FROM Procedure Call

A SQL Anywhere stored procedure can return a result set, and that result set can be treated just like a table in a FROM clause.

```
<procedure_reference>     ::= [ <owner_name> "." ] <procedure_name>
                              "(" [ <argument_list> ] ")"
                              [ WITH "(" <result_definition_list> ")" ]
                              [ [ AS ] <correlation_name> ]
<procedure_name>          ::= <identifier>
<argument_list>           ::= <argument> { "," <argument> }
<argument>                ::= <basic_expression>
                            | <parameter_name> "=" <basic_expression>
<parameter_name>          ::= see <parameter_name> in Chapter 8, "Packaging"
<result_definition_list>  ::= <result_definition> { "," <result_definition> }
<result_definition>       ::= <alias_name> <data_type>
<data_type>               ::= see <data_type> in Chapter 1, "Creating"
```

The advantage to using a stored procedure is that it can contain multiple statements whereas derived tables and views must be coded as a single query. Sometimes a difficult problem is made easier by breaking it into separate steps. For example, consider this convoluted request: Show all the products that contributed to the second- and third-best sales for a single color on a single day in the worst year for sales, using three of the ASADEMO database tables described in the previous section — product, sales_order, and sales_order_items.

A divide-and-conquer approach can be used to solve this problem:

- First, compute the worst year for total sales.
- Second, within that year, find the second- and third-best sales for a single color on a single day.
- Third, for those combinations of best color and order date, find the matching products; in other words, find the products with matching colors that were ordered on those dates.

Each of these steps has its challenges, but solving them separately is a lot easier than writing one single select to solve them all at once. And even if you could write one query to do everything, other people might have a lot of trouble understanding what you've written, and in some shops maintainability is more important than elegance.

A stored procedure called p_best_losers_in_worst_year performs the first two steps: One SELECT computes the total sales for each year, sorts the results in ascending order by sales amount, and takes the first year and stores it in a local variable called @worst_year. A second SELECT computes the total sales by color and date within @worst_year, sorts the results in descending order by sales amount, and returns the second and third rows (the "best losers") as the procedure result set.

The following shows what the procedure looks like. For more information about the CREATE PROCEDURE statement, see Section 8.9.

```
CREATE PROCEDURE p_best_losers_in_worst_year()
BEGIN
DECLARE @worst_year INTEGER;
```

```
-- Determine the worst year for total sales.

SELECT FIRST
        YEAR ( sales_order.order_date )
  INTO @worst_year
  FROM product
        INNER JOIN sales_order_items
            ON product.id = sales_order_items.prod_id
        INNER JOIN sales_order
            ON sales_order_items.id = sales_order.id
 GROUP BY YEAR ( sales_order.order_date )
 ORDER BY SUM ( sales_order_items.quantity * product.unit_price ) ASC;

-- Find the second- and third-best sales for a single color on a
-- single day in the worst year.

SELECT TOP 2 START AT 2
        product.color           AS best_color,
        sales_order.order_date AS best_day,
        SUM ( sales_order_items.quantity * product.unit_price ) AS sales_amount,
        NUMBER(*) + 1           AS rank
  FROM product
        INNER JOIN sales_order_items
            ON product.id = sales_order_items.prod_id
        INNER JOIN sales_order
            ON sales_order_items.id = sales_order.id
 WHERE YEAR ( sales_order.order_date ) = @worst_year
 GROUP BY product.color,
        sales_order.order_date
 ORDER BY SUM ( sales_order_items.quantity * product.unit_price ) DESC;
END;
```

The first SELECT in the procedure puts a single value into the variable @worst_year. The second query doesn't have an INTO clause, so its result set is implicitly returned to the caller when the procedure is called.

You can test this procedure in ISQL as follows:

```
CALL p_best_losers_in_worst_year();
```

Here are the second- and third-best color days, together with the sales amounts, as returned by the procedure call:

best_color	best_day	sales_amount	rank
Green	2001-03-24	1728.00	2
Black	2001-03-17	1524.00	3

The third step in the solution uses the procedure call as a table term in the FROM clause of a query to find the product details:

```
SELECT DISTINCT
        product.id,
        product.name,
        product.description,
        product.color,
        best_loser.rank
  FROM p_best_losers_in_worst_year() AS best_loser
        INNER JOIN product
            ON product.color = best_loser.best_color
        INNER JOIN sales_order_items
            ON product.id = sales_order_items.prod_id
        INNER JOIN sales_order
            ON sales_order_items.id   = sales_order.id
```

```
           AND sales_order.order_date = best_loser.best_day
ORDER BY best_loser.rank ASC,
        product.id ASC;
```

Here's how that SELECT works:

- The procedure reference p_best_losers_in_worst_year() is coded without the CALL keyword but with an empty argument list; those are the minimum requirements for a procedure call in a FROM clause.

- A correlation name, "best_loser," is defined, but isn't necessary; if you don't specify an explicit correlation name, the procedure name itself will be used as the correlation name in the rest of the query.

- The FROM clause then uses INNER JOIN operators to join rows in best_loser together with rows in the other three tables — product, sales_order_items, and sales_order — to find the combinations that match on color and order date.

- Finally, the select list returns columns from product plus the rank (second or third) from best_loser. The DISTINCT keyword is used because the same product may have been included in more than one sales order on the same day, and we're only interested in seeing each different product.

Here is the final result, which shows that one green product contributed to the second-best day, and three black products contributed to the third-best day:

```
id   name          description         color  rank
===  ============  =================   =====  ====
600  Sweatshirt    Hooded Sweatshirt   Green  2
302  Tee Shirt     Crew Neck           Black  3
400  Baseball Cap  Cotton Cap          Black  3
700  Shorts        Cotton Shorts       Black  3
```

A stored procedure can specify column names for its result set in one of two ways: by making sure each item in the select list has a column name or an alias name, or by specifying an explicit RESULT clause in the CREATE PROCEDURE statement. Both of those methods are optional, however, and that can cause problems for a stored procedure reference in a FROM clause. For example, if the expression NUMBER(*) + 1 didn't have the alias name "rank" explicitly specified in the procedure p_best_losers_in_worst_year presented above, the reference to best_loser.rank couldn't be used in the final select list.

Another solution is to add an explicit WITH list to the procedure reference in the FROM clause. This WITH list specifies the alias names and data types to be used for each column in the procedure result set, as far as this FROM clause is concerned. Even if the stored procedure specifies names for the columns in its result set, the WITH list names override those. Here is the above SELECT with an explicit WITH list that specifies two alias names that are different from the names the procedure returns:

```
SELECT DISTINCT
        product.id,
        product.name,
        product.description,
        product.color,
        best_loser.ranking
   FROM p_best_losers_in_worst_year()
        WITH ( best_color VARCHAR ( 6 ),
               best_day   DATE,
```

```
                    best_sales NUMERIC ( 15, 2 ),
                    ranking    INTEGER )
               AS best_loser
        INNER JOIN product
            ON product.color = best_loser.best_color
        INNER JOIN sales_order_items
            ON product.id = sales_order_items.prod_id
        INNER JOIN sales_order
            ON sales_order_items.id  = sales_order.id
            AND sales_order.order_date = best_loser.best_day
   ORDER BY best_loser.ranking ASC,
        product.id ASC;
```

A procedure reference in a FROM clause is executed exactly once, and the result set is materialized exactly once, if that procedure has an empty argument list or only receives constant arguments. This can be bad news or good news depending on your needs. If the procedure returns a lot of unnecessary rows, the query processor won't optimize the call and performance may be worse for a procedure reference than, say, for the equivalent view reference or derived table if one could be defined. On the other hand, knowing that the procedure will definitely be called exactly once, and the result set materialized, may help you solve some tricky problems.

In this discussion, *materialized* means the result set is fully evaluated and stored in memory or in the temporary file if memory is exhausted. Also, *constant argument* means an argument that doesn't change in value while the FROM clause is evaluated; literals fall into that category, as do program variables, and expressions involving literals and variables, but not references to columns in other tables in the FROM clause.

The next section talks about a procedure that receives a variable argument; i.e., a column from another table in the FROM clause.

3.8 LATERAL Procedure Call

If a column from another table is passed as an argument to a procedure reference in a FROM clause, that procedure reference must appear as part of a LATERAL derived table definition. Also, the other table must appear ahead of the LATERAL derived table definition and be separated from it by a comma rather than one of the join operators like INNER JOIN. This is a situation where the "comma join operator" must be used and the ON condition cannot be used.

Here is the general syntax for a LATERAL derived table:

```
<lateral_derived_table> ::= LATERAL
                    <subquery>
                    [ AS ] <correlation_name>
                    [ <derived_column_name_list> ]
                | LATERAL
                    "(" <table_expression> ")"
                    [ AS ] <correlation_name>
                    [ <derived_column_name_list> ]
```

Here is the simplified syntax for a join between a table and a procedure reference where a column from that table is passed as an argument; this is the only use of the comma join and the LATERAL keyword that is discussed in this book:

```
<typical_lateral_procedure_call> ::= <table_name> ","
                                    LATERAL "(" <procedure_name>
                                        "(" <table_name>.<column_name> ")" ")"
                                    AS <correlation_name>
```

Here is an example of a procedure that receives the customer id as an argument and returns a result set containing all the sales order information for that customer:

```
CREATE PROCEDURE p_customer_orders ( IN @customer_id INTEGER )
BEGIN
MESSAGE STRING ( 'DIAG ', CURRENT TIMESTAMP, ' ', @customer_id ) TO CONSOLE;
SELECT sales_order.order_date        AS order_date,
       product.name                  AS product_name,
       product.description           AS description,
       sales_order_items.quantity    AS quantity,
       product.unit_price
         * sales_order_items.quantity AS amount
  FROM sales_order
       INNER JOIN sales_order_items
              ON sales_order_items.id = sales_order.id
       INNER JOIN product
              ON product.id = sales_order_items.prod_id
 WHERE sales_order.cust_id = @customer_id
 ORDER BY order_date,
       product_name,
       description;
END;

CALL p_customer_orders ( 141 );
```

Here is the result of the CALL for customer id 141, using the ASADEMO database:

```
order_date  product_name  description   quantity  amount
==========  ============  =============  ========  ======
2000-11-19  Shorts        Cotton Shorts  36        540.00
2001-02-26  Baseball Cap  Cotton Cap     12        108.00
```

The following is an example where that procedure is called in a FROM clause in a select that specifies the company name, Mall Side Sports, instead of the customer id 141. The customer table is joined to the procedure call with the comma join operator, and the procedure call is called as part of a LATERAL derived table definition, because the customer.id column is passed as an argument.

```
SELECT customer.company_name,
       customer_orders.*
  FROM customer,
       LATERAL ( p_customer_orders ( customer.id ) ) AS customer_orders
 WHERE customer.company_name = 'Mall Side Sports'
 ORDER BY customer_orders.order_date,
       customer_orders.product_name,
       customer_orders.description;
```

Here is the final result; same data as before, plus the company name:

```
company_name     order_date  product_name  description    quantity  amount
===============  ==========  ============  =============  ========  ======
Mall Side Sports 2000-11-19  Shorts        Cotton Shorts  36        540.00
Mall Side Sports 2001-02-26  Baseball Cap  Cotton Cap     12        108.00
```

Note: The comma join operator should be avoided. The other join operators, like INNER JOIN, and the ON condition make FROM clauses much easier to understand. In this particular case, however, the comma join operator must be used, and it can be thought of as working like an INNER JOIN.

Tip: Procedure calls in FROM clauses may be called once or a million times, depending on how they're coded. You can easily confirm how many times a procedure is called by adding a MESSAGE statement like the one in the example above; each call will result in a line displayed in the database engine console.

3.9 **SELECT** List

The second step in the logical execution of a select is to evaluate all the select list items, except for aggregate function and NUMBER(*) calls, and append the values to each row in the virtual table that is returned by the FROM clause.

```
<select_list>        ::= <select_item> { "," <select_item> }
<select_item>        ::= "*"
                       | [ <owner_name> "." ] <table_name> "." "*"
                       | <correlation_name> "." "*"
                       | <expression>
                       | <expression> [ AS ] <select_item_alias>
<select_item_alias> ::= <alias_name>       -- very useful
                       | <string_literal> -- not so useful
<string_literal>     ::= a sequence of characters enclosed in single quotes
```

The asterisk "*" represents all the columns from all the tables in the FROM clause, in the order the tables were specified in the FROM clause, and for each table, in the order the columns were specified in the CREATE TABLE statement.

The "*" notation may be combined with other select list items; i.e., you aren't limited to SELECT * FROM .... This is sometimes useful for quick queries to "show me the product name column, plus all the other columns in the table in case I want to look at them" as in the following example:

```
SELECT product.name,
       *
  FROM product
       INNER JOIN sales_order_items
            ON sales_order_items.prod_id = product.id
       INNER JOIN sales_order
            ON sales_order.id = sales_order_items.id
 ORDER BY product.name,
       sales_order.order_date DESC;
```

You can qualify a table name with ".*" to represent all the columns in this particular table, in the order they were specified in the CREATE TABLE statement. There's no restriction on repetition in the select list. Here is an example of a query to "show me the product name, plus all the columns in sales_order_items, plus all the columns in all the tables in case I want to look at them":

```
SELECT product.name,
       sales_order_items.*,
       *
  FROM product
       INNER JOIN sales_order_items
            ON sales_order_items.prod_id = product.id
       INNER JOIN sales_order
```

```
                 ON sales_order.id = sales_order_items.id
ORDER BY product.name,
    sales_order.order_date DESC;
```

Tip: In application programs it is usually a better idea to explicitly list all the column names in the select list rather than use the asterisk "*" notation.

An individual item (i.e., something not using the asterisk "*" notation) in a select list may be assigned an alias name. This name may be used elsewhere in the select list and in other clauses to refer back to this select list item. In the case of a column name in a select list, the alias name is optional because with or without an alias name, the column name itself may be used to refer to that item. For a select list item that is an expression, an alias name is required if that select list item is to be referred to by name in another location.

Tip: The keyword AS may be optional but it should always be used when defining alias names to make it clear to the reader which is the alias name and which is the select list item.

Tip: Use identifiers as alias names, not string literals. Only the select list allows a string literal as an alias, and if you use that facility you can't refer to the alias from other locations. In all the other locations where alias names may be used (in derived table definitions, CREATE VIEW statements, and WITH clauses, for example), only identifiers may be used, and that's what you should use in the select list.

Individual items in the select list, such as expressions and column references, are explained in detail in the following sections.

3.10 Expressions and Operators

A select list can be more than asterisks and column names; you can use vastly more complex expressions as long as each one returns a single value when it is evaluated. In fact, the simple <column_reference> is almost lost in the syntax for <expression>:

```
<expression>        ::= <basic_expression>
                      | <subquery>
<basic_expression>  ::= <simple_expression>
                      | <if_expression>
                      | <case_expression>
<simple_expression> ::= "(" <basic_expression> ")"        -- Precedence:
                      | "-" <expression>                  -- 1. unary minus
                      | "+" <expression>                  -- 1. unary plus
                      | "~" <expression>                  -- 1. bitwise NOT
                      | <simple_expression> "&" <expression>  -- 2. bitwise AND
                      | <simple_expression> "|" <expression>  -- 2. bitwise OR
                      | <simple_expression> "^" <expression>  -- 2. bitwise XOR
                      | <simple_expression> "*" <expression>  -- 3. multiply
                      | <simple_expression> "/" <expression>  -- 3. divide
                      | <simple_expression> "+" <expression>  -- 4. add
                      | <simple_expression> "-" <expression>  -- 4. subtract
                      | <simple_expression> "||" <expression> -- 5. concatenate
                      | <column_reference>
                      | <variable_reference>
                      | <string_literal>
```

```
                                | <number_literal>
                                | <special_literal>
                                | NULL
                                | <function_call>
<column_reference>   ::= <column_name>
                                | <alias_name>
                                | [ <owner_name> "." ] <table_name> "." <column_name>
                                | <correlation_name> "." <column_name>
<variable_reference> ::= a reference to a SQL variable
<number_literal>     ::= integer, exact numeric or float numeric literal
<special_literal>    ::= see <special_literal> in Chapter 1, "Creating"
```

The syntax of an <expression> is more complex than it has to be to satisfy the needs of a select list item. That's because expressions can appear in many other places in SQL, and some of these other contexts place limitations on what may or may not appear in an expression. In particular, there are three kinds of expressions defined above:

■   First, there is the full-featured <expression>, which includes everything SQL Anywhere has to offer. That's the kind allowed in a select list, and that's what this section talks about.

■   The second kind is a <basic_expression>, which has everything an <expression> has except for subqueries. For example, a <case_expression> may not have a subquery appearing after the CASE keyword, and that's one context where <basic_expression> appears in the syntax.

■   The third kind is a <simple_expression>, which is like a <basic_expression> except it cannot begin with the IF or CASE keywords. For example, the message text parameter in the RAISERROR statement can't be any fancier than a <simple_expression>.

In reality, these are extremely subtle differences, unlikely to get in your way. From now on, as far as this book is concerned, an expression is just an expression and only the BNF will show the differences.

Tip: When using several arithmetic operators in a single expression, use parentheses to make the order of calculation clear. The default order when parentheses are not used is to perform multiplication and division first, and then addition and subtraction. Not everyone knows this or remembers it, so parentheses are a good idea if you want your code to be readable.

Following is an example of a SELECT that contains only one clause, the select list. The first and third expressions perform date arithmetic by subtracting one day from and adding one day to the special literal CURRENT DATE to compute yesterday's and tomorrow's dates. The last four select list items are subqueries that compute single values: the maximum value of product.unit_price, the number of rows in the product and sales_order tables, and the sum of all sales_order_items.quantity values.

```
SELECT CURRENT DATE - 1          AS yesterday,
       CURRENT DATE              AS today,
       CURRENT DATE + 1          AS tomorrow,
       ( SELECT MAX ( unit_price )
            FROM product )        AS max_price,
       ( SELECT COUNT(*)
            FROM product )        AS products,
       ( SELECT COUNT(*)
```

```
           FROM sales_order )         AS orders,
     ( SELECT SUM ( quantity )
           FROM sales_order_items ) AS items;
```

Here's what the result looks like:

yesterday	today	tomorrow	max_price	products	orders	items
===========	===========	===========	=========	========	======	=====
2003-10-17	2003-10-18	2003-10-19	24.00	10	648	28359

Note: The default FROM clause is actually "FROM SYS.DUMMY." For example, the statement "SELECT *" works, and returns a single row with a single column called dummy_col, with a zero value, which is exactly what the built-in read-only SYS.DUMMY table contains. That is why a SELECT with no FROM clause always returns a single row, as it does in the example above.

The following example uses some of the arithmetic operators to perform computations in the select list:

```
SELECT product.id,
       product.unit_price * product.quantity    AS stock_value,
       product.unit_price
         * ( SELECT SUM ( quantity )
                FROM sales_order_items
               WHERE sales_order_items.prod_id
                    = product.id )               AS sales_value,
       ( stock_value / sales_value ) * 100.00  AS percent
  FROM product
ORDER BY sales_value DESC;
```

Here's how it works: For every row in the product table, the unit_price is multiplied by the quantity to determine stock_value, the total value of stock on hand. Also, for each row in the product table, a subquery retrieves all the sales_order_items rows where prod_id matches product.id and computes the sum of all sales_order_items.quantity. This sum is multiplied by product.unit_price to compute the sales_value, total sales value for that product. Finally, a percentage calculation is performed on the results of the previous two calculations by referring to the alias names stock_value and sales_value. Here is what the result looks like, sorted in descending order by sales_value, when run against the ASADEMO database:

id	stock_value	sales_value	percent
===	===========	===========	========
600	936.00	73440.00	1.274510
700	1200.00	68040.00	1.763668
601	768.00	65376.00	1.174743
301	756.00	33432.00	2.261307
302	1050.00	30072.00	3.491620
400	1008.00	29502.00	3.416718
401	120.00	27010.00	.444280
300	252.00	21276.00	1.184433
500	252.00	18564.00	1.357466
501	196.00	17556.00	1.116427

Tip: You can use alias names just like cell names in a spreadsheet to build new expressions from the results of other expressions without repeating the code for those expressions. This feature is unique to SQL Anywhere: the ability to define an alias name and then refer to it somewhere else in the same query; e.g., in another select list item or in the WHERE clause.

3.10.1 IF and CASE Expressions

The IF and CASE keywords can be used to create expressions as well as to code IF-THEN-ELSE and CASE statements. The statements are discussed in Chapter 8, "Packaging," and the expressions are described here.

```
<if_expression> ::= IF <boolean_expression>
                       THEN <expression>
                       [ ELSE <expression> ]
                       ENDIF
```

The IF expression evaluates the <boolean_expression> to determine if it is TRUE, FALSE, or UNKNOWN. If the <boolean_expression> result is TRUE, the THEN <expression> is returned as the result of the IF. If the <boolean_expression> is FALSE, the ELSE <expression> is returned as the result of the IF. If there is no ELSE <expression>, or if the <boolean_expression> is UNKNOWN, then NULL is returned as the result of the IF.

Note that the THEN and ELSE expressions can be anything that the syntax of <expression> allows, including more nested IF expressions. Here is an example that displays 'Understocked' and 'Overstocked' for some products, and the empty string for the others:

```
SELECT product.id,
       product.quantity,
       IF product.quantity < 20
       THEN 'Understocked'
       ELSE IF product.quantity > 50
           THEN 'Overstocked'
           ELSE ''
           ENDIF
       ENDIF AS level
  FROM product
 ORDER BY product.quantity;
```

Here's what the result looks like when run against the ASADEMO database:

```
id   quantity  level
===  ========  ============
401  12        Understocked
300  28
501  28
601  32
500  36
600  39
301  54        Overstocked
302  75        Overstocked
700  80        Overstocked
400  112       Overstocked
```

For a discussion of TRUE, FALSE, UNKNOWN, and their relationship to NULL, see Section 3.12, "Boolean Expressions and the WHERE Clause."

The CASE expression comes in two forms:

```
<case_expression>        ::= <basic_case_expression>
                         | <searched_case_expression>

<basic_case_expression> ::= CASE <basic_expression>
                               WHEN <expression> THEN <expression>
                             { WHEN <expression> THEN <expression> }
                             [ ELSE <expression> ]
                             END
```

The first format evaluates the CASE <basic_expression> and compares it in turn to the value of each WHEN <expression>. This comparison implicitly uses the equals "=" operator. The result of this comparison may be TRUE, FALSE, or UNKNOWN. If a TRUE result is encountered, that's as far as the process gets; the corresponding THEN <expression> is evaluated and returned as the result of the CASE. If all the comparisons result in FALSE or UNKNOWN, then the ELSE <expression> is evaluated and returned; if there is no ELSE <expression>, then NULL is returned.

Following is an example where a basic CASE expression is used to convert the string values in sales_order.region into a number suitable for sorting. The result of the CASE expression is given an alias name, sort_order, and that alias name is referenced by both the WHERE clause and the ORDER BY clause.

```
SELECT CASE region
            WHEN 'Western' THEN 1
            WHEN 'Central' THEN 2
            WHEN 'Eastern' THEN 3
            ELSE 0
        END      AS sort_order,
        region,
        COUNT(*) AS orders
  FROM sales_order
 WHERE sort_order > 0
 GROUP BY region
 ORDER BY sort_order;
```

Here's the result; not only has an explicit sort order been defined, but all the orders outside those three regions have been excluded:

```
sort_order  region   orders
==========  =======  ======
1           Western  61
2           Central  224
3           Eastern  244
```

The second form of the CASE expression is more flexible; you are not limited to the implicit equals "=" operator, nor are you limited to a single CASE comparison value on the left side of all the WHEN comparisons.

```
<searched_case_expression> ::= CASE
                                  WHEN <boolean_expression> THEN <expression>
                                { WHEN <boolean_expression> THEN <expression> }
                                [ ELSE <expression> ]
                                END
```

Each WHEN <boolean_expression> is evaluated, in turn, to result in a TRUE, FALSE, or UNKNOWN result. As soon as a TRUE result is encountered, the search is over; the corresponding THEN <expression> is evaluated and returned as the result of the CASE. If all the results are FALSE or UNKNOWN, then the

ELSE <expression> is evaluated and returned; if there is no ELSE <expression>, then NULL is returned.

Here is an example that uses a searched CASE expression to specify three WHEN conditions that use AND and IN as well as simple comparisons. A second basic CASE expression is also used to translate the result of the first expression into a string title.

```
SELECT CASE
          WHEN sales_rep = 129
            AND region = 'Western'
               THEN 1
          WHEN region = 'Western'
               THEN 2
          WHEN region IN ( 'Eastern', 'Central' )
               THEN 3
          ELSE 0
        END AS sort_order,
        CASE sort_order
          WHEN 1 THEN 'Western 129'
          WHEN 2 THEN 'Other Western'
          WHEN 3 THEN 'Eastern and Central'
        END       AS breakdown,
        COUNT(*) AS orders
   FROM sales_order
  WHERE sort_order > 0
  GROUP BY sort_order
  ORDER BY sort_order;
```

Here's what the result looks like using the ASADEMO database:

```
sort_order  breakdown            orders
==========  =============        ======
1           Western 129          6
2           Other Western        55
3           Eastern and Central  468
```

3.11 Top 15 Scalar Built-in Functions

Function calls fall into four categories. First, there are references to user-defined functions created with the CREATE FUNCTION statement. Second, there are ordinary built-in functions like ABS() and SUBSTRING(), which look a lot like functions available in other languages. Third, there are a handful of special built-in functions, like CAST() and NUMBER(*), which work like ordinary built-in functions but have some unusual syntax in the argument lists. And finally, there are the aggregate built-in functions, which are in a whole world by themselves.

```
<function_call> ::= <user_defined_function_call>      -- scalar function
                  | <ordinary_builtin_function_call> -- scalar function
                  | <special_builtin_function_call>  -- scalar function
                  | <aggregate_builtin_function_call> -- aggregate function
<user_defined_function_call>     ::= <user_defined_function_name>
                                     "(" [ <function_argument_list> ] ")"
<user_defined_function_name>     ::= <identifier>
<function_argument_list>         ::= <expression> { "," <expression> }
<ordinary_builtin_function_call> ::= <ordinary_builtin_function_name>
                                     "(" [ <function_argument_list> ] ")"
<ordinary_builtin_function_name> ::= <identifier>
<special_builtin_function_call>  ::= CAST "(" <expression> AS <data_type> ")"
```

```
| NOW "( * )"
| NUMBER "( * )"
| PI "( * )"
| TODAY "( * )"
| TRACEBACK "( * )"
```

The first three categories are called scalar functions because they are executed once per row when they appear in a select list, as opposed to aggregate functions, which operate on multiple rows.

This section discusses the scalar built-in functions, both ordinary and special, with the exception of NUMBER(*), which is covered in Section 3.20. Aggregate functions are discussed in Section 3.14, and user-defined functions are covered in Section 8.10.

There are approximately 175 different built-in functions in SQL Anywhere 9; the number varies depending on whether you count functions like REPEAT() and REPLICATE() as being different (they aren't). One book can't do them all justice, and frankly, some of them aren't worth the effort; how much can you say about NOW(*) other than that it returns CURRENT TIMESTAMP?

It's not fair, however, to make fun of legacy artifacts like TODAY(*) and weird Transact-SQL abominations like CONVERT(). One of SQL Anywhere's strengths lies in its rich variety of built-in functions, all explained quite well in the SQL Anywhere Help file. This section presents some of the most useful, starting with (in the author's opinion) the top 15 in alphabetic order:

Table 3-1. Top 15 built-in scalar functions

Function	Description
CAST (p AS q)	Returns p after conversion to data type q.
COALESCE (p, q, …)	Returns the first non-NULL parameter.
LEFT (p, q)	Returns the leftmost q characters of string p.
LENGTH (p)	Returns the current length of string p.
LOCATE (p, q [, r])	Returns the first position of string q in string p, starting the search at r if it is specified.
LOWER (p)	Returns string p converted to lowercase.
LTRIM (p)	Returns string p with leading spaces removed.
REPEAT (p, q)	Returns q copies of string p concatenated together.
REPLACE (p, q, r)	Returns string p with all occurrences of string q replaced with string r.
RIGHT (p, q)	Returns the rightmost q characters of string p.
RTRIM (p)	Returns string p with trailing spaces removed.
STRING (p, …)	Returns a string consisting of each parameter converted to a string and concatenated together.
SUBSTR (p, q [, r])	Returns the substring of p starting at q for length r, or until the end of p if r is omitted.

Function	Description
TRIM (p)	Returns string p with leading and trailing spaces removed.
UPPER (p)	Returns string p converted to uppercase.

The **CAST** function performs a conversion from one data type to another. For example, CAST ('123' AS INTEGER) converts the string '123' into an INTEGER 123.

CAST will fail if there is an obvious data conversion error, but it also has some subtle limitations. For example, CAST (123.456 AS INTEGER) works just fine to truncate 123.456 and return 123, but CAST ('123.456' AS INTEGER) will fail; you have to do that conversion in two steps: CAST (CAST ('123.456' AS NUMERIC) AS INTEGER).

Nevertheless, CAST is very useful. Here's another example to show its flexibility:

```
CREATE TABLE t1 (
   key_1        UNSIGNED BIGINT NOT NULL,
   non_key_1    VARCHAR ( 100 ) NOT NULL,
   last_updated TIMESTAMP NOT NULL,
   PRIMARY KEY ( key_1 ) );

INSERT t1 VALUES ( 1, '123.45', '2003-10-19 15:32.25.123' );

SELECT CAST ( key_1 AS VARCHAR ( 1 ) )      AS a,
       CAST ( key_1 AS VARCHAR )            AS b,
       CAST ( non_key_1 AS NUMERIC ( 10, 2 ) ) AS c,
       CAST ( non_key_1 AS NUMERIC )        AS d,
       CAST ( last_updated AS DATE )        AS e,
       CAST ( last_updated AS TIME )        AS f
  FROM t1;
```

The result is shown below; note that the second CAST returns b as a VARCHAR (21) because that's the maximum size required for a BIGINT. Also, the fourth CAST returns d as NUMERIC (30, 6) because that's the default scale and precision for the NUMERIC data type. In general, CAST tries to do the right thing:

```
a    b    c       d          e          f
===  ===  ======  ==========  ==========  ============
'1'  '1'  123.45  123.450000  2003-10-19  15:32:25.123
```

You can use the EXPRTYPE function to verify what CAST is returning. Here is an example that proves b is returned as VARCHAR (21):

```
SELECT EXPRTYPE ( '
SELECT CAST ( key_1 AS VARCHAR ( 1 ) )      AS a,
       CAST ( key_1 AS VARCHAR )            AS b,
       CAST ( non_key_1 AS NUMERIC ( 10, 2 ) ) AS c,
       CAST ( non_key_1 AS NUMERIC )        AS d,
       CAST ( last_updated AS DATE )        AS e,
       CAST ( last_updated AS TIME )        AS f
  FROM t1
', 2 );
```

The **COALESCE** function, in spite of its strange name, is very simple and very useful: It evaluates each parameter from left to right and returns the first one that isn't NULL. COALESCE will accept two or more parameters but is most often called with exactly two: a column name and a value to be used when the column value is NULL. Here is an example that shows how non-NULL values can be substituted for NULL values in a table:

```
CREATE TABLE t1 (
    key_1       UNSIGNED BIGINT NOT NULL,
    non_key_1   VARCHAR ( 100 ) NULL,
    non_key_2   TIMESTAMP NULL,
    PRIMARY KEY ( key_1 ) );

INSERT t1 VALUES ( 2, NULL, NULL );

SELECT COALESCE ( non_key_1, 'empty' )            AS a,
       COALESCE ( non_key_2, CURRENT TIMESTAMP ) AS b
  FROM t1;
```

Here's the result of the SELECT:

```
a         b
=======   ========================
'empty'   2003-10-19 15:58:36.176
```

COALESCE can be used to eliminate the need for IS NOT NULL comparisons in WHERE clauses. It can also be used to eliminate the need for indicator variables in application programs by returning only non-NULL values from queries. This is helpful because NULL values can show up in your result sets even if every single column in every table is declared as NOT NULL. That's because all the OUTER JOIN operators produce NULL values to represent missing rows.

For example, a query in Section 3.6, "Multi-Table Joins," satisfied this request: "Show how many of each kind of shirt were sold to each customer in Washington, D.C., including combinations of product and customer that had no sales." The result contained NULL values for customer-product combinations with no sales. Here is that same query with COALESCE calls to turn NULL quantity and amount values into zeroes:

```
SELECT customer.company_name          AS company_name,
       product.name                   AS product_name,
       product.description            AS product_description,
       COALESCE (
           SUM ( sales_order_items.quantity ),
           0.00 )                     AS quantity,
       COALESCE (
           SUM ( product.unit_price
               * sales_order_items.quantity ),
           0.00 )                     AS amount
  FROM ( customer
       CROSS JOIN product )
       LEFT OUTER JOIN
       ( sales_order
         INNER JOIN sales_order_items
                ON sales_order_items.id = sales_order.id )
       ON  customer.id = sales_order.cust_id
       AND product.id  = sales_order_items.prod_id
 WHERE customer.state = 'DC'
   AND product.name LIKE '%shirt%'
 GROUP BY customer.company_name,
       product.name,
```

```
        product.description
ORDER BY customer.company_name,
        product.name,
        product.description;
```

Now there are zeroes in the result set to show which products had zero sales to which customers:

```
company_name              product_name  product_description  quantity  amount
========================  ============  ===================  ========  =======
Hometown Tee's            Sweatshirt    Hooded Sweatshirt    24         576.00
Hometown Tee's            Sweatshirt    Zipped Sweatshirt    0            0.00
Hometown Tee's            Tee Shirt     Crew Neck            0            0.00
Hometown Tee's            Tee Shirt     Tank Top             24         216.00
Hometown Tee's            Tee Shirt     V-neck               0            0.00
State House Active Wear   Sweatshirt    Hooded Sweatshirt    48        1152.00
State House Active Wear   Sweatshirt    Zipped Sweatshirt    48        1152.00
State House Active Wear   Tee Shirt     Crew Neck            0            0.00
State House Active Wear   Tee Shirt     Tank Top             0            0.00
State House Active Wear   Tee Shirt     V-neck               60         840.00
```

The LEFT, RIGHT, and SUBSTR functions all return substrings from a string parameter. The **LEFT** function counts characters from the beginning, the **RIGHT** function counts from the end, and the **SUBSTR** function uses a starting point and a length. If you omit the length parameter from the SUBSTR call, it takes all the characters up to the end of the string. All three are basic building blocks for string manipulation processes, and they all work just fine on LONG VARCHAR parameters. Here is an example to show some variations:

```
SELECT LEFT   ( '12345', 2 )    AS a,
       RIGHT  ( '12345', 2 )    AS b,
       SUBSTR ( '12345', 2, 3 ) AS c,
       SUBSTR ( '12345', 2 )    AS d;
```

Here are the results:

```
a      b      c       d
====   ====   =====   ======
'12'   '45'   '234'   '2345'
```

Note: All string functions in SQL Anywhere start counting string positions at 1, not 0. This is SQL, not C; there are no zero-based offsets or zero-byte string terminators.

The **LENGTH** function is another string manipulation building block; it returns the current length of the string parameter. For example, LENGTH (SUBSTR ('12345', 2)) returns 4.

The **LOCATE** function searches one string for the first occurrence of another string, returning the position of the other string if it is found and 0 if it isn't found. For example, LOCATE ('A=B+C', '=') returns 2.

Repeated LOCATE calls are made easy by an optional third parameter: the starting position for the search. For example, LOCATE ('=A=B+C', '=', 2) returns 3.

The LOCATE return value is always the character position relative to the full string, not relative to the starting position, which makes the return value useful in subsequent calls to SUBSTR. For example, the following SELECT returns 'B+C':

```
CREATE TABLE t1 (
    key_1        UNSIGNED BIGINT NOT NULL,
    non_key_1    VARCHAR ( 100 ) NOT NULL,
    PRIMARY KEY ( key_1 ) );

INSERT t1 VALUES ( 1, '=A=B+C' );

SELECT SUBSTR ( non_key_1,
                LOCATE ( non_key_1, '=', 2 ) + 1 )
    FROM t1;
```

The **LOWER** function converts the string parameter to all lowercase characters, and **UPPER** converts the parameter to uppercase. For example, LOWER ('Hello, World') returns 'hello, world' and UPPER ('Hello, World') returns 'HELLO, WORLD'.

The LTRIM, RTRIM, and TRIM functions all remove selected spaces from the string parameter and return the result. **LTRIM** removes leading spaces, **RTRIM** removes trailing spaces, and **TRIM** does both. For example, LTRIM (' AB CD ') returns 'AB CD ', RTRIM (' AB CD ') returns ' AB CD', and TRIM (' AB CD ') returns 'AB CD'. None of these functions touch spaces embedded in the interior of a string.

The **REPLACE** function changes all occurrences of one string into another and returns the result. For example, SELECT REPLACE (' Blah blah blah. ', ' ', '') removes all leading, trailing, and embedded spaces and returns 'Blahblahblah.'.

The **REPEAT** function takes the string parameter and returns the specified number of copies all concatenated together. For example, REPEAT ('AB', 3) returns 'ABABAB'. Like some of these other building block functions, REPEAT is more useful in conjunction with other functions than it is all by itself; this is shown in some of the examples using the STRING function that follow.

The **STRING** function doesn't look like much at first — all it does is take a variable number of parameters, convert them all to strings, concatenate all those strings together, and return the result. As it turns out, STRING is surprisingly useful, especially when combined with other functions and the fact that strings are effectively unlimited in length.

Here's an example where REPEAT is combined with STRING and RIGHT to convert decimal numbers into fixed-length, right-justified strings padded to the left with zeroes:

```
CREATE TABLE t1 (
    key_1        UNSIGNED BIGINT NOT NULL,
    non_key_1    NUMERIC ( 11, 2 ) NOT NULL,
    PRIMARY KEY ( key_1 ) );

INSERT t1 VALUES ( 1, 12345.78 );
INSERT t1 VALUES ( 2, 0.00 );
INSERT t1 VALUES ( 3, 12.34 );

SELECT RIGHT ( STRING ( REPEAT ( '0', 10 ), non_key_1 ), 10 ) AS a
    FROM t1
ORDER BY key_1;
```

Here's how it works: First, the REPEAT function produces a string of 10 zero characters. Then, STRING converts a non_key_1 value like 12345.78 into a string '12345.78' and appends it to the 10 zero characters to produce

'000000000012345.78'. Finally, the RIGHT function returns the rightmost 10 characters, or '0012345.78'. Here is what the whole result set looks like:

```
a
=============
'0012345.78'
'0000000.00'
'0000012.34'
```

Here's another example, which displays 'USER DBA at 2003-10-19 18:01:52.151' in the server console window:

```
MESSAGE STRING (
    'USER ',
    CURRENT USER,
    ' at ',
    CURRENT TIMESTAMP ) TO CONSOLE;
```

3.12 Boolean Expressions and the WHERE Clause

The syntax for the WHERE clause is the same as for the ON condition: Both keywords are followed by a <boolean_expression>. Boolean expressions can also be used in other locations; e.g., IF and CASE expressions and statements, HAVING and WHEN clauses, WHILE statements, and CHECK constraints all use boolean expressions. In reality, however, WHERE clauses tend to use more complex expressions than those other clauses and statements, and that's why the full syntax of <boolean_expression> is described here instead of somewhere else.

```
<where_clause>         ::= WHERE <boolean_expression> -- TRUE vs FALSE/UNKNOWN
<boolean_expression> ::= <predicate>                          -- Precedence:
                       | <boolean_expression> IS <truth_value>         -- 1
                       | <boolean_expression> IS NOT <truth_value>     -- 1
                       | NOT <boolean_expression>                      -- 1
                       | <boolean_expression> AND <boolean_expression>  -- 2
                       | <boolean_expression> OR <boolean_expression>   -- 3
                       | "(" <boolean_expression> ")"
                       | "(" <boolean_expression> "," <user_estimate> ")"
<predicate>            ::= <comparison_predicate>
                       | <exists_predicate>
                       | <in_predicate>
                       | <between_predicate>
                       | <null_test_predicate>
                       | <like_predicate>
                       | <trigger_predicate>
<truth_value>          ::= TRUE
                       | FALSE
                       | UNKNOWN
<user_estimate>        ::= number literal in the range 0.0 to 100.0
```

The WHERE clause is applied as the third step in the logical execution of a select, after the FROM clause and simple scalar select list items have been evaluated to produce a candidate result set. The <boolean_expression> is evaluated once for each row to return TRUE, FALSE, or UNKNOWN. If the boolean expression returns TRUE for a particular row, that row is left alone. If it returns FALSE or UNKNOWN for a row, that row is removed from the result set.

TRUE, FALSE, and UNKNOWN are boolean values in the special three-value logic system used by all relational database systems. The third value, UNKNOWN, is necessary because the result of most comparisons involving NULL are, in fact, unknown. For example, if X contains NULL, neither of the comparisons X = 0 or X <> 0 is TRUE. Neither of them is FALSE, either; they both return UNKNOWN.

> **Note:** You won't find "boolean expression" in the SQL Anywhere Help — look for "search condition" instead. The term "search condition" implies a repetitive act, which may apply to the WHERE clause but not to a simple IF statement, and that's why this book uses "boolean expression" instead.

Boolean expressions consist of the following:
- One or more predicates
- Boolean operators AND, OR, and NOT
- Truth value tests IS and IS NOT
- Parentheses to control the order of execution
- User estimates to influence the query optimizer

Predicates are the basic building blocks of a boolean expression; a predicate is the simplest expression that yields TRUE, FALSE, or UNKNOWN as its result. There are seven different kinds of predicates, each of which is discussed in the next seven sections. For the purposes of this section, simple comparison predicates of the form "X = Y" will be used to show how complex boolean expressions can be constructed from multiple predicates. Here is a table showing some simple predicates and the resulting truth values for different values of X:

```
                              X contains:
                         ======================
Predicate Examples       NULL      0       1
======================   =======  =====   =====
X = 0                    UNKNOWN  TRUE    FALSE
X = 1                    UNKNOWN  FALSE   TRUE
COALESCE ( X, 0 ) = 0    TRUE     TRUE    FALSE
COALESCE ( X, 0 ) = 1    FALSE    FALSE   TRUE
X <> 0                   UNKNOWN  FALSE   TRUE
X <> 1                   UNKNOWN  TRUE    FALSE
```

Here's how to read the first line of the table: If X contains NULL, the predicate X = 0 returns UNKNOWN. If X contains 0, the predicate returns TRUE. If X contains 1, the predicate returns FALSE.

> **Note:** TRUE, FALSE, and UNKNOWN are actual SQL Anywhere 9 keywords representing boolean or truth values. Unfortunately, however, there is no explicit BOOLEAN or TRUTH data type in SQL Anywhere 9. You can't declare a variable or column as BOOLEAN, so you can't directly store the value of a <boolean_ expression> in a variable or column. All you can do is use them as you calculate them, in WHERE clauses, ON conditions, and so on. Or use some other data type like BIT to hold 1 or 0, or VARCHAR (1) to hold 'Y' or 'N', and write code to indirectly calculate, store, and use values of those types. The IF and SET statements can be used for this purpose, and they're discussed in Chapter 8, "Packaging."

The IS and IS NOT operators can be used to test the result of a predicate or boolean expression. These operators have the advantage that they always return TRUE or FALSE, never UNKNOWN. Here are some examples showing the results of IS and IS NOT operators:

```
                          X contains:

                         ===================
Boolean Expression         NULL    0      1
========================   ======  =====  =====
( X = 0 ) IS TRUE          FALSE   TRUE   FALSE
( X = 0 ) IS FALSE         FALSE   FALSE  TRUE
( X = 0 ) IS UNKNOWN       TRUE    FALSE  FALSE
( X = 0 ) IS NOT TRUE      TRUE    FALSE  TRUE
( X = 0 ) IS NOT FALSE     TRUE    TRUE   FALSE
( X = 0 ) IS NOT UNKNOWN   FALSE   TRUE   TRUE
```

The IS UNKNOWN operator is rarely used because for most purposes, UNKNOWN is the same as FALSE. With a WHERE clause, for example, a row yielding either UNKNOWN or FALSE will be eliminated.

The NOT, AND, and OR operators can be used to change and combine intermediate TRUE, FALSE, and UNKNOWN results according to the following "truth tables." For example, if a <boolean_expression> results in TRUE, then NOT <boolean_expression> is FALSE. Note that you cannot actually code "NOT TRUE" in SQL Anywhere; the following tables are simply a shorthand for explaining what happens when you code something like "NOT X = 1":

```
        NOT          Result
    ===========      ======
    NOT TRUE         FALSE
    NOT FALSE        TRUE
    NOT UNKNOWN      UNKNOWN


         AND             Result
==================       ======
    TRUE AND TRUE        TRUE
    TRUE AND FALSE       FALSE
    TRUE AND UNKNOWN     UNKNOWN
   FALSE AND TRUE        FALSE
   FALSE AND FALSE       FALSE
   FALSE AND UNKNOWN     FALSE
 UNKNOWN AND TRUE        UNKNOWN
 UNKNOWN AND FALSE       FALSE
 UNKNOWN AND UNKNOWN     UNKNOWN


         OR              Result
==================       ======
    TRUE OR TRUE         TRUE
    TRUE OR FALSE        TRUE
    TRUE OR UNKNOWN      TRUE
   FALSE OR TRUE         TRUE
   FALSE OR FALSE        FALSE
   FALSE OR UNKNOWN      UNKNOWN
 UNKNOWN OR TRUE         TRUE
 UNKNOWN OR FALSE        UNKNOWN
 UNKNOWN OR UNKNOWN      UNKNOWN
```

3.12.1 **Comparison Predicates**

There are seven different kinds of predicates that can be used to construct a boolean expression. The first is a comparison involving a logical operator like "=" or "<":

```
<comparison_predicate> ::= <expression>
                            <comparison_operator>
                            <expression>
                        | <expression>
                            <comparison_operator>
                            <quantifier>
                            <subquery> -- single-column result set
<comparison_operator> ::= "="  -- equal to
                        | ">"  -- greater than
                        | "<"  -- less than
                        | ">=" -- greater than or equal to
                        | "<=" -- less than or equal to
                        | "<>" -- not equal to
                        | "!=" -- not equal to
                        | "!<" -- not less than
                        | "!>" -- not greater than
<quantifier>          ::= ANY  -- one or more
                        | SOME -- one or more
                        | ALL  -- every
```

A comparison predicate can involve two values, or a value and one of the quantifiers ANY, SOME, or ALL followed by a subquery that returns a single-column result set. Here's an example using two values and the equals operator:

```
CREATE TABLE t1 (
    key_1      UNSIGNED BIGINT NOT NULL,
    non_key_1  INTEGER NOT NULL,
    PRIMARY KEY ( key_1 ) );

INSERT t1 VALUES ( 1, 1 );
INSERT t1 VALUES ( 2, 2 );

SELECT *
  FROM t1
 WHERE t1.non_key_1 = 2;
```

Here's what the result set looks like:

```
key_1 non_key_1
===== =========
2     2
```

Here's an example using two tables and a subquery with the ANY quantifier:

```
CREATE TABLE t1 (
    key_1      UNSIGNED BIGINT NOT NULL,
    non_key_1  INTEGER NOT NULL,
    PRIMARY KEY ( key_1 ) );

CREATE TABLE t2 (
    key_1      UNSIGNED BIGINT NOT NULL,
    non_key_1  INTEGER NOT NULL,
    PRIMARY KEY ( key_1 ) );

INSERT t1 VALUES ( 3, 5 );
INSERT t1 VALUES ( 4, 6 );
```

```
INSERT t2 VALUES ( 11, 999 );
INSERT t2 VALUES ( 22, 50 );
COMMIT;

SELECT *
  FROM t1
 WHERE t1.non_key_1 = ANY ( SELECT t2.non_key_1 / 10
                              FROM t2 );
```

Here's how that WHERE clause works, at least logically: For each row returned by the FROM t1 clause, the single-column subquery (SELECT t2.non_key_1 / 10 FROM t2) is evaluated and searched to determine if one or more values are equal to t1.non_key_1. That comparison yields FALSE for one of the rows in t1, and TRUE for the other one. Here's the final result set:

```
key_1  non_key_1
=====  =========
3      5
```

The query optimizer doesn't actually do it that way. In fact, the whole select is turned into a join and the subquery is completely eliminated. You can see this for yourself by putting the select inside a string literal and passing it to the REWRITE function as follows:

```
SELECT REWRITE ( '
SELECT *
  FROM t1
 WHERE t1.non_key_1 = ANY ( SELECT t2.non_key_1 / 10
                              FROM t2 )' );
```

The REWRITE function shows you what the query optimizer does with your select; here's what it says in this case:

```
SELECT DISTINCT
       t1_1.key_1,
       t1_1.non_key_1
  FROM t2 as t2_1,
       t1 as t1_1
 WHERE t1_1.non_key_1 = t2_1.non_key_1 / 10;
```

The query optimizer rewrites queries for performance. That's good, because it means you can write your WHERE clauses in a way that makes sense to you; for example, if you want to use a subquery with the ANY quantifier, go ahead. Don't worry about performance, and don't struggle changing subqueries into joins.

3.12.2 EXISTS Predicates

The second kind of predicate is a test to see if any rows exist in a subquery:

```
<exists_predicate> ::= EXISTS "(" <query_expression> ")"
```

The exists predicate is especially useful with foreign key relationships. You can use it to find parent table rows that do, or do not, have any corresponding rows in a child table. Here is an example that shows which rows in the parent t1 have any corresponding rows in the child table t2, without actually displaying any data from t2:

```
CREATE TABLE t1 (
   key_1      INTEGER NOT NULL PRIMARY KEY,
   non_key_1  INTEGER NOT NULL );
```

```
CREATE TABLE t2 (
   key_1        INTEGER NOT NULL REFERENCES t1 ( key_1 ),
   key_2        INTEGER NOT NULL,
   non_key_1    INTEGER NOT NULL,
   PRIMARY KEY ( key_1, key_2 ) );

INSERT t1 VALUES ( 5, 5 );
INSERT t1 VALUES ( 6, 6 );
INSERT t1 VALUES ( 7, 7 );
INSERT t2 VALUES ( 6, 44, 77 );
INSERT t2 VALUES ( 6, 55, 88 );

SELECT *
  FROM t1
 WHERE EXISTS ( SELECT *
                  FROM t2
                 WHERE t2.key_1 = t1.key_1 );
```

This kind of subquery is often called a "correlated subquery" or "correlated subselect" because it contains a reference to a table in the outer query, and that outer reference is called a "correlation." Here's how it works, logically speaking: For every row in t1 the subquery is evaluated and checked to see if it returns any rows where t2.key_1 = t1.key_1. If the subquery doesn't return any rows, the EXISTS predicate returns FALSE and the row from t1 is discarded. Otherwise, EXISTS returns TRUE and the row from t1 is left alone. This process eliminates two of the rows in t1, leaving one behind to produce this final result set:

```
key_1  non_key_1
=====  =========
6      6
```

The NOT EXISTS predicate has the opposite effect:

```
SELECT *
  FROM t1
 WHERE NOT EXISTS ( SELECT *
                      FROM t2
                     WHERE t2.key_1 = t1.key_1 );
```

In this case, only childless rows from t1 are returned:

```
key_1  non_key_1
=====  =========
5      5
7      7
```

When you use EXISTS and NOT EXISTS, the subquery select list is immaterial. All the query engine has to do is determine if there are any rows in the subquery result, not what those rows actually are. That means SELECT * is perfectly okay and there is no advantage to coding SELECT 1 or anything else.

3.12.3 IN Predicates

The third kind of predicate tests to see if a value exists in a list or a single-column subquery:

```
<in_predicate> ::= <expression>
                   [ NOT ] IN
                   "(" <expression> "," <expression> { "," <expression> } ")"
                 | <expression>
```

```
                    [ NOT ] IN
                    "(" <basic_expression> ")"
               | <expression>
                    [ NOT ] IN
                    <subquery> -- single-column result set
```

Here is an example using IN with a list to show all the employees in the ASADEMO database with a first name of John, Paul, George, or Ringo:

```
SELECT emp_id,
       emp_fname,
       emp_lname
  FROM employee
 WHERE emp_fname IN ( 'John', 'Paul', 'George', 'Ringo' )
 ORDER BY emp_id;
```

Here's the final result set; three Johns and a Paul but no George or Ringo:

emp_id	emp_fname	emp_lname
======	=========	=========
318	John	Crow
862	John	Sheffield
1021	Paul	Sterling
1483	John	Letiecq

Here is another example using subqueries in two IN predicates to find all the employees whose first name is the same as someone else's last name, or vice versa:

```
SELECT emp_id,
       emp_fname,
       emp_lname
  FROM employee
 WHERE emp_fname IN ( SELECT emp_lname
                        FROM employee )
    OR emp_lname IN ( SELECT emp_fname
                        FROM employee )
 ORDER BY emp_id;
```

The final result set contains two rows, showing that "Scott" is the only name that appears as both first and last name in the employee table:

emp_id	emp_fname	emp_lname
======	=========	=========
501	David	Scott
1576	Scott	Evans

3.12.4 BETWEEN Predicates

The fourth kind of predicate tests one value to see if it falls in a range between two other values; the test is inclusive, meaning that it returns TRUE if the value being tested matches either of the end points.

```
<between_predicate> ::= <expression>
                        [ NOT ] BETWEEN
                        <expression> AND <expression>
```

The BETWEEN predicate is especially useful for date ranges. Here is an example that returns all sales_order rows where the order_date falls in the range 2000-01-03 to 2000-01-07:

```
SELECT id,
       cust_id,
       order_date
```

```
FROM sales_order
WHERE order_date BETWEEN '2000-01-03' and '2000-01-07'
ORDER BY order_date;
```

Here is the result, showing that a BETWEEN predicate includes the end points:

```
id    cust_id  order_date
====  =======  ==========
2065  164      2000-01-03
2126  136      2000-01-03
2127  142      2000-01-06
2135  205      2000-01-06
2129  166      2000-01-07
```

Tip: The performance of a range query can sometimes be improved by a clustered index on the column being compared. For more information about clustered indexes, see Section 10.7, "CREATE INDEX."

3.12.5 NULL Test Predicates

The fifth kind of predicate tests to see whether or not a value contains NULL:

```
<null_test_predicate> ::= <expression> IS [ NOT ] NULL
```

If you don't want to use COALESCE to change NULL values into non-NULL values, you may have to use a null test predicate to avoid problems. Here is an example that counts all the active employees by counting the rows where the termination_date is NULL:

```
SELECT COUNT(*) AS active
  FROM employee
 WHERE termination_date IS NULL;
```

The final result shows no turnover in the ASADEMO database because all of the rows in the employee table have NULL termination_date values:

```
active
======
75
```

3.12.6 LIKE Predicates

The sixth kind of predicate tests to see if a string value matches a pattern:

```
<like_predicate> ::= <expression>
                     [ NOT ] LIKE
                     <expression>
                     [ ESCAPE <expression> ]
```

The first <expression> in the LIKE predicate is the string value to be checked; this is usually a simple column reference. The second <expression> is a simple pattern that is usually coded as a string literal containing the text you're looking for plus the special characters shown in Table 3-2.

Table 3-2. Special characters in the LIKE predicate

Character	Description
%	Matches any string of zero or more characters.
_	Matches any single character.
[]	Matches a single character in the enclosed set.

Character	Description
[^]	Matches a single character not in the enclosed set.
-	Used to specify a range of characters in a set.

Here are some examples of LIKE predicates together with values that yield TRUE and FALSE for each predicate; note that string comparisons are case-insensitive by default:

```
                      TRUE for this    FALSE for this
LIKE Predicate        value of X       value of X
====================  ===============  ==============
X LIKE '%FRED%'       'Alfred Smith'   'Harry Potter'
X LIKE '%FRED'        'Smith, Alfred'  'Alfred Smith'
X LIKE '_a_'          'cat'            'aaaaa'
X LIKE '__[xyz]_'     'CAYA'           'YANK'
X LIKE '[A-Z][0-9]'   'a2'             '4F'
X LIKE '[^r]%'        'Alfred'         'Robert'
```

The "%" special character is by far the most popular. Here is an example that finds all employees with the string 'west' anywhere in the street address:

```
SELECT emp_id,
       street
  FROM employee
 WHERE street LIKE '%west%';
```

Here is the result using the ASADEMO database:

```
emp_id  street
======  ========================
409     190 Westmoreland Street
930     251 Westminster Street
1013    589 West Drive
```

Here is an example that displays a telephone directory for all employees whose last names begin with "D":

```
SELECT STRING ( emp_lname, ', ', emp_fname ) AS full_name,
       STRING ( '(', LEFT ( phone, 3 ), ') ',
                SUBSTR ( phone, 4, 3 ), '-',
                RIGHT ( phone, 4 ) ) AS phone
  FROM employee
 WHERE emp_lname LIKE 'd%'
 ORDER BY emp_lname,
       emp_fname;
```

Here is the result; note the use of STRING and other functions to format the output:

```
full_name          phone
=================  ==============
Davidson, Jo Ann   (617) 555-3870
Diaz, Emilio       (617) 555-3567
Dill, Marc         (617) 555-2144
Driscoll, Kurt     (617) 555-1234
```

The ESCAPE expression allows you to specify which single character will be interpreted as an escape character in the pattern. Any special character (percent, underscore, etc.) following an escape character will be treated as an ordinary data character. For example, LIKE '[a-z]%' normally matches a single alphabetic character followed by zero or more characters. If you want to match a single alphabetic character followed by an actual percent sign you can use '?' as the escape character and code it as LIKE '[a-z]?%' ESCAPE '?'. Here are some predicates to demonstrate how ESCAPE can make a difference:

```
predicate                           result
================================    =======
'x%' LIKE '[a-z]%'                  TRUE    -- % matches anything
'x%' LIKE '[a-z]?%' ESCAPE '?'      TRUE    -- ?% matches the %
'x'  LIKE '[a-z]%'                  TRUE    -- % matches anything
'x'  LIKE '[a-z]?%' ESCAPE '?'      FALSE   -- ?% looks for a %
```

3.12.7 Trigger Predicates

The seventh and final kind of predicate can only be used inside a trigger to determine what kind of operation caused the trigger to fire:

```
<trigger_predicate>   ::= INSERTING
                        | DELETING
                        | UPDATING [ "(" <column_name_literal> ")" ]
                        | UPDATE "(" <column_name> ")"
<column_name_literal> ::= string literal containing a <column_name>
<column_name>         ::= <identifier>
```

Here is an example that demonstrates each one of these trigger predicates, not in a WHERE clause, but in a CASE statement inside a trigger; the MESSAGE statement is used to display a diagnostic message on the database console:

```
CREATE TABLE t1 (
   key_1       INTEGER NOT NULL PRIMARY KEY,
   non_key_1   INTEGER NOT NULL,
   non_key_2   INTEGER NOT NULL,
   non_key_3   INTEGER NOT NULL );

CREATE TRIGGER triud_t1
   BEFORE INSERT, DELETE, UPDATE ON t1
   REFERENCING OLD AS old_t1 NEW AS new_t1
   FOR EACH ROW
BEGIN
   DECLARE @message VARCHAR ( 1000 );
   SET @message =
      CASE
         WHEN INSERTING               THEN 'Inserting t1'
         WHEN DELETING                THEN 'Deleting t1'
         WHEN UPDATING ( 'non_key_1' ) THEN 'Updating t1.non_key_1'
         WHEN UPDATE ( non_key_2 )    THEN 'Updating t1.non_key_2'
         WHEN UPDATING                THEN 'Updating other t1 column'
      END;
   MESSAGE @message TO CONSOLE;
END;

INSERT t1 VALUES ( 1, 1, 1, 1 );
UPDATE t1 SET non_key_1 = 2 WHERE key_1 = 1;
UPDATE t1 SET non_key_2 = 3 WHERE key_1 = 1;
UPDATE t1 SET non_key_3 = 4 WHERE key_1 = 1;
DELETE t1 WHERE key_1 = 1;
```

Here is what appears in the database engine window when the INSERT, UPDATE, and DELETE statements above are executed:

```
Inserting t1
Updating t1.non_key_1
```

```
Updating t1.non_key_2
Updating other t1 column
Deleting t1
```

For more information about the CASE and CREATE TRIGGER statements, see Chapter 8, "Packaging."

3.13 GROUP BY Clause

The GROUP BY clause comes in two forms: with and without the ROLLUP keyword. The first form consists of the GROUP BY keywords followed by a list of one or more expressions, with the most common expressions being simple references to column names. The second form starts with GROUP BY ROLLUP and is followed by the same list of expressions, but this time the list must be surrounded with parentheses.

```
<group_by_clause> ::= GROUP BY <group_by_list>
                    | GROUP BY ROLLUP "(" <group_by_list> ")"
<group_by_list>   ::= <expression> { "," <expression> }
```

Initially, both GROUP BY and GROUP BY ROLLUP perform exactly the same grouping process. This section talks about this initial grouping process, from now on simply called GROUP BY. The GROUP BY ROLLUP clause also performs a second step to add rollup rows to the candidate result set; that rollup step is separate, and is described in Section 3.15.

The GROUP BY clause is applied as the fourth step in the logical execution of a select, after the WHERE clause has finished eliminating unnecessary rows from the candidate result set. The main purpose behind GROUP BY is to enable the use of aggregate function calls; without an aggregate function call like SUM or COUNT, it's hard to tell GROUP BY from DISTINCT. For example, the following selects produce exactly the same results:

```
SELECT dept_id
  FROM employee
 GROUP BY dept_id
 ORDER BY dept_id;

SELECT DISTINCT dept_id
  FROM employee
 ORDER BY dept_id;
```

Here is the result set produced by both of those selects when run against the ASADEMO database:

```
dept_id
=======
100
200
300
400
500
```

Logically speaking, the GROUP BY clause segregates the rows into groups according to the values of the grouping expressions; all the rows with the same combination of values are placed into the same group. Any aggregate function calls in the select list are then calculated, once for each group. When that's done, each group can be reduced to a single row.

Note: For the purposes of comparing the values of grouping expressions, NULL values are considered to be the same. This is different from the way NULL values are usually treated: Comparisons involving NULL values have UNKNOWN results.

The GROUP BY clause may refer to select list items and to virtual columns that don't appear in the select list. Here is an example that groups employees in New York by manager and city and displays the count for each:

```
SELECT manager_id,
       COUNT(*)
  FROM employee
 WHERE state = 'NY'
 GROUP BY manager_id,
          city
 ORDER BY manager_id;
```

Here is the result; note that it is possible to group by a column that doesn't appear in the select list:

```
manager_id  COUNT(*)
==========  ========
501         2
501         1
902         1
1293        1
1576        3
```

In most cases it makes more sense to actually display the grouping expressions. Here is the same example with the city added to the select list:

```
SELECT manager_id,
       city,
       COUNT(*)
  FROM employee
 WHERE state = 'NY'
 GROUP BY manager_id,
          city
 ORDER BY manager_id;
```

Now you can see why there are two rows with manager_id = 501:

```
manager_id  city        COUNT(*)
==========  ==========  ========
501         Cornwall    2
501         Fort Henry  1
902         Cornwall    1
1293        Cornwall    1
1576        Cornwall    3
```

The use of a GROUP BY clause imposes a restriction on what can appear in the select list: If an expression in the select list doesn't also appear in the GROUP BY list, that expression must appear in an aggregate function call in the select list. For example, the following SELECT is invalid and produces the error message "Function or column reference to 'state' must also appear in a GROUP BY":

```
SELECT manager_id,
       state
  FROM employee
 GROUP BY manager_id
 ORDER BY manager_id;
```

However, it's okay to put state in the select list as long as it's in an aggregate function call. Here's an example that works because state is in a call to COUNT:

```
SELECT manager_id,
       COUNT ( DISTINCT state ) AS states
  FROM employee
 GROUP BY manager_id
 ORDER BY manager_id;
```

Here's the result that shows how many different states are home to employees that work for each manager:

```
manager_id  states
==========  ======
501         10
703         5
902         13
1293        7
1576        9
```

The COUNT function is discussed in the next section.

3.14 Aggregate Function Calls

Aggregate function calls may appear in the select list, the HAVING clause, and the ORDER BY clause.

```
<aggregate_builtin_function_call> ::= AVG "(" [ DISTINCT ] <expression> ")"
                                    | COUNT "( * )"
                                    | COUNT "(" [ DISTINCT ] <expression> ")"
                                    | GROUPING "(" <expression> ")"
                                    | LIST "(" <expression>
                                               [ "," <list_delimiter> ]
                                               [ <order_by_clause> ] ")"
                                    | MAX "(" <expression> ")"
                                    | MIN "(" <expression> ")"
                                    | STDDEV "(" <expression> ")"
                                    | STDDEV_POP "(" <expression> ")"
                                    | STDDEV_SAMP "(" <expression> ")"
                                    | SUM "(" [ DISTINCT ] <expression> ")"
                                    | VAR_POP "(" <expression> ")"
                                    | VAR_SAMP "(" <expression> ")"
                                    | VARIANCE "(" <expression> ")"
<list_delimiter> ::= string <expression> to place between LIST values
```

Logically speaking, all aggregate function calls (except calls to GROUPING) may be evaluated as soon as the grouping process described in the previous section is complete. The results of calls in the select list are placed in the candidate result set, whereas the results of calls in the HAVING clause are saved until that clause is processed; see Section 3.16, "HAVING Clause." This section talks about what the individual aggregate functions do.

The **AVG** function computes the average value within each group. Here is an example that computes the average salary within each department in the ASADEMO database:

```
SELECT dept_id,
       AVG ( salary ) AS average_salary
  FROM employee
```

```
GROUP BY dept_id
ORDER BY dept_id;
```

Here is the result set:

```
dept_id  average_salary
=======  ==============
100      58736.281364
200      48390.947368
300      59500.000000
400      43640.671875
500      33752.200000
```

Many of the aggregate functions allow the DISTINCT keyword. AVG (DISTINCT X) computes the average of all the different values of X; if two or more rows in a group have the same value of X, that value is only counted once as far as computing the average is concerned.

Note: You can also explicitly code the ALL keyword, as in AVG (ALL X), but that isn't shown in the syntax here because it's the default, and it simply states the obvious; e.g., compute the average of all X values in each group.

DISTINCT might not make much sense when you're talking about AVG, but it does make a difference. Here is the same SELECT as above, with DISTINCT used in the call to AVG, plus a COUNT(*) call to count the number of rows in each group, and a COUNT (DISTINCT salary) call to count the number of different salary values in each group:

```
SELECT dept_id,
       AVG ( DISTINCT salary )  AS average_distinct_salary,
       COUNT (*)                AS employee_count,
       COUNT ( DISTINCT salary ) AS distinct_salary_count
  FROM employee
GROUP BY dept_id
ORDER BY dept_id;
```

Following is the new result set; note that for dept_id = 100 there are 22 employees but only 21 different values of salary, and that's why AVG (DISTINCT salary) gives a slightly different result than AVG (salary) did earlier:

```
dept_id  average_distinct_salary  employee_count  distinct_salary_count
=======  =======================  ==============  =====================
100      57347.532857            22              21
200      48390.947368            19              19
300      59500.000000            9               9
400      43640.671875            16              16
500      33752.200000            9               9
```

The **COUNT** function comes in three useful formats: COUNT(*), which counts all the rows in the group; COUNT (X), which counts all the rows where X is not NULL; and COUNT (DISTINCT X), which counts all the different non-NULL values of X.

COUNT(*) is the only aggregate function that includes NULL values in the result; that's because it counts rows rather than operates on columns or expressions. For all the other aggregate functions, NULL values are not included in the calculations. For example, the following SELECT reports that the average of NULL, NULL, 100, and 200 is 150:

```
CREATE TABLE t1 (
   key_1         INTEGER NOT NULL PRIMARY KEY,
   non_key_1     INTEGER NULL );

INSERT t1 VALUES ( 1, NULL );
INSERT t1 VALUES ( 2, NULL );
INSERT t1 VALUES ( 3, 100 );
INSERT t1 VALUES ( 4, 200 );
COMMIT;

SELECT AVG ( non_key_1 )
   FROM t1;
```

If 150 makes sense to you, that's fine; it is the average of all the non-NULL values, or (100 + 200) divided by 2. However, if you want to include all the rows, you can use COALESCE to substitute a non-NULL value for rows containing NULL. The following query treats NULL as zero so it reports the average as 75 (300 divided by 4):

```
SELECT AVG ( COALESCE ( non_key_1, 0 ) )
   FROM t1;
```

Note that the last two examples don't have a GROUP BY clause. Normally, when there is no GROUP BY clause, there is no grouping; i.e., each row is its own group, and there is no removal of rows caused by the grouping process. In other words, SELECT * FROM employee returns all the rows in the employee table.

However, if you use one or more aggregate function references in the select list but don't use a GROUP BY clause, all the rows are treated as if they belong to one single group. It's as if you had coded GROUP BY 1. The literal 1 has the same value for every row, so they're all put in the same group. Instead of all the rows, you get exactly one row, which makes sense because you're asking for an aggregate computation. Here's the example above, with a GROUP BY 1 clause; the result is exactly the same, 75:

```
SELECT AVG ( COALESCE ( non_key_1, 0 ) )
   FROM t1
GROUP BY 1;
```

If you have one or more aggregate functions in the select list, but no GROUP BY, all references to columns in the select list must appear inside those aggregate function references. The following example violates that rule, and generates the error message "Function or column reference to 'emp_id' must also appear in a GROUP BY":

```
SELECT emp_id,
       COUNT(*)
   FROM employee;
```

The **MAX** and **MIN** functions operate on all data types, and they can be very efficient if there is an index on the column being referenced. For example, in the ASADEMO database the customer table has an ascending index called ix_cust_name on the lname column, so the ISQL Graphical Plan facility says the following SELECT uses an "index scan ... using index ix_cust_name":

```
SELECT MIN ( lname )
   FROM customer;
```

For more information about indexes and the ISQL Graphical Plan facility, see Section 10.5 in Chapter 10, "Tuning."

The **SUM** function calculates the sum of all the values of an expression for each group. The following example computes the payroll for each department in the ASADEMO database, plus the projected payroll after a 2% increase:

```
SELECT dept_id,
       SUM ( salary )       AS current_payroll,
       SUM ( salary * 1.02 ) AS projected_payroll
  FROM employee
 GROUP BY dept_id
 ORDER BY dept_id;
```

Here is the result:

```
dept_id  current_payroll  projected_payroll
=======  ===============  =================
100      1292198.190      1318042.15380
200      919428.000       937816.56000
300      535500.000       546210.00000
400      698250.750       712215.76500
500      303769.800       309845.19600
```

The SUM function can also be used for counting by exploiting the fact that a sum of ones is the same as a count. Here is an example that uses SUM and IF to count the number of women, men, employees under 55 years of age, and employees that are 55 and over:

```
SELECT SUM ( IF sex = 'F'
                THEN 1
                ELSE 0
              ENDIF )     AS women,
         SUM ( IF sex = 'M'
                THEN 1
                ELSE 0
              ENDIF )     AS men,
         SUM ( IF ( DATEDIFF ( YEAR, birth_date, CURRENT DATE )
                    - IF DATEFORMAT ( birth_date, 'mmdd' )
                            > DATEFORMAT ( CURRENT DATE, 'mmdd' )
                        THEN 1
                        ELSE 0
                      ENDIF ) < 55
                THEN 1
                ELSE 0
              ENDIF )     AS under_55,
         SUM ( IF ( DATEDIFF ( YEAR, birth_date, CURRENT DATE )
                    - IF DATEFORMAT ( birth_date, 'mmdd' )
                            > DATEFORMAT ( CURRENT DATE, 'mmdd' )
                        THEN 1
                        ELSE 0
                      ENDIF ) >= 55
                THEN 1
                ELSE 0
              ENDIF )     AS "55_and_over"
  FROM employee;
```

Here is the result for the ASADEMO database:

```
women  men  under_55  55_and_over
=====  ===  ========  ===========
34     41   63        12
```

Tip: This trick of using SUM to count things can be used to eliminate subqueries and even application program code. Here's how to work with it: Code an expression that returns 1 when you want something counted and 0 when you don't want that thing counted, and put that expression inside a call to SUM.

In addition to AVG, there are several other aggregate functions for statistical calculations shown in Table 3-3. All of them return DOUBLE values.

Table 3-3. Other statistical aggregate functions

Name	Description
STDDEV_POP	Standard deviation of a population.
STDDEV_SAMP	Standard deviation of a sample.
STDDEV	Same as STDDEV_SAMP.
VAR_POP	Statistical variance of a population.
VAR_SAMP	Statistical variance of a sample.
VARIANCE	Same as VAR_SAMP.

The **LIST** aggregate function is different from the others in that it doesn't return a single simple value but a string containing a formatted list of multiple values. The simplest form of LIST evaluates the expression for every row in a group, converts those values to strings, and concatenates them together into one long string with a comma (,) separating each value. Here is an example that produces a list of all the employee.state values for dept_id = 100:

```
SELECT LIST ( state ) AS states
  FROM employee
 WHERE dept_id = 100;
```

Here is the result; note that the list isn't sorted, and there are duplicates:

```
states
======
NY,UT,PA,UT,UT,NY,FL,CO,MI,FL,MI,WY,RI,IL,WY,UT,RI,TX,TX,TX,NY,UT
```

You can sort the list with an ORDER BY clause inside the LIST call:

```
SELECT LIST ( state ORDER BY state ) AS states
  FROM employee
 WHERE dept_id = 100;


states
======
CO,FL,FL,IL,MI,MI,NY,NY,NY,PA,RI,RI,TX,TX,TX,UT,UT,UT,UT,UT,WY,WY
```

You can order the list by something other than the list expression itself:

```
SELECT LIST ( state ORDER BY salary DESC ) AS different_states
  FROM employee
 WHERE dept_id = 100;


different_states
================
RI,TX,FL,MI,UT,UT,IL,MI,UT,FL,PA,UT,TX,CO,UT,NY,NY,RI,TX,WY,NY,WY
```

You can get rid of duplicate values with the DISTINCT keyword:

```
SELECT LIST ( DISTINCT state ORDER BY state ) AS different_states
  FROM employee
 WHERE dept_id = 100;

different_states
================
CO,FL,IL,MI,NY,PA,RI,TX,UT,WY
```

You can also change the LIST delimiter. Here a single space is included after the comma:

```
SELECT LIST ( DISTINCT state, ', ' ORDER BY state ) AS different_states
  FROM employee
 WHERE dept_id = 100;

different_states
================
CO, FL, IL, MI, NY, PA, RI, TX, UT, WY
```

Note that a comma separates the first two LIST parameters but not the ORDER BY clause.

Here is an example that exploits the LIST delimiter to produce a single string that contains an entire HTML document:

```
SELECT STRING (
          '<HTML><BODY><OL>\x0d\x0a',
          '   <LI>',
          LIST ( DISTINCT state,
                 '</LI>\x0d\x0a   <LI>'
                 ORDER BY state ),
          '</LI>\x0d\x0a',
          '</OL></BODY></HTML>' ) AS states_page
  FROM employee
 WHERE dept_id = 100;
```

The following shows what that string looks like. Note that the string includes embedded \x0d\x0a carriage return and linefeed pairs.

```
<HTML><BODY><OL>
   <LI>CO</LI>
   <LI>FL</LI>
   <LI>IL</LI>
   <LI>MI</LI>
   <LI>NY</LI>
   <LI>PA</LI>
   <LI>RI</LI>
   <LI>TX</LI>
   <LI>UT</LI>
   <LI>WY</LI>
</OL></BODY></HTML>
```

Tip: If the order of the LIST items is important to you, always use an ORDER BY clause even if you also use DISTINCT. There is no guaranteed natural order of LIST items; today sorting may be used to implement DISTINCT but tomorrow some other technique may be used.

If there are no rows in the candidate result set, the presence of an aggregate function call in the select list will cause one row to be included in the final result set. The LIST function will return the empty string, COUNT(*) will return 0, and other functions like MIN will return NULL values as shown in this example:

```
SELECT LIST ( dummy_col ), MIN ( dummy_col ), COUNT(*)
  FROM dummy
WHERE dummy_col <> 0;
```

The GROUPING aggregate function is discussed in the next section.

3.15 **GROUP BY ROLLUP Clause**

After the basic GROUP BY process is complete, the GROUP BY ROLLUP clause adds one or more additional rows to the candidate result set.

```
<group_by_clause> ::= GROUP BY <group_by_list>
                    | GROUP BY ROLLUP "(" <group_by_list> ")"
<group_by_list>   ::= <expression> { "," <expression> }
```

When you use the ROLLUP keyword, one level of additional summary rows is inserted for each grouping expression. The leftmost grouping expression yields a single grand total row, the second grouping expression produces one or more subtotal rows, the third grouping expression produces sub-subtotal rows, and so on.

Here's what these ROLLUP summary rows look like: One or more of the grouping expressions in the select list are replaced with NULL, with the number of NULL values determined by the level of subtotal. For example, all of the grouping expressions in the select list are replaced with NULL for the grand total ROLLUP row, and at the other end, only one is NULL in each of the lowest-level subtotal rows. The other columns in the select list, the ones using aggregate functions such as COUNT, SUM, and LIST, are recomputed over all underlying rows in all the groups.

Here is an example that computes the number of sales made to each customer in Ohio, by each salesperson, for the months of March, April, and May, 2000, using the ASADEMO database:

```
SELECT customer.id,
       sales_order.sales_rep,
       COUNT ( sales_order.sales_rep ) AS sales
  FROM ( SELECT *
           FROM customer
          WHERE customer.state IN ( 'OH' ) ) AS customer
         INNER JOIN
         ( SELECT *
             FROM sales_order
            WHERE sales_order.order_date
            BETWEEN '2000-03-01' AND '2000-05-31'  ) AS sales_order
         ON sales_order.cust_id = customer.id
 GROUP BY ROLLUP ( customer.id,
       sales_order.sales_rep )
 ORDER BY COALESCE ( customer.id, 99999999 ),
       COALESCE ( sales_order.sales_rep, 99999999 );
```

Without the ROLLUP keyword, the GROUP BY clause would produce five rows corresponding to the five different customer-salesperson combinations. With ROLLUP specified, five more rows are added to the result set — one subtotal row for each of the four customers showing the subtotal for all salespersons who made sales to that customer, and one grand total row showing the total for all the customers. In the subtotal rows the sales_rep column is NULL, and in the grand total row both customer.id and sales_rep are NULL.

```
id     sales_rep  sales
===    =========  =====
110    667        1
110    NULL       1     -- subtotal for customer 110
117    467        1
117    NULL       1     -- subtotal for customer 117
134    299        1
134    856        1
134    NULL       2     -- subtotal for customer 134
153    1142       1
153    NULL       1     -- subtotal for customer 153
NULL   NULL       5     -- grand total
```

Note: ROLLUP works for aggregate functions like MIN and LIST as well as SUM and COUNT, so the term "subtotal" isn't quite accurate. Also note that the fact that summary computations are based on the underlying rows rather than lower-level summary rows doesn't make a difference for most aggregate functions like LIST and COUNT, but it does affect the statistical functions like AVG and VARIANCE.

With most GROUP BY ROLLUP queries involving INNER JOIN operations it's easy to tell the subtotal and grand total rows apart from the other rows produced by the basic GROUP BY process. However, an OUTER JOIN operation can produce NULL values in the grouping columns, making it difficult to tell the GROUP BY rows apart from the ones added by the ROLLUP operation. For example, if the INNER JOIN in the SELECT above is changed to LEFT OUTER JOIN so that all the customers are included even if they didn't buy anything, the result set would look confusing:

```
id     sales_rep  sales
====   =========  =====
110    667        1
110    NULL       1
117    467        1
117    NULL       1
134    299        1
134    856        1
134    NULL       2
153    1142       1
153    NULL       1
155    NULL       0     -- is this a subtotal row?
155    NULL       0     -- ...or is this it?
162    NULL       0
162    NULL       0
167    NULL       0
167    NULL       0
NULL   NULL       5
```

The GROUPING aggregate function can be used in the select list to determine if a row was the result of the ROLLUP operation, and if so, whether it is a grand total row or one of the possibly several different levels of subtotals. For example, if a SELECT has GROUP BY ROLLUP (A, B, C), then GROUPING (A) will return 1 for the grand total row and 0 for all the others, GROUPING (B) will return 1 for the grand total and subtotal rows and 0 for all the others, and

GROUPING (C) will return 1 for the grand total, subtotal, and sub-subtotal rows and 0 for all the rest.

Here is the previous SELECT with calls to GROUPING used to produce formatted text instead of NULL in the ROLLUP rows:

```
SELECT IF GROUPING ( customer.id ) = 1
         THEN 'Grand Total'
         ELSE STRING ( customer.id )
       ENDIF                              AS customer_id,
       CASE
         WHEN GROUPING ( customer.id ) = 1
           THEN ''
         WHEN GROUPING ( sales_order.sales_rep ) = 1
           THEN 'Subtotal'
         ELSE STRING ( '', sales_order.sales_rep )
       END                                AS sales_rep,
       COUNT ( sales_order.sales_rep )    AS sales,
       LIST ( sales_order.id, ', ' )      AS order_ids
  FROM ( SELECT *
           FROM customer
          WHERE customer.state IN ( 'OH' ) ) AS customer
       LEFT OUTER JOIN
       ( SELECT *
           FROM sales_order
          WHERE sales_order.order_date
          BETWEEN '2000-03-01' AND '2000-05-31'  ) AS sales_order
       ON sales_order.cust_id = customer.id
 GROUP BY ROLLUP ( customer.id,
       sales_order.sales_rep )
ORDER BY customer_id,
       sales_rep;
```

Here is the result, showing how the GROUPING calls cleared up the confusion; also note that the LIST aggregate function works in ROLLUP summary rows as well as the basic GROUP BY rows:

customer_id	sales_rep	sales	order_ids
110	667	1	2231
110	Subtotal	1	2231
117	467	1	2238
117	Subtotal	1	2238
134	299	1	2177
134	856	1	2124
134	Subtotal	2	2124, 2177
153	1142	1	2171
153	Subtotal	1	2171
155		0	
155	Subtotal	0	
162		0	
162	Subtotal	0	
167		0	
167	Subtotal	0	
Grand Total		5	2231, 2238, 2124, 2177, 2171

Tip: When you don't want to count rows containing NULL values, use COUNT (<expression>) rather than COUNT(*). For example, COUNT (sales_order.sales_rep) in the SELECT above. If COUNT(*) had been used, the sales column would show the wrong value for rows that had no sales. Those rows would show 1 instead of 0 because COUNT(*) counts rows without regard to NULL values, and the error would have affected the ROLLUP summary rows as well.

Tip: When you want to convert an expression to string and get rid of NULL values at the same time without calling COALESCE, use the STRING ('', <expression>) function call instead; e.g., STRING ('', sales_order.sales_rep) in the SELECT above. This technique takes advantage of the fact that when NULL and non-NULL strings are concatenated with the "||" operator or the STRING function, the NULL strings are interpreted as non-NULL empty strings. Most operations involving NULL return NULL, but string concatenation isn't one of them.

3.16 HAVING Clause

The HAVING clause works exactly like the WHERE clause — to remove rows from the candidate result set. The difference, logically speaking, is that the HAVING clause is applied after all the GROUP BY and ROLLUP processing is completed, and it works by eliminating whole groups from the candidate result set as it exists at that point. That means the boolean expression in the HAVING clause may (and usually does) contain references to aggregate functions, whereas the WHERE clause may not.

```
<having_clause> ::= HAVING <boolean_expression>
```

The HAVING clause may also contain references to the grouping expressions; i.e., references to the expressions that appear in the GROUP BY clause. Following is an example of a SELECT that counts all the sales made by customers where the count is 10 or higher and the customer id is 200 or higher. Note that the predicate "sales >= 10" in the HAVING clause is actually a reference to the result of the aggregate function call COUNT(*) via the alias name sales.

```
SELECT customer.id  AS customer_id,
       COUNT(*)      AS sales
  FROM customer
       INNER JOIN sales_order
             ON sales_order.cust_id = customer.id
 GROUP BY customer_id
HAVING customer_id >= 200
   AND sales >= 10
 ORDER BY customer_id;
```

Here is the result using the ASADEMO database; note that COUNT(*) is okay in this select list because with an INNER JOIN you don't have to worry about counting NULL values:

```
customer_id  sales
===========  =====
201          11
204          11
209          10
```

Be careful how you code the HAVING clause when using GROUP BY ROLLUP because the NULL values in the summary rows may cause problems with the boolean expression. For example, if the above SELECT is changed to use GROUP BY ROLLUP (customer_id), the grand total summary row does not appear and the result set looks exactly the same as it does above. That's because the customer_id is NULL for the grand total ROLLUP row, causing the predicate "customer_id >= 200" to yield UNKNOWN, and that in turn causes the HAVING clause to yield UNKNOWN, and only rows that yield TRUE will survive.

One solution is to call COALESCE; another is to move "customer_id >= 200" into the WHERE clause so it is processed before the GROUP BY and HAVING clauses:

```
SELECT customer.id  AS customer_id,
       COUNT(*)     AS sales
  FROM customer
       INNER JOIN sales_order
             ON sales_order.cust_id = customer.id
 WHERE customer_id >= 200
 GROUP BY ROLLUP ( customer_id )
HAVING sales >= 10
 ORDER BY customer_id;
```

Now the ROLLUP summary row survives to be included in the final result set:

```
customer_id  sales
===========  =====
NULL         87
201          11
204          11
209          10
```

3.17 ORDER BY Clause

The ORDER BY clause is applied after the GROUP BY and HAVING clauses have been processed and sorts the candidate result groups by one or more explicit expressions and/or numbered select list items. The keywords ASC and DESC stand for ascending and descending, respectively, with ASC being the default.

```
<order_by_clause>    ::= ORDER BY <order_by_item> { "," <order_by_item> }
<order_by_item>      ::= <select_item_number> [ ASC | DESC ]
                       | <expression> [ ASC | DESC ]
<select_item_number> ::= integer literal in the range 1 to the number
                             of select list items
```

The select list item numbers refer to the ordinal positions of select list items; e.g., ORDER BY 1, 2, 3 for the first three select list items. This numbering also works for SELECT * as if the * had been coded as an explicit list of select items. For example, the following SELECT sorts the result set by emp_lname and then emp_fname because those are the fourth and third columns in the employee table in the ASADEMO database:

```
SELECT *
  FROM employee
ORDER BY 4, 3;
```

The syntax for <expression> allows it to be an integer literal, but in the case of ORDER BY an integer literal is interpreted not as an expression to be evaluated and used for sorting, but as an ordinal number to find a select list item. That doesn't take away anything useful since sorting by a fixed expression would have no effect on the order.

The explicit ORDER BY expressions may be, and often are, the same as select list items but they don't have to be. For example, you can sort a result set on a column that doesn't appear in the select list. You can also ORDER BY an aggregate function reference that doesn't appear anywhere else in the select.

There are limitations, however, on what you can accomplish. For example, if you GROUP BY column X you can't ORDER BY column Y. When used together with GROUP BY, the ORDER BY is really ordering the groups, and each group may contain multiple different values of Y, which means sorting on Y is an impossibility.

Here's a rule of thumb to follow: If you can't code something in the select list, you can't code it in the ORDER BY either. If you GROUP BY column X, you can't code Y in the select list, and therefore you can't ORDER BY Y. However, you can put SUM (Y) in the select list, so SUM (Y) is okay in the ORDER BY as well.

Here's an example that demonstrates how ORDER BY can produce a result set that is sorted on an expression that isn't included in the result set:

```
SELECT sales_order.order_date,
       COUNT(*) AS sales
  FROM sales_order
       INNER JOIN sales_order_items
               ON sales_order_items.id = sales_order.id
 WHERE sales_order.order_date BETWEEN '2000-04-01' AND '2000-11-30'
 GROUP BY sales_order.order_date
HAVING COUNT(*) >= 5
 ORDER BY SUM ( sales_order_items.quantity ) DESC;
```

The final result set doesn't look sorted, but it is; the first row shows the order date with the highest number of items sold, the second row represents the second highest number of items, and so on. The number of items isn't displayed, just the order date and number of orders, and that's why the sort order is not visibly apparent.

```
order_date  sales
==========  =====
2000-05-29  5      -- highest value of SUM ( sales_order_items.quantity )
2000-10-30  5
2000-04-02  7
2000-11-25  6
2000-11-19  5      -- lowest value of SUM ( sales_order_items.quantity )
```

Tip: Sorting by a column that doesn't appear in the result set isn't as pointless as it might appear; for example, the FIRST keyword can be used to pick the row at the top of an ORDER BY list, and that may be all you want.

Logically speaking, after the ORDER BY clause is processed, there is no longer any need to preserve multiple rows or extra columns inside the groups, and each group can be reduced to a single row consisting of select list items only. Even if no ORDER BY is present, this is still the point where groups become rows; for example, if a SELECT is part of a UNION it can't have its own ORDER BY clause, but the UNION works on rows rather than groups.

3.18 **SELECT DISTINCT**

If present, the SELECT DISTINCT keyword removes all duplication from the candidate result set.

```
<query_specification> ::= SELECT
                          [ DISTINCT ]
                          [ <row_range> ]
                          <select_list>
                          [ <select_into> ]
                          [ <from_clause> ]
                          [ <where_clause> ]
                          [ <group_by_clause> ]
                          [ <having_clause> ]
```

Note: You can explicitly code the ALL keyword, as in SELECT ALL * FROM employee, but that isn't shown in the syntax: It's the default, and it simply states the obvious; e.g., select all the rows.

A duplicate row is a row where all the select list items have the same values as the corresponding items in another row. The DISTINCT keyword applies to the whole select list, not just the first select list item that follows it. For each set of duplicate rows, all the rows are eliminated except one; this process is similar to the one used by GROUP BY.

For example, the following SELECT returns 13 rows when run against the ASADEMO database; without the DISTINCT keyword it returns 91:

```
SELECT DISTINCT
       prod_id,
       line_id
  FROM sales_order_items
 WHERE line_id >= 3
 ORDER BY prod_id,
       line_id;
```

Note: For the purposes of comparing values when processing the DISTINCT keyword, NULL values are considered to be the same. This is different from the way NULL values are usually treated: Comparisons involving NULL values have UNKNOWN results.

3.19 **FIRST and TOP**

The FIRST keyword or TOP clause can be used to limit the number of rows in the candidate result set. Logically speaking, this happens after the DISTINCT keyword has been applied.

```
<row_range>            ::= FIRST                    -- same as TOP 1
                         | TOP <maximum_row_count>
                           [ START AT <start_at_row_number> ]
<maximum_row_count>  ::= integer literal maximum number of rows to return
<start_at_row_number> ::= integer literal first row number to return
```

FIRST simply discards all the rows except the first one.

The TOP clause includes a maximum row count and an optional START AT clause. For example, if you specify TOP 4, only the first four rows survive, and all the others are discarded. If you specify TOP 4 START AT 3, only rows three, four, five, and six survive.

FIRST is sometimes used in a context that can't handle multiple rows; for example, a SELECT with an INTO clause that specifies program variables, or a subquery in a select list. If you think the select might return multiple rows, and you don't care which one is used, FIRST will guarantee only one will be returned. If you do care which row you get, an ORDER BY clause might help to sort the right row first.

Only integer literals are allowed in TOP and START; if you want to use variables you can use EXECUTE IMMEDIATE. Here is an example that calls a stored procedure to display page 15 of sales order items, where a "page" is defined as 10 rows:

```
CREATE PROCEDURE p_pagefull (
   @page_number INTEGER )
BEGIN
   DECLARE @page_size    INTEGER;
   DECLARE @start        INTEGER;
   DECLARE @sql          LONG VARCHAR;
   SET @page_size = 10;
   SET @start = 1;
   SET @start = @start + ( ( @page_number - 1 ) * @page_size );
   SET @sql = STRING (
      'SELECT TOP ',
      @page_size,
      ' START AT ',
      @start,
      ' * FROM sales_order ORDER BY order_date' );
   EXECUTE IMMEDIATE @sql;
END;

CALL p_pagefull ( 15 );
```

Following is the result set returned when that procedure call is executed on the ASADEMO database. For more information about the CREATE PROCEDURE and EXECUTE IMMEDIATE statements, see Chapter 8, "Packaging."

id	cust_id	order_date	fin_code_id	region	sales_rep
2081	180	2000-06-03	r1	Eastern	129
2241	123	2000-06-03	r1	Canada	856
2242	124	2000-06-04	r1	Eastern	299
2243	125	2000-06-05	r1	Central	667
2244	126	2000-06-08	r1	Western	129
2245	127	2000-06-09	r1	South	1142
2246	128	2000-06-10	r1	Eastern	195
2247	129	2000-06-11	r1	Eastern	690
2248	130	2000-06-12	r1	Central	1596
2029	128	2000-06-12	r1	Eastern	856

Retrieving data page by page is useful in some situations; e.g., web applications, where you don't want to keep a huge result set sitting around or a cursor open between interactions with the client.

> **Tip:** When you hear a request involving the words maximum, minimum, largest, or smallest, think of FIRST and TOP together with ORDER BY; that combination can solve more problems more easily than MAX or MIN.

3.20 NUMBER(*)

The NUMBER(*) function returns the row number in the final result set returned by a select. It is evaluated after FIRST, TOP, DISTINCT, ORDER BY, and all the other clauses have finished working on the result set. For that reason, you can only refer to NUMBER(*) in the select list itself, not the WHERE clause or any other part of the select that is processed earlier.

Here is an example that displays a numbered telephone directory for all employees whose last name begins with "D":

```
SELECT NUMBER(*) AS "#",
       STRING ( emp_lname, ', ', emp_fname ) AS full_name,
       STRING ( '(', LEFT ( phone, 3 ), ') ',
               SUBSTR ( phone, 4, 3 ), '-',
               RIGHT ( phone, 4 ) ) AS phone
  FROM employee
 WHERE emp_lname LIKE 'd%'
 ORDER BY emp_lname,
       emp_fname;
```

Here's what the result set looks like; note that the numbering is done after the WHERE and ORDER BY are finished:

```
# full_name          phone
= ================   ==============
1 Davidson, Jo Ann   (617) 555-3870
2 Diaz, Emilio       (617) 555-3567
3 Dill, Marc         (617) 555-2144
4 Driscoll, Kurt     (617) 555-1234
```

You can use NUMBER(*) together with ORDER BY to generate sequence numbers in SELECT INTO and INSERT with SELECT statements. This technique is sometimes a useful alternative to the DEFAULT AUTOINCREMENT feature. Here is an example that first creates a temporary table via SELECT INTO #t and inserts all the numbered names starting with "D," then uses an INSERT with SELECT to add all the numbered names starting with "E" to that temporary table, and finally displays the result sorted by letter and number:

```
SELECT NUMBER(*)            AS "#",
       LEFT ( emp_lname, 1 ) AS letter,
       STRING ( emp_fname, ' ', emp_lname ) AS full_name
  INTO #t
  FROM employee
 WHERE emp_lname LIKE 'D%'
 ORDER BY emp_lname,
       emp_fname;

INSERT #t
SELECT NUMBER(*)            AS "#",
       LEFT ( emp_lname, 1 ) AS letter,
       STRING ( emp_fname, ' ', emp_lname ) AS full_name
  FROM employee
 WHERE emp_lname LIKE 'E%'
```

```
ORDER BY emp_lname,
         emp_fname;

SELECT "#",
         full_name
  FROM #t
 ORDER BY letter,
          "#";
```

Here's what the final SELECT produces; there might be better ways to accomplish this particular task, but this example does demonstrate how NUMBER(*) can be used to preserve ordering after the original data used for sorting has been discarded:

```
#  full_name
=  =================
1  Jo Ann Davidson
2  Emilio Diaz
3  Marc Dill
4  Kurt Driscoll
1  Melissa Espinoza
2  Scott Evans
```

For more information about DEFAULT AUTOINCREMENT and SELECT INTO temporary tables, see Chapter 1, "Creating." For more information about the INSERT statement, see Chapter 2, "Inserting."

NUMBER(*) can also be used as a new value in the SET clause of an UPDATE statement; for more information, see Section 4.4, "Logical Execution of a Set UPDATE."

3.21 INTO Clause

The select INTO clause can be used for two completely different purposes: to create and insert rows into a temporary table whose name begins with a number sign (#), or to store values from the select list of a single-row result set into program variables. This section talks about the program variables; for more information about creating a temporary table, see Section 1.15.2.3, "SELECT INTO #table_name."

```
<select_into>                ::= INTO <temporary_table_name>
                             | INTO <select_into_variable_list>
<temporary_table_name>       ::= see <temporary_table_name> in Chapter 1, "Creating"
<select_into_variable_list>  ::= <non_temporary_identifier>
                                 { "," <non_temporary_identifier> }
<non_temporary_identifier>   ::= see <non_temporary_identifier> in
                                 Chapter 1, "Creating"
```

Here is an example that uses two program variables to record the name and row count of the table with the most rows; when run on the ASADEMO database it displays "SYSPROCPARM has the most rows: 1632" in the server console window:

```
BEGIN
    DECLARE @table_name VARCHAR ( 128 );
    DECLARE @row_count  BIGINT;

    CHECKPOINT;

    SELECT FIRST
```

```
        table_name,
        count
    INTO @table_name,
        @row_count
    FROM SYSTABLE
    ORDER BY count DESC;

  MESSAGE STRING (
     @table_name,
     ' has the most rows: ',
     @row_count ) TO CONSOLE;
END;
```

> **Note:**   The SYSTABLE.count column holds the number of rows in the table as
> of the previous checkpoint. The explicit CHECKPOINT command is used in the
> example above to make sure that SYSTABLE.count is up to date. The alternative,
> computing SELECT COUNT(*) for every table in order to find the largest number
> of rows, is awkward to code as well as slow to execute if the tables are large.

For more information about BEGIN blocks and DECLARE statements, see
Chapter 8, "Packaging."

3.22 **UNION, EXCEPT, and INTERSECT**

Multiple result sets may be compared and combined with the UNION,
EXCEPT, and INTERSECT operators to produce result sets that are the union,
difference, and intersection of the original result sets, respectively.

```
<select>              ::= [ <with_clause> ]          -- WITH...
                          <query_expression>        -- at least one SELECT...
                          [ <order_by_clause> ] -- ORDER BY...
                          [ <for_clause> ]          -- FOR...
<query_expression> ::= <query_expression> <query_operator> <query_expression>
                       | <subquery>
                       | <query_specification>
<query_operator>   ::= EXCEPT    [ DISTINCT | ALL ]
                       | INTERSECT [ DISTINCT | ALL ]
                       | UNION    [ DISTINCT | ALL ]
```

The comparisons involve all the columns in the result sets: If every column
value in one row in the first result set is exactly the same as the corresponding
value in a row in the second result set, the two rows are the same; otherwise
they are different. This means the rows in both result sets must have the same
number of columns.

> **Note:**   For the purpose of comparing rows when evaluating the EXCEPT,
> INTERSECT, and UNION operators, NULL values are treated as being the same.

The operation A EXCEPT B returns all the rows that exist in result set A and do
not exist in B; it could be called "A minus B." Note that A EXCEPT B is not
the same as B EXCEPT A.

A INTERSECT B returns all the rows that exist in both A and B, but not
the rows that exist only in A or only in B.

A UNION B returns all the rows from both A and B; it could be called "A
plus B."

The DISTINCT keyword ensures that no duplicate rows remain in the final result set, whereas ALL allows duplicates; DISTINCT is the default. The only way A EXCEPT ALL B could return duplicates is if duplicate rows already existed in A. The only way A INTERSECT ALL B returns duplicates is if matching rows are duplicated in both A and B. A UNION ALL B may or may not contain duplicates; duplicates could come from one or the other or both A and B.

Here is an example that uses the DISTINCT values of customer.state and employee.state in the ASADEMO database to demonstrate EXCEPT, INTERSECT, and UNION. Seven different selects are used, as follows:

- Distinct values of customer.state.
- Distinct values of employee.state.
- Customer states EXCEPT employee states.
- Employee states EXCEPT customer states.
- The "exclusive OR" (XOR) of customer and employee states: states that exist in one or the other table but not both.
- Customer states INTERSECT employee states.
- Customer states UNION employee states.

These selects use derived tables to compute the distinct state result sets, as well as the EXCEPT, INTERSECT, and UNION operations. The LIST function produces compact output, and the COUNT function computes how many entries are in each list.

```
SELECT COUNT(*) AS count,
       LIST ( state ORDER BY state ) AS customer_states
  FROM ( SELECT DISTINCT state
           FROM customer )
       AS customer;

SELECT COUNT(*) AS count,
       LIST ( state ORDER BY state ) AS employee_states
  FROM ( SELECT DISTINCT state
           FROM employee )
       AS employee;

SELECT COUNT(*) AS count,
       LIST ( state ORDER BY state ) AS customer_except_employee
  FROM ( SELECT state
           FROM customer
         EXCEPT
         SELECT state
           FROM employee )
       AS customer_except_employee;

SELECT COUNT(*) AS count,
       LIST ( state ORDER BY state ) AS employee_except_customer
  FROM ( SELECT state
           FROM employee
         EXCEPT
         SELECT state
           FROM customer )
       AS employee_except_customer;

SELECT COUNT(*) AS count,
       LIST ( state ORDER BY state ) AS customer_xor_employee
```

```
   FROM ( ( SELECT state
                FROM customer
             EXCEPT
             SELECT state
               FROM employee )
          UNION ALL
            ( SELECT state
                FROM employee
             EXCEPT
             SELECT state
               FROM customer ) )
        AS customer_xor_employee;

SELECT COUNT(*) AS count,
       LIST ( state ORDER BY state ) AS customer_intersect_employee
  FROM ( SELECT state
           FROM customer
         INTERSECT
         SELECT state
           FROM employee )
        AS customer_intersect_employee;

SELECT COUNT(*) AS count,
       LIST ( state ORDER BY state ) AS customer_union_employee
  FROM ( SELECT state
           FROM customer
         UNION
         SELECT state
           FROM employee )
        AS customer_intersect_employee;
```

Following are the results. Note that every SELECT produces a different count, and that the two EXCEPT results are different. In particular, the presence and absence of CA, AZ, and AB in the different lists illustrate the differences among EXCEPT, INTERSECT, and UNION.

```
count  LIST of states
=====  ==============
36     AB,BC,CA,CO,CT,DC,FL,GA,IA,IL,IN,KS,LA,MA,  -- customer_states
       MB,MD,MI,MN,MO,NC,ND,NJ,NM,NY,OH,ON,OR,PA,
       PQ,TN,TX,UT,VA,WA,WI,WY

16     AZ,CA,CO,FL,GA,IL,KS,ME,MI,NY,OR,PA,RI,TX,  -- employee_states
       UT,WY

23     AB,BC,CT,DC,IA,IN,LA,MA,MB,MD,MN,MO,NC,ND,  -- customer_except_employee
       NJ,NM,OH,ON,PQ,TN,VA,WA,WI

3      AZ,ME,RI                                    -- employee_except_customer

26     AB,AZ,BC,CT,DC,IA,IN,LA,MA,MB,MD,ME,MN,MO,  -- customer_xor_employee
       NC,ND,NJ,NM,OH,ON,PQ,RI,TN,VA,WA,WI

13     CA,CO,FL,GA,IL,KS,MI,NY,OR,PA,TX,UT,WY      -- customer_intersect_employee

39     AB,AZ,BC,CA,CO,CT,DC,FL,GA,IA,IL,IN,KS,LA,  -- customer_union_employee
       MA,MB,MD,ME,MI,MN,MO,NC,ND,NM,NY,OH,ON,
       OR,PA,PQ,RI,TN,TX,UT,VA,WA,WI,WY
```

Of the three operators EXCEPT, INTERSECT, and UNION, UNION is by far the most useful. UNION helps with the divide-and-conquer approach to problem solving: Two or more simple selects are often easier to write than one complex select. A UNION of multiple selects may also be much faster than one SELECT, especially when UNION is used to eliminate the OR operator from boolean expressions; that's because OR can be difficult to optimize but UNION is easy to compute, especially UNION ALL.

> **Tip:** UNION ALL is fast, so use it all the time, except when you can't. If you know the individual result sets don't have any duplicates, or you don't care about duplicates, use UNION ALL. Sometimes it's faster to eliminate the duplicates in the application than make the server do it.

Here is an example that displays a telephone directory for all customers and employees whose last name begins with "K." String literals 'Customer' and 'Employee' are included in the result sets to preserve the origin of the data in the final UNION ALL.

```
SELECT STRING ( customer.lname, ', ', customer.fname ) AS full_name,
       STRING ( '(', LEFT ( customer.phone, 3 ), ') ',
                SUBSTR ( customer.phone, 4, 3 ), '-',
                RIGHT ( customer.phone, 4 ) )          AS phone,
          'Customer'                                   AS relationship
   FROM customer
  WHERE customer.lname LIKE 'k%'
UNION ALL
SELECT STRING ( employee.emp_lname, ', ', employee.emp_fname ),
       STRING ( '(', LEFT ( employee.phone, 3 ), ') ',
                SUBSTR ( employee.phone, 4, 3 ), '-',
                RIGHT ( employee.phone, 4 ) ),
          'Employee'
   FROM employee
  WHERE employee.emp_lname LIKE 'k%'
  ORDER BY 1;
```

Here is the final result:

```
full_name          phone            relationship
================   =============    ============
Kaiser, Samuel     (612) 555-3409   Customer
Kelly, Moira       (508) 555-3769   Employee
King, Marilyn      (219) 555-4551   Customer
Klobucher, James   (713) 555-8627   Employee
Kuo, Felicia       (617) 555-2385   Employee
```

The INTO #table_name clause may be used together with UNION, as long as the INTO clause appears only in the first SELECT. Here is an example that creates a temporary table containing all the "K" names from customer and employee:

```
SELECT customer.lname AS last_name
  INTO #last_name
  FROM customer
 WHERE customer.lname LIKE 'k%'
UNION ALL
SELECT employee.emp_lname
  FROM employee
 WHERE employee.emp_lname LIKE 'k%';

SELECT *
  FROM #last_name
 ORDER BY 1;
```

Here are the contents of the #last_name table:

```
last_name
=========
Kaiser
Kelly
King
Klobucher
Kuo
```

For more information about creating temporary tables this way, see Section 1.15.2.3, "SELECT INTO #table_name."

The first query in a series of EXCEPT, INTERSECT, and UNION operations establishes the alias names of the columns in the final result set. That's not true for the data types, however; SQL Anywhere examines the corresponding select list items in all the queries to determine the data types for the final result set.

Tip: Be careful with data types in a UNION. More specifically, make sure each select list item in each query in a series of EXCEPT, INTERSECT, and UNION operations has exactly the same data type as the corresponding item in every other query in the series. If they aren't the same, or you're not sure, use CAST to force the data types to be the same. If you don't do that, you may not like what you get. For example, if you UNION a VARCHAR (100) with a VARCHAR (10) the result will be (so far, so good) a VARCHAR (100). However, if you UNION a VARCHAR with a BINARY the result will be LONG BINARY; that may not be what you want, especially if you don't like case-sensitive string comparisons.

3.23 CREATE VIEW

The CREATE VIEW statement can be used to permanently record a select that can then be referenced by name in the FROM clause of other selects as if it were a table.

```
<create_view>           ::= CREATE VIEW [ <owner_name> "." ] <view_name>
                            [ <view_column_name_list> ]
                            AS
                            [ <with_clause> ]       -- WITH...
                            <query_expression>      -- at least one SELECT...
                            [ <order_by_clause> ]   -- ORDER BY...
                            [ <for_xml_clause> ]
                            [ WITH CHECK OPTION ]
<view_column_name_list> ::= "(" [ <alias_name_list> ] ")"
```

Views are useful for hiding complexity; for example, here is a CREATE VIEW that contains a fairly complex SELECT involving the SQL Anywhere system tables:

```
CREATE VIEW v_parent_child AS
SELECT USER_NAME ( parent_table.creator )  AS parent_owner,
       parent_table.table_name             AS parent_table,
       USER_NAME ( child_table.creator )   AS child_owner,
       child_table.table_name              AS child_table
  FROM SYS.SYSFOREIGNKEY AS foreign_key
       INNER JOIN
          ( SELECT table_id,
                   creator,
                   table_name
```

```
                FROM SYS.SYSTABLE
                WHERE table_type = 'BASE' ) -- no VIEWs, etc.
         AS parent_table
         ON parent_table.table_id = foreign_key.primary_table_id
         INNER JOIN
            ( SELECT table_id,
                     creator,
                     table_name
                FROM SYS.SYSTABLE
                WHERE table_type = 'BASE' ) -- no VIEWs, etc.
         AS child_table
         ON  child_table.table_id = foreign_key.foreign_table_id;
```

The SYSTABLE table contains information about each table in the database, SYSFOREIGNKEY is a many-to-many relationship table that links parent and child rows in SYSTABLE, and USER_NAME is a built-in function that converts a numeric user number like 1 into the corresponding user id 'DBA'. The v_parent_child view produces a result set consisting of the owner and table names for the parent and child tables for each foreign key definition in the database. The INNER JOIN operations are required because SYSFOREIGNKEY doesn't contain the table names, just numeric table_id values; it's SYSTABLE that has the names we want.

Note: Every SQL Anywhere database comes with predefined views similar to this; for example, see SYSFOREIGNKEYS.

Following is a SELECT using v_parent_child to display all the foreign key relationships involving tables owned by 'DBA'. This SELECT is simple and easy to understand, much simpler than the underlying view definition.

```
SELECT parent_owner,
       parent_table,
       child_owner,
       child_table
  FROM v_parent_child
 WHERE parent_owner = 'DBA'
   AND child_owner = 'DBA'
 ORDER BY 1, 2, 3, 4;
```

Here is the result set produced by that SELECT when it's run against the ASADEMO database:

parent_owner	parent_table	child_owner	child_table
==============	==============	=============	===================
DBA	customer	DBA	sales_order
DBA	department	DBA	employee
DBA	employee	DBA	department
DBA	employee	DBA	sales_order
DBA	fin_code	DBA	fin_data
DBA	fin_code	DBA	sales_order
DBA	product	DBA	sales_order_items
DBA	sales_order	DBA	sales_order_items

Tip: Don't get carried away creating views. In particular, do not create a view for every table that simply selects all the columns with the aim of somehow isolating applications from schema changes. That approach doubles the number of schema objects that must be maintained, with no real benefit. A schema change either doesn't affect an application or it requires application maintenance, and an extra layer of obscurity doesn't help. And don't create views just to make column names more readable, use readable column names in the base tables themselves; hokey naming conventions are a relic of the past millennium and have no place in this new century.

Tip: Watch out for performance problems caused by excessive view complexity. Views are evaluated and executed from scratch every time a query that uses them is executed. For example, if you use views containing multi-table joins to implement a complex security authorization scheme that affects every table and every query, you may pay a price in performance. Views hide complexity from the developer but not the query optimizer; it may not be able to do a good job on multi-view joins that effectively involve dozens or hundreds of table references in the various FROM clauses.

A view can be used to UPDATE, INSERT, and DELETE rows if that view is updatable, insertable, and deletable, respectively. A view is updatable if it is possible to figure out which rows in the base tables must be updated; that means an updatable view cannot use DISTINCT, GROUP BY, UNION, EXCEPT, INTERSECT, or an aggregate function reference. A view is insertable if it is updatable and only involves one table. The same thing applies to a deletable rule: It must only have one table and be updatable.

The optional WITH CHECK OPTION clause applies to INSERT and UPDATE operations involving the view; it states that these operations will be checked against the view definition and only allowed if all of the affected rows would qualify to be selected by the view itself. For more information, see the SQL Anywhere Help; this book doesn't discuss updatable views except to present the following example:

```
CREATE TABLE parent (
   key_1        INTEGER NOT NULL PRIMARY KEY,
   non_key_1    INTEGER NOT NULL );

CREATE VIEW v_parent AS
SELECT *
  FROM parent;

CREATE TABLE child (
   key_1        INTEGER NOT NULL REFERENCES parent ( key_1 ),
   key_2        INTEGER NOT NULL,
   non_key_1    INTEGER NOT NULL,
   PRIMARY KEY ( key_1, key_2 ) );

CREATE VIEW v_child AS
SELECT *
  FROM child;

CREATE VIEW v_family (
   parent_key_1,
   parent_non_key_1,
   child_key_1,
   child_key_2,
```

```
       child_non_key_1 ) AS
SELECT parent.key_1,
       parent.non_key_1,
       child.key_1,
       child.key_2,
       child.non_key_1
  FROM parent
       INNER JOIN child
             ON child.key_1 = parent.key_1;

INSERT v_parent VALUES ( 1, 444 );
INSERT v_parent VALUES ( 2, 555 );
INSERT v_parent VALUES ( 3, 666 );

INSERT v_child VALUES ( 1, 77, 777 );
INSERT v_child VALUES ( 1, 88, 888 );
INSERT v_child VALUES ( 2, 99, 999 );
INSERT v_child VALUES ( 3, 11, 111 );

UPDATE v_family
   SET parent_non_key_1 = 1111,
       child_non_key_1  = 2222
 WHERE parent_key_1 = 1
   AND child_key_2  = 88;

DELETE v_child
 WHERE key_1 = 3
   AND key_2 = 11;

SELECT * FROM v_family
 ORDER BY parent_key_1,
          child_key_2;
```

The INSERT and DELETE statements shown above work because the v_parent
and v_child views are insertable, deletable, and updatable. However, the v_fam-
ily view is only updatable, not insertable or deletable, because it involves two
tables. Note that the single UPDATE statement changes one row in each of two
different tables. Here is the result set from the final SELECT:

parent_key_1	parent_non_key_1	child_key_1	child_key_2	child_non_key_1
1	1111	1	77	777
1	1111	1	88	2222
2	555	2	99	999

3.24 **WITH Clause**

The WITH clause may be used to define one or more local views. The WITH
clause is appended to the front of a query expression involving one or more
selects, and the local views defined in the WITH clause may be used in those
selects. The RECURSIVE keyword states that one or more of the local views
may be used in recursive union operations. The topic of recursive unions is covered in the next section.

```
<select>                 ::= [ <with_clause> ]        -- WITH...
                             <query expression>       -- at least one SELECT
                             [ <order_by_clause> ]    -- ORDER BY...
                             [ <for_clause> ]          -- FOR...
<with_clause>            ::= WITH [ RECURSIVE ] <local_view_list>
<local_view_list>       ::= <local_view> { "," <local_view> }
```

```
<local_view>                 ::= <local_view_name>
                                 [ <local_view_column_name_list> ]
                                 AS <subquery>
<local_view_name>            ::= <identifier>
<local_view_column_name_list> ::= "(" [ <alias_name_list> ] ")"
```

Note: The SQL Anywhere Help uses the term "temporary view" instead of "local view." Unlike temporary tables, however, these views may only be referenced locally, within the select to which the WITH clause is attached. The word "temporary" implies the view definition might persist until the connection drops. There is no such thing as CREATE TEMPORARY VIEW, which is why this book uses the phrase "local view" instead.

The WITH clause may be used to reduce duplication in your code: A single local view defined in the WITH clause may be referenced, by name, more than once in the FROM clause of the subsequent select. For example, the v_parent_child example from the previous section may be simplified to replace two identical derived table definitions with one local view called base_table. Note that there is no problem with having a WITH clause inside a CREATE VIEW; i.e., having a local view defined inside a permanent view.

```
CREATE VIEW v_parent_child AS
WITH base_table AS
       ( SELECT table_id,
                creator,
                table_name
          FROM SYS.SYSTABLE
         WHERE table_type = 'BASE' )
SELECT USER_NAME ( parent_table.creator ) AS parent_owner,
       parent_table.table_name            AS parent_table,
       USER_NAME ( child_table.creator )  AS child_owner,
       child_table.table_name             AS child_table
  FROM SYS.SYSFOREIGNKEY AS foreign_key
       INNER JOIN base_table
              AS parent_table
              ON parent_table.table_id = foreign_key.primary_table_id
       INNER JOIN base_table
              AS child_table
              ON child_table.table_id =  foreign_key.foreign_table_id;
```

You can only code the WITH clause in front of the outermost SELECT in a SELECT, CREATE VIEW, or INSERT statement. That isn't much of a restriction because you can still refer to the local view names anywhere down inside nested query expressions; you just can't code more WITH clauses inside subqueries.

3.24.1 Recursive UNION

The recursive union is a special technique that uses the WITH clause to define a local view based on a UNION ALL of two queries:

- The first query inside the local view is an "initial seed query" that provides one or more rows to get the process rolling.
- The second query contains a recursive reference to the local view name itself, and it appends more rows to the initial result set produced by the first query. The RECURSIVE keyword must appear in the WITH clause for the recursion to work.

The WITH clause as a whole appears in front of a third, outer query that also refers to the local view; it is this outer query that drives the whole process and produces an actual result set.

Here is the syntax for a typical recursive union:

```
<typical_recursive_union>      ::= WITH RECURSIVE <local_view_name>
                                    "(" <alias_name_list> ")"
                                    AS "(" <initial_query_specification>
                                        UNION ALL
                                            <recursive_query_specification> ")"
                                    <outer_query_specification>
                                    [ <order_by_clause> ]
                                    [ <for_clause> ]
<initial_query_specification>  ::= <query_specification> that provides seed rows
<recursive_query_specification> ::= <query_specification> that recursively
                                        refers to the <local_view_name>
<outer_query_specification>    ::= <query_specification> that refers to
                                        the <local_view_name>
```

Note: A recursive process is one that is defined in terms of itself. Consider the factorial of a number: The factorial of 6 is defined as 6 * 5 * 4 * 3 * 2 * 1, or 720, for example, so the formula for factorial may be written using a recursive definition: "factorial (n) = n * factorial (n – 1)." It's sometimes a convenient way to think about a complex process, and if you can code it the way you think about it, so much the better. SQL Anywhere allows you to code recursive functions like factorial. For more information about the CREATE FUNCTION statement, see Section 8.10 in Chapter 8, "Packaging." This section talks about a different kind of recursive process — the recursive union.

Recursive unions can be used to process hierarchical relationships in the data. Hierarchies in the data often involve self-referencing foreign key relationships where different rows in the same table act as child and parent for one another. These relationships are very difficult to handle with ordinary SQL, especially if the number of levels in the hierarchy can vary widely.

Figure 3-1 shows just such a relationship, an organization chart for a company with 14 employees where the arrows show the reporting structure (e.g., Briana, Calista, and Delmar all report to Ainslie, Electra reports to Briana, and so on).

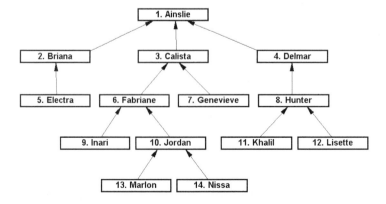

Figure 3-1. Organization chart

Following is a table definition plus the data to represent the organization chart in Figure 3-1; the employee_id column is the primary key identifying each employee, the manager_id column points to the employee's superior just like the arrows in Figure 3-1, and the name and salary columns contain data about the employee. Note that manager_id is set to 1 for employee_id = 1; that simply means Ainslie is at the top of the chart and doesn't report to anyone else within the company.

```
CREATE TABLE employee (
   employee_id  INTEGER NOT NULL,
   manager_id   INTEGER NOT NULL REFERENCES employee ( employee_id ),
   name         VARCHAR ( 20 ) NOT NULL,
   salary       NUMERIC ( 20, 2 ) NOT NULL,
   PRIMARY KEY ( employee_id ) );

INSERT INTO employee VALUES ( 1,  1,  'Ainslie',  1000000.00 );
INSERT INTO employee VALUES ( 2,  1,  'Briana',    900000.00 );
INSERT INTO employee VALUES ( 3,  1,  'Calista',   900000.00 );
INSERT INTO employee VALUES ( 4,  1,  'Delmar',    900000.00 );
INSERT INTO employee VALUES ( 5,  2,  'Electra',   750000.00 );
INSERT INTO employee VALUES ( 6,  3,  'Fabriane',  800000.00 );
INSERT INTO employee VALUES ( 7,  3,  'Genevieve', 750000.00 );
INSERT INTO employee VALUES ( 8,  4,  'Hunter',    800000.00 );
INSERT INTO employee VALUES ( 9,  6,  'Inari',     500000.00 );
INSERT INTO employee VALUES ( 10, 6,  'Jordan',    100000.00 );
INSERT INTO employee VALUES ( 11, 8,  'Khalil',    100000.00 );
INSERT INTO employee VALUES ( 12, 8,  'Lisette',   100000.00 );
INSERT INTO employee VALUES ( 13, 10, 'Marlon',    100000.00 );
INSERT INTO employee VALUES ( 14, 10, 'Nissa',     100000.00 );
```

Note: The employee table shown here is different from the employee table in the ASADEMO database.

Here is a SELECT that answers the question "Who are Marlon's superiors on the way up the chart to Ainslie?":

```
WITH RECURSIVE superior_list
   ( level,
     chosen_employee_id,
     manager_id,
     employee_id,
     name )
AS ( SELECT CAST ( 1 AS INTEGER ) AS level,
            employee.employee_id   AS chosen_employee_id,
            employee.manager_id    AS manager_id,
            employee.employee_id   AS employee_id,
            employee.name          AS name
        FROM employee
     UNION ALL
     SELECT superior_list.level + 1,
            superior_list.chosen_employee_id,
            employee.manager_id,
            employee.employee_id,
            employee.name
        FROM superior_list
            INNER JOIN employee
                    ON employee.employee_id = superior_list.manager_id
      WHERE superior_list.level <= 99
        AND superior_list.manager_id <> superior_list.employee_id )
```

```
SELECT superior_list.level,
       superior_list.name
  FROM superior_list
 WHERE superior_list.chosen_employee_id = 13
 ORDER BY superior_list.level DESC;
```

The final result set shows there are five levels in the hierarchy, with Jordan, Fabriane, and Calista on the path between Marlon and Ainslie:

```
level  name
=====  ========
5      Ainslie
4      Calista
3      Fabriane
2      Jordan
1      Marlon
```

Here's how the above SELECT works:

1. The WITH RECURSIVE clause starts by giving a name to the local view, superior_list, and a list of alias names for the five columns in that local view.

2. Each row in the view result set will contain information about one of Marlon's superiors on the path between Marlon and Ainslie. The end points will be included, so there will be a row for Marlon himself.

3. The level column in the view will contain the hierarchical level, numbered from 1 for Marlon at the bottom, 2 at the next level up, and so on.

4. The chosen_employee_id column will identify the employee of interest; in this case, it will be the fixed value 13 for Marlon because that's who the question asked about. In other words, every row will contain 13, and how this comes about is explained in point 10 below.

5. The manager_id column will identify the employee one level above this one, whereas employee_id and name will identify the employee at this level.

6. The first query in the UNION ALL selects all the rows from the employee table, and assigns them all level number 1. These rows are the bottom starting points for all possible queries about "Who are this employee's superiors?" This is the non-recursive "seed query," which gets the process going. In actual fact, there will only be one row generated by this query; how that is accomplished is explained in point 10 below.

7. The second query in the UNION ALL performs an INNER JOIN between rows in the employee table and rows that already exist in the superior_list result set, starting with the rows that came from the seed query. For each row already in superior_list, the INNER JOIN finds the employee row one level up in the hierarchy via "ON employee.employee_id = superior_list.manager_id." This recursive reference back to the local view itself is the reason for the RECURSIVE keyword on the WITH clause.

8. For each new row added to the result set by the second query in the UNION ALL, the level value is set one higher than the level in the row already in superior_list. The chosen_employee_id is set to the same value as the chosen_employee_id in the row already in superior_list. The other three columns — manager_id, employee_id, and name — are taken from the row in employee representing the person one level up in the hierarchy.

9. The WHERE clause keeps the recursion from running out of control. First of all, there is a sanity check on the level that stops the query when it hits the impossible number of 99. The second predicate in the WHERE clause, "superior_list.manager_id <> superior_list.employee_id," stops the recursion when Ainslie's row is reached; no attempt is made to look above her row when it shows up as one of the rows already existing in superior_list.

10. The outer SELECT displays all the rows in the superior_list where the chosen_employee_id is 13 for Marlon. The outer WHERE clause effectively throws away all the rows from the first query in the UNION ALL except the one for Marlon. It also excludes all the rows added by the second query in the UNION ALL except for the ones on the path above Marlon. The ORDER BY sorts the result in descending order by level so Ainslie appears at the top and Marlon at the bottom.

Tip: Always include a level number in a recursive union result set and a WHERE clause that performs a reasonableness check on the value. A loop in the data or a bug in the query may result in a runaway query, and it's a good idea to stop it before SQL Anywhere raises an error.

A CREATE VIEW statement can be used to store a complex recursive UNION for use in multiple different queries. The previous query can be turned into a permanent view by replacing the outer SELECT with a simple "SELECT *" and giving it a name in a CREATE VIEW statement, as follows:

```
CREATE VIEW v_superior_list AS
WITH RECURSIVE superior_list
   ( level,
     chosen_employee_id,
     manager_id,
     employee_id,
     name )
AS ( SELECT CAST ( 1 AS INTEGER ) AS level,
             employee.employee_id    AS chosen_employee_id,
             employee.manager_id     AS manager_id,
             employee.employee_id    AS employee_id,
             employee.name           AS name
        FROM employee
     UNION ALL
     SELECT superior_list.level + 1,
            superior_list.chosen_employee_id,
            employee.manager_id,
            employee.employee_id,
            employee.name
       FROM superior_list
            INNER JOIN employee
                  ON employee.employee_id = superior_list.manager_id
      WHERE superior_list.level <= 99
        AND superior_list.manager_id <> superior_list.employee_id )
SELECT *
  FROM superior_list;
```

The outer query from the previous example is now a much simpler standalone query using the view v_superior_list:

```
SELECT v_superior_list.level,
       v_superior_list.name
```

```
  FROM v_superior_list
WHERE v_superior_list.chosen_employee_id = 13
ORDER BY v_superior_list.level DESC;
```

That query produces exactly the same result set as before:

```
level   name
=====   ========
5       Ainslie
4       Calista
3       Fabriane
2       Jordan
1       Marlon
```

Following is another query that uses the same view in a different way. The LIST function shows all superiors on one line, and the WHERE clause eliminates Khalil's own name from the list.

```
SELECT LIST ( v_superior_list.name,
              ', then '
              ORDER BY v_superior_list.level ASC ) AS "Khalil's Superiors"
  FROM v_superior_list
WHERE v_superior_list.chosen_employee_id = 11
  AND v_superior_list.level > 1;
```

Here's the one-line result from the query above:

```
Khalil's Superiors
==================
Hunter, then Delmar, then Ainslie
```

Here is an example of a recursive union that can be used to answer top-down questions, including "What is the total salary of each employee plus all that employee's subordinates?"

```
CREATE VIEW v_salary_list AS
WITH RECURSIVE salary_list
   ( level,
     chosen_employee_id,
     manager_id,
     employee_id,
     name,
     salary )
AS ( SELECT CAST ( 1 AS INTEGER ) AS level,
            employee.employee_id  AS chosen_employee_id,
            employee.manager_id   AS manager_id,
            employee.employee_id  AS employee_id,
            employee.name         AS name,
            employee.salary       AS salary
       FROM employee
     UNION ALL
     SELECT salary_list.level + 1,
            salary_list.chosen_employee_id,
            employee.manager_id,
            employee.employee_id,
            employee.name,
            employee.salary
       FROM salary_list
            INNER JOIN employee
                    ON employee.manager_id = salary_list.employee_id
      WHERE salary_list.level <= 99
        AND employee.manager_id <> employee.employee_id )
SELECT *
  FROM salary_list;
```

This view works differently from the previous example; unlike v_superior_list, v_salary_list walks the hierarchy from the top down. The first query in the UNION ALL seeds the result set with all the employees as before, but the second query looks for employee rows further down in the hierarchy by using the condition "ON employee.manager_id = salary_list.employee_id" as opposed to the condition "ON employee.employee_id = superior_list.manager_id" in v_superior_list.

The following shows how v_salary_list can be used to compute the total payroll for each employee in the company. For each row in the employee table, a subquery computes the SUM of all v_salary_list.salary values where the chosen_employee_id matches employee.employee_id.

```
SELECT employee.name,
       ( SELECT SUM ( v_salary_list.salary )
           FROM v_salary_list
          WHERE v_salary_list.chosen_employee_id
              = employee.employee_id )          AS payroll
  FROM employee
ORDER BY 1;
```

Here's the final result set; at the top Ainslie's payroll figure is the sum of everyone's salary, and at the bottom Nissa's figure includes her own salary and no one else's:

```
name        payroll
=========   ==========
Ainslie     7800000.00
Briana      1650000.00
Calista     3250000.00
Delmar      1900000.00
Electra      750000.00
Fabriane    1600000.00
Genevieve    750000.00
Hunter      1000000.00
Inari        500000.00
Jordan       300000.00
Khalil       100000.00
Lisette      100000.00
Marlon       100000.00
Nissa        100000.00
```

3.25 UNLOAD TABLE and UNLOAD SELECT

The UNLOAD TABLE and UNLOAD SELECT statements are highly efficient ways to select data from the database and write it out to flat files.

```
<unload>            ::= <unload_table>
                      | <unload_select>
<unload_table>      ::= UNLOAD [ FROM ] TABLE [ <owner_name> "." ] <table_name>
                            TO <unload_filespec>
                            { <unload_table_option> }
<unload_select>     ::= UNLOAD <select_for_unload>
                            TO <unload_filespec>
                            { <unload_select_option> }
<select_for_unload> ::= [ <with_clause> ]
                            <query_expression>
                            [ <order_by_clause> ]
                            [ <for_xml_clause> ]
<unload_filespec>   ::= string literal file specification relative to the server
```

```
<unload_table_option>    ::= <unload_select_option>
                           | ORDER ( ON | OFF )            -- default ON
<unload_select_option>   ::= APPEND ( ON | OFF )           -- default OFF
                           | DELIMITED BY <unload_delimiter> -- default ','
                           | ESCAPE <escape_character>      -- default '\'
                           | ESCAPES ( ON | OFF )           -- default ON
                           | FORMAT ( ASCII | BCP )         -- default ASCII
                           | HEXADECIMAL ( ON | OFF )       -- default ON
                           | QUOTES ( ON | OFF )            -- default ON
<unload_delimiter>       ::= string literal 1 to 255 characters in length
<escape_character>       ::= string literal exactly 1 character in length
```

The first format, UNLOAD TABLE, is almost exactly like a limited form of the second format, UNLOAD SELECT. For example, the following two statements create identical files:

```
UNLOAD TABLE t1 TO 't1_a1.txt';
UNLOAD SELECT * FROM t1 TO 't1_a2.txt';
```

The UNLOAD TABLE statement does have one option, ORDER, that doesn't apply to UNLOAD SELECT. The rest of the options apply to both statements, and UNLOAD SELECT offers more flexibility. For those reasons, this section discusses the two statements together, with emphasis placed on UNLOAD SELECT.

The rules for coding the file specification in an UNLOAD statement are the same as the rules for the file specification in the LOAD TABLE statement; for more information, see Section 2.3, "LOAD TABLE."

The UNLOAD statements write one record to the output file for each row in the table or result set. Each record, including the last, is terminated by an ASCII carriage return and linefeed pair '\x0D\x0A'. Each column in the result set is converted to a string field value and appended to the output record in the order of the columns in the table or result set. The format of each output field depends on the original column data type and the various UNLOAD option settings.

The layout of the output file is controlled by the following UNLOAD options:

- **APPEND ON** specifies that the output records will be appended to the end of the file if it already exists; if the file doesn't exist a new one will be created. The default is APPEND OFF, to overwrite the file if it exists.
- **DELIMITED BY** can be used to change the output field delimiter; for example, DELIMITED BY '\x09' specifies that the output file is tab-delimited. DELIMITED BY '' may be used to eliminate field delimiters altogether. The default is DELIMITED BY ','.
- **ESCAPE CHARACTER** can be used to specify which single character will be used as the escape character in string literals in the output file; e.g., ESCAPE CHARACTER '!'. The default is ESCAPE CHARACTER '\'. Note that this option affects how the output data is produced; it doesn't have anything to do with the way escape characters in the output file specification are handled.
- **ESCAPES OFF** can be used to turn off escape character generation in output string literals. The default is ESCAPES ON, to generate escape characters. Once again, this option refers to the data in the file, not the file specification in the UNLOAD statement.

- **FORMAT BCP** specifies that the special Adaptive Server Enterprise Bulk Copy Program (bcp.exe) file format should be used for the output file. The default is FORMAT ASCII for ordinary text files. This book doesn't discuss the details of FORMAT BCP.

- **HEXADECIMAL OFF** turns off the generation of 0xnn-style unquoted binary string literals for binary string data. The default is HEXADECIMAL ON, to generate 0xnn-style output values.

- **ORDER OFF** can be used with UNLOAD TABLE to suppress the sorting of the output data. ORDER ON is the default, to sort the output data according to a clustered index if one exists, or by the primary key if one exists but a clustered index does not. ORDER ON has no effect if neither a clustered index nor a primary key exist. This sorting is primarily intended to speed up the process of reloading the file via LOAD TABLE. The ORDER option doesn't apply to the UNLOAD SELECT statement, but you can use the ORDER BY clause instead.

- **QUOTES OFF** specifies that all character string data will be written without adding leading and trailing single quotes and without doubling embedded single quotes. The default behavior, QUOTES ON, is to write character string data as quoted string literals.

Tip: When writing your own UNLOAD statements, don't bother with UNLOAD TABLE; use UNLOAD SELECT with ORDER BY. UNLOAD SELECT is worth getting used to because it's so much more flexible, and it's no harder to code when you want to do the same thing as UNLOAD TABLE. The only exception is when you want to dump a bunch of tables to files in sorted index order without having to code ORDER BY clauses; the ORDER ON default makes UNLOAD TABLE easier to use in this case.

Following is an example that shows the effect of the various UNLOAD options on values with different data types; the same data is written to five different text files using five different sets of options. Note that on each row in the table, the col_2 and col_3 values are actually the same; different formats are used in the INSERT VALUES clause to demonstrate that INSERT input formats have nothing to do with UNLOAD output formats.

```
CREATE TABLE t1 (
   key_1        INTEGER NOT NULL,
   col_2        VARCHAR ( 100 ) NULL,
   col_3        BINARY ( 100 ) NULL,
   col_4        DECIMAL ( 11, 2 ) NULL,
   col_5        DATE NULL,
   col_6        INTEGER NOT NULL,
   PRIMARY KEY ( key_1 ) );
INSERT t1 VALUES (
   1, 'Fred''s Here',         'Fred''s Here',     12.34, '2003-09-30', 888 );
INSERT t1 VALUES (
   2, 0x74776f0d0a6c696e6573, 'two\x0d\x0alines', 67.89, '2003-09-30', 999 );
COMMIT;
UNLOAD SELECT * FROM t1 ORDER BY key_1
   TO 't1_b1.txt';
UNLOAD SELECT * FROM t1 ORDER BY key_1
   TO 't1_b2.txt' ESCAPES OFF;
UNLOAD SELECT * FROM t1 ORDER BY key_1
   TO 't1_b3.txt' ESCAPES OFF QUOTES OFF;
```

```
UNLOAD SELECT * FROM t1 ORDER BY key_1
    TO 't1_b4.txt' HEXADECIMAL OFF ESCAPES OFF QUOTES OFF;
UNLOAD SELECT * FROM t1 ORDER BY key_1
    TO 't1_b5.txt' DELIMITED BY '' HEXADECIMAL OFF ESCAPES OFF QUOTES OFF;
```

Tip: If the order of output is important to you, be sure to use ORDER BY with UNLOAD SELECT. There is no guaranteed natural order of rows in a SQL Anywhere table, not even if there is a clustered index.

In the example above, the file t1_b1.txt was written with all the default option settings. This is the best choice for creating a file that can be successfully loaded back into a database via LOAD TABLE. Here's what the file looks like; note the quotes around the VARCHAR value, the doubled single quote, the escape characters, the 0xnn-style for the BINARY value, and the comma field delimiters:

```
1,'Fred''s Here',0x4672656427732048657265,12.34,2003-09-30,888
2,'two\x0d\x0alines',0x74776f0d0a6c696e6573,67.89,2003-09-30,999
```

The file t1_b2.txt was written with ESCAPES OFF. The following example show what the file looks like when displayed in Notepad or WordPad. Note that the embedded carriage return and linefeed pair '\x0d\x0a' in the VARCHAR column is not turned into an escape character sequence, but is placed in the output file as is to cause a real line break.

```
1,'Fred''s Here',0x4672656427732048657265,12.34,2003-09-30,888
2,'two
lines',0x74776f0d0a6c696e6573,67.89,2003-09-30,999
```

The file t1_b3.txt was written with ESCAPES OFF QUOTES OFF. Here's what the file looks like, with the leading and trailing single quotes gone and the embedded single quote no longer doubled:

```
1,Fred's Here,0x4672656427732048657265,12.34,2003-09-30,888
2,two
lines,0x74776f0d0a6c696e6573,67.89,2003-09-30,999
```

The file t1_b4.txt was written with HEXADECIMAL OFF ESCAPES OFF QUOTES OFF. The big difference now is that because of the HEXADECIMAL OFF setting the BINARY value is no longer output in the 0xnn-style. The BINARY values now look just like the VARCHAR values, and another embedded carriage return and linefeed pair is sent to the output file as is:

```
1,Fred's Here,Fred's Here,12.34,2003-09-30,888
2,two
lines,two
lines,67.89,2003-09-30,999
```

The file t1_b5.txt was written with DELIMITED BY '' HEXADECIMAL OFF ESCAPES OFF QUOTES OFF. This is the best choice for writing text "as is," without any extra formatting after the column values are converted to string; e.g., for writing text containing HTML or XML. Note that DELIMITED BY '' effectively eliminates field delimiters:

```
1Fred's HereFred's Here12.342003-09-30888
2two
linestwo
lines67.892003-09-30999
```

The UNLOAD statements work just like the STRING function as far as the conversion of each value to string for output is concerned. Various options, such as HEXADECIMAL ON and ESCAPES ON, perform further formatting after the conversion is complete, but if you turn all the options off the results from UNLOAD and STRING are the same. For example, the following SELECT returns string values that are exactly the same as the data written to the file t1_b5.txt above:

```
SELECT STRING (
          key_1,
          col_2,
          col_3,
          col_4,
          col_5,
          col_6 )
   FROM t1
   ORDER BY key_1;
```

An example in Section 3.14, "Aggregate Function Calls," showed how the STRING and LIST functions could be used to produce a string containing an entire HTML document. Here is that example again, this time using an UNLOAD SELECT to write the document to a file:

```
UNLOAD
SELECT STRING (
          '<HTML><BODY><OL>\x0d\x0a',
          '  <LI>',
          LIST ( DISTINCT state,
               '</LI>\x0d\x0a    <LI>'
               ORDER BY state ),
          '</LI>\x0d\x0a',
          '</OL></BODY></HTML>' ) AS states_page
   FROM employee
   WHERE dept_id = 100
   TO 'c:\\temp\\states_page.html' ESCAPES OFF QUOTES OFF;
```

Figure 3-2 shows what the c:\temp\states_page.html file looks like in Internet Explorer. Note that the HEXADECIMAL OFF option isn't needed because there is no BINARY value being written, and DELIMITED BY " isn't needed because there's only one field in the output record.

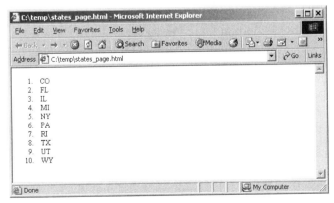

Figure 3-2. HTML written by UNLOAD SELECT

3.26 ISQL OUTPUT

The Interactive SQL utility (dbisql.exe, or ISQL) supports a statement that performs a similar function to UNLOAD SELECT but is profoundly different in many respects — the ISQL OUTPUT statement.

```
<isql_output>    ::= OUTPUT TO <output_file> { <output_option> }
<output_file>    ::= string literal file specification relative to the client
                   | double quoted file specification relative to the client
                   | unquoted file specification relative to the client
<output_option> ::= APPEND                            -- default overwrite
                   | COLUMN WIDTHS "(" <output_column_width_list> ")"
                   | DELIMITED BY <output_delimiter>          -- default ','
                   | ESCAPE CHARACTER <output_escape_character> -- default '\'
                   | FORMAT <output_format>            -- default ASCII
                   | HEXADECIMAL <hexadecimal_option> -- default ON
                   | QUOTE <output_quote> [ ALL ]     -- default 'quoted' strings
                                                      -- QUOTE '' for no quotes
                   | VERBOSE                           -- default data only
<output_column_width_list> ::= <output_column_width> { "," <output_column_width> }
<output_column_width>      ::= integer literal column width for FORMAT FIXED
<output_delimiter>         ::= string literal containing column delimiter string
<output_escape_character>  ::= string literal exactly 1 character in length
<output_format>            ::= string literal containing <output_format_name>
                             | double quoted <output_format_name>
                             | unquoted <output_format_name>
<output_format_name>       ::= ASCII    -- default
                             | DBASEII
                             | DBASEIII
                             | EXCEL
                             | FIXED
                             | FOXPRO
                             | HTML
                             | LOTUS
                             | SQL
                             | XML
<hexadecimal_option> ::= ON   -- default; 0xnn.. for binary strings
                       | OFF -- treat binary as character, with escape characters
                       | ASIS -- treat binary as character, no escape characters
<output_quote>       ::= string literal containing quote for string literals
```

The OUTPUT command only works as an ISQL command, and only when a result set is currently available to ISQL. This means OUTPUT is usually run together with a SELECT, as in the following example:

```
SELECT *
  FROM product
 WHERE name = 'Sweatshirt'
 ORDER BY id;
OUTPUT TO 'product.txt';
```

Here's what the product.txt file looks like when those statements are run against the ASADEMO database:

```
600,'Sweatshirt','Hooded Sweatshirt','Large','Green',39,24.00
601,'Sweatshirt','Zipped Sweatshirt','Large','Blue',32,24.00
```

Note: ISQL commands like OUTPUT and INPUT can't be nested inside BEGIN blocks. They can, however, be placed inside SQL command files and run together with other commands; in other words, they can be run in batch mode, but they can't be placed inside BEGIN blocks. That's because BEGIN blocks are sent to the database engine for execution; the database engine only understands SQL commands, not ISQL commands.

The rules for coding the file specification in an OUTPUT statement are the same as the rules for the file specification in the INPUT statement; for more information, see Section 2.4, "ISQL INPUT."

The big advantage OUTPUT has over UNLOAD SELECT is the variety of output formats — not just legacy formats like DBASEII, DBASEIII, EXCEL, FOXPRO, LOTUS, and SQL, but interesting ones like FIXED, HTML, and XML, as well as the default ASCII.

Here is a SELECT that retrieves two rows from the ASADEMO database, followed by OUTPUT statements that write three different kinds of files:

```
SELECT id,
       name,
       quantity,
       unit_price
  FROM product
 WHERE name = 'Sweatshirt'
 ORDER BY id;

OUTPUT TO 'c:\\temp\\product.dta' COLUMN WIDTHS ( 5, 15, 5, 7 ) FORMAT FIXED;
OUTPUT TO 'c:\\temp\\product.html' FORMAT HTML;
OUTPUT TO 'c:\\temp\\product.xml' FORMAT XML;
```

Here's what the FORMAT FIXED product.dta file looks like; each field is fixed length and there are no quotes, delimiters, or any formatting other than the conversion to string. Note that the INTEGER values id and quantity (e.g., 600 and 39) are right-justified, but the NUMERIC value unit_price (e.g., 24.00) is left-justified:

```
600Sweatshirt     3924.00
601Sweatshirt     3224.00
```

Figure 3-3 shows what the FORMAT HTML product.html file looks like in Internet Explorer; the data is displayed using an HTML <table> with headings and borders.

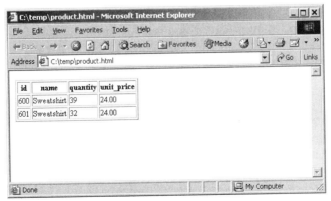

Figure 3-3. File written by OUTPUT FORMAT HTML

Figure 3-4 shows what the FORMAT XML product.xml file looks like in Internet Explorer; the data is structured using <resultset>, <row>, and <column> elements, the column names are coded as attributes of the <column> tags, and a DTD is embedded in the file.

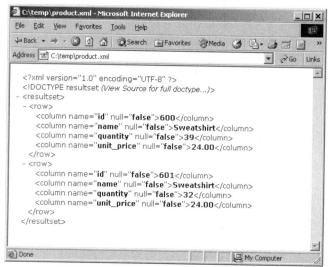

Figure 3-4. File written by OUTPUT FORMAT XML

The way OUTPUT works is controlled by several options:

■ **APPEND** specifies that the output records will be appended to the end of the file if it already exists; if the file doesn't exist a new one will be created. This option only applies to the ASCII, FIXED, and SQL formats. The default is to overwrite the file if it exists.

■ **COLUMN WIDTHS** may be used to provide a list of numeric column widths for FIXED format output. An explicit list of COLUMN WIDTHS should always be used with FORMAT FIXED. This book doesn't describe how the default widths are calculated when COLUMN WIDTHS is not specified or has too few values.

■ **DELIMITED BY** can be used to change the output field delimiter for ASCII format output. For example, DELIMITED BY '\x09' specifies that the output file is tab-delimited. DELIMITED BY '' may be used to eliminate field delimiters altogether. The default is DELIMITED BY ','.

■ **ESCAPE CHARACTER** can be used to specify which single character will be used as the escape character in string literals in ASCII format output; e.g., ESCAPE CHARACTER '!'. The default is ESCAPE CHARACTER '\'. Note that there is no ESCAPES OFF option, but HEXADECIMAL ASIS does the same thing.

■ **FORMAT FIXED** can be used to specify that each output field will have a fixed length, and that there will be no formatting other than conversion to string; i.e., there will be no field delimiters inserted, no escape characters generated, and no 0xnn-style formatting. FORMAT ASCII is the default.

FORMAT HTML and XML are presented in examples above but are not described in detail here. FORMAT DBASEII, DBASEIII, EXCEL, FOXPRO, LOTUS, and SQL are also available.

- **HEXADECIMAL OFF** can be used to format BINARY strings using escape characters in ASCII format output. For example, SELECT CAST ('1\\2\x0d\x0a3' AS BINARY) will be output as '1\\2\x0d\x0a3'. The default is HEXADECIMAL ON, which uses the 0xnn-style; e.g., SELECT CAST ('1\\2\x0d\x0a3' AS BINARY) will be output as 0x315c320d0a33. HEXADECIMAL ASIS can be used to turn off all reformatting of BINARY strings in ASCII format output. For example, SELECT CAST ('1\\2' AS BINARY) will be output as '1\2'. Note that string literal '1\\2' in the SELECT contains an escape character sequence \\ that is stored as a single backslash; the CAST function converts that string to BINARY, and HEXADECIMAL ASIS tells the OUTPUT command not to put the escape character back in.
  HEXADECIMAL ASIS also affects VARCHAR strings in ASCII format output. It turns off escape character generation for character strings just like ESCAPES OFF does for the UNLOAD statements. For example, SELECT '1\\2' will be output as '1\2', and SELECT '1\x0d\x0a2' will be output as '12' with a real line break between the 1 and the 2.
- **QUOTE** can be used to change the way output fields are "quoted" in ASCII format output; the quote character can be changed, and the ALL keyword may be used to force quoting of all output fields. For example, QUOTE "" will change the quote character to the double quote, and QUOTE "" ALL will put single quotes around all output fields; note that the string literal "" represents a single quote. The default is QUOTE "", to put single quotes around string fields. Note that the HEXADECIMAL option also affects what is quoted and what isn't.
  QUOTE " can be used to turn off quoting altogether; note that " represents the empty string. This also turns off the doubling of embedded quotes inside string values, so 'Fred''s Here' will appear as Fred's Here in the file.
- **VERBOSE** can be used to include extra diagnostic information in output, along with the actual data, when format ASCII, FIXED, or SQL is used. The default is to include only the data.

Tip: Be careful with BINARY data; make sure the output is actually what you want. You may want to call CAST to convert BINARY data to VARCHAR, especially with FORMAT FIXED.

Tip: Make sure the COLUMN WIDTHS option contains the same number of width numbers as there are columns in the result set to be OUTPUT. If you have too many or too few, you won't get any warning or error message; OUTPUT will apply the widths from left to right, ignore the extra widths, or calculate default widths for the missing entries.

Here is an example to show how various data types appear in FORMAT ASCII output when different option values are specified. The first OUTPUT statement uses all the defaults whereas the second OUTPUT turns off all the formatting except for conversion to string:

```
CREATE TABLE t1 (
   key_1        INTEGER NOT NULL,
   col_2        VARCHAR ( 100 ) NULL,
   col_3        BINARY ( 100 ) NULL,
   col_4        DECIMAL ( 11, 2 ) NULL,
   col_5        DATE NULL,
   col_6        INTEGER NOT NULL,
   PRIMARY KEY ( key_1 ) );

INSERT t1 VALUES (
   1, 'Fred''s Here',          'Fred''s Here',     12.34, '2003-09-30', 888 );
INSERT t1 VALUES (
   2, 0x74776f0d0a6c696e6573, 'two\x0d\x0alines', 67.89, '2003-09-30', 999 );
COMMIT;

SELECT * FROM t1 ORDER BY key_1;
OUTPUT TO 't1_c1.txt';
OUTPUT TO 't1_c2.txt' DELIMITED BY '' HEXADECIMAL ASIS QUOTE '';
```

Figure 3-5 shows what the result set looks like in ISQL.

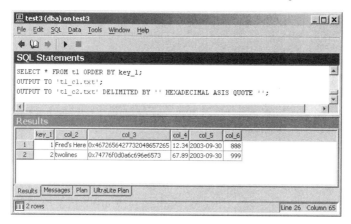

Figure 3-5. SELECT and OUTPUT in ISQL

Here's what the first file t1_c1.txt looks like; it contains field delimiters, quoted strings with escape characters, and a doubled embedded quote, plus 0xnn-style formatting for the BINARY data:

```
1,'Fred''s Here',0x4672656427732048657265,12.34,'2003-09-30',888
2,'two\x0d\x0alines',0x74776f0d0a6c696e6573,67.89,'2003-09-30',999
```

Here's the second file t1_c2.txt; no delimiters, no quotes, no escape characters, just the data presented as is including real line breaks:

```
1Fred's HereFred's Here12.342003-09-30888
2two
linestwo
lines67.892003-09-30999
```

Tip: For as-is output with no extra formatting, FORMAT ASCII DELIMITED BY " HEXADECIMAL ASIS QUOTE " beats FORMAT FIXED because the fields vary in width depending on the actual data after conversion to string. In other words, FORMAT ASCII can be made to behave more like the STRING function than FORMAT FIXED.

3.27 **Chapter Summary**

This chapter described how the various clauses of a SQL select work together to retrieve data and produce a final result set. A list of logical or imaginary steps was presented to clarify the relationships between the clauses and to provide answers to questions like "Why can't you call NUMBER(*) in the WHERE clause?" (Answer: The WHERE clause is executed before ORDER BY, and the rows must be sorted before NUMBER(*) can be calculated.)

Also covered in this chapter were expressions; boolean expressions; the UNION, EXCEPT, and INTERSECT operators; the CREATE VIEW statement; the WITH clause; recursive unions; and the UNLOAD and ISQL OUTPUT statements.

The next chapter moves on to the fourth step in the life cycle of a database: updating rows.

Chapter 4

Updating

4.1 Introduction

This chapter starts with a discussion of a simple UPDATE statement that
changes data in a single row in a single table, and then proceeds to a multi-row
UPDATE, also involving a single table. This is followed, in Section 4.4, with an
explanation of how more complex UPDATE statements involving multiple rows
in multiple tables operate, from a logical point of view. This explanation serves
to answer questions like "How can a single UPDATE change rows in more than
one table?" and "How can a single UPDATE change the same row more than
once?"

Section 4.4.1 describes the full syntax of the set-oriented UPDATE statement, with examples. Section 4.5 finishes up the chapter with the cursor-
oriented UPDATE, which tends to operate on single rows but can, in fact,
change more than one row in a single execution.

4.2 Single-Row UPDATE

The simplest, and perhaps the most common, form of the UPDATE statement is
used to change column values in a single row of a single table.

```
<typical_single_row_update> ::= UPDATE [ <owner_name> "." ] <table_name>
                                    <simple_set_clause>
                                    <single_row_where_clause>
<simple_set_clause>          ::= SET { <simple_set_item> "," }
                                    <simple_set_item>
<simple_set_item>            ::= <column_name> "=" <expression>
<single_row_where_clause>    ::= <where_clause> matching no more than 1 row
<owner_name>                 ::= <identifier>
<table_name>                 ::= <identifier>
<column_name>                ::= <identifier>
<identifier>                 ::= see <identifier> in Chapter 1, "Creating"
<expression>                 ::= see <expression> in Chapter 3, "Selecting"
<where_clause>               ::= see <where_clause> in Chapter 3, "Selecting"
```

A typical single-row UPDATE specifies one table name, a series of one or more
column assignments after the SET keyword, and a WHERE clause that matches
a single row in the table. Here is an example that changes the value of the
address column from '114 Pioneer Avenue' to '114 PIONEER AV' for the company row where the primary key id is 101, in the ASADEMO database:

```
UPDATE customer
   SET address = '114 PIONEER AV'
 WHERE id = 101;
```

For a description of the customer table in the ASADEMO database that ships with SQL Anywhere Studio 9, see Section 3.6, "Multi-Table Joins."

If the WHERE clause matches a row, and the SET clause specifies at least one new column value that is different from the current value, the UPDATE proceeds as follows: Any BEFORE UPDATE triggers associated with this table are fired, a row lock is obtained, the row is updated, the UPDATE is recorded in the transaction log, any AFTER UPDATE triggers are fired, and the SQLSTATE special literal is set to '00000' to indicate a completely normal condition. For more information about triggers, see Section 8.11, "CREATE TRIGGER," and for a discussion of locking, see Section 9.6, "Locks"

If the WHERE clause matches a row, but all the new column values are the same as the current values, the UPDATE proceeds as follows: Any BEFORE UPDATE triggers associated with this table are fired, a row lock is obtained but no update is performed, nothing is recorded in the transaction log, no AFTER UPDATE triggers are fired, and the SQLSTATE special literal is set to '00000'.

If the WHERE clause doesn't match any row, it isn't an error, but SQLSTATE is set to '02000' to indicate "row not found." In this case, no triggers are fired, no row lock is obtained, no update is performed, and nothing is recorded in the transaction log.

Note: These actions apply to multi-row updates as well, on a row-by-row basis. Two exceptions are SQLSTATE, which is set once for each execution of the UPDATE statement, and AFTER STATEMENT triggers, which are fired once per execution of the UPDATE statement.

Note: This book assumes the ISOLATION_LEVEL option is set to the default value of 0 for maximum performance and concurrency. Higher settings can change locking behavior; for example, the statement above that "no row lock is obtained" when the WHERE clause doesn't match any row isn't necessarily true when the ISOLATION_LEVEL is set to 3. For more information about isolation levels, see Section 9.7, "Blocks and Isolation Levels," in Chapter 9, "Protecting."

Here is an example showing the earlier UPDATE modified to make sure that the row is changed only if the current address value is still '114 Pioneer Avenue'. If the current value has been changed by some other process, the WHERE clause won't match any rows and SQLSTATE will be set to '02000':

```
UPDATE customer
   SET address = '114 PIONEER AV'
 WHERE id = 101
   AND address = '114 Pioneer Avenue';
```

This is a simple example of optimistic concurrency control whereby an application does not bother to lock a row between select and update, but instead checks to make sure that the row has not been changed by some other process before performing its own update.

Here is another example that updates the same row in the company table. This time, two columns are changed, the customer contact first and last names, and the WHERE clause specifies the company name instead of the primary key:

```
UPDATE customer
   SET fname = 'Fred',
```

```
         lname = 'Jones'
 WHERE company_name = 'The Power Group';
```

Tip: Watch out for single-row UPDATE statements that accidentally update more than one row, even the entire table. Make sure the WHERE clause refers to the primary key or a unique index, and that it specifies values for all the columns in that primary key or index if there are more than one.

4.3 Multi-Row UPDATE

As far as the syntax is concerned, there isn't any difference between a single-row and a multi-row UPDATE. In fact, a typical single-row UPDATE becomes a multi-row UPDATE by simply loosening up the WHERE clause or omitting it altogether.

```
<typical_multi_row_update> ::= UPDATE [ <owner_name> "." ] <table_name>
                                 <simple_set_clause>
                                 [ <multi_row_where_clause> ]
<multi_row_where_clause>   ::= <where_clause> matching zero or more rows
```

If the WHERE clause is omitted, every row in the table is changed. Here is an example that gives every employee a 5% raise; note that the expression on the right-hand side of a SET assignment may include references to current column values in the rows being updated. In this example, "SET salary = salary * 1.05" may be interpreted as "set the new value of the salary column in each row to the old value multiplied by 1.05":

```
UPDATE employee
  SET salary = salary * 1.05;
```

If a WHERE clause is included, and it matches two or more rows, the UPDATE is applied to all the matching rows. Here is an example that sets the termination date for everyone in department 100; in effect, the entire R&D department is fired:

```
UPDATE employee
  SET termination_date = CURRENT DATE
 WHERE dept_id = 100;
```

Tip: Be careful with multi-row UPDATE statements on large tables in a multi-user environment. The multi-row set-oriented UPDATE is a very powerful mechanism, but it will obtain an exclusive lock on every row it touches, and those locks will last at least as long as the UPDATE takes to execute. For example, an UPDATE that changes a million rows may take many minutes to complete, and the locks it obtains may prevent other users from getting their jobs done. It may also get halfway through and then be blocked itself by a lock held by another user, thus making a bad situation even worse. In this environment it may be more appropriate to use a cursor-oriented UPDATE in a fetch loop that executes a COMMIT from time to time to release locks. For more information about cursor fetch loops, see Chapter 6, "Fetching."

4.4 Logical Execution of a Set UPDATE

The full syntax of a set-oriented UPDATE includes a row range clause (FIRST or TOP), a table specification like the one described in Section 3.3, "FROM Clause," plus WHERE and ORDER BY clauses. This means the UPDATE statement can specify a multi-table join, and by extension, the SET clause can specify columns in more than one table.

```
<set_update> ::= UPDATE
                  [ <row_range> ]
                  <table_specification>
                  <set_clause>
                  [ <where_clause> ]
                  [ <order_by_clause> ]
```

The following sections describe the UPDATE clauses in detail, with examples. This section concentrates on the question "What does a multi-table UPDATE actually do?" It's an interesting question because, in fact, a single UPDATE can change the same row more than once, as well as changing multiple rows in multiple tables.

One way to explain what an UPDATE does is to describe a simple series of steps that could be used to perform the required functions. Like the steps described in Section 3.2, "Logical Execution of a SELECT," these are logical or imaginary steps, steps that "could be used," not the steps that are actually used.

Here's an overview of how an UPDATE is processed, step by step, from a logical point of view:

1. Start construction of a SELECT statement corresponding to the UPDATE: Copy the TOP or FIRST clause to the select list, copy the table expression from the UPDATE to the SELECT FROM clause, and copy the WHERE and ORDER BY clauses from the UPDATE to the SELECT.
2. Determine which base tables are being updated by the SET clause.
3. Put all the base table columns plus a call to NUMBER(*) into the select list. The NUMBER(*) call is needed if NUMBER(*) is used in any of the SET expressions.
4. Execute the SELECT to produce a candidate result set.
5. Apply the SET clause to the actual base table columns that appear in the candidate result set.

The rest of this section expands these steps in terms of a running example involving two simple tables and four rows:

```
CREATE TABLE t1 (
    key_1       UNSIGNED INTEGER NOT NULL PRIMARY KEY,
    non_key_1   INTEGER NOT NULL );

CREATE TABLE t2 (
    key_1       UNSIGNED INTEGER NOT NULL PRIMARY KEY,
    non_key_1   INTEGER NOT NULL );

INSERT t1 VALUES ( 1,   0 );
INSERT t1 VALUES ( 2,   0 );
INSERT t2 VALUES ( 1, 100 );
INSERT t2 VALUES ( 2, 100 );
```

Here's what the tables contain before the UPDATE:

```
t1.key_1  t1.non_key_1
========  ============
1         0
2         0
```

```
t2.key_1  t2.non_key_1
========  ============
1         100
2         100
```

The following UPDATE is a completely artificial example, only intended to demonstrate how the steps are applied. It includes a CROSS JOIN of table t1 with itself, followed by a CROSS JOIN with table t2. The SET clause refers to the NUMBER(*) function described in Section 3.20. A WHERE clause restricts the update to rows containing 0 in t1.non_key_1, and an ORDER BY clause ensures the values returned by NUMBER(*) are in order:

```
UPDATE t1
      CROSS JOIN t1 AS x
      CROSS JOIN t2
   SET t1.non_key_1 = NUMBER(*),
       t2.non_key_1 = NUMBER(*)
 WHERE t1.non_key_1 = 0
 ORDER BY t1.key_1 DESC,
       t2.key_1 DESC;
```

Here's what the tables look like after the UPDATE. All the rows in both tables have been updated, and although there are only two rows in each table it's clear the NUMBER(*) function returned much larger values; e.g., 4, 6, and 8:

```
t1.key_1  t1.non_key_1
========  ============
1         8
2         4

t2.key_1  t2.non_key_1
========  ============
1         8
2         6
```

Here's how that UPDATE is processed, with each logical step presented in more detail:

Step 1: The construction of a SELECT statement is started by copying the TOP or FIRST, WHERE, and ORDER BY clauses over to the SELECT, as well as copying the table expression from the UPDATE to the SELECT FROM clause. Here's what the unfinished SELECT looks like after this step:

```
SELECT ...
  FROM t1
       CROSS JOIN t1 AS x
       CROSS JOIN t2
 WHERE t1.non_key_1 = 0
 ORDER BY t1.key_1 DESC,
       t2.key_1 DESC;
```

Step 2: The base tables being updated are determined by inspecting the SET clause. A "base table" in this context is an actual table in the database; it can be a global permanent table, a local or global temporary table, or a proxy table, but it can't be a view, a derived table, or a procedure call. It is possible to write a SET clause that specifies columns in a view or a derived table, and in that case the underlying base tables that are actually being updated must be determined as part of this step; i.e., views and derived tables don't actually get updated, only real tables.

Note: You can update rows through a view only if that view qualifies as an updatable view; i.e., it does not use DISTINCT, GROUP BY, UNION, EXCEPT, INTERSECT, or an aggregate function reference. For more information about views, see Section 3.23, "CREATE VIEW."

In this example, there are two base tables — t1 and t2. This information is needed for the next step, and the fact that t1 appears twice in the join doesn't matter.

Step 3: All the base table columns, plus a call to NUMBER(*), are placed in the select list. Here's what the complete SELECT looks like, using the ".*" notation for each base table; note that simply coding "SELECT *" would not give the same result:

```
SELECT t1.*,
       t2.*,
       NUMBER(*)
  FROM t1
       CROSS JOIN t1 AS x
       CROSS JOIN t2
 WHERE t1.non_key_1 = 0
 ORDER BY t1.key_1 DESC,
       t2.key_1 DESC;
```

Also note that the join still looks the same; it's just the select list that's limited to base table columns. That's because an UPDATE can only change real columns, in real tables, so those are the only columns we're interested in, along with the NUMBER(*) function, since it can be used in the SET clause.

Step 4: The SELECT is executed to produce a candidate result set. Note that the WHERE and ORDER BY clauses are applied at this point, and the NUMBER(*) function references are evaluated, before the UPDATE SET clause is applied. Here is what the result set from the SELECT looks like; each row has been given a letter A, B, C, ... to identify it for the purposes of discussion:

```
   t1.key_1  t1.non_key_1  t2.key_1  t2.non_key_1  NUMBER(*)
   ========  ============  ========  ============  =========
A  2         0             2         100           1
B  2         0             2         100           2
C  2         0             1         100           3
D  2         0             1         100           4
E  1         0             2         100           5
F  1         0             2         100           6
G  1         0             1         100           7
H  1         0             1         100           8
```

Each row in the candidate result set contains columns from both t1 and t2. Also, because of the CROSS JOINs, each row from t1 appears in no less than four different rows in the candidate result set. The same is true of t2 — each row appears in the result four times.

Step 5: The SET clause is applied to the actual base table columns that appear in the candidate result set. Here's what the SET clause looks like:

```
SET t1.non_key_1 = NUMBER(*),
    t2.non_key_1 = NUMBER(*)
```

This process is performed for each row in the candidate result set. That means the SET clause is applied eight times, and since it involves two different tables, there are 16 separate row update operations.

Here's how it works for Row A, where NUMBER(*) returned 1: t1.non_key_1 is set to 1 for the row with t1.key_1 = 2, and t2.non_key_1 is set to 1 for the row with t2.key_1 = 2. That's the same as these two single-row UPDATE statements:

```
UPDATE t1 SET non_key_1 = 1 WHERE key_1 = 2;
UPDATE t2 SET non_key_1 = 1 WHERE key_1 = 2;
```

The following shows the full list of 16 row updates in the actual order that SQL Anywhere performs them; the order isn't important as long as the final answer is correct, and you can see that all the updates to t2 were applied before t1. Each row in t1 and each row in t2 is updated a total of four times; only the last UPDATE for each row counts, the ones marked "final."

```
UPDATE t2 SET non_key_1 = 1 WHERE key_1 = 2; -- Row A
UPDATE t2 SET non_key_1 = 2 WHERE key_1 = 2; -- Row B
UPDATE t2 SET non_key_1 = 3 WHERE key_1 = 1; -- Row C
UPDATE t2 SET non_key_1 = 4 WHERE key_1 = 1; -- Row D
UPDATE t2 SET non_key_1 = 5 WHERE key_1 = 2; -- Row E
UPDATE t2 SET non_key_1 = 6 WHERE key_1 = 2; -- Row F - final
UPDATE t2 SET non_key_1 = 7 WHERE key_1 = 1; -- Row G
UPDATE t2 SET non_key_1 = 8 WHERE key_1 = 1; -- Row H - final
UPDATE t1 SET non_key_1 = 1 WHERE key_1 = 2; -- Row A
UPDATE t1 SET non_key_1 = 2 WHERE key_1 = 2; -- Row B
UPDATE t1 SET non_key_1 = 3 WHERE key_1 = 2; -- Row C
UPDATE t1 SET non_key_1 = 4 WHERE key_1 = 2; -- Row D - final
UPDATE t1 SET non_key_1 = 5 WHERE key_1 = 1; -- Row E
UPDATE t1 SET non_key_1 = 6 WHERE key_1 = 1; -- Row F
UPDATE t1 SET non_key_1 = 7 WHERE key_1 = 1; -- Row G
UPDATE t1 SET non_key_1 = 8 WHERE key_1 = 1; -- Row H - final
```

Here's what t1 and t2 look like when all those updates are finished:

```
t1.key_1  t1.non_key_1
========  ============
1         8
2         4

t2.key_1  t2.non_key_1
========  ============
1         8
2         6
```

It's important to note that the original WHERE clause, "WHERE t1.non_key_1 = 0," didn't stop the 16 individual row updates from proceeding even though t1.non_key_1 quickly became non-zero. That's because the original WHERE clause is used to determine the candidate result set, and the actual updates performed by the SET clause "SET t1.non_key_1 = NUMBER(*)" come after that.

The same applies to the original ORDER BY clause; the actual update operations don't affect the ordering of the candidate result set because that is determined in an earlier step.

4.4.1 Set **UPDATE**

Here's the full syntax of the set-oriented UPDATE statement:

```
<set_update>          ::= UPDATE
                            [ <row_range> ]
                            <table_specification>
                            <set_clause>
                            [ <where_clause> ]
                            [ <order_by_clause> ]
<row_range>           ::= FIRST                      -- same as TOP 1
                          | TOP <maximum_row_count>
                            [ START AT <start_at_row_number> ]
<maximum_row_count>   ::= integer literal maximum number of rows to return
<start_at_row_number> ::= integer literal first row number to return
<table_specification> ::= see <table_specification> in Chapter 3, "Selecting"
<set_clause>          ::= SET { <set_item> "," }
                            <set_item>
<set_item>            ::= <column_reference> "=" <expression>
<column_reference>    ::= <column_name>
                          | <alias_name>
                          | [ <owner_name> "." ] <table_name> "." <column_name>
                          | <correlation_name> "." <column_name>
<order_by_clause>     ::= see <order_by_clause> in Chapter 3, "Selecting"
<alias_name>          ::= <identifier>
<correlation_name>    ::= <identifier>
```

A set-oriented UPDATE is free to update a single row in a single table or multiple rows in multiple tables. It can specify a join among tables that are to be updated and those that aren't. It can also involve views, derived tables, and procedure calls with the only real restriction that it must be possible, for the tables being updated, to determine exactly which rows are to be updated. That's why you can't code a GROUP BY clause in an UPDATE statement, for example, or update a view that is based on a UNION.

For example, the UPDATE presented in the previous section works exactly the same way when the tables t1 and t2 are referenced via a view, a procedure call, and a derived table as follows:

```
CREATE VIEW v1 AS
SELECT * FROM t1;

CREATE PROCEDURE p1()
BEGIN
   SELECT * FROM t1;
END;

UPDATE v1
      CROSS JOIN p1() AS x
      CROSS JOIN ( SELECT * FROM t2 ) AS d2
   SET v1.non_key_1 = NUMBER(*),
      d2.non_key_1 = NUMBER(*)
 WHERE v1.non_key_1 = 0
 ORDER BY v1.key_1 DESC,
      d2.key_1 DESC;
```

Tip: Don't use a comma-separated list of table names in a set-oriented UPDATE statement unless you actually want CROSS JOIN operations. For example, the example above does exactly the same thing if it's coded using commas like UPDATE v1, p1() AS x, (SELECT * FROM t2) AS d2.... This is an artificial example; in the real world CROSS JOINs aren't very popular, especially when they happen by accident.

Here is a more realistic example using the ASADEMO database: The following UPDATE gives a 10% raise to the employee with the most sales. This is a single-row, single-table UPDATE that involves a multi-table join; i.e., only a single row in the employee table is updated, but that row is determined by a fairly complex join. A derived table is used to determine which sales representative had the highest dollar amount of sales. Note that this UPDATE involves a GROUP BY, but that's okay because the SET clause only refers to the employee table, not any of the tables participating in the GROUP BY:

```
UPDATE employee
       INNER JOIN ( SELECT FIRST sales_order.sales_rep AS top_rep_id
                      FROM sales_order
                             INNER JOIN sales_order_items
                                    ON sales_order_items.id = sales_order.id
                             INNER JOIN product
                                    ON product.id = sales_order_items.prod_id
                           GROUP BY sales_order.sales_rep
                           ORDER BY SUM ( sales_order_items.quantity
                                              * product.unit_price ) DESC )
                    AS top_rep
                  ON top_rep.top_rep_id = employee.emp_id
   SET employee.salary = employee.salary * 1.1;
```

When that UPDATE runs it has exactly the same effect as this statement:

```
UPDATE employee SET salary = 43230.00 WHERE emp_id = 299; -- salary was 39300.00
```

You can't apply a SET clause to a table referenced via a procedure call, but that doesn't mean you can't use a procedure call in an UPDATE. Here is an example that calls a procedure to find one or more top performing salespeople (in this case, the top three) and give them all a 10% raise. This example uses the same GROUP BY as the previous UPDATE, but using a stored procedure has two advantages: First, it separates the complex join from the UPDATE to make the code easier to understand, and second, the procedure is more flexible because a variable TOP count is used instead of the fixed FIRST keyword:

```
CREATE PROCEDURE p_top_salespeople
  ( IN @top_count INTEGER )
  RESULT ( top_rep_id INTEGER )
BEGIN
  DECLARE @select LONG VARCHAR;

  SET @select = STRING (
     'SELECT TOP ', @top_count, ' sales_order.sales_rep
        FROM sales_order
             INNER JOIN sales_order_items
                    ON sales_order_items.id = sales_order.id
             INNER JOIN product
                    ON product.id = sales_order_items.prod_id
          GROUP BY sales_order.sales_rep
```

```
          ORDER BY SUM ( sales_order_items.quantity
                       * product.unit_price ) DESC' );

  EXECUTE IMMEDIATE @select;
END;

UPDATE employee
    INNER JOIN p_top_salespeople ( 3 )
            ON p_top_salespeople.top_rep_id = employee.emp_id
  SET employee.salary = employee.salary * 1.1;
```

When that UPDATE runs, it has exactly the same effect as the following three separate statements:

```
UPDATE employee SET salary = 43230.00 WHERE emp_id = 299;  -- salary was 39300.00
UPDATE employee SET salary = 38381.20 WHERE emp_id = 856;  -- salary was 34892.00
UPDATE employee SET salary = 49500.00 WHERE emp_id = 1142; -- salary was 45000.00
```

For more information about stored procedures and the EXECUTE IMMEDIATE statement, see Chapter 8, "Packaging."

You don't have to resort to views, derived tables, or procedure calls to make use of features like FIRST and ORDER BY; they're available in the UPDATE statement itself. Here is an example that gives a 5% salary cut to the two most junior employees in the Finance department:

```
UPDATE TOP 2
       employee
       INNER JOIN department
               ON department.dept_id = employee.dept_id
  SET employee.salary = employee.salary * 0.95
 WHERE department.dept_name = 'Finance'
 ORDER BY employee.start_date DESC;
```

When that UPDATE runs it has exactly the same effect as the following two statements:

```
UPDATE employee SET salary = 71630.00 WHERE emp_id = 1483; -- salary was 75400.00
UPDATE employee SET salary = 55983.50 WHERE emp_id = 1390; -- salary was 58930.00
```

Note: SQL Anywhere Studio permits a second form of set-oriented UPDATE using a separate FROM clause to specify the join conditions. This book doesn't discuss that form of UPDATE because it is confusing, even dangerous, to use if you make a mistake with correlation names, and it is limited to updating only one table. The UPDATE syntax described in this section is simple and straightforward: You specify the join conditions following the UPDATE keyword, and you specify the tables and columns to be updated in the SET clause.

4.5 UPDATE WHERE CURRENT OF Cursor

This section presents an overview of how a cursor-oriented UPDATE statement works.

```
<update_where_current_of_cursor> ::= UPDATE
                                     <table_or_view_list>
                                     <set_clause>
                                     <where_current_of_clause>
<table_or_view_list>            ::= { <table_or_view_reference> "," }
                                     <table_or_view_reference>
<table_or_view_reference>       ::= [ <owner_name> "." ] <table_name>
                                   | [ <owner_name> "." ] <view_name>
```

```
<where_current_of_clause>        ::= WHERE CURRENT OF <cursor_name>
<cursor_name> ::= <identifier> defined in a cursor DECLARE or FOR statement
```

When a cursor fetch loop is used to execute UPDATE statements using the
WHERE CURRENT OF clause, the same five steps listed in Section 4.4, "Logical Execution of a Set UPDATE," can be used to explain what happens. The
difference is the first four steps, those having to do with the construction of a
candidate result set, are now the responsibility of the SELECT statement that is
explicitly defined in the cursor declaration. Only the final step, the application
of the SET clause, is performed by the actual UPDATE statement.

This form of UPDATE does not use a FROM clause or any join operations;
those go in the cursor SELECT. The UPDATE does have to name the tables and
views being updated, and if there is more than one, a comma-separated list may
be used with no danger of that causing a CROSS JOIN; the list is simply that, a
list of table and view names.

Each time a cursor-oriented UPDATE is executed, it is only applied to a
single row in the cursor result set. It may, however, affect rows in more than one
base table if that's what the SET clause specifies.

Here is an example that performs exactly the same updates as the example
in Section 4.4. The cursor DECLARE defines a SELECT that uses exactly the
same table expression and WHERE and ORDER BY clauses, and the UPDATE
WHERE CURRENT OF statement uses exactly the same SET clause:

```
BEGIN
DECLARE @t1_key_1        INTEGER;
DECLARE @t1_non_key_1    INTEGER;
DECLARE @t2_key_1        INTEGER;
DECLARE @t2_non_key_1    INTEGER;
DECLARE @number          INTEGER;
DECLARE @SQLSTATE        VARCHAR ( 5 );

DECLARE cloop1 CURSOR FOR
SELECT t1.key_1,
       t1.non_key_1,
       t2.key_1,
       t2.non_key_1
  FROM t1
       CROSS JOIN t1 AS x
       CROSS JOIN t2
 WHERE t1.non_key_1 = 0
 ORDER BY t1.key_1 DESC,
       t2.key_1 DESC;

OPEN cloop1;

FETCH cloop1 INTO
   @t1_key_1,
   @t1_non_key_1,
   @t2_key_1,
   @t2_non_key_1;
SET @SQLSTATE = SQLSTATE;

SET @number = 0;

WHILE ( @SQLSTATE IN ( '00000', '01W04' ) ) LOOP
```

```
    SET @number = @number + 1;

    UPDATE t1, t2
       SET t1.non_key_1 = @number,
           t2.non_key_1 = @number
     WHERE CURRENT OF cloop1;

    FETCH cloop1 INTO
       @t1_key_1,
       @t1_non_key_1,
       @t2_key_1,
       @t2_non_key_1;
    SET @SQLSTATE = SQLSTATE;

END LOOP;
CLOSE cloop1;
END;
```

Tip: Use the much shorter FOR loop syntax whenever possible. The cursor loop shown above uses several local variables and separate DECLARE, OPEN, and FETCH statements. If you're writing a cursor loop in an application program such as the embedded SQL example shown in Section 6.2, "Cursor FETCH Loop," that's the kind of code you have to use. However, cursor loops written in SQL, like the one shown above, can use the simpler FOR loop described in Section 6.3, "Cursor FOR Loop."

When that loop runs, it has exactly the same effect as the following series of statements:

```
UPDATE t2 SET non_key_1 = 1 WHERE key_1 = 2; -- loop pass #1
UPDATE t1 SET non_key_1 = 1 WHERE key_1 = 2;
UPDATE t2 SET non_key_1 = 2 WHERE key_1 = 2; -- loop pass #2
UPDATE t1 SET non_key_1 = 2 WHERE key_1 = 2;
UPDATE t2 SET non_key_1 = 3 WHERE key_1 = 1; -- loop pass #3
UPDATE t1 SET non_key_1 = 3 WHERE key_1 = 2;
UPDATE t2 SET non_key_1 = 4 WHERE key_1 = 1; -- loop pass #4
UPDATE t1 SET non_key_1 = 4 WHERE key_1 = 2;
UPDATE t2 SET non_key_1 = 5 WHERE key_1 = 2; -- loop pass #5
UPDATE t1 SET non_key_1 = 5 WHERE key_1 = 1;
UPDATE t2 SET non_key_1 = 6 WHERE key_1 = 2; -- loop pass #6
UPDATE t1 SET non_key_1 = 6 WHERE key_1 = 1;
UPDATE t2 SET non_key_1 = 7 WHERE key_1 = 1; -- loop pass #7
UPDATE t1 SET non_key_1 = 7 WHERE key_1 = 1;
UPDATE t2 SET non_key_1 = 8 WHERE key_1 = 1; -- loop pass #8
UPDATE t1 SET non_key_1 = 8 WHERE key_1 = 1;
```

The exact order in which the rows are updated is different with the cursor loop, but the final contents of tables t1 and t2 are the same as the example in Section 4.4:

```
t1.key_1  t1.non_key_1
========  ============
1         8
2         4

t2.key_1  t2.non_key_1
========  ============
1         8
2         6
```

Note: The WHILE loop above tests for two different SQLSTATE values: 00000 indicates everything is normal, whereas 01W04 is a warning that a base table row being fetched has been changed since the last time it was fetched. In this example the warning is being ignored, but in some applications it may be a serious problem from a business point of view.

Cursor loops are described in more detail in Chapter 6, "Fetching."

4.6 Chapter Summary

This chapter described how to code single- and multi-row updates involving a single table, and explained how a multi-row, multi-table UPDATE works. The full syntax of the set-oriented UPDATE statement was described, and an overview of the cursor-oriented UPDATE WHERE CURRENT OF statement was presented.

The next chapter moves on to the fifth step in the life cycle of a database: deleting data.

Chapter 5

Deleting

5.1 Introduction

This chapter starts with typical single-row and multi-row DELETE statements involving a single table. These are followed, in Section 5.4, with an explanation of how complex DELETE statements involving joins of multiple tables operate from a logical point of view. This explanation serves to illustrate two important differences between UPDATE and DELETE: First, DELETE only affects rows in one single table, and second, DELETE can only affect a single row once.

Section 5.5.1 discusses the full syntax of the set-oriented DELETE together with some realistic examples. Section 5.5 describes the cursor-oriented DELETE WHERE CURRENT OF statement and how it can affect the execution of a cursor fetch loop. Section 5.6 discusses the efficient TRUNCATE TABLE, its side effects to watch out for, and a description of how TRUNCATE TABLE can be used even when you don't want to delete all the rows.

5.2 Single-Row DELETE

The simplest form of the DELETE statement is used to delete a single row from a single table.

```
<typical_single_row_delete> ::= DELETE [ <owner_name> "." ] <table_name>
                                       <single_row_where_clause>
<owner_name>                  ::= <identifier>
<table_name>                  ::= <identifier>
<single_row_where_clause>     ::= <where_clause> matching no more than 1 row
<identifier>                  ::= see <identifier> in Chapter 1, "Creating"
<where_clause>                ::= see <where_clause> in Chapter 3, "Selecting"
```

A typical single-row DELETE specifies the table name and a WHERE clause that matches a single row in the table. Here is an example that deletes a single sales order item where the primary key consists of id = 2015 and line_id = 4, in the ASADEMO database:

```
DELETE sales_order_items
  WHERE id = 2015
    AND line_id = 4;
```

For a description of the sales_order_items table in the ASADEMO database that ships with SQL Anywhere Studio 9, see Section 3.6, "Multi-Table Joins."

If the WHERE clause matches a row, the DELETE proceeds as follows: Any BEFORE DELETE triggers associated with this table are fired, a row lock is obtained, the row is deleted, the delete is recorded in the transaction log, any AFTER DELETE triggers are fired, and the SQLSTATE special literal is set to

'00000' to indicate a completely normal condition. For more information about triggers, see Section 8.11, "CREATE TRIGGER," and for a discussion of locking, see Section 9.6, "Locks."

If the WHERE clause doesn't match any row, it isn't an error, but SQLSTATE is set to '02000' to indicate "row not found." In this case, no triggers are fired, no row lock is obtained, no delete is performed, and nothing is recorded in the transaction log.

Note: These actions apply to multi-row deletes as well, on a row-by-row basis. Two exceptions are SQLSTATE, which is set once for each execution of the DELETE statement, and AFTER STATEMENT triggers, which are fired once per execution of the DELETE statement.

Note: This book assumes the ISOLATION_LEVEL option is set to the default value of 0 for maximum performance and concurrency. Higher settings can change locking behavior; for example, the statement above that "no row lock is obtained" when the WHERE clause doesn't match any row isn't necessarily true when the ISOLATION_LEVEL is set to 3. For more information about isolation levels, see Section 9.7, "Blocks and Isolation Levels."

Tip: Watch out for single-row DELETE statements that accidentally delete more than one row, even the entire table. Make sure the WHERE clause refers to the primary key or a unique index, and that it specifies values for all the columns in that primary key or index if there are more than one.

5.3 Multi-Row DELETE

There isn't much difference between a single-row and a multi-row DELETE. In fact, a typical single-row DELETE becomes a multi-row DELETE by simply loosening up the WHERE clause or omitting it altogether.

```
<typical_multi_row_delete> ::= DELETE [ <owner_name> "." ] <table_name>
                                [ <multi_row_where_clause> ]
<multi_row_where_clause>   ::= <where_clause> matching zero or more rows
```

If you omit the WHERE clause then all the rows in the table are deleted. Here's an example that deletes all 1,097 of the sales_order_items table:

```
DELETE sales_order_items;
```

Tip: TRUNCATE TABLE can be much faster than DELETE when you want to get rid of all the rows. For more information, see Section 5.6 later in this chapter.

Here's a less dramatic example, where all the sales order items for one sales order are deleted. The id column identifies the order and is part of the two-column primary key for the sales_order_items table:

```
DELETE sales_order_items
 WHERE id = 2015;
```

That statement deletes four rows, and as far as the table is concerned it is equivalent to running the following four single-row deletes:

```
DELETE sales_order_items WHERE id = 2015 AND line_id = 1;
DELETE sales_order_items WHERE id = 2015 AND line_id = 2;
```

```
DELETE sales_order_items WHERE id = 2015 AND line_id = 3;
DELETE sales_order_items WHERE id = 2015 AND line_id = 4;
```

Tip: If you want to delete most of the rows in a large table, it may be faster to copy the rows you want to save into a temporary table, use TRUNCATE TABLE to delete everything, and then copy the saved rows back. For more information, see Section 5.6.

5.4 Logical Execution of a Set DELETE

The full syntax of a set-oriented DELETE includes a row range clause (FIRST or TOP), a FROM clause with a table specification like the one described in Section 3.3, "FROM Clause," plus a WHERE clause. This means the DELETE statement can specify a multi-table join even though you can only delete rows from a single table.

```
<set_delete> ::= DELETE [ <row_range> ] [ FROM ]
                 <table_or_view_reference> [ AS <correlation_name> ]
                 <from_clause>
                 [ <where_clause> ]
```

The next section describes the DELETE clauses in more detail; this section concentrates on the question "What does a multi-table DELETE actually do?"

One way to explain what a DELETE does is to describe a simple series of steps that could be used to perform the required functions. Like the steps described in Section 3.2, "Logical Execution of a SELECT," these are logical or imaginary steps, steps that "could be used," not the steps that are actually used.

Here's an overview of how a DELETE is processed, step by step, from a logical point of view:

1. Start construction of a SELECT statement corresponding to the DELETE: Add the DISTINCT keyword, and copy the TOP or FIRST, FROM, and WHERE clauses over to the SELECT.
2. Determine which base table is being deleted.
3. Put all the columns from the base table being deleted into the select list.
4. Execute the SELECT to produce a candidate result set.
5. Delete the base table rows that appear in the candidate result set.

The rest of this section will expand these steps in terms of a running example involving one simple table and five rows:

```
CREATE TABLE t1 (
   key_1       UNSIGNED INTEGER NOT NULL PRIMARY KEY,
   non_key_1   INTEGER NOT NULL );

INSERT t1 VALUES ( 1, 1 );
INSERT t1 VALUES ( 2, 2 );
INSERT t1 VALUES ( 3, 3 );
INSERT t1 VALUES ( 4, 4 );
INSERT t1 VALUES ( 5, 5 );
```

The following DELETE is an artificial example to demonstrate how the steps are applied. The FROM clause contains a CROSS JOIN of t1 with itself, and the WHERE clause limits the candidate result set to rows with t1.key_1 = 2.

```
DELETE t1
  FROM t1
```

```
     CROSS JOIN t1 AS x
WHERE t1.key_1 = 2;
```

When that DELETE is executed it deletes exactly one row from t1, as if the following statement had been executed:

```
DELETE t1 WHERE key_1 = 2;
```

The following steps describe how that DELETE is processed, with each logical step presented in more detail.

Step 1: The construction of a SELECT statement is started by adding the DISTINCT keyword and copying the TOP or FIRST, FROM, and WHERE clauses over to the SELECT. In this case there isn't any TOP or FIRST clause, so here's what the unfinished SELECT looks like after this step:

```
SELECT DISTINCT ...
  FROM t1
       CROSS JOIN t1 AS x
WHERE t1.key_1 = 2;
```

Step 2: The base table being deleted is determined by inspecting the name following the DELETE keyword. A "base table" in this context is an actual table in the database, not a view. It is possible to code a view name after the DELETE keyword, and in that case the underlying base table that is actually being deleted must be determined in this step.

Note: You can delete rows through a view only if that view qualifies as an updatable view and it involves only one table. For more information about views, see Section 3.23, "CREATE VIEW."

In this example, the base table is t1. This information is needed for the next step, and the fact that t1 appears twice in the FROM clause doesn't matter.

Step 3: All the columns from the base table being deleted are placed in the select list. Here's what the SELECT looks like now, using the t1.* notation; note that simply coding SELECT * would not give the same result:

```
SELECT DISTINCT t1.*
  FROM t1
       CROSS JOIN t1 AS x
WHERE t1.key_1 = 2;
```

Note: If the table has a PRIMARY KEY constraint (as it does in this example) then only the primary key columns are required in the SELECT DISTINCT list because only those columns are required to find the rows to delete. The full select list t1.* is used to keep the example clear and simple.

Step 4: The SELECT is executed to produce a candidate result set. Note that if the SELECT had been coded as a SELECT *, the CROSS JOIN would have initially produced 25 rows, and the WHERE would only have whittled it down to five rows, but the SELECT DISTINCT t1.* produces only one row.

```
key_1  non_key_1
=====  =========
2      2
```

Step 5: The base table rows appearing in the candidate result set are deleted; in this example, that's equivalent to executing this single statement:

```
DELETE t1 WHERE key_1 = 2;
```

These steps illustrate two important differences between UPDATE and DELETE: DELETE only works on a single table, and you can only delete each row once, whereas UPDATE can work on more than one table and can change each row more than once.

5.4.1 Set DELETE

The set-oriented DELETE statement comes in two forms: with and without a FROM clause. Both forms may be used to delete multiple rows, but only from a single table; the FROM clause permits other tables to participate in the process that selects the rows to be deleted.

```
<set_delete>             ::= DELETE [ <row_range> ] [ FROM ]
                                 <table_or_view_reference> [ AS <correlation_name> ]
                                 <from_clause>
                                 [ <where_clause> ]
<simple_set_delete>      ::= DELETE [ <row_range> ] [ FROM ]
                                 <table_or_view_reference>
                                 [ <where_clause> ]
<row_range>              ::= FIRST
                           | TOP <row_count> [ START AT <row_number> ]
<row_count>              ::= integer literal maximum number of rows to return
<row_number>            ::= integer literal first row number to return
<table_or_view_reference> ::= [ <owner_name> "." ] <table_name>
                           | [ <owner_name> "." ] <view_name>
<view_name>             ::= <identifier>
<correlation_name>      ::= <identifier>
<from_clause>           ::= FROM <table_specification>
<table_specification>   ::= see <table_specification> in Chapter 3, "Selecting"
```

Tip: Don't use the optional FROM keyword that immediately follows the DELETE keyword; it just gets confused with the FROM clause. Save the keyword "FROM" to mean "here are the tables to be joined," which is what it stands for in other statements like SELECT and UPDATE.

Here is an example using four of the ASADEMO database tables as described in Section 3.6, "Multi-Table Joins": sales_order, sales_order_items, employee, and customer. The requirement is to delete all the old orders taken by two sales representatives who are no longer with the company, from two customers who are no longer in business. Specifically, the requirements are to delete all the sales_order and sales_order_items rows for orders taken up to December 31, 2000, by the employees Rollin Overbey and Philip Chin, from the customers The Power Group and Darling Associates.

Tip: When developing the code for a complex set-oriented DELETE, start by writing a prototype SELECT statement that displays the data to make sure you're getting the correct rows. You'll be able to test your FROM clause in ISQL, and you'll be able to change the SELECT into a DELETE quite easily.

Here is a SELECT statement that displays the data that's going to be deleted; the result set includes the primary key columns for sales_order (order_id) and sales_order_items (order_id and line_id) as well as the employee and customer names:

```
SELECT customer.id AS cust_id,
       customer.company_name,
       sales_order.id AS order_id,
       sales_order.order_date,
       employee.emp_id,
       STRING ( employee.emp_fname, ' ', employee.emp_lname ) AS emp_name,
       sales_order_items.line_id
  FROM customer
       INNER JOIN sales_order
               ON sales_order.cust_id = customer.id
       INNER JOIN employee
               ON employee.emp_id = sales_order.sales_rep
       INNER JOIN sales_order_items
               ON sales_order_items.id = sales_order.id
 WHERE STRING ( employee.emp_fname, ' ', employee.emp_lname )
          IN ( 'Rollin Overbey', 'Philip Chin' )
   AND customer.company_name
          IN ( 'The Power Group', 'Darling Associates' )
   AND sales_order.order_date <= '2000-12-31'
 ORDER BY 1, 2, 3, 4, 5, 6, 7;
```

Here's what the SELECT returns: data from 11 different sales_order_item rows in five different orders (five different values of order_id). It also shows that the correct company name, order date, and employee name are being selected.

cust_id	company_name	order_id	order_date	emp_id	emp_name	line_id
101	The Power Group	2001	2000-03-16	299	Rollin Overbey	1
101	The Power Group	2001	2000-03-16	299	Rollin Overbey	2
101	The Power Group	2001	2000-03-16	299	Rollin Overbey	3
101	The Power Group	2206	2000-04-16	299	Rollin Overbey	1
101	The Power Group	2206	2000-04-16	299	Rollin Overbey	2
101	The Power Group	2206	2000-04-16	299	Rollin Overbey	3
101	The Power Group	2206	2000-04-16	299	Rollin Overbey	4
101	The Power Group	2279	2000-07-23	299	Rollin Overbey	1
103	Darling Associates	2340	2000-09-25	299	Rollin Overbey	1
103	Darling Associates	2451	2000-12-15	129	Philip Chin	1
103	Darling Associates	2451	2000-12-15	129	Philip Chin	2

Two DELETE statements are required, one for sales_order and one for sales_order_items, because each DELETE can only affect a single table. The DELETE for sales_order_items must come first because it is the child table in a foreign key relationship with sales_order. Here's what the first DELETE looks like; it has exactly the same FROM and WHERE clauses as the SELECT above:

```
DELETE sales_order_items
  FROM customer
       INNER JOIN sales_order
               ON sales_order.cust_id = customer.id
       INNER JOIN employee
               ON employee.emp_id = sales_order.sales_rep
       INNER JOIN sales_order_items
               ON sales_order_items.id = sales_order.id
 WHERE STRING ( employee.emp_fname, ' ', employee.emp_lname )
          IN ( 'Rollin Overbey', 'Philip Chin' )
   AND customer.company_name
          IN ( 'The Power Group', 'Darling Associates' )
   AND sales_order.order_date <= '2000-12-31';
```

When that DELETE is executed, it performs exactly the same function as the following single-row DELETE statements:

```
DELETE sales_order_items WHERE id = 2001 AND line_id = 1;
DELETE sales_order_items WHERE id = 2001 AND line_id = 2;
DELETE sales_order_items WHERE id = 2001 AND line_id = 3;
DELETE sales_order_items WHERE id = 2206 AND line_id = 1;
DELETE sales_order_items WHERE id = 2206 AND line_id = 2;
DELETE sales_order_items WHERE id = 2206 AND line_id = 3;
DELETE sales_order_items WHERE id = 2206 AND line_id = 4;
DELETE sales_order_items WHERE id = 2279 AND line_id = 1;
DELETE sales_order_items WHERE id = 2340 AND line_id = 1;
DELETE sales_order_items WHERE id = 2451 AND line_id = 1;
DELETE sales_order_items WHERE id = 2451 AND line_id = 2;
```

The DELETE for sales_order looks almost the same, except that the INNER JOIN with sales_order_items must either be removed or changed to LEFT OUTER JOIN. The reason for that is because all the matching sales_order_items rows have already been deleted so an INNER JOIN will result in an empty result set and the DELETE will do nothing. Here's what the DELETE for sales_order looks like with the INNER JOIN with sales_order_items removed (there's no real point to using an OUTER JOIN):

```
DELETE sales_order
  FROM customer
        INNER JOIN sales_order
              ON sales_order.cust_id = customer.id
        INNER JOIN employee
              ON employee.emp_id = sales_order.sales_rep
 WHERE STRING ( employee.emp_fname, ' ', employee.emp_lname )
        IN ( 'Rollin Overbey', 'Philip Chin' )
   AND customer.company_name
        IN ( 'The Power Group', 'Darling Associates' )
   AND sales_order.order_date <= '2000-12-31';
```

The new FROM clause matches five rows; when that DELETE is executed it does exactly the same thing as these individual statements:

```
DELETE sales_order WHERE id = 2001;
DELETE sales_order WHERE id = 2206;
DELETE sales_order WHERE id = 2279;
DELETE sales_order WHERE id = 2340;
DELETE sales_order WHERE id = 2451;
```

The first four steps listed in Section 5.4, "Logical Execution of a Set DELETE," can be applied to the two set-oriented DELETE statements above to produce SELECT statements that will show the rows that are going to be deleted. Here are those two equivalent SELECT statements:

```
SELECT DISTINCT sales_order_items.*
  FROM customer
        INNER JOIN sales_order
              ON sales_order.cust_id = customer.id
        INNER JOIN employee
              ON employee.emp_id = sales_order.sales_rep
        INNER JOIN sales_order_items
              ON sales_order_items.id = sales_order.id
 WHERE STRING ( employee.emp_fname, ' ', employee.emp_lname )
        IN ( 'Rollin Overbey', 'Philip Chin' )
   AND customer.company_name
        IN ( 'The Power Group', 'Darling Associates' )
   AND sales_order.order_date <= '2000-12-31';
```

```
SELECT DISTINCT sales_order.*
  FROM customer
       INNER JOIN sales_order
               ON sales_order.cust_id = customer.id
       INNER JOIN employee
               ON employee.emp_id = sales_order.sales_rep
       INNER JOIN sales_order_items
               ON sales_order_items.id = sales_order.id
 WHERE STRING ( employee.emp_fname, ' ', employee.emp_lname )
         IN ( 'Rollin Overbey', 'Philip Chin' )
   AND customer.company_name
         IN ( 'The Power Group', 'Darling Associates' )
   AND sales_order.order_date <= '2000-12-31';
```

The following is an example where a view is used to select sales_order_items rows that are at least three years old, and a simple DELETE is then used to delete old rows where the quantity shipped was 12 or fewer. This DELETE doesn't need a FROM clause because there's no join involved, and a view is okay because it involves only one table and it doesn't use any features like GROUP BY or UNION.

```
CREATE VIEW v_old_items AS
SELECT *
  FROM sales_order_items
 WHERE ship_date < DATEADD ( YEAR, -3, CURRENT DATE );

DELETE v_old_items
 WHERE quantity <= 12;
```

That kind of DELETE is useful for purging old rows from the database; it can be repeatedly run, even every day, to delete rows that have become unwanted with the passing of time.

5.5 DELETE WHERE CURRENT OF Cursor

This section presents an overview of how a cursor-oriented DELETE statement works.

```
<delete_where_current_of_cursor> ::= DELETE <table_or_view_reference>
                                            <where_current_of_clause>
<where_current_of_clause>         ::= WHERE CURRENT OF <cursor_name>
<cursor_name> ::= <identifier> defined in a cursor DECLARE or FOR statement
```

When a cursor fetch loop is used to execute a DELETE statement using the WHERE CURRENT OF clause, the same five steps listed in Section 5.4, "Logical Execution of a Set DELETE," can be used to explain what happens. The difference is the first four steps, those having to do with the construction of a candidate result set, are now the responsibility of the SELECT statement that is explicitly defined in the cursor declaration. Only the final step, the row deletion, is performed by the actual DELETE statement.

This form of DELETE does not use a FROM clause or any join operations; those go in the cursor SELECT. The DELETE must name the table or view being deleted and the cursor being used.

Each time a cursor-oriented DELETE statement is executed, it deletes a single row in a single table. Here is an example that performs exactly the same delete as the example in Section 5.4; the cursor DECLARE defines a SELECT that uses exactly the same FROM and WHERE clauses:

```
CREATE TABLE t1 (
   key_1        UNSIGNED INTEGER NOT NULL PRIMARY KEY,
   non_key_1    INTEGER NOT NULL );

INSERT t1 VALUES ( 1, 1 );
INSERT t1 VALUES ( 2, 2 );
INSERT t1 VALUES ( 3, 3 );
INSERT t1 VALUES ( 4, 4 );
INSERT t1 VALUES ( 5, 5 );

BEGIN
DECLARE @t1_key_1        INTEGER;
DECLARE @t1_non_key_1    INTEGER;
DECLARE @SQLSTATE        VARCHAR ( 5 );

DECLARE cloop1 CURSOR FOR
SELECT t1.key_1,
       t1.non_key_1
   FROM t1
       CROSS JOIN t1 AS x
   WHERE t1.key_1 = 2;

OPEN cloop1;

FETCH cloop1 INTO
   @t1_key_1,
   @t1_non_key_1;
SET @SQLSTATE = SQLSTATE;

WHILE ( @SQLSTATE = '00000' ) LOOP

   DELETE t1
     WHERE CURRENT OF cloop1;

   FETCH cloop1 INTO
      @t1_key_1,
      @t1_non_key_1;
   SET @SQLSTATE = SQLSTATE;

END LOOP;
CLOSE cloop1;
END;
```

When that loop runs it has exactly the same effect as the following single
statement:

```
DELETE t1 WHERE key_1 = 2;
```

In fact, the WHILE loop makes only one pass before the FETCH sets the
SQLSTATE to '02000' indicating "row not found," even though the SELECT
specifies a CROSS JOIN that generates a candidate result set containing five
rows. The loop ends prematurely because the DELETE removes the base table
row that appears in every row in the candidate result set, and that effectively
wipes out the result set. For more information about cursor loops, see Chapter 6,
"Fetching."

5.6 TRUNCATE TABLE

The TRUNCATE TABLE statement deletes all the rows in a table, often much faster than the equivalent set-oriented DELETE statement.

```
<truncate_table> ::= TRUNCATE TABLE [ <owner_name> "." ] <table_name>
```

TRUNCATE TABLE comes in two versions: fast and slow. The fast form is used if two requirements are met: First, there must be no non-empty child tables, and second, the TRUNCATE_WITH_AUTO_COMMIT database option must be 'ON' (the default).

The first requirement means that the table being truncated cannot participate as the parent in any foreign key relationship where the child table contains any rows; there can be child tables, but they have to be empty for the fast form of TRUNCATE TABLE to be used.

The second requirement, that TRUNCATE_WITH_AUTO_COMMIT must be 'ON', is a bit confusing. It means that if the first requirement is met, TRUNCATE TABLE will perform a COMMIT when it is finished deleting rows. It also means, again only if the first requirement is met and if a transaction is already in progress before TRUNCATE TABLE is executed, that a COMMIT will be issued before it starts deleting rows. If the first requirement is not met, TRUNCATE TABLE will not issue either COMMIT even if TRUNCATE_WITH_AUTO_COMMIT is 'ON'.

The difference between fast and slow is striking. In one test, the fast version of TRUNCATE TABLE took 10 seconds to delete 50M of data in 30,000 rows. Both the slow version of TRUNCATE TABLE and the DELETE statement took four and a half minutes to do the same thing.

The fast version of TRUNCATE TABLE gets its speed from the fact that it takes several shortcuts. The first shortcut, which is also taken by the slow version, is that TRUNCATE TABLE does not fire any delete triggers. If you have critical application logic in a delete trigger, it won't get executed, and you may want to use another method to delete data.

This doesn't mean TRUNCATE TABLE bypasses foreign key checking; on the contrary, if you attempt to remove a row that is a parent in a foreign key relationship, the TRUNCATE TABLE statement will fail. That's true even if you coded ON DELETE CASCADE; the TRUNCATE TABLE operates as if you had specified ON DELETE RESTRICT, and you cannot use it to cascade deletes from parent to child tables. By definition, of course, the fast version of TRUNCATE TABLE won't violate referential integrity because if there are any child tables they must be empty; otherwise the fast version isn't used.

> **Note:** If a child table is non-empty, but contains only NULL values in the foreign key columns, it won't prevent TRUNCATE TABLE from executing successfully because there will be no referential integrity violations. It will, however, prevent the fast version of TRUNCATE TABLE from being used simply because the child table is non-empty. This combination of circumstances means that a setting of TRUNCATE_WITH_AUTO_COMMIT of 'ON' will not be honored, and TRUNCATE TABLE will not issue any commits.

The second shortcut, also taken by both the slow and fast forms of TRUNCATE TABLE, is that the individual deleted rows are not written to the transaction log file; just a record of the TRUNCATE TABLE command itself. This means that TRUNCATE TABLE should not be used on a table that is being uploaded via MobiLink if you want the deleted rows to be included in the upload stream. MobiLink determines which rows to upload by examining the transaction log, and rows deleted via TRUNCATE TABLE will be missed. For more information about MobiLink, see Chapter 7, "Synchronizing."

The third shortcut is only taken by the fast version of TRUNCATE TABLE. It does not acquire locks on the individual deleted rows but instead places an exclusive lock on the entire table. In most cases this will cause fewer problems for concurrency because the alternatives, DELETE or slow TRUNCATE TABLE, run slower and acquire locks on every row.

The fourth shortcut, also only taken by the fast version of TRUNCATE TABLE, is that extra space in the database file is not allocated for the rollback and checkpoint logs.

Note: If you delete and re-insert all the rows in a large table, using DELETE or the slow version of TRUNCATE TABLE, it is entirely possible for the database file to double or even triple in size because of all the space required to hold the rollback and checkpoint logs. For more information on these logs, see Section 9.11, "Logging and Recovery."

Tip: If you are willing to commit the change after deleting all the rows in a large table, and you want to avoid having the database file grow in size, execute explicit COMMIT and CHECKPOINT statements immediately after the DELETE or TRUNCATE TABLE. These statements will increase the chances that the database engine will be able to reuse or release the extra database file space that may have been allocated to accommodate the rollback and checkpoint logs during the deletion operation. In the case of a fast TRUNCATE TABLE, an explicit COMMIT is not necessary but it will do no harm, and it's sometimes hard to predict if you're going to get the fast or slow version. The same is true of the explicit CHECKPOINT; it may not be necessary because the database engine may decide on its own that it's time to do a CHECKPOINT, but in that case an extra CHECKPOINT will do no harm.

Note: CHECKPOINT statements can be expensive. Generally speaking, explicit CHECKPOINT statements are not required in application programs because the server does a good job of scheduling checkpoints to minimize their impact on performance. An explicit CHECKPOINT should never be used without careful consideration, especially in a busy multi-user environment.

Following is a table that shows how the actions performed by TRUNCATE TABLE depend on whether there are any rows in a child table, the TRUNCATE_WITH_AUTO_COMMIT setting, and whether or not a database transaction is already in progress. Note that of the eight combinations, only two result in the fast version of TRUNCATE TABLE being used. Also note that in two of the combinations, TRUNCATE_WITH_AUTO_COMMIT is 'ON' but no commits are performed.

```
Non-empty
  child       TRUNCATE_WITH  Transaction
  table?      _AUTO_COMMIT   in progress?              TRUNCATE TABLE Actions
=========    =============   =============   ==============================================
   Yes           'ON'            Yes                                   slow TRUNCATE
   Yes           'ON'            No                      BEGIN TRAN, slow TRUNCATE
   Yes           'OFF'           Yes                                  slow TRUNCATE
   Yes           'OFF'           No                      BEGIN TRAN, slow TRUNCATE
   No            'ON'            Yes          COMMIT, BEGIN TRAN, fast TRUNCATE, COMMIT
   No            'ON'            No                      BEGIN TRAN, fast TRUNCATE, COMMIT
   No            'OFF'           Yes                                  slow TRUNCATE
   No            'OFF'           No                      BEGIN TRAN, slow TRUNCATE
```

Note: This book assumes that the CHAINED database option is set to 'ON', and that is why BEGIN TRAN (short for BEGIN TRANsaction) operations are shown in the table above. The chained mode of operation means that any data manipulation operation like INSERT, UPDATE, DELETE, and TRUNCATE TABLE will implicitly start a database transaction if one isn't already started, and that transaction will not normally end until an explicit COMMIT or ROLLBACK is issued. Some commands, such as CREATE TABLE and the fast version of TRUNCATE TABLE, will perform a COMMIT as a side effect. For more information about transactions, see Section 9.3.

Here is an example that demonstrates how TRUNCATE TABLE works; first, two tables are created and one row is inserted into each:

```
CREATE TABLE t1 (
   key_1      UNSIGNED INTEGER NOT NULL PRIMARY KEY,
   non_key_1  INTEGER NOT NULL );

CREATE TABLE t2 (
   key_1      UNSIGNED INTEGER NOT NULL PRIMARY KEY,
   non_key_1  INTEGER NOT NULL );

INSERT t1 VALUES ( 1, 1 );
INSERT t2 VALUES ( 22, 22 );
COMMIT;
```

In the first test, TRUNCATE_WITH_AUTO_COMMIT is explicitly set to 'ON', the row in table t2 is updated, TRUNCATE TABLE is executed against table t1, and a ROLLBACK statement is executed:

```
SET EXISTING OPTION PUBLIC.TRUNCATE_WITH_AUTO_COMMIT = 'ON';
UPDATE t2 SET non_key_1 = 999;
TRUNCATE TABLE t1;
ROLLBACK;
```

After those statements are executed, t1 is empty and the value of t2.non_key_1 is 999; the TRUNCATE TABLE performed before-and-after COMMIT operations and the ROLLBACK statement was completely ignored, as is shown by the corresponding entries in the transaction log:

```
BEGIN TRANSACTION
UPDATE DBA.t2
   SET non_key_1=999
 WHERE key_1=22
COMMIT WORK
BEGIN TRANSACTION
```

```
truncate table t1
COMMIT WORK
```

If TRUNCATE_WITH_AUTO_COMMIT is 'OFF' the result is completely different; the ROLLBACK reverses the effects of the UPDATE and TRUNCATE TABLE statements, and the two tables contain the original rows:

```
SET EXISTING OPTION PUBLIC.TRUNCATE_WITH_AUTO_COMMIT = 'OFF';
UPDATE t2 SET non_key_1 = 999;
TRUNCATE TABLE t1;
ROLLBACK;
```

Here is what the transaction log looks like when TRUNCATE_WITH_AUTO_COMMIT is 'OFF':

```
BEGIN TRANSACTION
UPDATE DBA.t2
  SET non_key_1=999
 WHERE key_1=22
truncate table t1
ROLLBACK WORK
```

Not only is TRUNCATE TABLE often faster than DELETE when you want to delete all the rows, you can also use it to speed up the deletion of large numbers of rows even when you want to preserve some of them. A three-step technique can be used: First, copy the rows you want to save into a temporary table, then truncate the original table, and finally copy the saved rows back.

Here is an example of a table that was filled with 160M of data in 100,000 rows as part of a comparison of TRUNCATE TABLE with DELETE:

```
CREATE TABLE t1 (
   key_1         INTEGER NOT NULL PRIMARY KEY,
   inserted_date DATE NOT NULL DEFAULT CURRENT DATE,
   blob          LONG VARCHAR );
```

The following set-oriented DELETE took about one minute to delete 99.9% of the rows:

```
DELETE t1
 WHERE inserted_date < DATEADD ( DAY, -7, CURRENT DATE );
```

The following three statements performed exactly the same function in less than half the time (27 seconds):

```
SELECT *
  INTO #t1
  FROM t1
 WHERE inserted_date >= DATEADD ( DAY, -7, CURRENT DATE );

TRUNCATE TABLE t1;

INSERT t1
SELECT *
  FROM #t1;
```

Note: If the server crashes (because of a power failure, for example) immediately after the TRUNCATE TABLE in the example above, but before the final INSERT t1 finishes and a COMMIT is done, you will need to restore the database from a backup to recover the rows you want to keep. That's because the rows only exist in the temporary table and they won't be there after recovery.

For more information about the SELECT INTO method of creating and filling a temporary table, see Section 1.15.2.3, "SELECT INTO #table_name." For more information about using INSERT to copy data from one table to another, see Section 2.2.3, "INSERT Select All Columns."

> **Note:** Performance tests described in this book are not intended to be "benchmark quality," just reasonably fair comparisons of different techniques. The test above, for example, was run on a 933MHz Intel CPU with 512M of cache running Windows 2000, and the sa_flush_cache procedure was called before each test to ensure fairness.

5.7 Chapter Summary

This chapter described how to code simple DELETE statements that delete one or more rows from a single table and explained how a DELETE involving a multi-table join works. The full syntax of the set-oriented DELETE was described, followed by the cursor-oriented DELETE WHERE CURRENT OF and the TRUNCATE TABLE statement.

The next chapter turns to the subject of application logic written in SQL, with a discussion of cursor fetch loops.

Chapter 6

Fetching

6.1 Introduction

This chapter starts with an example of a cursor loop involving cursor DECLARE, OPEN, FETCH, and CLOSE statements as well as DELETE WHERE CURRENT OF. This example is shown in both SQL and C using embedded SQL and comes with a step-by-step explanation of how it works.

The next five sections describe the syntax of the three formats of the cursor DECLARE statement followed by the OPEN, CLOSE, and FETCH statements. The last section describes the cursor FOR loop, which can be used to simplify programming.

6.2 Cursor FETCH Loop

A *cursor loop* is a mechanism to deal with a multi-row result set one row at a time. Depending on the cursor type, it is possible to move forward and backward one or more rows, to move to a row at a specific position, and to update or delete the current row. Cursor loops are often used in application programs, either explicitly in the code or implicitly by the programming environment; for example, a call to the PowerBuilder DataWindow Retrieve function might look like a single operation but behind the scenes a cursor loop is used to fill the DataWindow buffer.

A cursor loop may also be coded inside a SQL stored procedure or other SQL programming block. It is constructed from several different SQL statements: some variable DECLARE statements, a WHILE loop, and statements to DECLARE, OPEN, FETCH, and CLOSE a cursor. The following is an example of a typical SQL cursor loop; this example is written to be short and simple while at the same time serving a useful purpose: to delete old rows from a table, limiting the total number of deletions to 1000 rows for each run and executing a COMMIT after every 100 deletions.

```
BEGIN
DECLARE @key_1          INTEGER;
DECLARE @non_key_1      VARCHAR ( 100 );
DECLARE @last_updated   TIMESTAMP;
DECLARE @SQLSTATE       VARCHAR ( 5 );
DECLARE @loop_counter   INTEGER;

DECLARE c_fetch NO SCROLL CURSOR FOR
SELECT TOP 1000
     t1.key_1,
     t1.non_key_1,
```

```
       t1.last_updated
   FROM t1
  WHERE t1.last_updated < DATEADD ( MONTH, -6, CURRENT DATE )
  ORDER BY t1.last_updated
 FOR UPDATE;

 OPEN c_fetch WITH HOLD;

 FETCH c_fetch INTO
    @key_1,
    @non_key_1,
    @last_updated;
 SET @SQLSTATE = SQLSTATE;

 SET @loop_counter = 0;

 WHILE @SQLSTATE = '00000' LOOP

    SET @loop_counter = @loop_counter + 1;
    MESSAGE STRING ( 'Deleting ',
                    @loop_counter, ', ',
                    @key_1, ', "',
                    @non_key_1, '", ',
                    @last_updated ) TO CONSOLE;

    DELETE t1 WHERE CURRENT OF c_fetch;
    IF MOD ( @loop_counter, 100 ) = 0 THEN
       COMMIT;
       MESSAGE STRING ( 'COMMIT after ', @loop_counter, ' rows.' ) TO CONSOLE;
    END IF;

    FETCH c_fetch INTO
       @key_1,
       @non_key_1,
       @last_updated;
    SET @SQLSTATE = SQLSTATE;

 END LOOP;
 CLOSE c_fetch;
 COMMIT;
 MESSAGE STRING ( 'Final COMMIT after ', @loop_counter, ' rows.' ) TO CONSOLE;
 END;
```

In the example above, the first three local variables — @key_1, @non_key_1, and @last_updated — are required to receive the column values returned by the cursor SELECT via the FETCH statements. The @SQLSTATE variable is used for checking the current state of execution, and @loop_counter is used to determine when to do a COMMIT.

The cursor DECLARE statement gives a name to the cursor, c_fetch, and uses the NO SCROLL keywords to indicate that the code won't be moving backward in the result set so SQL Anywhere is free to perform some kinds of optimization. The SELECT retrieves rows that are at least six months old, sorts them so the oldest rows appear first, and limits the number of rows returned to 1000. The FOR UPDATE keywords tell SQL Anywhere that the rows being retrieved may be changed; in this case, they are going to be deleted.

The OPEN statement starts the process by actually executing the SELECT defined in the cursor DECLARE. The WITH HOLD keywords tell SQL

Anywhere to hold the cursor open when a COMMIT is executed rather than implicitly closing the cursor.

The first FETCH statement retrieves the first row in the result set and copies the column values into the three local variables. The subsequent SET statement copies the value of SQLSTATE into the local variable @SQLSTATE. This kind of assignment is good practice because many SQL statements change SQLSTATE and this code only cares about the value set by the FETCH.

The WHILE statement starts the loop and runs it until there are no more rows; at that point @SQLSTATE will contain '02000'. The first MESSAGE statement inside the loop displays the current row.

The DELETE statement deletes the current row. For more information about the DELETE WHERE CURRENT OF cursor statement, see Section 5.5.

The IF statement after the DELETE shows how to use the MOD function to determine when multiples of 100 rows have been reached. MOD divides the first parameter by the second and returns the remainder; when the first parameter is exactly divisible by the second, the remainder is zero, so MOD (@loop_counter, 100) = 0 when @loop_counter is 100, 200, 300, and so on.

The next FETCH statement returns the second or later rows and fills in the three local variable with new column values. Eventually this FETCH will set SQLSTATE to '02000' for "row not found." After the loop ends, the cursor is closed and final COMMIT and MESSAGE statements are executed.

Here are the last few lines of MESSAGE output from the cursor loop above:

```
Deleting 998, 9003, "", 1979-05-11 10:04:07.389
Deleting 999, 9002, "", 1979-05-12 10:04:07.389
Deleting 1000, 9001, "", 1979-05-13 10:04:07.389
COMMIT after 1000 rows.
Done after 1000 rows.
```

Here is the same loop again, this time coded as a standalone C program using embedded SQL:

```
#include <stdio.h>
#include <stdlib.h>
#include <string.h>
#include "sqldef.h"
EXEC SQL INCLUDE SQLCA;
int main() {

EXEC SQL BEGIN DECLARE SECTION;
long    key_1;
char    non_key_1 [ 101 ];
char    last_updated [ 24 ];
EXEC SQL END DECLARE SECTION;

char    copy_SQLSTATE [ 6 ];
long    loop_counter;
ldiv_t loop_counter_ldiv;

db_init( &sqlca );
EXEC SQL CONNECT USING 'ENG=test6;DBN=test6;UID=DBA;PWD=SQL';

EXEC SQL DECLARE c_fetch NO SCROLL CURSOR FOR
SELECT TOP 1000
```

```
        t1.key_1,
        t1.non_key_1,
        DATEFORMAT ( t1.last_updated, 'yyyy-mm-dd hh:nn:ss.sss' )
    FROM t1
WHERE t1.last_updated < DATEADD ( MONTH, -6, CURRENT DATE )
ORDER BY t1.last_updated
FOR UPDATE;

EXEC SQL OPEN c_fetch WITH HOLD;

EXEC SQL FETCH c_fetch INTO
    :key_1,
    :non_key_1,
    :last_updated;
strcpy ( copy_SQLSTATE, SQLSTATE );

loop_counter = 0;

while ( strcmp ( copy_SQLSTATE, "00000" ) == 0 ) {

    loop_counter = loop_counter + 1;
    printf ( "Deleting %d, %d, '%s', %s\n",
        loop_counter,
        key_1,
        non_key_1,
        last_updated );

    EXEC SQL DELETE t1 WHERE CURRENT OF c_fetch;
    loop_counter_ldiv = ldiv ( loop_counter, 100L );
    if ( loop_counter_ldiv.rem == 0 ) {
        EXEC SQL COMMIT;
        printf ( "COMMIT after %d rows.\n", loop_counter );
    }

    EXEC SQL FETCH c_fetch INTO
        :key_1,
        :non_key_1,
        :last_updated;
    strcpy ( copy_SQLSTATE, SQLSTATE );

} // while...
EXEC SQL CLOSE c_fetch;
EXEC SQL COMMIT;
EXEC SQL DISCONNECT;
db_fini ( &sqlca );
printf ( "Done after %d rows.\n", loop_counter );
return ( 0 );
} // main
```

Note: This book doesn't cover embedded SQL in any great detail. The example above has been included because cursor fetch loops are very common in applications using various forms of embedded SQL statements, and the C version is representative of embedded SQL syntax found in other development environments, even PowerBuilder.

The next sections discuss the syntax of each component of a cursor fetch loop in detail.

6.2.1 **DECLARE CURSOR FOR Select**

A cursor may be defined as a select, as a USING clause referencing a string
variable that contains a select, or as a procedure CALL.

```
<declare_cursor> ::= <declare_cursor_for_select>
                   | <declare_cursor_using_select>
                   | <declare_cursor_for_call>
```

Here is the syntax for the first format:

```
<declare_cursor_for_select> ::= DECLARE <cursor_for_select>
<cursor_for_select> ::= <cursor_name>
                        [ <cursor_type> ]
                        CURSOR FOR
                        <select>
<cursor_name>       ::= <identifier> defined in a cursor DECLARE or FOR command
<identifier>        ::= see <identifier> in Chapter 1, "Creating"
<cursor_type>       ::= NO SCROLL      -- asensitive
                      | DYNAMIC SCROLL -- asensitive; default
                      | SCROLL         -- value-sensitive, keyset-driven
                      | INSENSITIVE    -- insensitive
                      | SENSITIVE      -- sensitive
<select>            ::= [ <with_clause> ]
                        <query_expression>
                        [ <order_by_clause> ]
                        [ <for_intent_clause> ]
<for_intent_clause> ::= FOR READ ONLY
                      | FOR UPDATE
<with_clause>       ::= see <with_clause> in Chapter 3, "Selecting"
<query_expression>  ::= see <query_expression> in Chapter 3, "Selecting"
<order_by_clause>   ::= see <order_by_clause> in Chapter 3, "Selecting"
```

The various clauses of a cursor DECLARE control the two main stages in the
life cycle of a cursor: The WITH clause, the query expression, and the ORDER
BY clause specify what the cursor result set looks like when the OPEN statement is executed, and the <cursor_type> and <for_intent_clause> specify how
the result set behaves as it is subsequently fetched and processed in the cursor
loop.

Even though the cursor DECLARE statement contains many elements that
specify executable behavior, it is not itself an executable statement. Each cursor
DECLARE must appear at the beginning of the BEGIN block before any executable statements. More than one cursor may be declared and used within one
block, but each cursor name must be unique within that block.

The WITH clause, query expression, and ORDER BY clause are all
described in Chapter 3, "Selecting."

The <cursor_type> indirectly specifies defaults for the following three cursor attributes:

- Scrollability controls the order in which rows can be fetched; in particular,
  it controls whether an earlier row can be fetched again after a later row has
  been fetched.
- Updatability controls whether or not UPDATE WHERE CURRENT OF
  and DELETE WHERE CURRENT OF statements can be used with this
  cursor, as well as the PUT statement in embedded SQL. Note that
  UPDATE, DELETE, and INSERT statements that operate directly on the
  underlying tables, without referring to the cursor by name, are always possible whether or not the cursor is updatable.

- Sensitivity controls whether or not changes made to the underlying tables while the cursor result set is being fetched will be made visible in the cursor result set itself. Cursor sensitivity applies to changes made by UPDATE WHERE CURRENT OF, DELETE WHERE CURRENT OF, and PUT statements applied to this cursor itself, as well as to changes made by other connections.

Cursor sensitivity is the most complex attribute of a cursor type; it can be described in terms of the following definitions:

- A cursor can be sensitive with respect to one kind of change, and insensitive with respect to another kind.
- *Membership sensitivity* controls whether or not changes to the values of columns specified in the cursor WHERE clause can cause a row to appear in the result set or to disappear from the result set.
- *Order sensitivity* controls whether or not changes to columns in the ORDER BY clause can cause a row to move to a different position in the result set, leaving behind a hole in the original position.
- *Value sensitivity* controls whether or not changes to the column values themselves are reflected in a row in the cursor result set.
- *Deletion sensitivity* controls whether or not, and how, the deletion of an underlying row is reflected in the result set.
- A *sensitive cursor* has a result set where every fetched row matches the cursor WHERE and ORDER BY clauses, and column values always agree with the underlying tables. An UPDATE may cause a row to appear, disappear, or change in position in the result set when it affects columns specified in the WHERE and ORDER BY clauses. A DELETE will cause the row to disappear from the result set as if it never existed.
- Note that higher settings of the ISOLATION_LEVEL connection option can effectively change sensitivity. For example, a sensitive cursor running at an isolation level of 3 may obtain locks that prevent changes from being made by other connections that would otherwise be reflected in the cursor result set. This topic is discussed further in Section 9.7, "Blocks and Isolation Levels."
- A *value-sensitive* or *keyset-driven* cursor is insensitive with respect to membership and order, and sensitive as far as values and deletions are concerned. An UPDATE affecting a column in the WHERE clause will not affect the membership of a row that has already been fetched, even if the WHERE clause no longer evaluates to TRUE for that row. Also, an UPDATE affecting a column in the ORDER BY clause will not cause the row to move to another position, although in both cases the changed column values will be visible if the row is fetched again.

  Two aspects of value-sensitive cursor behavior are worth mentioning: First, a DELETE creates a hole in the result set, and an attempt to fetch that row again will result in the error SQLSTATE 24503 'no current row of cursor'. The cursor remains open, however, and subsequent fetches will be processed, making this the only error condition that doesn't stop further processing of a cursor. Also, a value-sensitive cursor is sensitive with respect to row membership for an UPDATE that changes a primary key column, because that operation is treated as a DELETE followed by an INSERT.

- An *insensitive cursor* is insensitive with respect to membership, order, values, and deletions. In effect, a temporary copy of the entire result set is created when the cursor is opened. No subsequent changes to the underlying tables are reflected in the cursor result set.

- An *asensitive cursor* has undefined behavior as far as membership, order, value, and deletion sensitivity is concerned. SQL Anywhere is free to pick the most efficient execution method for the cursor without regard to sensitivity.

Here is how the five cursor types specify defaults for the three cursor attributes of scrollability, updatability, and sensitivity:

- **NO SCROLL** cursors do not permit backward scrolling; only FETCH NEXT, FETCH RELATIVE 0, and FETCH RELATIVE 1 operations are allowed. NO SCROLL cursors are updatable and asensitive by default.

- **DYNAMIC SCROLL** cursors allow all forms of scrolling; they are updatable and asensitive by default. DYNAMIC SCROLL is the default cursor type.

- **SCROLL** cursors allow all forms of scrolling and are updatable and value-sensitive by default.

- **INSENSITIVE** cursors allow all forms of scrolling and are read-only and insensitive by default.

- **SENSITIVE** cursors allow all forms of scrolling and are updatable and sensitive by default.

The <for_intent_clause> controls whether or not changes made by UPDATE WHERE CURRENT OF, DELETE WHERE CURRENT OF, and PUT statements are allowed for this cursor. FOR READ ONLY specifies that the cursor is not updatable, even if the declared cursor type implies that it is updatable (e.g., DYNAMIC SCROLL). Similarly, FOR UPDATE specifies that the cursor is updatable, even if the declared cursor type implies that it is read-only (e.g., INSENSITIVE). The <for_intent_clause> takes precedence over the cursor type; for example, a cursor declared as INSENSITIVE will actually be implemented as a value-sensitive cursor if the FOR UPDATE clause is specified.

Tip: The most efficient kinds of cursors are NO SCROLL and DYNAMIC SCROLL, together with FOR READ ONLY.

Host variable substitution is possible in cursor DECLARE statements as long as the variable exists and has a value when the block containing the cursor DECLARE is entered. This can be done with nested BEGIN blocks where the variable is declared and initialized in the outer block and the cursor DECLARE is coded inside the inner block. It can also be done with a stored procedure. Here is an example of a procedure containing a cursor DECLARE that includes a reference to a parameter value. The following procedure and CALL statement perform the same work as the example shown earlier in Section 6.2, "Cursor FETCH Loop":

```
CREATE PROCEDURE p_delete_oldest ( IN @age_in_months INTEGER )
BEGIN
```

```
DECLARE @key_1        INTEGER;
DECLARE @non_key_1    VARCHAR ( 100 );
DECLARE @last_updated TIMESTAMP;
DECLARE @SQLSTATE     VARCHAR ( 5 );
DECLARE @loop_counter INTEGER;

DECLARE c_fetch NO SCROLL CURSOR FOR
SELECT TOP 1000
       t1.key_1,
       t1.non_key_1,
       t1.last_updated
  FROM t1
 WHERE t1.last_updated < DATEADD ( MONTH, -@age_in_months, CURRENT DATE )
 ORDER BY t1.last_updated
FOR UPDATE;

OPEN c_fetch WITH HOLD;

FETCH c_fetch INTO
   @key_1,
   @non_key_1,
   @last_updated;
SET @SQLSTATE = SQLSTATE;

SET @loop_counter = 0;

WHILE @SQLSTATE = '00000' LOOP
   SET @loop_counter = @loop_counter + 1;
   DELETE t1 WHERE CURRENT OF c_fetch;
   IF MOD ( @loop_counter, 100 ) = 0 THEN
      COMMIT;
   END IF;
   FETCH c_fetch INTO
      @key_1,
      @non_key_1,
      @last_updated;
   SET @SQLSTATE = SQLSTATE;
END LOOP;
CLOSE c_fetch;
COMMIT;
END; -- p_delete_oldest

CALL p_delete_oldest ( 6 );
```

A cursor DECLARE can specify a query involving all the features described in
Chapter 3, "Selecting," including the WITH clause, multiple selects, and operators like UNION. The following is a cursor fetch loop based on the first
example from Section 3.24.1, "Recursive UNION." This query answers the
question "Who are Marlon's superiors on the way up the chart to Ainslie?" and
the output is the same as shown in Section 3.24.1:

```
BEGIN
DECLARE @level        INTEGER;
DECLARE @name         VARCHAR ( 20 );
DECLARE @SQLSTATE     VARCHAR ( 5 );
DECLARE @loop_counter INTEGER;

DECLARE c_fetch NO SCROLL CURSOR FOR
WITH RECURSIVE superior_list
   ( level,
     chosen_employee_id,
```

```
        manager_id,
        employee_id,
        name )
AS ( SELECT CAST ( 1 AS INTEGER )  AS level,
            employee.employee_id   AS chosen_employee_id,
            employee.manager_id    AS manager_id,
            employee.employee_id   AS employee_id,
            employee.name          AS name
       FROM employee
     UNION ALL
     SELECT superior_list.level + 1,
            superior_list.chosen_employee_id,
            employee.manager_id,
            employee.employee_id,
            employee.name
       FROM superior_list
            INNER JOIN employee
                    ON employee.employee_id = superior_list.manager_id
      WHERE superior_list.level <= 99
        AND superior_list.manager_id <> superior_list.employee_id )
SELECT superior_list.level,
       superior_list.name
  FROM superior_list
 WHERE superior_list.chosen_employee_id = 13
 ORDER BY superior_list.level DESC
FOR READ ONLY;

OPEN c_fetch WITH HOLD;
FETCH c_fetch INTO
   @level,
   @name;
SET @SQLSTATE = SQLSTATE;
SET @loop_counter = 0;
WHILE @SQLSTATE = '00000' LOOP
   SET @loop_counter = @loop_counter + 1;
   MESSAGE STRING ( @level, ' ', @name ) TO CONSOLE;
   FETCH c_fetch INTO
      @level,
      @name;
   SET @SQLSTATE = SQLSTATE;
END LOOP;
CLOSE c_fetch;
END;
```

6.2.2 DECLARE CURSOR USING Select

The query used for a cursor can be stored in a string variable, and that variable can appear in a cursor DECLARE after the USING keyword:

```
<declare_cursor_using_select> ::= DECLARE <cursor_using_select>
<cursor_using_select>         ::= <cursor_name>
                                  [ <cursor_type> ]
                                  CURSOR USING
                                  <cursor_select_variable>
<cursor_select_variable>      ::= string <identifier> already containing a <select>
```

Here is the example from Section 6.2, "Cursor FETCH Loop," after modifications to use a variable containing the SELECT. An outer BEGIN block has been added to declare and initialize the string variable @select. Note that the FOR UPDATE clause is part of the cursor select, rather than the outer cursor DECLARE statement, so it is included in the string value:

```
BEGIN -- outer block
DECLARE @select LONG VARCHAR;
SET @select = '
SELECT TOP 1000
        t1.key_1,
        t1.non_key_1,
        t1.last_updated
  FROM t1
 WHERE t1.last_updated < DATEADD ( MONTH, -6, CURRENT DATE )
 ORDER BY t1.last_updated
FOR UPDATE';

BEGIN -- inner block
DECLARE @key_1          INTEGER;
DECLARE @non_key_1      VARCHAR ( 100 );
DECLARE @last_updated   TIMESTAMP;
DECLARE @SQLSTATE       VARCHAR ( 5 );
DECLARE @loop_counter   INTEGER;

DECLARE c_fetch NO SCROLL CURSOR USING @select;

OPEN c_fetch WITH HOLD;
FETCH c_fetch INTO
    @key_1,
    @non_key_1,
    @last_updated;
SET @SQLSTATE = SQLSTATE;
SET @loop_counter = 0;
WHILE @SQLSTATE = '00000' LOOP
   SET @loop_counter = @loop_counter + 1;
   DELETE t1 WHERE CURRENT OF c_fetch;
   IF MOD ( @loop_counter, 100 ) = 0 THEN
      COMMIT;
      MESSAGE STRING ( 'COMMIT after ', @loop_counter, ' rows.' ) TO CONSOLE;
   END IF;
   FETCH c_fetch INTO
       @key_1,
       @non_key_1,
       @last_updated;
   SET @SQLSTATE = SQLSTATE;
END LOOP;
CLOSE c_fetch;
COMMIT;
END; -- inner block
END; -- outer block
```

The USING clause can be used to dynamically construct the entire cursor select, and it is especially useful inside stored procedures where various components like table names, column names, and WHERE clauses can be passed as parameters.

6.2.3 DECLARE CURSOR FOR CALL

A cursor DECLARE can specify a procedure CALL instead of a SELECT. This form of cursor is implicitly read only; the FOR UPDATE clause is not permitted:

```
<declare_cursor_for_call> ::= DECLARE <cursor_for_call>
<cursor_for_call> ::= <cursor_name>
                        [ <cursor_type> ]
                        CURSOR FOR CALL [ <owner_name> "." ] <procedure_name>
```

```
                        [ <argument_list> ]
<owner_name>       ::= <identifier>
<procedure_name>   ::= <identifier>
<argument_list>    ::= { <argument> "," } <argument>
<argument>         ::= <basic_expression>
                     | <parameter_name> "=" <basic_expression>
<basic_expression> ::= see <basic_expression> in Chapter 3, "Selecting"
                       -- an expression that is not a subquery
<subquery>         ::= see <subquery> in Chapter 3, "Selecting"
<parameter_name>   ::= <identifier> defined as a parameter in the procedure
```

Once again here is the example from Section 6.2, "Cursor FETCH Loop," this time using a procedure CALL. The DELETE WHERE CURRENT OF has been changed to an ordinary DELETE with a WHERE clause that explicitly specifies the primary key value; just because a cursor is not updatable doesn't mean updates are impossible.

```
CREATE PROCEDURE p_oldest ( IN @age_in_months INTEGER )
BEGIN
SELECT TOP 1000
       t1.key_1,
       t1.non_key_1,
       t1.last_updated
  FROM t1
 WHERE t1.last_updated < DATEADD ( MONTH, -@age_in_months, CURRENT DATE )
 ORDER BY t1.last_updated;
END;

BEGIN
DECLARE @key_1         INTEGER;
DECLARE @non_key_1     VARCHAR ( 100 );
DECLARE @last_updated  TIMESTAMP;
DECLARE @SQLSTATE      VARCHAR ( 5 );
DECLARE @loop_counter  INTEGER;

DECLARE c_fetch NO SCROLL CURSOR FOR CALL p_oldest ( 6 );

OPEN c_fetch WITH HOLD;

FETCH c_fetch INTO
   @key_1,
   @non_key_1,
   @last_updated;
SET @SQLSTATE = SQLSTATE;

SET @loop_counter = 0;

WHILE @SQLSTATE = '00000' LOOP
   SET @loop_counter = @loop_counter + 1;
   DELETE t1
    WHERE t1.key_1 = @key_1;
   IF MOD ( @loop_counter, 100 ) = 0 THEN
      COMMIT;
   END IF;
   FETCH c_fetch INTO
      @key_1,
      @non_key_1,
      @last_updated;
   SET @SQLSTATE = SQLSTATE;
END LOOP;
CLOSE c_fetch;
```

```
COMMIT;
END;
```

6.2.4 OPEN and CLOSE Cursor

The OPEN statement actually executes the query defined by the cursor DECLARE. The CLOSE statement can be used to close the cursor after processing is complete.

```
<open_cursor>      ::= OPEN <cursor_name>
                       [ WITH HOLD ]
                       [ <isolation_level> ]
<isolation_level> ::= ISOLATION LEVEL 0
                   | ISOLATION LEVEL 1 -- prevent dirty reads
                   | ISOLATION LEVEL 2 -- also prevent non-repeatable reads
                   | ISOLATION LEVEL 3 -- also prevent phantom rows
<close_cursor>     ::= CLOSE <cursor_name>
```

The WITH HOLD clause lets you issue a COMMIT without the cursor being implicitly closed. By default, a COMMIT statement will close any open cursors, and a subsequent FETCH will fail.

The ISOLATION LEVEL clause sets the isolation level for all operations involving this cursor. It overrides the current setting of the ISOLATION_LEVEL connection option. For more information about isolation levels, see Section 9.7, "Blocks and Isolation Levels."

The cursor OPEN statement can detect a number of exceptional conditions that are treated as warnings rather than errors. One of these warning conditions sets the SQLSTATE to '01S02', which means one or more attributes of the cursor have been changed to be different from the attributes specified or implied by the cursor DECLARE. An example of this is when an INSENSITIVE cursor type is used together with FOR UPDATE in the DECLARE. By default these warning conditions are ignored by SQL Anywhere when an OPEN statement is executed inside a procedure or BEGIN block; if you want to detect them, or treat them as errors, you have to add code to do that. Here is an example of an OPEN statement followed by an IF statement that turns any SQLSTATE other than '00000' into an error:

```
OPEN c_fetch WITH HOLD;
IF SQLSTATE <> '00000' THEN
   RAISERROR 20000 STRING ( 'Cursor OPEN SQLSTATE = ', SQLSTATE )
END IF;
```

For more information about the RAISERROR statement, see Section 9.5.2, "RAISERROR and CREATE MESSAGE."

6.2.5 FETCH Cursor

The FETCH statement is used to move to a particular position in the cursor result set, retrieve the column values from that row if one exists at that position, and assign those values to host variables.

```
<fetch_cursor>      ::= FETCH [ <cursor_positioning> ] <cursor_name>
                        INTO <fetch_into_list>
                        [ FOR UPDATE]
<cursor_positioning> ::= NEXT    -- default, same as RELATIVE 1
                      | FIRST   -- same as ABSOLUTE 1
                      | LAST    -- same as ABSOLUTE -1
```

```
                    | PRIOR    -- same as RELATIVE -1
                    | ABSOLUTE <move_to_row_number>
                    | RELATIVE <move_to_row_offset>
<move_to_row_number> ::= positive or negative numeric <simple_expression>
<move_to_row_offset> ::= positive or negative numeric <simple_expression>
<simple_expression>  ::= see <simple_expression> in Chapter 3, "Selecting"
                    -- not a subquery and does not start with IF or CASE
<fetch_into_list> ::= { <non_temporary_identifier> "," } <non_temporary_identifier>
<non_temporary_identifier> ::= see <non_temporary_identifier> in Chapter 1, "Creating"
```

A cursor position may or may not correspond to an actual row in the result set. When a cursor is first opened it is positioned prior to the first row, and it is possible for the position to return to that point later. It is also possible for the cursor to move to a position after the last row, or to a position that was once occupied by a row that no longer exists. If a FETCH moves to a position that doesn't correspond to an actual row, the INTO clause is ignored and the SQLSTATE is set to the "row not found" warning value '02000'.

The various cursor positioning keywords work as follows:

- **NEXT** is the default; it moves to the next position in the cursor result set. When a cursor is first opened it is positioned before the first row so the first FETCH NEXT operation will move to the first row.
- **FIRST** moves to the first position.
- **LAST** moves to the last position.
- **PRIOR** moves to the previous position.
- **ABSOLUTE** moves to the specified position. The first row is numbered 1, the second row 2, and so on. FETCH ABSOLUTE 1 is the same as FETCH FIRST.
- **RELATIVE** moves the specified number of positions forward for a positive number or backward for a negative number. FETCH RELATIVE 1 is the same as FETCH NEXT, and FETCH RELATIVE –1 is the same as FETCH PRIOR.

There is only one position that is treated as being "prior to the first row" and one position that is "after the last row." For example, if a cursor contains five rows, a FETCH ABSOLUTE –999 will move prior to the first row, and a subsequent FETCH NEXT will move to the first row. Similarly, a FETCH ABSOLUTE +999 followed by a FETCH PRIOR will move to the last row.

Depending on the cursor type, it is possible for a repeated FETCH to detect that one or more columns in the row have changed since the last time that row was fetched. This is treated as a warning and the SQLSTATE is set to '01W04'.

The INTO clause specifies one or more variables to receive column values from the fetched row. The list of variables in the INTO clause must match the cursor DECLARE select list in number and order. If a row does not exist at the fetched position, the variables are not changed.

6.3 Cursor FOR Loop

The FOR loop can be used to simplify coding of a cursor loop. It combines the cursor DECLARE and WHILE loop into a single FOR statement; it eliminates the OPEN, CLOSE, and FETCH statements; and it implicitly defines local variables to receive column values fetched from each row.

The FOR loop comes in two formats: with and without a label that may be used as a target for a LEAVE statement.

```
<for_cursor_loop>          ::= FOR <for_name>
                               AS <cursor_declaration>
                               DO
                                   <for_loop_body_statements>
                               END FOR
                           | <for_label> ":"
                               FOR <for_name>
                               AS <cursor_declaration>
                               DO
                                   <for_loop_body_statements>
                               END FOR [ <for_label> ]
<for_name>                 ::= <identifier>
<cursor_declaration>       ::= <cursor_for_select>
                           | <cursor_using_select>
                           | <cursor_for_call>
<for_loop_body_statements> ::= statements that may refer to select
                               list items by name
<for_label>       ::= <identifier> that may be used in a <leave_statement>
<leave_statement> ::= see <leave_statement> in Chapter 8, "Packaging"
```

Here is the example from Section 6.2, "Cursor FETCH Loop," coded to use a FOR loop instead of all those DECLARE, OPEN, FETCH, and WHILE statements:

```
BEGIN
DECLARE @loop_counter  INTEGER;
SET @loop_counter = 0;
FOR f_fetch
AS c_fetch NO SCROLL CURSOR FOR
SELECT TOP 1000
        t1.key_1       AS @key_1,
        t1.non_key_1   AS @non_key_1,
        t1.last_updated AS @last_updated
  FROM t1
WHERE t1.last_updated < DATEADD ( MONTH, -6, CURRENT DATE )
ORDER BY t1.last_updated
FOR UPDATE
DO
   SET @loop_counter = @loop_counter + 1;
   MESSAGE STRING ( 'Deleting ',
                    @loop_counter, ', ',
                    @key_1, ', "',
                    @non_key_1, '", ',
                    @last_updated ) TO CONSOLE;
   DELETE t1 WHERE CURRENT OF c_fetch;
   IF MOD ( @loop_counter, 100 ) = 0 THEN
      COMMIT;
   END IF;
END FOR;
COMMIT;
END;
```

Only one variable is explicitly declared in the above code: @loop_counter is just used to determine when to perform a COMMIT and it isn't really part of the cursor processing. Three other variables are implicitly created by the cursor definition in the FOR statement: @key_1, @non_key_1, and @last_updated get their names and data types from the columns in the SELECT list.

Tip: Always specify alias names for columns in a FOR loop SELECT list, and make these alias names different from the column names themselves. The SELECT list items are used to implicitly create local variables to hold values fetched from the rows in the cursor, and by default the column names are used as variable names. This can lead to problems if you want to add SQL statements inside the cursor loop that refer to the same table; in those statements any reference to a variable name would be interpreted as a reference to the column name instead. The "@" prefix is handy for making it clear which are the variables and which are the columns, as shown in the example above.

Here is the code from Section 6.2.3, "DECLARE CURSOR FOR CALL," simplified with a FOR loop. In this case a different alias name like @key_1 is absolutely necessary. If the alias name @key_1 wasn't used, the DELETE statement would be written as DELETE t1 WHERE t1.key_1 = key_1, and it would delete all the rows in t1 because key_1 would be interpreted as the column name within the context of the DELETE:

```
CREATE PROCEDURE p_oldest ( IN @age_in_months INTEGER )
BEGIN
SELECT TOP 1000
        t1.key_1        AS @key_1,
        t1.non_key_1    AS @non_key_1,
        t1.last_updated AS @last_updated
  FROM t1
  WHERE t1.last_updated < DATEADD ( MONTH, -@age_in_months, CURRENT DATE )
  ORDER BY t1.last_updated;
END;

BEGIN
DECLARE @loop_counter  INTEGER;
SET @loop_counter = 0;
FOR f_fetch
AS c_fetch NO SCROLL CURSOR FOR CALL p_oldest ( 6 )
DO
   SET @loop_counter = @loop_counter + 1;
   MESSAGE STRING ( 'Deleting ',
                    @loop_counter, ', ',
                    @key_1, ', "',
                    @non_key_1, '", ',
                    @last_updated ) TO CONSOLE;
   DELETE t1
     WHERE t1.key_1 = @key_1;
   IF MOD ( @loop_counter, 100 ) = 0 THEN
      COMMIT;
   END IF;
END FOR;
COMMIT;
END;
```

The string variable and the USING clause can also be used with the FOR loop; e.g., the example shown in Section 6.2.2, "DECLARE CURSOR USING Select," can be rewritten as a FOR loop.

6.4 Chapter Summary

This chapter showed how to code cursor loops using DECLARE, OPEN, FETCH, and CLOSE statements. Examples were included to show the different DECLARE formats using an inline query, a string variable containing the query, and a procedure call. Equivalent examples were also included to show how the cursor FOR loop simplifies the SQL code.

The next chapter switches to a different topic: the distribution of data into multiple databases and the synchronization of these databases with MobiLink.

Chapter 7

Synchronizing

7.1 Introduction

Distribution of data is the physical storage of data in different locations with access provided to the necessary data regardless of its location. Sometimes data is distributed for historical reasons; for example, when separate applications use different software and hardware. Sometimes data is distributed for a specific purpose: to speed up access by moving it closer to the end user, to improve reliability in the face of network failure, or because network connections are only occasionally available.

SQL Anywhere Studio 9 offers four ways to implement distributed data: proxy tables, Replication Server, SQL Remote, and MobiLink.

Proxy tables provide real-time access to data in different locations as if it were all stored in one database. This feature is described in Section 1.14, "Remote Data Access."

Replication Server provides near-real-time copying of data among a small number of databases. SQL Anywhere Studio 9 ships with the components you need to make use of Replication Server, but not Replication Server itself, and for that reason it isn't covered in this book.

SQL Remote and MobiLink both work by occasionally copying data between a single consolidated database and a virtually unlimited number of remote databases. Both products ship with SQL Anywhere Studio 9, and both are fully supported by iAnywhere Solutions. This chapter only discusses MobiLink, and in particular MobiLink as it is used with ASA remote databases; UltraLite databases can be used with MobiLink but the subject of UltraLite is not covered in this book.

The term "replication" is used to describe what SQL Remote does, as opposed to "synchronization" for MobiLink. The difference is that MobiLink guarantees that the consolidated and remote database are "in synch" at the point data is transferred, whereas with SQL Remote there are communication delays that prevent that guarantee.

And that's why this chapter is called "Synchronizing" instead of "Replicating" or "Distributing."

7.2 How MobiLink Works

MobiLink software consists of two main components: a client and a server. The client initiates a synchronization session by connecting to a remote database, gathering all the rows changed since the previous synchronization, and uploading those rows to the server. The server then applies the uploaded changes to the consolidated database, selects rows to be downloaded, and sends those rows to the client. Finally, the client applies the downloaded changes to the remote database and sends an acknowledgment back to the server.

Many thousands of remote databases, each with its own copy of the MobiLink client component, may be synchronized with a single consolidated database.

MobiLink is very powerful and very flexible, but not particularly easy to set up. Effective use requires an understanding of its architecture, described here in terms of its main characteristics.

MobiLink is designed for central administration. The original design was oriented towards a mobile workforce with no "remote DBA" available for hands-on maintenance of the remote databases. MobiLink has since been used for large, stationary remote databases but the orientation remains the same: Most administrative functions are performed on the consolidated database.

MobiLink supports occasional connections rather than continuous operations. MobiLink synchronization is characterized by high latency or long time lags between data entry and transmission to other databases. Synchronizations are typically run once or twice a day — every few minutes is even possible — and so can be part of an automated schedule, but MobiLink is not intended for continuous real-time replication.

Entire rows are transmitted rather than differences or changes. Multiple changes to the same row will be transmitted as a single, final copy of the row rather than individual updates. This applies to both upload and download although the details are very different.

MobiLink is optimized for large numbers of low-volume synchronizations. This is another result of the orientation towards a mobile workforce. MobiLink can and has been used to transmit millions of rows in a single synchronization but there is a price to be paid. In particular, the entire upload and download streams are each applied as single transactions with single commit operations. A large synchronization can cause concurrency problems at both ends; a giant download might as well be run as a standalone process.

Synchronization is session-based rather than file- or message-based. MobiLink software connects to both the consolidated and remote databases during the synchronization process, and all changes are applied during the session rather than stored and forwarded for later application. At the point the synchronization process reaches completion the two databases are known to be "in synch."

Synchronization is hierarchical rather than peer-to-peer. Changes to be passed from one remote database to another remote database must first be uploaded to the consolidated database in one session, and then downloaded to the other remote database in a later session, rather than passed directly.

MobiLink works with different kinds of consolidated databases. ASA, Sybase ASE, Oracle, Microsoft SQL Server, and IBM DB2 UDB are all officially supported, and other software has been used successfully. The limiting factors are the capabilities of the ODBC drivers and database stored procedure languages.

Tip: The proxy table feature supports other database applications in addition to MobiLink. If MobiLink can't be used directly with your central database software, set up an ASA consolidated database and use proxy tables to transfer data to and from the other database. This approach has its limitations, not to mention the extra coding effort required, and it isn't covered in detail in this book; nevertheless, it does work to extend synchronization to other kinds of databases.

MobiLink only works with ASA and UltraLite remote databases. This book doesn't cover UltraLite, so only remote databases using ASA are discussed.

MobiLink works well with heterogeneous databases. Not only can different software be used for remote and consolidated databases, but the schema can be different as well. The table and column names can be different, the numbers of columns can be different, even the level of normalization can be different. For example, you can download data from two different consolidated tables into one remote table, and vice versa, and with careful scripting you can do the same on the upload side.

The synchronization process is asymmetrical. The MobiLink client and server components use completely different techniques for processing the upload and download streams. In particular, there are four different processes, all using different techniques: the creation of the upload stream by the client component, the application of the upload stream by the server, the creation of the download stream by the server, and the application of the download stream by the client.

The upload stream is automatically constructed from the transaction log. The MobiLink client reads the transaction log to find which rows have been inserted, updated, or deleted since the previous successful synchronization. It then builds the upload stream using the final versions of those rows, and sends them marked as "inserts," "updates," or "deletes." It is this characteristic more than any other that limits MobiLink to ASA and UltraLite remote databases: Proprietary information about the transaction log is required and that is not available for databases like Oracle.

The upload stream is applied to the consolidated database by scripts that you write. You have to write one script for each kind of operation applied to each table — insert, update, and delete, if they are expected, as well as scripts to handle update conflicts if you expect those as well. A discussion of upload scripts starts in Section 7.6.4.1, "Handling Uploaded Inserts."

The download stream is constructed from the consolidated database by scripts that you write. You have to write one script for each table to select all the rows to be inserted and updated on the remote database, and if necessary, another script to delete rows from the remote table. A discussion of download scripts starts in Section 7.6.4.6, "Downloading Inserts and Updates."

The download stream is automatically filtered to remove any rows that were just uploaded. This makes it easier to write the download scripts because you don't have to worry about excluding those rows to reduce unnecessary network traffic — it's done for you.

The download stream is automatically applied to the remote database. Inserts and updates are not identified as such in the download stream, but are matched against the remote database by primary key: If a row with that key already exists, the downloaded row is applied as an update; otherwise it is inserted. Deleted rows are downloaded separately; they are identified as deletes and are handled as such. This implies that MobiLink requires all tables in the remote database to have primary keys. That agrees with Rule Number 2 of relational databases presented in Chapter 1, and it's an absolute requirement for MobiLink.

By default, the MobiLink client automatically resolves referential integrity violations caused by changes downloaded to the remote database. This automatic resolution sometimes causes downloaded changes to be silently ignored, and sometimes causes existing rows to be deleted as if ON CASCADE DELETE had been specified. The main reason for this behavior is to reduce administrative effort even when mistakes are made. This topic is discussed further in Section 7.6.4.8, "Handling Download Errors."

MobiLink requires you to write a multitude of scripts. For even a simple implementation without a lot of complex business rules affecting synchronization, and without large schema differences between the consolidated and remote databases, writing and testing all the MobiLink scripts is a labor-intensive process. However, it is these scripts that give MobiLink its great power and flexibility; you can use them to solve complex problems and accommodate great differences in database design.

MobiLink synchronization is driven by the remote database schema. MobiLink upload and download scripts are named for tables in the remote database even though the scripts execute on the consolidated database. Uploaded rows are applied to the consolidated database in an order that would preserve referential integrity as it is defined on the remote database, not the consolidated database. In other words, the upload stream is sorted according to the foreign key order on the remote database: Parent rows are inserted first and deleted last, and so on.

MobiLink scripts run on the consolidated database and have no access to the remote database. MobiLink synchronization might be session-based but that doesn't mean your code has access to both databases at the same time; it doesn't. The MobiLink scripts might be named for tables on the remote database but the scripts themselves only have access to tables on the consolidated database. This can be a huge source of initial confusion when the schema is different between the consolidated and remote databases, but once understood it's easy to deal with.

MobiLink scripts may be written in Java, .Net languages like C#, as well as the SQL supported by the consolidated database software. The examples in this book are all written in SQL for SQL Anywhere 9.

MobiLink does not offer any form of system-wide locking. There's nothing to stop you from inserting two rows with the same primary key on two different remote databases or from applying different updates to the same row on two different databases. These rows will cause problems when they are uploaded to the consolidated database. You must design your application so these errors and conflicts do not occur, or you must write scripts to handle them. In particular, primary key collisions must be avoided.

Failure handling is done at the level of upload and download streams. If processing of the upload stream fails, all the uploaded changes to the consolidated database are rolled back and synchronization stops before the download process begins. If synchronization is reattempted after a failure during upload, the entire upload stream will be reconstructed, and the whole process will be repeated as if it had never been attempted before. You never have to write any special code to handle the reconstruction of the upload stream because the MobiLink client program does it for you.

If the upload stream is successful, all the uploaded changes are committed and the download process begins. If the processing of the download stream fails, all the downloaded changes to the remote database are rolled back. If synchronization is reattempted after a failure during download, the original upload stream will not be reconstructed because it was successfully applied during the previous synchronization. The original download stream, however, will be reconstructed because it was not applied successfully in the previous attempt. This reconstruction of the download stream is your responsibility; in most applications this is easy to do, but in some special situations extra code is required to make sure reconstruction is correct; this topic is discussed further in Section 7.6.4.8, "Handling Download Errors."

Communication errors are reliably detected as synchronization failures, and the failure handling described above is used. Database errors are handled as synchronization failures by default, but you can write code to skip the rows that are causing the errors as well as reporting the errors by writing diagnostic information to a table.

Update conflicts occur when the same row is updated differently on different databases, and the updated rows are uploaded to the consolidated database. Conflicts are not errors, and by default they are handled silently: The last uploaded row wins, replacing all the other versions of that row. By definition, update conflicts only occur on the consolidated database, and that's the only place they can be detected. You can override the default action by providing scripts that handle or resolve the conflicts in whatever manner your application requires; see Section 7.6.4.4, "Handling Upload Conflicts" for more information.

MobiLink scripts are event driven. Each script is invoked in response to a single event. For example, the upload_insert script for table t is invoked each time an uploaded row marked for "insert" is received from remote table t. All the script has to do is handle the row, usually via INSERT to the corresponding table on the consolidated database.

MobiLink events exist on four levels: row, table, session, and connection. The Help talks about two levels, table and connection, where "table events" encompass the row- and table-level events discussed in this book, and "connection events" encompass session- and connection-level events.

A row-level event occurs once for each row or set of rows in an upload or download stream. For example, the upload_insert event for table t handles a single uploaded insert from table t, and the download_cursor event for table t generates a result set of inserts and updates for downloading into the remote table t. Row-level scripts are the most common, and you have to write at least one of them or nothing will happen during synchronization.

A table-level event occurs once for each table in an upload or download stream, but does not explicitly deal with actual rows of data. For example, the begin_upload event for table t is invoked just before the first uploaded row for table t is processed. Most of these events are rarely used.

A session-level event occurs once for each synchronization session from a single remote database. For example, the begin_download event is invoked after the upload stream is processed and just before the download stream is generated. A few of these events are regularly used to handle administrative tasks.

A connection-level event occurs once for each connection that the MobiLink server establishes with the consolidated database. The MobiLink server can reuse the same connection for multiple sessions, one after the other, so connection-level events cannot be used for processing that is specific to a single session. These events are often just used to create temporary tables and global variables for use in other events.

If you leave out the script for a particular event, a default action will be taken. In almost every case this action is "do nothing." For example, if there is no upload_insert script for table t then all uploaded inserts for table t will be skipped when they arrive at the consolidated database. Only the error-handling events actually do something if there is no script: They roll back the current transaction and end the session.

7.3 The MobiLink ASA Client

The MobiLink client for ASA remote databases is called dbmlsync.exe. It usually runs on the same machine as the remote database engine, and it controls the synchronization process between the remote and consolidated databases. It can be executed to perform a single synchronization and then shut down, or it can be left running continuously to perform multiple synchronizations according to a predetermined schedule.

The MobiLink client can also be launched by the new server-initiated synchronization feature, but even then it is still in control; it is dbmlsync.exe that starts the actual synchronization process.

When dbmlsync.exe is executed it immediately connects to the remote database to determine which tables and columns are to be synchronized. It also combines various command-line parameters with values stored in the remote database to determine the full set of options controlling synchronization. When it's time to perform a synchronization, it scans one or more remote database transaction log files to build the upload stream, and then connects to the MobiLink server.

At this point dbmlsync is acting as a client of two servers: It has a database connection with the remote database and a network connection with the MobiLink server.

After connecting to the MobiLink server, dbmlsync sends the upload stream and waits for the MobiLink server to apply the upload and perform a commit on the consolidated database and then build the download stream.

After this point the order of events depends on the setting of the SendDownloadACK extended option. If SendDownloadACK is 'OFF' (the default) the MobiLink server builds the download stream, immediately performs another commit on the consolidated database, and then sends the download stream. The MobiLink client applies the download stream to the remote database, performs a commit on the remote database, and disconnects from the MobiLink server and the remote database.

If SendDownloadACK is 'ON' the MobiLink server builds the download stream, sends it, and waits for an acknowledgment before performing the second commit. The MobiLink client applies the download stream to the remote database, does a commit on the remote database, and sends an acknowledgment to the MobiLink server. The MobiLink server now performs the second commit on the consolidated database, and the MobiLink client disconnects from the MobiLink server and the remote database. The SendDownloadACK extended option is described in more detail in sections 7.4.4, "The DBMLSYNC Command Line," and 7.6.4.8, "Handling Download Errors."

7.4 MobiLink Client Setup

Four commands are required to get the MobiLink client running. The first three are CREATE PUBLICATION to define which tables and columns are to be synchronized, CREATE SYNCHRONIZATION USER to uniquely identify the remote database, and CREATE SYNCHRONIZATION SUBSCRIPTION to link the publication with the remote database. The fourth command is the dbmlsync command line itself.

```
<MobiLink_client_setup>        ::= <create_publication>
                                 | <create_synch_user>
                                 | <create_synch_subscription>
                                 | <dbmlsync_command>
                                 | <store_publication_defaults>
```

There is an optional fifth command, a special version of CREATE SYNCHRONIZATION SUBSCRIPTION, which can be used to store default values for various options at the publication level.

Note: Earlier versions of MobiLink used a different method to set up a remote database for synchronization. This book doesn't discuss the earlier method, so the following statements are not covered here: CREATE SYNCHRONIZATION DEFINITION, CREATE SYNCHRONIZATION SITE, and CREATE SYNCHRONIZATION TEMPLATE.

7.4.1 CREATE PUBLICATION

The CREATE PUBLICATION statement assigns a name to a list of articles, or tables and columns, that are to be considered for synchronization. This statement is only executed on the remote database, not on the consolidated database, and it refers to tables and columns on the remote database.

```
<create_publication> ::= CREATE PUBLICATION <publication>
                         "(" <article_list> ")"
<publication>        ::= [ <owner_name> "." ] <publication_name>
<publication_name>   ::= <identifier>
```

```
<article_list>      ::= { <article> "," } <article>
<article>           ::= TABLE [ <owner_name> "." ] <table_name>
                        [ "(" [ <column_list> ] ")" ]
                        [ <where_clause> ]
<column_list>       ::= { <column_name> "," } <column_name>
```

All tables to be included in the publication must be explicitly named in an article. The column lists, however, are optional. If a column list is omitted then all columns in that table are assumed.

The order of columns in a column list isn't important. The structure of the uploaded and downloaded rows is determined by the column order in the CREATE TABLE statement on the remote database.

The order of tables in the article list doesn't matter either. The upload stream is applied to the consolidated database in an order that would preserve referential integrity as defined on the remote database, and the download stream is applied to the remote database with referential integrity checking deferred until the final commit.

Tip: The TableOrder extended option can be used to change the order of the upload stream. That can help if the foreign key structure is different on the consolidated database or you have problems with foreign key cycles.

If a table or column does not appear in any publication that is actually used for synchronization, then that table or column won't be synchronized. That's one way to implement column partitioning; by including some tables and columns and leaving others out, you can define tables and columns where the values exist only on the remote database and are never uploaded or downloaded.

Different publications can contain different sets of tables, and you can synchronize these publications at different times to achieve different goals. However, if the same table appears in more than one publication, the same set of columns in that table must be specified. If you want to synchronize different columns at different times, you have to put those columns in different tables. For example, if you want to synchronize a large blob column only when the MobiLink client has a fast, cheap local connection to the MobiLink server but not when a slow or expensive long-distance connection is used, then put the blob in a separate table all by itself.

A WHERE clause is permitted on each table in a publication. This facility is rarely used with MobiLink, but it can be used to determine which rows are to be uploaded. This is a way to implement row partitioning, by specifying which rows are to be uploaded and which ones are to exist only on the remote database. The WHERE clause does not affect the download stream; all downloaded rows will be accepted whether or not they match the WHERE clause in the publication.

Here is an example of a publication called p1 that explicitly specifies the column names for two tables:

```
CREATE PUBLICATION p1 (
   TABLE t1 ( key_1,
              key_2,
              non_key_1,
              non_key_2 ),
```

```
TABLE t2 ( key_1,
          non_key_1 ) );
```

Tip: Consider specifying explicit column lists even for tables where all the columns are synchronized. This may increase the amount of maintenance work, but it does force you to check the publication whenever the schema changes. Schema changes can be disruptive to synchronization, and it's always important to check every aspect of the MobiLink setup.

7.4.2 CREATE SYNCHRONIZATION USER

The CREATE SYNCHRONIZATION USER statement defines a globally unique MobiLink user name for this remote database. Each remote database being synchronized with one consolidated database must have a different MobiLink user name. This name is a "database identifier," which has nothing at all to do with database user ids, permissions, or ownerships.

```
<create_synch_user>        ::= CREATE SYNCHRONIZATION USER
                                <MobiLink_user_list>
                                [ TYPE <MobiLink_protocol> ]
                                [ ADDRESS <MobiLink_protocol_parameters> ]
                                [ OPTION <extended_option_list> ]
<MobiLink_user_list>       ::= { <MobiLink_user> "," } <MobiLink_user>
<MobiLink_user>            ::= <identifier>
<MobiLink_protocol>        ::= http
                             | https
                             | tcpip
                             | ActiveSync
<MobiLink_protocol_parameters> ::= string literal 'keyword=value;...'
<extended_option_list>     ::= { <extended_option> "," } <extended_option>
<extended_option>          ::= <extended_option_name> "=" <extended_option_value>
<extended_option_name>     ::= dbmlsync extended option keyword; see Table 7-3
<extended_option_value>    ::= dbmlsync extended option value; see Table 7-3
```

The CREATE SYNCHRONIZATION USER statement may also be used to provide various parameters used by dbmlsync. There are actually four different locations where you can do this; the other three are described in the next three sections: 7.4.3, "CREATE SYNCHRONIZATION SUBSCRIPTION," 7.4.4, "The DBMLSYNC Command Line," and 7.4.5, "SYSSYNC and Publication Defaults."

Here is an example of a typical CREATE SYNCHRONIZATION USER statement:

```
CREATE SYNCHRONIZATION USER "1"
   TYPE tcpip
   ADDRESS 'host=mobilink.risingroad.com'
   OPTION ConflictRetries='2';
```

The TYPE clause defines TCP/IP as the communication protocol to be used between the MobiLink client and server. The ADDRESS clause specifies the network location of the MobiLink server; examples of host addresses include localhost for the same computer, 192.1.1.50 for a server nearby on the LAN, and 64.7.134.118 (or mobilink.risingroad.com) for a server somewhere out on the Internet. The OPTION clause defines an extended synchronization option: ConflictRetries sets a limit on the number of times a download will be reattempted if it conflicts with changes made by another connection. These and other parameters are described in more detail in section 7.4.4.

Historically, the synchronization user has been confused with the actual user of a remote database because there was a one-to-one relationship between them in early implementations. The confusion persists because the field is called "MobiLink user name" in all the documentation, including this book, and there is a MobiLink script called authenticate_user, which can be used to implement security checking during synchronization.

Tip: To increase flexibility and reduce administrative duties, use the MobiLink user name to uniquely identify the remote database, not any actual person using the database. If you need to authenticate the actual user during synchronization, use the authenticate_parameters script instead of authenticate_user. This makes it easier for different people to use the same remote database, and for one person to use multiple remote databases, without making synchronization more complicated.

Tip: To simplify administrative duties even further, make the MobiLink user name the same as the GLOBAL_DATABASE_ID option setting. It's okay to use numeric strings like "1" and "2" in CREATE SYNCHRONIZATION USER.

It is possible to define more than one MobiLink user for each remote database, with all values being unique across all remote databases. Having multiple MobiLink users is one way to define different sets of data to be synchronized at different times. This technique is rarely used, however, because there are simpler ways to achieve this flexibility. In most applications, including the examples in this book, each remote database is identified by one single MobiLink user.

Tip: To reduce the manual effort required to set up each remote database, use EXECUTE IMMEDIATE and UUIDTOSTR (NEWID()) before the first synchronization to execute a CREATE SYNCHRONIZATION USER command that defines a universally unique identifier as the MobiLink user name. If the resulting values are too monstrously ugly for your tastes, use a DEFAULT AUTOINCREMENT column on the consolidated database to generate a numeric replacement value, send the new value down as part of the first synchronization, and then run DROP and CREATE SYNCHRONIZATION USER on the remote database to put it into effect. It's tricky code, but it does help to achieve zero administration effort at setup time.

7.4.3 CREATE SYNCHRONIZATION SUBSCRIPTION

A MobiLink subscription is a link between a single publication and a single MobiLink user name. The CREATE SYNCHRONIZATION SUBSCRIPTION statement lets you create these links on the remote database one at a time, or in bulk by specifying multiple publication and MobiLink user names.

```
<create_synch_subscription> ::= CREATE SYNCHRONIZATION SUBSCRIPTION
                                  TO <publication_list>
                                  FOR <MobiLink_user_list>
                                  [ TYPE <MobiLink_protocol> ]
                                  [ ADDRESS <MobiLink_protocol_parameters> ]
                                  [ OPTION <extended_option_list> ]
<publication_list>            ::= { <publication> "," } <publication>
```

The following example creates a single subscription: The remote database identified by MobiLink user name "1" subscribes to all the tables and columns listed in publication p1:

```
CREATE SYNCHRONIZATION SUBSCRIPTION TO p1 FOR "1"
    TYPE tcpip
    ADDRESS 'port=2439'
    OPTION LockTables='OFF',
           FireTriggers='ON',
           SendTriggers='ON',
           ScriptVersion='1',
           SendDownloadACK='ON';
```

If the example above had listed three publications and four MobiLink user names, a total of 12 different subscriptions would have been created, one for each combination. In the real world, however, subscriptions are created one at a time in separate CREATE SYNCHRONIZATION SUBSCRIPTION statements. Most remote databases only have one MobiLink user name, and they often have only one or two publications, so there's no real need to create 12 subscriptions at once.

The TYPE, ADDRESS, and OPTION clauses may be used to provide various parameters used by dbmlsync. These parameters are described in more detail in the next section.

7.4.4 The DBMLSYNC Command Line

The MobiLink client program dbmlsync.exe can be launched via Start > Run, from an operating system command file, from within an application program, or even from a stored procedure or event inside the database. You can also use the new server-initiated synchronization feature to launch dbmlsync via the listener program.

Here is an example of a Windows batch file that executes dbmlsync:

```
"%ASANY9%\win32\dbmlsync.exe" -c "DSN=remo" -o c:\temp\dbmlsync.txt -vnosu -x
```

Tip: Use %ASANY9% in your batch files to explicitly specify SQL Anywhere 9 program locations. This is easier than hard-coding the whole path. It is also safer than relying on the PATH, which may have entries for different versions of SQL Anywhere. The SQL Anywhere Studio 9 setup process creates the ASANY9 environment variable to contain the software installation path; e.g., C:\Program Files\Sybase\SQL Anywhere 9.

Here is an example from a PowerBuilder application running on Windows; all the options are hard-coded except for the MobiLink server address in ls_address:

```
ls_address = 'host=localhost'
li_RC = Run ( '"C:\Program Files\Sybase\SQL Anywhere 9\win32\dbmlsync.exe" ' &
    + '-ap "test1,test2" -c "DSN=remo" -e adr=~'' &
    + ls_address &
    + '~' -k -o c:\temp\dbmlsync.txt -vnorsu -x' )
```

Here is a similar example from an embedded Visual Basic application running on a PocketPC:

```
intRC = CreateProcess("\windows\dbmlsync.exe", "-c ""dsn=handheld""" -e adr='" _
    & strHost _
```

```
& "';sa='OFF' -d -k -o \Temp\dbmlsync.txt -pd dbsock9.dll -vnosu -x", _
 0, 0, 0, 0, 0, 0, 0, 0)
```

Here is an example where dbmlsync is executed from a stored procedure running inside the remote database itself:

```
SET @address = 'host=localhost';
CALL xp_cmdshell ( STRING (
 '"%ASANY9%\win32\dbmlsync.exe" -ap "test1,test2" -c "DSN=remo"  -e adr=''',
 @address,
 ''' -k -o c:\temp\dbmlsync.txt -vnosu -x' ) );
```

Here is the format of the dbmlsync command line as coded in a Windows batch file; the format in other environments is subject to the rules for coding strings and line separators:

```
<dbmlsync_command> ::= dbmlsync <dbmlsync_option_list> [ <transaction_log_folder> ]
<dbmlsync_option_list>      ::= <dbmlsync_option> { <dbmlsync_option> }
<dbmlsync_option>           ::= <dbmlsync_connection_option>
                             | <dbmlsync_interface_option>
                             | <dbmlsync_session_option>
                             | <dbmlsync_extended_options>
<dbmlsync_connection_option> ::= -c remote database connection-string
<dbmlsync_interface_option> ::= option affecting interface behavior; see Table 7-1
<dbmlsync_session_option>   ::= option affecting synchronization; see Table 7-2
<dbmlsync_extended_options> ::= -e options for all synchronizations; see Table 7-3
                             | -eu options for one -n publication; see Table 7-3
<transaction_log_folder>   ::= folder containing old and/or current log files
```

Only the remote database connection string is required on the dbmlsync command line itself. All the others are optional or can be specified inside the remote database itself using the CREATE SYNCHRONIZATION USER and CREATE SYNCHRONIZATION SUBSCRIPTION statements.

Note: If different values for the same option are specified in different places, the simple rule is that the value on the dbmlsync command line takes precedence. The full story of precedence appears in Section 7.4.5, "SYSSYNC and Publication Defaults."

The full explanation of what each option is for and how it works can be found in the SQL Anywhere 9 Help file. For your reference an overview is presented here. Table 7-1 shows the options that have more to do with the external interface of dbmlsync than with its internal workings. Options that control the internal synchronization process are listed in Tables 7-2 and 7-3, the difference being that Table 7-3 expands on the -e and -eu options from Table 7-2.

Tip: Don't panic! You can safely accept the default values for almost all the dbmlsync options. Or to put it another way: If you don't understand a particular option, don't touch it. And if you want to know which ones to study, start with the options in the examples earlier in this section.

Table 7-1. DBMLSYNC options affecting behavior

Option	Description
-a	Do not prompt for input again on error
-dl	Display log messages on the console

Option	Description
-is	Ignore schedule
-k	Close window on completion
-l	List available extended options
-o logfile	Write diagnostic trace to text file
-os size	Maximum size of trace file
-ot logfile	Truncate and write diagnostic trace to text file
-p	Disable logscan polling
-pd dllname;...	Get past bug in PocketPC; e.g. -pd dbsock8.dll
-pi	Ping MobiLink server
-pp number	Logscan polling period
-q	Run in minimized window
-urc row-estimate	Estimate of the rows that will be uploaded
-v[levels]	Verbose operation: -v+cpnorsu
-wc classname	Windows CE class name for ActiveSync synchronization
-x	Rename and restart the transaction log

Table 7-2. DBMLSYNC options affecting synchronization

Option	Description
-ap "value,..."	Upload application-defined parameters
-ba filename	Apply download file
-bc filename	Create download file
-be string	Add string to download file
-bg	Make download file suitable for new remotes
-d	Drop conflicting connections
-ds	Download-only synchronization
-e "opt=value;..."	Extended options; same as OPTION clause; see Table 7-3
-eu "opt=value;..."	Extended options for one publication; see Table 7-3
-eh	Ignore errors that occur in hook functions
-ek key	Encryption key
-ep	Prompt for encryption key
-i filename	SQL command file to execute after synchronization

Option	Description
-mn password	New MobiLink password
-mp password	MobiLink password
-n name,...	Publication name(s) to synchronize
-ra	Retry upload from remote progress if it is after consolidated
-rb	Retry upload from remote progress if it is before consolidated
-sc	Reload schema information before each synchronization.
-u ml_username	MobiLink user name to synchronize
-uo	Upload only

Table 7-3. DBMLSYNC extended options -e and -eu

Abbreviated Keyword	Default	Long Keyword and Description
adr='network-parms;...'		CommunicationAddress; same as ADDRESS clause
cr=number	–1	ConflictRetries; –1 for indefinite
ctp=sync-type	tcpip	CommunicationType; same as OPTION clause
dbs=number[K|M]	1M (CE 32K)	DownloadBufferSize
dir=path		OfflineDirectory; same as <transaction_log_folder>
ds={ON|OFF}	OFF	DownloadOnly
eh={ON|OFF}	OFF	IgnoreHookErrors
el=number[K|M]	32K	ErrorLogSendLimit; for uploading trace
ft={ON|OFF}	ON	FireTriggers; should download fire triggers
hrt=number[K|M]	1M	HoverRescanThreshold; for scheduled sessions
inc=number[K|M]		Increment; size of upload, default single
isc={ON|OFF}	OFF	IgnoreScheduling
lt={ON|OFF}	ON	LockTables
mem=number[K|M]	1M	Memory; for building upload stream
mn=new-password		NewMobiLinkPwd

Abbreviated Keyword	Default	Long Keyword and Description
mp=password		MobiLinkPwd
p={ON|OFF}	OFF	DisablePolling; for log scan
pp=number[S|M|H|D]	1M	PollingPeriod; for log scan
sa={ON|OFF}	OFF	SendDownloadACK; new default in version 9
sch=schedule		Schedule; for synchronizations
scn={ON|OFF}	OFF	SendColumnNames; for dbmlsrv9 -za, -ze
st={ON|OFF}	OFF	SendTriggers; to upload trigger actions
sv=version-name	default	ScriptVersion; identifies MobiLink scripts
tor=table,...		TableOrder; order in upload stream
uo={ON|OFF}	OFF	UploadOnly
v={ON|OFF}	OFF	Verbose; like -v+ for most information
vm={ON|OFF}	OFF	VerboseMin; like -vm for minimum trace
vn={ON|OFF}	OFF	VerboseRowCounts; like -vn
vo={ON|OFF}	OFF	VerboseOptions; like -vo
vr={ON|OFF}	OFF	VerboseRowValues; like -vr
vs={ON|OFF}	OFF	VerboseHooks; like -vs for hook trace
vu={ON|OFF}	OFF	VerboseUpload; like -vu for upload trace

There is overlap within the list of dbmlsync options itself, as well as between the dbmlsync command line and the CREATE SYNCHRONIZATION USER and CREATE SYNCHRONIZATION SUBSCRIPTION statements. For example, the <transaction_log_folder> may be specified all by itself at the end of the dbmlsync command line, or inside the -e option as dir=path or OffLineDirectory=path.

When dbmlsync runs it needs to know which subscriptions for which MobiLink user are to be processed. This is easy if there is only one user, one publication, and one subscription, but it gets more complicated if there are multiple users and subscriptions.

Note: All subscriptions in a single run of dbmlsync must be for the same synchronization user.

The dbmlsync -n parameter may be used to identify one or more publications, the -u parameter may be used to identify the synchronization user, and the subscriptions are determined as follows:

- If there is only one synchronization user in the remote database and the dbmlsync -n and -u parameters are not specified, then all subscriptions for that user are processed. This is the most common usage; none of the examples earlier in this section need the -n or -u options.

- If there is only one synchronization user in the remote database, the dbmlsync -n parameter may be used to identify one or more publications. The single user plus the chosen publication name(s) are used to determine which subscription(s) are to be processed.

- If there is only one synchronization user in the remote database, the dbmlsync -u parameter is redundant; if it is specified, it must name that single user.

- If there are multiple synchronization users in the remote database, the dbmlsync -u parameter must be specified to identify the synchronization user for this session.

- If there are multiple synchronization users in the remote database and the dbmlsync -n parameter is not specified, then all subscriptions for the chosen user are processed.

- If there are multiple synchronization users in the remote database, the dbmlsync -n parameter may be used to identify one or more publications. The chosen user plus the chosen publication(s) are used to determine which subscription(s) are to be processed.

7.4.5 SYSSYNC and Publication Defaults

When dbmlsync options are stored in the database via CREATE SYNCHRONIZATION USER and CREATE SYNCHRONIZATION SUBSCRIPTION statements, they are placed in the SYSSYNC system table. In particular, the values from the OPTION, ADDRESS, and TYPE clauses are stored in the SYSSYNC option, server_connect, and server_conn_type columns respectively:

```
CREATE TABLE SYS.SYSSYNC (
    sync_id             UNSIGNED INT NOT NULL,
    type                CHAR ( 1 ) NOT NULL,  -- 'D' for MobiLink
    publication_id      UNSIGNED INT NULL,    -- points to SYSPUBLICATON
    progress            NUMERIC ( 20 ) NULL,
    site_name           CHAR ( 128 ) NULL,    -- MobiLink user name
    "option"            LONG VARCHAR NULL,    -- OPTION clause
    server_connect      LONG VARCHAR NULL,    -- ADDRESS clause
    server_conn_type    LONG VARCHAR NULL,    -- TYPE clause
    last_download_time  TIMESTAMP NULL,
    last_upload_time    TIMESTAMP NOT NULL DEFAULT 'jan-1-1900',
    created             NUMERIC ( 20 ) NULL,
    log_sent            NUMERIC ( 20 ) NULL,
    generation_number   INTEGER NOT NULL DEFAULT 0,
    extended_state      VARCHAR ( 1024 ) NOT NULL DEFAULT '',
    PRIMARY KEY ( sync_id ) );
```

SYSSYNC contains three kinds of rows:

- A "subscription" row where the MobiLink user name is stored in the site_name column and the publication_id points to a row in the SYSPUBLICATION table. One of these rows is inserted for every subscription created with CREATE SYNCHRONIZATION SUBSCRIPTION.
- A "user" row where the MobiLink user name is stored in the site_name column but the publication_id is empty. One of these rows is inserted for every MobiLink user created with CREATE SYNCHRONIZATION USER.
- A "publication defaults" row where the site_name is empty but the publication_id is filled in. This row is optional. It is not created by CREATE PUBLICATION but with a special form of CREATE SYNCHRONIZATION SUBSCRIPTION described later in this section.

When dbmlsync runs, it gathers option values from six different locations. Three of these locations are on the dbmlsync command line itself, and the other three are all in SYSSYNC. If different values for the same option appear in more than one place, the value with the highest precedence is used according to this list:

- Values in the -eu command line option take precedence over values from all other locations.
- Values in the -e command line option are second in precedence.
- Values in other command line options are third in precedence.
- Options stored in the SYSSYNC "subscription" row by CREATE SYNCHRONIZATION SUBSCRIPTION are fourth in precedence.
- Options stored in the SYSSYNC "user" row by CREATE SYNCHRONIZATION USER statement are fifth in precedence.
- Options stored in the "publication defaults" row in SYSSYNC come last in precedence.

The SYSSYNC "publication defaults" row is optional. It is created by a special form of the CREATE SYNCHRONIZATION SUBSCRIPTION statement that specifies the publication(s) but leaves out the MobiLink user name(s):

```
<store_publication_defaults> ::= CREATE SYNCHRONIZATION SUBSCRIPTION
                                 TO <publication_list>
                                 [ TYPE <MobiLink_protocol> ]
                                 [ ADDRESS <MobiLink_protocol_parameters> ]
                                 [ OPTION <extended_option_list> ]
```

The following example specifies option values to be used when the publication p1 is involved in a synchronization, but only when different values for the same options are not specified anywhere else:

```
CREATE SYNCHRONIZATION SUBSCRIPTION TO p1
   TYPE tcpip
   ADDRESS 'host=localhost'
   OPTION ConflictRetries='2';
```

It is possible for one run of dbmlsync to execute more than one synchronization session if different publications are named in separate -n options. All the sessions must have the same synchronization user, but each of the sessions can use different extended options if different values have been specified at the subscription or publication levels. Here's how it works: When dbmlsync -n p1 -n p2 is specified, two separate sessions are executed, and the extended options are determined separately for each sessions. If dbmlsync -n p1,p2 is specified, one session is executed, and the extended options determined for the subscription to publication p1 are also used for p2. To use the options specified for the subscription to p2 instead, specify dbmlsync -n p2,p1.

7.5 **The MobiLink Server**

The MobiLink server is called dbmlsrv9.exe. It can be run on the same machine as the consolidated database server, or on a separate but nearby machine to spread the load. It is often started as a Windows service or Unix daemon and left running continuously to service synchronization requests from MobiLink clients.

When dbmlsrv9.exe is started it immediately makes one connection to the consolidated database. It then makes a number of worker threads available for incoming synchronization requests from MobiLink clients. When the first synchronization session is started on one of these threads, another connection with the consolidated database is established. That connection remains open when the session is completed, and the same connection is used again for the next session on the same thread. This process is called connection pooling, where the same connection is used over and over again, and the overhead of opening and closing database connections is reduced.

If two MobiLink clients perform synchronizations one after the other, in single file, they will use the same worker thread on the MobiLink server and the same connection to the database. If two or more MobiLink clients start synchronizing before the other clients are finished, each will get its own worker thread, and the server will start another connection to the consolidated database for each worker thread being used. When all the threads are busy, new synchronization requests must wait until one is free.

The MobiLink server uses ODBC to connect to the consolidated database. The choice of ODBC driver is critical to the success of MobiLink synchronizations. It is very important to use the driver recommended in the SQL Anywhere 9 documentation, and it may be different from the driver provided by the database vendor; e.g., Oracle.

Tip: To find out about recommended ODBC drivers for MobiLink go to http://www.ianywhere.com/developer/technotes/odbc_mobilink.html or use the following search string in Google: mobilink recommended odbc driver site:ianywhere.com.

When a synchronization session starts, dbmlsrv9.exe is acting as both a server and a client. It is a server as far as the MobiLink client dbmlsync.exe is concerned, and it is a client of the consolidated database server. The order of upload and download processing is described earlier in Section 7.3, "The MobiLink ASA Client."

7.6 MobiLink Server Setup

The MobiLink server is controlled by scripts that you write and store in the consolidated database. These scripts are stored as strings inside the ml_script table, and they are not compiled or checked for syntax until they are executed by the MobiLink server during the synchronization process.

```
<store_MobiLink_script> ::= <store_MobiLink_connection_script>
                          | <store_MobiLink_session_script>
                          | <store_MobiLink_table_script>
                          | <store_MobiLink_row_script>
```

Two stored procedures are provided to make it easier to save the scripts. One of the procedures is for connection- and session-level scripts that are not associated with any particular table and the other is for table- and row-level scripts that require a table name.

Note: This book divides MobiLink events into four different classifications: connection, session, table, and row. The SQL Anywhere 9 documentation uses two classifications: connection and table.

7.6.1 Connection-Level Scripts

Connection-level events are only executed once per connection, and because of connection pooling multiple sessions may follow one after the other on the same connection. That means connection-level events aren't much use for anything other than creating temporary variables and tables for use in other scripts.

Here's the syntax for storing a connection-level script:

```
<store_MobiLink_connection_script> ::= CALL ml_add_connection_script
                                         ( <script_version>,
                                           <connection_script_name>,
                                           <MobiLink_script> )
<script_version>            ::= string value from 1 to 128 characters long
<connection_script_name> ::= 'begin_connection'
                           | 'begin_connection_autocommit'
                           | 'end_connection'
<MobiLink_script>           ::= string containing consolidated database SQL code
```

Note: This book shows MobiLink scripts written in SQL for consolidated database using SQL Anywhere 9. It doesn't cover scripts written in other languages like Java or C#, or other consolidated databases like Oracle or Microsoft SQL Server.

Here is an example of a begin_connection script that creates a global variable called @g_session_started:

```
CALL ml_add_connection_script ( '1', 'begin_connection',
'CREATE VARIABLE @g_session_started TIMESTAMP;' );
```

The "script version" is a string value under your control that you can use to identify different versions of the MobiLink scripts on the consolidated database. Different versions of the same script can coexist as long as this script version value is different for each set of scripts. The script version can contain anything you want; for example, '1', 'Version 1', and 'Intermec Beta Version 0.105.B' are all valid. Most projects start out with a single value for script version.

Note: The script version is one of the options determined when dbmlsync runs. Usually one script version is used for all the scripts in one run, but you can use different script versions for different subscriptions if you tell dbmlsync to run them in separate sessions. You do this by naming the publications in separate -n parameters, as in dbmlsync -n p1 -n p2.

7.6.2 Session-Level Scripts

MobiLink session-level scripts are defined using the same stored procedure, but there are a lot more events to consider, and they are a lot more useful than connection-level events:

```
<store_MobiLink_session_script> ::= CALL ml_add_connection_script
                                   ( <script_version>,
                                     <session_script_name>,
                                     <MobiLink_script> )
<session_script_name>           ::= 'authenticate_parameters'
                                 | 'authenticate_user'
                                 | 'authenticate_user_hashed'
                                 | 'begin_download'
                                 | 'begin_publication'
                                 | 'begin_synchronization'
                                 | 'begin_upload'
                                 | 'download_statistics'
                                 | 'end_download'
                                 | 'end_publication'
                                 | 'end_synchronization'
                                 | 'end_upload'
                                 | 'handle_error'
                                 | 'handle_odbc_error'
                                 | 'modify_last_download_timestamp'
                                 | 'modify_next_last_download_timestamp'
                                 | 'modify_user'
                                 | 'prepare_for_download'
                                 | 'report_error'
                                 | 'report_odbc_error'
                                 | 'synchronization_statistics'
                                 | 'time_statistics'
                                 | 'upload_statistics'
```

Most session-level scripts execute once per synchronization session; e.g., modify_user, begin_upload, and begin_download. A few may be called more than once; e.g., time_statistics, and handle_error if it sets the return code to "skip the row and continue." For more information about the handle_error script, see Section 7.6.4.5, "Handling Upload Errors."

Here is an example of a session-level begin_synchronization script coded as a call to a stored procedure:

```
CALL ml_add_connection_script ( '1', 'begin_synchronization',
'CALL ml_begin_synchronization ( ? )' );

CREATE PROCEDURE ml_begin_synchronization (
  IN @ml_username    VARCHAR ( 128 ) )
BEGIN
  INSERT session_history ( ml_username, details )
  VALUES ( @ml_username, 'begin_synchronization' );
END;
```

Most events are passed parameters such as the MobiLink user name and the date/time of the previous successful download. These parameters are positional and must be coded as question marks in the script. In the example above there is one "?" parameter representing @ml_username. The SQL Anywhere 9 Help file describes all the parameters in detail.

Tip: Write session- and table-level scripts as stored procedure calls. This lets you turn the positional "?" parameter placeholders into named parameters such as @ml_username in the example above. Stored procedure calls also keep the scripts themselves small, and they let you use the same procedures with different script versions for scripts that remain the same. There's one more advantage: CREATE PROCEDURE will catch syntax errors at compile time. If you put all the code in the MobiLink script, the errors won't be detected until run time.

Tip: Name your stored procedures after the scripts that call them, using a common prefix such as "ml_." That makes it easier to find the procedure you're looking for when you have a lot of them, and keeps the MobiLink-related procedures separate from application and system procedures. For example, the procedure called from the begin_synchronization script is easier to find if it's named ml_begin_synchronization.

Tip: Use the Sybase Central "Test Scripts" facility to catch some basic mistakes (see Figure 7-1). Connect to the consolidated database using the MobiLink Synchronization 9 plug-in, click the right mouse button on the Connection Scripts folder in the left pane, and then select Test Scripts. This facility is no substitute for thorough testing with real data but it's nice to catch syntax errors early.

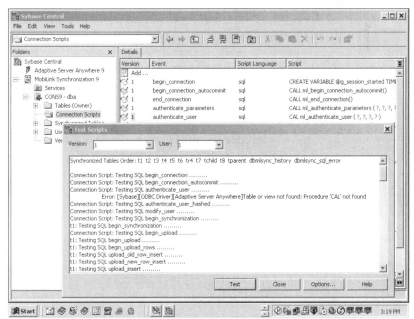

Figure 7-1. Sybase Central MobiLink Test Scripts window

7.6.3 **Table-Level Scripts**

MobiLink table-level events are associated with a particular table, and a different stored procedure is provided to store the scripts. There are 18 different table-level events, and if you code scripts for all of them in a hundred-table database, you would end up with 1,800 different scripts. None of them are required, however, and in most applications none of them are used.

```
<store_MobiLink_table_script> ::= CALL ml_add_table_script
                                    ( <script_version>,
                                      <remote_table_name>,
                                      <table_script_name>,
                                      <MobiLink_script> )
<remote_table_name>         ::= string containing remote database table name
<table_script_name>         ::= 'begin_download'
                              | 'begin_download_deletes'
                              | 'begin_download_rows'
                              | 'begin_synchronization'
                              | 'begin_upload'
                              | 'begin_upload_deletes'
                              | 'begin_upload_rows'
                              | 'download_statistics'
                              | 'end_download'
                              | 'end_download_deletes'
                              | 'end_download_rows'
                              | 'end_synchronization'
                              | 'end_upload'
                              | 'end_upload_deletes'
                              | 'end_upload_rows'
                              | 'synchronization_statistics'
                              | 'time_statistics'
                              | 'upload_statistics'
```

Here is an example of a table-level script that records how many times every table-level and row-level event occurs for table t1:

```
CALL ml_add_table_script  ( '1', 't1', 'time_statistics',
'CALL ml_time_statistics_by_table ( ?, ?, ?, ?, ?, ?, ? )' );

CREATE PROCEDURE ml_time_statistics_by_table (
  IN @ml_username  VARCHAR ( 128 ),
  IN @table        VARCHAR ( 128 ),
  IN @event_name   VARCHAR ( 128 ),
  IN @num_calls    INTEGER,
  IN @min_time     INTEGER,
  IN @max_time     INTEGER,
  IN @total_time   INTEGER )
BEGIN
  INSERT session_history ( ml_username, details )
  VALUES ( @ml_username,
     STRING ( @table, ' - ', @event_name, ' ', @num_calls ) );
END; -- ml_time_statistics_by_table
```

Because time_statistics is a table-level event you must write one script for each table you want to handle. In this case, however, the table name is also passed to the script at run time. This redundant information is actually helpful because it means you can write one stored procedure and call it from all the scripts. Here's the script for table t2:

```
CALL ml_add_table_script ( '1', 't2', 'time_statistics',
'CALL ml_time_statistics_by_table ( ?, ?, ?, ?, ?, ?, ? )' );
```

7.6.4 **Row-Level Scripts**

MobiLink row-level events are where all the real action takes place. You need separate scripts to handle uploaded inserts, updates, and deletes: upload_insert, upload_update, and upload_delete. Downloaded inserts and updates are generated by one script (download_cursor) and downloaded deletes by another (download_delete_cursor). Other scripts are used to handle conflicts between rows uploaded from different remote databases.

The same stored procedure, ml_add_table_script, is used to store row-level scripts as was used earlier for table-level scripts.

```
<store_MobiLink_row_script> ::= CALL ml_add_table_script
                                  ( <script_version>,
                                    <remote_table_name>,
                                    <row_script_name>,
                                    <MobiLink_script> )
<row_script_name>           ::= 'download_cursor'
                              | 'download_delete_cursor'
                              | 'resolve_conflict'
                              | 'upload_delete'
                              | 'upload_fetch'
                              | 'upload_insert'
                              | 'upload_new_row_insert'
                              | 'upload_old_row_insert'
                              | 'upload_update'
```

You only write scripts for the operations you expect to be performed. For example, if nothing ever gets deleted, you never have to write upload_delete or download_delete_cursor scripts.

Note: Earlier versions of MobiLink used a different method to handle the upload stream. It is still available, but this book doesn't discuss the earlier method, and that means these events are not covered here: upload_cursor, new_row_cursor, and old_row_cursor.

7.6.4.1 **Handling Uploaded Inserts**

The upload_insert row-level event is fired once on the consolidated database for each row that was inserted on the remote database and then uploaded by dbmlsync.

Note: A row that was inserted on the remote database after the previous synchronization and then updated is uploaded as a single insert of the final version.

A typical upload_insert script simply inserts the row into the corresponding table on the consolidated database.

```
<typical_upload_insert>    ::= INSERT <consolidated_table_name>
                                  "(" { <column_name> "," }
                                      <column_name> ")"
                                  VALUES "(" { "?," } "?" ")"
<consolidated_table_name> ::= a table that exists on the consolidated database
```

The following is an example that shows that each column being uploaded is represented as one "?" parameter placeholder in the script; these column placeholders appear in the order of the columns in the CREATE TABLE on the remote database.

```
CALL ml_add_table_script ( '1', 't1', 'upload_insert', '
INSERT t1
        ( key_1,
          key_2,
          non_key_1,
          non_key_2 )
VALUES ( ?,
         ?,
         ?,
         ? )' );
```

7.6.4.2 Handling Uploaded Updates

The upload_update row-level event is fired once on the consolidated database for each row that was updated on the remote database and then uploaded by dbmlsync.

Note: A row that was deleted and re-inserted on the remote database after the previous synchronization is uploaded as an update, not an insert or delete.

A typical upload_update script simply updates the row in the corresponding table on the consolidated database.

```
<typical_upload_update>         ::= UPDATE <consolidated_table_name>
                                    SET { <non_primary_key_column_name> "= ?," }
                                        <non_primary_key_column_name> "= ?"
                                    WHERE <primary_key_column_name> "= ?"
                                    { AND <primary_key_column_name> "= ?" }
<non_primary_key_column_name> ::= a column that is not in the primary key
<primary_key_column_name>     := a column in the primary key
```

Here is an example that shows that the "?" placeholders for the non-primary key columns come first, followed by the primary key columns, so they can be placed correctly in the SET and WHERE clauses:

```
CALL ml_add_table_script ( '1', 't1', 'upload_update', '
UPDATE t1
   SET non_key_1 = ?,
       non_key_2 = ?
WHERE key_1 = ?
  AND key_2 = ?' );
```

You can substitute a stored procedure call for an UPDATE in an upload_update script if you want to add extra processing logic. The tricky part is to get the parameters in the right order: non-primary key columns first, in remote CREATE TABLE order, then the primary key columns, again in remote CREATE TABLE order.

In other words, you can replace this:

```
CALL ml_add_table_script ( '1', 't3', 'upload_update', '
UPDATE t3
   SET non_key_1 = ?
WHERE key_1 = ?
' );
```

with this:

```
CALL ml_add_table_script  ( '1', 't3', 'upload_update', '
CALL ml_upload_update_t3 ( ?, ? )
' );

CREATE PROCEDURE ml_upload_update_t3 (
  IN @non_key_1    INTEGER,
  IN @key_1        UNSIGNED BIGINT )
BEGIN
  -- This code does the same thing, but more
  -- complex logic could easily be used here.
  UPDATE t3
    SET non_key_1 = @non_key_1
   WHERE key_1 = @key_1;
END;
```

Tip: Don't put a COMMIT or ROLLBACK in any of your MobiLink scripts, don't call any stored procedures that contain COMMIT or ROLLBACK commands, and don't execute any statements that cause implicit commits, such as TRUNCATE TABLE or DROP INDEX. The MobiLink server is responsible for transaction processing during synchronization. In particular, when an error occurs, the MobiLink server has to be able to roll back the entire upload or download stream so it can be safely repeated on the next synchronization.

Tip: Don't forget to COMMIT after calling ml_add_connection_script or ml_add_table_script. If you forget, locks may be held on the MobiLink system tables that prevent the next synchronization session from proceeding. This is different from the tip "don't put a COMMIT inside your script"; it's a suggestion to "do a COMMIT after adding a script."

7.6.4.3 Handling Uploaded Deletes

The upload_delete row-level event is fired once on the consolidated database for each row that was deleted on the remote database and then uploaded by dbmlsync.

Note: A row that was updated and deleted on the remote database after the previous synchronization is uploaded as a single delete. A row that was inserted and then deleted is not uploaded at all, since it never existed on the consolidated database and doesn't exist now on the remote database.

A typical upload_delete script simply deletes the row from the corresponding table on the consolidated database.

```
<typical_upload_delete> ::= DELETE <consolidated_table_name>
                            WHERE <primary_key_column_name> "= ?"
                            { AND <primary_key_column_name> "= ?" }
```

This example shows that "?" placeholders for the primary key columns are the only ones required in an upload_delete script:

```
CALL ml_add_table_script ( '1', 't1', 'upload_delete', '
DELETE t1
WHERE key_1 = ?
  AND key_2 = ?' );
```

Tip: If you don't want a particular type of operation to be applied to the consolidated database, just leave that script out. For example, if you want inserts and updates to be applied but not deletes, leave out the upload_delete script. The deletes will still be uploaded but they will be ignored by the MobiLink server.

7.6.4.4 Handling Upload Conflicts

In general, an upload conflict is anything that causes a resolve_conflict event to occur for a single uploaded row. This definition is vague for a reason: An upload conflict isn't just a problem to be dealt with; it is a powerful programming tool. Upload conflicts come in two flavors: natural conflicts and forced conflicts, and a forced conflict can be anything you want it to be. This section will discuss natural conflicts first, then forced conflicts.

A *natural conflict* is caused by the same row being updated on different remote databases and then uploaded to the consolidated database. It can also occur if the same row is updated on the consolidated database and on a remote database, and then that row is uploaded from the remote database to the consolidated.

Some applications don't have conflicts; the databases are set up so it's impossible for the same row to be updated on more than one database. Other applications don't care; the default action of "last uploaded update wins" is okay. But many applications have special business-related rules that must be followed when a conflict occurs. For these applications, the conflicts must first be detected and then dealt with, and each of those actions require more MobiLink scripts to be written.

Every uploaded update consists of two copies of the row: the old column values as they existed on the remote database before the row was updated, and the new column values that the upload_update script would normally apply to the consolidated database. A natural conflict is detected by comparing the old values being uploaded, not with the new values, but with the values as they currently exist on the consolidated database. If they are the same, there is no conflict, and the upload_update script proceeds to apply the new values.

If the uploaded old remote values are different from the current consolidated values, a natural conflict exists, and it can be detected in one of two ways.

First, if you write an upload_fetch script for the table with the conflicts, MobiLink will use that script to do the conflict check on each uploaded update. If no conflict is detected, the row will be passed over to the upload_update script for processing. When a conflict is detected the upload_update event is not fired; what happens instead is discussed a bit later, but right now this discussion is concentrating on how conflicts are detected.

The upload_fetch script should be a SELECT that specifies all the columns in the select list and a WHERE clause that lists all the primary key columns. As with other MobiLink scripts, it names tables and columns that exist on the consolidated database but the column order must match the CREATE TABLE column order on the remote database.

```
<typical_upload_fetch>    ::= SELECT { <column_name> "," }
                                     <column_name>
                              FROM <current_values_table_name>
```

```
                              WHERE <primary_key_column_name> "= ?"
                            { AND <primary_key_column_name> "= ?" }
<current_values_table_name> ::= the target table on the consolidated database
```

The following is an example of an upload_fetch script; it's up to you to write the SELECT to tell MobiLink how to retrieve the current column values from the consolidated database, and it's up to the MobiLink server to actually execute the SELECT and then compare the values with the old column values uploaded from the remote database.

```
CALL ml_add_table_script ( '1', 't2', 'upload_fetch', '
SELECT key_1,
       key_2,
       non_key_1,
       non_key_2
  FROM t2
 WHERE key_1 = ?
   AND key_2 = ?' );
```

There is an alternative to the upload_fetch script: If the upload_update script includes all the non-key columns in the WHERE clause as well as the primary key columns, this extended upload_update script is used by MobiLink to detect a conflict. If a conflict is detected, the extended upload_update script will not actually apply the update. If no conflict is detected, the extended upload_update will proceed as it normally does.

```
<typical_extended_upload_update> ::= UPDATE <consolidated_table_name>
                                       SET { <non_primary_key_column_name> "= ?," }
                                           <non_primary_key_column_name> "= ?"
                                     WHERE <primary_key_column_name> "= ?"
                                     { AND <primary_key_column_name> "= ?" }
                                       AND <non_primary_key_column_name> "= ?"
                                     { AND <non_primary_key_column_name> "= ?" }
```

Here is an example of an extended upload_update that can detect a natural conflict just like the earlier upload_fetch; the primary key columns come first in the WHERE clause, then the non-key columns:

```
CALL ml_add_table_script ( '1', 't2', 'upload_update', '
UPDATE t2
   SET non_key_1 = ?,
       non_key_2 = ?
 WHERE key_1 = ?
   AND key_2 = ?
   AND non_key_1 = ?
   AND non_key_2 = ?' );
```

If you write both upload_fetch and extended upload_update scripts, it doesn't hurt, but it's a waste of your effort to code the longer WHERE clause in the upload_update; it will be the upload_fetch that detects the conflicts.

Note: The same extended WHERE clause is available for the upload_delete script as well, where predicates involving all the non-key columns can be appended.

Detecting a conflict is just the first part of the process. Actually doing something about it requires three more scripts: upload_new_row_insert, upload_old_row_insert, and resolve_conflict. The first two scripts allow you to store the old and new uploaded values, usually in temporary tables. The resolve_conflict script is where you put the code that deals with the conflict.

```
<typical_upload_old_row_insert> ::= INSERT <old_values_table_name>
                                    "(" { <column_name> "," }
                                        <column_name> ")"
                                    VALUES "(" { "?," } "?" ")"
<old_values_table_name> ::= a temporary table to hold the uploaded before-images
<typical_upload_new_row_insert> ::= INSERT <new_values_table_name>
                                    "(" { <column_name> "," }
                                        <column_name> ")"
                                    VALUES "(" { "?," } "?" ")"
<new_values_table_name> ::= a temporary table to hold the uploaded after-images
```

The upload_old_row_insert event is fired once for each conflict, and it is passed the old value of each column in the uploaded update row. Similarly, the upload_new_row_insert is passed the new column values. The resolve_conflict script is then fired, and if you have saved the old and new values, you now have access to all three versions of the row: old, new, and current.

The following example implements a business rule that requires multiple conflicting updates to be merged by accumulating both changes and applying the result to the consolidated database. The upload_old_row_insert script inserts a row into the t2_old temporary table, the upload_new_row_insert script inserts a row into t2_new, and the resolve_conflict script joins all three tables to calculate the final values of the non_key_1 and non_key_2 columns. A stored procedure is used to keep the script short.

```
CALL ml_add_table_script ( '1', 't2', 'upload_old_row_insert', '
INSERT t2_old
       ( key_1,
         key_2,
         non_key_1,
         non_key_2 )
VALUES ( ?, ?, ?, ? )' );

CALL ml_add_table_script ( '1', 't2', 'upload_new_row_insert', '
INSERT t2_new
       ( key_1,
         key_2,
         non_key_1,
         non_key_2 )
VALUES ( ?, ?, ?, ? )' );

CALL ml_add_table_script ( '1', 't2', 'resolve_conflict',
'CALL ml_resolve_conflict_t2 ( ?, ? )' );

CREATE PROCEDURE ml_resolve_conflict_t2 (
   IN @ml_username    VARCHAR ( 128 ),
   IN @table_name     VARCHAR ( 128 ) )
BEGIN
   UPDATE t2
      SET t2.non_key_1 = t2.non_key_1 - t2_old.non_key_1 + t2_new.non_key_1,
          t2.non_key_2 = t2.non_key_2 - t2_old.non_key_2 + t2_new.non_key_2
      FROM t2
      JOIN t2_old
        ON t2.key_1 = t2_old.key_1
       AND t2.key_2 = t2_old.key_2
      JOIN t2_new
        ON t2.key_1 = t2_new.key_1
```

```
          AND t2.key_2 = t2_new.key_2;
    DELETE t2_new;
    DELETE t2_old;
END;
```

Tip: Don't forget to delete the rows from the temporary tables when they are no longer needed so they won't get processed over and over again as later conflicts are handled.

Tip: You can put the conflict resolution logic for several different tables into a single procedure if you want. The table name is passed to the resolve_conflict event as one of the parameters so your code can decide which action to take.

Note: If an ordinary upload_update script exists but there is no upload_fetch script, a conflict will not be detected and the upload_update will be executed. This is the "last uploaded update wins" scenario. If an upload_fetch script does exist together with an ordinary upload_update script but there are no conflict resolution scripts, an uploaded update that is in conflict will be ignored. This is the "first update wins" scenario, where the update could have come from a prior upload or it could have been made directly to the consolidated database.

The entire process of natural conflict detection and resolution can be merged into a single stored procedure called from an extended upload_update script. The following example shows an extended upload_update script and a procedure ml_upload_update_t2 that replace all the scripts in the previous example; i.e., the following code replaces the previous upload_update, upload_old_row_insert, upload_new_row_insert, and resolve_update scripts and the ml_resolve_conflict_t2 procedure. One "?" parameter value is passed from the extended upload_update script to the procedure for each new non-key value, each primary key column, and each old non-key value:

```
CALL ml_add_table_script ( '1', 't2', 'upload_update', '
CALL ml_upload_update_t2 ( ?, ?, ?, ?, ?, ? )' );
CREATE PROCEDURE ml_upload_update_t2 (
  IN @non_key_1    INTEGER,
  IN @non_key_2    INTEGER,
  IN @key_1        UNSIGNED BIGINT,
  IN @key_2        INTEGER,
  IN @old_non_key_1 INTEGER,
  IN @old_non_key_2 INTEGER )
BEGIN
  UPDATE t2
    SET t2.non_key_1 = t2.non_key_1 - @old_non_key_1 + @non_key_1,
        t2.non_key_2 = t2.non_key_2 - @old_non_key_2 + @non_key_2
    WHERE t2.key_1 = @key_1
      AND t2.key_2 = @key_2;
END;
```

A *forced conflict* occurs when three conditions are satisfied: First, an uploaded insert, delete, or update is received. Second, there are no upload_insert, upload_delete, upload_update, or upload_fetch scripts for that table. Finally, upload_old_row_insert and upload_new_row_insert scripts do exist; a resolve_conflict script may also exist but it is optional.

When a forced conflict occurs for an uploaded insert, the upload_new_row_insert event will receive the new row from the remote database. The resolve_conflict script is then executed, but not the upload_old_row_insert event. If your scripts insert rows into temporary tables as in the previous example, the resolve_conflict script will be able to determine it was fired by an uploaded insert because t2_new contains one row while t2_old is empty.

When a forced conflict occurs for an uploaded delete, the upload_old_row_insert event will receive the entire deleted row from the remote database. The resolve_conflict script is then executed, but not the upload_new_row_insert event. When the resolve_conflict script is executed there will be one row in t2_old but t2_new will be empty.

When a forced conflict occurs for an uploaded update, both of the upload_old_row_insert and upload_new_row_insert events will be fired, and when the resolve_conflict script is executed there will be one row in t2_old and one row in t2_new.

You can use these three events to solve complex synchronization problems, such as dealing with differences in database design between the consolidated and remote databases. Rows from different tables can be combined into one and vice versa: Changes made to one table can be spread across multiple tables. Actions performed on the remote database can be altered when they reach the consolidated one; for example, updates and deletes can be changed into inserts to record everything as a detailed audit trail. This kind of logic is possible because all three sets of data are available when a forced conflict occurs: the old and new rows from the remote database and the current row on the consolidated database.

7.6.4.5 Handling Upload Errors

An upload error is different from a conflict in two ways: There is no built-in mechanism to silently handle an error, and the default action is to roll back the upload and stop the synchronization session. Changing this behavior isn't easy, and that's why it's important to prevent errors from occurring in the first place.

The most common upload error is a coding mistake in a synchronization script. These are usually easy to repair, and because the whole upload was rolled back you can just fix the script on the consolidated database and run the synchronization session over again.

Tip: Watch out for characteristic errors when modifying your database design. A "characteristic error" is a mistake you make because of the way the software is designed. In this case, because MobiLink requires you to write several different scripts for the same table, it's easy to forget one of them when the table layout changes. For example, when adding or removing columns in a table, check these scripts: upload_insert, upload_update, upload_fetch, upload_old_row_insert, upload_new_row_insert, and download_cursor. Also check the list of columns in the CREATE SYNCHRONIZATION PUBLICATION statement. If you are modifying the primary key definition, also check the upload_update, upload_delete, and download_delete_cursor scripts, as well as the shadow table and delete trigger. Shadow tables are discussed in Section 7.6.4.7, "Downloading Deletes."

Tip: Always test synchronization after even the simplest schema change. Construct a pair of test databases and a set of simple test cases that exercise all of the MobiLink scripts, plus a "read me" file describing how to run the test and check the results. Do not rely on user-oriented regression testing to exercise all the scripts or to catch subtle problems. Testing is very important with MobiLink scripts because even basic syntax errors won't be discovered until the scripts are executed.

More serious upload errors involve the actual data, such as a duplicate primary key or a referential integrity violation. In most applications the best approach is to design the databases so these errors don't happen. The DEFAULT GLOBAL AUTOINCREMENT feature and GLOBAL_DATABASE_ID option can be used to guarantee unique primary keys, for example; see Section 1.8.2 for more information.

Referential integrity violations won't happen if the same foreign key relationships exist on both the remote and consolidated databases and you remember to include all the necessary tables in the CREATE PUBLICATION statement. Schema differences require more work on your part, perhaps involving the TableOrder extended option described in Section 7.4.1, "CREATE PUBLICATION," or forced conflict scripts described in Section 7.6.4.4, "Handling Upload Conflicts."

When push comes to shove, however, some applications require non-stop operations even in the face of upload errors. One approach is to skip the bad data and carry on with the rest, which is possible with the handle_error script. The following example shows how to skip all errors:

```
CALL ml_add_connection_script ( '1', 'handle_error',
'CALL ml_handle_error ( ?, ?, ?, ?, ? )' );

CREATE PROCEDURE ml_handle_error (
   INOUT  @action_code    INTEGER,
   IN     @error_code     INTEGER,
   IN     @error_message  LONG VARCHAR,
   IN     @ml_username    VARCHAR ( 128 ),
   IN     @table          VARCHAR ( 128 ) )
BEGIN
   SET @action_code = 1000; -- skip row and continue
END;
```

You can easily write a more sophisticated handle_error script to take different actions depending on which errors occur and which tables are involved. The action code parameter defaults to 3000, which means roll back the upload and stop the synchronization session. This is also the default action when no handle_error script is present. Other values include 1000, shown above, to skip the uploaded row causing the error and carry on with the rest of the upload, and 4000 to roll back the upload and shut down the server entirely.

One way to record all the errors for later analysis is to run the MobiLink server with the -o option to write all the error message to a text file. Another way is to insert the error information into your own table on the consolidated database. You can do this in two places: the handle_error script and the report_error script. The advantage to putting your INSERT in the report_error script is that it will run on a separate connection and will be committed immediately, so the row will still be there if the upload is rolled back. An INSERT in the handle_error script will be rolled back if the action code is set to 3000 or 4000 now or at some later point before the upload is committed.

The following is an example of a report_error script together with the table it uses. The error_code column is defined as VARCHAR instead of INTEGER so this table can also be used in the report_ODBC_error script that receives an alphanumeric SQLSTATE instead of a number.

```
CREATE TABLE ml_error (
    ml_username     VARCHAR ( 128 ) NOT NULL,
    inserted_at     TIMESTAMP NOT NULL DEFAULT TIMESTAMP,
    unique_id       UNSIGNED BIGINT NOT NULL DEFAULT AUTOINCREMENT,
    action_code     INTEGER NOT NULL,
    error_code      VARCHAR ( 100 ) NOT NULL,
    error_message   LONG VARCHAR NOT NULL,
    table_name      VARCHAR ( 128 ) NOT NULL,
    PRIMARY KEY ( ml_username, inserted_at, unique_id ) );

CALL ml_add_connection_script ( '1', 'report_error',
'CALL ml_report_error ( ?, ?, ?, ?, ? )' );

CREATE PROCEDURE ml_report_error (
    IN @action_code     INTEGER,
    IN @error_code      INTEGER,
    IN @error_message   LONG VARCHAR,
    IN @ml_username     VARCHAR ( 128 ),
    IN @table           VARCHAR ( 128 ) )
BEGIN
    INSERT ml_error
    VALUES ( @ml_username,
             DEFAULT,
             DEFAULT,
             @action_code,
             CAST ( COALESCE ( @error_code, 0 ) AS VARCHAR ( 100 ) ),
             COALESCE ( @error_message, '' ),
             COALESCE ( @table, '' ) );
END;
```

Here is what the ml_error row looks like after a primary key violation has been skipped:

```
'1', '2003 07 28 16:55:54.710000', 8, 1000, '-193',
'ODBC: [Sybase][ODBC Driver][Adaptive Server Anywhere]Integrity
    constraint violation: Primary key for table ''t1'' is not
    unique (ODBC State = 23000, Native error code = -193)', 't1'
```

Tip: If all you want to do is record diagnostic information about the first error encountered and then let the session roll back and stop, leave out the handle_error script and use only a report_error script like the one above.

Another way to handle upload errors is to change the basic scripts that receive the uploaded rows. For example, you can use the ON EXISTING SKIP clause on the INSERT statement in an upload_insert script to skip any rows that have primary key violations. Or use ON EXISTING UPDATE to change the failing INSERT into an UPDATE that will work. These techniques only work on a SQL Anywhere consolidated database, of course; for Oracle and other software you must work harder, perhaps using forced conflict scripts as described in Section 7.6.4.4, "Handling Upload Conflicts."

7.6.4.6 Downloading Inserts and Updates

Unlike the upload stream, the download stream is entirely under your control as the author of the MobiLink scripts. Downloaded deletes are discussed in the next section; this section describes how to construct the insert and update portion of the download stream.

For each table to be downloaded, you must write a download_cursor script that selects all the rows from the consolidated database that must be inserted or updated on the remote database. You don't have to worry about which rows need to be inserted and which ones updated; that's all taken care of by dbmlsync when it receives the download stream. Here's how that works: If the primary key of a downloaded row matches the primary key of a row that already exists on the remote database, dbmlsync treats it as a downloaded update. If the primary key doesn't match any row on the remote database, it's processed as an insert. This is sometimes called an "upsert" for "update-or-insert as required."

Tip: Don't ever update the primary key value of any row involved in MobiLink synchronization, and don't delete and immediately re-insert a row with the same primary key value. MobiLink depends on the primary key values to determine which rows are being inserted, updated, and deleted. If your application requires key values to change, make that key a separate UNIQUE constraint on the table, and add a DEFAULT GLOBAL AUTOINCREMENT column as the PRIMARY KEY. A row can only be tracked reliably in a distributed database environment if it has a primary key that never changes; otherwise there is chaos.

The simplest download_cursor script is "SELECT * FROM t," which sends all the columns and rows down to the remote. New rows are automatically inserted by dbmlsync, old rows are updated, and in effect a "snapshot" of the entire consolidated table is downloaded. This is often called "snapshot synchronization." If the table is treated as read-only on the remote database, and if rows aren't deleted from the consolidated, snapshot synchronization works to replace the entire contents of the table on the remote database with every synchronization.

Snapshot synchronization may work for small, rapidly changing tables, but for large tables it generates too much network traffic. A more common technique is to download only those rows that have been inserted or updated on the consolidated database since the last download. If you put a TIMESTAMP DEFAULT TIMESTAMP column in your consolidated table, you can make use of the last_download parameter passed to the download_cursor script as the first "?" placeholder. This is called a "timestamp download":

```
<typical_download_cursor> ::= SELECT { <column_name> "," }
                                     <column_name>
                              FROM <consolidated_table_name>
                              WHERE <when_updated_column_name> "> ?"
<when_updated_column_name> ::= a TIMESTAMP column with DEFAULT TIMESTAMP
```

The following is an example of a simple table and the corresponding timestamp-based download_cursor script. Every time a row is inserted into t1, or updated, the last_updated column gets set to CURRENT TIMESTAMP by the special DEFAULT TIMESTAMP feature. This column only appears in the WHERE clause, not the SELECT list; it is not included on the remote database because it isn't needed there. The only reason last_updated exists on the consolidated database is to control the download_cursor script.

```
CREATE TABLE t1 (
    key_1        UNSIGNED BIGINT NOT NULL DEFAULT GLOBAL AUTOINCREMENT ( 1000000 ),
    key_2        INTEGER NOT NULL DEFAULT 0,
    non_key_1    VARCHAR ( 100 ) NOT NULL DEFAULT '',
    non_key_2    VARCHAR ( 100 ) NOT NULL DEFAULT '',
    last_updated TIMESTAMP NOT NULL DEFAULT TIMESTAMP,
    PRIMARY KEY ( key_1, key_2 ) );

CALL ml_add_table_script ( '1', 't1', 'download_cursor', '
SELECT key_1,
       key_2,
       non_key_1,
       non_key_2
  FROM t1
 WHERE last_updated > ?' );
```

Note: The initial value for the last_download parameter is 1900-01-01.

You can join data from different tables in a download_cursor script, you can select rows based on complex WHERE clauses, you can do just about anything that's required to build the desired result set to be applied to the named table in the remote database. The only rule you must follow is that the same number of columns must appear in the SELECT list as in the CREATE PUBLICATION for that table, with the same or compatible data types in the same order as they exist in the CREATE TABLE on the remote database. In many cases that's easy because the tables look the same on both databases and all the columns are being synchronized.

In some applications, however, the schema is different, and/or different sets of rows must be downloaded to different remote databases. MobiLink provides some assistance for these special cases by providing the MobiLink user name for the current synchronization session as the second parameter to the download_cursor script. You can partition the data for different remote databases by storing the MobiLink user name in a database column and referring to this parameter as the second "?" placeholder in the WHERE clause.

Tip: You can call a stored procedure from a download_cursor script, as long as that procedure returns a single result set that meets the download requirements of the table on the remote database.

Here is a short but intricate example that demonstrates some of the freedom you have when writing a download_cursor script:

```
CALL ml_add_table_script ( '1', 'tr4', 'download_cursor', '
SELECT tc3.key_3,
       tc2.non_key_1,
       tc3.non_key_1
  FROM tc1
  JOIN tc2 ON tc1.key_1 = tc2.key_1
  JOIN tc3 ON tc2.key_1 = tc3.key_1 AND tc2.key_2 = tc3.key_2
 WHERE tc3.last_update > ?                -- last_download
   AND tc1.db_id      = CAST ( ? AS BIGINT ) -- ML_username' );
```

Here's how the example works:

1. The script is for downloading data to a table named tr4 on the remote database. There is no table with that name on the consolidated database, but that doesn't matter as long as the script builds a result set that matches tr4.

2. The SELECT joins three tables on the consolidated database, tc1, tc2, and tc3, all of which have different names and schemas from the remote table tr4. MobiLink scripts have no access to the remote database; they can only refer to tables on the consolidated database. Here is what the three tables on the consolidated database look like:

```
CREATE TABLE tc1 ( -- on the consolidated database
    key_1        BIGINT NOT NULL,
    db_id        BIGINT NOT NULL,
    PRIMARY KEY ( key_1 ) );

CREATE TABLE tc2 ( -- on the consolidated database
    key_1        BIGINT NOT NULL,
    key_2        BIGINT NOT NULL,
    non_key_1    BIGINT NOT NULL,
    PRIMARY KEY ( key_1, key_2 ),
    FOREIGN KEY ( key_1 ) REFERENCES tc1 );

CREATE TABLE tc3 ( -- on the consolidated database
    key_1        BIGINT NOT NULL,
    key_2        BIGINT NOT NULL,
    key_3        BIGINT NOT NULL UNIQUE,
    non_key_1    BIGINT NOT NULL,
    last_update  TIMESTAMP NOT NULL DEFAULT TIMESTAMP,
    PRIMARY KEY ( key_1, key_2, key_3 ),
    FOREIGN KEY ( key_1, key_2 ) REFERENCES tc2 );
```

3. The SELECT list picks three columns from tc2 and tc3 in the order that matches the requirements of tr4. This is a critical point: The CREATE PUBLICATION names the columns in tr4 that are to be synchronized, the CREATE TABLE for tr4 specifies the column order, and the download_cursor SELECT must agree. Here is what the table and publication look like on the remote database:

```
CREATE TABLE tr4 ( -- on the remote database
    key_1        BIGINT NOT NULL,
    non_key_1    BIGINT NOT NULL,
    non_key_2    BIGINT NOT NULL,
    PRIMARY KEY ( key_1 ) );

CREATE PUBLICATION p1 (
    TABLE tr4 ( key_1,
                non_key_1,
                non_key_2 ) );
```

4. The FROM clause in the download_cursor script joins tr1, tr2, and tr3 according to their foreign key relationships. This is an example of denormalization: The download_cursor is flattening the multi-level hierarchy on the consolidated database into a single table on the remote database.

5. The WHERE clause implements the timestamp download technique as discussed earlier: tc3.last_update > ?.

6. The WHERE clause also uses a second "?" placeholder to limit the result set to rows that match on the MobiLink user name: tc1.db_id = CAST (?

AS BIGINT). The db_id column could be stored in every table that is downloaded, but it is often sufficient to store it in a parent table and use a join to find it.

7. Neither of the columns named in the WHERE clause are being downloaded. In fact, one of the tables (tc1) isn't named in the SELECT list at all.

8. The CAST function is used to make it clear that numeric MobiLink user names are used in this application, even though the data type for MobiLink user names is VARCHAR (128).

Tip: If you don't need the last download parameter, but you do want to refer to the MobiLink user name parameter in your download_cursor script, you can skip over the last download parameter with a dummy expression that always evaluates as TRUE; for example, '... WHERE ? IS NOT NULL AND db_id = ?'. This is necessary because the "?" placeholders are positional in nature; you can leave them both out or just code the first one, but if you need the second one you must code both of them.

Tip: If you want to send overlapping sets of rows to different remote databases, you can store the MobiLink user name in a separate many-to-many relationship table that relates MobiLink user names to the primary key values of the rows you wish to download. These relationships can be as flexible and complex as you require them to be, as long as you can code the appropriate SELECT in the download_cursor.

7.6.4.7 Downloading Deletes

It is particularly difficult to download deletions from the consolidated to the remote database with MobiLink. The problem arises from the fact that after a row is deleted from the consolidated database, there is no longer any record of its existence when the next synchronization session occurs. Unlike the upload process, the download is not built from the transaction log. It is up to your code to specify which rows must be deleted from which remote databases.

There are a number of solutions to this problem, the first one being the simplest: Don't delete anything. For some applications that's not as silly as it sounds; sometimes data must be archived for a long time for business reasons, and disk space is so cheap that "a long time" can be implemented as "indefinitely."

Another solution is to have the application get rid of old data on the remote database. With this technique only inserts and updates are downloaded, not deletes, and it's up to your application to decide when a row must be deleted. A problem with this technique is that deletes explicitly done on the remote database will be recorded in the transaction log and will be included in the upload stream built by dbmlsync. You may or may not want these deletes to be repeated on the consolidated; if not, you can simply leave out the upload_delete script for that table, but that doesn't eliminate the unwanted network traffic.

To get around this problem you can temporarily suppress the uploading of deletes with a special command: STOP SYNCHRONIZATION DELETE. This tells SQL Anywhere 9 that from now on, for the current connection, any deletes recorded in the transaction log will be completely ignored when dbmlsync runs.

The START SYNCHRONIZATION DELETE command can be used to return behavior to normal.

Here is an example showing how two-year-old rows can be deleted from the remote database without uploading the deletes to the consolidated database or worrying about how to download deletes:

```
STOP SYNCHRONIZATION DELETE;
DELETE t7
 WHERE t7.last_updated < DATEADD ( year, -2, CURRENT TIMESTAMP );
START SYNCHRONIZATION DELETE;
```

Note: The STOP SYNCHRONIZATION DELETE command can have unexpected effects. For example, if you insert a row on the remote database and then immediately delete it while STOP SYNCHRONIZATION DELETE is in effect, that row will be uploaded as an insert by the next synchronization even though it no longer exists on the remote database. The reason is that dbmlsync processes the transaction log, and it picks up the insert but ignores the delete because of the STOP SYNCHRONIZATION DELETE command.

The third way to delete rows from the remote database is to write a MobiLink download_delete_cursor script for each table to be processed. That script must produce a result set containing the primary key values for every row to be deleted from the remote database; this result set is included in the download stream and is processed by dbmlsync.

That raises a difficult question: How do you produce a result set containing the primary keys of rows that no longer exist? A popular approach is to insert a row in a separate "shadow table" every time a row is deleted. The shadow table contains the primary key columns from the original table, plus a "when deleted" timestamp column, but does not need any of the other non-key columns. This shadow table is then used in the download_delete_cursor to download the primary keys of rows that no longer exist.

```
<typical_download_delete_cursor> ::= SELECT { <primary_key_column_name> "," }
                                            <primary_key_column_name>
                                     FROM <shadow_table_name>
                                     WHERE <when_deleted_column_name> "> ?"
<shadow_table_name>         ::= [ <owner_name> "." ] <table_name>
<when_deleted_column_name> ::= a TIMESTAMP column with DEFAULT CURRENT TIMESTAMP
```

Here is an example of a typical download_delete_cursor script for the table t1; it selects rows that have been inserted in the DELETED_t1 shadow table since the previous synchronization session:

```
CALL ml_add_table_script ( '1', 't1', 'download_delete_cursor', '
SELECT key_1,
       key_2
 FROM DELETED_t1
WHERE deleted_on > ? -- last_download ' );
```

Here's what the shadow table looks like; the deleted_on column is included in the primary key to handle the situation of the same primary key being inserted and deleted more than once on the consolidated database:

```
CREATE TABLE DELETED_t1 (
   key_1       UNSIGNED BIGINT NOT NULL,
   key_2       INTEGER NOT NULL,
   deleted_on  TIMESTAMP NOT NULL DEFAULT CURRENT TIMESTAMP,
```

```
PRIMARY KEY ( key_1,
              key_2,
              deleted_on ) );
```

Here's how the shadow table is maintained by a trigger that inserts a row in DELETED_t1 every time a row is deleted from t1:

```
CREATE TRIGGER trd_ml_t1 BEFORE DELETE ON t1
  REFERENCING OLD AS old_t1
  FOR EACH ROW
BEGIN
  INSERT DELETED_t1
  VALUES ( old_t1.key_1, old_t1.key_2, DEFAULT );
END; -- trd_ml_t1
```

Rows in the shadow table can themselves be deleted when they have been downloaded to all remote databases. You can determine this by checking the MobiLink system table called ml_subscription; it records the last_download_time for every remote database, and any shadow table row that was inserted before the oldest last_download_time is no longer needed.

Here is an example of a begin_publication script that performs a cleanup of any old rows in the shadow table:

```
CALL ml_add_connection_script ( '1', 'begin_publication',
'CALL ml_begin_publication ( ?, ?, ?, ?, ? )' );

CREATE PROCEDURE ml_begin_publication (
  INOUT @generation_number  INTEGER,
  IN    @ml_username        VARCHAR ( 128 ),
  IN    @publication_name   VARCHAR ( 128 ),
  IN    @last_upload        TIMESTAMP,
  IN    @last_download      TIMESTAMP )
BEGIN
  DECLARE @oldest_download  TIMESTAMP;
  SELECT MIN ( ml_subscription.last_download_time )
    INTO @oldest_download
    FROM ( SELECT a.last_download_time
             FROM ml_subscription AS a
             WHERE a.publication_name = @publication_name
             AND a.progress = ( SELECT MAX ( b.progress )
                                  FROM ml_subscription AS b
                                  WHERE b.user_id = a.user_id
                                  AND b.publication_name = @publication_name ) )
        AS ml_subscription ( last_download_time );
  DELETE DELETED_t1
    WHERE DELETED_t1.deleted_on < @oldest_download;
END; -- ml_begin_publication
```

Note: The SELECT to get @oldest_download is complex because it must examine only the "active" rows in ml_subscription, not the older "inactive" rows that represent subscriptions that have been dropped and replaced. For more information about ml_subscription, see Section 7.7, "The MobiLink System Tables."

Note: The begin_synchronization event is the earliest point in time where ml_subscription.last_download_time is guaranteed to be the most up-to-date value regardless of the setting of SendDownloadACK. However, the begin_publication event is a better place for this code because it receives the publication name as a parameter and begin_synchronization does not.

The shadow table approach is popular because it is quite efficient. It also requires no changes to the way your applications work or to the way ad hoc queries are written; shadow tables are hidden from everyone. However, shadow tables are quite verbose: You must create one new table, one new trigger, and one new MobiLink script for every table to be handled this way.

Shadow tables can be avoided altogether by adding a "deleted flag" to every table, and turning that flag "on" instead of actually deleting the row. Here is what a download_delete_cursor might look like using this technique:

```
CALL ml_add_table_script ( '1', 't1', 'download_delete_cursor', '
SELECT key_1,
       key_2
  FROM t1
 WHERE deleted = 'Y'
   AND last_updated > ? -- last_download' );
```

The deleted flag approach avoids the separate shadow table and trigger, and uses similar logic in the begin_publication script to actually delete rows that are no longer needed for downloading. The big disadvantage is that application programs must be carefully written to skip over deleted rows. End users must also be careful when writing ad hoc reports and other queries. In many environments the deleted flag approach is an invitation to catastrophe.

A special variant of the download_delete_cursor is available if you want to delete all the table's rows on the remote database: Simply select a single row consisting of a NULL value for each primary key column.

```
<typical_download_delete_truncate>  ::= SELECT { NULL, }
                                               NULL
```

The following download_delete_cursor script will delete all the rows in t1; this technique is useful for data that is gathered on the remote database but is no longer required after it is uploaded.

```
CALL ml_add_table_script ( '1', 't1', 'download_delete_cursor', '
SELECT NULL,
       NULL' );
```

Tip: You can use a truncate variant of a download_delete_cursor to purge tables that only exist on the remote database. Just leave out all other scripts for this table except the download_delete_cursor, which selects NULL values. Rows will be uploaded but ignored, and nothing will be downloaded except the special NULL download_delete_cursor row.

7.6.4.8 Handling Download Errors

One type of download error is detected by the MobiLink server long before the data reaches the remote database. For example, if a downloaded value does not match the column definition on the remote database, because it's the wrong data type or NULL when it shouldn't be, the MobiLink server will roll back the download process on the consolidated database as follows:

```
E. 08/17 11:56:26. <1.5> [1]: Error: [-10038] A downloaded value for table t8
   (column #3) was either too big or invalid for the remote schema type
...
I. 08/17 12:35:51. <1.5> [1]: ROLLBACK Transaction: end_download
```

The MobiLink client will also roll back the download process on the remote database:

```
I. 08/17 12:35:59. ROLLBACK
E. 08/17 12:35:59. SQLCODE from MobiLink server is: -10038
E. 08/17 12:35:59. Message: A downloaded value for table t8 (column #3) was either
   too big or invalid for the remote schema type.  Table Name: t8
I. 08/17 12:35:59. Download stream processing failed
```

Another type of download error is not detected until the data reaches the remote database. For example, a column value that is valid on the consolidated database but violates a UNIQUE constraint on the remote database will be detected as an error by the MobiLink client as follows:

```
E. 08/21 09:42:35. SQL statement failed: (-196) Index 't8 UNIQUE (unique_1)' for
   table 't8' would not be unique
```

By default, this error causes the download to fail on the remote database and all the changes are rolled back. However, if the SendDownloadACK extended option is 'OFF' (the default) the MobiLink server is not told about this failure, and the download processing on the server side is committed. This raises two difficult questions affecting administration: First, how do you find out about the error in order to fix it? Second, how do you get the next synchronization to resend the download stream with the repair?

The first question is difficult if no one calls in to report a problem or you don't have access to the remote computer. However, it is possible to set up the remote database so it will automatically record download errors and upload that information on the next synchronization.

MobiLink offers a feature called "hook procedures" in the remote database, which are similar to the MobiLink events and scripts in the consolidated database. These stored procedures have special names associated with specific events that occur on the remote database during synchronization. Initially, none of these procedures exist, in the same way MobiLink scripts don't exist on the consolidated database until you write them. But like MobiLink scripts, if you code one of these procedures with its special name, it will be called when the corresponding event occurs.

One of these hook procedures is called sp_hook_dbmlsync_download_fatal_sql_error, and it gets called when a SQL statement fails during the download stage. Like the report_error event on the consolidated database, this hook procedure is executed on a separate connection. That means any changes made to the remote database in this procedure are committed even if the whole download stream is going to be rolled back.

When sp_hook_dbmlsync_download_fatal_sql_error is called, it receives a lot of information about the error, including the SQL error code, table name, MobiLink user name, and publication name. You can insert this information into your own table on the remote database, and if you put that table in the publication, a record of the error will be uploaded during the next synchronization.

Here is an example of an error table on the remote database; you will also need to define a corresponding table on the consolidated database and provide an upload_insert script:

```
CREATE TABLE dbmlsync_sql_error (
   ml_username  VARCHAR ( 128 ) NOT NULL,
   inserted_at  TIMESTAMP NOT NULL DEFAULT TIMESTAMP,
   unique_id    UNSIGNED BIGINT NOT NULL DEFAULT GLOBAL AUTOINCREMENT ( 1000000 ),
   publication_name        VARCHAR ( 128 ) NOT NULL,
```

```
table_name              VARCHAR ( 128 ) NOT NULL,
sql_error_code          VARCHAR ( 10 ) NOT NULL,
script_version          VARCHAR ( 128 ) NOT NULL,
PRIMARY KEY ( ml_username, inserted_at, unique_id ) );
```

Each hook procedure receives its own set of parameters, but not in the usual way. Instead, a strange little temporary table called #hook_dict is created and filled by the MobiLink client just before calling the hook procedure. Each parameter is represented by a separate row in #hook_dict. Each row contains two string columns, "name" and "value", with "value" containing the actual parameter value and "name" containing the parameter name. The parameter names are all documented in the SQL Anywhere 9 Help file, and you can retrieve the corresponding values via singleton SELECT statements.

For example, the expression (SELECT value FROM #hook_dict WHERE name = 'SQL error code') will return a single string value containing an error code like '-196'. If five parameters are passed to a particular hook procedure, and you want to get all five values, you have to code five separate SELECTs.

Note: There is a related hook procedure, sp_hook_dbmlsync_download_sql_ error, which allows you to fix errors and continue processing. This is not recommended because an error affecting one row may cause dbmlsync to skip all the rows for that table. The default action, when you don't write an sp_hook_ dbmlsync_download_sql_error procedure at all, is to call sp_hook_dbmlsync_ download_fatal_sql_error if it exists and then roll back the download. And that's the recommended approach; don't bother with sp_hook_dbmlsync_down- load_sql_error.

Here is what a download fatal error hook procedure looks like; it is similar to the ml_report_error procedure described in Section 7.6.4.5, "Handling Upload Errors":

```
CREATE PROCEDURE sp_hook_dbmlsync_download_fatal_sql_error()
BEGIN
   INSERT dbmlsync_sql_error VALUES (
      ( SELECT value FROM #hook_dict WHERE name = 'MobiLink user' ),
      DEFAULT,
      DEFAULT,
      ( SELECT value FROM #hook_dict WHERE name = 'publication_0' ),
      ( SELECT value FROM #hook_dict WHERE name = 'table name' ),
      ( SELECT value FROM #hook_dict WHERE name = 'SQL error code' ),
      ( SELECT value FROM #hook_dict WHERE name = 'script version' ) );
END; -- sp_hook_dbmlsync_download_fatal_sql_error
```

Tip: Be careful coding #hook_dict parameter names. Some of them have underscores separating words, like 'publication_0', and some of them have spaces like 'MobiLink user'. Also note that the first (or only) publication is num- bered with a zero instead of one. If you make a mistake coding a parameter name, you won't get an error; you'll just get a NULL value because no matching row exists in #hook_dict.

Now you can determine when a download has failed on a remote database by looking at the dbmlsync_sql_error table on the consolidated database. In the example above, where a column value violated a UNIQUE constraint on the remote database, one way to fix the problem is to change the value on the con- solidated database. That brings up the second question: How do you make sure the next download contains all the other rows that were rolled back earlier, plus the repaired row?

With download_cursor scripts that use the timestamp download technique, the answer is easy: Just run the synchronization again. The last_download parameter will be the same as it was in the previous synchronization, so the same rows will be selected for the download stream. The last_download parameter comes from the MobiLink client, and it doesn't get changed by a failed download.

More complex download techniques might have a problem, however, if the previous download was committed on the consolidated database but rolled back on the remote database. For example, different remote databases may contain different partitions or subsets of rows from the consolidated database, and the previous download may have been an attempt to change partitions by deleting the old subset and inserting the new subset. If the download failed on the remote but succeeded on the consolidated, the consolidated database may contain incorrect information that the partition has been changed when it fact it has not. When the next synchronization is done, your MobiLink scripts may have to detect the earlier failure and take special action to ensure the same partition change is sent in the next download stream.

Tip: Your MobiLink scripts on the consolidated database can determine if the previous download failed on the remote database even if SendDownloadACK is 'OFF', and even if you don't use a hook procedure to record the error. Simply compare the @last_upload and @last_download parameters in the begin_publication script. If @last_upload is larger than @last_download, it means the previous download failed on the remote database even though the server might have thought everything was okay. This allows you to leave SendDownloadACK set to 'OFF' to reduce the load on the MobiLink server and on the consolidated database, which is especially helpful if the remote databases are running on slower computers. For more information and a detailed example, see Section 7.7, "The MobiLink System Tables."

Note: The technique described in the previous tip only works for two-way synchronizations and does not apply when the UploadOnly extended option is in effect. This whole chapter assumes that all synchronization sessions are two-way; upload-only and download-only synchronizations are not discussed.

A third type of download error is detected by the MobiLink client and silently handled by default. Referential integrity violations caused by the download stream are avoided by automatically deleting all the rows in the child or dependent tables that are causing the violations. This is done regardless of how the foreign keys are defined on the remote database, and regardless of whether the offending rows are being downloaded or already exist on the remote database.

For example, if the tables tparent and tchild have a parent-child relationship, and a download_delete_cursor sends a delete for a row in tparent, the MobiLink client will automatically delete all the corresponding rows in tchild. A message is produced in the MobiLink client diagnostic log, but it isn't treated as an error; the download is committed:

```
I. 08/21 17:18:38. Resolving referential integrity violations on table tchild,
   role tparent
```

```
I. 08/21 17:18:38. delete from "DBA"."tchild" from "DBA"."tchild" ft where not
   exists ( select * from "DBA"."tparent" pt where  ( ft."key_1" = pt."key_1"
   or ft."key_1" is NULL ) )
I. 08/21 17:18:38. 1 rows deleted.
I. 08/21 17:18:38. COMMIT
```

In other words, the foreign key relationship is handled as if ON DELETE CASCADE was specified even if you explicitly specify ON DELETE RESTRICT. The same thing happens if you download a child row that has no corresponding parent row. The MobiLink client will first insert the new child row, then delete it using the same kind of logic shown in the message above.

If this behavior comes as a shock, you can change it. Simply add the following one-line hook procedure to the remote database; the MobiLink client will see that this procedure exists and will call it whenever it detects a referential integrity error:

```
CREATE PROCEDURE sp_hook_dbmlsync_download_ri_violation()
BEGIN
   RAISERROR 19999;
END;
```

When this particular sp_hook_dbmlsync_download_ri_violation procedure is called, the RAISERROR statement will force the MobiLink client to roll back the download stream as follows:

```
I. 08/22 10:21:22. execute "DBA".sp_hook_dbmlsync_download_ri_violation
E. 08/22 10:21:22. SQL statement failed: (-19999) RAISERROR executed:
E. 08/22 10:21:22. Error while executing hook procedure
   sp_hook_dbmlsync_download_ri_violation.
I. 08/22 10:21:22. ROLLBACK
I. 08/22 10:21:22. Download stream processing failed
I. 08/22 10:21:22. Sending a failure status to the MobiLink server.
```

If you want to save a record of diagnostic information about referential integrity violations in the download stream, you can write another hook procedure called sp_hook_dbmlsync_download_log_ri_violation. This procedure also gets executed when the MobiLink client detects a violation, but it runs on a separate connection so anything it inserts into the database will be automatically committed even if the rest of the download is going to be rolled back.

Here is an example of a remote database table for recording referential integrity violations and the corresponding sp_hook_dbmlsync_download_log_ri_violation procedure to fill it:

```
CREATE TABLE dbmlsync_ri_violation (
   ml_username  VARCHAR ( 128 ) NOT NULL,
   inserted_at  TIMESTAMP NOT NULL DEFAULT TIMESTAMP,
   unique_id    UNSIGNED BIGINT NOT NULL DEFAULT GLOBAL AUTOINCREMENT ( 1000000 ),
   publication_name      VARCHAR ( 128 ) NOT NULL,
   foreign_key_table_name VARCHAR ( 128 ) NOT NULL,
   primary_key_table_name VARCHAR ( 128 ) NOT NULL,
   role_name             VARCHAR ( 128 ) NOT NULL,
   script_version        VARCHAR ( 128 ) NOT NULL,
   PRIMARY KEY ( ml_username, inserted_at, unique_id ) );

CREATE PROCEDURE sp_hook_dbmlsync_download_log_ri_violation()
BEGIN
   INSERT dbmlsync_ri_violation VALUES (
      ( SELECT value FROM #hook_dict WHERE name = 'MobiLink user' ),
      DEFAULT,
```

```
    DEFAULT,
    ( SELECT value FROM #hook_dict WHERE name = 'publication_0' ),
    ( SELECT value FROM #hook_dict WHERE name = 'Foreign key table' ),
    ( SELECT value FROM #hook_dict WHERE name = 'Primary key table' ),
    ( SELECT value FROM #hook_dict WHERE name = 'Role name' ),
    ( SELECT value FROM #hook_dict WHERE name = 'script version' ) );
END; -- sp_hook_dbmlsync_download_log_ri_violation
```

A fourth type of download error also involves a referential integrity violation, but this time it is not silently handled. If a referential integrity error is detected that involves a table that is not being synchronized, it is diagnosed as a fatal error and sp_hook_dbmlsync_download_fatal_sql_error is called. For example, if a parent table is included in the publication but the child table is not, and an attempt is made to download a delete for a parent row that has a corresponding child row, that attempt will fail; dbmlsync does not silently delete the child row because it is not part of the synchronization process.

Because this type of error is not detected until the end of the download stream is reached and the final commit is attempted, the table name passed to sp_hook_dbmlsync_download_fatal_sql_error will be empty. That's the bad news — your hook procedures won't help you pinpoint the problem. The good news is, at least you find out there is a problem even if you don't write any hook procedures.

7.7 The MobiLink System Tables

The MobiLink client and server components maintain information about the state of synchronization in system tables on both the remote and consolidated database. The most important of these tables are SYSSYNC on the remote database and ml_subscription on the consolidated database. Here's what they look like:

```
CREATE TABLE SYS.SYSSYNC (
    sync_id            UNSIGNED INT NOT NULL,
    type               CHAR ( 1 ) NOT NULL,
    publication_id     UNSIGNED INT NULL,
    progress           NUMERIC ( 20 ) NULL,
    site_name          CHAR ( 128 ) NULL,
    "option"           LONG VARCHAR NULL,
    server_connect     LONG VARCHAR NULL,
    server_conn_type   LONG VARCHAR NULL,
    last_download_time TIMESTAMP NULL,
    last_upload_time   TIMESTAMP NOT NULL DEFAULT 'jan-1-1900',
    created            NUMERIC ( 20 ) NULL,
    log_sent           NUMERIC ( 20 ) NULL,
    generation_number  INTEGER NOT NULL DEFAULT 0,
    extended_state     VARCHAR ( 1024 ) NOT NULL DEFAULT '',
    PRIMARY KEY ( sync_id ) );

CREATE TABLE dbo.ml_subscription (
    user_id            INTEGER NOT NULL,
    subscription_id    VARCHAR ( 128 ) NOT NULL,
    progress           NUMERIC ( 20 ) NOT NULL DEFAULT 0,
    publication_name   VARCHAR ( 128 ) NOT NULL DEFAULT '',
    last_upload_time   TIMESTAMP NOT NULL DEFAULT '1900/01/01 00:00:00',
    last_download_time TIMESTAMP NOT NULL DEFAULT '1900/01/01 00:00:00',
    PRIMARY KEY ( user_id,
                  subscription_id ) );
```

As discussed earlier in Section 7.4.5, "SYSSYNC and Publication Defaults," the SYSSYNC table contains one special row for each subscription. That row can be identified by a 'D' in the type column and non-null values in publication_id and site_name. The publication_id column points to the row in SYSPUBLICATION containing the corresponding publication name, and site_name contains a MobiLink user name that is unique to this remote database. In most cases there is only one site_name value for each remote database, and often there is only one publication, which means there is often only one "subscription row" in SYSSYNC. The sync_id column is an artificial primary key, and for the subscription row it should be thought of as a "subscription id."

On the consolidated database there is a matching row in the ml_subscription table. The user_id column points to a row in the ml_user table containing the corresponding MobiLink user name for that remote database, and that name matches SYSSYNC.site_name. The ml_subscription.subscription_id column contains the remote database SYSSYNC.sync_id value after conversion to string. In many cases there is exactly one row in ml_subscription for each remote database; if a remote database has two different subscriptions for different sets of tables, there will be two rows in ml_subscription.

The subscription row in SYSSYNC also holds important information about the state of synchronization between the consolidated and remote databases. The progress column contains the byte offset in the remote database transaction log file that was reached during the last successful upload. This value is also uploaded and stored in the ml_subscription table on the consolidated database to facilitate double-checking before the next synchronization starts. If the values match, the next synchronization will start scanning the remote transaction log at that point.

If the values don't match, there may or may not be a problem. The default action is to use the log offset value stored in the ml_subscription.progress column on the consolidated database. If that offset can't be found in the remote database transaction log, or it is not a valid offset, then there really is a problem. You might be able to use the dbmlsync -ra or -rb options to solve it, you might be able to modify the ml_subscription value to match, you might solve the problem by deleting the row in ml_subscription, or you might have to drop and recreate the subscription on the remote database to start synchronization afresh.

The SYSSYNC.last_download_time column contains the date and time of the previous successful download. This date and time is relative to the consolidated database server, not the remote server. It is calculated immediately after the previous upload stream was committed, before the download stream processing began, so it is earlier than any consolidated database changes that might have been made after the previous download began. As such, it is very useful for determining which rows have changed since the last download, and it is made available as a parameter to MobiLink scripts for this purpose. The value is stored here, in the SYSSYNC table on the remote database, as well as in the ml_subscription table on the consolidated database.

SYSSYNC also contains the last_upload_time column holding the date and time of the previous successful upload. This value is relative to the date and time on the consolidated database server, and it is also stored in the ml_subscription table. If the last download worked, last_upload_time will be less than last_download_time because the upload stream is processed before the download. If the previous upload worked but the download failed, last_upload_time will be greater than last_download_time.

Here is a query you can run on the remote database to show these columns:

```
SELECT SYSSYNC.site_name,
       SYSSYNC.sync_id,
       SYSSYNC.progress,
       SYSPUBLICATION.publication_name,
       SYSSYNC.last_upload_time,
       SYSSYNC.last_download_time
  FROM SYSPUBLICATION
  JOIN SYSSYNC
    ON SYSPUBLICATION.publication_id = SYSSYNC.publication_id
 WHERE SYSSYNC.type = 'D'
   AND SYSSYNC.publication_id IS NOT NULL
   AND SYSSYNC.site_name IS NOT NULL;
```

Here is the corresponding query for the consolidated database; if everything is working these two queries should show the same values for the same subscriptions:

```
SELECT ml_user.name,
       ml_subscription.subscription_id,
       ml_subscription.progress,
       ml_subscription.publication_name,
       ml_subscription.last_upload_time,
       ml_subscription.last_download_time
  FROM ml_user
  JOIN ( SELECT a.user_id,
                a.subscription_id,
                a.progress,
                a.publication_name,
                a.last_upload_time,
                a.last_download_time
           FROM ml_subscription AS a
          WHERE a.progress = ( SELECT MAX ( b.progress )
                                 FROM ml_subscription AS b
                                WHERE b.user_id = a.user_id
                                  AND b.publication_name = a.publication_name ) )
         AS ml_subscription
    ON ml_user.user_id = ml_subscription.user_id;
```

The second query is complex because the ml_subscription table is not automatically purged of old data when a subscription is dropped and recreated on a remote database. Instead, a new row with the same user_id and publication_name but a different subscription_id is inserted into ml_subscription on the next synchronization. This new row is the "active" row and it is the only row that has meaningful data. The other rows are "inactive" and no longer useful. The active rows have the largest value in the progress column for each combination of user_id and publication_name.

On the consolidated database, the ml_subscription.last_upload_time and last_download_time columns are filled in at different times. The last_upload_time column is updated as soon as the upload stream is committed, and you can query the new value in the prepare_for_download and later MobiLink scripts on the same synchronization, as well as the scripts on the next synchronization up to end_upload.

If the SendDownloadACK extended option is 'OFF' (the default), the last_download_time column is not updated until the next synchronization starts; it is then available to be queried in all the MobiLink scripts. If SendDownloadACK is 'ON', the last_download_time column is updated as soon as the download acknowledgement is received and you can query the new value in the end_publication script on the same synchronization, as well as in the scripts on the next synchronization up to end_download.

You can compare ml_subscription.last_upload_time and last_download_time to determine if the previous upload worked but the download failed. However, you must make this comparison during one of the MobiLink upload scripts, no later than end_upload. After that the last_upload_time has its new value and a comparison would not be valid.

The best place to compare ml_subscription.last_upload_time and last_download_time is in the begin_publication script. In fact, you don't even need to query the database because the begin_publication script provides the values for the current subscription as parameters.

Following is an example of a begin_publication script that determines if the previous download failed or not, regardless of the setting of SendDownloadACK. It also handles the case where there has been no synchronization yet.

```
CALL ml_add_connection_script ( '1', 'begin_publication',
CALL ml_add_connection_script ( '1', 'begin_publication',
'CALL ml_begin_publication ( ?, ?, ?, ?, ? )' );

CREATE PROCEDURE ml_begin_publication (
  INOUT @generation_number  INTEGER,
  IN    @ml_username        VARCHAR ( 128 ),
  IN    @publication_name   VARCHAR ( 128 ),
  IN    @last_upload        TIMESTAMP,
  IN    @last_download      TIMESTAMP )
BEGIN
  IF @last_upload > '1900-01-01 00:00:00' THEN
    IF @last_upload > @last_download THEN
      MESSAGE STRING (
        'Previous download FAILED for subscription to publication "',
        @publication_name,
        '" by MobiLink User "',
        @ml_username,
        '".' ) TO CONSOLE;
    ELSE
      MESSAGE STRING (
        'Previous download SUCCEEDED for subscription to publication "',
        @publication_name,
        '" by MobiLink user "',
        @ml_username,
        '".' ) TO CONSOLE;
    END IF
  ELSE
    MESSAGE STRING (
      'This is the FIRST SYNCHRONIZATION for subscription to publication "',
      @publication_name,
      '" by MobiLink user "',
      @ml_username,
      '".' ) TO CONSOLE;
  END IF;
END;
```

Note: The begin_publication script is the same place where the purging of shadow table rows takes place in the example shown in Section 7.6.4.7, "Downloading Deletes." That example required a SELECT from ml_subscription, however, because the oldest download for all remote databases had to be determined, not just for the current remote database.

7.8 MobiLink Monitor

The MobiLink Monitor is an administration tool that shows what's happening on a running MobiLink server. It doesn't have access to the MobiLink clients running on the remote databases but it does show you all about the consolidated database side of synchronization sessions in both graphic and text modes.

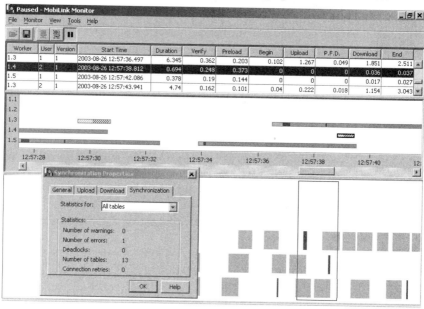

Figure 7-2. MobiLink Monitor

The MobiLink Monitor display consists of three panes. The details pane at the top is a scrolling list of all the synchronization sessions that have started since the monitor connected to the MobiLink server. The chart pane in the middle shows those same sessions in a vivid color-coded display that slides from left to right as time passes. The overview pane at the bottom shows a much larger view of all the sessions without the detail of the other two panes.

Here's a description of what you see in Figure 7-2:

■ The top pane includes the MobiLink user name ("User") for each session, the exact starting time ("Start Time"), and the elapsed time in seconds for the whole session ("Duration"). Columns containing zeroes usually indicate that the corresponding MobiLink script is not defined or there was some kind of problem.

- The middle pane shows each synchronization as a colored bar with different colors used to represent different stages in the upload and download processes. By default, shades of green are used for the upload stage and shades of red are used for the download.

- The middle pane shows about 10 seconds worth of sessions; you can change the range with the View > Go To menu option.

- The bottom pane shows the full time period since the monitor started gathering statistics. The box outline in the bottom pane corresponds to the time period shown in the middle pane. This box shrinks in size as time goes on because the bottom pane represents a longer time period whereas the middle pane represents a fixed amount of time.

- Failed sessions show up with cross-hatching in the middle pane and bright red in the bottom pane.

- Successful sessions are shown with solid colors in the chart pane and dull gray in the bottom pane.

- You can click on the pause button to freeze the middle and bottom panes even while the monitor is still gathering statistics. This lets you scroll left and right to look for problems and investigate individual sessions. New sessions continue to show up in the top pane, and when you turn off pausing the middle and bottom panes immediately return to live display.

- The middle and bottom panes have one line for each "worker thread" executing on the MobiLink server. Each worker thread handles one synchronization session at a time. Overlapping sessions from different remote databases will be assigned to different worker threads so they can be processed in parallel to improve throughput.

- You can double-click on a colored bar to see more information about an individual session. The colored bar will then be displayed with a heavy outline to show that it has been selected. The corresponding line in the top pane will also be selected, and a pop-up Synchronization Properties window will appear, as shown in Figure 7-2.

- The various tabs in the Synchronization Properties window show row counts, error counts, and other detailed information about the selected session.

Figure 7-2 shows that a failed synchronization on worker thread 1.4 has been selected. The Synchronization Properties window shows that one error was detected. The top pane shows it is a session for MobiLink user name "2" that began at 12:57:38. You can use these three pieces of information (worker thread, MobiLink user name, and time) to find the explanation in the MobiLink server diagnostic text file:

```
I. 08/26 12:57:39. <thread 1.4>: ASA synchronization request from: 2 (version: 1)
E. 08/26 12:57:39. <1.4> [2]: Error: [-10053] The user name '2' is already
   synchronizing.  Concurrent synchronizations using the same user name are
   not allowed
...
I. 08/26 12:57:39. <1.4> [2]: ROLLBACK Transaction: begin_synchronization
```

In this case two overlapping synchronization sessions were started from the same remote database, and that isn't permitted. Here's what the error looked like from the MobiLink client's point of view:

```
I. 08/26 12:57:39. Waiting for MobiLink to apply upload
I. 08/26 12:57:39. Download stream: received 10 bytes from MobiLink Server.
E. 08/26 12:57:39. The MobiLink user 2 was already being synchronized. Concurrent
   synchronizations for the same user are not allowed.
...
E. 08/26 12:57:40. Download aborted
```

7.9 Chapter Summary

This chapter described how the MobiLink synchronization client and server programs work to distribute data among a single consolidated database and a large number of remote databases. Also discussed were the remote database setup involving publications and subscriptions as well as the many options available to control MobiLink client execution. MobiLink server scripts for processing the upload stream, generating the download stream, and handling conflicts were explained.

Some techniques for handling errors during the upload and download stages were described, as well as the details of MobiLink system tables, which record the state of synchronization. The MobiLink Monitor was also presented.

The next chapter moves to the topic of packaging SQL code into modules stored in the database itself: procedures, functions, triggers, and events.

Chapter 8

Packaging

8.1 Introduction

This chapter describes how to gather SQL statements into BEGIN blocks that include local declarations and exception handling logic. These BEGIN blocks can then be executed directly or stored in the database as modules for later execution. Stored SQL modules take the form of procedures that are called, functions that are referenced in expressions, and triggers that are automatically fired by INSERT, UPDATE, and DELETE operations.

SQL Anywhere also supports events that execute asynchronously on separate connections; events can be fired automatically according to a schedule, when certain conditions occur, or explicitly by TRIGGER EVENT statements.

Also described in this chapter are the multi-statement control structures IF, CASE, and WHILE for implementing complex logic inside BEGIN blocks. The EXECUTE IMMEDIATE statement lets you create and execute SQL statements on the fly, and the CREATE VARIABLE statement lets you pass data among all the modules executing on a connection.

8.2 BEGIN Block

The BEGIN block is used to encapsulate SQL statements together with local declarations and exception handling logic. BEGIN blocks are used to construct SQL modules stored in the database (procedures, functions, triggers, and events) as well as batches of statements for direct execution from a client application like ISQL.

The BEGIN block comes in two formats — with and without a label that may be used as a target for a LEAVE statement:

```
<begin_block>        ::= BEGIN [ [ NOT ] ATOMIC ]
                           [ <declaration_list> ]
                           [ <statement_list> ]
                           [ <exception_handler> ]
                         END
                     | <begin_label> ":"
                         BEGIN [ [ NOT ] ATOMIC ]
                           [ <declaration_list> ]
                           [ <statement_list> ]
                           [ <exception_handler> ]
                         END [ <begin_label> ]
<begin_label>        ::= <identifier> that may be used in a <leave_statement>
<identifier>         ::= see <identifier> in Chapter 1, "Creating"
<leave_statement>    ::= LEAVE <begin_label>
                     | LEAVE <for_label>
```

```
              | LEAVE <while_label>
<for_label>        ::= see <for_label> in Chapter 6, "Fetching"
```

The ATOMIC and NOT ATOMIC keywords determine whether the default mode of execution for the BEGIN block will be atomic or non-atomic. An atomic operation is one that executes completely or not at all; if a statement fails inside an atomic BEGIN block, causing the block to terminate abnormally, all database changes made by code inside the BEGIN block will be undone. COMMIT and ROLLBACK statements are not allowed inside an atomic BEGIN block because they would contradict the atomic nature of the block as a whole.

In a non-atomic block of code each statement is treated as its own execution unit, and a failure of one of the statements may not undo database changes made by other statements.

Note: The ROLLBACK TO SAVEPOINT statement is allowed within an atomic operation, with limitations; for more information see Section 9.4, "Savepoints and Subtransactions."

NOT ATOMIC is the default. However, the actual mode of execution is determined at execution time; if a BEGIN block is executed as part of a larger atomic operation, the inner BEGIN block is subject to the restrictions of an atomic operation described above. This is true even if the NOT ATOMIC keywords are explicitly specified on the inner BEGIN block. All triggers fall into this category; all INSERT, UPDATE, and DELETE statements are atomic operations so the triggers they fire are included in those atomic operations. Another example is a BEGIN block in a procedure that is called from an outer procedure using the ATOMIC keyword; it doesn't matter how the inner BEGIN block is coded, it executes as part of an atomic operation.

DECLARE statements can be placed at the front of a BEGIN block, before any executable statements, to create local variables, cursors, named exception conditions, and local temporary tables. Cursor DECLARE statements are described in Chapter 6, "Fetching," and temporary tables are described in Section 1.15.2, "Local Temporary Tables." Exception conditions are explained in the next section in this chapter.

```
<declaration_list>              ::= <declaration> ";" { <declaration> ";" }
<declaration>                   ::= <declare_local_variable>
                                  | <declare_cursor>
                                  | <declare_exception_name>
                                  | <declare_local_temporary_table>
<declare_local_variable>        ::= DECLARE <local_variable_name> <data_type>
<local_variable_name>           ::= <identifier>
<data_type>                     ::= see <data_type> in Chapter 1, "Creating"
<declare_cursor>                ::= see <declare_cursor> in Chapter 6, "Fetching"
<declare_local_temporary_table> ::= see <declare_local_temporary_table> in
                                        Chapter 1, "Creating"
```

A local variable defined at the front of a BEGIN block is created when the block is entered and destroyed when the block terminates. The scope of a local variable includes all the executable statements in the same BEGIN block, as well as all statements in any nested BEGIN blocks.

There is no nesting of scope. The same variable name cannot be used for a local variable declared inside a nested BEGIN block, nor can it appear as the name of an implicit local variable created by a cursor FOR loop. (For more information about the cursor FOR loop, see Section 6.3, "Cursor FOR Loop.") However, a local variable with the same name as a column may be hidden or invisible within a SQL statement that refers to the table containing that column. Here is an example that demonstrates what can happen when a variable and column share the same name "scope":

```
CREATE TABLE t1 (
    key_1    INTEGER NOT NULL,
    scope    VARCHAR ( 1 ) NOT NULL,
    PRIMARY KEY ( key_1 ) );

INSERT t1 VALUES ( 1, 'B' );

BEGIN
    DECLARE scope VARCHAR ( 1 );
    SET scope = 'A';
    MESSAGE STRING ( 'scope #1: ', scope ) TO CONSOLE;
    MESSAGE STRING ( 'scope #2: ',
        ( SELECT scope FROM t1 WHERE key_1 = 1 ) ) TO CONSOLE;
    MESSAGE STRING ( 'scope #3: ', scope ) TO CONSOLE;
END;
```

The first and third MESSAGE statements display the value 'A', whereas the second MESSAGE statement displays 'B' because the SELECT statement refers to the column t1.scope rather than the variable scope.

Tip: Use the character @ at the front of local variable names so they won't be confused with column names; e.g., DECLARE @scope VARCHAR (1).

The BEGIN block statement list is optional, as are the declaration list and the exception handler. If present, the statement list consists of one or more executable statements with multiple statements separated by semicolons.

```
<statement_list>        ::= <executable_statement>
                         | <statement_list> ";" <executable_statement>
                         | <statement_list> ";"
<executable_statement> ::= anything except DECLARE and EXCEPTION
```

BEGIN blocks are most often used to create procedures, triggers, and other modules stored inside the database, but they can also be used by application programs. Here is an example of a PowerBuilder script that sends a BEGIN block to the database server for execution:

```
string ls_sql

ls_sql &
    = "BEGIN " &
    + "   DECLARE @x VARCHAR ( 100 ); " &
    + "   SET @x = 'Hello, World'; " &
    + "   MESSAGE STRING ( @x ) TO CONSOLE; " &
    + "END;"

EXECUTE IMMEDIATE :ls_sql USING SQLCA;
```

8.3 Exception Handler

Each BEGIN block may contain an exception handler placed at the end of the block. An exception handler consists of the keyword EXCEPTION followed by one or more WHEN clauses. Each WHEN keyword is followed by the names of one or more exception conditions, the keyword THEN, and one or more executable statements. When one of those named exceptions occurs anywhere in the executable statements ahead of the exception handler, the flow of control transfers immediately to the statements in the corresponding WHEN clause, and after they finish executing the BEGIN block is terminated.

Each exception condition named in a WHEN clause corresponds to a single five-character value of SQLSTATE, and that name must be defined at the front of the BEGIN block with a special form of the DECLARE statement. Here is the syntax for that DECLARE statement, and for the exception handler:

```
<declare_exception_name>  ::= DECLARE <exception_name>
                                  EXCEPTION FOR SQLSTATE <sqlstate_error_value>
<exception_name>          ::= <identifier> to use in an <exception_handler>
<sqlstate_error_value>    ::= string literal containing SQLSTATE error value
<exception_handler>       ::= EXCEPTION <when_exception_list>
<when_exception_list>     ::= <when_exception> { <when_exception> }
<when_exception>          ::= WHEN <exception_name_list>
                                  THEN <statement_list>
                            | WHEN OTHERS
                                  THEN <statement_list>
<exception_name_list>     ::= <exception_name> { "," <exception_name> }
```

Here is a very simple example that displays "Data conversion error!" when you run it:

```
BEGIN
DECLARE @date            DATE;
DECLARE @sqlstate_53018 EXCEPTION FOR SQLSTATE '53018';
SET @date = 'xxx';
EXCEPTION
   WHEN @sqlstate_53018 THEN
      MESSAGE STRING ( 'Data conversion error!' ) TO CLIENT;
END;
```

The keyword OTHERS may be used instead of a list of named exception conditions to create a WHEN clause that corresponds to any exception that isn't named in an earlier WHEN clause. There should only be one WHEN OTHERS clause, and it should be the last WHEN clause, because any WHEN clause appearing after the first WHEN OTHERS will never be executed.

Since there are over 500 different kinds of exceptions, a WHEN OTHERS clause is a real time-saver. Here is an example that traps a division-by-zero exception and displays "SQLSTATE = 22012":

```
BEGIN
DECLARE @number          INTEGER;
DECLARE @date            DATE;
DECLARE @sqlstate_53018 EXCEPTION FOR SQLSTATE '53018';
SET @number = 1 / 0;
SET @date = 'xxx';
EXCEPTION
   WHEN @sqlstate_53018 THEN
      MESSAGE STRING ( 'Data conversion error!' ) TO CLIENT;
```

```
WHEN OTHERS THEN
    MESSAGE STRING ( 'SQLSTATE = ', SQLSTATE ) TO CLIENT;
END;
```

If you just want to trap and diagnose all exceptions, without special logic for any particular exception condition, a single WHEN OTHERS clause is all you need. The ERRORMSG function can be called in the WHEN OTHERS clause to get the exact error message that would have been displayed if there was no exception handler at all. Here is an example that displays "Cannot convert xxx to a timestamp":

```
BEGIN
DECLARE @date DATE;
SET @date = 'xxx';
EXCEPTION
    WHEN OTHERS THEN
        MESSAGE ERRORMSG() TO CLIENT;
END;
```

It is not easy to display both the SQLSTATE and ERRORMSG() values inside a WHEN clause because a reference to one may set the other to the default value; i.e., a reference to SQLSTATE may set ERRORMSG() to the empty string, and a reference to ERRORMSG() may set SQLSTATE to '00000'. Also, a BEGIN block inside the WHEN clause will set both to their default values.

The solution requires two local variables in the outer BEGIN block, plus a single statement that captures both the SQLSTATE and ERRORMSG() values as soon as the WHEN clause is executed. A simple SELECT statement with an INTO clause may be used for this purpose. Here is a BEGIN block showing how it's done:

```
BEGIN
DECLARE @date      DATE;
DECLARE @sqlstate  VARCHAR ( 5 );
DECLARE @errormsg  VARCHAR ( 32767 );
SET @date = 'xxx';
EXCEPTION
    WHEN OTHERS THEN
        SELECT SQLSTATE, ERRORMSG() INTO @sqlstate, @errormsg;
        MESSAGE STRING ( 'SQLSTATE = ', @sqlstate ) TO CLIENT;
        MESSAGE STRING ( 'ERRORMSG() = ', @errormsg ) TO CLIENT;
END;
```

When that BEGIN block is executed it displays the following information about the exception:

```
SQLSTATE = 53018
ERRORMSG() = Cannot convert xxx to a timestamp
```

Not all of the 576 non-zero SQLSTATE values will be detected by an exception handler; Table 8-1 shows 32 values that are treated as warnings and cannot be handled by a WHEN clause even if they are explicitly named and defined in a DECLARE. If you want to trap these warnings you have to add code that explicitly checks for these SQLSTATE values immediately after the executable statements that might raise them. An example of that kind of check is shown in Section 6.2.4, "OPEN and CLOSE Cursor."

Table 8-1. Warning conditions by SQLSTATE

SQLSTATE	SQLCODE	Warning Message
01000	200	Warning
01003	109	Null value eliminated in aggregate function
01004	101	Value truncated
01S02	121	Cursor option values changed
01W01	124	Invalid data conversion: NULL was inserted for column '%1' on line %2
01W02	102	Using temporary table
01W03	103	Invalid data conversion
01W04	104	Row has been updated since last time read
01W05	105	Procedure has completed
01W06	106	Value for column '%1' in table '%2' has changed
01W07	107	Language extension detected in syntax
01W08	111	Statement cannot be executed
01W09	112	More information required
01W10	110	Transaction log backup page only partially full
01W11	113	Database option '%1' for user '%2' has an invalid setting
01W12	114	Character set translation to '%1' cannot be performed; '%2' is used instead
01W13	115	Database server cannot convert data from/to character set '%1'; conversion may not be correct
01W14	116	Language '%1' is not supported, '%2' will be used
01W15	117	Unsupported character set '%1' and unsupported language '%2'; language used is '%3' instead
01W16	118	Illegal user selectivity estimate specified
01W17	120	'%1' is an unknown option
01W18	122	The result returned is non-deterministic
01W19	123	Database created without any schema
01W20	129	Plan may contain virtual indexes
01W21	130	A row could not be converted to the new schema format

SQLSTATE	SQLCODE	Warning Message
01W23	132	Cannot output the histogram for string column '%1'
01WC1	125	An invalid multi-byte input character was encountered
01WC2	126	An invalid multi-byte output character was encountered
01WC3	127	An input character could not be converted to database character set and simple substitution took place
01WC4	128	An output character could not be converted to the application character set and simple substitution took place
02000	100	Row not found
WB011	119	Unable to open backup log '%1'

8.4 Assignment Statement

The assignment statement can be used to copy data values into three types of targets: local variables, connection-level variables, and fields in row-level trigger structures.

```
<assignment_statement> ::= SET <assignment_target> "=" <expression>
<assignment_target>     ::= <local_variable_name>
                          | <connection_variable_name>
                          | <row_structure_name> "." <column_name>
<expression>            ::= see <expression> in Chapter 3, "Selecting"
```

Here is an example of several assignment statements using local variables as targets:

```
BEGIN
DECLARE @a INTEGER;
DECLARE @b TIMESTAMP;
DECLARE @c BIGINT;
DECLARE @d VARCHAR ( 7 );
DECLARE @e LONG BINARY;
SET @a = 1;
SET @b = CURRENT TIMESTAMP;
SET @c = ( SELECT COUNT(*) FROM customer )
       + ( SELECT COUNT(*) FROM customer );
SET @d = IF DOW ( CURRENT DATE ) IN ( 1, 7 )
            THEN 'weekend'
            ELSE 'weekday'
         ENDIF;
SET @e = xp_read_file ( 'hello.txt' );
END;
```

For more information about connection-level variables, see Section 8.14, "CREATE VARIABLE," and for structures in triggers, see Section 8.11, "CREATE TRIGGER." Expressions are described in Section 3.10, "Expressions and Operators."

8.5 **IF Statement**

The IF statement can be used to control which statements are executed inside a
BEGIN block. Each IF statement consists of a boolean expression, a THEN
clause, zero or more ELSEIF clauses, an optional ELSE clause, and the
keywords END IF to terminate the IF.

```
<if_statement>        ::= IF <boolean_expression> THEN
                            [ <statement_list> ]
                          { ELSEIF <boolean_expression> THEN
                              [ <statement_list> ] }
                          [ ELSE
                              [ <statement_list> ] ]
                          END IF
<boolean_expression> ::= see <boolean_expression> in Chapter 3, "Selecting"
```

When the IF statement is executed, the first boolean expression is evaluated. If
the result is TRUE, the statements in the THEN clause are executed and the rest
of the clauses are skipped. If the result is FALSE or UNKNOWN, the boolean
expression in each successive ELSEIF clause is evaluated until a TRUE result is
found; in that case the statements in the ELSEIF clause are executed and the rest
of the clauses are skipped. If the result of every boolean expression is FALSE or
UNKNOWN, the statements in the ELSE clause are executed if one is present.

Here is an example that displays "ELSEIF" because the result of evaluating
"@x IS NULL" is TRUE:

```
BEGIN
   DECLARE @x INTEGER;
   SET @x = NULL;
   IF @x = 1 THEN
      MESSAGE 'THEN' TO CLIENT;
   ELSEIF @x IS NULL THEN
      MESSAGE 'ELSEIF' TO CLIENT;
   ELSE
      MESSAGE 'ELSE' TO CLIENT;
   END IF;
END;
```

If @x contained 1, the example above would display "THEN," and if @x contained 2 it would display "ELSE." Boolean expressions and TRUE, FALSE, and
UNKNOWN values are described in Section 3.12, "Boolean Expressions and
the WHERE Clause."

IF statements can be nested within one another; e.g., any statement in the
THEN, ELSEIF, or ELSE clauses can be another IF statement with a corresponding END IF. Also, there is no need to use BEGIN and END keywords
around the statements in the THEN, ELSEIF, and ELSE clauses. Here is an
example of nested IF statements:

```
BEGIN
   DECLARE @message VARCHAR ( 100 );
   IF DATEFORMAT ( CURRENT DATE, 'MMDD' ) = '1225' THEN
      SET @message = 'It''s Christmas Day';
      IF DOW ( CURRENT DATE ) IN ( 1, 7 ) THEN
         SET @message = @message + ' on a weekend.';
      ELSE
         SET @message = @message + ' on a weekday.';
      END IF;
```

```
ELSEIF DOW ( CURRENT DATE ) IN ( 1, 7 ) THEN
   SET @message = 'It''s just another weekend.';
ELSE
   SET @message = 'It''s just another weekday.';
END IF;
MESSAGE @message TO CLIENT;
END;
```

8.6 **CASE Statement**

The CASE statement provides two alternatives to an IF with multiple ELSEIF clauses.

```
<case_statement> ::= <basic_case_statement>
                   | <searched_case_statement>
```

Both forms consist of the CASE keyword, one or more WHEN clauses, an optional ELSE clause, and the keywords END CASE to terminate the CASE statement.

The first form of the CASE statement contains an expression after the CASE keyword, and each WHEN clause specifies a constant value, followed by the keyword THEN and one or more statements. The CASE expression is evaluated once and then compared with the constant value in each successive WHEN clause. As soon as there is a match, the statements in that WHEN clause are executed and the rest of the clauses are skipped.

```
<basic_case_statement> ::= CASE <expression>
                             WHEN <when_constant> THEN
                                  [ <statement_list> ]
                             { WHEN <when_constant> THEN
                                  [ <statement_list> ] }
                             [ ELSE
                                  [ <statement_list> ] ]
                             END CASE
<when_constant>        ::= <string_literal>
                         | [ "-" ] <number_literal>
                         | <special_literal>
                         | NULL
<string_literal>      ::= a sequence of characters enclosed in single quotes
<number_literal>      ::= integer, exact numeric or float numeric literal
<special_literal>     ::= see <special_literal> in Chapter 1, "Creating"
```

The constant in each WHEN clause can take the form of a literal or the NULL keyword. In the first case the comparison is interpreted as the boolean expression "<expression> = <when_constant>"; in the latter case the comparison is interpreted as "<expression> IS NULL."

The boolean expression for each successive WHEN clause is evaluated until a TRUE result is found; in that case the statements after the corresponding THEN are executed and the rest of the clauses are skipped. If the result of every boolean expression is FALSE or UNKNOWN, the statements in the ELSE clause are executed if it is present.

Here is an example that displays "CASE #3" because the result of evaluating "@x IS NULL" is TRUE:

```
BEGIN
   DECLARE @x INTEGER;
   SET @x = NULL;
   CASE @x
```

```
        WHEN 1 THEN
            MESSAGE 'CASE #1' TO CLIENT;
        WHEN -2 THEN
            MESSAGE 'CASE #2' TO CLIENT;
        WHEN NULL THEN
            MESSAGE 'CASE #3' TO CLIENT;
        ELSE
            MESSAGE 'CASE ELSE' TO CLIENT;
    END CASE;
END;
```

If @x contained 1, the example above would display "CASE #1," if @x contained –2, it would display "CASE #2," and if @x contained some other non-NULL value, it would display "CASE ELSE."

The other form of the CASE statement omits the expression after the CASE keyword and instead uses complete boolean expressions in each WHEN clause. Each of these boolean expressions is evaluated until a TRUE result is found; in that case the statements after the corresponding THEN are executed and the rest of the clauses are skipped. If the result of every boolean expression is FALSE or UNKNOWN, the statements in the ELSE clause are executed if one is present.

```
<searched_case_statement> ::= CASE
                    WHEN <boolean_expression> THEN
                        [ <statement_list> ]
                    { WHEN <boolean_expression> THEN
                        [ <statement_list> ] }
                    [ ELSE
                        [ <statement_list> ] ]
                    END CASE
```

Here is the previous example, changed to use the second form of the CASE statement.

```
BEGIN
    DECLARE @x INTEGER;
    SET @x = NULL;
    CASE
        WHEN @x = 1 THEN
            MESSAGE 'CASE #1' TO CLIENT;
        WHEN @x = -2 THEN
            MESSAGE 'CASE #2' TO CLIENT;
        WHEN @x IS NULL THEN
            MESSAGE 'CASE #3' TO CLIENT;
        ELSE
            MESSAGE 'CASE ELSE' TO CLIENT;
    END CASE;
END;
```

The second form of the CASE statement is more flexible because you aren't limited to a single <expression> and a series of constants; instead, each <boolean_expression> can involve completely different values and operators, just like the ELSEIF clause described in the previous section.

8.7 WHILE Loop

The WHILE loop consists of a boolean expression, followed by the LOOP keyword, one or more executable statements, and the keywords END LOOP to terminate the loop. The WHILE loop comes in two formats — with and without a label that may be used as a target for a LEAVE statement:

```
<while_loop>  ::= WHILE <boolean_expression> LOOP
                     [ <statement_list> ]
                  END LOOP
                | <while_label> ":"
                  WHILE <boolean_expression> LOOP
                     [ <statement_list> ]
                  END LOOP [ <while_label> ]
<while_label> ::= <identifier> that may be used in a <leave_statement>
```

When a WHILE loop is encountered during execution, the boolean expression is evaluated. If the result is FALSE or UNKNOWN, the statements between the keywords LOOP and END LOOP are skipped and control passes to the statement following the END LOOP. If the result is TRUE, the statements between the keywords LOOP and END LOOP are executed and control then passes back to the beginning of the WHILE. The boolean expression is evaluated a second time, and if it's still TRUE the statements are executed again and control passes back to the beginning again. This process is repeated until the result of the boolean expression is FALSE or UNKNOWN, at which point control passes to the statement after the END LOOP.

Here is an example of a WHILE loop that executes 10 times:

```
BEGIN
   DECLARE @loop_counter INTEGER;
   SET @loop_counter = 1;
   WHILE @loop_counter <= 10 LOOP
      MESSAGE STRING ( 'Loop pass # ', @loop_counter ) TO CLIENT;
      SET @loop_counter = @loop_counter + 1;
   END LOOP;
END;
```

Here is a WHILE loop that runs until some other connection inserts a row into the table called go_ahead; the WAITFOR statement pauses for three seconds so the loop doesn't spin so fast it uses up all the CPU time. In effect, this loop waits until some other connection gives it the go-ahead to proceed with other work:

```
BEGIN
   WHILE NOT EXISTS ( SELECT * FROM go_ahead ) LOOP
      WAITFOR DELAY '00:00:03';
   END LOOP;
END;
```

8.8 EXECUTE IMMEDIATE

The EXECUTE IMMEDIATE statement can be used inside a BEGIN block to execute SQL statements that are themselves constructed at execution time.

```
<execute_immediate> ::= EXECUTE IMMEDIATE { <execute_option> } <basic_expression>

<execute_option>    ::= WITH QUOTES ON      -- double quotes delimit identifiers
                      | WITH QUOTES         -- same as WITH QUOTES ON
                      | WITH QUOTES OFF     -- default; QUOTED_IDENTIFIER applies
                      | WITH ESCAPES ON     -- default; transform escape sequences
                      | WITH ESCAPES OFF    -- ignore escape sequences
                      | WITH RESULT SET ON  -- allow result set
                      | WITH RESULT SET OFF -- default; do not allow result set

<basic_expression>  ::= see <basic_expression> in Chapter 3, "Selecting"
                        -- an expression that is not a subquery
```

When an EXECUTE IMMEDIATE statement is executed, the expression is evaluated as a string containing one or more SQL statements, and the contents of that string are executed. Several options control how the string expression is interpreted and how it is executed, as follows:

- **WITH QUOTES ON** specifies that pairs of double quotes embedded inside the string expression are to be interpreted as delimiting identifiers.
- **WITH QUOTES OFF** is the default; it specifies that pairs of double quotes embedded inside the string expression are to be interpreted according to the current value of the QUOTED_IDENTIFIER option. If the QUOTED_IDENTIFIER option has been set to 'OFF', then double quote characters are interpreted as delimiting string literals, just like single quote characters. If QUOTED_IDENTIFIER is 'ON', the default, then strings like "t1" are interpreted as identifiers rather than embedded string literals. If the QUOTED_IDENTIFIER option has been set to 'OFF', but you want embedded strings in double quotes to be treated as identifiers in EXECUTE IMMEDIATE, use WITH QUOTES ON.
- **WITH ESCAPES OFF** specifies that backslash characters in the string expression will not be treated as escape characters when the EXECUTE IMMEDIATE statement is executed.
- **WITH ESCAPES ON** is the default; it specifies that backslash characters embedded in the string expression may be interpreted as escape characters when the EXECUTE IMMEDIATE statement is executed. For example, \\ will be changed to a single backslash character, and \n will be changed to a new line character.
- **WITH RESULT SET ON** specifies that the EXECUTE IMMEDIATE statement is allowed to return one or more result sets.
- **WITH RESULT SET OFF** is the default; it specifies that the EXECUTE IMMEDIATE does not return any result sets.

The EXECUTE IMMEDIATE statement can be used to execute a SELECT that returns a result set. Here is an example that displays all the rows in the employee table when you run it in ISQL:

```
BEGIN
   DECLARE @table_name VARCHAR ( 128 );
   SET @table_name = 'employee';
   EXECUTE IMMEDIATE WITH RESULT SET ON STRING ( 'SELECT * FROM ', @table_name );
END;
```

More than one SQL statement can be executed at once. The following example displays two result sets when you run it in ISQL:

```
BEGIN
   EXECUTE IMMEDIATE WITH RESULT SET ON
      'SELECT * FROM employee; SELECT * FROM customer';
END;
```

You can even declare local variables inside an EXECUTE IMMEDIATE as long as you include a BEGIN block. The following example displays "Hello":

```
BEGIN
   EXECUTE IMMEDIATE STRING ( '
      BEGIN
         DECLARE @x VARCHAR ( 10 );
         SET @x = ''Hello'';
```

```
        MESSAGE @x TO CLIENT;
    END;' );
END;
```

The WITH ESCAPES OFF option can be used to suppress the parsing of string literal escape characters when the EXECUTE IMMEDIATE statement parses the string expression that is passed to it. This doesn't mean you don't need to use the "\" escape character in string literals, it just means you don't have to double-up the escape characters when using EXECUTE IMMEDIATE.

The default is WITH ESCAPES ON. Here is an example that demonstrates the problem:

```
BEGIN
    DECLARE @sql LONG VARCHAR;
    SET @sql = 'UNLOAD TABLE t1 TO ''C:\\temp\\new_t1.txt''';
    EXECUTE IMMEDIATE @sql;
END;
```

When this example is run in ISQL, the string literal 'UNLOAD TABLE t1 TO "C:\\temp\\new_t1.txt'" is parsed by SQL Anywhere before it is assigned to @sql; the backslash character is treated as an escape character, and each pair of backslashes is interpreted as a single backslash. When @sql is passed to EXECUTE IMMEDIATE it is parsed again, the backslash characters are again treated as escape characters, and the \n pair is interpreted as a new line character; the statement fails with the following two-line error message:

```
Cannot access file 'C:\temp
ew_t1.txt' -- Invalid argument
```

The WITH ESCAPES OFF clause suppresses the second parsing of escape characters. The following code works okay:

```
BEGIN
    DECLARE @sql LONG VARCHAR;
    SET @sql = 'UNLOAD TABLE t1 TO ''C:\\temp\\new_t1.txt''';
    EXECUTE IMMEDIATE WITH ESCAPES OFF @sql;
END;
```

The default WITH ESCAPES ON requires a multitude of backslashes, as follows:

```
BEGIN
    DECLARE @sql LONG VARCHAR;
    SET @sql = 'UNLOAD TABLE t1 TO ''C:\\\\temp\\\\new_t1.txt''';
    EXECUTE IMMEDIATE @sql;
END;
```

Note that it is not possible to suppress all parsing of escape characters. The following example fails with the same error message as above because SQL Anywhere parses the string literal before passing it to EXECUTE IMMEDIATE, and even though the WITH ESCAPES OFF option is specified the \n pair has already been turned into a new line character.

```
BEGIN
    EXECUTE IMMEDIATE WITH ESCAPES OFF 'UNLOAD TABLE t1 TO ''C:\temp\new_t1.txt''';
END;
```

Note: In some contexts an EXECUTE IMMEDIATE statement will fail with the syntax error "Procedure 'IMMEDIATE' not found." When that happens, just place a BEGIN block around the EXECUTE IMMEDIATE statement.

8.9 CREATE PROCEDURE, CALL, and RETURN

The CREATE PROCEDURE statement lets you store a BEGIN block in the database for later execution via the CALL statement. Here is the syntax for the CREATE PROCEDURE, CALL, and RETURN statements:

```
<create_procedure>        ::= CREATE PROCEDURE [ <owner_name> "." ] <procedure_name>
                              "(" [ <parameter_list> ] ")"
                              [ RESULT "(" <result_set_column_list> ")" ]
                              <begin_block>
<owner_name>              ::= <identifier>
<procedure_name>          ::= <identifier>
<parameter_list> ::= <parameter_specification> { "," <parameter_specification> }
<parameter_specification> ::= [ <parameter_disposition> ]
                                  <parameter_name>
                                  <data_type>
                                  [ <parameter_default> ]
<parameter_disposition>   ::= IN
                            | OUT
                            | INOUT  -- default
<parameter_name>          ::= <identifier>
<parameter_default>       ::= DEFAULT <expression>
<result_set_column_list>  ::= <result_set_column> { "," <result_set_column> }
<result_set_column>       ::= <identifier> <data_type>

<call_statement>          ::= [ <return_code> "=" ]
                              CALL [ <owner_name> "." ] <procedure_name>
                              [ "(" [ <call_argument_list> ] ")" ]
<return_code>             ::= <identifier> variable ready to receive an INTEGER value
<call_argument_list> ::= <call_argument> { "," <call_argument> }
<call_argument>           ::= <basic_expression>
                            | <parameter_name> "=" <basic_expression>

<return_statement>        ::= RETURN [ <expression> ]
```

Note: It is possible to create a procedure in SQL Anywhere that doesn't specify code in a BEGIN block but instead refers to a procedure written in another language and stored externally in a Windows .dll, a Netware .nlm, or a Unix shared library. It is also possible to replace the BEGIN block with a reference to a stored procedure in a different database. Neither of these techniques is discussed in this book; for more information see the SQL Anywhere Help.

The combination of owner name and procedure name must be unique among all procedures and user-defined functions in the database; for more information about functions, see Section 8.10, "CREATE FUNCTION."

The parameter list is optional in the CREATE PROCEDURE statement but the parentheses aren't; if the procedure doesn't expect any parameters you still have to code an empty list with (). You can, however, omit the parentheses from the CALL statement.

A procedure can return one or more result sets, as well as a single INTEGER return code. Here is an example of a procedure that returns one result set plus a return code, together with the table that the procedure refers to and a BEGIN block containing a CALL:

```
CREATE TABLE t1 (
   key_1       INTEGER NOT NULL,
   non_key_1   VARCHAR ( 100 ) NOT NULL DEFAULT '',
```

```
      PRIMARY KEY ( key_1 ) );

CREATE PROCEDURE p1()
BEGIN
   SELECT * FROM t1;
   RETURN 999;
END;

BEGIN
   DECLARE @return_code INTEGER;
   INSERT t1 VALUES ( 1, 'A' );
   @return_code = CALL p1;
   SELECT @return_code;
END;
```

Here's what the results look like when the code above is executed in ISQL; two result sets are displayed, one from the CALL statement and one from the SELECT @return_code:

```
key_1  non_key_1
=====  =========
1       'A'

@return_code
============
999
```

The RETURN statement is optional in a procedure. If one is used, the return value expression is optional; if a return value expression is specified, it is converted to the INTEGER data type because that's all a procedure can return. If the procedure doesn't execute a RETURN statement that specifies an explicit return code value, the return code is set to zero.

Each parameter in the CREATE PROCEDURE parameter list can have four components: an optional parameter disposition, a required parameter name and data type, and an optional DEFAULT value.

The parameter disposition can be one of three keywords:

- **IN** means the parameter is read-only. The corresponding argument value is passed into the procedure when it is called, but any change made to the parameter will not be reflected in the argument when the procedure returns.
- **OUT** means the parameter is return-only. The corresponding argument value is ignored when the procedure is called, and so is any DEFAULT value that is specified for the parameter; the parameter starts out as NULL when the procedure is called. However, any value assigned to the parameter is passed back to the corresponding argument when the procedure returns.
- **INOUT** is the default; it means the corresponding argument value is passed into the procedure, and any change to the parameter value will be passed back to the argument when the procedure returns.

If an expression is passed as an argument to an OUT or INOUT parameter, any change to the parameter value is discarded when the procedure returns. The OUT and INOUT parameter dispositions only work if the corresponding argument is a simple variable.

Each parameter name must be unique as far as parameter and local variable names inside the procedure are concerned. The data type for each parameter must be one of the types described in Section 1.5, "Data Types."

The DEFAULT clause can be used with an IN or INOUT parameter to specify a default value to be assigned to the parameter if the corresponding argument in the CALL statement is omitted. The DEFAULT clause has no effect for an OUT parameter, and it may not make much sense for an INOUT parameter because the default would only take effect if there's no argument to receive the output value.

Here is an example to show how the parameter dispositions and DEFAULT values work; the argument values are displayed before and after the CALL, and the parameters are displayed on entry to the procedure and just before the exit:

```
CREATE PROCEDURE p1 (
    IN    @p_in    VARCHAR ( 1 ) DEFAULT 'X',
    OUT   @p_out   VARCHAR ( 1 ) DEFAULT 'Y',
    INOUT @p_inout VARCHAR ( 1 ) DEFAULT 'Z' )
BEGIN
    SELECT 'entry' AS point, @p_in, @p_out, @p_inout;
    SET @p_in    = 'P';
    SET @p_out   = 'Q';
    SET @p_inout = 'R';
    SELECT 'exit' AS point, @p_in, @p_out, @p_inout;
END;

BEGIN
    DECLARE @in    VARCHAR ( 1 );
    DECLARE @out   VARCHAR ( 1 );
    DECLARE @inout VARCHAR ( 1 );
    SET @in    = 'A';
    SET @out   = 'B';
    SET @inout = 'C';
    SELECT 'before' AS point, @in, @out, @inout;
    CALL p1 ( @in, @out, @inout );
    SELECT 'after' AS point, @in, @out, @inout;
END;
```

The following shows what the four SELECT statements display; since arguments are specified for all the parameters, all the DEFAULT values are ignored. Also, the input value of the IN parameter is passed to the procedure but the return value is ignored; the input value of the OUT parameter is ignored but the return value is passed back; and the INOUT parameter both receives the input value and returns the output value back to the corresponding argument.

```
point   @in  @out  @inout
======  ===  ====  ======
before  A    B     C
entry   A    NULL  C
exit    P    Q     R
after   A    Q     R
```

Because all the parameters have DEFAULT values, all the arguments can be omitted from the CALL as follows:

```
CALL p1;
```

The following shows what the four SELECT statements display when no arguments are specified; the DEFAULT values are assigned to the IN and INOUT parameters but ignored for the OUT parameter. Also, none of the parameter values are passed back to the caller because there are no arguments to receive them in the CALL.

```
point   @in  @out  @inout
======  ===  ====  ======
before  A    B     C
entry   X    NULL  Z
exit    P    Q     R
after   A    B     C
```

The correspondence between arguments and parameters is usually determined by position: The first argument corresponds to the first parameter, the second argument to the second parameter, and so on. There is also an alternative method where the correspondence is specified by parameter name using the "<parameter_name> = <basic_expression>" argument format in the CALL. When this format is used, leading arguments can be omitted and the order of arguments can be changed. Here is a CALL to the above procedure where the first argument is omitted and the other two are rearranged; the DEFAULT value is applied to the IN parameter and the OUT and INOUT output values are returned to the correct arguments:

```
CALL p1 ( @p_inout = @inout, @p_out = @out );
```

Mixed formats can be used for the arguments, but once the format switches to "<parameter_name> = <basic_expression>" that's what has to be used for the rest of the argument list. Here is a CALL using both formats:

```
CALL p1 ( @in, @p_inout = @inout, @p_out = @out );
```

A procedure can return one or more result sets to the caller; this is done with one or more SELECT statements that don't have INTO clauses. Single or multiple result sets may also be returned to a calling procedure for later return from that procedure via cascading CALL statements.

If a procedure returns one result set, or two or more result sets that have the same number of columns, a RESULT clause can be used in the CREATE PROCEDURE statement to explicitly specify the returned column names and data types; data conversions will be performed if necessary.

Following is an example showing two procedures: p1 returns two results sets, and p2 returns the two result sets from p1 plus a third result set of its own. The RESULT clause forces a conversion of '9' to an INTEGER column for the final return.

```
CREATE PROCEDURE p1()
BEGIN
   SELECT 1, 2, 3;
   SELECT 4, 5, 6;
END;

CREATE PROCEDURE p2()
RESULT ( a INTEGER, b INTEGER, c INTEGER )
BEGIN
   CALL p1();
   SELECT 7, 8, '9';
END;

CALL p2();
```

Note: Multiple result sets can be displayed by ISQL, but this book doesn't discuss programming techniques for handling a single procedure call that returns two or more result sets to a client application.

If a procedure returns only one result set, with or without a RESULT clause, it can be called in the FROM clause of a query; for more information, see Section 3.7, "SELECT FROM Procedure Call."

Tip: When in doubt, use a RESULT clause to specify names and data types of a procedure result set. If the RESULT clause is omitted, the names and data types of the returned columns are determined by the SELECT statement itself, and the results are sometimes unexpected (e.g., for expressions in the SELECT list).

By default, an exception that occurs inside a procedure is immediately passed back to the caller. The following example shows a procedure that is called from a BEGIN block that contains an exception handler plus a SET statement that causes a data conversion error:

```
CREATE PROCEDURE p1()
BEGIN
    DECLARE @date      DATE;
    MESSAGE STRING ( 'Before error' ) TO CONSOLE;
    SET @date = 'xxx';
    MESSAGE STRING ( 'After error' ) TO CONSOLE;
END;

BEGIN
    DECLARE @sqlstate  VARCHAR ( 5 );
    DECLARE @errormsg  VARCHAR ( 32767 );
    MESSAGE STRING ( 'Before call' ) TO CONSOLE;
    CALL p1();
    MESSAGE STRING ( 'After call' ) TO CONSOLE;
EXCEPTION
    WHEN OTHERS THEN
        SELECT SQLSTATE, ERRORMSG() INTO @sqlstate, @errormsg;
        MESSAGE 'Error handled outside procedure' TO CONSOLE;
        MESSAGE STRING ( 'SQLSTATE = ', @sqlstate ) TO CONSOLE;
        MESSAGE STRING ( 'ERRORMSG() = ', @errormsg ) TO CONSOLE;
END;
```

The following shows what the output looks like: The final MESSAGE statement in the procedure is bypassed because the exception is immediately passed back to the caller where it is handled by the WHEN OTHERS clause in the exception handler.

```
Before call
Before error
Error handled outside procedure
SQLSTATE = 53018
ERRORMSG() = Cannot convert xxx to a timestamp
```

If a procedure contains an exception handler, that exception handler gets control and the caller doesn't see any information about the exception. Here is the code from the example above, with the exception handler moved inside the procedure:

```
CREATE PROCEDURE p1()
BEGIN
    DECLARE @sqlstate  VARCHAR ( 5 );
    DECLARE @errormsg  VARCHAR ( 32767 );
    DECLARE @date      DATE;
    MESSAGE STRING ( 'Before error' ) TO CONSOLE;
    SET @date = 'xxx';
```

```
      MESSAGE STRING ( 'After error' ) TO CONSOLE;
EXCEPTION
   WHEN OTHERS THEN
      SELECT SQLSTATE, ERRORMSG() INTO @sqlstate, @errormsg;
      MESSAGE 'Error handled inside procedure' TO CONSOLE;
      MESSAGE STRING ( 'SQLSTATE = ', @sqlstate ) TO CONSOLE;
      MESSAGE STRING ( 'ERRORMSG() = ', @errormsg ) TO CONSOLE;
END;

BEGIN
   DECLARE @sqlstate  VARCHAR ( 5 );
   DECLARE @errormsg  VARCHAR ( 32767 );
   MESSAGE STRING ( 'Before call' ) TO CONSOLE;
   CALL p1();
   SELECT SQLSTATE, ERRORMSG() INTO @sqlstate, @errormsg;
   MESSAGE STRING ( 'After call' ) TO CONSOLE;
   MESSAGE STRING ( 'SQLSTATE = ', @sqlstate ) TO CONSOLE;
   MESSAGE STRING ( 'ERRORMSG() = ', @errormsg ) TO CONSOLE;
END;
```

Here is the output; the exception handler inside the procedure immediately gets control when the exception occurs, and the SQLSTATE is set back to '00000' when the procedure returns to the caller:

```
Before call
Before error
Error handled inside procedure
SQLSTATE = 53018
ERRORMSG() = Cannot convert xxx to a timestamp
After call
SQLSTATE = 00000
ERRORMSG() =
```

If another exception occurs within an exception handler inside a procedure, that second exception is passed back to the caller. Here is the code from above, modified to include two errors and two exception handlers:

```
CREATE PROCEDURE p1()
BEGIN
   DECLARE @sqlstate  VARCHAR ( 5 );
   DECLARE @errormsg  VARCHAR ( 32767 );
   DECLARE @date      DATE;
   MESSAGE STRING ( 'Before error' ) TO CONSOLE;
   SET @date = 'xxx';
   MESSAGE STRING ( 'After error' ) TO CONSOLE;
EXCEPTION
   WHEN OTHERS THEN
      SELECT SQLSTATE, ERRORMSG() INTO @sqlstate, @errormsg;
      MESSAGE 'Error handled inside procedure' TO CONSOLE;
      MESSAGE STRING ( 'SQLSTATE = ', @sqlstate ) TO CONSOLE;
      MESSAGE STRING ( 'ERRORMSG() = ', @errormsg ) TO CONSOLE;
      SET @undefined = 0;
END;

BEGIN
   DECLARE @sqlstate  VARCHAR ( 5 );
   DECLARE @errormsg  VARCHAR ( 32767 );
   MESSAGE STRING ( 'Before call' ) TO CONSOLE;
   CALL p1();
   MESSAGE STRING ( 'After call' ) TO CONSOLE;
EXCEPTION
   WHEN OTHERS THEN
```

```
          SELECT SQLSTATE, ERRORMSG() INTO @sqlstate, @errormsg;
          MESSAGE 'Error handled outside procedure' TO CONSOLE;
          MESSAGE STRING ( 'SQLSTATE = ', @sqlstate ) TO CONSOLE;
          MESSAGE STRING ( 'ERRORMSG() = ', @errormsg ) TO CONSOLE;
END;
```

The following shows what the output looks like; the inner exception handler gets control and displays information about the first exception, then the second exception is passed back to the caller where its details are displayed by the second exception handler.

```
Before call
Before error
Error handled inside procedure
SQLSTATE = 53018
ERRORMSG() = Cannot convert xxx to a timestamp
Error handled outside procedure
SQLSTATE = 42W14
ERRORMSG() = Variable '@undefined' not found
```

For more information about handling exceptions, see Section 9.5.1, "SIGNAL and RESIGNAL," and Section 9.5.2, "RAISERROR and CREATE MESSAGE."

8.10 CREATE FUNCTION

The CREATE FUNCTION statement can be used to create a user-defined function that behaves just like many of the built-in scalar functions like ABS() and SUBSTRING(); i.e., it accepts zero or more read-only parameters, returns a single value, and can be referenced in an expression.

```
<create_function> ::= CREATE FUNCTION
                      [ <owner_name> "." ] <user_defined_function_name>
                      "(" [ <function_parameter_list> ] ")"
                      RETURNS <data_type>
                      <function_characteristic>
                      <begin_block> -- should RETURN a value
<user_defined_function_name> ::= <identifier>
<function_parameter_list>   ::= <function_parameter> { "," <function_parameter> }
<function_parameter>        ::= [ IN ]
                                  <parameter_name> <data_type>
                                  [ <parameter_default> ]
<function_characteristic>   ::= DETERMINISTIC          -- default
                                | NOT DETERMINISTIC
<user_defined_function_call> ::= <user_defined_function_name>
                                  "(" [ <function_argument_list> ] ")"
<function_argument_list>    ::= <expression> { "," <expression> }
```

Functions are expected to return values, so the CREATE FUNCTION statement requires a RETURNS clause to specify the data type of the return value. That's not the only difference between functions and procedures; here's a list of characteristics that make a function different from a procedure:

- The only parameter disposition allowed is IN, and that's the default; OUT and INOUT parameters aren't allowed.
- A function cannot return a result set or have a RESULT clause.
- The default return value is NULL instead of zero.
- The correspondence between arguments and parameters is strictly positional.

■ A function can be defined as DETERMINISTIC or NOT
DETERMINISTIC.

Note: A function can be invoked by a CALL statement just like a procedure,
and in that case none of the differences in the above list apply. However, this
book doesn't discuss the subject of using CALL to invoke a function. If you want a
procedure, use CREATE PROCEDURE.

Here is an example of a function that calculates the factorial of a number,
together with a SELECT that uses the built-in table RowGenerator to call the
function 10 times; note that this function calls itself recursively:

```
CREATE FUNCTION factorial ( IN @n UNSIGNED BIGINT )
RETURNS UNSIGNED BIGINT
BEGIN
    DECLARE @f UNSIGNED BIGINT;
    CASE
        WHEN @n <= 1 THEN SET @f = 1;
        WHEN @n > 20 THEN SET @f = 0; -- too big
        ELSE SET @f = @n * factorial ( @n - 1 );
    END CASE;
    RETURN @f;
END;

SELECT row_num AS n,
       factorial ( n )
  FROM RowGenerator
 WHERE row_num <= 10
 ORDER BY row_num;
```

Here's what the output looks like:

```
n    factorial(n)
==   ============
1    1
2    2
3    6
4    24
5    120
6    720
7    5040
8    40320
9    362880
10   3628800
```

Note: RowGenerator is a simple little table containing 255 rows numbered 1
to 255. It's very handy for generating multi-row result sets out of thin air, like in
the example above.

The DEFAULT clause can be used with a function parameter to specify a
default value to be assigned to the parameter if the corresponding argument is
omitted from the function reference. The correspondence between arguments
and parameters is strictly determined by position in a function reference: The
first argument corresponds to the first parameter, the second argument to the
second parameter, and so on; there is no alternative "<parameter_name> =
<basic_expression>" method for specifying a function argument. That means
argument values can only be omitted from the right; e.g., if a function has two

parameters with DEFAULT values, you can omit both arguments, or specify the first argument and omit the second, but you cannot omit the first argument and specify the second, nor can you change the order of the arguments.

Here is an example of a function that expects two parameters but is only passed one argument; in addition, this function has a RETURNS clause but no actual RETURN statement:

```
CREATE FUNCTION f1 (
    @p1    VARCHAR ( 1 ) DEFAULT 'X',
    @p2    VARCHAR ( 1 ) DEFAULT 'Y' )
RETURNS VARCHAR ( 1 )
BEGIN
   MESSAGE STRING ( 'entry ', @p1, ' ', @p2 ) TO CONSOLE;
   SET @p1 = 'P';
   SET @p2 = 'Q';
   MESSAGE STRING ( 'exit   ', @p1, ' ', @p2 ) TO CONSOLE;
END;

BEGIN
   DECLARE @a1     VARCHAR ( 1 );
   DECLARE @return VARCHAR ( 1 );
   SET @a1 = 'A';
   MESSAGE STRING ( 'before ', @a1 ) TO CONSOLE;
   SET @return = f1 ( @a1 );
   MESSAGE STRING ( 'after  ', @a1 ) TO CONSOLE;
   MESSAGE STRING ( 'return ', COALESCE ( @return, 'NULL' ) ) TO CONSOLE;
END;
```

Here's what the output looks like. The first parameter receives the value from the function call but the second one gets a DEFAULT value; also, the return value is NULL:

```
before A
entry  A Y
exit   P Q
after  A
return NULL
```

A function is said to be deterministic if the input parameter values uniquely determine what the return value will be; in other words, the same inputs will always yield the same output. In SQL Anywhere, functions are assumed to be deterministic by default. That implies that SQL Anywhere doesn't have to actually execute the function again if it is called with the same parameter values; it can use the return value that was calculated by the previous call, and that in turn can save time and improve performance.

A function is said to be non-deterministic if the return value can vary for the same input parameters, or if the function performs some side effect such as updating a table. This kind of function should have the keywords NOT DETERMINISTIC explicitly specified in the CREATE PROCEDURE statement to force SQL Anywhere to actually call the function every time a reference to it is encountered during execution. Otherwise, the wrong return value may be used or the expected side effect may not happen.

Here is an example of a NOT DETERMINISTIC function that is expected to return a random value no matter what the input parameter is:

```
CREATE FUNCTION f1 ( @n INTEGER )
RETURNS INTEGER
```

```
NOT DETERMINISTIC
BEGIN
   RETURN CAST ( RAND() * 10000 AS INTEGER );
END;

SELECT row_num, f1 ( 1 )
  FROM RowGenerator
 ORDER BY row_num;
```

Here are the first five rows produced by the SELECT that calls the function; this output is correct:

```
row_num  f1(1)
=======  =====
1        4775
2        4864
3        4285
4        8194
5        6299
```

Without the NOT DETERMINISTIC clause, the output looks like the following. SQL Anywhere has assumed that the return value will be the same because the input parameter never changes.

```
row_num  f1(1)
=======  =====
1        9842
2        9842
3        9842
4        9842
5        9842
```

For the purposes of comparing old and new parameter values passed to DETERMINISTIC functions, SQL Anywhere treats string values as being case sensitive. Here is the function from above, without the NOT DETERMINISTIC clause, modified to receive a VARCHAR (1) parameter, and called twice with 'A' and 'a':

```
CREATE FUNCTION f1 ( @s VARCHAR ( 1 ) )
RETURNS INTEGER
BEGIN
   RETURN CAST ( RAND() * 10000 AS INTEGER );
END;

SELECT f1 ( 'A' ), f1 ( 'a' );
```

By default, SQL Anywhere string comparisons are case insensitive, so the result of the boolean expression 'A' = 'a' is TRUE. In this case, however, the two function calls return different return values because 'A' and 'a' are regarded as being different:

```
f1('A')  f1('a')
=======  =======
7648     4417
```

Tip: Don't count on a user-defined function being executed any particular number of times if you call it from a FROM, WHERE, or HAVING clause, whether or not it's defined as DETERMINISTIC. That's because SQL Anywhere is free to optimize queries by rewriting them in different forms, and it's very difficult to predict how many times each portion of the final query will be executed, if at all.

8.11 **CREATE TRIGGER**

A *trigger* is a special kind of BEGIN block that is stored in the database. Each trigger is associated with a single table, and it is automatically executed, or fired, whenever a specified INSERT, UPDATE, or DELETE operation is performed on that table. Triggers come in three basic flavors, depending on when they are fired: for each row operation before it is performed, for each row after the operation is performed, or once after an entire INSERT, UPDATE, or DELETE statement is completed.

```
<create_trigger> ::= <create_before_row_trigger>
                   | <create_after_row_trigger>
                   | <create_after_statement_trigger>
```

Here is the full syntax of the first form, the "before row" trigger:

```
<create_before_row_trigger> ::= CREATE TRIGGER <trigger_name>
                                BEFORE
                                <fired_by>
                                [ ORDER <order_number> ]
                                ON [ <owner_name> "." ] <table_name>
                                [ <referencing_as_structures> ]
                                FOR EACH ROW
                                [ WHEN "(" <boolean_expression> ")" ]
                                <begin_block>
<trigger_name>               ::= <identifier>
<fired_by>                   ::= <simple_fired_by> { "," <simple_fired_by> }
                               | UPDATE OF <column_name> { "," <column_name> }
<simple_fired_by>            ::= INSERT
                               | DELETE
                               | UPDATE
<column_name>                ::= <identifier>
<order_number>               ::= integer literal in the range 1 to 32767
<table_name>                 ::= <identifier>
<referencing_as_structures>  ::= REFERENCING { <as_structure> } <as_structure>
<as_structure>               ::= OLD AS <row_structure_name>
                               | NEW AS <row_structure_name>
<row_structure_name>         ::= <identifier> naming the single row structure
```

The CREATE TRIGGER statement is quite complex; here's how to put one together, clause by clause, for a before row trigger:

- The **trigger name** must be unique for the associated table. Each trigger must also be uniquely identified by the time it is fired, the reason it is fired, the order it is fired, and the table to which it applies; these characteristics are all defined by clauses described below.

- The **BEFORE** keyword specifies the time this trigger is fired; it is part of what identifies this trigger as a "before row" trigger.

- The **<fired_by>** clause specifies the reason this trigger is fired; it must consist of one or more of the keywords INSERT, UPDATE, and DELETE, or a single UPDATE OF clause followed by a comma-separated list of column names. The keywords INSERT, UPDATE, and DELETE mean this trigger will be fired for every INSERT, UPDATE, and/or DELETE operation respectively. The UPDATE OF clause means this trigger will be fired only when an UPDATE operation specifies one of the named columns.

- The **ORDER** clause specifies the order in which different triggers fire. This clause is only required for two or more triggers that fire at the same time, for the same reason, and for the same table; e.g., two before row INSERT triggers.

■ The **ON** table name clause is required to identify a single table; the table's owner name is optional. Triggers have the same owners as their associated tables; in fact, each trigger can be regarded as an attribute of its table, just like a foreign key or other constraint, and it cannot exist apart from that table.

■ The **REFERENCING** clause can name one or two structures by which code in the WHEN clause and the BEGIN block can refer to the old and new versions of the row. The OLD AS structure implicitly contains one field for each column in the row as it exists in the database before the operation that fired the trigger is performed, and the NEW AS structure contains the row as it will exist after the operation. These old and new row structures are the only place in SQL Anywhere where structured data other than tables is implemented. By default, these structures do not exist and you have to use the REFERENCING clause to define them; the OLD AS structure can be defined for a trigger that is fired by DELETE and UPDATE operations, and the NEW AS structure can be defined for triggers fired by INSERT and UPDATE operations.

■ The **FOR EACH ROW** clause specifies how often this trigger is fired; it is the other part of what identifies this trigger as a "before row" trigger. For example, a single SQL statement that affects 1000 rows will cause an associated before row trigger to fire 1000 times.

■ The optional **WHEN** clause lets you specify a boolean expression to further limit the conditions under which the trigger will actually be fired. The boolean expression can refer to fields (columns) in the old and new structures defined in the REFERENCING clause described above; the BEGIN block will be executed for each row that matches the other requirements and has a TRUE result when the boolean expression is evaluated.

Note: The REFERENCING OLD AS structure can only be defined for an INSERT trigger if that trigger can also be fired by a DELETE or UPDATE operation. Similarly, the NEW AS structure can only be defined for a DELETE trigger if that trigger can also be fired by an INSERT or UPDATE operation. Defining them doesn't necessarily mean they exist when the trigger is fired, however. When a trigger is fired by an INSERT operation, only the NEW AS structure will actually be created and any reference to the OLD AS structure will fail. Correspondingly, when a trigger is fired by a DELETE, only the OLD AS structure will be created. When a trigger is fired by an UPDATE operation, both the OLD AS and NEW AS structures exist.

Here is an example of a very simple before row trigger, plus four SQL statements that will fire this trigger a total of six times:

```
CREATE TABLE t1 (
   key_1        INTEGER NOT NULL PRIMARY KEY,
   non_key_1    VARCHAR ( 100 ) NOT NULL );

CREATE TRIGGER triud_t1
BEFORE INSERT, DELETE, UPDATE
ON t1
```

```
FOR EACH ROW
BEGIN
  MESSAGE STRING ( 'Trigger triud_t1 fired.' ) TO CONSOLE;
END;

INSERT t1 VALUES ( 1, 'first row' );
INSERT t1 VALUES ( 2, 'second row' );
UPDATE t1 SET non_key_1 = 'xxx';
DELETE t1;
```

Here's what the output looks like; because this trigger was defined as FOR EACH ROW, it was fired once by each INSERT, twice by the single UPDATE statement, and twice by the DELETE for a total of six times:

```
Trigger triud_t1 fired.
Trigger triud_t1 fired.
Trigger triud_t1 fired.
Trigger triud_t1 fired.
Trigger triud_t1 fired.
Trigger triud_t1 fired.
```

Here's an example of the same trigger, modified to execute different code depending on which kind of SQL operation fired the trigger:

```
CREATE TRIGGER triud_t1
BEFORE INSERT, DELETE, UPDATE
ON t1
FOR EACH ROW
BEGIN
  CASE
     WHEN INSERTING THEN MESSAGE 'Inserting t1.' TO CONSOLE;
     WHEN UPDATING  THEN MESSAGE 'Updating t1.' TO CONSOLE;
     WHEN DELETING  THEN MESSAGE 'Deleting t1.' TO CONSOLE;
  END CASE;
END;

INSERT t1 VALUES ( 1, 'first row' );
INSERT t1 VALUES ( 2, 'second row' );
UPDATE t1 SET non_key_1 = 'xxx';
DELETE t1;
```

Here's the output; for more information about the special trigger predicates INSERTING, DELETING and UPDATING, see Section 3.12.7, "Trigger Predicates."

```
Inserting t1.
Inserting t1.
Updating t1.
Updating t1.
Deleting t1.
Deleting t1.
```

Tip: Use IF and CASE statements, not IF and CASE expressions, when referring to the special trigger predicates INSERTING, DELETING, and UPDATING in insert and delete triggers. That's because the REFERENCING OLD AS structure is undefined when an INSERT fires the trigger, and the NEW AS row structure is undefined when a DELETE fires the trigger. The THEN and ELSE expressions in IF and CASE expressions are always parsed, even if they are not evaluated, and an undefined row structure will cause an error. The same is not true for IF and CASE statements; not only are the THEN and ELSE branches not evaluated if they are not chosen, they are not even parsed. And that's why IF and CASE statements work in a situation like this, whereas IF and CASE expressions will fail.

An UPDATE that specifies new column values that are the same as old column values will still fire a before row UPDATE trigger; the same is true of an UPDATE that refers to a column named in the UPDATE OF clause but doesn't specify a different value. Also, the row structures contain all the column values from the old and new rows, even columns excluded from an UPDATE OF list, and all those other columns can be named in the WHEN clause. Here is an example of a before row trigger with both an UPDATE OF clause and a WHEN clause, plus code that changes the final values for all the non-key columns:

```
CREATE TABLE t1 (
    key_1       INTEGER NOT NULL PRIMARY KEY,
    non_key_1   VARCHAR ( 100 ) NOT NULL,
    non_key_2   VARCHAR ( 100 ) NOT NULL );

CREATE TRIGGER triud_t1
BEFORE UPDATE OF non_key_1
ON t1
REFERENCING OLD AS old_t1
          NEW AS new_t1
FOR EACH ROW
WHEN ( old_t1.non_key_2 = 'xxx' )
BEGIN
    MESSAGE 'Updating t1...' TO CONSOLE;
    MESSAGE STRING ( '  Old row:    ',
        old_t1.key_1, ', ',
        old_t1.non_key_1, ', ',
        old_t1.non_key_2 ) TO CONSOLE;
    MESSAGE STRING ( '  New row:    ',
        new_t1.key_1, ', ',
        new_t1.non_key_1, ', ',
        new_t1.non_key_2 ) TO CONSOLE;
    SET new_t1.non_key_1 = 'ccc';
    SET new_t1.non_key_2 = 'ddd';
    MESSAGE STRING ( '  Final row: ',
        new_t1.key_1, ', ',
        new_t1.non_key_1, ', ',
        new_t1.non_key_2 ) TO CONSOLE;
END;

INSERT t1 VALUES ( 1, 'ppp', 'aaa' );
INSERT t1 VALUES ( 2, 'qqq', 'bbb' );
UPDATE t1 SET non_key_2 = 'xxx' WHERE key_1 = 1;
UPDATE t1 SET non_key_1 = 'zzz' WHERE key_1 = 2;
UPDATE t1 SET non_key_1 = 'yyy';
SELECT * FROM t1 ORDER BY key_1;
```

The first UPDATE above doesn't fire the trigger because the SET clause specifies a column that isn't named in the trigger's UPDATE OF clause. The second UPDATE doesn't fire the trigger because the old value of t1.non_key_2 is 'bbb' and that doesn't match the trigger's WHEN clause. The third update changes both rows in t1, but only the update to the first row fires the trigger because that's the only update that matches both the UPDATE OF and WHEN clauses. The code inside the trigger then changes both non-key column values and displays all three versions of the row: old, new, and final. Here's what that display looks like:

```
Updating t1...
  Old row:  1, ppp, xxx
```

```
New row:   1, yyy, xxx
Final row: 1, ccc, ddd
```

Here's what the final SELECT shows after all the updates are complete:

```
key_1  non_key_1  non_key_2
=====  =========  =========
1      'ccc'      'ddd'
2      'yyy'      'bbb'
```

Tip: The before row form of CREATE TRIGGER is very popular because it is the easiest to code. For example, it is possible to modify the new row in a before row UPDATE trigger without worrying about endless recursion. Updates made in the other two kinds of trigger must be made directly to the associated table rather than to a row structure; that nested update may recursively fire the same trigger, requiring extra code to make sure the recursion doesn't run away.

The syntax for the second form of trigger differs only by one word: The keyword AFTER specifies that this trigger is fired after the row operation is complete:

```
<create_after_row_trigger> ::= CREATE TRIGGER <trigger_name>
                               AFTER
                               <fired_by>
                               [ ORDER <order_number> ]
                               ON [ <owner_name> "." ] <table_name>
                               [ <referencing_as_structures> ]
                               FOR EACH ROW
                               [ WHEN "(" <boolean_expression> ")" ]
                               <begin_block>
```

After row triggers work almost the same way as before row triggers, with three differences:

- An after row UPDATE trigger is not fired for a row where no column values actually changed in value.
- An after row UPDATE OF trigger is not fired for a row where none of the columns named in the UPDATE OF clause actually changed in value.
- It is not possible to modify the values in the REFERENCING NEW AS structure because it's too late, the row operation has already been performed.

The syntax for the third form of trigger uses the keywords AFTER and FOR EACH STATEMENT to define a trigger that is fired once after the triggering INSERT, UPDATE, or DELETE statement is finished operating on all the rows it affects:

```
<create_after_statement_trigger> ::= CREATE TRIGGER <trigger_name>
                                     AFTER
                                     <fired_by>
                                     [ ORDER <order_number> ]
                                     ON [ <owner_name> "." ] <table_name>
                                     [ <referencing_as_tables> ]
                                     [ FOR EACH STATEMENT ]
                                     <begin_block>
<referencing_as_tables> ::= REFERENCING { <as_table> } <as_table>
<as_table>              ::= OLD AS <as_table_name>
                         | NEW AS <as_table_name>
<as_table_name>         ::= <identifier> naming a read-only temporary table
```

Here's a list of characteristics that make an after statement trigger different from an after row trigger:

■ The REFERENCING OLD AS and NEW AS clauses define multi-row temporary tables as opposed to single-row structures.

■ The REFERENCING OLD AS temporary table contains the rows affected by the statement that caused the trigger to fire, as they existed in the database before the triggering statement executed.

■ The REFERENCING NEW AS temporary table contains the rows affected by the statement that caused the trigger to fire, as they exist in the database after the triggering statement finished but before the trigger itself began executing.

■ The REFERENCING NEW AS temporary table itself is read-only, although it can be used in a join in an UPDATE statement inside the trigger.

■ The WHEN clause is not allowed in an after statement trigger.

■ The REFERENCING OLD AS and NEW AS temporary tables can be empty if the triggering statement doesn't actually affect any rows in the table. An after statement trigger is always fired if the other criteria are met; e.g., an UPDATE OF trigger is fired if the UPDATE statement contains a SET clause that specifies at least one of the columns named in the trigger's UPDATE OF clause, even if the UPDATE statement's WHERE clause didn't match any rows.

■ The REFERENCING OLD AS and NEW AS temporary tables in an after statement UPDATE or UPDATE OF trigger won't contain any rows where the column values didn't actually change. This means the temporary tables can be empty or can contain fewer rows than the UPDATE statement's WHERE clause matched.

The rules for when an after statement trigger is fired, and if so, how many rows appear in the REFERENCING OLD AS and NEW AS temporary tables, are rather complex. Following are two tables that summarize the rules, and include the before row and after row triggers as well. Each table entry answers two questions: "Is this trigger fired, yes or no?" and "For an after statement trigger, how many rows appear in the REFERENCING temporary tables?" For simplicity, the tables assume an UPDATE statement that matches either one or zero rows.

The first table is for an ordinary UPDATE trigger, one that doesn't use the special UPDATE OF clause. Whether or not this class of trigger is fired depends on whether or not the WHERE clause matches any rows, and whether or not the SET clause specifies any column values that are different.

```
UPDATE Trigger Fired?
   WHERE clause matches row:    yes         yes          no
   SET clause specifies value:  different   same         n/a
                                ==========  ===========  ===========
     BEFORE UPDATE ROW          yes         yes          no
     AFTER UPDATE ROW           yes         no           no
     AFTER UPDATE STATEMENT     yes, 1 row  yes, 0 rows  yes, 0 rows
```

The second table is for a trigger with an UPDATE OF clause. Whether or not this class of trigger is fired depends on whether or not the WHERE clause matches any rows, whether or not the SET clause names any columns also named in the UPDATE OF clause, and whether or not the SET clause specifies any column values that are different.

```
UPDATE OF Trigger Fired?
    WHERE clause matches row:      yes         yes         yes   no          no
    SET clause matches UPDATE OF:  yes         yes         no    yes         no
    SET clause specifies value:    different   same        -     -           -
                                   ==========  =========== ====  =========== ====
        BEFORE UPDATE OF ROW       yes         yes         no    no          no
        AFTER UPDATE OF ROW        yes         no          no    no          no
        AFTER UPDATE OF STATEMENT  yes, 1 row  yes, 0 rows no    yes, 0 rows no
```

Following is an example of an after statement trigger that is fired by an UPDATE statement that matches two rows. The trigger BEGIN block includes cursor FOR loops and MESSAGE statements to display the entire contents of the REFERENCING OLD AS and NEW AS temporary tables.

This trigger also contains an UPDATE statement that overrides the changes made by the triggering UPDATE statement by directly updating the table again. This will fire the trigger recursively, so the trigger takes the following two steps to prevent runaway recursion. First, the UPDATE statement inside the trigger includes a WHERE clause that won't match any rows that have already been changed by a previous trigger execution. Second, the first statement in the trigger BEGIN block is an IF that checks how many rows are in the REFERENCING OLD AS temporary table. If that temporary table is empty (which will happen if it is fired by an UPDATE that doesn't match any rows), the LEAVE statement terminates the trigger before it has a chance to fire itself again.

```
CREATE TABLE t1 (
    key_1        INTEGER NOT NULL PRIMARY KEY,
    non_key_1    VARCHAR ( 100 ) NOT NULL,
    non_key_2    VARCHAR ( 100 ) NOT NULL );

CREATE TRIGGER tru_t1
AFTER UPDATE OF non_key_1
ON t1
REFERENCING OLD AS old_t1
            NEW AS new_t1
FOR EACH STATEMENT
this_trigger:
BEGIN
    MESSAGE 'Updating t1...' TO CONSOLE;
    IF NOT EXISTS ( SELECT * FROM old_t1 ) THEN
        MESSAGE '...no rows updated.' TO CONSOLE;
        LEAVE this_trigger;
    END IF;

    FOR f1 AS c1 NO SCROLL CURSOR FOR
    SELECT old_t1.key_1        AS @key_1,
           old_t1.non_key_1    AS @non_key_1,
           old_t1.non_key_2    AS @non_key_2
      FROM old_t1
    ORDER BY old_t1.key_1
    DO
        MESSAGE STRING ( ' Old row:  ',
            @key_1, ', ',
            @non_key_1, ', ',
            @non_key_2 ) TO CONSOLE;
```

```
  END FOR;

  FOR f2 AS c2 NO SCROLL CURSOR FOR
  SELECT new_t1.key_1        AS @key_1,
         new_t1.non_key_1    AS @non_key_1,
         new_t1.non_key_2    AS @non_key_2
    FROM new_t1
   ORDER BY new_t1.key_1
  DO
     MESSAGE STRING ( '  New row:   ',
        @key_1, ', ',
        @non_key_1, ', ',
        @non_key_2 ) TO CONSOLE;
  END FOR;


  UPDATE t1
        INNER JOIN new_t1
              ON new_t1.key_1 = t1.key_1
     SET t1.non_key_1 = 'ccc',
         t1.non_key_2 = 'ddd'
   WHERE t1.non_key_1 <> 'ccc'
      OR t1.non_key_2 <> 'ddd';

  FOR f4 AS c4 NO SCROLL CURSOR FOR
  SELECT t1.key_1          AS @key_1,
         t1.non_key_1      AS @non_key_1,
         t1.non_key_2      AS @non_key_2
    FROM t1
        INNER JOIN new_t1
              ON new_t1.key_1 = t1.key_1
   ORDER BY t1.key_1
  DO
     MESSAGE STRING ( 'Final row: ',
        @key_1, ', ',
        @non_key_1, ', ',
        @non_key_2 ) TO CONSOLE;
  END FOR;

END;

INSERT t1 VALUES ( 1, 'ppp', 'aaa' );
INSERT t1 VALUES ( 2, 'qqq', 'bbb' );
UPDATE t1 SET non_key_1 = 'yyy';
SELECT * FROM t1 ORDER BY key_1;
```

Note: A runaway trigger will run for quite a while, firing itself over and over again many times, but SQL Anywhere will eventually detect an error and set the SQLSTATE to '42W29' for "Procedure or trigger calls have nested too deeply."

The MESSAGE output shows that the trigger is fired three times, once by the outer UPDATE, once by the UPDATE in the first trigger execution that changes the rows a second time, and once for the UPDATE in the second trigger execution that doesn't match any rows:

```
Updating t1...
  Old row:   1, ppp, aaa
  Old row:   2, qqq, bbb
  New row:   1, yyy, aaa
  New row:   2, yyy, bbb
```

```
Updating t1...
  Old row:  1, yyy, aaa
  Old row:  2, yyy, bbb
  New row:  1, ccc, ddd
  New row:  2, ccc, ddd
Updating t1...
...no rows updated.
Final row: 1, ccc, ddd
Final row: 2, ccc, ddd
Final row: 1, ccc, ddd
Final row: 2, ccc, ddd
```

The output from the SELECT shows the final contents of the table:

key_1	non_key_1	non_key_2
=======	===========	===========
1	'ccc'	'ddd'
2	'ccc'	'ddd'

Triggers can be used for complex integrity checks and for calculations in a denormalized database design. For example, here is a trigger that updates a running total in a parent table every time a row in a child table is inserted, updated, or deleted. For every INSERT, the inserted value in child.non_key_3 is added to the corresponding parent.non_key_3; for every DELETE, the deleted value is subtracted; and every UPDATE subtracts the old value and adds the new value.

```
CREATE TRIGGER tr_child
BEFORE INSERT, DELETE, UPDATE
ORDER 1 ON child
REFERENCING OLD AS old_child
            NEW AS new_child
FOR EACH ROW
BEGIN
   CASE
      WHEN INSERTING THEN
         UPDATE parent
            SET parent.non_key_3
               = parent.non_key_3
               + new_child.non_key_3
            WHERE parent.key_1 = new_child.key_1;
      WHEN UPDATING THEN
         UPDATE parent
            SET parent.non_key_3
               = parent.non_key_3
               - old_child.non_key_3
               + new_child.non_key_3
            WHERE parent.key_1 = old_child.key_1;
      WHEN DELETING THEN
         UPDATE parent
            SET parent.non_key_3
               = parent.non_key_3
               - old_child.non_key_3
            WHERE parent.key_1 = old_child.key_1;
   END CASE;
END;
```

Tip: Avoid writing triggers. They're hard to code, hard to understand, hard to test, hard to debug, and prone to errors and performance problems. SQL Anywhere has many features you can use to avoid writing triggers: primary and foreign key constraints, UNIQUE constraints, CHECK constraints, computed columns, and DEFAULT values like TIMESTAMP, LAST USER, AUTOINCREMENT and GLOBAL AUTOINCREMENT, all of which are described in Chapter 1, "Creating."

8.12 CREATE EVENT

An *event* is a special kind of BEGIN block that is stored in the database. Each event may be associated with a named occurrence or condition that SQL Anywhere can detect or a schedule that SQL Anywhere can follow. An event is somewhat like a trigger in that it can be automatically executed by SQL Anywhere. Unlike a trigger, however, an event is not associated with any table in the database, and it can be explicitly executed as well as fired automatically.

Events come in three basic flavors: typed events that are associated with a named condition or event type, scheduled events that are executed according to a clock and calendar schedule, and user-defined events that are explicitly executed via the TRIGGER EVENT statement described in Section 8.13.

```
<create_event> ::= <create_typed_event>
                 | <create_scheduled_event>
                 | <create_user_defined_event>
```

A typed event is associated with one of 14 different conditions or event types. Most of these event types are associated with specific occurrences that SQL Anywhere can detect and react to as soon as they occur; e.g., "Connect" represents a user connection being successfully established. Four of these event types — DBDiskSpace, LogDiskSpace, ServerIdle, and TempDiskSpace — require active polling, which is done by SQL Anywhere every 30 seconds.

```
<create_typed_event> ::= CREATE EVENT <event_name>
                            TYPE <event_type>
                            [ <event_where_clause> ]
                            HANDLER <begin_block>
<event_name>        ::= <identifier>
<event_type>        ::= BackupEnd           -- backup completed
                      | "Connect"           -- user connected OK
                      | ConnectFailed       -- user connection failed
                      | DatabaseStart       -- database started
                      | DBDiskSpace         -- checked every 30 seconds
                      | "Disconnect"        -- user disconnected
                      | GlobalAutoincrement -- near end of range
                      | GrowDB              -- database file extended
                      | GrowLog             -- transaction log extended
                      | GrowTemp            -- temporary file extended
                      | LogDiskSpace        -- checked every 30 seconds
                      | "RAISERROR"         -- RAISERROR issued
                      | ServerIdle          -- checked every 30 seconds
                      | TempDiskSpace       -- checked every 30 seconds
```

The event WHERE clause may be used to limit the conditions under which a typed event is actually executed. Different event types have different measurements associated with them, available through calls to the built-in EVENT_CONDITION function. The WHERE clause can be used to compare these measurements to literal values in a simple boolean expression using numeric comparison predicates and the AND operator:

```
<event_where_clause>       ::= WHERE <event_predicate> { AND <event_predicate> }
<event_predicate>          ::= EVENT_CONDITION "(" <event_condition_name> ")"
                                 <event_comparison_operator>
                                 <event_condition_value>
<event_condition_name>     ::= 'DBFreePercent'     -- for DBDiskSpace
                             | 'DBFreeSpace'       -- for DBDiskSpace, in MB
                             | 'DBSize'            -- for GrowDB, in MB
                             | 'ErrorNumber'       -- for "RAISERROR"
                             | 'IdleTime'          -- for ServerIdle, in seconds
                             | 'Interval'          -- for all, in seconds
                             | 'LogFreePercent'    -- for LogDiskSpace
                             | 'LogFreeSpace'      -- for LogDiskSpace, in MB
                             | 'LogSize'           -- for GrowLog, in MB
                             | 'RemainingValues'   -- for GlobalAutoincrement
                             | 'TempFreePercent'   -- for TempDiskSpace
                             | 'TempFreeSpace'     -- for TempDiskSpace, in MB
                             | 'TempSize'          -- for GrowTemp, in MB
<event_comparison_operator> ::= "="
                             | "<"
                             | ">"
                             | "!="
                             | "<="
                             | ">="
<event_condition_value>    ::= integer literal value for comparison
```

Note: The CREATE EVENT statement has other keywords you can read about in the SQL Anywhere Help. The DISABLE keyword may be used to create an event that won't be automatically executed, no matter what, until an ALTER EVENT statement specifies ENABLE; by default events are enabled, and the ALTER EVENT statement isn't discussed in this book. Also, the AT CONSOLIDATED and AT REMOTE clauses can be used to control where events will be executed in a SQL Remote environment; this book doesn't discuss SQL Remote, just MobiLink, so these AT clauses aren't covered either.

Only the string literal <event_condition_name> values listed above can be used as EVENT_CONDITION parameters. They aren't case sensitive, but they are checked for syntax; any spelling mistake or attempt to use an expression will cause the CREATE EVENT statement to fail.

The EVENT_CONDITION return value is numeric. Except for 'Interval', each event condition name only applies to one event type; EVENT_CONDITION returns zero for any event condition name that is used with an event type to which it doesn't apply.

The EVENT_CONDITION function can only be called in the WHERE clause as shown above; if you need the same information inside the event's BEGIN block you can call the EVENT_PARAMETER function.

EVENT_PARAMETER accepts all the same condition names as EVENT_CONDITION, plus some additional predefined parameters listed here:

```
<event_parameter_function_call> ::= EVENT_PARAMETER
                                      "(" <event_parameter_name_string> ")"
<event_parameter_name_string>   ::= string expression containing an
                                      <event_parameter_name>
<event_parameter_name>          ::= DBFreePercent    -- from EVENT_CONDITION
```

```
                                  | DBFreeSpace
                                  | DBSize
                                  | ErrorNumber
                                  | IdleTime
                                  | Interval
                                  | LogFreePercent
                                  | LogFreeSpace
                                  | LogSize
                                  | RemainingValues
                                  | TempFreePercent
                                  | TempFreeSpace
                                  | TempSize
                                  | AppInfo          -- more predefined names
                                  | ConnectionID
                                  | DisconnectReason
                                  | EventName
                                  | Executions
                                  | NumActive
                                  | ScheduleName
                                  | TableName
                                  | User
                                  | <user_defined_event_parameter_name>
<user_defined_event_parameter_name> ::= <identifier>
```

The argument to EVENT_PARAMETER is a string containing the name of an event parameter; e.g., EVENT_PARAMETER ('User') will return the user id that invoked this event. Unlike the argument to EVENT_CONDITION, EVENT_PARAMETER can be passed an expression as long as the result of that expression is one of the predefined parameter names listed above, or a user-defined parameter name.

The EVENT_PARAMETER return value is VARCHAR (254); alphanumeric and numeric values are all returned as strings. The default values are the empty string '' for predefined alphanumeric parameters, '0' for predefined numeric parameters, and NULL for user-defined parameters that haven't been given a value in a TRIGGER EVENT statement. For more information about user-defined parameters, see Section 8.13, "TRIGGER EVENT."

Here is an example of a ServerIdle typed event handler that uses a WHERE clause to start executing as soon as the server has been idle for 60 seconds:

```
CREATE EVENT ev_ServerIdle
TYPE ServerIdle
WHERE EVENT_CONDITION ( 'IdleTime' ) >= 60
HANDLER BEGIN
   MESSAGE STRING (
      'The server has been idle for ',
      EVENT_PARAMETER ( 'IdleTime' ),
      ' seconds.' ) TO CONSOLE;
END;
```

Here is the output produced by that event handler; SQL Anywhere polls for this kind of event every 30 seconds, and the WHERE clause prevented the event handler from executing at the first 30-second point:

```
The server has been idle for 60 seconds.
The server has been idle for 90 seconds.
The server has been idle for 120 seconds.
The server has been idle for 150 seconds.
The server has been idle for 180 seconds.
The server has been idle for 210 seconds.
```

```
The server has been idle for 240 seconds.
The server has been idle for 270 seconds.
```

The CREATE EVENT statement can only be executed by a user with DBA privileges. When the event executes, it not only executes with the privileges of that user, but it opens a separate connection to the database using that user id. This separate connection executes asynchronously; in other words, the execution of the event's BEGIN block is not coordinated with the execution of code running on any other connection, including a connection that may have directly caused this event to be executed.

Tip: Watch the engine console window for errors detected inside event handlers; for example "Handler for event 'ev_ServerIdle' caused SQLSTATE '52003'" means "column not found." Because a separate internal connection is used for each event execution, there is no "client application" to receive an error message when one is produced by an event's BEGIN block, so SQL Anywhere has nowhere else to send it other than the console window. Even if you use ISQL and TRIGGER EVENT statements to test your events, you'll have to go looking for the error messages; they won't appear in ISQL's Message pane.

Here is an example that demonstrates the separate connection and its asynchronous nature. First of all, the following CREATE EVENT is executed by a user called "Admin1"; MESSAGE statements are included to display the connection number and user id for the event itself. Also, two EVENT_PARAMETER calls display the connection number and user of the other connection, the one that causes this event to be executed.

```
CREATE EVENT ev_Connect
TYPE "Connect"
HANDLER BEGIN
   MESSAGE STRING ( 'Connection event...' );
   MESSAGE STRING ( 'Event connection:     ', CONNECTION_PROPERTY ( 'Number' ) );
   MESSAGE STRING ( 'Event user:           ', CURRENT USER );
   MESSAGE STRING ( 'Triggering connection: ', EVENT_PARAMETER( 'ConnectionID' ) );
   MESSAGE STRING ( 'Triggering user:       ', EVENT_PARAMETER( 'User' ) );
   MESSAGE STRING ( CURRENT TIMESTAMP, ' ', CURRENT USER, ' Event waiting...' );
   WAITFOR DELAY '00:00:30';
   MESSAGE STRING ( CURRENT TIMESTAMP, ' ', CURRENT USER, ' ...event complete.' );
END;
```

The second step of this example is for a user called "User1" to connect to the database, and then immediately run this statement:

```
MESSAGE STRING ( CURRENT TIMESTAMP, ' ', CURRENT USER, ' Connected OK.' );
```

Here's what the display looks like; the first six MESSAGE statements inside the event run as soon as User1 connects to the database. At that point a WAITFOR statement causes the event to pause for 30 seconds; just because the connection event is still running, however, doesn't mean that User1's connection is delayed. Instead, User1 can run the "Connected OK" MESSAGE statement right away, long before the connection event executes the last MESSAGE statement and finishes.

```
Connection event...
Event connection:       200824710
Event user:             ADMIN1
Triggering connection: 1778456925
Triggering user:        User1
```

```
2004-01-11 12:29:29.157 ADMIN1 Event waiting...
2004-01-11 12:29:31.661 User1 Connected OK.
2004-01-11 12:29:59.240 ADMIN1 ...event complete.
```

Typed events are reentrant and can be executed in parallel; in the above example, a second connection can fire the same event a second time before the first execution has finished.

Tip: The CURRENT USER inside an event is the event's creator, not the user id of a connection that caused this event to execute. Be careful when calling CONNECTION_PROPERTY inside an event; if you want the properties of some other connection you must explicitly provide that connection number.

Tip: Don't create two typed events for the same type, unless you don't care in which order they are executed. Not only is there no documentation specifying the order in which they will be started, since events run asynchronously there's no guarantee that the event that started first won't finish last.

Scheduled events don't have TYPE or WHERE clauses, but do have one or more SCHEDULE items:

```
<create_scheduled_event>     ::= CREATE EVENT <event_name>
                                     <event_schedule_list>
                                     HANDLER <begin_block>
<event_schedule_list>        ::= <event_schedule_item> { "," <event_schedule_item> }
<event_schedule_item>        ::= SCHEDULE [ <event_schedule_item_name> ]
                                     <event_start_times>
                                     [ <event_repeat_every> ]
                                     [ <event_on_days> ]
                                     [ START DATE <event_start_date> ]
<event_schedule_item_name> ::= <identifier> -- required for multiple schedule items
<event_start_times>          ::= START TIME <first_scheduled_time>
                                 | BETWEEN <first_scheduled_time> AND <ending_time>
<first_scheduled_time>       ::= string literal starting time
<ending_time>                ::= string literal time after which event doesn't occur
<event_repeat_every>         ::= EVERY <schedule_interval> HOURS
                                 | EVERY <schedule_interval> MINUTES
                                 | EVERY <schedule_interval> SECONDS
<schedule_interval>          ::= integer literal number of hours, minutes, or seconds
<event_on_days>              ::= ON "(" <day_name>   { "," <day_name>   ")" }
                                 | ON "(" <day_number> { "," <day_number> ")" }
<day_name>                   ::= string literal weekday name
<day_number>                 ::= integer literal day in the month
<event_start_date>           ::= string literal starting date
```

Each event SCHEDULE item may contain the following components:

- An **identifier** can be used to name a schedule item. This name is available at execution time via EVENT_PARAMETER ('ScheduleName') so the event handler code can determine which schedule item caused the event to fire, and it is required if the event has more than one SCHEDULE item.
- The **START TIME** clause specifies the exact time at which the event is to be fired for the first time.
- The **BETWEEN** clause specifies two times: the time the event is to fire for the first time (just like START TIME), plus the time after which the event is not fired.

■ The **EVERY** clause specifies that the event is to be fired more than once, and how often in terms of an interval measured in hours, minutes, and seconds.

■ The **ON** clause specifies on which named days of the week, or numbered days of the month, the event is to be fired.

■ The **START DATE** clause specifies the exact date on which the event is to be fired for the first time.

If both the EVERY and ON clauses are omitted, the event is fired once. If EVERY is specified and ON is omitted, a default ON clause specifying all possible days is assumed. If EVERY is omitted and ON is specified, the event is fired once on each specified day. If both EVERY and ON are specified, the event is fired at the calculated times on the specified days.

Here is an example using all the clauses in two SCHEDULE items:

```
CREATE EVENT ev_repeater
SCHEDULE sched_10
    START TIME '14:40:01'
    EVERY 10 SECONDS
    ON ( 'Monday', 'Sunday', 'Tuesday' )
    START DATE '2004-01-11',
SCHEDULE sched_17
    BETWEEN '14:40:02' AND '20:00'
    EVERY 17 SECONDS
    ON ( 'Wednesday', 'Sunday' )
    START DATE '2004-01-11'
HANDLER BEGIN
    MESSAGE STRING (
        'Event ',
        EVENT_PARAMETER ( 'EventName' ),
        ' fired at ',
        CURRENT TIMESTAMP,
        ' because of schedule ',
        EVENT_PARAMETER ( 'ScheduleName' ) ) TO CONSOLE;
END;
```

Here is the display that shows that the schedule item named "sched_10" caused the event to fire at the START TIME of 14:40:01, then according to the EVERY 10 SECONDS clause at 14:40:11, :21, :31, and so on. It also shows that the schedule item named "sched_17" caused the event to fire at the initial BETWEEN time of 14:40:02, then according to the EVERY 17 SECONDS clause at 14:40:19, :36, :53, and so on.

```
Event ev_repeater fired at 2004-01-11 14:40:01.048 because of schedule sched_10
Event ev_repeater fired at 2004-01-11 14:40:02.050 because of schedule sched_17
Event ev_repeater fired at 2004-01-11 14:40:11.083 because of schedule sched_10
Event ev_repeater fired at 2004-01-11 14:40:19.014 because of schedule sched_17
Event ev_repeater fired at 2004-01-11 14:40:21.017 because of schedule sched_10
Event ev_repeater fired at 2004-01-11 14:40:31.051 because of schedule sched_10
Event ev_repeater fired at 2004-01-11 14:40:36.079 because of schedule sched_17
Event ev_repeater fired at 2004-01-11 14:40:41.096 because of schedule sched_10
Event ev_repeater fired at 2004-01-11 14:40:51.030 because of schedule sched_10
Event ev_repeater fired at 2004-01-11 14:40:53.033 because of schedule sched_17
Event ev_repeater fired at 2004-01-11 14:41:01.055 because of schedule sched_10
Event ev_repeater fired at 2004-01-11 14:41:10.088 because of schedule sched_17
```

Repetitions of a scheduled event are executed serially even if the schedule indicates an apparent overlap. This can result in an actual interval different from the one specified in the EVERY clause. For example, if an event is specified with

EVERY 10 SECONDS but it takes 15 seconds to complete execution each time it is fired, every second interval point will be missed and the actual schedule will be the same as if EVERY 20 SECONDS had been specified.

The time to execute an event is not determined by continuously watching the system clock, but is calculated as an elapsed time to wait before firing the event. For a one-time event this calculation is done when the CREATE EVENT or ALTER EVENT statement is executed, and again if the database is stopped and restarted before the event fires; the same is true for the first time a repetitive event is fired. For a later firing of a repetitive event, the calculation is done when the previous execution is finished, and again if the database is stopped and restarted.

Note: If the calculated elapsed time is more than one hour, SQL Anywhere forces a recalculation after one hour; this recalculation is repeated after each hour until the remaining elapsed time is less than one hour. This makes sure an event will fire at the expected clock-on-the-wall time when the server clock automatically changes to and from daylight saving time.

Tip: When changing the system clock to test that a scheduled event actually occurs at some specific time, such as midnight, DROP and CREATE the event, or ALTER it, after changing the system clock; you can also stop and start the server. If you change the system clock time while the server is running, and don't do something to force SQL Anywhere to recalculate the elapsed time for a scheduled event, the next time it fires may not agree with the CURRENT TIMESTAMP.

Typed and scheduled events can work together to automate administrative tasks. Here is an example of a scheduled event that performs a database backup and renames the transaction log every weekday and Sunday at midnight, plus a typed event that reorganizes a table as soon as the backup is complete:

```
CREATE EVENT ev_backup
SCHEDULE
   START TIME '00:00:00'
   ON ( 'Monday', 'Tuesday', 'Wednesday', 'Thursday', 'Friday', 'Sunday' )
HANDLER BEGIN
   MESSAGE STRING (
      EVENT_PARAMETER ( 'EventName' ),
      ' started at ',
      CURRENT TIMESTAMP ) TO CONSOLE;
   BACKUP DATABASE DIRECTORY 'c:\\backup'
      TRANSACTION LOG RENAME MATCH
      WITH COMMENT 'ev_backup';
   MESSAGE STRING (
      EVENT_PARAMETER ( 'EventName' ),
      ' finished at ',
      CURRENT TIMESTAMP ) TO CONSOLE;
END;

CREATE EVENT ev_reorganize
TYPE BackupEnd
HANDLER BEGIN
   MESSAGE STRING (
      EVENT_PARAMETER ( 'EventName' ),
      ' started at ',
      CURRENT TIMESTAMP ) TO CONSOLE;
```

```
REORGANIZE TABLE t1;
REORGANIZE TABLE t1 PRIMARY KEY;
MESSAGE STRING (
    EVENT_PARAMETER ( 'EventName' ),
    ' finished at ',
    CURRENT TIMESTAMP ) TO CONSOLE;
END;
```

The following shows what the output looks like; at midnight the ev_backup event fires and executes the BACKUP DATABASE statement, which in turn forces a number of checkpoint operations as it proceeds. As soon as the backup is complete, the ev_reorganize event is fired because it was defined with TYPE BackupEnd; this event executes two REORGANIZE TABLE statements that also force checkpoints.

```
ev_backup started at 2004-01-12 00:00:00.003
Starting checkpoint of "test8" (test8.db) at Mon Jan 12 2004 00:00
Finished checkpoint of "test8" (test8.db) at Mon Jan 12 2004 00:00
Starting checkpoint of "test8" (test8.db) at Mon Jan 12 2004 00:00
Finished checkpoint of "test8" (test8.db) at Mon Jan 12 2004 00:00
Starting checkpoint of "test8" (test8.db) at Mon Jan 12 2004 00:00
Finished checkpoint of "test8" (test8.db) at Mon Jan 12 2004 00:00
ev_backup finished at 2004-01-12 00:00:01.044
ev_reorganize started at 2004-01-12 00:00:01.044
Starting checkpoint of "test8" (test8.db) at Mon Jan 12 2004 00:00
Finished checkpoint of "test8" (test8.db) at Mon Jan 12 2004 00:00
Starting checkpoint of "test8" (test8.db) at Mon Jan 12 2004 00:00
Finished checkpoint of "test8" (test8.db) at Mon Jan 12 2004 00:00
ev_reorganize finished at 2004-01-12 00:00:01.124
```

Note that it isn't the ev_backup event that fires ev_reorganize, it is the BACKUP statement inside ev_backup. If the ev_backup event contained time-consuming code after the BACKUP statement, the ev_reorganize event will start before ev_backup is finished. This cascading of events is similar to cascading triggers, where a second trigger is fired by an INSERT, UPDATE, or DELETE statement contained in the first trigger.

For more information about the BACKUP DATABASE statement, see Section 9.12, "Backup." For more information about the REORGANIZE TABLE statement, see Section 10.6.3, "Table Reorganization."

A user-defined event is created with no TYPE, WHERE, or SCHEDULE clauses:

```
<create_user_defined_event> ::= CREATE EVENT <event_name>
                                HANDLER <begin_block>
```

The only way to execute a user-defined event is by using a TRIGGER EVENT statement; user-defined events are never automatically fired by SQL Anywhere. A user-defined event is like a procedure in the sense that the TRIGGER EVENT statement is like the CALL statement, with the difference being that a procedure is executed synchronously on the same connection as the CALL, whereas an event runs asynchronously on its own connection. User-defined events and the TRIGGER EVENT statement are discussed in more detail in the next section.

8.13 TRIGGER EVENT

The TRIGGER EVENT statement can be used to test typed and scheduled events, as well as to fire user-defined events on demand as part of regular processing.

```
<trigger_event>                ::= TRIGGER EVENT <event_name>
                                   [ <event_parameter_list> ]
<event_parameter_list>         ::= "(" <event_parameter_assignment> { ","
                                   <event_parameter_assignment> } ")"
<event_parameter_assignment> ::= <event_parameter_name> "=" <event_parameter_value>
<event_parameter_value>        ::= string expression up to 254 characters in length
```

The TRIGGER EVENT statement forces the event to execute regardless of what the event's TYPE, WHERE, or SCHEDULE clauses say. For example, the following statement will fire the ev_backup event described in the previous section even if it isn't midnight yet:

```
TRIGGER EVENT ev_backup;
```

The TRIGGER EVENT statement allows values to be passed to the event; these values may be obtained by calls to EVENT_PARAMETER inside the event's BEGIN block. Here is an example of an event that will be used to demonstrate various TRIGGER EVENT statements; the ev_DBDiskSpace event displays the DBFreePercent and DBFreeSpace parameters:

```
CREATE EVENT ev_DBDiskSpace
   TYPE DBDiskSpace
   WHERE EVENT_CONDITION ( 'DBFreePercent' ) < 20
HANDLER BEGIN
   MESSAGE STRING ( 'ev_DBDiskSpace started at ', CURRENT TIMESTAMP );
   MESSAGE STRING ( 'DBFreePercent: ', EVENT_PARAMETER ( 'DBFreePercent' ) );
   MESSAGE STRING ( 'DBFreeSpace  : ', EVENT_PARAMETER ( 'DBFreeSpace' ) );
END;
```

Under normal conditions, once the DBFreeSpace measurement falls below 20%, SQL Anywhere will execute this event every 30 seconds. Here's what the output looks like:

```
ev_DBDiskSpace started at 2004-01-12 13:39:56.495
DBFreePercent: 9
DBFreeSpace  : 2664
```

Here is a TRIGGER EVENT that provides a value for DBFreePercent but not DBFreeSpace:

```
TRIGGER EVENT ev_DBDiskSpace ( DBFreePercent = '15' );
```

Here is the corresponding output; SQL Anywhere doesn't automatically provide any parameter values when TRIGGER EVENT is used, so DBFreeSpace is zero, the default for numeric predefined parameters:

```
ev_DBDiskSpace started at 2004-01-12 13:40:30.564
DBFreePercent: 15
DBFreeSpace  : 0
```

Here is an example that provides values for both measurements:

```
TRIGGER EVENT ev_DBDiskSpace ( DBFreePercent = '15', DBFreeSpace = '111' );
```

Here is the resulting output; when you use TRIGGER EVENT you have to provide a value for every parameter that's important to the event handler:

```
ev_DBDiskSpace started at 2004-01-12 13:41:09.710
DBFreePercent: 15
DBFreeSpace  : 111
```

Parameters named in the TRIGGER EVENT statement may be the same as the ones returned by calls to EVENT_CONDITION in the event's WHERE clause. However, the WHERE clause is ignored by TRIGGER EVENT, and the event will still be executed even if values that otherwise wouldn't match the WHERE clause are specified in the TRIGGER EVENT. Here is a TRIGGER EVENT statement that sets a parameter to a value that doesn't match the WHERE clause:

```
TRIGGER EVENT ev_DBDiskSpace ( DBFreePercent = '50', DBFreeSpace = '111' );
```

Here is the corresponding output:

```
ev_DBDiskSpace started at 2004-01-12 13:41:40.975
DBFreePercent: 50
DBFreeSpace  : 111
```

Any and all of the event condition and event parameter names can be specified in a TRIGGER EVENT statement for any event, and any string value up to 254 characters may be specified. SQL Anywhere doesn't perform any error checking at all on the values passed by TRIGGER EVENT; for example, you can pass 'xxx' to DBFreePercent even though that parameter is always numeric when an event is executed normally.

Tip: TRIGGER EVENT is not a very good test of a typed event with or without a WHERE clause, or an event with a SCHEDULE clause. That's because the TRIGGER EVENT statement creates a completely artificial test environment that may or may not reflect reality. To perform an adequate test, you should set up the actual conditions that cause the event to execute and check to make sure the event really does run as expected.

Note: A TRIGGER EVENT statement does not affect the time at which the next automatically scheduled execution of an event will occur.

TRIGGER EVENT can be used to execute a user-defined event, and even pass user-defined parameters to the event's BEGIN block. This technique can be used to run a block of code asynchronously on a separate connection. Here is an example of an event that runs in the background to generate test data; the number of rows to insert is provided by a call to EVENT_PARAMETER that returns the value of a user-defined parameter called @row_count:

```
CREATE EVENT ev_generate
HANDLER BEGIN
   DECLARE @row_count INTEGER;
   DECLARE @row_counter INTEGER;
   SET TEMPORARY OPTION BACKGROUND_PRIORITY = 'ON';
   MESSAGE STRING ( 'ev_generate started at ', CURRENT TIMESTAMP );
   SET @row_count = CAST ( EVENT_PARAMETER ( '@row_count' ) AS INTEGER );
   SET @row_counter = 0;
   WHILE @row_counter < @row_count LOOP
      SET @row_counter = @row_counter + 1;
```

```
      INSERT t1 VALUES (
         @row_counter,
         CAST ( RAND() * 1000000 AS INTEGER ) );
      IF MOD ( @row_counter, 10000 ) = 0 THEN
         COMMIT;
         MESSAGE STRING ( 'ev_generate COMMIT at ', CURRENT TIMESTAMP );
      END IF;
   END LOOP;
   COMMIT;
   MESSAGE STRING ( 'ev_generate ended at ', CURRENT TIMESTAMP );
END;
```

Here is an example of a TRIGGER EVENT that requests 100,000 rows of test data, followed by a MESSAGE statement to show when control is regained by this connection:

```
TRIGGER EVENT ev_generate ( @row_count = '100000' );
MESSAGE STRING ( 'Control regained after TRIGGER EVENT at ', CURRENT TIMESTAMP );
```

The resulting output shows that control was immediately returned to the connection that executed the TRIGGER EVENT statement, while the ev_generate event continued to run in the background:

```
ev_generate started at 2004-01-12 17:26:14.940
Control regained after TRIGGER EVENT at 2004-01-12 17:26:14.980
ev_generate COMMIT at 2004-01-12 17:26:16.112
ev_generate COMMIT at 2004-01-12 17:26:17.063
ev_generate COMMIT at 2004-01-12 17:26:18.034
ev_generate COMMIT at 2004-01-12 17:26:18.946
ev_generate COMMIT at 2004-01-12 17:26:19.817
ev_generate COMMIT at 2004-01-12 17:26:20.718
ev_generate COMMIT at 2004-01-12 17:26:21.670
ev_generate COMMIT at 2004-01-12 17:26:22.541
ev_generate COMMIT at 2004-01-12 17:26:24.414
ev_generate COMMIT at 2004-01-12 17:26:25.465
ev_generate ended at 2004-01-12 17:26:25.465
```

The parameter names specified in a TRIGGER EVENT statement may look like local variables but in fact they have nothing to do with any other names in the surrounding code. Here is an example to demonstrate that fact; this event calls EVENT_PARAMETER to get the value of the user-defined parameter called '@p', then assigns that value to a local variable also called @p, and displays the result:

```
CREATE EVENT ev_test
HANDLER BEGIN
   DECLARE @p VARCHAR ( 128 );
   SET @p = COALESCE ( EVENT_PARAMETER ( '@p' ), 'NULL' );
   MESSAGE STRING ( '@p passed to event: ', @p );
END;
```

Here is some code that executes TRIGGER EVENT (@p = @v) to pass a value into the event. This code also has a local variable called @p, but in this context the local variable @p has nothing to do with the @p named in the TRIGGER EVENT.

```
BEGIN
   DECLARE @p VARCHAR ( 128 );
   DECLARE @v VARCHAR ( 254 );
   SET @p = 'hello';
   SET @v = 'world';
   MESSAGE STRING ( '@p before event:    ', @p );
```

```
   TRIGGER EVENT ev_test ( @p = @v );
   MESSAGE STRING ( '@p after event:     ', @p );
END;
```

Here is the resulting display; the local variable @p in the outer BEGIN block is unaffected by the parameter specification @p = @v in the TRIGGER EVENT statement:

```
@p before event:    hello
@p passed to event: world
@p after event:     hello
```

8.14 CREATE VARIABLE

The CREATE VARIABLE statement may be used to create a connection-level variable in SQL Anywhere. This kind of variable is also called a "global variable" because once it is created, it can be referenced by any SQL code running on the same connection; this includes procedures, triggers, and SQL statements passed to SQL Anywhere from a client application, but not events.

```
<create_connection_variable> ::= CREATE VARIABLE
                        <connection_variable_name> <data_type>
<connection_variable_name>  ::= <identifier>
<data_type>                 ::= see <data_type> in Chapter 1, "Creating"
```

Once a connection-level variable has been created, it continues to exist until it is explicitly dropped or the connection ends. Connection-level variables are not truly "global" in nature, however, since variables created by different connections are completely separate; even if they have the same names, they can have different data types and values.

The VAREXISTS function may be used to determine whether or not a particular connection-level variable exists. VAREXISTS expects one string parameter containing the name of the connection-level variable, and it returns 1 if the variable exists or 0 if it doesn't. Here is an example of code that drops a connection-level variable if it already exists, and then creates it:

```
IF VAREXISTS ( '@g_user_id' ) = 1 THEN
   DROP VARIABLE @g_user_id;
END IF;
CREATE VARIABLE @g_user_id VARCHAR ( 128 );
```

A local variable with the same name as a connection-level variable may be declared inside a BEGIN block, and it will hide the connection-level variable from view for the duration. In the following example three SELECT statements display 'xxx', 'yyy', and 'xxx' to show that the connection-level variable is not visible inside the BEGIN block:

```
CREATE VARIABLE @g_user_id VARCHAR ( 128 );
SET @g_user_id = 'xxx';
SELECT @g_user_id;
BEGIN
   DECLARE @g_user_id VARCHAR ( 128 );
   SET @g_user_id = 'yyy';
   SELECT @g_user_id;
END;
SELECT @g_user_id;
```

8.15 Chapter Summary

This chapter described how to write BEGIN blocks that contain multiple SQL statements, including IF, CASE, and WHILE control structures, local declarations, and exception handling logic. The four kinds of stored SQL modules built from BEGIN blocks were explained: stored procedures, functions, triggers, and events.

Also described were the EXECUTE IMMEDIATE statement for the dynamic creation and execution of SQL commands, and the CREATE VARIABLE statement used to define connection-level variables.

The next chapter switches direction entirely, from constructing a database to protecting your investment from disaster.

Chapter 9

Protecting

9.1 Introduction

This is the chapter on crashing, bashing, and thrashing, and the prevention thereof. In other words, it's all about protecting your database from Very Bad Things.

Section 9.2 is devoted to the SET OPTION statement, not because that statement is devoted to protection, but because many database and connection options do control aspects of protection and safety.

Section 9.3 discusses transaction control using BEGIN TRANSACTION, COMMIT, and ROLLBACK, and how transaction processing is influenced by the server-side CHAINED option and client-side autocommit mode.

Section 9.4 describes how SQL Anywhere implements nested subtransactions using the SAVEPOINT, RELEASE SAVEPOINT, and ROLLBACK TO SAVEPOINT statements.

The "Error Handling" subsections discuss various ways that SQL code can explicitly inform client applications about problems: SIGNAL, RAISERROR, and ROLLBACK TRIGGER.

Sections 9.6 through 9.7 discuss how locks, blocks, and isolation levels protect the database from inconsistencies caused by different connections working on the same data at the same time. Section 9.8 describes two kinds of deadlock: the cyclical kind caused by two or more connections blocking each other, and the "all threads blocked" variety when there are too many blocked connections for SQL Anywhere to handle. Section 9.9 discusses mutexes, or mutual exclusion operations, and how they can hurt performance in a multiple CPU environment.

Section 9.10 describes how database user ids are created with the GRANT CONNECT statement. The next three subsections show how other forms of GRANT are used to give various privileges to individual user ids, including permission to select and update tables and views and execute stored procedures and functions. Subsection 9.10.4 continues the discussion of privileges with the GRANT RESOURCE, GRANT DBA, and GRANT REMOTE DBA. Subsection 9.10.5 explains how user groups can be used to simplify both administration and SQL programming.

Section 9.11 describes how logging and recovery works in SQL Anywhere, including discussions of the transaction log, checkpoint log, and rollback log. Section 9.12 shows how to set up database backup procedures, Section 9.13

describes how to restore a database from a backup, and Section 9.14 shows how to validate backup files to make sure they'll work when you need them.

9.2 Options

Many aspects of SQL Anywhere's behavior are controlled by built-in parameters called options. This section describes how these options are stored, and how you can change their values, together with some examples. Other examples may be found elsewhere in this chapter, and in other chapters, where particular options are important to the subjects being discussed.

Two basic kinds of options exist: global and local. Global options apply to the database or server as a whole rather than an individual connection; for example, the AUDITING option can be used to enable and disable the auditing feature in the database, and the effect is the same for all connections. Local options, on the other hand, apply to individual connections; for example, the BACKGROUND_PRIORITY option may be used to lower or raise the priority of an individual connection while it is running.

Most options are local in nature; the few global options are listed in Table 9-1.

Table 9-1. Global options

Option Name
ANSI_PERMISSIONS
AUDITING
AUDITING_OPTIONS
CHECKPOINT_TIME
DATABASE_AUTHENTICATION
GLOBAL_DATABASE_ID
JAVA_NAMESPACE_SIZE
JAVA_PAGE_BUFFER_SIZE
LOGIN_MODE
MAX_HASH_SIZE
MAX_WORK_TABLE_HASH_SIZE
MIN_PASSWORD_LENGTH
MIN_TABLE_SIZE_FOR_HISTOGRAM
OPTIMIZATION_WORKLOAD
PINNED_CURSOR_PERCENT_OF_CACHE
PRESERVE_SOURCE_FORMAT
RECOVERY_TIME

Option Name
RI_TRIGGER_TIME
TRUNCATE_DATE_VALUES
TRUNCATE_TIMESTAMP_VALUES
TRUNCATE_WITH_AUTO_COMMIT

Note: The SQL Anywhere Help uses a different classification scheme rather than global versus local. The Help identifies options according to their overall purpose; i.e., Transact SQL compatibility options, ISQL options, ANSI compatibility options, and so on. This book uses the global versus local classification to help describe how the various SET OPTION statements work.

Different values can exist for the same option at up to four different levels in the following hierarchy:

■ **Internal system default values** exist for all global and local options that are critical to the operation of SQL Anywhere. These values cannot be changed, but they can be overridden by values specified at a lower level in this hierarchy. These values are used only if the corresponding public values have been deleted; this book assumes that public default values always exist, so these internal system values aren't discussed in any further detail.

■ **Public default values** exist for global and local options and are stored in the SYSOPTION catalog table. For global options, these are the values that apply. For local options, these values are used if explicit values have not been specified at a lower level in this hierarchy; i.e., "public" means everyone, as opposed to an individual user or connection.

■ **User default values** are optional, and they may exist only for local options. User default values are associated with individual user ids, and they are also stored in the SYSOPTION table. Initially, in a new database, no user default values exist in SYSOPTION.

■ **Current values** of local options are initialized when a connection is established, and they may be changed temporarily. Current values are not stored in the SYSOPTION table.

Note: Every time a new connection is established, SQL Anywhere calls the sp_login_environment built-in procedure, which in turn calls the sp_tsql_environment procedure if the communication protocol is TDS. The sp_tsql_environment procedure explicitly sets several options in order to maintain Transact SQL compatibility. The TDS protocol is used for connections using Sybase Open Connect libraries or JDBC with Sybase jConnect. If you happen to be using TDS but you aren't interested in Transact SQL compatibility, you should look up "sp_tsql_environment" in the SQL Anywhere Help and make sure the option values it sets are the ones you want. However, if you use ODBC, OLE DB, or embedded SQL to connect to the database, you don't have to worry about sp_tsql_environment, as it isn't called.

Note: After ISQL connects to the database, it explicitly sets some options for its own purposes. ISQL options are described in the SQL Anywhere Help, and they aren't discussed in detail in this book.

You can change option values at the public, user, and current levels using three different forms of the SET OPTION statement:

```
<set_option> ::= <set_public_default_option>
               | <set_user_default_local_option>
               | <set_temporary_local_option>
```

Here is the syntax for changing global and local options at the public level:

```
<set_public_default_option> ::= SET [ EXISTING ] OPTION
                                PUBLIC "." <option_name> "=" [ <option_value> ]
<option_name>  ::= <identifier> -- usually the name of an existing option
<option_value> ::= string literal to be stored as the option value
                 | numeric literal to be stored as a string value
                 | <identifier> to be stored, as is, as a string value
                 | ON  -- stored as 'ON'
                 | OFF -- stored as 'OFF'
                 | NULL -- to delete the entry at this level
<identifier>   ::= see <identifier> in Chapter 1, "Creating"
```

Note: The <option_value> syntax described above is used with all three formats of the SET OPTION statement. However, the NULL value is rarely if ever used at the public default level; it should probably only be used at the lower user and current levels to delete the values specified at those levels. Also, you can't delete a PUBLIC default value if a value exists at the user level.

Note: The <option_value> may be omitted altogether in all three formats of the SET OPTION statement, and when it is omitted it is the same as specifying the NULL value: The effect is to delete the entry at the corresponding level. Explicit NULL values will be shown in this book.

Most public default option settings don't need to be changed; one of SQL Anywhere's greatest strengths is that most default settings have been carefully chosen and you don't need to fiddle with them.

There are some candidates for change, however; here are some examples of SET statements that may be used to permanently change the public settings to different values:

```
SET EXISTING OPTION PUBLIC.ANSI_INTEGER_OVERFLOW        = 'ON';
SET EXISTING OPTION PUBLIC.CLOSE_ON_ENDTRANS            = 'OFF';
SET EXISTING OPTION PUBLIC.FLOAT_AS_DOUBLE              = 'ON';
SET EXISTING OPTION PUBLIC.MIN_TABLE_SIZE_FOR_HISTOGRAM = '100';
SET EXISTING OPTION PUBLIC.STRING_RTRUNCATION           = 'ON';
```

Here is what these settings mean:

- ANSI_INTEGER_OVERFLOW = 'ON' means that an INSERT statement that attempts to store an out-of-range value in an integer column will raise an error instead of storing an incorrect value.
- CLOSE_ON_ENDTRANS = 'OFF' prevents a cursor from being closed as a side effect of a COMMIT or ROLLBACK operation.
- FLOAT_AS_DOUBLE = 'ON' forces the CREATE TABLE statement to interpret the FLOAT data type as DOUBLE instead of SINGLE when it doesn't have an explicit precision specified.

- MIN_TABLE_SIZE_FOR_HISTOGRAM = '100' forces SQL Anywhere to maintain performance statistics for small tables.
- STRING_RTRUNCATION = 'ON' means that an INSERT statement that attempts to truncate non-blank characters from the right end of a string value will raise an error instead of silently truncating those characters to make the value fit in a column.

The EXISTING keyword is optional but highly recommended; it prevents SQL Anywhere from interpreting a spelling mistake in the option name as the name of a new option.

> **Note:**   It is possible to create user-defined options, but that topic isn't discussed in this book. A user-defined option is one with an option name that is different from any of the predefined options.

The second format of the SET statement may be used to set, change, and delete local options at the user level.

```
<set_user_default_local_option>
   ::= SET OPTION <user_id> "." <option_name> "=" [ <option_value> ]

<user_id> ::= <identifier>
```

If a non-NULL option value is specified, a row in the SYSOPTION table corresponding to the user name and option name is inserted if it doesn't exist already or updated if it already exists. If NULL is specified as the option value, the corresponding row in the SYSOPTION is deleted if it exists; otherwise no action is taken.

Here is an example that sets the BLOCKING option to 'OFF' for a user that will be performing time-critical processing:

```
SET OPTION User1.BLOCKING = 'OFF';
```

> **Note:**   This section concentrates on how to set options; for more information on the BLOCKING option in particular, see Section 9.7, "Blocks and Isolation Levels."

The third format of the SET statement may be used to change the current value of a local option:

```
<set_temporary_local_option> ::= SET TEMPORARY OPTION
                        <option_name> "=" [ <option_value> ]
```

The SET TEMPORARY OPTION doesn't affect the contents of the SYSOPTION table. If a non-NULL option value is specified, that value immediately goes into effect for the current connection. If NULL is specified for the option value, the current setting reverts to the value that was in effect prior to any other SET TEMPORARY OPTION statement that was executed for this option.

When you change the public setting of a global option, it takes effect immediately for all users and connections; that's the nature of a global option. At the other extreme, changes to local options, no matter how they are made, never affect the current setting in effect on other connections that are already open. In other words, there's nothing you can do to a local option on one connection that will immediately affect the setting on a different connection that's already running.

The rules are quite complex, however, for the effect a change to a local option has on the current connection; the effect may or may not be immediate. The end result depends on what kind of SET statement is executed, the current contents of the SYSOPTION table, and whether the SET statement specifies NULL or a non-NULL option value. The following example shows 14 consecutive changes to the same local option, ANSI_INTEGER_OVERFLOW, made on one connection to a new database. Initially, the public setting is the default 'OFF', there is no setting for DBA in the SYSOPTION table, and the current setting when the user DBA connects is 'OFF' because it is initialized to the public setting.

Here is a numbered list of the 14 consecutive SET statements with each result shown in the right-hand column:

```
                                                           Current Setting for
#    Statement                                             This Connection
==   =======================================================  ===================
1    SET EXISTING OPTION PUBLIC.ANSI_INTEGER_OVERFLOW = 'ON'     On
2    SET OPTION DBA.ANSI_INTEGER_OVERFLOW            = 'OFF'     Off
3    SET EXISTING OPTION PUBLIC.ANSI_INTEGER_OVERFLOW = 'ON'     Off
4    SET OPTION DBA.ANSI_INTEGER_OVERFLOW            = NULL      On
5    SET EXISTING OPTION PUBLIC.ANSI_INTEGER_OVERFLOW = 'OFF'    Off
6    SET OPTION DBA.ANSI_INTEGER_OVERFLOW            = 'ON'      On
7    SET TEMPORARY OPTION ANSI_INTEGER_OVERFLOW      = 'OFF'     Off
8    SET OPTION DBA.ANSI_INTEGER_OVERFLOW            = 'ON'      On
9    SET EXISTING OPTION PUBLIC.ANSI_INTEGER_OVERFLOW = 'OFF'    On
10   SET TEMPORARY OPTION ANSI_INTEGER_OVERFLOW      = NULL      On
11   SET OPTION DBA.ANSI_INTEGER_OVERFLOW            = NULL      Off
12   SET TEMPORARY OPTION ANSI_INTEGER_OVERFLOW      = 'ON'      On
13   SET EXISTING OPTION PUBLIC.ANSI_INTEGER_OVERFLOW = 'OFF'    On
14   SET TEMPORARY OPTION ANSI_INTEGER_OVERFLOW      = NULL      Off
```

Here's how those changes worked; some of the results may be surprising, including the fact that identical SET statements may have different effects on the current setting:

1. The new public setting went into effect immediately because there was no user or temporary setting in effect.
2. Changes to the user setting for the currently connected user always go into effect immediately.
3. The new public setting did not change the current setting because a user setting is in effect.
4. The public setting went into effect because the user setting was deleted.
5. The new public setting went into effect immediately for the same reason as change 1 above.
6. The new user setting went into effect immediately because they always do.
7. Temporary changes always go into effect immediately.
8. The new user setting went into effect, as usual, even though a temporary change had been made.
9. The new public setting did not change the current setting for the same reason as change 3 above.
10. Deleting the temporary setting had no effect.

11. Deleting the user setting caused the current setting to revert to the public setting.
12. Like in change 7, temporary settings always go into effect immediately.
13. The new public setting did not change the current setting, this time because there was a temporary setting.
14. This time, deleting the public setting caused the current setting to revert to the public setting.

Tip: Keep option settings simple. Change public and user default settings once, ahead of time, and don't change them on the fly. Instead, use SET TEMPORARY OPTION statements to make changes during processing. Also, don't use the NULL value to revert to old settings; specify new values explicitly.

9.3 Transactions

A database transaction is a sequence of SQL statements that are treated as an single unit for the purposes of correctly satisfying a request while ensuring database integrity. Transaction design is an important part of application design, and it has profound effects on database performance as well as correctness and integrity.

A transaction must satisfy four requirements: It must be atomic, consistent, isolated, and durable, or "ACID" for short.

- **Atomic:** All of the database changes made by the transaction must be completed when the transaction finishes successfully; if the transaction fails, none of the changes are to be made to the database. A failure at any point during the transaction causes the entire transaction to fail; a failure may be explicitly forced by a SQL statement such as ROLLBACK or caused implicitly by an external event such as a system crash. For example, if a transaction inserts a sales_order row in the ASADEMO database, together with one or more corresponding sales_order_item rows, a failure during the transaction means that none of those rows exist when the transaction is completed.

- **Consistent:** All constraints on the data must be satisfied when the transaction is completed. These include constraints maintained by application programs as well as constraints defined within the database schema.

- **Isolated:** Separate transactions must not change the same data at the same time; all changes must be isolated from one another. The smallest unit of isolation with SQL Anywhere is the row. Isolation may be taken further when considering whether different transactions may even see the effects of changes made by other transactions; the ISOLATION_LEVEL option applies to this aspect, and is discussed later in this chapter. As far as updates are concerned, however, isolation is not optional; once a transaction has changed a row in a table, SQL Anywhere does not permit any other transaction from changing the same row until the first transaction is completed.

- **Durable:** All database changes made by a transaction that finishes successfully must be persistent; subsequent failures must not affect the changes made by this transaction. In other words, a COMMIT must be permanent.

For example, a transaction may insert a sales_order row in the ASADEMO database, together with one or more corresponding sales_order_item rows. This transaction is atomic because all of the inserted rows will exist in the database if the transaction succeeds, and none of them will remain if the transaction fails. This transaction is consistent because it satisfies the application constraint that for every sales_order row, at least one corresponding sales_order_item row must also exist; it also satisfies the database foreign key constraint that every sales_order_item row must have a single corresponding sales_order row. This transaction is isolated because no other database connection can delete or update the inserted rows until the transaction is successfully completed. This transaction is durable because, once it is successfully completed, the inserted rows remain in the database.

Each transaction has a beginning and an end, and is run within the context of a single connection. One connection may execute more than one transaction, but only one after another in a serial fashion. Different transactions may run at the same time on different connections, and they can affect one another, but a single transaction does not span more than one connection.

Note: Individual non-compound SQL statements are atomic in nature, which means that if the statement fails, any changes it has already made to the database are automatically undone. This applies to single INSERT, UPDATE, and DELETE statements that operate on more than one row; if one of these statements fail after affecting one or more rows, all of its effects are automatically undone. This activity is separate from transaction control; the failure of one statement does not automatically cause a transaction to roll back. The atomic nature of SQL statements is implemented internally via savepoints, which are discussed in Section 9.4, "Savepoints and Subtransactions."

Three different SQL statements may be used to explicitly control when transactions begin and end: BEGIN TRANSACTION, COMMIT, and ROLLBACK. This control is not absolute in all cases; a ROLLBACK statement always ends a transaction, but a BEGIN TRANSACTION doesn't necessarily start a transaction, nor does a COMMIT necessarily end one.

```
<begin_transaction> ::= BEGIN TRAN        -- all forms are equivalent
                      | BEGIN TRANSACTION
                      | BEGIN TRAN <transaction_name>
                      | BEGIN TRANSACTION <transaction_name>
<transaction_name>  ::= <identifier>      -- not used for any purpose

<commit>            ::= COMMIT             -- all forms are equivalent
                      | COMMIT WORK
                      | COMMIT TRAN
                      | COMMIT TRANSACTION
                      | COMMIT TRAN <transaction_name>
                      | COMMIT TRANSACTION <transaction_name>

<rollback>         ::= ROLLBACK           -- all forms are equivalent
                      | ROLLBACK WORK
                      | ROLLBACK TRAN
                      | ROLLBACK TRANSACTION
                      | ROLLBACK TRAN <transaction_name>
                      | ROLLBACK TRANSACTION <transaction_name>
```

> **Tip:** Don't bother with the transaction name parameters on the BEGIN TRANSACTION, COMMIT, or ROLLBACK statements; they have no effect in SQL Anywhere. Also, the different formats for each statement are equivalent. The full syntax is shown here because these different formats sometimes appear in documentation and utility program output, and they often lead to unnecessary confusion.

SQL Anywhere has two modes of transaction control, called "chained mode" and "unchained mode."

- In *chained mode* a transaction is implicitly started by any INSERT, UPDATE, or DELETE statement, or any SELECT statement that acquires locks. This transaction ends when an explicit COMMIT or ROLLBACK statement is executed or when the transaction fails.
- In *unchained mode* a transaction may be explicitly started by a BEGIN TRANSACTION statement; such a transaction ends when an explicit COMMIT or ROLLBACK statement is executed, or when the transaction fails. If no BEGIN TRANSACTION statement is executed, each statement is run as its own transaction, with an implicit commit if it works and an implicit rollback if it fails.

Here is a simple example of two UPDATE statements run in chained mode; the SET TEMPORARY OPTION CHAINED = 'ON' statement is used to clearly document that chained mode is in effect:

```
SET TEMPORARY OPTION CHAINED = 'ON';
UPDATE t1 SET non_key_1 = 'xxx' WHERE key_1 = 1;
UPDATE t1 SET non_key_1 = 'yyy' WHERE key_1 = 2;
COMMIT;
```

The transaction log file may be examined to determine when transactions begin and end; the dbtran.exe utility program can be used to translate the log file into readable SQL statements. Here is a command line that executes dbtran.exe, using the options -a to include all operations including uncommitted ones, -c to specify the connection parameters, -s to produce UPDATE statements in the ANSI format, and -y to overwrite the output file without confirmation. The final parameter is the file specification for the output text file, test9_log.sql.

```
"%ASANY9%\win32\dbtran.exe" -a -c "DSN=test9" -s -y test9_log.sql
```

Here's what the output looks like for the UPDATE and COMMIT statements shown above; the BEGIN TRANSACTION entry shows that a transaction was started before the first UPDATE:

```
--BEGIN TRANSACTION-1001-0000402114
BEGIN TRANSACTION
go
--UPDATE-1001-0000402115
UPDATE DBA.t1
   SET non_key_1='xxx'
 WHERE key_1=1
go
--UPDATE-1001-0000402126
UPDATE DBA.t1
   SET non_key_1='yyy'
 WHERE key_1=2
go
--COMMIT-1001-0000402137
```

```
COMMIT WORK
go
```

Here are the same two UPDATE statements, run in unchained mode with no explicit COMMIT:

```
SET TEMPORARY OPTION CHAINED = 'OFF';
UPDATE t1 SET non_key_1 = 'xxx' WHERE key_1 = 1;
UPDATE t1 SET non_key_1 = 'yyy' WHERE key_1 = 2;
```

This time the dbtran.exe output shows two separate BEGIN TRANSACTION and COMMIT operations were performed:

```
--BEGIN TRANSACTION-1001-0000402237
BEGIN TRANSACTION
go
--UPDATE-1001-0000402238
UPDATE DBA.t1
   SET non_key_1='xxx'
 WHERE key_1=1
go
--COMMIT-1001-0000402249
COMMIT WORK
go
--BEGIN TRANSACTION-1001-0000402250
BEGIN TRANSACTION
go
--UPDATE-1001-0000402251
UPDATE DBA.t1
   SET non_key_1='yyy'
 WHERE key_1=2
go
--COMMIT-1001-0000402262
COMMIT WORK
go
```

Applications using unchained mode have no control over the design or scope of transactions unless they issue explicit BEGIN TRANSACTION statements. Here is the previous example, modified to take control and force both UPDATE statements to be included in one transaction:

```
SET TEMPORARY OPTION CHAINED = 'OFF';
BEGIN TRANSACTION;
UPDATE t1 SET non_key_1 = 'xxx' WHERE key_1 = 1;
UPDATE t1 SET non_key_1 = 'yyy' WHERE key_1 = 2;
COMMIT;
```

The dbtran.exe output for unchained mode using an explicit BEGIN TRANSACTION looks exactly the same as it did for the first example using chained mode above; one BEGIN TRANSACTION, two UPDATE statements, and a single COMMIT:

```
--BEGIN TRANSACTION-1001-0000402314
BEGIN TRANSACTION
go
--UPDATE-1001-0000402315
UPDATE DBA.t1
   SET non_key_1='xxx'
 WHERE key_1=1
go
--UPDATE-1001-0000402326
UPDATE DBA.t1
   SET non_key_1='yyy'
```

```
WHERE key_1=2
go
--COMMIT-1001-0000402337
COMMIT WORK
go
```

Note: The BEGIN TRANSACTION entry in the dbtran.exe output serves to mark the point when a transaction was actually started, not the point when an explicit BEGIN TRANSACTION statement was executed. That might sound pedantic, but it's important when reading the output from dbtran.exe: An explicit BEGIN TRANSACTION statement in the application code may or may not correspond to a BEGIN TRANSACTION entry in the transaction log, regardless of the transaction mode.

Chained mode is sometimes called manual mode because it requires explicit COMMIT and ROLLBACK statements to mark the end of transactions. Unchained mode is sometimes called autocommit mode because each successful statement is automatically committed when no explicit BEGIN TRANSACTION statement has been executed. However, there are two kinds of autocommit mode:

■ *Server-side autocommit mode* is the kind implemented by the SQL Anywhere database engine when you set the CHAINED option 'OFF' to get unchained mode as described above, and you don't execute explicit BEGIN TRANSACTION statements. Transactions are started and ended automatically, inside the database engine, and there are no BEGIN TRANSACTION, COMMIT, or ROLLBACK statements coming from the client side.

■ *Client-side autocommit mode* is implemented by the client database interface software such as ODBC and JDBC. When the interface AutoCommit flag is set, an explicit COMMIT statement is sent to SQL Anywhere after each INSERT, UPDATE, and DELETE statement. If server-side autocommit is also in force, these extra COMMIT statements have no effect because by the time they arrive, SQL Anywhere has already done a commit. If server-side autocommit is not in force, then the COMMIT statements sent by client-side autocommit will have an effect.

The following table shows what happens when a single UPDATE statement is issued by a PowerBuilder application using ODBC, under the four combinations of server-side and client-side autocommit settings. The first column shows the client-side SQLCA.AutoCommit setting used by the PowerBuilder application when connecting via ODBC to the database. The second column shows the server-side setting of the CHAINED option used by SQL Anywhere. The third column shows the SQL statements that were actually sent across the client server interface from ODBC to SQL Anywhere. The fourth column shows what internal operations were performed by SQL Anywhere, as recorded in the transaction log:

Client-side ODBC AutoCommit	Server-side CHAINED Mode	Statements Sent	Operations Performed
FALSE	OFF	UPDATE	Begin, update, commit
TRUE	OFF	UPDATE, COMMIT	Begin, update, commit

TRUE	ON	UPDATE, COMMIT	Begin, update, commit
FALSE	ON	UPDATE	Update

Autocommit mode is in effect for the first three combinations shown above; it doesn't matter much if it's client-side or server-side autocommit, the important fact is that each database change is treated as a transaction by itself. With autocommit in effect it is impossible for an application transaction to span more than one INSERT, UPDATE, or DELETE statement.

Tip: Never use autocommit. Always take explicit control of transaction design in your applications. Use the settings shown on the last line of the table above: Always set the CHAINED option 'ON', set any client-side AutoCommit flag to FALSE, and explicitly execute a COMMIT or ROLLBACK statement when it is time to finish a transaction.

SQL Anywhere may or may not actually perform a commit operation when it executes a COMMIT statement; this depends on the current value of a built-in connection-level variable called @@TRANCOUNT. If @@TRANCOUNT is 0 or 1 when a COMMIT statement is executed, SQL Anywhere will perform a commit; if @@TRANCOUNT is 2 or higher, the COMMIT statement will be ignored. Here are the details of how @@TRANCOUNT gets changed and used:

- @@TRANCOUNT is set to 0 when a connection is started, and is set back to 0 whenever a transaction is finished.
- In unchained mode, each explicit BEGIN TRANSACTION statement increases @@TRANCOUNT by 1.
- In chained mode, if @@TRANCOUNT is 0 when an implicit transaction is being started, it isn't immediately changed, but the next explicit BEGIN TRANSACTION statement will set @@TRANCOUNT to 2. Subsequent BEGIN TRANSACTION statements increase @@TRANCOUNT by 1.
- In chained mode, if an explicit BEGIN TRANSACTION statement is executed before a transaction is implicitly started, @@TRANCOUNT is set to 1; subsequent BEGIN TRANSACTION statements increase @@TRAN-COUNT by 1.
- In both chained and unchained modes, each COMMIT statement decreases @@TRANCOUNT by 1 until it reaches 0. If @@TRANCOUNT reaches 0 when a COMMIT statement is executed, an actual commit operation is performed: All the transaction's database changes are made permanent, all the locks held by the transaction are released, and the transaction is ended. If @@TRANCOUNT does not reach 0 when a COMMIT statement is executed, nothing more is done; as far as the outstanding database changes and locks are concerned, the COMMIT is ignored, and the transaction is still in progress.
- In both chained and unchained modes, a ROLLBACK statement sets @@TRANCOUNT to 0, rolls back all the transaction's database changes, releases all the locks, and ends the transaction. This happens regardless of the current value of @@TRANCOUNT.

The term "nested transaction" is sometimes used when @@TRANCOUNT rises to 2 or higher. That term is misleading, however, because only the outermost transaction has any meaning as far as database changes and locks are concerned. When @@TRANCOUNT rises to 2 or higher, a COMMIT statement does absolutely nothing except lower the @@TRANCOUNT value. A nested transaction implies that changes made in an inner transaction may be made permanent while changes made in the outer transaction are rolled back, and that simply is not possible in SQL Anywhere; there is no such thing as a nested transaction.

Tip: Don't use the BEGIN TRANSACTION statement at all. Use chained mode: Let SQL Anywhere start each transaction implicitly, use explicit COMMIT and ROLLBACK statements to end each transaction, and don't disable COMMIT statements with extra BEGIN TRANSACTION statements.

The following is an example of a simple transaction; a parent row is inserted in the sales_order table in the ASADEMO database, and a corresponding child row is inserted in the sales_order_items table. The first INSERT starts the transaction. If both INSERT statements work okay, the transaction ends with a COMMIT; if a foreign key violation is detected, the SQLSTATE will be set to '23503' and the exception handler will end the transaction with a ROLLBACK.

```
BEGIN
   DECLARE @errormsg VARCHAR ( 32767 );
   DECLARE error_23503 EXCEPTION FOR SQLSTATE '23503';

   INSERT sales_order ( id, cust_id, order_date, fin_code_id, region, sales_rep )
      VALUES ( 1, 101, CURRENT DATE, 'r1', 'Eastern', 299 );

   INSERT sales_order_items ( id , line_id, prod_id, quantity, ship_date )
      VALUES ( 1, 1, 999, 12, DATEADD ( DAY, 1, CURRENT DATE ) );

   COMMIT;
   MESSAGE 'COMMIT OK.' TO CONSOLE;

EXCEPTION
   WHEN error_23503 THEN
      SET @errormsg = ERRORMSG();
      ROLLBACK;
      MESSAGE 'ROLLBACK after error.' TO CONSOLE;
      MESSAGE STRING ( 'ERRORMSG() = ', @errormsg ) TO CONSOLE;
END;
```

In this particular case, the prod_id value of 999 causes a foreign key violation and the transaction ends with a ROLLBACK. Here's the output from the MESSAGE statements:

```
ROLLBACK after error.
ERRORMSG() = No primary key value for foreign key 'ky_prod_id' in
   table 'sales_order_items'
```

For more information about the tables in the ASADEMO database, see Section 3.6, "Multi-Table Joins." For more information about the BEGIN block and exception handlers, see Sections 8.2 and 8.3 in Chapter 8, "Packaging."

Tip: When designing transactions, watch out for any SQL statement that performs a commit as a side effect. Any statement that updates the SQL Anywhere system catalog tables falls into this category, and if a transaction is in progress it will be ended. For example, statements like SET OPTION, GRANT, and CREATE SYNCHRONIZATION USER all perform commits, and so do CREATE TABLE and CREATE INDEX when used on global permanent and global temporary tables. The LOAD TABLE statement also performs a commit, and so does TRUNCATE TABLE if the fast form is used; for more information about TRUNCATE TABLE, see Section 5.6. Some statements that affect schema don't perform commits, however; CREATE DATABASE doesn't, probably because it doesn't affect the current database, and neither does any statement involving a local temporary table. Also, the SET TEMPORARY OPTION statement doesn't do a commit so it's possible to change connection options while a transaction is in progress.

9.4 Savepoints and Subtransactions

Savepoints provide a flexible way to implement partial rollbacks. A *savepoint* is a point in time that marks the beginning of a subtransaction during the processing of a transaction on the current connection. Subtransactions can be rolled back without rolling back or ending the whole transaction, but they cannot be committed without committing and ending the whole transaction.

```
<savepoint>            ::= SAVEPOINT [ <savepoint_name> ]
<savepoint_name>       ::= <identifier> -- for use in RELEASE and ROLLBACK

<rollback_to_savepoint> ::= ROLLBACK TO SAVEPOINT [ <savepoint_name> ]

<release_savepoint>    ::= RELEASE SAVEPOINT [ <savepoint_name> ]
```

The SAVEPOINT statement creates a savepoint, and it can specify an optional savepoint name. Nested subtransactions may be created by subsequent SAVEPOINT statements, and they may be given names.

A savepoint may be active or inactive. An active savepoint is one that has been established by a SAVEPOINT statement and has not yet been made inactive by a subsequent RELEASE SAVEPOINT, ROLLBACK TO SAVEPOINT, ROLLBACK, or COMMIT statement.

The ROLLBACK TO SAVEPOINT statement rolls back all the changes made since a particular active savepoint, and then makes that savepoint inactive. If the ROLLBACK TO SAVEPOINT statement doesn't specify a savepoint name, then it implicitly refers to the most recently established active savepoint. The ROLLBACK TO SAVEPOINT statement may name a savepoint, and in that case all changes made since that savepoint are rolled back, and the named savepoint plus all active savepoints that were established since the named savepoint are made inactive.

RELEASE SAVEPOINT doesn't roll back any changes; it just makes a savepoint inactive. If the RELEASE SAVEPOINT statement doesn't specify a savepoint name, then it implicitly refers to the most recently established active savepoint. The RELEASE SAVEPOINT statement may name a savepoint, and in that case the named savepoint plus all active savepoints that were established since the named savepoint are made inactive.

It is an error to execute a ROLLBACK TO SAVEPOINT or RELEASE SAVEPOINT statement that refers to an inactive savepoint.

The ROLLBACK and COMMIT statements both end the whole transaction as well as all the subtransactions; all the savepoints are made inactive.

Here is a simple table that will be used in the next three examples of savepoint processing; note that each example starts with the same values in the two rows shown here, not the values that existed at the end of the previous example:

```
CREATE TABLE t1 (
   key_1          INTEGER NOT NULL PRIMARY KEY,
   non_key_1      VARCHAR ( 100 ) NOT NULL );

INSERT t1 VALUES ( 1, 'AAA' );
INSERT t1 VALUES ( 2, 'BBB' );
COMMIT;
```

The first example shows a transaction consisting of two updates to row #1, one update to row #2, and a savepoint; the ROLLBACK TO SAVEPOINT statement rolls back the second update to row #1 but not the first one. Also, since the ROLLBACK TO SAVEPOINT statement does not end the transaction or affect SQL statements that follow it, the update to row #2 and the COMMIT proceed normally.

```
UPDATE t1 SET non_key_1 = '1' WHERE key_1 = 1;
SAVEPOINT;
UPDATE t1 SET non_key_1 = '2' WHERE key_1 = 1;
ROLLBACK TO SAVEPOINT;
UPDATE t1 SET non_key_1 = 'XXX' WHERE key_1 = 2;
COMMIT;
SELECT * FROM t1;
```

Here is the output from the final SELECT; it shows that the first update to row #1 and the update to row #2 were committed, but not the second update to row #1:

```
key_1  non_key_1
=====  =========
1      '1'
2      'XXX'
```

The second example shows a nested savepoint, with the code indented to show the nesting; note that the ROLLBACK TO SAVEPOINT statement implicitly refers to the second SAVEPOINT statement.

```
UPDATE t1 SET non_key_1 = '3' WHERE key_1 = 1;
SAVEPOINT;
   UPDATE t1 SET non_key_1 = '4' WHERE key_1 = 1;
   SAVEPOINT;
      UPDATE t1 SET non_key_1 = '5' WHERE key_1 = 1;
   ROLLBACK TO SAVEPOINT;
   UPDATE t1 SET non_key_1 = 'YYY' WHERE key_1 = 2;
COMMIT;
SELECT * FROM t1;
```

The output from the SELECT shows that the ROLLBACK TO SAVEPOINT statement rolled back the third update to row #1 but not the first two; also, the update to row #2 proceeded normally:

```
key_1  non_key_1
=====  =========
1      '4'
2      'YYY'
```

The third example shows savepoints with names; as the script proceeds to update row #1 in table t1, four nested savepoints are established. The ROLLBACK TO SAVEPOINT s7 statement reaches back to the second savepoint to roll back all the changes made since then; the savepoint name makes it unnecessary to explicitly deal with the intervening savepoints. The script then updates row #2 and ends the transaction with a COMMIT.

```
UPDATE t1 SET non_key_1 = '6' WHERE key_1 = 1;
SAVEPOINT s6;
   UPDATE t1 SET non_key_1 = '7' WHERE key_1 = 1;
   SAVEPOINT s7;
      UPDATE t1 SET non_key_1 = '8' WHERE key_1 = 1;
      SAVEPOINT s8;
         UPDATE t1 SET non_key_1 = '9' WHERE key_1 = 1;
         SAVEPOINT s9;
            UPDATE t1 SET non_key_1 = '10' WHERE key_1 = 1;
   ROLLBACK TO SAVEPOINT s7;
   UPDATE t1 SET non_key_1 = 'ZZZ' WHERE key_1 = 2;
COMMIT;
SELECT * FROM t1;
```

The output from the SELECT shows that the last three updates to row #1 were all rolled back, but the other changes were committed:

```
key_1   non_key_1
=====   =========
1       '7'
2       'ZZZ'
```

The RELEASE SAVEPOINT statement makes it possible for the relationship among different savepoints to match the SQL module call structure. If each module starts with a SAVEPOINT statement and ends with a ROLLBACK TO SAVEPOINT or RELEASE SAVEPOINT statement, then different modules may be called consecutively without creating nested subtransactions, but if one module contains a nested call to another, a nested subtransaction will be created.

The following is another example where the first UPDATE is placed within its own subtransaction by SAVEPOINT and RELEASE SAVEPOINT statements. The second UPDATE is placed inside a second, consecutive, subtransaction; this subtransaction is not nested within the first one because the previous RELEASE SAVEPOINT statement ended the first subtransaction. The third UPDATE is placed inside a third subtransaction, but this one is nested inside the second one. The third subtransaction is ended by a RELEASE SAVEPOINT statement, and the second subtransaction is ended by a ROLLBACK TO SAVEPOINT statement; because the third subtransaction is nested, all the changes made by the second and third subtransactions are rolled back.

```
CREATE TABLE t1 (
   key_1        INTEGER NOT NULL PRIMARY KEY,
   non_key_1    VARCHAR ( 100 ) NOT NULL,
   non_key_2    VARCHAR ( 100 ) NOT NULL,
   non_key_3    VARCHAR ( 100 ) NOT NULL );

INSERT t1 VALUES ( 1, 'AAA', 'BBB', 'CCC' );
COMMIT;

SAVEPOINT;
```

```
   UPDATE t1 SET non_key_1 = 'xxx' WHERE key_1 = 1;
RELEASE SAVEPOINT;
SAVEPOINT;
   UPDATE t1 SET non_key_2 = 'yyy' WHERE key_1 = 1;
   SAVEPOINT;
      UPDATE t1 SET non_key_3 = 'zzz' WHERE key_1 = 1;
   RELEASE SAVEPOINT;
ROLLBACK TO SAVEPOINT;
COMMIT;
SELECT * FROM t1;
```

The output from the SELECT shows that the change made by the first subtransaction was committed, but not the changes made by the second and third subtransactions:

```
key_1   non_key_1   non_key_2   non_key_3
=====   =========   =========   =========
1       'xxx'       'BBB'       'CCC'
```

Savepoints can be used to used to simplify the design of single-user applications that allow the user to undo changes. The application can execute SAVEPOINT statements and then directly update the database rather than saving changes to be applied later; if the user decides to undo a change, the application can execute a ROLLBACK TO SAVEPOINT statement. Different combinations of consecutive and nested subtransactions can be used to accommodate different application dialogs. This technique is not appropriate for a multi-user environment because it implies that locks are held for a long time as the user decides what to do, and long-running transactions can cause contention between different users. In a single-user environment, however, locks don't matter as much; there are no other users to worry about.

Tip: In a multi-user environment, never give the user control of the keyboard or mouse between the time a transaction starts and the time it ends with a COMMIT or ROLLBACK. Database changes cause rows to be locked, and locks can prevent other users from getting their work done; transactions should be as short as possible. In particular, when an error is detected, execute a ROLLBACK statement before rather than after displaying a diagnostic message to the user.

Note: Even though the terms "single-user" and "multi-user" are commonly used, "single-connection" and "multi-connection" would be more accurate because it's the connections that count as far as transactions and locks are concerned, not users. This is true even if all the connections specify the same user id, and even if there is only one application running; when there is more than one connection to the database, transactions may overlap.

Note: Savepoints are used internally by SQL Anywhere to implement the atomic nature of non-compound SQL statements and atomic BEGIN blocks. These internal savepoints aren't visible to client applications, but they are what cause all of the effects of a failed INSERT, UPDATE, or DELETE statement to be automatically undone without necessarily affecting the transaction in progress.

9.5 Error Handling

SQL Anywhere offers several methods by which a SQL module can interrupt itself to handle a user-defined exception or error. These methods include the SIGNAL and RESIGNAL statements discussed in the next section, and the RAISERROR and ROLLBACK TRIGGER statements discussed in the two sections after that.

9.5.1 SIGNAL and RESIGNAL

The SIGNAL and RESIGNAL statements explicitly raise an exception condition using a specified value of SQLSTATE:

```
<signal_exception>    ::= SIGNAL <exception_name>
<exception_name>      ::= see <exception_name> in Chapter 8, "Packaging"
<resignal_exception>  ::= RESIGNAL
```

Note: For an introduction to exception handlers inside procedures and other BEGIN blocks, see Section 8.3, "Exception Handler."

The SIGNAL statement can be used to explicitly raise any predefined SQLSTATE value, such as '23503' for a foreign key violation. It can also be used to raise a user-defined SQLSTATE value in the range '99000' to '99999'.

When a SIGNAL statement is executed, any statements after the SIGNAL statement are skipped and control is immediately transferred to the exception handler in the current BEGIN block. If there is no exception handler, the current block is terminated and the exception is passed to the exception handler in the calling or outer BEGIN block; if that block doesn't have an exception handler either, the exception is passed onward until an exception handler is found or it reaches the client application as an error.

Note: The SIGNAL statement doesn't do anything with SQLSTATE values that are defined as "warnings," only those defined as "errors." In other words, a SIGNAL statement will be ignored if it refers to any of the SQLSTATE values listed in Table 8-1, "Warning conditions by SQLSTATE," in Section 8.3, "Exception Handler."

By default, if an exception is handled by a WHEN clause in an exception handler, SQLSTATE is reset to '00000' and the exception is not passed on. The RESIGNAL statement may be used inside a WHEN clause to override this behavior: Execution of the WHEN clause is terminated and the exception is passed to the calling or outer BEGIN block. This means that an exception may be processed in stages; for example, an inner block may gather diagnostic information about a problem while still passing the exception back to the client application.

The following is an example that shows how SIGNAL and RESIGNAL work. The procedure p_error1 is called by p_error2, and p_error2 is called by the outer BEGIN block. When p_error1 gets control, it executes a SIGNAL statement to set SQLSTATE to a user-defined exception '99001'. Since p_error1 doesn't have an exception handler, control is passed to the exception handler in the calling block, p_error2. The WHEN clause in p_error2 then executes a

RESIGNAL statement to pass the exception onward to the outer BEGIN block; along the way, several MESSAGE statements trace the flow of control.

```
CREATE PROCEDURE p_error1 ()
BEGIN
   DECLARE error_99001 EXCEPTION FOR SQLSTATE '99001';
   MESSAGE 'p_error1 before SIGNAL' TO CONSOLE;
   SIGNAL error_99001;
   MESSAGE 'p_error1 after SIGNAL' TO CONSOLE;
END;

CREATE PROCEDURE p_error2 ()
BEGIN
   DECLARE error_99001 EXCEPTION FOR SQLSTATE '99001';
   MESSAGE 'p_error2 before CALL p_error1' TO CONSOLE;
   CALL p_error1();
   MESSAGE 'p_error2 after CALL p_error1' TO CONSOLE;
EXCEPTION
   WHEN error_99001 THEN
      MESSAGE STRING ( 'p_error2 WHEN error_99001' ) TO CONSOLE;
      RESIGNAL;
END;

BEGIN
   DECLARE error_99001 EXCEPTION FOR SQLSTATE '99001';
   MESSAGE 'Before CALL p_error2' TO CONSOLE;
   CALL p_error2();
   MESSAGE 'After CALL p_error2' TO CONSOLE;
EXCEPTION
   WHEN error_99001 THEN
      MESSAGE STRING ( 'Outer WHEN error_99001' ) TO CONSOLE;
END;
```

Here is what the output looks like; not all of the MESSAGE statements are executed because once an exception is raised, the normal flow of control is disrupted:

```
Before CALL p_error2
p_error2 before CALL p_error1
p_error1 before SIGNAL
p_error2 WHEN error_99001
Outer WHEN error_99001
```

For more information about the BEGIN block and exception handlers, see Sections 8.2 and 8.3 in Chapter 8, "Packaging."

Here is an example of a stored procedure that is called from a Java program; this stored procedure returns a result set and then executes a SIGNAL statement to raise a user-defined exception:

```
CREATE PROCEDURE p1()
RESULT (
   key_1 INTEGER,
   non_key_1 VARCHAR ( 100 ) )
BEGIN
   DECLARE error_99001 EXCEPTION FOR SQLSTATE '99001';
   MESSAGE 'p1 before SELECT';
   SELECT key_1,
          non_key_1
     FROM t1
    ORDER BY key_1;
   MESSAGE 'p1 after SELECT';
   SIGNAL error_99001;
```

```
   MESSAGE 'p1 after SIGNAL';
END;
```

Here is the CatchError.java application that calls the stored procedure p1:

```java
import java.sql.*;
public class CatchError {
  public static void main( String args[] ) {
    try {
      String driver = "ianywhere.ml.jdbcodbc.IDriver";
      Class.forName ( driver );
      String url = "jdbc:odbc:driver=Adaptive Server Anywhere 9.0;"
                 + "ENG=test9;DBN=test9;UID=DBA;PWD=SQL";
      Connection conn = DriverManager.getConnection ( url );
      String sql =  "CALL p1()" ;
      Statement stmtSql = conn.createStatement();
      stmtSql.execute ( sql );
      ResultSet result = stmtSql.getResultSet();
      while ( result.next() ) {
        Integer key_1 = new Integer ( result.getInt ( 1 ) );
        String non_key_1 = result.getString ( 2 );
        System.out.println (
           "key_1 = "
           + key_1.toString()
           + ", non_key_1 = '"
           + non_key_1
           + "'");
      } // while
      Statement stmtMsg = conn.createStatement();
      String message =  "MESSAGE 'CatchError.java after display'" ;
      stmtMsg.execute ( message );
      stmtSql.getMoreResults();
    } // try
    catch ( SQLException e ) {
      Integer errorCode;
      errorCode = new Integer ( e.getErrorCode() );
      System.out.println ( "SQLState:  " + e.getSQLState() );
      System.out.println ( "ErrorCode: " + errorCode.toString() );
      System.out.println ( "Message:   " + e.getMessage() );
      System.out.println ( "Stack trace..." );
      e.printStackTrace();
    }
    catch ( Exception e ) {
      System.out.println ( "Error: " + e.getMessage() );
      e.printStackTrace();
    }
  } // main
} // class CatchError
```

The CatchError.java application above uses the new high-performance iAnywhere JDBC driver that ships with SQL Anywhere. After connecting to the database, it calls the java.sql.Statement.execute() method to CALL the stored procedure p1. Then it displays the rows in the result set, executes a SQL MESSAGE statement to record its progress in the database console window, and finally calls the getMoreResults() method to force the stored procedure p1 to execute the SQL statements following the SELECT statement. In this example the call to getMoreResults is critical because the SIGNAL statement follows the SELECT; without the getMoreResults() call the SIGNAL statement wouldn't be executed. Two catch blocks are included in the application, one to catch any SQL errors and a second block to catch other kinds of errors.

Here is a Windows batch file that compiles and executes the Java application; the Sun JDK 1.4.2_03 versions of the javac.exe compiler and java.exe runtime utility are used, and the CLASSPATH is set to the current folder plus the file specification of the iAnywhere JDBC driver jodbc.jar:

```
C:\j2sdk1.4.2_03\bin\javac.exe CatchError.java
SET CLASSPATH=.;%ASANY9%\java\jodbc.jar
C:\j2sdk1.4.2_03\bin\java.exe CatchError
```

The following is the output displayed by the Java application; the result set is followed by the output from the first catch block. Note that the user-defined SQLSTATE of '99001' has been turned into the SQLState HY000, which means "driver-specific error," and the SQL ErrorCode has been set to –297, which means "user-defined error."

```
key_1 = 1, non_key_1 = 'AAA'
key_1 = 2, non_key_1 = 'BBB'
SQLState: HY000
ErrorCode: -297
Message:    [Sybase][ODBC Driver][Adaptive Server Anywhere]User-defined exception
 signaled
Stack trace...
java.sql.SQLException: [Sybase][ODBC Driver][Adaptive Server Anywhere]User-defined
exception signaled
        at ianywhere.ml.jdbcodbc.IStatement.getMoreResults(Native Method)
        at CatchError.main(CatchError.java:27)
```

The following is the output that was displayed in the database console window; note that the Java application message "CatchError.java after display" was produced before the stored procedure produced the message "p1 after SELECT." This shows that the call to getMoreResults is necessary to reach that part of the stored procedure containing the SIGNAL statement because it followed the SELECT.

```
p1 before SELECT
CatchError.java after display
p1 after SELECT
```

9.5.2 **RAISERROR and CREATE MESSAGE**

When compared with the SIGNAL and RESIGNAL statements, the RAISERROR statement is quite polite; SIGNAL rudely interrupts processing and immediately transfers control to an exception handler, whereas RAISERROR simply records some diagnostic information and carries on with the next statement. Later SQL statements may check this diagnostic information and take action if it's been filled in, but that's entirely optional; in most cases this information is simply passed back to the client application.

The RAISERROR statement comes in four formats:

```
<raiserror> ::= RAISERROR <message_number>
            | RAISERROR <message_number> <message_text>
            | RAISERROR <message_number> <message_text> "," <substitution_list>
            | RAISERROR <high_message_number> "," <substitution_list>
<message_number> ::= integer literal in the range 17000 to 99999
              | <identifier> of an integer variable in the same range
<message_text>   ::= <simple_expression> -- which may contain %nn! placeholders
<simple_expression>  ::= see <simple_expression> in Chapter 3, "Selecting"
                 -- not a subquery and does not start with IF or CASE
<substitution_list>  ::= { <substitution_value> "," } <substitution_value>
```

```
<substitution_value>    ::= <simple_expression>
<high_message_number> ::= integer literal in the range 20000 to 99999
                        | <identifier> of an integer variable in the same range
```

The first format of RAISERROR just specifies a message number in the range 17000 to 99999; this number may be an integer literal or a variable, but it can't be an expression. Here is an example of a simple RAISERROR statement:

```
RAISERROR 17000;
```

Figure 9-1 shows the dialog box that appears when that RAISERROR is executed in ISQL; the message "RAISERROR executed:" is displayed but no other message text is included.

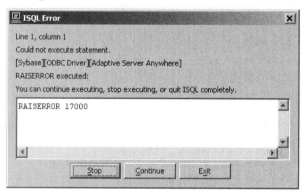

Figure 9-1. RAISERROR dialog box in ISQL

If the message number is in the high range of 20000 to 99999, then the CREATE MESSAGE statement may be used ahead of time to store a text message that will be automatically displayed by RAISERROR. The CREATE MESSAGE statement inserts a row in the SQL Anywhere catalog table called SYSUSERMESSAGES.

```
<create_message>  ::= CREATE MESSAGE <high_message_number> AS <message_literal>
<message_literal> ::= string literal up to 255 bytes in length
```

Here is an example of a CREATE MESSAGE statement, followed by a SELECT to show where the message text is stored:

```
CREATE MESSAGE 20000 AS 'Demonstration message.';
SELECT *
  FROM SYSUSERMESSAGES
  WHERE error = 20000;
```

Here is what the resulting row in SYSUSERMESSAGES looks like:

```
error  uid  description               langid
=====  ===  ========================  ======
20000   1    'Demonstration message.'   0
```

Tip: Use the SET TEMPORARY OPTION ON_ERROR = 'CONTINUE' statement to temporarily change the special ISQL ON_ERROR option when using ISQL to test SQL scripts containing RAISERROR statements. However, don't make that change permanent because it may cause real errors to go unnoticed.

Here is an example of a RAISERROR statement that will display the message text stored in SYSUSERMESSAGES; the special ISQL option ON_ERROR has been temporarily set to 'CONTINUE' to let ISQL carry on after a RAISERROR is executed without popping up a dialog box:

```
SET TEMPORARY OPTION ON_ERROR = 'CONTINUE';
RAISERROR 20000;
```

Here is what appears in the Messages tab of the ISQL Results pane when the RAISERROR statement is executed; note that the message text "Demonstration message." has automatically appeared:

```
Line 1, column 1
Could not execute statement.
[Sybase][ODBC Driver][Adaptive Server Anywhere]
RAISERROR executed:  Demonstration message.
(Continuing after error)
```

The second format of the RAISERROR statement explicitly provides the message text as well as the message number; in this case the specified message text will override anything stored in the SYSUSERMESSAGES table. Here is an example using the same message number as above but with different message text; note that there is no comma between the message number and the message text:

```
RAISERROR 20000 'Different message.';
```

This time, ISQL displays:

```
RAISERROR executed:  Different message.
```

The third format of the RAISERROR statement uses a message text parameter containing special numbered placeholders of the form %n!, and the message text is followed by a comma-separated list of values to be substituted for the placeholders; the first substitution value replaces the placeholder %1!, the second value replaces %2!, and so on. Here is an example with two placeholders; notice that commas must be used after the message text:

```
RAISERROR 20000 'Diagnostic number = %1!, string = "%2!".', 999, 'AAA';
```

Here's what the resulting output looks like in ISQL:

```
RAISERROR executed:  Diagnostic number = 999, string = "AAA".
```

The fourth format of the RAISERROR statement omits the message text but includes the list of substitution values; in this case a CREATE MESSAGE statement must be used to store a message containing the placeholders %n!. Here is an example of a CREATE MESSAGE to store the same message text that was used in the previous example, together with a RAISERROR that produces exactly the same output as above; note that in this format a comma appears after the message number in the RAISERROR:

```
CREATE MESSAGE 20000 AS 'Diagnostic number = %1!, string = "%2!".';
RAISERROR 20000, 999, 'AAA';
```

The message text stored in SYSUSERMESSAGES is limited to 255 bytes. However, SQL Anywhere will only include 233 characters after the prefix "RAISERROR executed:" when the message is displayed or returned to an application program, and that limit applies to the message after any placeholders have been replaced.

After a RAISERROR statement has been executed, SQL processing continues normally; the message number is available to other SQL statements in the built-in connection-level variable @@ERROR and the message text is available by calling the built-in function ERRORMSG(). BEGIN block exception handlers won't get executed; if the SQL code needs to handle errors flagged by the RAISERROR statement, then the @@ERROR variable must be explicitly checked.

Tip: Do not change the default setting of the option CONTINUE_AFTER_ RAISERROR; leave it set to 'ON' so that RAISERROR statements inside BEGIN blocks will behave as described in this section.

Following is an example of two stored procedures and an outer BEGIN block. The BEGIN block calls p_error2, p_error2 calls p_error1, and then p_error1 executes a RAISERROR statement; along the way the value of @@ERROR is checked, and various MESSAGE statements display the progress in the database console window. The RAISERROR statement uses variables for the message number and the substitution values to show that all the diagnostic information can be determined at execution time; the syntax even allows an expression to be used for the message text in a RAISERROR statement.

```
CREATE PROCEDURE p_error1 ()
BEGIN
   DECLARE @error INTEGER;
   DECLARE @diagnostic_number INTEGER;
   DECLARE @diagnostic_string VARCHAR ( 10 );
   MESSAGE 'p_error1 before RAISERROR';
   SET @error = 20000;
   SET @diagnostic_number = 999;
   SET @diagnostic_string = 'AAA';
   RAISERROR @error
      'Diagnostic number = %1!, string = "%2!".',
      @diagnostic_number,
      @diagnostic_string;
   MESSAGE 'p_error1 after RAISERROR';
EXCEPTION
   WHEN OTHERS THEN
      MESSAGE STRING ( 'p_error1 exception handler' );
END;

CREATE PROCEDURE p_error2 ()
BEGIN
   MESSAGE 'p_error2 before CALL p_error1';
   CALL p_error1();
   MESSAGE 'p_error2 after CALL p_error1';
   IF @@ERROR <> 0 THEN
      MESSAGE 'Error detected in p_error2...';
      MESSAGE STRING ( '   @@ERROR   = ', @@ERROR );
      MESSAGE STRING ( '   ERRORMSG() = ', ERRORMSG() );
   END IF;
EXCEPTION
   WHEN OTHERS THEN
      MESSAGE STRING ( 'p_error2 exception handler' );
END;

BEGIN
   MESSAGE 'Before CALL p_error2';
```

```
    CALL p_error2();
    MESSAGE 'After CALL p_error2';
    IF @@ERROR <> 0 THEN
       MESSAGE 'Error detected in outer block...';
       MESSAGE STRING ( '   @@ERROR    = ', @@ERROR );
       MESSAGE STRING ( '   ERRORMSG() = ', ERRORMSG() );
    END IF;
EXCEPTION
    WHEN OTHERS THEN
       MESSAGE STRING ( 'Outer block exception handler' );
END;
```

Here is the output from the example above; note that execution continued normally after each CALL and the RAISERROR, that the values of @@ERROR and ERRORMSG() were preserved as execution proceeded, and that none of the EXCEPTION handlers were executed:

```
p_error2 before CALL p_error1
p_error1 before RAISERROR
p_error1 after RAISERROR
p_error2 after CALL p_error1
Error detected in p_error2...
   @@ERROR    = 20000
   ERRORMSG() = RAISERROR executed:  Diagnostic number = 999, string = "AAA".
After CALL p_error2
Error detected in outer block...
   @@ERROR    = 20000
   ERRORMSG() = RAISERROR executed:  Diagnostic number = 999, string = "AAA".
```

Here is another example of a stored procedure called from a Java application; the application is the same as the one shown earlier, CatchError.java, but the stored procedure has been changed to execute a RAISERROR statement instead of SIGNAL:

```
CREATE PROCEDURE p1()
RESULT (
   key_1 INTEGER,
   non_key_1 VARCHAR ( 100 ) )
BEGIN
   DECLARE @error INTEGER;
   DECLARE @diagnostic_number INTEGER;
   DECLARE @diagnostic_string VARCHAR ( 10 );

   MESSAGE 'p1 before SELECT';
   SELECT key_1,
          non_key_1
     FROM t1
    ORDER BY key_1;
   MESSAGE 'p1 after SELECT';

   SET @error = 20000;
   SET @diagnostic_number = 999;
   SET @diagnostic_string = 'AAA';
   RAISERROR @error
      'Diagnostic number = %1!, string = "%2!".',
      @diagnostic_number,
      @diagnostic_string;
   MESSAGE 'p1 after RAISERROR';

END;
```

The following output is displayed by the Java application shown earlier,
CatchError.java, when the new version of the procedure p1 has been stored in
the database. As before, the result set is followed by the output from the first
catch block, and the same value of SQLState is displayed: HY000 for "driver-
specific error." This time, however, the SQL ErrorCode has been set to –20000,
which is the negative value of the message number specified in the
RAISERROR statement. Also, the full version of the RAISERROR message is
displayed, including the diagnostic data; this shows that RAISERROR is more
powerful than SIGNAL when it comes to passing information back to a client
application.

```
key_1 = 1, non_key_1 = 'AAA'
key_1 = 2, non_key_1 = 'BBB'
SQLState:  HY000
ErrorCode: -20000
Message:   [Sybase][ODBC Driver][Adaptive Server Anywhere]RAISERROR executed:
Diagnostic number = 999, string = "AAA".
Stack trace...
java.sql.SQLException: [Sybase][ODBC Driver][Adaptive Server Anywhere]RAISERROR
executed:  Diagnostic number = 999, string = "AAA".
        at ianywhere.ml.jdbcodbc.IStatement.getMoreResults(Native Method)
        at CatchError.main(CatchError.java:27)
```

Here is the output that was displayed in the database console window when
CatchError.java called the new procedure p1. Unlike the previous test that used
a SIGNAL statement, execution of this procedure continued after the
RAISERROR statement was executed. However, the getMoreResults() call is
still required to force the statements following the SELECT to be executed at
all.

```
p1 before SELECT
CatchError.java after display
p1 after SELECT
p1 after RAISERROR
```

Here is an example of an EXCEPTION handler that can be used inside a
BEGIN block to turn exceptions into RAISERROR messages; this code has the
advantage that the original SQLCODE, SQLSTATE, and ERRORMSG() values
are all preserved inside the error message passed back to the client application:

```
CREATE PROCEDURE p1()
RESULT (
   key_1 INTEGER,
   non_key_1 VARCHAR ( 100 ) )
BEGIN
   DECLARE @sqlcode   INTEGER;
   DECLARE @sqlstate  VARCHAR ( 5 );
   DECLARE @errormsg  VARCHAR ( 32767 );
   DECLARE error_99001 EXCEPTION FOR SQLSTATE '99001';
   SIGNAL error_99001;
EXCEPTION
   WHEN OTHERS THEN
      SELECT SQLCODE, SQLSTATE, ERRORMSG()
         INTO @sqlcode, @sqlstate, @errormsg;
      RAISERROR 99999
         'SQLCODE = %1!, SQLSTATE = %2!, ERRORMSG() = %3!',
         @sqlcode, @sqlstate, @errormsg;
END;
```

Here is the output displayed by the Java application CatchError.java when it calls the procedure shown above; now the original SQLSTATE '99001' is available to the client application:

```
SQLState:  HY000
ErrorCode: -99999
Message:   [Sybase][ODBC Driver][Adaptive Server Anywhere]RAISERROR executed:
SQLCODE = -297, SQLSTATE = 99001, ERRORMSG() = User-defined exception signaled
```

This technique also works for built-in SQLSTATE exceptions; the error message returned to the client contains all the original diagnostic information available at the point of error. Here is the output displayed by the Java application CatchError.java when the exception handler shown above is used inside a procedure that raises a data conversion exception when it is called:

```
SQLState:  HY000
ErrorCode: -99999
Message:   [Sybase][ODBC Driver][Adaptive Server Anywhere]RAISERROR executed:
SQLCODE = -157, SQLSTATE = 53018, ERRORMSG() = Cannot convert xxx to a timestamp
```

9.5.3 ROLLBACK TRIGGER

The ROLLBACK TRIGGER statement can be used inside a trigger to perform two vastly different operations: either silently roll back the inner triggering operation and then continue processing as if nothing happened, or roll back the outer triggering operation and return an error to the client application. Here's the syntax for the two operations; the first format does the silent rollback and the second format returns an error:

```
<rollback_trigger> ::= ROLLBACK TRIGGER
                     | ROLLBACK TRIGGER WITH <raiserror>
```

The following is an example of the silent local rollback using ROLLBACK TRIGGER; table t1 doesn't have any trigger, table t2 has an update trigger that contains an UPDATE affecting table t3, and table t3 has an update trigger that contains the ROLLBACK TRIGGER statement. The transaction consists of two UPDATE statements to change tables t1 and t2, followed by a COMMIT.

```
CREATE TABLE t1 (
   key_1        INTEGER NOT NULL PRIMARY KEY,
   non_key_1    VARCHAR ( 100 ) NOT NULL );

CREATE TABLE t2 (
   key_2        INTEGER NOT NULL PRIMARY KEY,
   non_key_2    VARCHAR ( 100 ) NOT NULL );

CREATE TABLE t3 (
   key_3        INTEGER NOT NULL PRIMARY KEY,
   non_key_3    VARCHAR ( 100 ) NOT NULL );

INSERT t1 VALUES ( 1, 'AAA' );
INSERT t2 VALUES ( 1, 'AAA' );
INSERT t3 VALUES ( 1, 'AAA' );
COMMIT;

CREATE TRIGGER tru_t2 BEFORE UPDATE ON t2
FOR EACH ROW
BEGIN
   UPDATE t3 SET non_key_3 = 'ZZZ' WHERE key_3 = 1;
```

```
END;

CREATE TRIGGER tru_t3 BEFORE UPDATE ON t3
FOR EACH ROW
BEGIN
   ROLLBACK TRIGGER;
END;

UPDATE t1 SET non_key_1 = 'XXX' WHERE key_1 = 1;
UPDATE t2 SET non_key_2 = 'YYY' WHERE key_2 = 1;
COMMIT;

SELECT * FROM t1;
SELECT * FROM t2;
SELECT * FROM t3;
```

Note: Except where otherwise noted, the CHAINED option is set to the default 'ON' for all the examples in this book. For more information about the CHAINED option, see Section 9.3, "Transactions."

When the script above is executed, the ROLLBACK TRIGGER performs a rollback that affects only the operation that directly fired the trigger; in this case the UPDATE to table t3 is rolled back. However, the update to table t2 is not affected because it didn't directly fire the trigger containing the ROLLBACK TRIGGER; instead, it fired a trigger on table t2, which in turn fired the trigger on table t3. Also, the update to table t1 is not affected by the ROLLBACK TRIGGER; the three SELECT statements show that tables t1 and t2 were updated but not t3.

```
key_1  non_key_1
=====  =========
1      'XXX'

key_2  non_key_2
=====  =========
1      'YYY'

key_3  non_key_3
=====  =========
1      'AAA'
```

The second form of ROLLBACK TRIGGER merges the RAISERROR statement with the ROLLBACK TRIGGER statement. Here is one of the triggers from the previous example, modified to add WITH RAISERROR to the ROLLBACK TRIGGER:

```
CREATE TRIGGER tru_t3 BEFORE UPDATE ON t3
FOR EACH ROW
BEGIN
   ROLLBACK TRIGGER WITH RAISERROR 99999 'ROLLBACK TRIGGER in tru_t3';
END;
```

The following ISQL test script shows the effect of the new trigger; the ISQL option ON_ERROR is set to 'CONTINUE' so ISQL will keep going after the error, and the UPDATE statements are wrapped in a BEGIN block so ISQL will treat them as a single executable batch to be passed to SQL Anywhere. MESSAGE statements are included to show which SQL statements are executed and which ones are bypassed.

```
SET TEMPORARY OPTION ON_ERROR = 'CONTINUE';
BEGIN
    MESSAGE '1';
    UPDATE t1 SET non_key_1 = 'XXX' WHERE key_1 = 1;
    MESSAGE '2';
    UPDATE t2 SET non_key_2 = 'YYY' WHERE key_2 = 1;
    MESSAGE '3';
    COMMIT;
    MESSAGE '4';
END;
MESSAGE '5';

SELECT * FROM t1;
SELECT * FROM t2;
SELECT * FROM t3;
```

When the script above was executed, the following message appeared in the ISQL Messages tab:

```
RAISERROR executed:  ROLLBACK TRIGGER in tru_t3
```

The following output appeared in the database console window; it shows that the COMMIT was not executed because the second UPDATE statement had an error. That error caused SQL Anywhere to bypass the remaining statements in the BEGIN block and return control to the client, ISQL.

```
1
2
5
```

The three SELECT statements show that, unlike the previous example, the change to table t2 was rolled back as well as the change to t3; this form of ROLLBACK TRIGGER rolls back the change that fired the outer trigger as well as the nested trigger. However, the change to table t1 is still in effect; both forms of ROLLBACK TRIGGER perform partial rollbacks, and the change to t1 was not included.

```
key_1  non_key_1
=====  =========
1      'XXX'

key_2  non_key_2
=====  =========
1      'AAA'

key_3  non_key_3
=====  =========
1      'AAA'
```

It is important to note that when the script shown above finished executing, a transaction was still in effect. It is up to the client (ISQL) whether to execute a COMMIT or ROLLBACK; the change to table t1 is still in an uncommitted state even though the changes to t2 and t3 have been rolled back.

The two forms of the ROLLBACK TRIGGER statement provide a partial contradiction to the earlier statement that in SQL Anywhere "there is no such thing as a nested transaction." Specifically, there is no such thing as a partial commit; when people talk about nested transactions, they are usually thinking about partial commits, which aren't supported. However, a limited form of partial rollbacks is supported by ROLLBACK TRIGGER, and by an even more flexible facility that was described in Section 9.4, "Savepoints and Subtransactions."

9.6 Locks

In order to improve overall productivity, different transactions are allowed to overlap one another in a multi-user environment. For example, if SQL Anywhere has processed an UPDATE and is waiting to receive the next SQL command that is part of the same transaction, and a SELECT that is part of a different transaction arrives in the meantime, it will try to process the SELECT immediately. If SQL Anywhere only worked on one transaction at a time, no one would get any work done; in reality, the database engine can switch back and forth among hundreds of overlapping transactions in a busy environment.

The ability of SQL Anywhere to process overlapping transactions is called *concurrency*, and it may conflict with two of the basic requirements of a transaction: consistency and isolation. For example, if two overlapping transactions were allowed to update the same row, the requirement that changes made by different transactions must be isolated from one another would be violated. Another example is a transaction design that requires data to remain unchanged between retrieval and update in order for the final result to be consistent; that requirement would be violated by an overlapping transaction that changed the data after the first transaction retrieved it, even if the second transaction committed its change before the first transaction performed its update.

SQL Anywhere uses locks to preserve isolation and consistency while allowing concurrency. A *lock* is a piece of data stored in an internal table maintained by SQL Anywhere. Each lock represents a requirement that must be met before a particular connection can proceed with its work, and logically it is implemented as a temporary relationship between that connection and a single row or table. While it exists, a lock serves to prevent any other connection from performing certain operations on that table or row.

When a lock is needed by a connection in order to proceed, it is said to be requested by that connection. If SQL Anywhere creates the lock, the request is said to be granted, the lock is said to be acquired, and the work of that connection can proceed. If SQL Anywhere does not create the lock because some other conflicting lock already exists, the request is said to be blocked, the lock cannot be acquired, and the connection cannot proceed.

Locks fall into two broad categories: short-term and long-term. A *short-term lock* is only held for the duration of a single SQL statement or less, whereas a *long-term lock* is held for a longer period, usually until the end of a transaction. This chapter concentrates on the discussion of long-term locks because short-term locks are not visible from an administrative point of view. Unless otherwise noted, the term "lock" means "long-term lock" in this chapter.

The built-in procedure sa_locks can be used to show all the locks held at a given point in time. Here is an example of a call:

```
CALL sa_locks();
```

The following shows what the output from sa_locks looks like; each entry represents one or more locks associated with a particular table or row. The connection column identifies the connection that is holding the locks, the user_id column contains the user id that was used to make the connection, the table_name shows which table the locks are associated with, the lock_type identifies the different kinds of locks represented by this entry, and the lock_name column is an internal row identifier or NULL for an sa_locks entry that is associated with an entire table.

connection	user_id	table_name	lock_type	lock_name
508116521	DBA	DBA.t1	E	473
508116521	DBA	DBA.t3b	EPA*	4294967836
508116521	DBA	DBA.t1b	EPA0000	4294967834
508116521	DBA	DBA.t1u	EPA0001	12884902403
508116521	DBA	DBA.t1n	EPT	528
508116521	DBA	DBA.t3	S	4294967821
508116521	DBA	DBA.t1	SPA0000	1095216660986
508116521	DBA	DBA.t1u	SPA0001	1095216661028
508116521	DBA	DBA.t3n	SPT	553
508116521	DBA	DBA.e4b	E	NULL
508116521	DBA	DBA.e4	EPT	NULL
508116521	DBA	DBA.t2n	S	NULL
508116521	DBA	DBA.e1b	SAT	NULL
508116521	DBA	DBA.e3	SPAT	NULL
508116521	DBA	DBA.t2b	SPT	NULL

Here is what the various characters in the lock_type column mean for lines in the sa_locks output that have non-NULL row identifiers in the lock_name column:

- "E" represents an *exclusive row write lock*. This kind of lock won't be granted if any other connection has an exclusive row write lock or a shared row read lock on the row. Once an exclusive row write lock has been acquired, no other connection can obtain any kind of lock on the row.

- "S" represents a *shared row read lock*. This kind of lock may coexist with other shared row read locks on the same row that have been granted to other connections.

- "P" represents an *insert, or anti-phantom, row position lock*, which reserves the right to insert a row in the position immediately ahead of the row identified by the lock_name column. The row position is determined in one of three ways: with respect to the order of a particular index, with respect to the order of a sequential table scan, or with respect to all index and sequential orderings on the table. An exclusive row write lock or a shared read row lock is always granted at the same time as an insert row position lock.

- "A" represents an *anti-insert, or phantom, row position lock*, which prevents any other connection from inserting a row in the position immediately ahead of the row identified by the lock_name column. The row position is determined in the same manner as for an insert lock. An exclusive row write lock or a shared read row lock is always granted at the same time as an anti-insert row position lock. Also, anti-insert and insert locks may be granted at the same time; e.g., the combinations "EPA" and "SPA" mean that three locks associated with the same row are represented by one entry in the sa_locks output.

- A four-digit integer like 0000 or 0001 identifies the index used to determine the row ordering for insert and anti-insert row position locks.

- "T" specifies that a sequential table scan is used to determine the row ordering for insert and anti-insert row position locks.
- The asterisk (*) specifies that the insert and anti-insert locks apply to all index and sequential orders.

Here is what the various characters in the lock_type column mean for lines in the sa_locks output that have NULL values in the lock_name column:

- "E" represents an exclusive table schema lock.
- "S" represents a shared table schema lock.
- "PT" represents a table contents update intent lock.
- "AT" represents a table contents read lock.
- "PAT" represents a combination of two table contents locks: update intent and read.

Here are all the combinations of lock_type and lock_name from the earlier example of sa_locks output, together with a description of the locks they represent according to the definitions given above:

Table 9-2. lock_type and lock_name combinations

lock_type	lock_name	Description
E	473	Exclusive row write lock
EPA*	4294967836	Exclusive row write lock, plus insert and anti-insert row position locks with respect to all orders
EPA0000	4294967834	Exclusive row write lock, plus insert and anti-insert row position locks with respect to index 0000
EPA0001	12884902403	Exclusive row write lock, plus insert and anti-insert row position locks with respect to index 0001
EPT	528	Exclusive row write lock, plus anti-insert row position lock with respect to sequential order
S	4294967821	Shared row read lock
SPA0000	1095216660986	Shared row read lock, plus insert and anti-insert row position locks with respect to index 0000
SPA0001	1095216661028	Shared row read lock, plus insert and anti-insert row position locks with respect to index 0001
SPT	553	Shared row read lock, plus anti-insert row position lock with respect to sequential order
E	(NULL)	Exclusive table schema lock
EPT	(NULL)	Exclusive table schema lock, plus update intent table contents lock

lock_type	lock_name	Description
S	(NULL)	Shared table schema lock
SAT	(NULL)	Shared table schema lock, plus table contents read lock
SPAT	(NULL)	Shared table schema lock, plus table contents read and update intent locks
SPT	(NULL)	Shared table schema lock, plus table contents update intent lock

A single connection isn't prevented from obtaining different kinds of locks on the same table or row; conflicts only arise between different connections. For example, one connection cannot obtain an insert lock on a row position while another connection has an anti-insert lock on the same row position, but a single connection can obtain both kinds of locks on the same position.

When a lock is no longer needed by a connection, it is said to be released, and SQL Anywhere deletes the entry from the internal lock table. Most locks persist from the time they are acquired by a connection until the next time that connection performs a COMMIT or ROLLBACK operation. However, some locks are released earlier, and others can last longer. For example, a read lock that is acquired by a FETCH operation in order to ensure cursor stability at isolation level 1 will be released as soon as the next row is fetched. Also, the exclusive table lock acquired by a LOCK TABLE statement using the WITH HOLD clause will persist past a COMMIT; indeed, if the table is dropped and recreated, the table lock will be resurrected automatically, and it won't released until the connection is dropped. Cursor stability is discussed in the following section, as are some performance improvements made possible by the LOCK TABLE statement.

For all practical purposes, however, all row locks acquired during a transaction are held until the transaction ends with a COMMIT or ROLLBACK, and at that point all the locks are released. This is true of statements that fail as well as those that succeed. Single SQL statements like INSERT, UPDATE, and DELETE are atomic in nature, which means that if the statement fails, any changes it made to the database will be automatically undone. That doesn't apply to the locks, however; any locks obtained by a failed statement will persist until the transaction ends.

9.7 Blocks and Isolation Levels

A *block* occurs when a connection requests a lock that cannot be granted. By default, a block causes the blocked connection to wait until all conflicting locks are released. The database option BLOCKING may be set to 'OFF' so that a blocked operation will be immediately cancelled and an error will be returned to the blocked connection. The cancellation of a blocked operation does not imply an automatic rollback, however; the affected connection may proceed forward and it still holds any locks it may have acquired earlier, including locks acquired during earlier processing of the failed statement.

The number of locks held at any one time by a single connection can vary from zero to several million. The actual number depends on two main factors: the kinds of SQL operations performed during the current transaction and the setting of the ISOLATION_LEVEL database option for the connection when each operation was performed. Some operations, such as UPDATE, require locks regardless of the isolation level. Other operations, such as SELECT, may or may not require locks depending on the isolation level.

The *isolation level* is a number 0, 1, 2, or 3, which represents the degree to which this connection will be protected from operations performed by other connections.

- **Isolation level 0** prevents overlapping data changes, data retrievals overlapping with schema changes, and deadlock conditions. Figures 9-2 through 9-5 and 9-20 show how overlapping transactions are affected by isolation level 0.
- **Isolation level 1** prevents dirty reads and cursor instability, in addition to the protection provided by isolation level 0. Figures 9-6 through 9-9 demonstrate the effects of isolation level 1.
- **Isolation level 2** prevents non-repeatable reads and update instability, in addition to the protection provided by isolation levels 0 and 1. Figures 9-10 through 9-13 show how repeatable reads and update stability is achieved at isolation level 2.
- **Isolation level 3** prevents phantom rows and a particular form of lost update, in addition to the protection provided by isolation levels 0, 1, and 2. Figures 9-14 through 9-17 demonstrate the effects of isolation level 3.

Isolation levels 2 and 3 result in the largest number of locks and the highest level of protection at the cost of the lowest level of concurrency. Figures 9-18 and 9-19 show how high isolation levels affect concurrency.

9.7.1 Isolation Level 0

Isolation level 0 is the default; it results in the fewest number of locks and the highest degree of concurrency at the risk of allowing inconsistencies that would be prevented by higher isolation levels.

Figure 9-2 is the first of several demonstrations of locks and blocks, all of which involve two connections, one table, and various values of isolation level. Here is the script used to create and fill the table with five rows; this script is the starting point for Figures 9-2 through 9-20:

```
CREATE TABLE DBA.t1 (
    k1      INTEGER NOT NULL PRIMARY KEY,
    c1      VARCHAR ( 100 ) NOT NULL );

INSERT t1 VALUES ( 1, 'clean' );
INSERT t1 VALUES ( 3, 'clean' );
INSERT t1 VALUES ( 5, 'clean' );
INSERT t1 VALUES ( 7, 'clean' );
INSERT t1 VALUES ( 9, 'clean' );
COMMIT;
```

Figure 9-2 shows what happens when Connection A updates a row and then Connection B attempts to update and delete the same row before Connection A executes a COMMIT or ROLLBACK; both operations performed by

Connection B are blocked because Connection A has an exclusive write lock on that row.

	Connection A	Connection B	Comment	c1 Value	Locks Held by A & B
1	SET TEMPORARY OPTION ISOLATION_LEVEL = 0				
2		SET TEMPORARY OPTION ISOLATION_LEVEL = 0			
3	UPDATE t1 SET c1 = 'winner' WHERE k1 = 5				A Write (E) A Schema (S)
4		UPDATE t1 SET c1 = 'loser' WHERE k1 = 5	Blocked: 42W18 User 'A' has the row in 't1' locked		A Write (E) A Schema (S) B Schema (S)
5		DELETE t1 WHERE k1 = 5	Blocked: 42W18 User 'A' has the row in 't1' locked		A Write (E) A Schema (S) B Schema (S)

Figure 9-2. UPDATE blocks UPDATE, DELETE

Here is a description of the six columns appearing in Figure 9-2 and the other figures to follow:

■ The **step number 1, 2, 3...** lists the order in which each separate SQL command was performed on one or the other of the two connections. Steps 1 and 2 in each figure show what value of ISOLATION_LEVEL is explicitly set for each connection. For the purposes of Figure 9-2, the isolation level doesn't matter; an UPDATE always blocks an UPDATE or a DELETE.

■ The **Connection A** column shows each SQL statement executed on one of the connections.

■ **Connection B** shows the SQL statements executed on the other connection.

■ The **Comment** column describes any interesting situation that arises when this step is completed. In Figure 9-2 it shows that Connection B is blocked from executing the UPDATE and DELETE statements in Steps 4 and 5. For the purposes of all but one of these figures, the BLOCKING option is set to 'OFF' for both connections so there's no waiting; a blocked statement is immediately cancelled and the SQLSTATE is set to '42W18' to indicate an error. Note that a block doesn't cause a rollback or release any locks.

■ The **c1 Value** column contains the value of the t1.c1 column for steps that SELECT or FETCH a particular row. This value is important in later figures but not in Figure 9-2.

■ The column **Locks Held by A & B** shows all the locks held by Connection A and B after each step is executed. This column shows the locks as they exist at this point in time, not necessarily the locks that were acquired by this step. For example, the write lock that first appears in Step 3 was acquired by that step and persists through Steps 4 and 5. The letter A or B preceding the description of each lock shows which connection holds the lock.

Simplified lock descriptions are shown in the Locks Held by A & B column because the purpose of these figures is to explain how locks, blocks, and isolation levels affect concurrency and consistency, not to explain the inner workings of lock management in SQL Anywhere. Here's a list of the simplified descriptions and what they mean in terms of the definitions from Section 9.6:

■ **Write (E)** is used to represent an exclusive row write lock.

- **Read (S)** is used to represent a shared row read lock.
- **Anti-insert (S)** is used to represent the combination of a shared row read lock and an anti-insert row position lock.
- **Anti-insert + Insert (S)** is used to represent the combination of three locks: a shared row read lock plus anti-insert and insert row position locks.
- **Schema (S)** is used to represent a shared table schema lock, with or without a table contents update intent lock.

Note: Chained mode is assumed for Figures 9-2 through 9-20, and the transaction starting and ending points aren't explicitly shown. Chained mode is described in Section 9.3, "Transactions"; it means that transactions are implicitly started by the first INSERT, UPDATE, or DELETE statement, or SELECT statement that acquires locks, shown in the Connection A and Connection B columns. These transactions end when an explicit COMMIT or ROLLBACK statement is executed.

Figure 9-3 shows that a row deleted by Connection A cannot be re-inserted by Connection B before Connection A commits the change. This is true regardless of the isolation level. Connection A must be able to roll back the delete, thus effectively re-inserting the row itself; if Connection B was allowed to re-insert the row, Connection A's rollback would cause a primary key conflict. What does happen is that Connection B's insert is blocked; Connection A holds a write lock on the row, as well as an anti-insert lock to prevent other connections from re-inserting the row. It also holds an insert lock so that it can re-insert the row in the case of a rollback. Connection B is free to wait or reattempt the insert later; if Connection A commits the change, Connection B can then insert the row, but if Connection A rolls back the delete, Connection B's insert will fail.

	Connection A	Connection B	Comment	c1 Value	Locks Held by A & B
1	SET TEMPORARY OPTION ISOLATION LEVEL = 0				
2		SET TEMPORARY OPTION ISOLATION LEVEL = 0			
3	DELETE t1 WHERE k1 = 5				A Write (E) A Anti-insert + Insert (S) A Schema (S)
4		INSERT t1 VALUES (5, 'reinserted')	Blocked: 42W18 User 'A' has the row in 't1' locked		A Write (E) A Anti-insert + Insert (S) A Schema (S) B Schema (S)

Figure 9-3. DELETE blocks INSERT

The scenario shown in Figure 9-3 depends on the existence of a primary key in table t1. If there had been no primary key, Connection A would not have obtained the anti-insert and insert locks in Step 3, there would have been no block in Step 4, and Connection B would have been able to insert the row.

Figure 9-4 shows that a row inserted by Connection A cannot be updated or deleted by Connection B until Connection A commits the change, regardless of the isolation level. Connection A has complete control over the new row until it does a commit or rollback; until that point, Connection A must be free to perform other operations on that row without interference, and an update or delete by Connection B would certainly fall into that category. As with Figure 9-3, Connection B is free to wait or reattempt the operations later. If Connection A commits, subsequent update and delete operations will work; if Connection A rolls back the insert, Connection B won't be able to do an update or delete.

	Connection A	Connection B	Comment	c1 Value	Locks Held by A & B
1	SET TEMPORARY OPTION ISOLATION LEVEL = 0				
2		SET TEMPORARY OPTION ISOLATION LEVEL = 0			
3	INSERT t1 VALUES (4, 'new')				A Write (E) A Schema (S)
4		UPDATE t1 SET c1 = 'different' WHERE k1 = 4	Blocked: 42W18 User 'A' has the row in 't1' locked		A Write (E) A Schema (S) B Schema (S)
5		DELETE t1 WHERE k1 = 4	Blocked: 42W18 User 'A' has the row in 't1' locked		A Write (E) A Schema (S) B Schema (S)

Figure 9-4. INSERT blocks UPDATE, DELETE

Figure 9-5 shows that a simple SELECT, even at isolation level 0, obtains a schema lock on the table. These locks have no effect on any other connection except to prevent schema changes; in this example, the SELECT by Connection A prevents Connection B from creating an index. Applications running at isolation level 0 rarely do commits after retrieving rows; in a busy environment that can mean most tables are subject to perpetual schema locks, making schema changes a challenge. The opposite effect is even more dramatic: Once a schema change begins, no other connection can do anything with the affected table until the schema change is complete. Schema changes during prime time are not recommended, and the locks and blocks they cause aren't discussed any further in this book.

	Connection A	Connection B	Comment	c1 Value	Locks Held by A & B
1	SET TEMPORARY OPTION ISOLATION LEVEL = 0				
2		SET TEMPORARY OPTION ISOLATION LEVEL = 0			
3	SELECT c1 INTO @c1 FROM t1 WHERE k1 = 5			clean	A Schema (S)
4		CREATE INDEX xc1 ON t1 (c1)	Blocked: 42W18 User 'A' has the row in 't1' locked		A Schema (S)
5	COMMIT				
6		CREATE INDEX xc1 ON t1 (c1)	Unblocked		

Figure 9-5. SELECT blocks schema change

9.7.2 Isolation Level 1

Figure 9-6 shows the first example of interconnection interference that is permitted at isolation level 0: the *dirty read*. In Step 3 Connection A updates a row that is immediately read by Connection B in Step 4. This is called a "dirty read" because the change by Connection A has not been committed yet; if that change is eventually rolled back, it means that Connection B is working with dirty data at Step 4.

Connection A	Connection B	Comment	c1 Value	Locks Held by A & B
1 SET TEMPORARY OPTION ISOLATION LEVEL = 0				
2	SET TEMPORARY OPTION ISOLATION LEVEL = 0			
3 UPDATE t1 SET c1 = 'dirty' WHERE k1 = 5				A Write (E) A Schema (S)
4	SELECT c1 INTO @c1 FROM t1 WHERE k1 = 5	Dirty read	dirty	A Write (E) A Schema (S) B Schema (S)
5 ROLLBACK				B Schema (S)
6	SELECT c1 INTO @c1 FROM t1 WHERE k1 = 5	Original value	clean	B Schema (S)

Figure 9-6. Dirty read permitted at isolation level = 0

Figure 9-7 shows how dirty reads are prevented for a connection running at isolation level 1. The SELECT at Step 4 is blocked because Connection A has a write lock on that row, and a write lock blocks a read at isolation level 1. SQL Anywhere blocks dirty reads altogether, rather than implementing a solution that returns some older, unchanged value that doesn't actually exist anymore.

Connection A	Connection B	Comment	c1 Value	Locks Held by A & B
1 SET TEMPORARY OPTION ISOLATION LEVEL = 0				
2	SET TEMPORARY OPTION ISOLATION LEVEL = 1			
3 UPDATE t1 SET c1 = 'dirty' WHERE k1 = 5				A Write (E) A Schema (S)
4	SELECT c1 INTO @c1 FROM t1 WHERE k1 = 5	Blocked: 42W18 User 'A' has the row in 't1' locked		A Write (E) A Schema (S) B Schema (S)
5 ROLLBACK				B Schema (S)
6	SELECT c1 INTO @c1 FROM t1 WHERE k1 = 5	Unblocked	clean	B Schema (S)

Figure 9-7. Dirty read prevented at isolation level = 1

Figure 9-7 shows that no extra long-term locks are required to prevent dirty reads. The reason Connection B was blocked in Step 4 is because it attempted to get a short-term lock on the row for the duration of the SELECT, and that attempt ran afoul of Connection A's write lock. This short-term lock does not appear in the Locks Held by A & B column because it was not granted, and sa_locks only shows the locks that are granted at the instant the sa_locks is called (in these examples, at the end of each step). Short-term locks are the mechanism whereby dirty reads are prevented at isolation level 1.

A dirty read is not necessarily a bad thing; it depends on the application. For example, if one connection updates column X and then another connection reads column Y from the same row, that might not be considered a "dirty read" from an application point of view, but nevertheless it is prevented by isolation level 1. Another point to consider is the fact that most updates are committed, not rolled back; just because a change has not been committed yet doesn't necessarily mean the data is incorrect from an application point of view.

Figure 9-8 shows another form of interference that's allowed at isolation level 0: *cursor instability*. At Step 7, Connection B has fetched the row with k1 = 5, and in Steps 8 and 9 that row is changed by Connection A and the change is immediately committed. When Connection B updates the same row in Step 10, it isn't blocked because Connection A doesn't hold a write lock on that row anymore. However, the change made by Connection A isn't the one that's expected. The SET c1 = c1 + 'er' clause doesn't change "clean" to "cleaner," it changes "dirty" to "dirtyer"; the final incorrect (unlucky?) result is shown in Step 13. This form of interference is called "cursor instability" because another connection is allowed to change a row that was most recently fetched in a cursor loop.

	Connection A	Connection B	Comment	c1 Value	Locks Held by A & B
1	SET TEMPORARY OPTION ISOLATION LEVEL = 0				
2		SET TEMPORARY OPTION ISOLATION LEVEL = 0			
3		DECLARE cur1 CURSOR FOR SELECT k1, c1 FROM t1 ORDER BY k1 FOR READ ONLY			
4		OPEN cur1			B Schema (S)
5		FETCH cur1 INTO @k1, @c1	clean		B Schema (S)
6		FETCH cur1 INTO @k1, @c1	clean		B Schema (S)
7		FETCH cur1 INTO @k1, @c1	clean		B Schema (S)
8	UPDATE t1 SET c1 = 'dirty' WHERE k1 = 5		Allowed		A Write (E) A Schema (S) B Schema (S)
9	COMMIT				B Schema (S)
10		UPDATE t1 SET c1 = c1 + 'er' WHERE k1 = 5	Unstable		B Write (E) B Schema (S)
11		CLOSE cur1			B Write (E) B Schema (S)
12		COMMIT			
13		SELECT c1 INTO @c1 FROM t1 WHERE k1 = 5	Incorrect result	dirtyer	B Schema (S)

Figure 9-8. Cursor stability not ensured at isolation level = 0

Figure 9-9 shows how isolation level 1 guarantees cursor stability; once the row has been fetched by Connection B in Step 7, the update by Connection A in Step 8 is blocked. Now the update by Connection B in Step 9 has the expected result: "clean" is changed to "cleaner" as shown in Step 11.

Cursor stability is implemented at isolation level 1 by the read locks established for each fetch; for example, the read lock acquired by Connection B in Step 7 blocks Connection A's attempt to acquire a write lock in Step 8.

Each of these read locks is released as soon as the next row is fetched and a new read lock is acquired on that row. This early release of cursor stability read locks is an exception to the rule of thumb that "all row locks are held until the end of a transaction."

	Connection A	Connection B	Comment	c1 Value	Locks Held by A & B
1	SET TEMPORARY OPTION ISOLATION LEVEL = 0				
2		SET TEMPORARY OPTION ISOLATION LEVEL = 1			
3		DECLARE cur1 CURSOR FOR SELECT k1, c1 FROM t1 ORDER BY k1 FOR READ ONLY			
4		OPEN cur1			B Schema (S)
5		FETCH cur1 INTO @k1, @c1	clean		B Read (S) B Schema (S)
6		FETCH cur1 INTO @k1, @c1	clean		B Read (S) B Schema (S)
7		FETCH cur1 INTO @k1, @c1	clean		B Read (S) B Schema (S)
8	UPDATE t1 SET c1 = 'dirty' WHERE k1 = 5		Blocked: 42W18 User 'B' has the row in 't1' locked		A Schema (S) B Read (S) B Schema (S)
9		UPDATE t1 SET c1 = c1 + 'er' WHERE k1 = 5	Stable		A Schema (S) B Write (E) B Read (S) B Schema (S)
10		CLOSE cur1			A Schema (S) B Write (E) B Schema (S)
11		SELECT c1 INTO @c1 FROM t1 WHERE k1 = 5	Interim result	cleaner	A Schema (S) B Write (E) B Schema (S)
12		COMMIT			A Schema (S)
13	UPDATE t1 SET c1 = 'dirty' WHERE k1 = 5		Unblocked		A Write (E) A Schema (S)
14	COMMIT				
15	SELECT c1 INTO @c1 FROM t1 WHERE k1 = 5		Final result	dirty	A Schema (S)

Figure 9-9. Cursor stability ensured at isolation level = 1

The scenario in Figure 9-9 continues through Step 15 to show that Connection A can eventually make its change once Connection B releases the read lock. Locks, blocks, and isolation levels only affect overlapping transactions; they don't protect against changes made by non-overlapped or serialized transactions.

Locks and blocks also don't protect against changes made by the same transaction. For example, a single transaction may have two different cursors open at the same time and any locks obtained by one cursor won't prevent changes made by the other cursor from interfering with it.

9.7.3 Isolation Level 2

Figure 9-10 shows a form of interference called a *non-repeatable read*, which can occur at isolation level 0 and 1. Connection A retrieves the same row twice, in Steps 3 and 6, and gets two different results; the reason is that Connection B updated that row and committed its change inbetween the two SELECT statements executed by Connection A.

	Connection A	Connection B	Comment	c1 Value	Locks Held by A & B
1	SET TEMPORARY OPTION ISOLATION LEVEL = 1				
2		SET TEMPORARY OPTION ISOLATION LEVEL = 1			
3	SELECT c1 INTO @c1 FROM t1 WHERE k1 = 5		clean		A Schema (S)
4		UPDATE t1 SET c1 = 'different' WHERE k1 = 5	Allowed		A Schema (S) B Write (E) B Schema (S)
5		COMMIT			A Schema (S)
6	SELECT c1 INTO @c1 FROM t1 WHERE k1 = 5		Not repeated	different	A Schema (S)

Figure 9-10. Repeatable read not ensured at isolation level <= 1

The non-repeatable read shown in Figure 9-10 happens even though the isolation level has been set to 1: There is no remaining write lock in Step 6 so the mechanism that prevented the dirty read in Figure 9-7 doesn't come into play. Also, the SELECT statement in Step 3 didn't acquire a long-term read lock like the FETCH did in Figure 9-9, so cursor stability doesn't help either.

Note that Connection A did obtain a short-term lock in Step 3 of Figure 9-10, in order to prevent dirty reads. However, that short-term lock was released when the SELECT statement finished so it didn't block Connection B from getting the write lock in Step 4.

Figure 9-11 shows that an isolation level of 2 or higher is required to guarantee that reads are repeatable: At isolation level 2 Connection A gets a read lock on the row retrieved in Step 3, and that read lock prevents Connection B from getting a write lock in Step 4. Now the second SELECT in Step 5 returns the same value as it did before.

	Connection A	Connection B	Comment	c1 Value	Locks Held by A & B
1	SET TEMPORARY OPTION ISOLATION LEVEL = 2				
2		SET TEMPORARY OPTION ISOLATION LEVEL = 1			
3	SELECT c1 INTO @c1 FROM t1 WHERE k1 = 5		clean		A Read (S) A Schema (S)
4		UPDATE t1 SET c1 = 'different' WHERE k1 = 5	Blocked: 42W18 User 'A' has the row in 't1' locked		A Read (S) A Schema (S) B Schema (S)
5	SELECT c1 INTO @c1 FROM t1 WHERE k1 = 5		Repeated result	clean	A Read (S) A Schema (S) B Schema (S)
6	COMMIT				B Schema (S)
7		UPDATE t1 SET c1 = 'different' WHERE k1 = 5	Unblocked		B Write (E) B Schema (S)
8		COMMIT			
9	SELECT c1 INTO @c1 FROM t1 WHERE k1 = 5		Final result	different	A Read (S) A Schema (S)

Figure 9-11. Repeatable read ensured at isolation level = 2

Steps 6 through 9 in Figure 9-11 show once again that serialized transactions aren't affected by isolation levels: Connection B is able to perform its UPDATE as soon as Connection A releases its read lock.

Figure 9-12 shows another form of interference that can happen at isolation level 0 or 1: the *unstable update*. In Step 3 Connection B selects the value "clean," then in Steps 4 and 5 Connection A updates the value to "dirty" and commits the change. In Step 6 Connection B is able to update the same row because Connection A no longer holds a write lock. Because this second update uses the SET c1 = c1 + 'er' clause, the final value in Step 8 is "dirtyer"; from Connection B's point of view, the current value of c1 is "clean" so the new value should be "cleaner."

	Connection A	Connection B	Comment	c1 Value	Locks Held by A & B
1	SET TEMPORARY OPTION ISOLATION_LEVEL = 1				
2		SET TEMPORARY OPTION ISOLATION_LEVEL = 1			
3		SELECT c1 INTO @c1 FROM t1 WHERE k1 = 5	clean		B Schema (S)
4	UPDATE t1 SET c1 = 'dirty' WHERE k1 = 5		Allowed		A Write (E) A Schema (S) B Schema (S)
5	COMMIT				B Schema (S)
6		UPDATE t1 SET c1 = c1 + 'er' WHERE k1 = 5	Unstable		B Write (E) B Schema (S)
7		COMMIT			
8		SELECT c1 INTO @c1 FROM t1 WHERE k1 = 5	Incorrect result	dirtyer	B Schema (S)

Figure 9-12. UPDATE stability not ensured at isolation level < − 1

If the UPDATE in Step 6 of Figure 9-12 was changed to SET c1 = @c1 + 'er', where @c1 is the variable holding the column value retrieved in Step 3, the final value in Step 8 would be "cleaner." This would be the expected result from Connection B's point of view, but not according to Connection A. In this case the inconsistency is a form of *lost update*, where one transaction's update is lost because another transaction is allowed to perform its own update based on earlier data; from Connection A's point of view, the final result should be "dirty" rather than "cleaner" or "dirtyer."

Figure 9-13 shows how isolation level 2 can be used to prevent the unstable read; it also prevents the form of lost update described above. The mechanism is the same as the one used in Figure 9-11 to ensure a repeatable read: A connection running at isolation level 2 gets a read lock on each row it retrieves, and this read lock prevents any other connection from getting a write lock.

	Connection A	Connection B	Comment	c1 Value	Locks Held by A & B
1	SET TEMPORARY OPTION ISOLATION LEVEL = 1				
2		SET TEMPORARY OPTION ISOLATION LEVEL = 2			
3		SELECT c1 INTO @c1 FROM t1 WHERE k1 = 5	clean		B Read (S) B Schema (S)
4	UPDATE t1 SET c1 = 'dirty' WHERE k1 = 5		Blocked: 42W18 User 'B' has the row in 't1' locked		A Schema (S) B Read (S) B Schema (S)
5		UPDATE t1 SET c1 = c1 + 'er' WHERE k1 = 5	Stable		A Schema (S) B Write (E) B Schema (S)
6		SELECT c1 INTO @c1 FROM t1 WHERE k1 = 5	Interim result	cleaner	A Schema (S) B Write (E) B Schema (S)
7		COMMIT			A Schema (S)
8	UPDATE t1 SET c1 = 'dirty' WHERE k1 = 5		Unblocked		A Write (E) A Schema (S)
9	COMMIT				
10		SELECT c1 INTO @c1 FROM t1 WHERE k1 = 5	Final result	dirty	B Read (S) B Schema (S)

Figure 9-13. UPDATE stability ensured at isolation level = 2

9.7.4 Isolation Level 3

Figure 9-14 shows a form of interference that can occur at isolation level 0, 1, or 2: the *phantom row*. In Step 3 Connection A retrieves a single row that matches a particular selection criteria, and in Step 6 retrieves a completely different row using exactly the same SELECT statement. This new, phantom row was inserted by Connection B, and the insert was committed in Steps 4 and 5. Connection A did obtain a read lock in Step 3 because it's running at isolation level 2, but that read lock did nothing to prevent a new row from being inserted.

	Connection A	Connection B	Comment	c1 Value	Locks Held by A & B
1	SET TEMPORARY OPTION ISOLATION LEVEL = 2				
2		SET TEMPORARY OPTION ISOLATION LEVEL = 2			
3	SELECT FIRST c1 INTO @c1 FROM t1 WHERE k1 < 7 ORDER BY k1 DESC		clean		A Read (S) A Schema (S)
4		INSERT t1 VALUES (6, 'phantom')	Allowed		A Read (S) A Schema (S) B Write (E) B Schema (S)
5		COMMIT			A Read (S) A Schema (S)
6	SELECT FIRST c1 INTO @c1 FROM t1 WHERE k1 < 7 ORDER BY k1 DESC		Phantom row	phantom	A Read (S) A Read (S) A Schema (S)

Figure 9-14. Phantom row permitted at isolation level <= 2

Figure 9-15 shows how isolation level 3 can be used to prevent the appearance of phantom rows. In Step 3 Connection A acquires anti-insert locks that prevent the subsequent insertion of any rows that would satisfy the selection criteria. This causes Connection B to be blocked in Step 4, which in turn prevents the phantom row from appearing in Step 5.

Connection A	Connection B	Comment	c1 Value	Locks Held by A & B
1 SET TEMPORARY OPTION ISOLATION LEVEL = 3				
2	SET TEMPORARY OPTION ISOLATION LEVEL = 2			
3 SELECT FIRST c1 INTO @c1 FROM t1 WHERE k1 < 7 ORDER BY k1 DESC		clean		A Anti-insert (S) A Anti-insert (S) A Schema (S)
4	INSERT t1 VALUES (6, 'phantom')	Blocked: 42W18 User 'A' has the row in 't1' locked		A Anti-insert (S) A Anti-insert (S) A Schema (S) B Schema (S)
5 SELECT FIRST c1 INTO @c1 FROM t1 WHERE k1 < 7 ORDER BY k1 DESC		Old row	clean	A Anti-insert (S) A Anti-insert (S) A Schema (S) B Schema (S)
6 COMMIT				B Schema (S)
7	INSERT t1 VALUES (6, 'phantom')	Unblocked		B Write (E) B Schema (S)
8	COMMIT			
9 SELECT FIRST c1 INTO @c1 FROM t1 WHERE k1 < 7 ORDER BY k1 DESC		New row	phantom	A Anti-insert (S) A Anti-insert (S) A Schema (S)

Figure 9-15. Phantom row prevented at isolation level = 3

Tip: Watch out for COMMIT statements inside cursor fetch loops run at high isolation levels. Just because the WITH HOLD clause is used to keep the cursor open when a COMMIT is executed doesn't mean that any row locks are being held past the COMMIT; they aren't. If a high isolation level is being used to protect the processing inside the cursor loop from interference caused by SQL statements run on other connections, each COMMIT cancels the protection provided by all the locks acquired up to that point.

Figure 9-16 shows another form of interference that can occur at isolation level 0, 1, or 2: the *suppressed update*. In Step 3 Connection A deletes a single row, and in Step 4 Connection B attempts to update the same row. At isolation level 2 or lower, there's no problem with this update, other than the fact it doesn't do anything: the WHERE clause doesn't match any rows.

Connection A	Connection B	Comment	c1 Value	Locks Held by A & B
1 SET TEMPORARY OPTION ISOLATION LEVEL = 2				
2	SET TEMPORARY OPTION ISOLATION LEVEL = 2			
3 DELETE t1 WHERE k1 = 5				A Write (E)
				A Anti-insert + Insert (S)
				A Schema (S)
4	UPDATE t1 SET c1 = 'different' WHERE k1 = 5	Suppressed		A Write (E)
				A Anti-insert + Insert (S)
				A Schema (S)
				B Schema (S)
5	COMMIT			A Write (E)
				A Anti-insert + Insert (S)
				A Schema (S)
6 ROLLBACK				
7	SELECT c1 INTO @c1 FROM t1 WHERE k1 = 5	Original value	clean	B Read (S)
				B Schema (S)

Figure 9-16. DELETE suppresses UPDATE at isolation level <= 2

Much earlier, Figure 9-3 showed that a DELETE always blocks a subsequent INSERT of the same row in overlapping transactions; it's clear from Figure 9-16, however, that a DELETE doesn't block a subsequent UPDATE by a different connection, it just turns it into a "do nothing" operation.

In Step 6 of Figure 9-16, Connection A rolls back the deletion to restore the original value "clean" in column c1. From Connection B's point of view, however, the value returned by the SELECT in Step 7 should be "different," and it's not.

Tip: Don't confuse "no error" with "worked OK" when checking the result of an UPDATE. An application can use SELECT @@ROWCOUNT to retrieve the integer number of rows that were actually affected by an UPDATE, and take action if the number is zero when it shouldn't be. The value of @@ROWCOUNT should be retrieved immediately after the UPDATE since subsequent SQL statements, including SELECT, may change its value.

Figure 9-17 shows how isolation level 3 prevents the problem of a suppressed update by blocking the update of a row that has been deleted by an overlapping transaction. Now the blocked connection can choose to wait or re-attempt the update later, as shown in Step 6. In this situation, the difference between isolation levels 2 and 3 doesn't lie in the number of locks obtained but in the lock that wasn't obtained; in Step 4 of Figure 9-17 Connection B attempted to obtain an anti-insert lock on the gap left by the missing row, and it was blocked by the fact that Connection A held an insert lock on the same gap.

Connection A	Connection B	Comment	c1 Value	Locks Held by A & B
1 SET TEMPORARY OPTION ISOLATION LEVEL = 2				
2	SET TEMPORARY OPTION ISOLATION LEVEL = 3			

3 DELETE t1
   WHERE k1 = 5
				A Write (E)
				A Anti-insert +
				    Insert (S)
				
				A Schema (S)

4	UPDATE t1 SET c1 = 'different' WHERE k1 = 5	Blocked: 42W18 User 'A' has the row in 't1' locked		A Write (E) A Anti-insert + Insert (S) A Schema (S) B Schema (S)
5 ROLLBACK				B Schema (S)
6	UPDATE t1 SET c1 = 'different' WHERE k1 = 5	Unblocked		B Write (E) B Schema (S)
7	COMMIT			
8	SELECT c1 INTO @c1 FROM t1 WHERE k1 = 5	Updated value	different	B Read (S) B Schema (S)

Figure 9-17. DELETE blocks UPDATE at isolation level = 3

Note: These figures only show locks that have been granted; i.e., they don't explicitly show the locks that aren't obtained because the connections attempting to obtain them are blocked by locks that already exist. For example, the anti-insert lock that wasn't obtained by Connection B in Step 4 of Figure 9-17 isn't shown; the built-in procedure sa_locks doesn't show missing locks, and that procedure was used to construct these figures. In this particular case, if Connection A performed a COMMIT between Steps 3 and 4, the UPDATE performed by Connection B in Step 4 would successfully obtain an anti-insert lock on the gap left by the deleted row, and a call to sa_locks would show that lock.

Note: The difference between Figures 9-16 and 9-17 is due to the isolation level used by Connection B, not Connection A. In other words, Connection A would still obtain write, anti-insert, and insert locks in Step 3 even if it had been using isolation level 0.

SELECT statements run at isolation level 2 and 3 can obtain a surprisingly large number of locks. For example, when the following query is run against the ASADEMO database using isolation level 0 or 1, it only acquires a single unobtrusive schema lock even though it returns 75 rows. However, at isolation level 2 it acquires 75 read locks in addition to the schema lock, one read lock for every row returned; that means no other connection can update any of those rows until the locks are released by a COMMIT or ROLLBACK.

```
SELECT *
  FROM sales_order_items
 WHERE quantity = 48;
```

Figure 9-18 shows another query that acquires a large number of locks at isolation level 2. All that the SELECT in Step 3 does is count the number of rows in table t1, but it also gets a read lock on every single row in the table. That blocks the update attempted by Connection B in Step 4; in fact, it blocks any attempt by any other connection to update or delete any row in the table.

	Connection A	Connection B	Comment	c1 Value	Locks Held by A & B
1	SET TEMPORARY OPTION ISOLATION LEVEL = 2				
2		SET TEMPORARY OPTION ISOLATION LEVEL = 0			
3	SELECT COUNT(*) INTO @c1 FROM t1		Single value	5	A Read (S) A Read (S) A Read (S) A Read (S) A Read (S) A Schema (S)
4		UPDATE t1 SET c1 = 'different' WHERE k1 = 5	Blocked: 42W18 User 'A' has the row in 't1' locked		A Read (S) A Read (S) A Read (S) A Read (S) A Read (S) A Schema (S) B Schema (S)

Figure 9-18. Example of extreme locking at isolation level = 2

Tip: Keep transactions short, especially when using isolation levels 2 and 3. Sometimes a SELECT can be placed in its own transaction, separate from other SQL statements, with a COMMIT right after the SELECT to reduce the time that locks are held.

A SELECT at isolation level 3 acquires anti-insert locks for each table in the query as follows:

■   If an index scan is used to satisfy the selection criteria for the table, one anti-insert lock is acquired to prevent an insert ahead of each row that is read, plus one extra anti-insert lock is acquired to prevent an insert at the end of the result set. That's why Figure 9-15 shows two anti-insert locks appearing in Step 3: one lock for the row that was retrieved using the primary key index on the column k1, plus the extra lock.

■   If an index scan isn't used for the table, either because no index exists or because SQL Anywhere can't use any of the indexes to satisfy the selection criteria, one anti-insert lock will be acquired for each and every row in the table, plus one extra lock at the end. If there was no index on column k1, Step 3 in Figure 9-15 would show that six anti-insert locks were acquired because the table t1 contains five rows.

The effect of isolation level 3 can be quite dramatic. For example, when the following SELECT is run against the ASADEMO database it returns only 75 rows but, since there are 1097 rows in the table and no index on the quantity column, it obtains 1098 anti-insert locks. This simple query blocks all other connections from inserting, updating, or deleting any rows at all in the sales_order_items table until these locks are released by a COMMIT or ROLLBACK:

```
SET TEMPORARY OPTION ISOLATION_LEVEL = '3';
SELECT *
  FROM sales_order_items
  WHERE quantity = 48;
```

More locks are usually acquired with isolation level 3 because SQL Anywhere obtains a lock on every row that is examined, whereas with isolation level 2 a lock is acquired on a row only if it contributes to the final result set. This difference is most evident when a sequential scan is required.

Figure 9-19 shows another example of extreme locking at isolation level 3: The SELECT in Step 3 doesn't return anything, yet it acquires an anti-insert lock on every single row in the table.

	Connection A	Connection B	Comment	c1 Value	Locks Held by A & B
1	SET TEMPORARY OPTION ISOLATION_LEVEL = 3				
2		SET TEMPORARY OPTION ISOLATION_LEVEL = 0			
3	SELECT FIRST c1 INTO @c1 FROM t1 WHERE c1 <> 'clean' ORDER BY c1		Empty result		A Anti-insert (S)
					A Anti-insert (S)
					A Anti-insert (S)
					A Anti-insert (S)
					A Anti-insert (S)
					A Anti-insert (S)
					A Schema (S)
4		UPDATE t1 SET c1 = 'different' WHERE k1 = 5	Blocked: 42W18 User 'A' has the row in 't1' locked		A Anti-insert (S)
					A Anti-insert (S)
					A Anti-insert (S)
					A Anti-insert (S)
					A Anti-insert (S)
					A Anti-insert (S)
					A Schema (S) B Schema (S)

Figure 9 19. Example of extreme locking at isolation level = 3

Tip: It's okay to dynamically change the setting of the ISOLATION_LEVEL database option during the execution of a transaction. A high level can be set before executing SQL statements that need a high level of protection from interference, and a lower level can be set for statements that don't need so much protection and therefore don't need so many locks. You can even specify different isolation levels for different tables in the same query by using "table hints" like NOLOCK and READCOMMITTED in the FROM clause; for more details about the syntax, see Section 3.3, "FROM Clause."

The LOCK TABLE statement, together with the IN EXCLUSIVE MODE clause, can be used to greatly reduce the number of locks acquired on a single table. For example, if the table t2 contains 100,000 rows, the following SELECT statement will acquire 100,002 locks because of the way isolation level 3 works:

```
SET TEMPORARY OPTION ISOLATION_LEVEL = '3';
SELECT COUNT(*)
   FROM t2;
```

The addition of the LOCK TABLE statement, as follows, reduces the number of locks to exactly one:

```
SET TEMPORARY OPTION ISOLATION_LEVEL = '3';
LOCK TABLE t2 IN EXCLUSIVE MODE;
SELECT COUNT(*)
   FROM t2;
```

The LOCK TABLE statement also helps update operations, even at lower isolation levels. For example, the following UPDATE statement changes every one

of the 100,000 rows in the table t2, and in one test it ran three times faster with
the addition of the LOCK TABLE statement:

```
SET TEMPORARY OPTION ISOLATION_LEVEL = '0';
LOCK TABLE t2 IN EXCLUSIVE MODE;
UPDATE t2 SET non_key_1 = 'xxx';
```

Great care should be taken, however, with LOCK TABLE statements in
multi-user environments: Make sure that transactions using LOCK TABLE are
committed as soon as possible.

9.8 Deadlock

Figure 9-20 shows an example of a condition known as *cyclical deadlock*. Steps
1 and 3 set the isolation level to 0 for both connections to show that a cyclical
deadlock can happen at any isolation level, and Steps 2 and 4 set the
BLOCKING option to 'ON' to force each connection to wait when blocked by a
lock held by the other connection rather than immediately raising an exception.

	Connection A	Connection B	Comment	c1 Value	Locks Held by A & B
1	SET TEMPORARY OPTION ISOLATION_LEVEL = 0				
2	SET TEMPORARY OPTION BLOCKING = 'ON'				
3		SET TEMPORARY OPTION ISOLATION_LEVEL = 0			
4		SET TEMPORARY OPTION BLOCKING = 'ON'			
5	UPDATE t1 SET c1 = 'changed by A' WHERE k1 = 1		A gets lock		A Write (E) A Schema (S)
6		UPDATE t1 SET c1 = 'changed by B' WHERE k1 = 3	B gets lock		A Write (E) A Schema (S) B Write (E) B Schema (S)
7	UPDATE t1 SET c1 = 'changed by A' WHERE k1 = 3		A blocked		A Write (E) A Schema (S) B Write (E) B Schema (S)
8		UPDATE t1 SET c1 = 'changed by B' WHERE k1 = 1	Deadlock: 40001 Deadlock detected		A Write (E) A Schema (S) B Write (E) B Schema (S)
9		ROLLBACK	A unblocked		A Write (E) A Write (E) A Schema (S)
10		SELECT c1 INTO @c1 FROM t1 WHERE k1 = 1	Final result	changed by A	A Write (E) A Write (E) A Schema (S) B Schema (S)
11		SELECT c1 INTO @c1 FROM t1 WHERE k1 = 3	Final result	changed by A	A Write (E) A Write (E) A Schema (S) B Schema (S)

Figure 9-20. Cyclical deadlock at isolation level = 0

Note: Most applications should use the default value of the BLOCKING
option, which is 'ON'. Most blocks are short-lived, and waiting for eventual success is easier than reacting to an immediate failure. Earlier figures assume the
value is 'OFF' simply to demonstrate how locking and blocking works.

In Steps 5 and 6 of Figure 9-20, each connection updates a row, and then in Step 7 Connection A tries to update the same row that Connection B updated in Step 6; this blocks Connection A from proceeding. In Step 8 Connection B tries to update the same row that Connection A updated back in Step 5; at this point SQL Anywhere detects a cyclical deadlock condition: Connection A is blocked and waiting for Connection B to release its locks, and Connection B is blocked and waiting for Connection A to finish. This circle or cycle of blocks is called a cyclical deadlock; neither connection can proceed, so rather than let them both wait forever SQL Anywhere automatically cancels the update in Step 8 and tells Connection B about the problem with SQLSTATE '40001'.

By default, SQL Anywhere extends its handling of the cyclical deadlock SQLSTATE '40001' in a special way: If SQLSTATE is still set to '40001' when processing of the current operation is complete, SQL Anywhere automatically executes a ROLLBACK operation on that connection before returning to the client application. This default behavior can be avoided by using a BEGIN block with an exception handler that catches the SQLSTATE '40001' and doesn't execute a RESIGNAL statement to pass the exception onward; in this case SQLSTATE will be set back to '00000' before returning to the client application and SQL Anywhere won't execute the automatic ROLLBACK. With or without this ROLLBACK, the affected connection is free to proceed; with the ROLLBACK, the other connection is also free to proceed because the lock that was blocking it is gone, whereas without the ROLLBACK the other connection remains blocked. For more information about BEGIN blocks with exception handlers, see Section 8.3, "Exception Handler." For more information about the RESIGNAL statement and more examples of exception handlers, see Sections 9.5.1 and 9.5.2.

Note: SQL Anywhere doesn't execute an automatic ROLLBACK for any other SQLSTATE, just '40001'. And it doesn't have to be an actual cyclical deadlock condition; a SIGNAL statement that sets SQLSTATE to '40001' will also cause the automatic ROLLBACK unless an exception handler or some other logic sets SQLSTATE to some other value before the current operation is complete.

In the example shown in Figure 9-20, an explicit ROLLBACK is shown separately as Step 9; all of the changes made by Connection B are rolled back. This allows Connection A to immediately proceed as shown by the second write lock it acquired in Step 9. The SELECT statements in Steps 10 and 11 confirm that Connection A was the winner in this cyclical deadlock conflict.

Cyclical deadlocks are fairly rare in SQL Anywhere because row locks are used for most operations; there is no such thing as a page lock in SQL Anywhere, and row locks are never "escalated" into table locks, even when they number in the millions.

Many cyclical deadlocks can be avoided by designing transactions to always perform the same operations in the same order when executed on different connections. For example, the cyclical deadlock in Figure 9-20 was caused by overlapping transactions updating the same rows in a different order. If they had updated the same rows in the same order, one connection would simply have been blocked until the other one finished and then it too would have proceeded to completion with no danger of a cyclical deadlock.

Cyclical deadlocks are more likely at higher isolation levels simply because there are more locks to cause blocks. For example, two connections that SELECT the same row at isolation level 2 or 3 will both obtain shared read row locks on that row; see Step 3 in Figure 9-11 for an example of a shared read row lock at isolation level 2. If both of those connections then attempt to UPDATE that row, one will be blocked and the other will cause a cyclical deadlock error. In this scenario, one solution is to have each connection perform the UPDATE first, and then the SELECT; the first connection that performs the UPDATE will be able to proceed whereas the other connection will be blocked right away, and a deadlock will not occur.

Tip: Set the BLOCKING_TIMEOUT option to a non-zero value for a connection that can easily repeat its work in the event of a cyclical deadlock. The default value of BLOCKING_TIMEOUT is 0, which means "wait forever." If a cyclical deadlock occurs involving one or more connections where BLOCKING_TIMEOUT has been set to some non-zero value, the connection with the smallest non-zero value will be chosen to receive the error. This could be useful if one connection is making important updates that should be allowed to proceed, and another connection is producing a report that could easily be re-executed later.

A different kind of deadlock, called *thread deadlock*, occurs when all operating system tasks or execution threads available to the SQL Anywhere engine are occupied with connections that are blocked. Internally, the SQL Anywhere engine uses thread pooling where the number of connections can exceed the number of threads; at any given point some connections are idle and no work is being performed for them on any thread, while each active connection is executing on one thread. When a connection becomes idle it will release its thread back into the pool of free threads for use on another connection. However, when an active connection becomes blocked, it does not release its thread; when all threads become occupied with blocked connections the condition called thread deadlock arises. At this point no work can proceed; rather than let all the threads wait forever, SQL Anywhere automatically cancels one of the blocked operations and tells the connection about the problem with SQLSTATE '40W06' and the error message "All threads are blocked."

By default, the SQL Anywhere network server dbsrv9.exe has 20 threads in its pool, and the personal server dbeng9.exe has 10 threads. This doesn't limit the number of simultaneous connections that can be handled, but it does limit the number of connections that can be actively processed at one time. Also, with a large number of busy connections that acquire a large number of locks and experience frequent blocks, thread deadlock is possible.

Here is a query that uses the built-in sa_conn_info procedure to display all the blocked connections and the connections that are blocking them:

```
SELECT NUMBER(*) AS "#",
       Name,
       UserId,
       Number,
       BlockedOn
  FROM sa_conn_info() AS conn1
 WHERE BlockedOn <> 0
    OR EXISTS ( SELECT *
                  FROM sa_conn_info() AS conn2
```

```
                   WHERE conn2.BlockedOn = conn1.Number )
ORDER BY BlockedOn,
        Name,
        UserId,
        Number;
```

The following example shows the output from the query above on a server that supports 20 threads and had 25 different connections attempting to update the same row in the same table at the same time. One connection was successful in performing the update and the next 19 attempts were blocked; the 21st attempt resulted in thread deadlock and was cancelled, as were the remaining 4 attempts. The output below shows the 19 blocked connections plus the connection blocking them:

```
#   Name  UserId  Number       BlockedOn   LockName
==  ====  ======  ===========  =========   ========
1   C01   C01     1447092880   0           0
2   C02   C02     2016944313   1447092880  445
3   C03   C03     1579014964   1447092880  445
4   C04   C04     1141085615   1447092880  445
5   C05   C05     439312098    1447092880  445
6   C06   C06     571234182    1447092880  445
7   C07   C07     133304833    1447092880  445
8   C08   C08     1710937048   1447092880  445
9   C09   C09     265226917    1447092880  445
10  C10   C10     835078350    1447092880  445
11  C11   C11     1842859132   1447092880  445
12  C12   C12     1273007699   1447092880  445
13  C13   C13     954498130    1447092880  445
14  C14   C14     703156266    1447092880  445
15  C15   C15     1382749      1447092880  445
16  C20   C20     1524349563   1447092880  445
17  C21   C21     1404929783   1447092880  445
18  C22   C22     1974781216   1447092880  445
19  C23   C23     384646697    1447092880  445
20  C24   C24     516568781    1447092880  445
```

Here's what's in the columns shown above: The # column provides row numbering, the Name and UserID columns contain the connection name and user id, and the Number column uniquely identifies each connection with a number. The BlockedOn column shows the connection number of the connection that is blocking this one, and the LockName uniquely identifies the lock responsible for the block. If a connection isn't blocked, BlockedOn and LockName are zero.

As noted earlier, SQL Anywhere sets the SQLSTATE to '40W06' when it cancels an operation because it detected a thread deadlock. In this case SQL Anywhere does not execute the automatic ROLLBACK described earlier in the discussion of cyclical deadlock. However, from an application point of view the SQLSTATE may be the same as that returned for a cyclical deadlock: '40001'. That's because SQLSTATE values go through a translation process for certain client interfaces, including ODBC; these alternate SQLSTATE values are documented in the SQL Anywhere Help. Figure 9-21 shows the Help description for thread deadlock: The SQLCODE is -307 and the SQLSTATE inside the engine is '40W06', but the SQLSTATE returned to applications using an ODBC Version 2 or Version 3 interface is changed to '40001' as shown by the items labeled "ODBC 2 State" and "ODBC 3 State."

ASA Error Messages
Database Error Messages
Alphabetic list of error messages
All threads are blocked

Item	Value
SQLCODE	-307
Constant	SQLE_THREAD_DEADLOCK
SQLSTATE	40W06
Sybase error code	1205
ODBC 2 State	40001
ODBC 3 State	40001

Probable cause

You attempted to read or write a row and it is locked by
another user. Also, all other threads (see the -gn server
option) are blocked waiting for a lock to be released.

*Figure 9-21. SQL Anywhere Help for
SQLSTATE '40W06'*

Thread deadlock can sometimes indicate a busy server that simply needs more threads; the dbsrv9 -gn command line option can be used to increase the number of threads. However, thread deadlock may be evidence of an application design flaw where too many connections are competing for an artificially scarce resource. In the previous example, it's clear that all 19 blocked connections are trying to get at exactly same database object; it's unlikely that all these different users are really trying to do the same work at the same time, and increasing the number of available threads may simply increase the number of blocked connections.

For example, an application that updates a single row in a single table to compute the next available primary key value instead of using DEFAULT AUTOINCREMENT can easily result in thread deadlock when too many connections collide trying to calculate new primary keys. From a business point of view these connections are doing different work; the thread deadlock is artificial, caused by a design flaw.

9.9 Mutexes

The SQL Anywhere engine can use multiple CPUs to handle SQL operations. Each operation is handled by one CPU rather than split across multiple CPUs, but it is possible for SQL Anywhere to handle requests from more than one connection at the same time.

Ideally, *n* CPUs should be able to handle *n* simultaneous requests in the same amount of time that one CPU could handle one request. For example, if one CPU handles one request in 10 seconds then two CPUs should be able to handle two such requests in 10 seconds.

In reality, that's impossible; there's always overhead, and two simultaneous requests will take longer than 10 seconds. If you get them through SQL Anywhere in 12 or 13 seconds, that's still a lot better than the 20 seconds it would take for a single CPU.

However, if the two requests take 20 seconds, then you've got a big problem with overhead, and you're not seeing any benefit from the extra CPU at all. If two requests take longer than 20 seconds, you've got a huge problem: You'd be better off without the extra CPU.

Problems with multiple CPU overhead can be caused by *mutexes*, or mutual exclusion operations. A mutex is a mechanism used by multi-threaded programs such as SQL Anywhere to protect shared internal data structures from conflicts and corruption. Mutexes are similar to row locks, with the following differences:

- Mutexes occur more frequently than locks.
- Mutexes don't last as long as locks.
- Mutexes can affect read-only queries that aren't subject to locks or blocks.
- Mutexes are a bigger issue with multiple CPUs than with a single CPU.
- Convoys can occur where more time is spent waiting for mutexes than getting productive work done.
- There are no tools to display mutexes or directly measure contention caused by mutexes.
- Request-level logging may be used to look for SQL statements that behave poorly on multiple CPUs.

A convoy occurs when different connections need repeated access to the same internal data structure. If the amount of time spent working on the data is small relative to the amount of time spent checking and waiting for mutexes, the situation may arise where only one connection is working on the data and all the others are waiting. The connection at the head of the line gets a bit of work done, yields control to another connection, and then tries to get access to the same data again; now it has to rejoin the convoy and wait its turn again. In this situation, overall throughput can be worse on multiple CPUs than with a single CPU.

Tip: Don't go looking for problems you don't have. Convoys on mutexes are rarely the cause of performance problems. Mutexes themselves are very common; they are used in all multi-threaded software, not just SQL Anywhere, and they are generally harmless.

If you have a contention problem and you've eliminated locks and blocks as the likely cause, you can use SQL Anywhere's request-level logging facility to look for circumstantial evidence of mutexes. Here's how the technique works:

1. Use a workload that demonstrates that throughput is worse when using multiple CPUs, or at least not nearly as good as expected.
2. Turn request-level logging on and run the workload from a single connection. For more information on this facility, see Section 10.2, "Request-Level Logging."
3. Run the built-in procedure sa_get_request_times to analyze the request-level logging file and save the results in the built-in temporary table satmp_request_time. Copy the contents of satmp_request_time to another table with the same schema so it can be used in Step 7.
4. Turn request-level logging off, and delete the output file in preparation for the next step.

5. Turn request-level logging on again and run the workload simultaneously from more than one connection.
6. Repeat Step 3 and save the contents of satmp_request_time from the second test in a different table.
7. Compare the data from Steps 3 and 6. Look for SQL statements that took longer to process when run from multiple connections in Step 5 than they did when run from one connection in Step 2. Mutexes may or may not be at fault, but these statements are worth looking at because they're the ones hurting throughput.

Problems with throughput on multiple CPUs can sometimes be solved by changing the way the applications work. In particular:

- Avoid referencing the same small subset of rows at the same time on many different connections.
- Avoid retrieving the same data in the same order many times on each connection.

One approach is to copy this actively read data to the client rather than repeatedly retrieving it. Another approach is to copy it to a global temporary table so that it effectively becomes different data, local to each connection.

9.10 GRANT CONNECT

In SQL Anywhere a connection is a link between a client application and a single database. In order to establish a connection in the first place, and then perform any useful work, the client application must provide a user id and a password. That user id and its password must be defined ahead of time and stored in the SYSUSERPERM catalog table. Each new SQL Anywhere database contains exactly one such user id and password when it is created: DBA and SQL. For some applications that's all you need to know, and it's safe to skip ahead to Section 9.11, "Logging and Recovery."

The GRANT statement is used to create user ids and permit them to do the following:

- Connect to the database
- Select rows from a table
- Insert rows into a table
- Update rows in a table
- Delete rows from a table
- Execute a procedure or function
- Own tables and other objects
- Create tables and views
- Create indexes and foreign keys in a table
- Alter the schema of a table
- Grant privileges to other user ids
- Act as a group
- Inherit privileges as a member of a group
- Perform administrative tasks
- Use a Windows integrated login to connect to the database

Here's how the GRANT statement can be used to create user ids and give them permission to connect to the database:

```
<create_user>              ::= GRANT CONNECT TO <user_id_list>
                                 [ IDENTIFIED BY <positional_password_list> ]
<user_id_list>             ::= <user_id> { "," <user_id> }
<positional_password_list> ::= <password> { "," <password> }
<password>                 ::= <identifier> -- to be used as a password
                             | string literal containing a password
                             | empty string literal
                             | empty string in double quotes
```

The user id list can contain one or more SQL Anywhere identifiers. The IDENTIFIED BY clause is optional, and if present it specifies passwords to be assigned to the user ids. When multiple user ids and passwords are specified the correspondence is positional; i.e., the first password in the list is assigned to the first user id, the second password to the second user id, and so on.

A user id must have a password in order to connect to the database. That password can be the empty string, but it has to be explicitly specified in the IDENTIFIED BY clause. Here are some examples of GRANT statements that create new user ids; A, B, "C 2", and E can be used to connect to the database because they have passwords, but D cannot connect because it doesn't have a password:

```
GRANT CONNECT TO A, B, "C 2" IDENTIFIED BY SQL, '', 'QWER ASDF';
GRANT CONNECT TO D;
GRANT CONNECT TO E IDENTIFIED BY "";
```

Note: This book assumes all databases are created as case-insensitive, which is the default. This means that password values are case-insensitive as well; e.g., even if you define a password in uppercase as shown above, it's okay to specify the lowercase equivalent when using it to connect. However, with a case-sensitive database, password values are case-sensitive when connecting, although user ids remain case-insensitive.

As shown above, user ids must be coded as SQL Anywhere identifiers with or without double quotes, but password strings may be coded using several different formats: as identifiers with or without double quotes, as string literals surrounded by single quotes, and as empty strings surrounded by double quotes.

Following are four ISQL command lines that can be used to connect to a database with the user ids A, B, "C 2", and E defined above. Note that the user id and password values are coded as is inside the -c connection string; no delimiters are required around "C 2", 'QWER ASDF', or the empty string used as a password for user ids B or E.

```
"%ASANY9%\win32\dbisql.exe" -c "ENG=test9;DBN=test9;UID=A;PWD=sql;CON=A"
"%ASANY9%\win32\dbisql.exe" -c "ENG=test9;DBN=test9;UID=B;PWD=;CON=B"
"%ASANY9%\win32\dbisql.exe" -c "ENG=test9;DBN=test9;UID=C 2;PWD=QWER ASDF"
"%ASANY9%\win32\dbisql.exe" -c "ENG=test9;DBN=test9;UID=E;PWD="
```

Tip: Use the CON connection parameter to specify a "connection name" when connecting to the database, as shown in the first and second ISQL command lines above. The connection name is available to an application program via the built-in function call CONNECTION_PROPERTY ('Name') and it is included in the information returned by the built-in procedure sa_conn_info. Connection names can be used to differentiate between connections that are using the same user id, and when used with ISQL they are displayed in the title bar. Figure 9-22 shows that the connection names A and B make it clear which task bar item is which, whereas the task bar title for user id E is cluttered up with the server name.

Figure 9-22. Connection names appear in ISQL task bar titles.

The terms "user," "user id," and "user name" are often used interchangeably to refer to the identifier named in GRANT and other SQL statements. Inside the SQL Anywhere catalog, however, there is a distinction between the user_id and user_name columns in the SYSUSERPERM table. The SYSUSERPERM.user_name column contains the unique alphanumeric identifier strings such as 'DBA', 'SYS', and 'bcarter', whereas the user_id column contains unique unsigned integer values such as 1 and 101.

The SYSUSERPERM.user_id values are assigned by SQL Anywhere when the GRANT statement is executed for a new user, and it is these values, not the string user_name values, that appear in related columns in other catalog tables. For example, the SYSTABLE.creator column contains these numeric user_id values to identify each table's owner. SQL Anywhere offers several ways to manipulate these user id and name values:

- CURRENT USER returns the currently connected SYSUSERPERM.user_name; e.g., 'DBA'.
- USER_NAME() is the same as CURRENT USER.
- USER_ID() returns the currently connected SYSUSERPERM.user_id; for example, 1.
- USER_NAME (1) converts a numeric user_id to the corresponding user_name; e.g., 'DBA'.

- USER_ID ('DBA') converts a user_name to the corresponding numeric user_id; e.g., 1.
- USER_ID (CURRENT USER) is the same as USER_ID().

The GRANT CONNECT statement can also be used to change the password of a particular user id or remove it altogether. Special permission is required to change the password of a user id other than the one used for the current connection, but the password of the currently connected user id can always be changed; in other words, you have to have "database administrator" authority to change other people's passwords, but you can always change your own.

Here is an example of a GRANT statement that can be used on a connection established with user id B; this statement changes the password for user id B, and although the current connection can proceed, the next connection using B must specify the new password:

```
GRANT CONNECT TO B IDENTIFIED BY ASDFASDF;
```

Tip: Use the GRANT CONNECT statement without a password to disable an existing user id, rather than REVOKE CONNECT. The REVOKE statement is the opposite of GRANT, and it can be used to remove specific privileges from a user id. However, think twice before executing REVOKE CONNECT because it deletes the user id completely. If that user id is named as the owner of any tables, all those tables and the data in them plus any triggers and indexes will also disappear, along with any procedures and functions owned by that user id. This tip is an exception to the rule that statements like REVOKE and DROP aren't covered in this book; for more information, see the REVOKE statement in the SQL Anywhere Help.

Tip: Watch out for self-destructing user ids. For example, if B is the user id for the current connection, the statement GRANT CONNECT TO B without an IDENTIFIED BY clause removes the password so B can't be used to connect anymore. The current connection can proceed, but subsequent attempts to connect will fail until someone else uses a GRANT to define a password for B.

Tip: Don't use the built-in user id "dbo" for your own purposes. In SQL Anywhere, dbo is an actual user id rather than a special alias for "database owner" like it is in Adaptive Server Anywhere or Microsoft SQL Server, so it may be tempting to use it as the owner of new tables. Resist that temptation, however, because some application development software restricts the use of "dbo" in the same way it restricts the use of the special system user id "SYS."

9.10.1 Table Privileges

The user ids that have been specified so far can't do much until they obtain more permissions. In particular, a user id with no password has only one ability: It can be named as the owner of tables and other database objects; it can't be used to create those tables, or even look at them, because it can't be used to connect in the first place.

A user id with a password can do a bit more: Besides connecting, it can be used to browse most of the system catalog tables. However, in order to run queries and perform other operations on tables owned by other users, more permissions are required; the following form of the GRANT statement can be used to satisfy that requirement:

```
<grant_table_privileges> ::= GRANT <table_privileges>
                                ON [ <owner_name> "." ] <table_name>
                                TO <user_id_list>
                                [ WITH GRANT OPTION ]
<table_privileges>  ::= ALL
                    |  <table_privilege> { "," <table_privilege> }
<table_privilege>   ::= ALTER
                    |  DELETE
                    |  INDEX [ "(" [ <column_name_list> ] ")" ]
                    |  INSERT
                    |  REFERENCES [ "(" [ <column_name_list> ] ")" ]
                    |  SELECT [ "(" [ <column_name_list> ] ")" ]
                    |  UPDATE [ "(" [ <column_name_list> ] ")" ]
<owner_name>        ::= <identifier>
<table_name>        ::= <identifier>
<column_name_list>  ::= <column_name> { "," <column_name> }
<column_name>       ::= <identifier>
```

The following example shows a table created and initialized by a connection
using the user id DBA, together with a GRANT CONNECT statement to create
the user id A; these objects will serve as the starting point for the examples that
follow:

```
CREATE TABLE t1 (
    key_1       INTEGER NOT NULL,
    key_2       INTEGER NOT NULL,
    non_key_1   VARCHAR ( 100 ) NOT NULL,
    non_key_2   VARCHAR ( 100 ) NOT NULL,
    PRIMARY KEY ( key_1, key_2 ) );

INSERT t1 VALUES ( 1, 1, 'xxx', 'yyy' );
INSERT t1 VALUES ( 1, 2, 'xxx', 'yyy' );
GRANT CONNECT TO A IDENTIFIED BY SQL;
```

Note: In this book, phrases like "executed by user id X" and "performed by
X" are sometimes used as shorthand for "executed on a connection established
with user id X."

Table 9-3 shows examples of GRANT statements and the SQL statements they
allow. The first column numbers each example, while the second column shows
GRANT statements executed by the user id DBA; each of these GRANT statements gives permission for user id A to perform a specific operation on the table
DBA.t1. The third column shows examples of the corresponding SQL statements that user id A is now able to perform.

Table 9-3. GRANT statement examples

#	GRANT These Privileges...	To Allow These Statements...
1.	GRANT ALTER ON t1 TO A;	ALTER TABLE DBA.t1 ADD non_key_3 VARCHAR (100) DEFAULT '';
2.	GRANT DELETE ON t1 TO A;	DELETE DBA.t1;

3.	GRANT SELECT (key_1, key_2)
	    ON t1 TO A;
	GRANT DELETE ON t1 TO A;
		DELETE DBA.t1
		    WHERE key_1 = 1
		    AND key_2 = 1;

#	GRANT These Privileges...	To Allow These Statements...
4.	GRANT INSERT ON t1 TO A;	INSERT DBA.t1 (key_1, key_2, non_key_1, non_key_2) VALUES (1, 3, 'aaa', 'bbb');
5.	GRANT REFERENCES ON t1 TO A;	CREATE INDEX x1 ON DBA.t1 (non_key_1);
6.	GRANT SELECT (non_key_2) ON t1 TO A;	SELECT non_key_2 FROM DBA.t1;
7.	GRANT UPDATE (non_key_2) ON t1 TO A;	UPDATE DBA.t1 SET non_key_2 = 'ppp';

Example 1 in Table 9-3 allows user id A to execute ALTER TABLE statements that change the schema of DBA.t1. This is an unusual privilege to have by itself since it doesn't extend to any of the less dramatic operations; e.g., permission to ALTER a table doesn't automatically come with permission to SELECT any data, let alone UPDATE any rows.

Example 2 shows that permission to DELETE is required in order to DELETE from a table.

Example 3 shows that permission to DELETE isn't enough to be able to DELETE a single row. In this particular case, permission to SELECT the columns t1.key_1 and t1.key_2 is also required in order to specify those columns in the WHERE clause of the DELETE statement.

Example 4 shows that permission to INSERT is required in order to INSERT a row. It is unusual, but possible, for a user id to be able to INSERT rows without being able to SELECT them.

Example 5 shows that the REFERENCES or INDEX privilege is required in order to create an index on DBA.t1. Like the ALTER privilege, REFERENCES is an unusual privilege to possess by itself.

Example 6 shows a very common privilege: permission to SELECT some or all the columns in a table. This permission is also required in order to name columns in WHERE, FROM, and other clauses as well as in the select list. If the column name list is omitted or an empty column name list "()" is specified in the GRANT SELECT statement, permission to SELECT all the columns is implied.

Example 7 in Table 9-3 shows that UPDATE permission is required in order to name some or all of the columns in the SET clause of an UPDATE statement.

Note: Depending on the context, various combinations of privileges may be required to execute certain SQL statements, including CREATE TRIGGER, LOAD TABLE, UNLOAD SELECT, UNLOAD TABLE, and some forms of ALTER TABLE. For example, in order to use ALTER TABLE to create a foreign key relationship, ALTER privilege on the child table and REFERENCES privilege on the parent table are both required. For more information, see the descriptions of the individual statements in the SQL Anywhere Help.

Different privileges may be combined in a single GRANT statement; the following example permits user id A to select and delete rows in DBA.t1 but not to perform any other operation:

```
GRANT SELECT, DELETE ON DBA.t1 TO A;
```

The keyword ALL is shorthand for all the privileges; for example, the following two GRANT statements perform the same function:

```
GRANT ALL ON DBA.t1 TO A;
GRANT ALTER, DELETE, INSERT, REFERENCES, SELECT, UPDATE ON DBA.t1 TO A;
```

The WITH GRANT OPTION clause may be used to permit the user id to grant the named privileges to other user ids. For example, user id DBA can execute the following statement to give user id A all of the ALTER, DELETE, INSERT, REFERENCES, SELECT, and UPDATE privileges on the table DBA.t1, as well as permission to pass those privileges on to other user ids in turn:

```
GRANT ALL ON DBA.t1 TO A WITH GRANT OPTION;
```

User id A can now execute the following statement to grant SELECT privilege on the same table to user id E; note that the SELECT privilege is a subset of the privileges that were granted to A. Also note that this statement could include the WITH GRANT OPTION as well, and if that was the case user id E would also be able to grant the SELECT privilege to other user ids:

```
GRANT SELECT ON DBA.t1 TO E;
```

Note: With ownership comes permission. For example, if user id A is named as the owner of table t1, regardless of who actually created the table, user id A has permission to perform any operation on that table as well as the permission to grant privileges on that table to other user ids. This is more or less the same as if the statement GRANT ALL ON A.t1 to A WITH GRANT OPTION had been executed; it's not exactly the same, however, and the difference between privilege and permission is explained in Section 9.10.5, "GRANT GROUP."

9.10.2 View Privileges

Privileges may be granted on views as well as tables, using the following form of the GRANT statement:

```
<grant_view_privileges> ::= GRANT <view_privileges>
                                  ON [ <owner_name> "." ] <view_name>
                                  TO <user_id_list>
                                  [ WITH GRANT OPTION ]
<view_privileges>        ::= ALL
                           | <view_privilege> { "," <view_privilege> }
<view_privilege>         ::= DELETE
                           | INSERT
                           | SELECT
                           | UPDATE [ <column_name_list> ]
<view_name>              ::= <identifier>
```

Granting privileges on a view instead of the underlying tables gives a higher degree of control over which operations are allowed. In particular, a view can be used to grant row-level privileges in addition to the column-level privileges offered by the GRANT statement.

The following example shows a view created and initialized by a connection using the user id DBA, together with a GRANT CONNECT statement to create the user id B. The view v1 is based on the table t1 shown in an earlier example, and it specifies a WHERE clause that only matches rows where t1.key_2 = 1. This view and the user id B will serve as the starting point for the examples that follow.

```
CREATE VIEW v1 AS
SELECT *
  FROM t1
 WHERE key_2 = 1
  WITH CHECK OPTION;

GRANT CONNECT TO B IDENTIFIED BY SQL;
```

For more information about creating views, see Section 3.23, "CREATE VIEW."

Table 9-4 shows some examples of GRANT statements involving the view DBA.v1. The second column shows GRANT statements executed by the user id DBA, and the third column shows some corresponding SQL statements that user id B is now able to perform.

Table 9-4. GRANT statement examples with views

#	GRANT These Privileges...	To Allow These Statements...
1.	GRANT DELETE ON v1 TO B;	DELETE DBA.v1;
2.	GRANT INSERT ON v1 TO B;	INSERT DBA.v1 (key_1, key_2, non_key_1, non_key_2) VALUES (2, 1, 'aaa', 'bbb');
3.	GRANT SELECT ON v1 TO B;	SELECT * FROM DBA.v1;

4.	GRANT UPDATE (non_key_1)
	  ON v1 TO B;
		UPDATE DBA.v1
		  SET non_key_1 = 'zzz';

5.	GRANT UPDATE (non_key_1)
	  ON t1 TO B;
		UPDATE DBA.v1
		  SET non_key_1 = 'zzz';

Example 1 in Table 9-4 shows that the DELETE privilege is required in order to DELETE rows from a view. In this case, the DELETE statement only deletes the row where key_2 = 1 in the underlying table DBA.t1 because that's what the WHERE clause in the view specifies.

Example 2 shows that permission to INSERT is required in order to INSERT a row in a view. Only the value 1 can be specified for the column key_2 because the WITH CHECK OPTION in the view definition specifies that new rows inserted into this view must satisfy the WHERE clause.

Example 3 shows that the SELECT privilege gives permission to SELECT all the columns in a table. Unlike the SELECT privilege on a table, a column name list cannot be specified for a view. The SELECT privilege is also required in order to name columns in WHERE, FROM, and other clauses in SELECT, UPDATE, and other statements.

Example 4 shows that UPDATE permission is required in order to name some or all of the columns in the SET clause of an UPDATE statement. If the column name list is omitted or an empty column name list "()" is specified in the GRANT UPDATE statement, permission to UPDATE all the columns is implied. In this case, the UPDATE statement only updates the row where key_2 = 1 in the underlying table DBA.t1 because that's what the WHERE clause in the view specifies, and the WITH CHECK OPTION clause was included in the view definition.

Example 5 in Table 9-4 shows that permission to use an underlying table extends to a view defined on that table; this means you don't have to worry about granting permission to use a view if permission to use the underlying tables has already been granted. The opposite is not true; for example, the GRANT UPDATE on the view DBA.v1 as shown in example 4 does not permit user id B to explicitly specify the table DBA.t1 in an UPDATE statement.

The keyword ALL is shorthand for all the privileges that apply to views, and the WITH GRANT OPTION works with view as well as table privileges.

9.10.3 Execution Privileges

The following form of the GRANT statement is used to give permission to execute procedures and functions:

```
<grant_execute_privilege>      ::= GRANT EXECUTE ON [ <owner_name> "." ]
                                     <procedure_name>
                                     TO <user_id_list>
                                   GRANT EXECUTE ON [ <owner_name> "." ]
                                     <user_defined_function_name>
                                     TO <user_id_list>
<procedure_name>               ::= see <procedure_name> in Chapter 8, "Packaging"
<user_defined_function_name>   ::= see <user_defined_function_name>
                                     in Chapter 8, "Packaging"
```

The following example shows a procedure created by user id DBA, together with a GRANT EXECUTE statement to allow user id B to call the procedure:

```
CREATE PROCEDURE p1()
BEGIN
   SELECT *
     FROM t1
     WHERE key_2 = 1;
END;

GRANT CONNECT TO C IDENTIFIED BY SQL;
GRANT EXECUTE ON p1 TO C;
```

SQL statements inside a procedure or function are executed with the permissions of the user id that is the owner of that procedure or function, not the permissions of the user id calling the procedure or function. This isn't a confusing restriction but an important feature that enables a high degree of control over the operations that a particular user id may perform.

For example, the GRANT EXECUTE statement shown above gives user id C the ability to retrieve a subset of rows from table t1 without granting SELECT permission on the table as a whole. It's okay for user id C to execute the first statement below because it's okay for C to CALL p1, and it's okay for DBA to

SELECT from DBA.t1; however, the second statement fails because C is not allowed to directly SELECT from DBA.t1:

```
CALL DBA.p1();       -- OK
SELECT * FROM DBA.t1; -- fails
```

User id C can also be used to execute the following statement; it may be written as a SELECT but for the purposes of determining permissions, a procedure reference in a FROM clause is the same as a CALL statement:

```
SELECT * FROM DBA.p1(); -- OK
```

In some security-conscious environments, all INSERT, UPDATE, and DELETE operations are placed inside stored procedures, and GRANT EXECUTE privileges are the only permissions given to user ids. Those stored procedures can perform all sorts of extra editing and auditing functions, and the technique can be used to put a stop to ad hoc updates using general-purpose tools such as Excel while still allowing users to make the changes they're supposed to.

SQL statements inside a trigger are executed with the permissions of the user id named as the owner of the corresponding table. If different permissions are needed, one alternative is to move the contents of the trigger into a procedure owned by a user id that has the necessary permissions, and then call that procedure from the trigger.

Note: The statements inside a procedure, function, or trigger execute with permissions of the owner, not the privileges of the owner. The difference between permission and privilege is discussed in Section 9.10.5, "GRANT GROUP."

SQL statements inside an event are executed with the permissions of the owner of that event. In the case of an event, the owner is the same as the creator, and the owner must have the all-encompassing DBA privilege when the event is fired. In effect, events can do anything; the DBA privilege is discussed in the next section.

9.10.4 Special Privileges

Three kinds of special privileges are available:
- The RESOURCE privilege permits a user id to be used to create its own tables and other database objects.
- The DBA privilege (not to be confused with the DBA user id) permits a user id to perform any operation supported by SQL Anywhere.
- The REMOTE DBA privilege is the same as the DBA privilege, but only within certain contexts.

Here is the format of the GRANT statement that is used to grant the RESOURCE privilege:

```
<grant_resource_privilege> ::= GRANT RESOURCE TO <user_id_list>
```

The RESOURCE privilege permits a user to CREATE and DROP tables, views, procedures, and functions where that user id is either explicitly or implicitly named as the owner of those objects. In other words, a user id with RESOURCE privilege can create its own tables.

As noted earlier, ownership implies permission. For example, if user id A makes use of the RESOURCE privilege to create table A.t1, the user id A also has permission to perform any other operation on that table as well as the permission to grant privileges on that table to other user ids. These extra permissions come automatically to user id A without the need to explicitly GRANT them as privileges; there's a subtle difference between permissions and privileges, and it's discussed further in Section 9.10.5, "GRANT GROUP."

The RESOURCE privilege does not permit a user id to create a database object with some other user id named as the owner; for that, the special DBA privilege is required. Table 9-5 shows the difference between RESOURCE, DBA, and some other privileges in terms of the minimum privilege required for a user id to execute various CREATE statements.

Table 9-5. Privileges required to execute CREATE statements

CREATE Statement	Minimum Privilege Required
CREATE DATABASE	DBA; see Help for exceptions
CREATE DATATYPE	RESOURCE
CREATE DBSPACE	DBA
CREATE EVENT	DBA; also required for TRIGGER EVENT
CREATE EXISTING TABLE	RESOURCE
CREATE EXTERNLOGIN	DBA; see Help for exceptions
CREATE FUNCTION	RESOURCE
CREATE INDEX	REFERENCES
CREATE MESSAGE	RESOURCE
CREATE PROCEDURE	RESOURCE
CREATE PUBLICATION	DBA
CREATE SERVER	DBA
CREATE SERVICE	DBA
CREATE STATISTICS	DBA
CREATE SUBSCRIPTION	DBA
CREATE SYNCHRONIZATION USER	DBA
CREATE TABLE	RESOURCE
CREATE TRIGGER	ALTER
CREATE VARIABLE	Allowed for any connection
CREATE VIEW	RESOURCE and SELECT

Here's how the DBA privilege is granted:

```
<grant_dba_privilege> ::= GRANT DBA TO <user_id_list>
```

There is no privilege more powerful than DBA. It's the privilege held by the user id also called DBA when a new SQL Anywhere database is created. If security is of no concern to you then that's the only privilege, and the only user id, you'll ever need.

Tip: Create one or more extra user ids with the DBA privilege. These extra user ids will provide backup protection against accidental loss of DBA privileges; at all times there must be at least one user id available with the DBA privilege.

If you do care about security, but you also need to permit a more or less publicly available user id to perform some of the operations that normally require DBA privilege, the special REMOTE DBA privilege may help. Here is the format of the GRANT statement that is used to grant the REMOTE DBA privilege:

```
<grant_remote_dba_privilege> ::= GRANT REMOTE DBA TO <user_id_list>
```

A user id with REMOTE DBA privilege can be used to connect to the database from the following programs:

- dbmlsync.exe — MobiLink synchronization client
- dbvalid.exe — database validation utility
- dbbackup.exe — database backup utility

A connection made with a user id that has the REMOTE DBA privilege can execute the DROP CONNECTION, VALIDATE TABLE, and VALIDATE INDEX statements.

Here is an example of a user id that has no privileges other than REMOTE DBA plus the ability to connect to the database:

```
GRANT CONNECT TO SYNCH IDENTIFIED BY SQL;
GRANT REMOTE DBA TO SYNCH;
```

The user id SYNCH can't be used to SELECT data from an application program or ISQL, let alone change anything, but it can be used to run the MobiLink synchronization client as shown in this command line:

```
"%ASANY9%\win32\dbmlsync.exe" -c "ENG=remo;DBN=remo;UID=SYNCH;PWD=SQL"
```

9.10.5 GRANT GROUP

The GROUP privilege can be used to solve two problems: It can make it easier to assign combinations of privileges to large numbers of user ids, and it can eliminate the need to explicitly specify owner names when referring to tables and views.

In SQL Anywhere a user group is just a user id with the GROUP privilege. Here is the format of the GRANT statement that can be used to turn an ordinary user id into a group:

```
<create_user_group> ::= GRANT GROUP TO <group_name_list>
<group_name_list>   ::= <user_id_list> -- users which are also groups
```

Here is the syntax for the GRANT statement that places other user ids in a group:

```
<add_user_to_group> ::= GRANT MEMBERSHIP IN GROUP <group_name_list>
                              TO <user_id_list>
```

The following privileges are inherited through group membership:
- Table privileges ALTER, DELETE, INSERT, REFERENCES, SELECT, and UPDATE
- View privileges DELETE, INSERT, SELECT, and UPDATE
- EXECUTE privilege on procedures and functions
- MEMBERSHIP in a group

The following privileges are not inherited through group membership:
- RESOURCE
- DBA
- REMOTE DBA
- GROUP
- WITH GRANT OPTION on table and view privileges

Note that group MEMBERSHIP is inherited, but not the GROUP privilege. For example, if user id A is a member of group CHILD, and CHILD is a member of group PARENT, then A is also a member of group PARENT and can inherit privileges from PARENT. However, user id A is not a group itself; it does not inherit the GROUP privilege from CHILD or PARENT.

Also note that the privilege implied by WITH GRANT OPTION clause is not inherited through group membership. For example, just because user group G has been granted a privilege with the WITH GRANT OPTION clause specified, it doesn't mean that members of that group can automatically grant that privilege to other user ids.

The following example shows a series of GRANT statements executed by the DBA user id; these statements set up a group with 10 members:

```
GRANT CONNECT TO READ_ONLY;
GRANT GROUP TO READ_ONLY;
GRANT SELECT ON t1 TO READ_ONLY;
GRANT SELECT ON t2 TO READ_ONLY;
GRANT SELECT ON t3 TO READ_ONLY;
GRANT MEMBERSHIP IN GROUP READ_ONLY TO A, B, C, D, E, F, G, H, I, J;
GRANT SELECT ON t4 TO READ_ONLY;
GRANT SELECT ON t5 TO READ_ONLY;
GRANT SELECT ON t6 TO READ_ONLY;
```

Here's how the those nine GRANT statements work:
- The GRANT CONNECT statement creates the user id READ_ONLY. This user id doesn't have a password so it can't be used to connect to the database; this is common practice with user ids that are only going to be used as groups.
- The GRANT GROUP statement allows the READ_ONLY user id to be used as a group; i.e., READ_ONLY can appear in GRANT MEMBERSHIP statements.
- The next three GRANT SELECT statements give SELECT privilege on the tables DBA.t1 through DBA.t3 to READ_ONLY. Since READ_ONLY can't be used to connect, it can't be used to actually SELECT anything; these privileges are granted only so they can be passed on to other user ids through their group membership.
- The GRANT MEMBERSHIP statement places the 10 user ids A through J into the group called READ_ONLY. These user ids automatically inherit the SELECT privileges that have been granted to READ_ONLY.

- The last three GRANT SELECT statements show that privileges may be granted to the group before or after members are added; these privileges go into effect immediately for all the group members.

Now all 10 user ids have permission to execute the following statement:

```
SELECT * FROM DBA.t1;
```

The main advantage to user groups is the fact that it's easier to grant multiple privileges to one user id (the group) than it is to grant them to many individual user ids (the members).

Another advantage to user groups is that they make combinations of privileges easier to assign. For example, the following GRANT statements executed by DBA set up a second group called DATA_ENTRY; members of this group can perform INSERT and UPDATE operations on the tables DBA.t1 and DBA.t3:

```
GRANT CONNECT TO DATA_ENTRY;
GRANT GROUP TO DATA_ENTRY;
GRANT INSERT, UPDATE ON t1 TO DATA_ENTRY;
GRANT INSERT, UPDATE ON t3 TO DATA_ENTRY;
GRANT MEMBERSHIP IN GROUP DATA_ENTRY TO A, E, H;
```

Since the user ids A, E, and H are now members of both groups READ_ONLY and DATA_ENTRY, they can perform all three operations — SELECT, INSERT, and UPDATE — on the tables DBA.t1 and DBA.t3. A, E, and H are still limited to SELECT operations on the other tables, however, and the other user ids still can't do anything except SELECT on any of the tables.

Another advantage to user groups is that they can eliminate the need to explicitly specify owner names when referring to tables and views. For example, even though the GRANT statements shown above give user id A permission to SELECT from the table DBA.t1, if it tries to execute the following statement it will get an error "Table 't1' not found":

```
SELECT * FROM t1;
```

However, if the user id DBA executes the following GRANT statements, it is no longer necessary for user id A to qualify the table name "t1" with the owner name "DBA":

```
GRANT GROUP TO DBA;
GRANT MEMBERSHIP IN GROUP DBA TO A;
```

Now it's okay for the user id A to execute the following SELECT:

```
SELECT * FROM t1;
```

Note: As discussed earlier, DBA privileges are not inherited through group membership.

When a SQL statement is executed, SQL Anywhere must determine the fully qualified name for each reference to a table or view that omits the owner name. Here are the steps that accomplish that task:

1. If there is a local temporary table with a matching name, then the search is over; the temporary table is the one to use.

2. If there is a global temporary or permanent table or view with a matching name that is owned by the current user id, then the search is over; that's the table or view to use.
3. If there is exactly one table or view with a matching name that is owned by some group that the current user id is a member of, then the search is over; that table or view is the one to use. This search isn't affected by any hierarchical relationships that might exist among the groups that the current user id is a member of; all the groups are treated equally by the search.
4. If more than one table or view with a matching name is found in Step 3, each owned by a different group that the current user id is a member of, it's an error: "Table 'x' is ambiguous."
5. If no table or view with a matching name is found, it's an error: "Table 'x' not found."

This chapter uses the words "permission" and "privilege" more or less interchangeably; they are, however, different as the following points explain:
■   The permission to perform some operation is required before a user id can perform that operation.
■   A privilege is something that is explicitly granted via the GRANT statement or inherited through group membership.
■   A privilege implies one or more permissions. For example, a user id with the SELECT privilege has permission to SELECT from that table, and a user id with the DBA privilege has permission to do anything.
■   The reverse of the above point is not true: A permission does not necessarily imply the corresponding privilege. For example, the owner of a table automatically has permission to SELECT from that table but does not have the SELECT privilege unless it is explicitly granted.
■   Privileges are not implied by other privileges. For example, a user id with the DBA privilege does not automatically have the SELECT privilege on any table even though it has permission to SELECT from any table.
■   Privileges, not permissions, are inherited through group membership.

The last point is the reason it's safe to make a user id a member of the DBA group: The DBA user id doesn't have any privilege other than DBA, and the DBA privilege is not inherited through group membership. Therefore, a member of the DBA group doesn't actually inherit any more privileges at all. All it gets is the ability to leave out the owner name when referring to tables owned by DBA.

9.11 Logging and Recovery

SQL Anywhere provides efficient and reliable mechanisms for recovering from data loss and inconsistencies caused by execution and file failure. This section describes the basic recovery mechanism built-in to the database engine to handle problems caused by execution failure. The next two sections describe backup and restore procedures that extend the basic mechanism to cover file failure.

During execution, database data may be stored in seven different locations:
■   Cache in memory
■   Database files on disk, including other dbspace files

- Transaction log file on disk
- Optional mirror log file on disk
- Checkpoint log in the database file
- Rollback log in the cache and database file
- Temporary file on disk

Most of those data storage locations are critical to the basic recovery mechanism; each is described here.

The *cache* contains table and index pages that have been read from the database files into memory. The cache is always up to date; to be specific, logical database changes made by SQL statements are immediately reflected in the table and index pages in the cache, including both committed and uncommitted changes.

The *database files* contain table and index pages, and the SYSTEM dbspace database file may also contain checkpoint log and rollback log pages. Changed table and index pages are written to the physical database files before and during a checkpoint; they are not necessarily written to the physical database files when the logical database changes are first made by SQL statements, or even when a COMMIT statement is executed. In fact, there is no direct correspondence between COMMIT operations and data in the physical database files; uncommitted changes may be written to the database files while committed changes may not be written immediately.

The database files are up to date after a checkpoint; to be specific, all table and index pages in the physical database files are guaranteed to be up to date with respect to data in the cache whenever a checkpoint is completed.

Note that the physical database files may contain uncommitted changes; the uncommitted data is visible to any connection running at isolation level 0 and blocked from view by any connection running at a higher isolation level. For more information about isolation levels, see Section 9.7, "Blocks and Isolation Levels."

The *transaction log file*, also known as the *redo log*, contains a sequential record of logical changes made to the database since this log file was created. Both committed and uncommitted changes may be written to the physical transaction log file, and they may be written before a COMMIT is executed on the corresponding connection. COMMIT and CHECKPOINT operations are recorded in the transaction log as well as other changes.

Note: This discussion assumes that a transaction log is being used; a transaction log improves performance as well as increasing reliability. This discussion also assumes that the setting of the DELAYED_COMMIT database option remains 'OFF', the default, which also ensures reliability.

The transaction log file is up to date after a COMMIT; to be specific, the changes made by a particular transaction are guaranteed to be written to the physical transaction log by the time control is returned to the connection after a COMMIT ending that transaction is successfully completed. In fact, all changes, committed or otherwise, are guaranteed to be written to the transaction log whenever a COMMIT is performed on any connection.

The transaction log file is used in the second step of the recovery process discussed later in this section.

The transaction log contains the minimum data required for complete recovery. Although the process might be slow, the entire database could be rebuilt from scratch by initializing an empty database and applying the transaction log to it.

The *mirror log file* is an optional copy of the transaction log file. When a mirror log is specified, it is automatically maintained as an identical, redundant copy of the transaction log file. The mirror log does not automatically participate in the recovery process, but can be substituted for the transaction log during the recovery process if the transaction log is lost or damaged.

The *checkpoint log*, also known as the *page level undo log*, contains a sequential record of before images or unchanged copies of database table, index, and rollback log pages that have been changed since the last checkpoint. Each checkpoint log page is written to the physical database file just before the corresponding modified table, index, or rollback log page is written to the file for the first time since the previous checkpoint. Each checkpoint log page only needs to be written once, even if the corresponding page is changed multiple times, because only one copy of the unchanged page is needed.

The checkpoint log is always up to date; to be specific, checkpoint log pages only exist in the database file, and they are only created when the corresponding modified table and index pages are also written to the database file. Note that a checkpoint log is empty immediately after a checkpoint is performed, and it is non-empty only between checkpoints.

The checkpoint log pages are written at the end of the SYSTEM dbspace database file during execution, and they may be moved as the file grows to ensure they remain at the end of the file. The data in the checkpoint log is discarded when a checkpoint is successfully completed, and the space is recovered when the database is shut down.

The checkpoint log makes it possible for the database server to delay writing updated table and index pages back to the database files, rather than writing them every time a COMMIT is executed. Since the changes are guaranteed to be present in the transaction log whenever a COMMIT is executed, they won't be lost in the event the server stops running before writing all the changed pages back to the database files. The delay in writing pages to the database files results in better overall performance because more efficient disk operations can be used. However, if the server stops running at some point between two checkpoints, the table and index pages in the database files may be in an unstable or inconsistent state; some may be up to date and others may be out of date. That's why the checkpoint log exists, for use in the first step of the recovery process discussed later in this section.

A *rollback log*, also known as an *undo log* or *row level undo log*, is maintained for each connection to hold a sequential record of the reverse operations that would undo the logical changes made to the database by this connection since the last COMMIT or ROLLBACK was executed on the connection.

The rollback log pages are stored in the SYSTEM dbspace database file, together with table and data pages, and they are written to the physical database file before and during a checkpoint. They are not necessarily written to the physical database file when the logical database changes are first made by SQL statements. Note that rollback log pages are included in the checkpoint log.

The rollback log is up to date after a checkpoint; to be specific, all current rollback log pages in the physical database file are guaranteed to be up to date whenever a checkpoint is completed.

The data in a rollback log may include changes made before and after a checkpoint; there is no correspondence between a checkpoint and the end of any particular transaction.

The data in a rollback log is used during normal operation to roll back the changes when a ROLLBACK is executed on the connection, and it is then discarded. It is also discarded when a COMMIT is executed on the connection.

The rollback logs are also used in the third step of the recovery process.

The *temporary file* is used for temporary data, including temporary table data and indexes on temporary tables. It is never used to hold permanent table or index pages, checkpoint log pages, or rollback log pages.

Changes to temporary tables are not recorded in the transaction log, nor do they cause any pages to be written to the checkpoint log. However, changes to temporary tables do cause entries to be written to the rollback log unless the NOT TRANSACTIONAL clause is specified when the table is created.

Temporary table changes recorded in the rollback log are only used during the normal ROLLBACK process and are not processed during the recovery process; i.e., temporary tables are not recreated by the recovery process.

The *recovery process* is performed by the database engine to repair inconsistencies in the data when a database is started. This recovery process is performed in the following situations:

- Automatically, when a database is started after it was stopped without a final successful checkpoint.
- Automatically, when a backup copy of a database is started, if that backup copy was created while the original database was running; the online backup process is described in the next section.
- Explicitly, when a database is started with the -a parameter to request that a transaction log be applied.
- Explicitly, when a database is started with the -f parameter to request that the database be started without a transaction log.

Here's what the database engine displays in the console window when performing a recovery process:

```
Starting database "test9" (E:\test9\test9.db) at Sat Feb 21 2004 12:15
Database recovery in progress
    Last checkpoint at Sat Feb 21 2004 12:14
    Checkpoint log...
    Transaction log: test9.log...
    Rollback log...
    Checkpointing...
Starting checkpoint of "test9" (test9.db) at Sat Feb 21 2004 12:15
Finished checkpoint of "test9" (test9.db) at Sat Feb 21 2004 12:15
Recovery complete
```

There are four steps to the recovery process:

1. The pages in the checkpoint log are used to overwrite all the corresponding changed table, index, and rollback log pages to restore the database to the

way it was at the previous successful checkpoint. Note that at this point there may be uncommitted changes in the database, and for each uncommitted transaction there will be a rollback log that is up to date with respect to the previous successful checkpoint.

2. All the logical redo operations recorded in the transaction log file since the previous successful checkpoint are applied to restore the database to the way it was when it was shut down. This process also recreates the portions of the rollback logs corresponding to changes made after the previous successful checkpoint. Note that any COMMIT and ROLLBACK operations performed during this stage wipe out the rollback logs for the corresponding transactions, and further uncommitted changes will cause new rollback logs to be created for these new transactions.

3. All the logical undo operations recorded in the remaining rollback logs are applied to the database to roll back any uncommitted active transactions and bring the database to a valid consistent state. Note that for a long-running uncommitted transaction, that rollback log may include undo operations from before and after the previous successful checkpoint; the portion of the rollback log from before the previous successful checkpoint is restored in the first step above, and the portion from after the previous checkpoint is reconstructed in the second step.

4. A checkpoint is performed, and the database is now ready for use. If the recovery process had been started with the -a or -f parameter, the database engine shuts down automatically at this point, and can be restarted without the -a or -f parameter to resume normal operations.

9.12 **Backup**

SQL Anywhere offers several different facilities for creating backup copies of databases. The following five sections describe how those facilities can be used to create these five different kinds of backups:

- A full offline image backup of the database and transaction log files made while the database is not running.
- A full online image backup of the database and log files made while the database is running.
- A differential online backup of the log file that has been in use since the last full backup.
- An incremental online backup of the log file that has only been in use since the previous backup operation.
- A live log backup that continuously copies transaction log data to a file on a remote computer.

9.12.1 **Full Offline Image Backup**

A *full offline image backup* is a file copy of the database and transaction log files that is made while the database is not running. Normal operating system file copy commands are used to create the backup files. A full offline image backup is appropriate when it is possible to shut the database down and there is sufficient room to make a complete copy of both the database and transaction log files.

Note: Making a backup copy of the transaction log isn't absolutely necessary if the database was stopped normally, because the final checkpoint that was performed as the database was stopped ensures that the backup copy of the database file reflects all the activity recorded in the transaction log. However, if the database was stopped without a final checkpoint, a full restore requires the backup transaction log. It's always safe, and often necessary, to include the transaction log in any backup operation, and this section doesn't discuss "database-only" backups.

The examples in this section use a database file named test9.db, which has both a transaction log (test9.log) and a mirror log (test9.mlg); the mirror log is stored on a different physical disk drive from the transaction log and database file to reduce the impact of a disk failure.

Here are the Windows command lines that are used to create this database and then start the database server:

```
"%ASANY9%\win32\dbinit.exe" -m C:\mirror\test9.mlg -p 4096 test9.db
"%ASANY9%\win32\dbsrv9.exe" -x tcpip test9.db
```

The -m parameter tells dbinit.exe to create a mirror log for this database, the -p parameter tells dbinit to use a 4K page size for the database, and the -x parameter tells dbsrv9.exe that TCP/IP is the only client-server protocol to be used in addition to the default "shared memory" local connection protocol.

Except where noted otherwise, the commands shown in this section are run on the main or primary computer where the database server is located. The starting folder for command execution is "E:\test9", which is where the current database and transaction log files are located. The mirror log is in "C:\mirror" on the main computer, and the backup files are placed in a "G:\bkup" folder on a different, remote computer. The G: drive is mapped to the "remote_test9" folder on the other computer. The full path to "G:\bkup" in UNC format is "\\Dell180\DELL180G\remote_test9\bkup".

Tip: It's okay, and probably a good idea, to put backup files on a different computer. However, all the files used by the database engine during normal request processing must be on physical drives that are locally attached to the same CPU that's running the engine. Do not put the database, transaction log, mirror log, or temporary files on a different computer, no matter how fast the LAN might be.

Here is an example of a Windows batch file that performs a full offline image backup:

```
SET CONNECTION="ENG=test9;DBN=test9;UID=dba;PWD=sql"
"%ASANY9%\win32\dbisql.exe" -c %CONNECTION% STOP ENGINE test9 UNCONDITIONALLY
RENAME G:\bkup\test9.db  old_test9.db
RENAME G:\bkup\test9.log old_test9.log
RENAME G:\bkup\test9.mlg old_test9.mlg
IF EXIST G:\bkup\test9.db  GOTO ERROR
IF EXIST G:\bkup\test9.log GOTO ERROR
IF EXIST G:\bkup\test9.mlg GOTO ERROR
COPY test9.db           G:\bkup\test9.db
COPY test9.log          G:\bkup\test9.log
COPY C:\mirror\test9.mlg G:\bkup\test9.mlg
ECHO N | COMP test9.db G:\bkup\test9.db
IF ERRORLEVEL 1 GOTO ERROR
```

```
ECHO N | COMP test9.log G:\bkup\test9.log
IF ERRORLEVEL 1 GOTO ERROR
ECHO N | COMP C:\mirror\test9.mlg G:\bkup\test9.mlg
IF ERRORLEVEL 1 GOTO ERROR
ERASE G:\bkup\old_test9.db
ERASE G:\bkup\old_test9.log
ERASE G:\bkup\old_test9.mlg
"%ASANY9%\win32\dbsrv9.exe" -x tcpip test9.db
GOTO END
:ERROR
PAUSE Backup process failed.
:END
```

Tip: To get help for Windows commands, open a command or "DOS prompt" window and type HELP. You can also type the command name, as in HELP IF. If that doesn't work in your version of Windows, try the /? option, as in IF /?.

Here's how that batch file works to perform a full offline image backup:

- The SET command defines a local environment variable to hold the connection string for use in the next command.
- The second command line runs ISQL in batch mode to execute a STOP ENGINE statement to stop the database engine called test9 without waiting for any currently connected users to disconnect. For more information about the STOP ENGINE statement and running a SQL statement on the ISQL command line, see the SQL Anywhere Help.
- The three RENAME commands rename the previous backup files so they won't be overwritten if they already exist. These files are deleted later in the process if everything goes well.
- The three IF EXIST commands check to make sure the RENAME commands worked okay; they stop the whole process if any of the original file names are still in use.
- The three COPY commands copy the .db, .log, and .mlg files to a folder called bkup on a different computer.
- The next six commands compare the original files with the fresh backup copies. Each "ECHO N |" pipes a single "N" character to the corresponding COMP command to provide an automatic response to the prompt "Compare more files (Y/N) ?". The COMP commands compare the files, and the IF ERRORLEVEL commands stop the whole process if the COMP commands set the return code to 1 or higher.
- The three ERASE commands get rid of the old backup files that were renamed earlier.
- The next command starts the database engine again, using the current database and transaction log files.
- The last four lines display an error message or skip over it, depending on what happens.

9.12.2 Full Online Image Backup

It is possible to back up a database while it is still running by using the dbbackup.exe program or the BACKUP DATABASE statement. Examples in this section will only show the BACKUP DATABASE statement for online backups because it is more flexible: it can be run from ISQL, from application programs, and from inside scheduled events. For more information about scheduled events, see Section 8.12, "CREATE EVENT."

A backup created by the BACKUP DATABASE statement is called an "online backup" as opposed to the "offline backup" described earlier. One important difference is that the online backup copies of the database and transaction log files may not agree with each other because users may continue to make changes to the database while the backup is proceeding; this affects the restore procedures discussed in Section 9.13.

The BACKUP DATABASE statement has two formats: One is used to create separate image copies of the .db and .log files, and the other format is used to create a single "archive" file. The archive file form of BACKUP DATABASE is described in the SQL Anywhere Help.

Here is the syntax of the online image file BACKUP DATABASE statement:

```
<backup_database_to_image_files> ::= BACKUP DATABASE { <image_option> }
<image_option>        ::= DIRECTORY <image_destination> -- required
                        | DBFILE ONLY               -- these two clauses
                        | TRANSACTION LOG ONLY      --   are mutually exclusive
                        | TRANSACTION LOG RENAME
                        | TRANSACTION LOG RENAME MATCH -- conflicts with TRUNCATE
                        | TRANSACTION LOG TRUNCATE  -- overrides RENAME
                        | WAIT BEFORE START         -- these two clauses may
                        | WAIT AFTER END            --   be used together
                        | WITH COMMENT <backup_comment>
<image_destination> ::= string literal path and folder
<backup_comment>    ::= string literal to put in %ASANY9%\win32\backup.syb
```

The BACKUP DATABASE statement must be run on a connection to the database that is to be backed up, with a user id that has REMOTE DBA or DBA privilege. Different options can be used to perform different kinds of online image backups, including the following:

- A full online image backup creates backup copies of the database and transaction files.
- A differential online log backup backs up transaction log entries made since the last full backup.
- An incremental online log backup backs up transaction log entries made since the last full or incremental backup.

A *full online image backup* uses the dbbackup.exe program or the BACKUP DATABASE statement to create separate backup copies of the database file and the transaction log file while the database is still running. The backup process performs a checkpoint operation when it starts, and the database backup file is an image of the database at that point; the transaction log backup file, however, is an image of the transaction log as it exists at the end of the backup process.

Although users may continue to update the database, no changes are made to the database file while it is being copied. Changes are made in cache only, and if the cache becomes full a temporary file will be used. This means that the resulting transaction log backup file may contain more recent data than the corresponding database backup file; a full restore requires both backup files because SQL Anywhere must perform the recovery process as described in Section 9.11.

Following is an example of a BACKUP DATABASE statement that creates a full online image backup; only the DIRECTORY clause has been specified because it's required for all image BACKUP DATABASE statements. The DBFILE ONLY and TRANSACTION LOG ONLY clauses have both been omitted on purpose so SQL Anywhere will include the database and transaction log; that's what makes this a full backup. All the other clauses have been omitted as well, for simplicity.

```
BACKUP DATABASE DIRECTORY 'G:\bkup';
```

Here's how the various BACKUP DATABASE clauses work:

- The DIRECTORY clause specifies the folder where the backup files will be written.
- DBFILE ONLY specifies that only the database files will be backed up; this option is not discussed further because the transaction log is too important.
- The TRANSACTION LOG ONLY clause specifies that only the transaction log file is backed up; this clause is for differential and incremental online log backups, described in the next two sections.
- TRANSACTION LOG RENAME will close and rename the current transaction log file as YYMMDDXX.LOG when the backup is complete, and start a new transaction log file with the original name. YYMMDD is today's date and XX is AA for the first backup today, AB for the second, and so on. Either TRANSACTION LOG RENAME or TRANSACTION LOG RENAME MATCH is used for incremental online log backups, described later in this chapter; TRANSACTION LOG RENAME MATCH is recommended.
- TRANSACTION LOG RENAME MATCH is the same as TRANSACTION LOG RENAME, except that the backup copy of the current transaction log file will also be renamed to YYMMDDXX.LOG to match the renamed version of the current transaction log. By default, the backup copy of the current transaction log has the same name as the current transaction log, so repeated BACKUP DATABASE statements will overwrite old backup copies. With the MATCH keyword, two permanent YYMMDDXX.LOG copies of the backup log file are created, one in the current folder and one in the backup folder.
- TRANSACTION LOG TRUNCATE specifies that the transaction log file will be closed and deleted when the BACKUP DATABASE statement is complete, and a new transaction log file will be started with the original name. A backup copy of the transaction log will be made in the folder specified by the DIRECTORY clause, but it too will have the original file name. The TRANSACTION LOG RENAME clauses are more flexible, so TRANSACTION LOG TRUNCATE won't be discussed further.
- The WAIT BEFORE START clause instructs SQL Anywhere to wait until every transaction has ended with a COMMIT or ROLLBACK operation. The resulting database backup file won't contain any information in the rollback logs; this is useful if you want to start the database backup file in read-only mode to run a validation check; however, if different connections keep starting new, overlapping transactions, WAIT BEFORE START will

cause the backup process to wait indefinitely before getting underway. The validation process is discussed in Section 9.14.

- The WAIT AFTER END clause instructs SQL Anywhere to wait until every transaction has ended with a COMMIT or ROLLBACK operation before finishing the backup of the transaction log file. If different connections keep starting new, overlapping transactions, WAIT AFTER END will cause the backup process to wait indefinitely before finishing. The WAIT AFTER END clause only takes effect when the current log file is being renamed or truncated; otherwise, it has no effect and the backup finishes without waiting.

  Both WAIT BEFORE START and WAIT AFTER END can be specified for the same BACKUP DATABASE statement, and they can both have an effect because new transactions can start after the backup has started but before it ends. Note that changes made by these transactions will not be included in the database backup file, but they may be included in the transaction log backup file; in fact, they will be included in the transaction log backup file if WAIT AFTER END is specified.

- The WITH COMMENT clause may be used to specify a string literal to be included in the message that the backup operation appends to the text file backup.syb file located in the same folder as the database engine; for Windows, the default location is C:\Program Files\Sybase\SQL Anywhere 9\win32\backup.syb. This file is updated whether or not you use the WITH COMMENT clause; here is an example that uses it:

```
BACKUP DATABASE DIRECTORY 'G:\bkup' WITH COMMENT 'Ad hoc';
```

Here is what that statement added to the backup.syb file:

```
BACKUP, 2.0, test9.db, ASAn, '2004-03-17 09:29:00.000', DBA, Full, Imag, G:\bkup,
   'Ad hoc'
```

9.12.3 Differential Online Log Backup

A *differential online log backup* uses dbbackup.exe or the BACKUP DATABASE statement to create a backup copy of the transaction log while the database is still running. The word "differential" means that the current transaction log that is being backed up has been in use at least since the last full backup was created, and contains all the changes made since that point. A repeated differential backup makes the previous differential backup copy of the transaction log unnecessary, because the new differential backup contains all its data plus the changes made since then. A full restore requires the previous full online image backup of the database file and transaction log, plus the most recent differential backup copy of the transaction log.

A differential online log BACKUP DATABASE statement specifies the TRANSACTION LOG ONLY clause but leaves out the TRANSACTION LOG RENAME and TRANSACTION LOG RENAME MATCH clauses. Here is an example of three BACKUP DATABASE statements: one full online image backup to get the process started, followed by two successive differential online log backups:

```
BACKUP DATABASE DIRECTORY 'G:\bkup' WITH COMMENT 'Start';
BACKUP DATABASE DIRECTORY 'G:\bkup' TRANSACTION LOG ONLY WITH COMMENT 'Diff 1';
BACKUP DATABASE DIRECTORY 'G:\bkup' TRANSACTION LOG ONLY WITH COMMENT 'Diff 2';
```

Here are the entries added to the backup.syb file by the three BACKUP DATABASE statements above:

```
BACKUP, 2.0, test9.db, ASAn, '2004-03-17 09:31:00.000', DBA, Full, Imag, G:\bkup,
    'Start'
BACKUP, 2.0, test9.db, ASAn, '2004-03-17 09:31:00.000', DBA, LGFO, Imag, G:\bkup,
    'Diff 1'
BACKUP, 2.0, test9.db, ASAn, '2004-03-17 09:31:00.000', DBA, LGFO, Imag, G:\bkup,
    'Diff 2'
```

Each time a differential online log backup is executed, it makes a new backup copy of the current transaction log, and this fresh copy overwrites any previous backup copy that was created. The current transaction log is left alone, and continues to grow as more updates are performed.

9.12.4 Incremental Online Log Backup

An *incremental online log backup* also uses dbbackup.exe or the BACKUP DATABASE statement to create a backup copy of the transaction log while the database is still running. The word "incremental" means that the current transaction log that is being backed up has only been in use since the previous backup operation; at that point a new, empty transaction log file was created. An incremental backup copy of the transaction log only contains changes made since the previous backup operation. A full restore requires the previous full online image backup of the database file and transaction log, plus all the incremental backup copies of the transaction log.

An incremental online log BACKUP DATABASE statement specifies the TRANSACTION LOG ONLY clause plus the TRANSACTION LOG RENAME or TRANSACTION LOG RENAME MATCH clause. Here is an example of three BACKUP DATABASE statements: one full online image backup to get the process started, followed by two successive incremental online log backups. All three BACKUP DATABASE statements use the TRANSACTION LOG RENAME MATCH clause so the current transaction log is backed up, closed, renamed, and restarted each time:

```
BACKUP DATABASE DIRECTORY 'G:\bkup'
   TRANSACTION LOG RENAME MATCH;

BACKUP DATABASE DIRECTORY 'G:\bkup'
   TRANSACTION LOG ONLY
   TRANSACTION LOG RENAME MATCH;

BACKUP DATABASE DIRECTORY 'G:\bkup'
   TRANSACTION LOG ONLY
   TRANSACTION LOG RENAME MATCH;
```

Here are the relevant files after the above three BACKUP DATABASE statements were executed:

```
test9.db                  - current database file
test9.log                 - fresh current transaction log file
040317AA.LOG              - renamed transaction log file from 1st backup
040317AB.LOG              - renamed transaction log file from 2nd backup
040317AC.LOG              - renamed transaction log file from 3rd backup

C:\mirror\test9.mlg       - fresh current mirror log file
C:\mirror\040317AA.MLG    - renamed mirror log file from 1st backup
C:\mirror\040317AB.MLG    - renamed mirror log file from 2nd backup
```

```
C:\mirror\040226AC.MLG   - renamed mirror log file from 3rd backup

G:\bkup\test9.db         - backup database file from 1st backup
G:\bkup\040317AA.LOG     - backup transaction log file from 1st backup
G:\bkup\040317AB.LOG     - backup transaction log file from 2nd backup
G:\bkup\040317AC.LOG     - backup transaction log file from 3rd backup
```

Note: The BACKUP DATABASE command renames and restarts the current mirror log file in the same way it does the current transaction log file, but it does not make a backup copy of the mirror log file. That's okay: The mirror log files are really just copies of the corresponding transaction logs anyway, and three copies are probably sufficient.

9.12.5 Live Log Backup

A *live log backup* uses dbbackup.exe to continuously copy transaction log data to a file on a remote computer. The live log backup file will lag behind the current transaction log on the main computer, but not by much, especially if the two computers are connected by a high-speed LAN. If other backup files are written to the remote computer, and a live log backup file is maintained, it is possible to use that remote computer to start the database in case the entire main computer is lost; only a small amount of data will be lost due to the time lag between the current transaction log and the live log backup.

The following is an example of a Windows batch file that starts dbbackup.exe on the remote computer; this batch file is executed on that computer, and the startup folder is remote_test9, the same folder that is mapped to the G: drive on the main computer as described earlier. A local environment variable CONNECTION is used to hold the connection string for dbbackup to use, and the LINKS parameter allows dbbackup.exe to reach across the LAN to make a connection to the database running on the main computer. The -l parameter specifies that the live log backup is to be written to a file called live_test9.log in the folder remote_test9\bkup. The last parameter, bkup, meets the requirement for the backup folder to be specified at the end of every dbbackup command line.

```
SET CONNECTION="ENG=test9;DBN=test9;UID=dba;PWD=sql;LINKS=TCPIP(HOST=TSUNAMI)"
"%ASANY9%\win32\dbbackup.exe" -c %CONNECTION% -l bkup\live_test9.log bkup
```

Here's what the dbbackup.exe displays in the command window after it has been running on the remote computer for a while; three successive BACKUP DATABASE commands have been run on the main computer, and then some updates have been performed on the database:

```
Adaptive Server Anywhere Backup Utility Version 9.0.1.1751
   (1 of 1 pages, 100% complete)
   (1 of 1 pages, 100% complete)
Transaction log truncated by backup -- restarting ...
   (1 of 1 pages, 100% complete)
   (1 of 1 pages, 100% complete)
Transaction log truncated by backup -- restarting ...
   (1 of 1 pages, 100% complete)
   (1 of 1 pages, 100% complete)
Transaction log truncated by backup -- restarting ...
   (1 of 1 pages, 100% complete)
   (2 of 2 pages, 100% complete)
   (3 of 3 pages, 100% complete)
```

```
(4 of 4 pages, 100% complete)
Live backup of transaction log waiting for next page...
```

When a backup operation on the main computer renames and restarts the current transaction log, the dbbackup.exe program running on the remote computer erases the contents of the live log backup file and starts writing to it again. That's okay; it just means the live log backup is just a live copy of the current transaction log, which has also been restarted. If the other backup operations, performed on the main computer, write their backup files to the remote computer, then everything necessary to start the database is available on the remote computer.

Note: It is okay for backup operations, including live log backups, to write output files across the LAN to disk drives that are attached to a different computer from the one running the database engine. However, the active database, transaction log, mirror log, and temporary files must all be located on disk drives that are locally attached to the computer running the engine; LAN I/O is not acceptable. In this context, the mirror log is not a "backup file" but an active, albeit redundant, copy of the active transaction log.

The next section shows how the files created by the backup examples in this section can be used to restore the database after a failure.

9.13 **Restore**

A *restore* is the process of replacing the current database file with a backup copy, performing any necessary recovery process to get the database up and running, and then applying any necessary transaction logs to bring the database up to date.

Tip: There's no such thing as an automated restore. You can automate the backup process, and you probably should, but any restore requires careful study and attention.

Here is a broad outline of the steps involved in restoring a database, followed by several examples:
1. Don't panic.
2. Plan ahead: Determine what backup files are available and which ones are going to be used, in what steps and in what order.
3. Rename or copy any file that is going to be overwritten; this is very important because mistakes are easy to make when restoring a database... especially since Step 1 is often difficult to accomplish.
4. Restore the database and/or apply the transaction log files according to the plan developed in Steps 2 and 3.

Example 1: The current database and transaction log are both unusable, and the most recent backup was a full offline image backup of both the database and transaction log as described at the beginning of this section. Here is the Windows batch file that performed the backup; it created the backup files that will be used in the restore, G:\bkup\test9.db and G:\bkup\test9.log, plus a backup of the mirror log:

```
SET CONNECTION="ENG=test9;DBN=test9;UID=dba;PWD=sql"
"%ASANY9%\win32\dbisql.exe" -c %CONNECTION% STOP ENGINE test9 UNCONDITIONALLY
RENAME G:\bkup\test9.db  old_test9.db
RENAME G:\bkup\test9.log old_test9.log
RENAME G:\bkup\test9.mlg old_test9.mlg
IF EXIST G:\bkup\test9.db  GOTO ERROR
IF EXIST G:\bkup\test9.log GOTO ERROR
IF EXIST G:\bkup\test9.mlg GOTO ERROR
COPY test9.db            G:\bkup\test9.db
COPY test9.log           G:\bkup\test9.log
COPY C:\mirror\test9.mlg G:\bkup\test9.mlg
ECHO N | COMP test9.db G:\bkup\test9.db
IF ERRORLEVEL 1 GOTO ERROR
ECHO N | COMP test9.log G:\bkup\test9.log
IF ERRORLEVEL 1 GOTO ERROR
ECHO N | COMP C:\mirror\test9.mlg G:\bkup\test9.mlg
IF ERRORLEVEL 1 GOTO ERROR
ERASE G:\bkup\old_test9.db
ERASE G:\bkup\old_test9.log
ERASE G:\bkup\old_test9.mlg
"%ASANY9%\win32\dbsrv9.exe" -x tcpip test9.db
GOTO END
:ERROR
PAUSE Backup process failed.
:END
```

In this situation the best you can hope for is to restore the database to the state it was in at the time of the earlier backup; any updates made since that point are lost. Here is a Windows batch file that performs the simple full restore for Example 1:

```
ATTRIB -R test9.db
ATTRIB -R test9.log
ATTRIB -R C:\mirror\test9.mlg
RENAME test9.db            old_test9.db
RENAME test9.log           old_test9.log
RENAME C:\mirror\test9.mlg old_test9.mlg
COPY G:\bkup\test9.db  test9.db
COPY G:\bkup\test9.log test9.log
COPY G:\bkup\test9.mlg C:\mirror\test9.mlg
"%ASANY9%\win32\dbsrv9.exe" -o ex_1_console.txt -x tcpip test9.db
```

Here's how the batch file works for Example 1:

- The three ATTRIB commands reset the "read-only" setting on the .db, .log, and .mlg files so they can be renamed.
- The three RENAME commands follow the rule to "rename or copy any file that's going to be overwritten."
- The three COPY commands restore the backup .db, .log, and .mlg files from the remote computer backup folder back to the current and mirror folders. Restoring the mirror log file isn't really necessary, and the next few examples aren't going to bother with it.
- The last command starts the engine again, using the database and transaction log files that were just restored. The -o option specifies that the database console window messages should also be written to a file.

Example 2: The current database is unusable but the current transaction file is still available, and the most recent backup was a full online image backup of both the database and transaction log as described earlier in this section. The

following statement performed the backup and created G:\bkup\test9.db and
G:\bkup\test9.log:

```
BACKUP DATABASE DIRECTORY 'G:\bkup';
```

In this case, the backup database file is copied back from the backup folder, and
the current transaction log file is applied to the database to bring it forward to a
more recent state. All the committed transactions will be recovered, but any
changes that were uncommitted at the time of failure will be lost. Here is a Windows batch file that will perform the restore for Example 2:

```
ATTRIB -R test9.db
RENAME test9.db old_test9.db
COPY test9.log old_test9.log
COPY G:\bkup\test9.db test9.db
"%ASANY9%\win32\dbsrv9.exe" -o ex_2_console.txt test9.db -a G:\bkup\test9.log
"%ASANY9%\win32\dbsrv9.exe" -o ex_2_console.txt test9.db -a test9.log
"%ASANY9%\win32\dbsrv9.exe" -o ex_2_console.txt -x tcpip test9.db
```

Here's how the batch file works for Example 2:

■ The ATTRIB command resets the "read-only" setting on the current .db
file. In this example the current .log file is left alone.

■ The RENAME command and the first COPY follow the rule to "rename or
copy any file that's going to be overwritten"; the database file is going to be
overwritten with a backup copy, and the current transaction log is eventually going to be updated when the server is started in the final step.

■ The second COPY command restores the backup .db file from the remote
computer backup folder back to the current folder.

■ The next command runs dbsrv9.exe with the option "-a G:\bkup\test9.log,"
which applies the backup .log file to the freshly restored .db file. All the
committed changes that exist in that .log file but are not contained in the
database itself are applied to the database; this step is required because an
online BACKUP statement performed the original backup, and the backup
transaction log may be more up to date than the corresponding backup database file. When the database engine is run with the -a option, it operates as
if it were a batch utility program and stops as soon as the roll forward process is complete.

■ The second-to-last command runs dbsrv9.exe with the option "-a test9.log,"
which applies the current .log file to the database. This will bring the database up to date with respect to committed changes made after the backup.

■ The last command starts the engine again, using the restored .db file and
current .log file.

Note: In most restore procedures, the backup transaction log file that was
created at the same time as the backup database file is the first log that is
applied using the dbsrv9 -a option, as shown above. In this particular example
that step isn't necessary because the current transaction log contains everything
that's necessary for recovery. In other words, the dbsrv9.exe command with the
option "-a G:\bkup\test9.log" could have been omitted; it does no harm, however, and it is shown here because it usually is necessary.

Here is some of the output that appeared in the database console window during
the last three steps of Example 2:

```
I. 03/17 09:21:27. Adaptive Server Anywhere Network Server Version 9.0.0.1270
...
I. 03/17 09:21:27. Starting database "test9" ... at Wed Mar 17 2004 09:21
I. 03/17 09:21:27. Database recovery in progress
I. 03/17 09:21:27.    Last checkpoint at Wed Mar 17 2004 09:17
I. 03/17 09:21:27.    Checkpoint log...
I. 03/17 09:21:27.    Transaction log: G:\bkup\test9.log...
I. 03/17 09:21:27.    Rollback log...
I. 03/17 09:21:27.    Checkpointing...
I. 03/17 09:21:27. Starting checkpoint of "test9" ... at Wed Mar 17 2004 09:21
I. 03/17 09:21:27. Finished checkpoint of "test9" ... at Wed Mar 17 2004 09:21
I. 03/17 09:21:27. Recovery complete
I. 03/17 09:21:27. Database server stopped at Wed Mar 17 2004 09:21
...
I. 03/17 09:21:27. Starting database "test9" ... at Wed Mar 17 2004 09:21
I. 03/17 09:21:27. Database recovery in progress
I. 03/17 09:21:27.    Last checkpoint at Wed Mar 17 2004 09:21
I. 03/17 09:21:27.    Checkpoint log...
I. 03/17 09:21:27.    Transaction log: test9.log...
I. 03/17 09:21:27.    Rollback log...
I. 03/17 09:21:27.    Checkpointing...
I. 03/17 09:21:28. Starting checkpoint of "test9" ... at Wed Mar 17 2004 09:21
I. 03/17 09:21:28. Finished checkpoint of "test9" ... at Wed Mar 17 2004 09:21
I. 03/17 09:21:28. Recovery complete
I. 03/17 09:21:28. Database server stopped at Wed Mar 17 2004 09:21
...
I. 03/17 09:21:28. Starting database "test9" ... at Wed Mar 17 2004 09:21
I. 03/17 09:21:28. Transaction log: test9.log
I. 03/17 09:21:28. Transaction log mirror: C:\mirror\test9.mlg
I. 03/17 09:21:28. Starting checkpoint of "test9" ... at Wed Mar 17 2004 09:21
I. 03/17 09:21:28. Finished checkpoint of "test9" ... at Wed Mar 17 2004 09:21
I. 03/17 09:21:28. Database "test9" (test9.db) started at Wed Mar 17 2004 09:21
I. 03/17 09:21:28. Database server started at Wed Mar 17 2004 09:21
...
I. 03/17 09:21:36. Now accepting requests
```

The restore shown above recovers all the committed changes made up to the point of failure, because they were all contained in the transaction log. It is also possible to recover uncommitted changes if they are also in the transaction log, and that will be true if a COMMIT had been performed on any other connection after the uncommitted changes had been made; in other words, any COMMIT forces all changes out to the transaction log.

Following is an example of how the dbtran.exe utility may be used to analyze a transaction log file and produce the SQL statements corresponding to the changes recorded in the log. The -a option tells dbtran.exe to include uncommitted operations in the output, and the two file specifications are the input transaction log file and the output text file.

```
"%ASANY9%\win32\dbtran.exe" -a old_test9.log old_test9.sql
```

Here is an excerpt from the output text file produced by the dbtran.exe utility; it contains an INSERT statement that may be used in ISQL if you want to recover this uncommitted operation:

```
--INSERT-1001-0000385084
INSERT INTO DBA.t1(key_1,non_key_1)
VALUES (9999,'Lost uncommitted insert')
```

Example 3: The current database is unusable but the current transaction file is still available, and the backups consist of an earlier full online image backup that renamed and restarted the transaction log, followed by two incremental log backups. Here are the statements that created the backups:

```
BACKUP DATABASE DIRECTORY 'G:\bkup'
   TRANSACTION LOG RENAME MATCH;

BACKUP DATABASE DIRECTORY 'G:\bkup'
   TRANSACTION LOG ONLY
   TRANSACTION LOG RENAME MATCH;

BACKUP DATABASE DIRECTORY 'G:\bkup'
   TRANSACTION LOG ONLY
   TRANSACTION LOG RENAME MATCH;
```

In this case, the backup database file must be copied back from the remote backup folder, and then a whole series of transaction logs must be applied to bring the database forward to a recent state. Here is a Windows batch file that will perform the restore for Example 3:

```
ATTRIB -R test9.db
RENAME test9.db old_test9.db
COPY test9.log old_test9.log
COPY G:\bkup\test9.db
"%ASANY9%\win32\dbsrv9.exe" -o ex_3_console.txt test9.db -a G:\bkup\040317AA.LOG
"%ASANY9%\win32\dbsrv9.exe" -o ex_3_console.txt test9.db -a G:\bkup\040317AB.LOG
"%ASANY9%\win32\dbsrv9.exe" -o ex_3_console.txt test9.db -a G:\bkup\040317AC.LOG
"%ASANY9%\win32\dbsrv9.exe" -o ex_3_console.txt test9.db -a test9.log
"%ASANY9%\win32\dbsrv9.exe" -o ex_3_console.txt -x tcpip test9.db
```

Here's how the batch file works for Example 3:

- The ATTRIB command resets the "read-only" setting on the current .db file.
- The RENAME command and the first COPY follow the rule to "rename or copy any file that's going to be overwritten." Note that if everything goes smoothly, all these "old*.*" files can be deleted.
- The second COPY command copies the backup .db file from the backup folder back to the current folder.
- The next three commands run dbsrv9.exe with the -a option to apply the oldest three transaction log backups in consecutive order.
- The second-to-last command runs dbsrv9.exe with -a to apply the current transaction log to bring the database up to date as far as committed transactions are concerned.
- The last command starts the engine again, using the restored .db file and current .log file.

Here is some of the output that appeared in the database console window during the five dbsrv9.exe steps in Example 3:

```
I. 03/17 09:44:00. Starting database "test9" ... at Wed Mar 17 2004 09:44
...
I. 03/17 09:44:00.    Transaction log: G:\bkup\040317AA.LOG...
...
I. 03/17 09:44:01. Starting database "test9" ... at Wed Mar 17 2004 09:44
...
I. 03/17 09:44:01.    Transaction log: G:\bkup\040317AB.LOG...
...
I. 03/17 09:44:01. Starting database "test9" ... at Wed Mar 17 2004 09:44
...
I. 03/17 09:44:01.    Transaction log: G:\bkup\040317AC.LOG...
```

```
...
I. 03/17 09:44:01. Starting database "test9" ... at Wed Mar 17 2004 09:44
...
I. 03/17 09:44:02.    Transaction log: test9.log...
...
I. 03/17 09:44:02. Starting database "test9" ... at Wed Mar 17 2004 09:44
I. 03/17 09:44:02. Transaction log: test9.log
...
I. 03/17 09:44:10. Now accepting requests
```

Example 4: The main computer is unavailable, and the backups are the same as shown in Example 3, with the addition of a live log backup running on the remote computer. Here are the commands run on the remote computer to start the live log backup:

```
SET CONNECTION="ENG=test9;DBN=test9;UID=dba;PWD=sql;LINKS=TCPIP(HOST=TSUNAMI)"
"%ASANY9%\win32\dbbackup.exe" -c %CONNECTION% -l bkup\live_test9.log bkup
```

Here are the statements run on the main computer to create the backups:

```
BACKUP DATABASE DIRECTORY 'G:\bkup'
   TRANSACTION LOG RENAME MATCH;

BACKUP DATABASE DIRECTORY 'G:\bkup'
   TRANSACTION LOG ONLY
   TRANSACTION LOG RENAME MATCH;

BACKUP DATABASE DIRECTORY 'G:\bkup'
   TRANSACTION LOG ONLY
   TRANSACTION LOG RENAME MATCH;
```

In this case, the restore process must occur on the remote computer. Here is a Windows batch file that will perform the restore for Example 4:

```
COPY bkup\test9.db
COPY bkup\live_test9.log test9.log
"%ASANY9%\win32\dbsrv9.exe" -o ex_4_console.txt test9.db -a bkup\040317AD.LOG
"%ASANY9%\win32\dbsrv9.exe" -o ex_4_console.txt test9.db -a bkup\040317AE.LOG
"%ASANY9%\win32\dbsrv9.exe" -o ex_4_console.txt test9.db -a bkup\040317AF.LOG
"%ASANY9%\win32\dbsrv9.exe" -o ex_4_console.txt test9.db -a test9.log
"%ASANY9%\win32\dbsrv9.exe" -o ex_4_console.txt -x tcpip test9.db
```

Here's how the batch file works for Example 4:

- The first COPY command copies the backup .db file from the backup folder to the current folder. Note that the backup folder is simply referred to as "bkup" rather than "G:\bkup" because all these commands are run on the remote computer.
- The second COPY command copies the live log backup from the backup folder to the current folder, and renames it to "test9.log" because it's going to become the current transaction log.
- The next three commands run dbsrv9.exe with the -a option to apply the oldest three transaction log backups in consecutive order.
- The second-to-last command runs dbsrv9.exe with -a to apply the current transaction log, formerly known as the live log backup file. This brings the database up to date as far as all the committed transactions that made it to the live log backup file are concerned.
- The last command starts the engine again, using the restored .db file and current .log file. Clients can now connect to the server on the remote

computer; this may or may not require changes to the connection strings used by those clients, but that issue isn't covered here.

9.14 Validation

If you really want to make sure your database is protected, every backup database file and every backup transaction log should be checked for validity as soon as it is created.

There are two ways to check the database: Run the dbvalid.exe utility program, or run a series of VALIDATE TABLE and VALIDATE INDEX statements. Both of these methods require that the database be started.

Following are two Windows batch files that automate the process of running dbvalid.exe. The first batch file, called copy_database_to_validate.bat, makes a temporary copy of the database file so that the original copy remains undisturbed by the changes made whenever a database is started. It then uses dblog.exe with the -n option to turn off the transaction log and mirror log files for the copied database, runs dbsrv9.exe with the -f option to force recovery of the copied database without the application of any log file, and finally starts the copied database using dbsrv9.exe:

```
ATTRIB -R temp_%1.db
COPY /Y %1.db temp_%1.db
"%ASANY9%\win32\dblog.exe" -n temp_%1.db
"%ASANY9%\win32\dbsrv9.exe" -o console.txt temp_%1.db -f
"%ASANY9%\win32\dbsrv9.exe" -o console.txt temp_%1.db
```

The second Windows batch file, called validate_database_copy.bat, runs dbvalid.exe on the temporary copy of the database:

```
@ECHO OFF
SET CONNECTION="ENG=temp_%1;DBN=temp_%1;UID=dba;PWD=sql"
ECHO ***** DBVALID %CONNECTION% >>validate.txt
DATE /T >>validate.txt
TIME /T >>validate.txt
"%ASANY9%\win32\dbvalid.exe" -c %CONNECTION% -f -o validate.txt
IF NOT ERRORLEVEL 1 GOTO OK
ECHO ON
REM ***** ERROR: DATABASE IS INVALID *****
GOTO END
:OK
ECHO ON
ECHO OK >>validate.txt
```

Here's how the validate_database_copy.bat file works:

- The ECHO OFF command cuts down on the display output.
- The SET command creates a local environment variable to hold the connection string.
- The ECHO, DATE, and TIME commands start adding information to the validate.txt file.
- The next command runs dbvalid.exe with the -f option to perform a full check of all tables and the -o option to append the display output to the validate.txt file. The -c option is used to connect to a running database, which in this case is a temporary copy of the original database.
- The IF command checks the return code from dbvalid.exe. A return code of zero means everything is okay, and any other value means there is a

problem. The IF command can be interpreted as follows: "if not (return code >= 1) then go to the OK label, else continue with the next command."

- The remaining commands display "ERROR" or "DATABASE IS OK," depending on the return code.

Here is an example of how the two batch files above are executed, first for a valid database and then for a corrupted database. Both batch files take the file name portion of the database file name as a parameter, with the .db extension omitted:

```
copy_database_to_validate valid_test9
validate_database_copy valid_test9

copy_database_to_validate invalid_test9
validate_database_copy invalid_test9
```

Here's what validate_database_copy.bat displayed for the database that was okay:

```
Adaptive Server Anywhere Validation Utility Version 9.0.0.1270
No errors reported
E:\validate>ECHO OK  1>>validate.txt
E:\validate>REM ***** DATABASE IS OK *****
```

Here is what validate_database_copy.bat displayed for the database with a problem, in particular an index that has become corrupted:

```
Adaptive Server Anywhere Validation Utility Version 9.0.0.1270
Validating DBA.t1
Run time SQL error - Index "x1" has missing index entries
1 error reported
E:\validate>REM ***** ERROR: DATABASE IS INVALID *****
```

Here is the contents of the validate.txt file after the above two runs of validate_database_copy.bat; it records the database connection parameters, date, time, and validation results:

```
***** DBVALID "ENG=temp_valid_test9;DBN=temp_valid_test9;UID=dba;PWD=sql"
Wed 03/17/2004
 8:19a
Adaptive Server Anywhere Validation Utility Version 9.0.0.1270
No errors reported
OK
***** DBVALID "ENG=temp_invalid_test9;DBN=temp_invalid_test9;UID=dba;PWD=sql"
Wed 03/17/2004
 8:19a
Adaptive Server Anywhere Validation Utility Version 9.0.0.1270
Run time SQL error - Index "x1" has missing index entries
1 error reported
```

Here is the syntax for the VALIDATE TABLE statement:

```
<validate_table> ::= VALIDATE TABLE [ <owner_name> "." ] <table_name>
                     [ <with_check> ]

<with_check>    ::= WITH DATA CHECK    -- adds data checking
                  | WITH EXPRESS CHECK -- adds data, quick index checking
                  | WITH INDEX CHECK   -- adds full index checking
                  | WITH FULL CHECK    -- adds data, full index checking
```

In the absence of any WITH clause, the VALIDATE TABLE statement performs some basic row and index checks. The various WITH clauses extend the checking as follows:

- **WITH DATA CHECK** performs extra checking of blob pages.
- **WITH EXPRESS CHECK** performs the WITH DATA checking plus some more index checking.
- **WITH INDEX CHECK** performs the same extensive index checking as the VALIDATE INDEX statement, on every index for the table.
- **WITH FULL CHECK** is the most thorough; it combines the WITH DATA and WITH INDEX checking.

Here is an example of a VALIDATE TABLE statement that was run against the same database that had the error detected by dbvalid.exe in the previous example:

```
VALIDATE TABLE t1;
```

The VALIDATE TABLE statement above set the SQLSTATE to '40000' and produced the same error message: "Run time SQL error — Index "x1" has missing index entries."

The VALIDATE INDEX statement checks a single index for validity; in addition to the basic checks, it confirms that every index entry actually corresponds to a row in the table, and if the index is on a foreign key it ensures the corresponding row in the parent table actually exists.

There are two different formats for VALIDATE INDEX, one for a primary key index and one for other kinds of indexes. Here is the syntax:

```
<validate_primary_key> ::= VALIDATE INDEX
                            [ [ <owner_name> "." ] <table_name> "." ]
                            <table_name>
<validate_other_index> ::= VALIDATE INDEX
                            [ [ <owner_name> "." ] <table_name> "." ]
                            <index_name>
<index_name>           ::= <identifier>
```

Here is an example of a VALIDATE INDEX statement that checks the primary key index of table t1; this index is okay so this statement sets SQLSTATE to '00000':

```
VALIDATE INDEX DBA.t1.t1;
```

Here is an example of a VALIDATE INDEX statement that checks an index named x1 on the table t1. When it is run against the same database as the previous VALIDATE TABLE example, this statement also sets the SQLSTATE to '40000' and produces the same error message about missing index entries:

```
VALIDATE INDEX t1.x1;
```

Here is an example of a VALIDATE INDEX statement that checks a foreign key with a role name of fk2 on table t2:

```
VALIDATE INDEX t2.fk2;
```

In this case, the foreign key column value in one row of the table has been corrupted, and the VALIDATE INDEX produces the following error message:

```
Run time SQL error — Foreign key "fk2" for table "t2" is invalid
because primary key or unique constraint "t1" on table "t1" has missing
entries
```

A transaction log file can be checked for validity by using the dbtran.exe utility to attempt to translate the log into SQL commands. If the attempt succeeds, the log is okay; if the attempt fails, the log is not usable for recovery purposes.

Following is an example of a Windows batch file called check_log.bat that may be called from a command line that specifies a transaction log file specification as a parameter. This batch file runs dbtran.exe with the -o option to append error messages to a text file called validate.txt, the -y option to overwrite the output SQL file, the %1 notation to represent the batch file parameter value, and the output SQL file called dummy.sql.

```
ECHO OFF
ECHO ***** DBTRAN %1 >>validate.txt
DATE /T >>validate.txt
TIME /T >>validate.txt
"%ASANY9%\win32\dbtran.exe" -o validate.txt -y %1 dummy.sql
IF NOT ERRORLEVEL 1 GOTO OK
ECHO ON
REM ***** ERROR: LOG IS INVALID *****
GOTO END
:OK
ECHO ON
ECHO OK >>validate.txt
REM ***** LOG IS OK *****
:END
```

Here are two Windows command lines that call check_log.bat, once for a transaction log that is okay and once for a log that has been corrupted:

```
CALL check_log 040226AB.LOG
CALL check_log 040226AC.LOG
```

The first call to check_log.bat above will display "***** LOG IS OK *****" and the second call will display "***** ERROR: LOG IS INVALID *****." Here's what the validate.txt file contains after those two calls:

```
***** DBTRAN 040226AB.LOG
Fri 02/27/2004
10:17a
Adaptive Server Anywhere Log Translation Utility Version 9.0.0.1270
Transaction log "040226AB.LOG" starts at offset 0000380624
Transaction log ends at offset 0000385294
OK
***** DBTRAN 040226AC.LOG
Fri 02/27/2004
10:17a
Adaptive Server Anywhere Log Translation Utility Version 9.0.0.1270
Transaction log "040226AC.LOG" starts at offset 0000380624
Log file corrupted (invalid operation)
Corruption of log starts at offset 0000385082
Log operation at offset 0000385082 has bad data at offset 0000385083
```

9.15 Chapter Summary

This chapter covered various techniques and facilities that are used to protect the integrity of SQL Anywhere databases.

Section 9.2 discussed local and global database options and how values can exist at four different levels: internal default values, public defaults, user defaults, and the values currently in use on a particular connection.

Section 9.3 presented the "ACID" properties of a transaction — atomicity, consistency, isolation, and durability. It also discussed the details of transaction control using BEGIN TRANSACTION, COMMIT, and ROLLBACK as well as server-side and client-side autocommit modes.

Section 9.4 described savepoints and how they can be used to implement a form of nested subtransaction that allows partial rollbacks.

Sections 9.5 and its subsections showed how to explicitly report problems back to client applications using the SIGNAL, RESIGNAL, RAISERROR, CREATE MESSAGE, and ROLLBACK TRIGGER statements.

Sections 9.6 through 9.7 covered locks, blocks, the trade-off between database consistency and concurrency, and how higher isolation levels can prevent inconsistencies at the cost of lower overall throughput. Section 9.8 discussed cyclical deadlock, thread deadlock, how SQL Anywhere handles them, and how you can fix the underlying problems. Section 9.9 described how mutexes can reduce throughput in a multiple CPU environment.

The next section and its subsections described the relationship between connections, user ids, and privileges, and showed how various forms of the GRANT statement are used to create user ids and give various privileges to these user ids. Subsection 9.10.5 showed how privileges can be inherited via user groups, how permissions differ from privileges, and how user groups can be used to eliminate the need to explicitly specify the owner name when referring to tables and views.

Section 9.11 described various aspects of logging and recovery, including how the transaction, checkpoint, and recovery logs work, what happens during COMMIT and CHECKPOINT operations, and how the logs are used when SQL Anywhere starts a database. The last three sections, 9.12 through 9.14, described database backup and restore procedures and how to validate backup files to make sure they're usable if you need to restore the database.

The next chapter moves from protection to performance: It presents various methods and approaches you can use to improve the performance of SQL Anywhere databases.

Chapter 10

Tuning

10.1 Introduction

"More computing sins are committed in the name of efficiency (without necessarily achieving it) than for any other single reason — including blind stupidity."

William Wulf of Carnegie-Mellon University wrote that in a paper called "A Case Against the GOTO" presented at the annual conference of the ACM in 1972. Those words apply just as well today, to all forms of misguided optimization, including both programs and databases.

Here is another quote, this one more practical because it is more than an observation made after the fact — it is a pair of rules you can follow. These rules come from the book *Principles of Program Design* by Michael A. Jackson, published in 1975 by Associated Press:

Rules on Optimization

Rule 1. Don't do it.

Rule 2. (for experts only) Don't do it yet.

The point is it's more important for an application and a database to be correct and maintainable than it is to be fast, and many attempts to improve performance introduce bugs and increase maintenance effort. Having said that, it is the subject of this chapter: methods and approaches, tips, and techniques you can use to improve the performance of SQL Anywhere databases — if you have to. If nobody's complaining about performance, then skip this chapter; if it ain't broke, don't fix it.

The first topic is request-level logging, which lets you see which SQL statements from client applications are taking all the database server's time. Sometimes that's all you need, to find that "Oops!" or "Aha!" revelation pointing to a simple application change that makes it go much faster. Other times, the queries found by looking at the request-level log can be studied further using other techniques described in this chapter.

The next topic is the Index Consultant, which can be used to determine if your production workload would benefit from any additional indexes. If you have stored procedures and triggers that take time to execute, the section on the Execution Profiler shows how to find the slow bits inside those modules, detail not shown by the request-level logging facility or Index Consultant. The section on the Graphical Plan talks about how to examine individual queries for performance problems involving SQL Anywhere's query engine.

Section 10.6 and its subsections are devoted to file, table, and index fragmentation and ways to deal with it. Even though indexes are discussed throughout this chapter, a separate section is devoted to the details of the CREATE INDEX statement. Another section covers the many database performance counters that SQL Anywhere maintains, and the last section gathers together a list of tips and techniques that didn't get covered in the preceding sections.

10.2 Request-Level Logging

The SQL Anywhere database engine offers a facility called request-level logging that creates a text file containing a trace of requests coming from client applications. This output can be used to determine which SQL statements are taking the most time so you can focus your efforts where they will do the most good.

Here is an example of how you can call the built-in stored procedure sa_server_option from ISQL to turn on request-level logging. The first call specifies the output text file and the second call starts the logging:

```
CALL sa_server_option ( 'Request_level_log_file', 'C:\\temp\\rlog.txt' );
CALL sa_server_option ( 'Request_level_logging', 'SQL+hostvars' );
```

The sa_server_option procedure takes two string parameters: the name of the option you want to set and the value to use.

In the first call above, the file specification 'C:\\temp\\rlog.txt' is relative to the computer running the database server. Output will be appended to the log file if it already exists; otherwise a new file will be created.

Tip: Leave the request-level logging output file on the same computer as the database server; don't bother trying to put it on another computer via a UNC format file specification. You can copy it later for analysis elsewhere or analyze it in place on the server.

The second call above opens the output file, starts the recording process, and sets the level of detail to be recorded. The choices for level of detail are 'SQL' to show SQL statements in the output file, 'SQL+hostvars' to include host variable values together with the SQL statements, and 'ALL' to include other non-SQL traffic that comes from the clients to the server. The first two settings are often used for analyzing performance, whereas 'ALL' is more useful for debugging than performance analysis because it produces an enormous amount of output.

Logging can be stopped by calling sa_server_option again, as follows:

```
CALL sa_server_option ( 'Request_level_logging', 'NONE' );
```

The 'NONE' option value tells the server to stop logging and to close the text file so you can open it with a text editor like WordPad.

Tip: Don't forget to delete the log file or use a different file name if you want to run another test without appending the data to the end of an existing file.

Here is an excerpt from a request-level logging file produced by a short test run against two databases via four connections; the log file grew to 270K containing over 2,400 lines in about four minutes, including the following lines produced for a single SELECT statement:

```
12/04 17:43:18.073 ** REQUEST conn: 305282592  STMT_PREPARE         "SELECT *
   FROM child AS c   WHERE c.non_key_4 LIKE '0000000007%';  "
12/04 17:43:18.073 ** DONE     conn: 305282592  STMT_PREPARE         Stmt=65548
12/04 17:43:18.074 ** REQUEST conn: 305282592  STMT_EXECUTE         Stmt=-1
12/04 17:43:18.074 ** WARNING conn: 305282592  code: 111 "Statement cannot be executed"
12/04 17:43:18.074 ** DONE     conn: 305282592  STMT_EXECUTE
12/04 17:43:18.075 ** REQUEST conn: 305282592  CURSOR_OPEN          Stmt=65548
12/04 17:43:18.075 ** DONE     conn: 305282592  CURSOR_OPEN          Crsr=65549
12/04 17:43:58.400 ** WARNING conn: 305282592  code: 100 "Row not found"
12/04 17:43:58.401 ** REQUEST conn: 305282592  CURSOR_CLOSE         Crsr=65549
12/04 17:43:58.401 ** DONE     conn: 305282592  CURSOR_CLOSE
12/04 17:43:58.409 ** REQUEST conn: 305282592  STMT_DROP            Stmt=65548
12/04 17:43:58.409 ** DONE     conn: 305282592  STMT_DROP
```

The excerpt above shows the full text of the incoming SELECT statement plus the fact that processing started at 17:43:18 and ended at 17:43:58.

Note: The overhead for request-level logging is minimal when only a few connections are active, but it can be heavy if there are many active connections. In particular, setting 'Request_level_logging' to 'ALL' can have an adverse effect on the overall performance for a busy server. That's because the server has to write all the log data for all the connections to a single text file.

There is good news and bad news about request-level logging. The bad news is that the output file is difficult to work with, for several reasons. First, the file is huge; a busy server can produce gigabytes of log data in a very short time. Second, the file is verbose; information about a single SQL statement issued by a client application is spread over multiple lines in the file. Third, the text of each SQL statement appears all on one line without any line breaks (the SELECT above is wrapped to fit on the page, but in the file it doesn't contain any line breaks). Fourth, connection numbers aren't shown, just internal connection handles like "305282592," so it's difficult to relate SQL statements back to the originating applications. Finally, elapsed times are not calculated for each SQL statement; i.e., it's up to you to figure out the SELECT above took 40 seconds to execute.

The good news is that SQL Anywhere includes several built-in stored procedures that can be used to analyze and summarize the request-level logging output. The first of these, called sa_get_request_times, reads the request-level logging output file and performs several useful tasks: It reduces the multiple lines recorded for each SQL statement into a single entry, it calculates the elapsed time for each SQL statement, it determines the connection number corresponding to the connection handle, and it puts the results into a built-in GLOBAL TEMPORARY TABLE called satmp_request_time.

Here's the schema for satmp_request_time:

```
CREATE GLOBAL TEMPORARY TABLE dbo.satmp_request_time (
   req_id        INTEGER NOT NULL,
   conn_id       UNSIGNED INT NULL,
   conn_handle   UNSIGNED INT NULL,
   stmt_num      INTEGER NULL,
   millisecs     INTEGER NOT NULL,
   stmt_id       INTEGER NULL,
```

```
stmt        LONG VARCHAR NOT NULL,
prefix      LONG VARCHAR NULL,
PRIMARY KEY ( req_id ) )
ON COMMIT PRESERVE ROWS;
```

Each row in satmp_request_time corresponds to one SQL statement. The req_id column contains the first line number in the request-level logging file corresponding to that SQL statement and can be used to sort this table in chronological order. The conn_id column contains the actual connection number corresponding to the handle stored in conn_handle. The stmt_num column contains the internal "statement number" from the entries that look like "Stmt=65548" in the request-level logging file. The stmt_id and prefix columns aren't filled in by the sa_get_request_times procedure. The two most useful columns are stmt, which contains the actual text of the SQL statement, and millisecs, which contains the elapsed time.

Here is an example of a call to sa_get_request_times for the request-level logging file shown in the previous excerpt, together with a SELECT to show the resulting satmp_request_time table; the 2,400 lines of data in the text file are reduced to 215 rows in the table:

```
CALL sa_get_request_times ( 'C:\\temp\\rlog.txt' );

SELECT req_id,
       conn_id,
       conn_handle,
       stmt_num,
       millisecs,
       stmt
  FROM satmp_request_time
ORDER BY req_id;
```

Here is what the first three rows of satmp_request_time look like, plus the row corresponding to the SELECT shown in the previous excerpt:

req_id	conn_id	conn_handle	stmt_num	millisecs	stmt
5	1473734206	305182584	65536	3	'SELECT @@version, if ''A''...
11	1473734206	305182584	65537	6	'SET TEMPORARY OPTION ...
17	1473734206	305182584	65538	0	'SELECT connection_property...
...					
1297	1939687630	305282592	65548	40326	'SELECT * FROM child ...

Tip: If you want to match up rows in the satmp_request_time table with lines in the raw input file, you can either use the line number in the req_id column or the stmt_num values. For example, you can use WordPad to do a "find" on "Stmt=65548" to search the log file for the lines corresponding to the fourth row shown above. Be careful, however, if the server has multiple databases running because the statements on each database are numbered independently; the same statement numbers will probably appear more than once.

Here is another SELECT that shows the top 10 most time-consuming statements:

```
SELECT TOP 10
       millisecs,
       stmt
  FROM satmp_request_time
ORDER BY millisecs DESC;
```

Here's what the resulting output looks like:

```
millisecs  stmt
=========  ============================================================
111813     'SELECT c.key_1,         c.key_2,        c.non_key_3, ...
41195      'SELECT *    FROM child AS c  WHERE c.non_key_4 LIKE ''0000000005%''; '
40326      'SELECT *    FROM child AS c  WHERE c.non_key_4 LIKE ''0000000007%''; '
19595      'SELECT p.key_1,         p.non_key_3,     p.non_key_5 ...
17674      'call "dba".p_non_key_3'
257        'call "dba".p_parent_child'
218        'SELECT c.key_1,         c.key_2,        c.non_key_3, ...
217        'SELECT c.key_1,         c.key_2,        c.non_key_3, ...
216        'SELECT c.key_1,         c.key_2,        c.non_key_3, ...
216        'SELECT c.key_1,         c.key_2,        c.non_key_3, ...
```

Tip: You don't have to run these stored procedures and queries on the same database or server that was used to create the request-level log file. Once you've got the file, you can move it to another machine and analyze it there. Every SQL Anywhere database contains the built-in procedures like sa_get_request_times and the tables like satmp_request_time; even a freshly created empty database can be used to analyze a request-level log file from another server.

A second built-in stored procedure, called sa_get_request_profile, does all the same processing as sa_get_request_times plus four extra steps. First, it summarizes the time spent executing COMMIT and ROLLBACK operations into single rows in satmp_request_time. Second, it fills in the satmp_request_time.prefix column with the leading text from "similar" statements; in particular, it eliminates the WHERE clauses. Third, it assigns each row a numeric stmt_id value, with the same values assigned to rows with matching prefix values. Finally, the data from the satmp_request_time table is copied and summarized into a second table, satmp_request_profile.

Here is an example of a call to sa_get_request_profile for the request-level logging file shown in the previous excerpt, together with a SELECT to show the resulting satmp_request_profile table; the 2,400 lines of data in the text file are now reduced to 17 rows in this new table:

```
CALL sa_get_request_profile ( 'C:\\temp\\rlog.txt' );
SELECT *
  FROM satmp_request_profile;
```

Here is what the result set looks like; the satmp_request_profile.uses column shows how many times a SQL statement matching the corresponding prefix was executed, and the total_ms, avg_ms, and max_ms columns show the total time spent, the average time for each statement, and the maximum time spent executing a single statement respectively:

stmt_id	uses	total_ms	avg_ms	max_ms	prefix
1	2	3	1	2	'SELECT @@version, if ''A''<>''a'' then...
2	2	31	15	19	'SET TEMPORARY OPTION Time_format = ...
3	2	1	0	1	'SELECT connection_property(...
4	2	1	0	1	'SELECT db_name()'
5	2	1	0	1	'SELECT @@SERVERNAME'
6	2	8	4	6	'SELECT (SELECT width FROM ...
7	2	28	14	15	'SELECT DISTINCT if domain_name = ...
8	97	10773	111	133	'SELECT customer.company_name, ...
9	1	17674	17674	17674	'call "dba".p_non_key_3'

```
10    10    113742   11374   111813   'SELECT c.key_1,          c.key_2, ...
11    2     81521    40760   41195    'SELECT *      FROM child AS c     '
12    30    21056    701     19595    'SELECT p.key_1,          p.non_key_3, ...
13    28    3067     109     174      'SELECT *      FROM parent AS p    '
14    15    1457     97      257      'call "dba".p_parent_child'
15    15    1304     86      148      'call "dba".p_parent_child_b'
16    1     0        0       0        'CALL sa_server_option ( ...
17    2     0        0       0        'COMMIT'
```

This summary of time spent executing similar SQL statements may be just what
you need to identify where the time-consuming operations are coming from in
the client applications. Sometimes that's enough to point to a solution; for
example, an application may be executing the wrong kind of query or performing an operation too many times, and a change to the application code may
speed things up.

More often, however, the right kind of query is being executed; it's just taking too long, and you need more information about the SQL statement than just
its "prefix." In particular, you may want to see an entire SELECT together with
its WHERE clause so you can investigate further. And you'd like to see the
SELECT in a readable format.

SQL Anywhere offers a third built-in stored procedure, sa_statement_text,
which takes a string containing a SELECT statement and formats it into separate lines for easier reading. Here's an example of a call to sa_statement_text
together with the result set it returns:

```
CALL sa_statement_text
   ( 'SELECT * FROM child AS c WHERE c.non_key_4 LIKE ''0000000007%''' );

stmt_text
=======================================
SELECT *
       FROM child AS c
WHERE c.non_key_4 LIKE ''0000000007%''
```

As it stands, sa_statement_text isn't particularly useful because it's written as a
procedure rather than a function, and it returns a result set containing separate
rows rather than a string containing line breaks. However, sa_statement_text can
be turned into such a function as follows:

```
CREATE FUNCTION f_formatted_statement ( IN @raw_statement LONG VARCHAR )
RETURNS LONG VARCHAR
NOT DETERMINISTIC
BEGIN
   DECLARE @formatted_statement LONG VARCHAR;
   SET @formatted_statement = '';
   FOR fstmt AS cstmt CURSOR FOR
   SELECT sa_statement_text.stmt_text AS @formatted_line
     FROM sa_statement_text ( @raw_statement )
   DO
      SET @formatted_statement = STRING (
         @formatted_statement,
         '\x0d\x0a',
         @formatted_line );
   END FOR;
   RETURN @formatted_statement;
END;
```

The above user-defined function f_formatted_statement takes a raw, unformatted SQL statement as an input parameter and passes it to the sa_statement_text procedure. The formatted result set returned by sa_statement_text is processed, row by row, in a cursor FOR loop that concatenates all the formatted lines together with leading carriage return and linefeed characters '\x0d\x0a'. For more information about cursor FOR loops, see Chapter 6, "Fetching," and for a description of the CREATE FUNCTION statement, see Chapter 8, "Packaging."

Here is an example of a call to f_formatted_statement in an UNLOAD SELECT statement that produces a text file:

```
UNLOAD SELECT f_formatted_statement
    ( 'SELECT * FROM child AS c WHERE c.non_key_4 LIKE ''0000000007%''' )
TO 'C:\\temp\\sql.txt' QUOTES OFF ESCAPES OFF;
```

Here's what the file looks like; even though f_formatted_statement returned a single string value, the file contains four separate lines (three lines of text plus a leading line break):

```
SELECT *
      FROM child AS c
WHERE c.non_key_4 LIKE '0000000007%'
```

The new function f_formatted_statement may be combined with a call to sa_get_request_times to create the following procedure, p_summarize_request_times:

```
CREATE PROCEDURE p_summarize_request_times ( IN @log_filespec LONG VARCHAR )
BEGIN
   CALL sa_get_request_times ( @log_filespec );
   SELECT NUMBER(*)                                          AS stmt_#,
          COUNT(*)                                           AS uses,
          SUM ( satmp_request_time.millisecs )               AS total_ms,
          CAST ( ROUND ( AVG ( satmp_request_time.millisecs ),
                         0 ) AS BIGINT )                     AS avg_ms,
          MAX ( satmp_request_time.millisecs )               AS max_ms,
          f_formatted_statement ( satmp_request_time.stmt ) AS stmt
     FROM satmp_request_time
    GROUP BY satmp_request_time.stmt
   HAVING total_ms >= 100
    ORDER BY total_ms DESC;
END;
```

The p_summarize_request_times procedure above takes the request-level logging output file specification as an input parameter and passes it to the sa_get_request_times built-in procedure so the satmp_request_time table will be filled. Then a SELECT statement with a GROUP BY clause summarizes the time spent by each identical SQL statement (WHERE clauses included). A call to f_formatted_statement breaks each SQL statement into separate lines. The result set is sorted in descending order by total elapsed time, and the NUMBER(*) function is called to assign an artificial "statement number" to each row. The HAVING clause limits the output to statements that used up at least 1/10th of a second in total.

Following is an example of how p_summarize_request_times can be called in an UNLOAD SELECT ... FROM clause to produce a formatted report in a file. For more information about UNLOAD SELECT, see Section 3.25, "UNLOAD TABLE and UNLOAD SELECT."

```
UNLOAD
SELECT STRING ( '-- Statement ',
                stmt_#,
                ': ',
                uses,
                ' uses, ',
                total_ms,
                ' ms total, ',
                avg_ms,
                ' ms average, ',
                max_ms,
                ' ms maximum time ',
                stmt,
                '\x0d\x0a' )
  FROM p_summarize_request_times ( 'C:\\temp\\rlog.txt' )
TO 'C:\\temp\\rlog_summary.txt' QUOTES OFF ESCAPES OFF;
```

The resulting text file, rlog_summary.txt, contained information about 12 different SQL statements. Here's what the first five look like, four SELECT statements and one procedure call:

```
-- Statement 1: 1 uses, 111813 ms total, 111813 ms average, 111813 ms maximum time
SELECT c.key_1,
       c.key_2,
       c.non_key_3,
       c.non_key_5
  FROM child AS c
WHERE c.non_key_5 BETWEEN '1983-01-01'
AND   '1992-01-01 12:59:59'
ORDER BY c.non_key_5;

-- Statement 2: 1 uses, 41195 ms total, 41195 ms average, 41195 ms maximum time
SELECT *
  FROM child AS c
WHERE c.non_key_4 LIKE '0000000005%';

-- Statement 3: 1 uses, 40326 ms total, 40326 ms average, 40326 ms maximum time
SELECT *
  FROM child AS c
WHERE c.non_key_4 LIKE '0000000007%';

-- Statement 4: 1 uses, 19595 ms total, 19595 ms average, 19595 ms maximum time
SELECT p.key_1,
       p.non_key_3,
       p.non_key_5
  FROM parent AS p
WHERE p.non_key_5 BETWEEN '1983-01-01'
AND   '1992-01-01 12:59:59'
ORDER BY p.key_1;

-- Statement 5: 1 uses, 17674 ms total, 17674 ms average, 17674 ms maximum time
call "dba".p_non_key_3
```

Statement 5 in the example above shows that the request-level log gives an overview of the time spent executing procedures that are called directly from the client application, but it contains no information about where the time is spent inside those procedures. It also doesn't contain any information about triggers, or about nested procedures that are called from within other procedures or triggers. For the details about what's going on inside procedure and triggers, you can use the Execution Profiler described in Section 10.4.

Request-level logging is often used to gather information about all the SQL operations hitting a server, regardless of which client connection they're coming from or which database is being used by that connection. For instance, the example above involved four different connections and two databases running on one server.

It is possible, however, to filter the request-level log output to include only requests coming from a single connection. This may be useful if a server is heavily used and there are many connections all doing the same kind of work. Rather than record many gigabytes of repetitive log data or be forced to limit the time spent gathering data, a single representative connection can be monitored for a longer period of time.

To turn on request-level logging for a single connection, first you need to know its connection number. The sa_conn_info stored procedure may be used to show all the connection numbers currently in use, as follows:

```
SELECT sa_conn_info.number AS connection_number,
       sa_conn_info.userid AS user_id,
       IF connection_number = CONNECTION_PROPERTY ( 'Number' )
          THEN 'this connection'
          ELSE 'different connection'
       ENDIF AS relationship
  FROM sa_conn_info();
```

Not only does the result set show all the connections and their user ids, but it also identifies which one is the current connection:

```
connection_number  user_id   relationship
=================  ========  =====================
1864165868         DBA       this connection
286533653          bcarter   different connection
856385086          mkammer   different connection
383362151          ggreaves  different connection
```

The built-in stored procedure sa_server_option can be used to filter request-level logging by connection; the first parameter is the option name 'Requests_for_connection' and the second parameter is the connection number.

Here are the procedure calls to start request-level logging for a single connection; in this case the connection number 383362151 is specified. Also shown is the procedure call to stop logging:

```
CALL sa_server_option ( 'Request_level_log_file', 'C:\\temp\\rlog_single.txt' );
CALL sa_server_option ( 'Requests_for_connection', 383362151 );
CALL sa_server_option ( 'Request_level_logging', 'SQL+hostvars' );
-- Requests from connection 383362151 will now be logged.
CALL sa_server_option ( 'Request_level_logging', 'NONE' );
```

Here is the procedure call that turns off filtering of the request-level logging at the connection level:

```
CALL sa_server_option ( 'Requests_for_connection', -1 );
```

Tip: Don't forget to CALL sa_server_option ('Requests_for_connection', –1) to turn off filtering. Once a specific connection number is defined via the 'Requests_for_connection' call to sa_server_option, it will remain in effect until the connection number is changed by another call, the server is restarted, or –1 is used to turn off filtering.

You can also call sa_server_option to filter request-level logging by database. First, you need to know the database number of the database you're interested in; the following SELECT shows the number and names of all the databases running on a server:

```
SELECT sa_db_properties.number AS database_number,
       sa_db_properties.value  AS database_name,
       IF database_number = CONNECTION_PROPERTY ( 'DBNumber' )
          THEN 'this database'
          ELSE 'different database'
       ENDIF AS relationship
  FROM sa_db_properties()
 WHERE sa_db_properties.PropName = 'Name'
 ORDER BY database_number;
```

The result set shows which database is which, as well as which database is being used by the current connection:

```
database_number   database_name   relationship
===============   =============   ==================
0                 asademo         different database
1                 volume          this database
```

The stored procedure sa_server_option can be used to filter request-level logging by database; the first parameter is 'Requests_for_database' and the second parameter is the database number.

Here are the procedure calls to start request-level logging for a single database; in this case the database number 0 is specified. Also shown is the procedure call to stop logging:

```
CALL sa_server_option ( 'Request_level_log_file', 'C:\\temp\\rdb.txt' );
CALL sa_server_option ( 'Requests_for_database', 0 );
CALL sa_server_option ( 'Request_level_logging', 'SQL+hostvars' );
-- Requests against database 0 will now be logged.
CALL sa_server_option ( 'Request_level_logging', 'NONE' );
```

Here is the procedure call that turns off filtering of the request-level logging at the database level:

```
CALL sa_server_option ( 'Requests_for_database', -1 );
```

Tip: Don't forget to CALL sa_server_option ('Requests_for_database', −1) to turn off filtering. Also, watch out for connection filtering when combined with database filtering; it is easy to accidentally turn off request-level logging altogether by specifying an incorrect combination of filters.

10.3 Index Consultant

When the request-level logging output indicates that several different queries are taking a long time, and you think they might benefit from additional indexes, you can use the Index Consultant to help you figure out what to do.

To use the Index Consultant on a running database, connect to that database with Sybase Central, select the database in the tree view, right-click to open the pop-up menu, and click on Index Consultant... (see Figure 10-1).

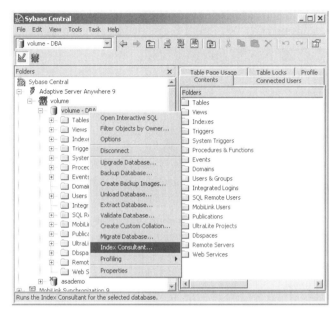

Figure 10-1. Starting the Index Consultant from Sybase Central

The Index Consultant operates as a wizard. The first window lets you begin a new analysis and give it a name in case you choose to save it for later study (see Figure 10-2).

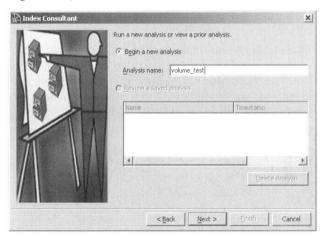

Figure 10-2. Beginning a new Index Consultant analysis

When you click on the Next button in the first wizard window, it displays the status window shown in Figure 10-3. From this point onward, until you click on the Done button, the Index Consultant session will watch and record information about all the queries running on the database. If you're running a workload manually, now is the time to start it from another connection; if there already is work being done on the database from existing connections, it will be monitored by the Index Consultant.

Figure 10-3. Capturing a new Index Consultant workload

From time to time the Captured Queries count will increase to show you that it's really doing something. When you are satisfied that the Index Consultant has seen a representative sample of queries (see Figure 10-4), press the Done button to stop the data capture.

Figure 10-4. Index Consultant capturing done

Before the Index Consultant starts analyzing the data it's just captured, you have to answer some questions about what you want it to do. The first questions have to do with indexes (see Figure 10-5): Do you want it to look for opportunities to create clustered indexes, and do you want it to consider dropping existing indexes if they didn't help with this workload?

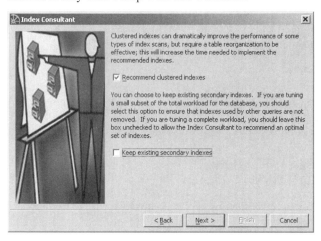

Figure 10-5. Setting index options for the Index Consultant

The next Index Consultant window asks about disk storage (see Figure 10-6):
Do you want it to consider indexes of unlimited size, or do you want to keep
things within limits?

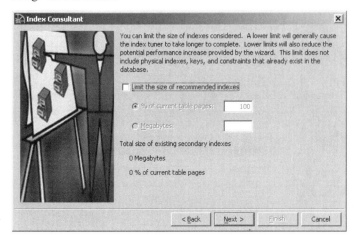

Figure 10-6. Setting disk space options for the Index Consultant

When you click on the Next button after answering the questions, the Index
Consultant will analyze the workload and display the status window shown in
Figure 10-7.

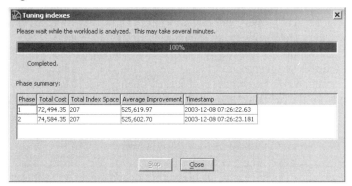

Figure 10-7. Index Consultant analyzing a workload

The next window displayed by the Index Consultant wizard shows the details of
the analysis, including the Recommended Indexes tab shown in Figure 10-8.

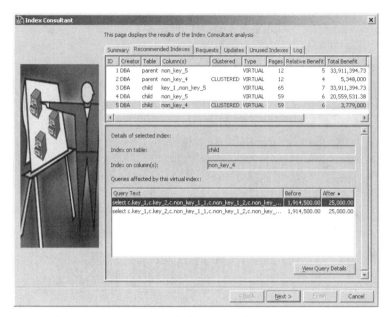

Figure 10-8. Indexes recommended by the Index Consultant

Not only does the Recommended Indexes tab show the indexes it thinks you need, it also shows the queries that would be affected by each new index. You can select a particular query associated with one of the new indexes and press the View Query Details button to see more information about it.

The last window displayed by the Index Consultant wizard is the Recommended Indexes script shown in Figure 10-9. This script contains DROP INDEX commands for any indexes that aren't being used, CREATE INDEX commands for the new ones, plus a REORGANIZE TABLE command for each new clustered index so that table's rows will be re-sorted in the clustered index order. You can press the Save button to save the script in a text file for later use, or press Run Script to make the changes right away.

Tip: Use meaningful names for all your indexes; good names will help you later, when you're trying to remember why the indexes were created in the first place. The Index Consultant generates index names for the Recommended Indexes script shown in Figure 10-9; if index names based on the workload analysis name aren't what you want, you can change them before pressing the Run Script button.

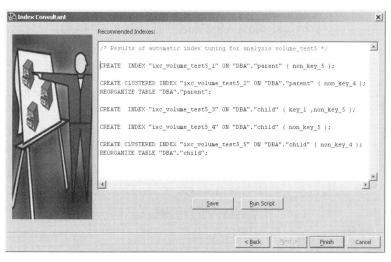

Figure 10-9. Index Consultant Recommended Indexes script

10.4 Execution Profiler

The Execution Profiler is a feature that shows where the time is being spent down inside stored procedures, functions, and triggers. To use the Execution Profiler on a running database, connect to that database with Sybase Central, select the database in the tree view, right-click to open the pop-up menu, and click on Profiling > Start Profiling (see Figure 10-10).

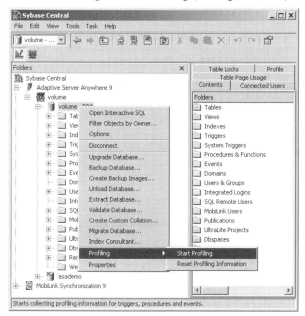

Figure 10-10. Starting the Execution Profiler from Sybase Central

From this point forward, until you click on Profiling > Stop Profiling, SQL Anywhere will gather information about how much time is spent executing each statement inside each stored procedure and trigger in the database.

To see the profile information, select the database in the Sybase Central tree view and click on the Profile tab; at this point you may have to press F5 to refresh the display. The Profile tab will show a list of all the procedures, functions, and triggers that were executed while the profiler was running (see Figure 10-11).

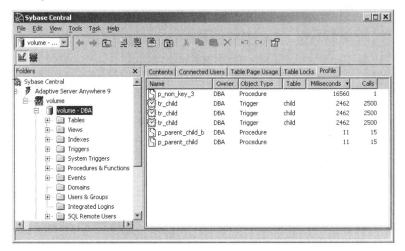

Figure 10-11. Execution Profiler's list of procedure and triggers

Note: The Execution Profiler gathers information inside the database that is being profiled. Unlike request-level logging, you don't have the option of moving the data to another computer and using a different engine to analyze it; you have to remain connected to the database that was profiled.

To see where the time was spent inside a stored procedure or trigger, double-click on its entry in the Profile tab. For example, Figure 10-12 shows the SQL code for the p_non_key_3 procedure together with the amount of time spent executing each statement; in this case 16.5 seconds was spent executing the UPDATE statement.

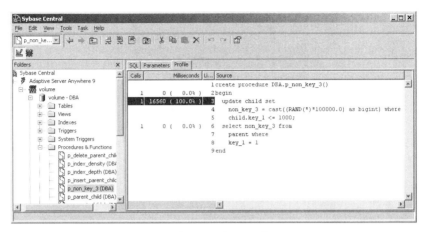

Figure 10-12. Execution profile of a stored procedure

Not all the time spent executing the UPDATE statement in the p_non_key_3 procedure was actually spent updating the child table; some of it was spent in the tr_child trigger that was fired once for each child row being updated. Figure 10-13 shows that 2.5 seconds was spent executing a different UPDATE statement inside tr_child; this UPDATE statement affects the parent table instead of the child.

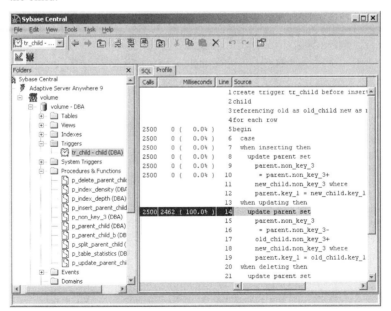

Figure 10-13. Execution profile of a trigger

10.5 **Graphical Plan**

The Graphical Plan is a feature that displays the "execution plan" that SQL Anywhere chooses for a particular query, whether it is a straightforward SELECT or an INSERT, UPDATE, or DELETE involving a query. The execution plan is very important to performance; SQL Anywhere usually chooses the best plan possible given the current state of affairs in the database, but sometimes that choice isn't very good. By looking at the details of the execution plan you can often see what's going wrong and determine changes to the schema or to the query itself that will lead to a better plan and better performance.

The Graphical Plan is displayed by ISQL; the first step is to set a few options by choosing the ISQL menu options Tools > Options and then clicking on Plan to get the options window shown in Figure 10-14.

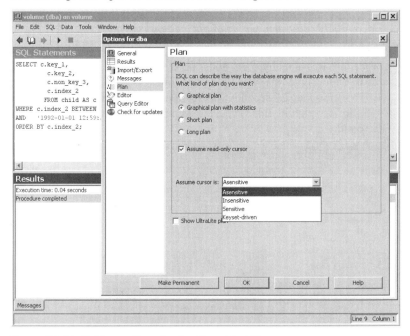

Figure 10-14. Setting options for the Graphical Plan

Here are the options that have been chosen in Figure 10-14:

- The **Graphical plan with statistics** radio button has been selected to gather actual run-time statistics as well as estimates. This option will cause ISQL to actually execute the query, although the result set won't be displayed.
- The **Assume read-only cursor** check box has been checked to mimic the kind of cursor that was used in the actual application program from which the query came. The default is to generate a plan for an updatable cursor, which may be both different and less efficient than the plan used for a read-only cursor.

- The **Assume cursor is: Asensitive** setting has been chosen for the same reason: to use the same kind of cursor processing that was used for the actual application.

- The **Show UltraLite plan** check box has been unchecked to speed up the plan display. An UltraLite plan is very helpful for optimizing queries in UltraLite applications, but that doesn't apply to the examples in this book.

Tip: Be sure to check the Assume read-only cursor check box for any SELECT statement that is really being used in a read-only manner in your application. It can make a huge difference in the plan that ISQL displays and it's important to get the correct information when you're trying to improve performance.

You can display the Graphical Plan by pasting the query into the SQL Statements pane of ISQL and then pressing Shift+F5 or choosing the menu options SQL > Get Plan. For example, here is the most time-consuming SQL statement from an earlier example in Section 10.2, "Request-Level Logging," where the p_summarize_request_times stored procedure was used to display the SQL code for several slow statements:

```
-- Statement 1: 1 uses, 111813 ms total, 111813 ms average, 111813 ms maximum time
SELECT c.key_1,
       c.key_2,
       c.non_key_3,
       c.non_key_5
    FROM child AS c
WHERE c.non_key_5 BETWEEN '1983-01-01'
AND    '1992-01-01 12:59:59'
ORDER BY c.non_key_5;
```

Figure 10-15 shows that same statement, in ISQL, with the Graphical Plan displayed in the Plan tab of the Results pane. The left side of the pane shows the graphical overview as four icons: The SELECT icon represents the query as a whole, the Work icon represents the temporary work table used to produce the result set, the Sort icon represents the sorting done for the ORDER BY, and the icon labeled "c" represents the process required to select rows from the child table. The right side of the pane shows the details for the currently selected icon: In this case the details corresponding to the "c" icon shows that the child table is being scanned sequentially, and that SQL Anywhere estimated that this query would return all 25,000 rows in the child table.

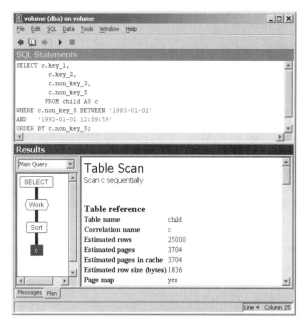

Figure 10-15. Graphical Plan for SELECT table scan

A great deal of information is available in the Graphical Plan display by scrolling down through the statistical data. For example, Figure 10-16 shows that only 748 rows were actually returned by this query, and that the predicate in the WHERE clause matched only 2.99% of the rows. Predicates that are highly

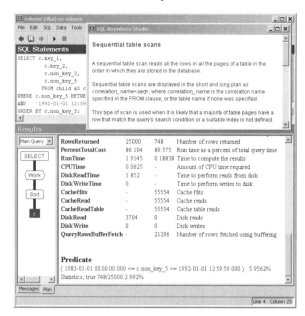

Figure 10-16. Graphical Plan statistics, predicate, and Help

selective often benefit from the existence of an index; i.e., if there were an index
on the non_key_5 column, the execution plan might look completely different,
and performance might be a lot better.

Figure 10-16 also shows the context-sensitive ISQL Help window that can
be displayed by pressing the right mouse button and selecting Help in the
pop-up menu. In this case the Help window describes what it means when a
table scan is used, and mentions that it is often used when "a suitable index is
not defined."

The Graphical Plan display may also be used for INSERT, UPDATE, and
DELETE statements. Figure 10-17 shows the plan for the UPDATE statement
that was copied and pasted from the Execution Profiler display shown earlier in
Figure 10-12.

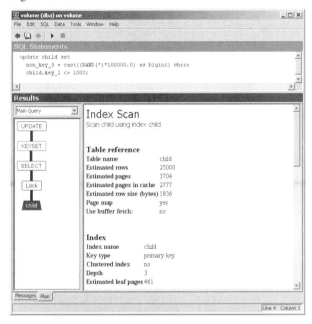

Figure 10-17. Graphical Plan for UPDATE index scan

Figure 10-17 shows that a keyset-driven cursor is used to implement this
multi-row UPDATE statement, and that the primary key index was used to find
the rows in the child table.

You can save the graphical plan in an XML file for later display by selecting the File > Save As menu option in ISQL and setting the Save as type to
XML (*.XML). These XML files contain all the information gathered for the
original plan display. They can be displayed later, in ISQL, without having
access to the original database.

You can also create these graphical plan XML files without using ISQL.
The built-in GRAPHICAL_PLAN function may be used to analyze a string containing a SQL statement and return another string containing the graphical plan
in XML format. You can use GRAPHICAL_PLAN together with UNLOAD
SELECT to save the execution plans for statements contained within stored procedures and triggers. Here is what the syntax looks like:

```
<write_graphical_plan_to_file> ::= UNLOAD SELECT GRAPHICAL_PLAN
                                   "(" <string_containing_SQL_statement> ","
                                       <statistics_level> ","
                                       <cursor_type_parameter> ","
                                       <update_status> ")"
                                   TO <xml_output_filespec> ESCAPES OFF QUOTES OFF
<string_containing_SQL_statement> ::= string literal or variable containing query
<statistics_level>            ::= 0 -- estimates only
                                | 1 -- include summarized actual statistics
                                | 2 -- include detailed actual statistics
<cursor_type_parameter>       ::= 'asensitive'
                                | 'insensitive'
                                | 'sensitive'
                                | 'keyset-driven'
<update_status>               ::= 'READ-ONLY'
                                | 'FOR UPDATE'
<xml_output_filespec> ::= string literal file specification relative to the server
```

This is a useful technique for capturing information about statements that use a host variable whose values are determined at run time. Here is an example of a stored procedure containing a SELECT with a WHERE clause that refers to a procedure parameter:

```
CREATE PROCEDURE p_test_temp ( IN @from_date TIMESTAMP )
BEGIN
SELECT c.key_1,
       c.key_2,
       c.non_key_3,
       c.non_key_5
  FROM child AS c
 WHERE c.non_key_5 BETWEEN @from_date
   AND '1992-01-01 12:59:59'
 ORDER BY c.non_key_5;
END;
```

Here are the step-by-step instructions for adding an UNLOAD SELECT GRAPHICAL_PLAN statement to a procedure:

1. Copy and paste the SELECT so that it appears twice, and modify the second copy as follows.
2. Surround the SELECT with single quotes and double any embedded quotes to make a valid string literal containing the SELECT.
3. If there are any host variables, break up the string literal and use a call to the STRING function to insert the actual host variable values into the string at run time. This may require the addition of more doubled single quotes to surround the host variable values; e.g., quotes around timestamp literals.
4. Wrap the SELECT with the rest of the keywords: the GRAPHICAL_PLAN call and its parameters, the UNLOAD SELECT keywords, the TO file specification, and the ESCAPES OFF and QUOTES OFF options.

Following is what the above procedure looks like after the UNLOAD SELECT GRAPHICAL_PLAN has been added. At run time, the SELECT statement is computed as a string value and passed to GRAPHICAL_PLAN, which then returns a string containing the execution plan in XML format, and that string is written to the file c:\temp\plan_for_embedded_select.xml.

```
CREATE PROCEDURE p_test_temp ( IN @from_date TIMESTAMP )
BEGIN
```

```
SELECT c.key_1,
       c.key_2,
       c.non_key_3,
       c.non_key_5
  FROM child AS c
WHERE c.non_key_5 BETWEEN @from_date
  AND '1992-01-01 12:59:59'
ORDER BY c.non_key_5;

UNLOAD SELECT GRAPHICAL_PLAN ( STRING (
'SELECT c.key_1,
        c.key_2,
        c.non_key_3,
        c.non_key_5
   FROM child AS c
  WHERE c.non_key_5 BETWEEN ''',
@from_date,
''' AND ''1992-01-01 12:59:59''
  ORDER BY c.non_key_5;' ),
2, 'asensitive', 'READ-ONLY' )
TO 'c:\\temp\\plan_for_embedded_select.xml' ESCAPES OFF QUOTES OFF;
END;
```

After the procedure is executed the resulting file plan_for_embedded_select.xml
may be viewed in ISQL by selecting the File > Open menu option and setting
Files of type to XML (*.XML).

10.6 Fragmentation and Reorganization

There are three distinct kinds of fragmentation that can adversely affect performance no matter how carefully you write SQL statements to be efficient: file, table, and index fragmentation. These three kinds of fragmentation, and four different techniques that can be used to deal with it, are discussed in the following sections:

- File fragmentation and disk defragmentation utilities.
- Table fragmentation and the physical organization of data on pages.
- Table reorganization via SQL statements.
- Index fragmentation and how depth and density affects performance.
- Index reorganization via SQL statements.
- Database, or table and index, reorganization using unload and reload.

10.6.1 File Fragmentation

If the physical database file is stored on a heavily fragmented disk drive, the time spent gathering up data from separate locations can slow processing down a great deal. The DB_PROPERTY built-in function can be used to determine if file fragmentation is affecting the database file, as follows:

```
SELECT DB_PROPERTY ( 'DBFileFragments' ) AS db_file_fragments;
```

Anything more than one fragment is less than ideal; large numbers are very bad. Solutions to disk fragmentation depend on the operating system; Figure 10-18 shows what the Windows 2000 Disk Defragmenter utility has to say about one hard drive containing a SQL Anywhere database that was split across 13,556 fragments.

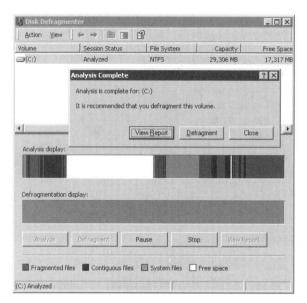

Figure 10-18. Windows 2000 Disk Defragmenter analysis

Disk fragmentation should be dealt with before other kinds of fragmentation. Some operating systems come with disk defragmentation programs, and separate utilities are available for those that don't.

Tip: Some disk defragmentation programs only work well on existing files, not free space, which means you should run them after the files have been created. For example, if you run the Windows 2000 Disk Defragmenter and then create a large database file, that file may be heavily fragmented; the proper order is to create the database first and then run the Disk Defragmenter.

If you anticipate database growth you should preallocate free space in the database file before defragmenting the disk. This will ensure that contiguous space is reserved for the database file before the disk becomes fragmented again. The ALTER DBSPACE command can be used for this; here is the syntax:

```
<add_space_to_database_file> ::= ALTER DBSPACE <database_file_reference>
                                     ADD <number_of_units> [ <units> ]
<database_file_reference>    ::= SYSTEM    -- primary database .DB file
                               | TRANSLOG  -- transaction .LOG file
                               | TEMPORARY -- temporary file for this database
                               | <identifier> -- the DBSPACE name of a secondary
                                                 database file
<number_of_units>            ::= integer literal number of <units> to add
<units>                      ::= PAGES -- default
                               | KB
                               | MB
                               | GB
                               | TB
```

Here is an example that adds 100 megabytes of space to a running database; a command like this only takes a short time to run, in this case a few seconds:

```
ALTER DBSPACE SYSTEM ADD 100 MB;
```

You can use the built-in stored procedure sa_disk_free_space to determine how much space is available on the disks holding each of the physical files. Here is a query that shows the free disk space together with the file specification for each file; the name column will contain "SYSTEM" for the main database file, "Transaction Log" for the .log file, "Transaction Log Mirror" for the mirror log, "Temporary File" for the temporary file, and the name used in the corresponding CREATE DBSPACE statements for any secondary dbspace files:

```
SELECT sa_disk_free_space.dbspace_name                          AS name,
       sa_disk_free_space.free_space                            AS bytes,
       CAST ( TRUNCNUM ( bytes / ( 1024 ), 0 ) AS BIGINT )      AS KB,
       CAST ( TRUNCNUM ( bytes / ( 1024 * 1024 ), 0 ) AS BIGINT )   AS MB,
       CAST ( TRUNCNUM ( bytes / ( 1024 * 1024 * 1024 ), 0 ) AS BIGINT ) AS GB,
       CASE name
           WHEN 'SYSTEM'                 THEN DB_PROPERTY ( 'File' )
           WHEN 'Transaction Log'        THEN DB_PROPERTY ( 'LogName' )
           WHEN 'Transaction Log Mirror' THEN DB_PROPERTY ( 'LogMirrorName' )
           WHEN 'Temporary File'         THEN DB_PROPERTY ( 'TempFileName' )
           ELSE ( SELECT SYSFILE.file_name
                    FROM SYSFILE
                   WHERE SYSFILE.dbspace_name = name )
       END AS file
  FROM sa_disk_free_space();
```

Here is an example of what the output looks like; the name and free space amounts come from the sa_disk_free_space procedure, whereas the file specifications come from the SYSFILE table for the secondary dbspace "extend" and from the built-in DB_PROPERTY function for the other files:

```
name                     bytes         KB         MB      GB  file
=================        ===========   ========   =====   ==  ====================
SYSTEM                   3546898432    3463768    3382    3   e:\\xdb\\demo.db
extend                   12201697280   11915720   11636   11  c:\\xtend\\extend.db
Transaction Log          12201697280   11915720   11636   11  c:\\xlog\\demo.log
Transaction Log Mirror   3546898432    3463768    3382    3   e:\\xmirror\\demo.mlg
Temporary File           3546898432    3463768    3382    3   e:\\xtemp\\asat0000.tmp
```

Note: The free_space number reported by sa_disk_free_space is the amount of free space on the disk, outside of any particular file, not free space inside the database file itself. That means sa_disk_free_space reports the same free_space number for all database files that reside on the same disk.

Note: Each running database has its own separate temporary file, which is automatically created when necessary and deleted when it is no longer needed.

10.6.2 Table Fragmentation

Even if the disk isn't fragmented, and all the database files are contained in contiguous areas on the disk, the actual table data inside the database can be highly fragmented. Like disk fragmentation, table fragmentation can slow down performance and it is worth investigating.

When a new row is inserted, it is placed in a contiguous area on a single page. If there is not enough free space on a page that already contains data from other rows, an empty page is taken. If the row is larger than one page or contains one or more long columns that contain 255 or more bytes, the row is split across two or more pages, but those are the only conditions that prevent a new row from being inserted entirely within a single page.

Note: Data for different tables is never stored on the same page. Also, the table's PCTFREE setting is honored when a new row is inserted: If the free space on a page containing existing data would sink below the PCTFREE setting when inserting a new row, that page is not chosen for the new row. In other words, the PCTFREE free space may be consumed by an UPDATE later on, but an INSERT leaves it alone. For more information about PCTFREE, see Section 1.12, "Free Space."

Subsequent UPDATE operations may cause a row to grow beyond its original page. That can happen for two reasons: First, one or more short columns grow in size by an amount larger than the free space remaining on the page, and second, one or more long columns grow to 255 bytes or longer. In the first case, the row splits because it won't fit. In the second case, a blob column causes a split as soon as it grows to 255 bytes.

Row splits are generally a bad thing, especially row splits caused by short columns. Row splits lead to table fragmentation, and heavy table fragmentation can slow down processing a great deal, affecting both SELECT operations that must gather together the split rows and UPDATE operations that must spend time handling new splits.

SQL Anywhere offers some facilities for measuring table fragmentation, and these measurements are based on the following definitions:

- A *short column* is any column that can't grow beyond 254 bytes in length, whereas a *long column* can hold more. Both kinds of columns can cause fragmentation, and the kind of fragmentation caused by short columns is often worse.
- A *row segment* is all or part of one row that is contained on one page, excluding the portions of long columns beyond 254 bytes. A row may have one or more row segments.
- A *table page* is a page containing the leading row segments of one or more rows of data.
- The placement of each leading row segment on a page is *immutable*. That means once the leading row segment for a row has been inserted on a particular table page, subsequent UPDATE operations never move that leading row segment to a different page. In other words, an UPDATE may cause parts of the row to be moved to other row segments on other pages because they no longer fit on this page, but the first part of the row always remains on its original table page. The only exception to this is the REORGANIZE TABLE statement, discussed in the next section in this chapter.
- A *row continuation* is that part of a row that does not fit in the leading row segment, excluding the portions of long columns beyond 254 bytes. A row continuation consists of one or more row segments. Row continuations are caused by short column row splits.

- A *blob continuation* is that part of a row containing the portion of a single long column that has grown longer than 254 bytes. Each long column is treated separately, with its own blob continuation for the overflow data. Blob continuations are caused by long column row splits. Note that a column that is exactly 255 bytes in length requires a blob continuation, but that blob continuation is empty of data; the first 255 bytes of each long column is always stored together with the short columns in one of the row segments.

- An *extension page* is a page containing data for row and/or blob continuations. Extension pages are sometimes referred to as the "blob arena" but they are not limited to blobs. Unlike table pages, data on extension pages is dynamically rearranged so that each row continuation is stored contiguously in column order. Also, each blob continuation is managed independently and is stored contiguously. However, SQL Anywhere does not use table bitmaps to efficiently locate extension pages; table bitmaps are only used for table pages.

Tip: If your UPDATE performance grinds to a halt, it might not have anything to do with execution plans or indexes. It might be caused by short columns that are growing in size, causing more row splits in an already heavily fragmented table. SQL Anywhere might be spending a lot of time shuffling pages around to keep the row continuation data in contiguous order.

The built-in sa_table_fragmentation stored procedure can be used to show the average number of row segments per row for each table. Here is an example of how to call sa_table_fragmentation to show all the tables owned by DBA:

```
CHECKPOINT;
SELECT *
  FROM sa_table_fragmentation ( owner_name = 'DBA' );
```

Note: Explicit CHECKPOINT statements are not normally required but in this case one is used to force SQL Anywhere to store up-to-date row counts in the SYSTABLE system catalog table so they can be reported by sa_table_fragmentation.

Here is an example of the output from sa_table_fragmentation; the segs_per_row column shows the average number of row segments per row. A segs_per_row value of 1 is as good as it gets, and any value much above 1 indicates a high degree of fragmentation; e.g., a value of 1.5 means that half of the rows are partitioned. Three of the tables listed here have very high values of segs_per_row: child, parent, and twide. On average, almost every row in the child and parent tables has row continuations caused by short column row splits, and the single row in the twide table has been split several times. Only the normal and tblob tables have no row continuations; their segs_per_row values of 1.0 are ideal:

```
TableName   rows    row_segments   segs_per_row
=========   =====   ============   ============
child       25000   49073          1.96292
normal      1       1              1.0
parent      5000    9999           1.9998
```

```
tblob      1      1           1.0
twide      1      4           4.0
```

Note: A call to sa_table_fragmentation can take a long time and require a lot of disk I/O, especially for large, fragmented tables with many pages that are not currently in the cache.

Another useful built-in procedure is called sa_table_stats; it shows the number of table pages and extension pages for each table, as follows:

```
SELECT sa_table_stats.table_name      AS table_name,
       sa_table_stats.count           AS rows,
       sa_table_stats.table_page_count AS table_pages,
       sa_table_stats.ext_page_count  AS ext_pages
  FROM sa_table_stats()
 WHERE sa_table_stats.creator = 'DBA'
 ORDER BY table_name;
```

The following shows what the output from sa_table_stats looks like for the same tables as the earlier example; as expected, the three tables that had a lot of row continuations also have a large number of extension pages: child, parent, and twide. However, the tblob table also has a large number of extension pages, 104, even though it didn't show up earlier as having any row continuations; that's because tblob contains a long column that required a blob continuation rather than a row continuation.

```
table_name  rows    table_pages  ext_pages
==========  =====   ===========  =========
child       25000   3704         49073
normal      1       1            1
parent      5000    360          10013
tblob       1       1            104
twide       1       1            3
```

Here is a procedure that combines the output of both the sa_table_fragmentation and sa_table_stats procedures so you can see the data about row segments and extension pages side by side:

```
CREATE PROCEDURE p_table_fragmentation ( IN @owner_name VARCHAR ( 128 ) )
RESULT ( table_name       VARCHAR ( 128 ),
         rows             UNSIGNED INTEGER,
         row_segments     UNSIGNED BIGINT,
         segments_per_row DOUBLE,
         table_pages      UNSIGNED BIGINT,
         extension_pages  UNSIGNED BIGINT )
BEGIN
SELECT *
  INTO #sa_table_fragmentation
  FROM sa_table_fragmentation ( owner_name = @owner_name );

SELECT #sa_table_fragmentation.TableName      AS table_name,
       #sa_table_fragmentation.rows           AS rows,
       #sa_table_fragmentation.row_segments   AS row_segments,
       #sa_table_fragmentation.segs_per_row   AS segments_per_row,
       sa_table_stats.table_page_count        AS table_pages,
       sa_table_stats.ext_page_count          AS extension_pages
  FROM #sa_table_fragmentation
       INNER JOIN sa_table_stats()
           ON sa_table_stats.table_name = #sa_table_fragmentation.TableName
 WHERE sa_table_stats.creator = @owner_name
```

```
ORDER BY table_name;
END;
SELECT * FROM p_table_fragmentation ( 'DBA' );
```

Following is the output from the call to p_table_fragmentation showing the same five tables. Tables where segments_per_row is large but extension_pages more or less matches row_segments (in this case child, parent, twide) probably have fragmentation caused by row continuations, whereas tables where the segments_per_row is 1 or close to it but have a comparatively large number of extension pages (tblob) probably have fragmentation caused by blob continuations.

table_name	rows	row_segments	segments_per_row	table_pages	extension_pages
child	25000	49073	1.96292	3704	49073
normal	1	1	1.0	1	1
parent	5000	9999	1.9998	360	10013
tblob	1	1	1.0	1	104
twide	1	4	4.0	1	3

Note: The sa_table_stats procedure is currently undocumented and it is primarily intended to report on the current contents of the cache. In the p_table_fragmentation procedure above, sa_table_stats is only being called to obtain information about table and extension pages. That information is not available immediately after database startup because the cache hasn't been populated yet, and that's why the call to sa_table_fragmentation is placed first in the procedure: It forces the cache to be populated so the subsequent call to sa_table_stats will return useful information.

Following is yet another query that reports 'Fragmentation!' for tables where these conditions are satisfied: when the average number of segments per row is 1.05 or larger, and/or when the ratio of extension pages to row segments is 2 or larger. The first condition detects table fragmentation caused by row continuations and the second attempts to detect fragmentation caused by blob continuations. Both of the numbers 1.05 and 2 are arbitrary thresholds that can be changed, perhaps to match actual values measured when performance begins to degrade.

```
SELECT table_name,
       segments_per_row,
       CAST ( IF rows = 0
                THEN 0
                ELSE CAST ( extension_pages AS DOUBLE ) / row_segments
              ENDIF AS FLOAT ) AS extension_pages_per_segment,
       IF segments_per_row >= 1.05
          THEN 'Fragmentation!'
          ELSE IF extension_pages_per_segment >= 2
                 THEN 'Fragmentation!'
                 ELSE ''
               ENDIF
       ENDIF AS fragmentation
  FROM p_table_fragmentation ( 'DBA' )
ORDER BY table_name;
```

Here's what the 'Fragmentation!' report looks like — nice and easy to read and interpret; only the normal table escapes detection:

```
table_name  segments_per_row  extension_pages_per_segment  fragmentation
==========  ================  ===========================  =============
child       1.96292           1.0                          Fragmentation!
normal      1.0               1.0
parent      1.9998            1.0014001                    Fragmentation!
tblob       1.0               104.0                        Fragmentation!
twide       4.0               0.75                         Fragmentation!
```

Note: Extension pages may be used for both row continuations and blob continuations, and there is no accurate way of determining which is which. The 'Fragmentation' query above isn't perfect, but it probably won't miss too many tables that are causing trouble, and it probably won't give too many false warnings.

10.6.3 Table Reorganization

One way to deal with table fragmentation is to periodically use the REORGANIZE TABLE statement. Here is the syntax:

```
<reorganize_table> ::= REORGANIZE TABLE [ <owner_name> "." ] <table_name>
```

The REORGANIZE TABLE statement rebuilds all the table pages by deleting and re-inserting rows. If a clustered index exists, then it is used to determine the order in which the rows are inserted; otherwise the order is determined by the primary key. That means REORGANIZE TABLE won't work for a table that has neither a primary key nor a clustered index.

The REORGANIZE TABLE process works by deleting and re-inserting rows in large groups while holding an exclusive lock on the table. When it finishes with a group of rows, it releases the lock to allow other processes to proceed if they've been blocked by the reorganization process. After a while the reorganization process will obtain the table lock again and proceed with the next group. This process won't completely kill performance for other connections but it may reduce concurrency on a busy server, so running REORGANIZE TABLE during the busiest time of the day might not be a good idea.

Tip: Execute the following statement just before starting a long-running REORGANIZE TABLE statement: SET TEMPORARY OPTION BACKGROUND_PRIORITY = 'ON'. This tells SQL Anywhere that this connection should give up control more often to allow other higher-priority connections to get some work done. In fact, this tip isn't just for REORGANIZE TABLE — it applies to any connection that does a lot of work but doesn't need rapid response.

The REORGANIZE TABLE statement does not cause any triggers to fire, and it does not write anything to the transaction log; from a logical point of view it isn't changing any data, just moving it around on different pages. It does cause the checkpoint log to grow, however, because database pages are changing and they must be written to the database file at the next checkpoint.

The form of REORGANIZE TABLE used in this section does not affect any of the indexes associated with the table. For more information about index fragmentation, see the next section in this chapter.

Here is an example of REORGANIZE TABLE followed by a call to p_table_fragmentation to show the effect:

```
REORGANIZE TABLE child;
CHECKPOINT;
SELECT * FROM p_table_fragmentation ( 'DBA' );
```

Here is what p_table_fragmentation reports for the child table, both before and after the REORGANIZE TABLE. The segments_per_row value drops to a perfect 1.0, indicating that all the row continuations have been eliminated. Also, the number of extension pages has dropped by half, with the remaining extension pages required for blob continuations:

table_name	rows	row_segments	segments_per_row	table_pages	extension_pages	
child	25000	49073	1.96292	3704	49073	-- BEFORE
child	25000	25000	1.0	25001	25008	-- AFTER

Several techniques may be used to avoid table fragmentation in the first place, or at least minimize its effects:

- Don't insert empty rows and immediately update them with non-empty values. If the real values are available at the point of INSERT, use them.
- Avoid inserting NULL values in columns that will be later updated with non-NULL values. A NULL column value takes up no space at all, so updating it with any non-NULL value will always cause the row to grow in size.
- Avoid inserting short or empty strings if they will be later updated with longer values. Insert the real values, or pad the initial value with blanks.
- Do not repeatedly update large numbers of rows so they grow in size with each update. That kind of processing is almost guaranteed to result in a heavily fragmented table, and the update process will probably become slower and slower with each repetition, eventually running about as fast as continental drift.
- Specify a larger PCTFREE value for tables whose rows are likely to grow in size when short columns are updated. For more information about PCTFREE, see Section 1.12, "Free Space."
- Place frequently used short columns near the front of the row so that even if a row split occurs, those columns will remain on the table page instead of way out on an extension page.

10.6.4 Index Fragmentation

Index fragmentation is both different from and similar to file and table fragmentation. Index fragmentation has different causes, it is measured differently, and it has different solutions. On the other hand, the effect of index fragmentation on performance is similar to that of file and table fragmentation: All of them are bad.

Index entries are stored in pages just like table data. Every index starts with a single page at the top (level 1), and that page will most certainly reside in the cache. As more entries are added, a wide and shallow tree structure of pages is constructed, consisting of two or more levels. The number of levels is called the depth; the larger this value, the slower the index becomes because extra disk I/O is required to move from a page at one level to another page one level down.

If all the pages are full of index entries and the tree is nicely balanced, performance will be reasonable. The depth of the index will be governed by the size of the index entries and the page size of the database. However, if the index becomes unbalanced, and/or pages become partially empty, the index depth may be greater than is required by the data. When this happens, the index is fragmented and performance suffers.

A couple of built-in stored procedures are available to measure index fragmentation. One of these is called sa_index_levels; here is an example of a call that displays all the indexes on tables owned by DBA:

```
SELECT *
  FROM sa_index_levels ( owner_name = 'DBA' )
 ORDER BY sa_index_levels.TableName,
       sa_index_levels.IndexName;
```

Following is the resulting output from sa_index_levels for a sample database; it shows the primary key indexes for five tables plus one foreign key index. The fact that the child table primary key index has three levels is not a good sign; the database page size is 4K, the primary key is a narrow INTEGER column, and there are only 25,000 rows in the table so two levels should be sufficient, and the extra level may double the disk I/O required to use this index.

```
TableName  IndexName  Levels
=========  =========  ======
child      child      3       -- child table primary key index
child      parent     2       -- child table foreign key index
normal     normal     1       -- normal table primary key index
parent     parent     2       -- parent table primary key index
tblob      tblob      1       -- tblob table primary key index
twide      twide      1       -- twide table primary key index
```

Tip: A two-level index is okay, three levels is bad, and four is astonishingly bad.

The other built-in stored procedure is called sa_index_density; it reports the density of each index, which is a measure of how full each index page is on average. It also reports the number of leaf pages in each index, which is the number of index pages that contain index entries. Here is an example of how to call sa_index_density:

```
SELECT *
  FROM sa_index_density ( owner_name = 'DBA' )
 ORDER BY sa_index_density.TableName,
       sa_index_density.IndexName;
```

A density close to 1.0 is good, whereas a density of 0.25 is very bad. Here's what the output from sa_index_density looks like for the six indexes. The density of the child table primary key index is less than 0.25, which means that on average each page is mostly empty; that explains why that index has three levels instead of two:

```
TableName  IndexName  LeafPages  Density
=========  =========  =========  ========
child      child      461        0.249984
child      parent     218        0.263677
normal     normal     1          0.014893
parent     parent     34         0.478322
```

```
tblob     tblob     1       0.014893
twide     twide     1       0.014893
```

The following procedure joins the output from sa_index_levels and
sa_index_density in a more convenient display. It also adds the row count from
SYSTABLE, and calculates a "concerns" column to warn about potential
problems:

```
CREATE PROCEDURE p_index_fragmentation ( IN @owner_name VARCHAR ( 128 ) )
RESULT ( table_name    VARCHAR ( 128 ),
         index_name    VARCHAR ( 128 ),
         rows          UNSIGNED BIGINT,
         leaf_pages    UNSIGNED INTEGER,
         levels        INTEGER,
         density       NUMERIC ( 8, 6 ),
         concerns      VARCHAR ( 100 ) )
BEGIN
SELECT sa_index_levels.TableName    AS table_name,
       sa_index_levels.IndexName    AS index_name,
       SYSTABLE.count               AS rows,
       sa_index_density.LeafPages   AS leaf_pages,
       sa_index_levels.Levels       AS levels,
       sa_index_density.Density     AS density,
       STRING (
          IF levels > 2
             THEN 'deep'
             ELSE ''
          ENDIF,
          IF levels > 1 AND density < 0.5
             THEN IF levels > 2
                     THEN ', low density'
                     ELSE 'low density'
                  ENDIF
             ELSE ''
          ENDIF ) AS concerns
  FROM sa_index_levels ( owner_name = @owner_name )
       INNER JOIN sa_index_density ( owner_name = @owner_name )
            ON sa_index_density.TableName = sa_index_levels.TableName
            AND sa_index_density.IndexName = sa_index_levels.IndexName
       INNER JOIN SYSTABLE
            ON SYSTABLE.table_name = sa_index_density.TableName
WHERE USER_NAME ( SYSTABLE.creator ) = 'DBA'
ORDER BY table_name,
         index_name;
END;
```

Here is a sample call to p_index_fragmentation; the CHECKPOINT statement
is used to force the storage of up-to-date row count values in the
SYSTABLE.count column:

```
CHECKPOINT;
CALL p_index_fragmentation ( 'DBA' );
```

Here's what the output from p_index_fragmentation looks like; the "concerns"
column contains the word 'deep' if the number of levels is greater than 2, and
the phrase 'low density' appears when the density is less than 0.5 for an index
with more than one level:

```
table_name  index_name  rows   leaf_pages  levels  density   concerns
==========  ==========  =====  ==========  ======  ========  =================
child       child       25000  461         3       0.249984  deep, low density
child       parent      25000  218         2       0.263677  low density
```

normal	normal	1	1	1	0.014893	
parent	parent	5000	34	2	0.478322	low density
tblob	tblob	1	1	1	0.014893	
twide	twide	1	1	1	0.014893	

SQL Anywhere doesn't rebalance indexes when rows are deleted; that's the single largest cause of index fragmentation, and that's how the child and parent table indexes above got to be that way. Large indexes that have too many levels and too many partially filled index pages will cause performance problems every time they're used to satisfy a query.

10.6.5 Index Reorganization

The following three forms of the REORGANIZE TABLE statement can be used to reorganize indexes:

```
<reorganize_index> ::= REORGANIZE TABLE [ <owner_name> "." ] <table_name>
                           PRIMARY KEY
                     | REORGANIZE TABLE [ <owner_name> "." ] <table_name>
                           FOREIGN KEY <constraint_or_role_name>
                     | REORGANIZE TABLE [ <owner_name> "." ] <table_name>
                           INDEX <index_name>
<constraint_or_role_name> ::= <identifier> used as CONSTRAINT or role name
<identifier>              ::= see <identifier> in Chapter 1, "Creating"
```

The first form uses the keywords PRIMARY KEY to specify that the primary key index is to be reorganized. The second form specifies the keywords FOREIGN KEY together with the role name for a foreign key relationship to specify that a foreign key index is to be reorganized. The third form uses the keyword INDEX together with an index name to specify that a regular non-key index is to be reorganized. Although they all say "REORGANIZE TABLE," none of these statements touch the table data; even if the index is clustered, only the index pages themselves are affected, not the table pages.

Note: The third form of REORGANIZE TABLE may also be used to reorganize the index that's automatically created for a UNIQUE constraint. For example, if the child table had a constraint defined as UNIQUE (key_2, key_3), then the following statement will reorganize the associated index: REORGANIZE TABLE child INDEX "child UNIQUE (key_2,key_3)". Don't bother trying to predict what index name to use; simply call the sa_index_density procedure described in the previous section to find out what it's called.

Here is an example of three REORGANIZE TABLE statements that can be used to reorganize the three fragmented indexes described in the previous section. By default, the role name of a foreign key is the same as the name of the other table (the parent) in the relationship; in this case, the table called child has a foreign key relationship with a table that is actually named "parent," so that's the role name used in the second REORGANIZE TABLE:

```
REORGANIZE TABLE child PRIMARY KEY;
REORGANIZE TABLE child FOREIGN KEY parent;
REORGANIZE TABLE parent PRIMARY KEY;
```

Here is what a call to the p_index_fragmentation procedure displays for the three indexes after they have been reorganized; the number of leaf pages has dropped and the density has increased because the index entries have been packed to fill up the pages, the number of levels has dropped from three to two for the child table foreign key index, and the "concerns" column no longer reports any problems:

```
table_name  index_name  rows   leaf_pages  levels  density   concerns
==========  ==========  =====  ==========  ======  ========  ==================
child       child       25000  111         2       1.001269
child       parent      25000  56          2       0.993517
parent      parent      5000   16          2       1.003250
```

Using REORGANIZE TABLE to reorganize an index is not nearly as time-consuming as reorganizing the table itself, so it may not have an adverse effect on the performance of other connections. It works by rebuilding the index from scratch rather than moving index entries around on the index pages. In other words, it may be okay to reorganize an index on a busy server.

10.6.6 Database Reorganization with Unload/Reload

The ultimate, brute-force technique for reorganizing an entire database is to unload all the data, recreate the database from scratch, and then reload all the data. This is also the only way to reduce the amount of disk space used by the database file; other techniques may reorganize data inside the file but they cannot reduce the file size.

The following steps can be used to perform a database reorganization via unload/reload; these steps assume some time is available to take the database offline:

1. Disconnect all other users from the old database.
2. Unload the old database with dbunload.exe.
3. Stop the old database.
4. Back-up and remove the old database.
5. Create a new database file with dbinit.exe.
6. Start the new database.
7. Increase the size of the new database file with ALTER DBSPACE in ISQL.
8. Defragment the hard drive.
9. Examine and edit the reload.sql file if necessary.
10. Load the new database by running reload.sql via ISQL.
11. Check to make sure everything's okay.
12. Make the new database available.

Here are the steps described in more detail:

Step 1: Disconnect all other users from the old database. You are going to unload all the data and delete the entire database, and you don't want to include changes made on other connections that are going to be rolled back, or miss changes that are made and committed after a table has been unloaded. Also, the unload process may be blocked by locks held by other connections, and vice versa.

Tip: In a network environment, one way to prevent other users from connecting to a database is to stop the network server dbsrv9.exe and restart the database file using the standalone engine dbeng9.exe. The standalone engine doesn't allow network connections.

Here is an example of a Windows batch file to start a database using dbeng9.exe; the -x none parameter speeds engine startup by only loading support for shared memory connections (no TCP/IP, etc.):

```
"%ASANY9%\win32\dbeng9.exe" -x none volume.db
```

Step 2: Run the SQL Anywhere dbunload.exe program to create an unloaded data file in text format for each table, as well as a reload.sql command file to be used later to load that data into a new database. If possible, the disk drive used to hold the unloaded data files should be a different physical drive from the one used to hold the database file itself; that will speed up the unload and reload processes.

Following is an example of a Windows batch file to run dbunload.exe. The -c parameter is required to specify how dbunload.exe is to connect to the database. An ODBC DSN is used here for convenience, but the program only uses it to find other connection parameters; it doesn't actually use ODBC for the connection. The -r option provides the file specification of the .sql command file to be used later to reload the database; this file specification is relative to the computer used to run dbunload.exe. The final parameter is the drive and folder to be used to receive the text .dat files holding the unloaded table data; this parameter is relative to the computer running the database, not the computer running dbunload.exe. In this case, dbunload.exe is run on the same computer as the database engine to make everything fast and simple, and the same folder, c:\temp, is used to receive the reload.sql file and all the unloaded data files:

```
"%ASANY9%\win32\dbunload.exe" -c "DSN=volume" -j 3 -r c:\temp\reload.sql c:\temp
```

The resulting reload.sql file contains all the CREATE TABLE and other statements necessary to completely recreate the database schema. It also contains one LOAD TABLE statement for each table, referencing the .dat file that dbunload.exe created to hold the table's data. Here is an excerpt from an actual reload.sql file showing the LOAD TABLE statement for a table called "parent" that refers to the file c:\temp\428.dat:

```
LOAD TABLE "DBA"."parent" ("key_1", "non_key_1_1", "non_key_1_2", "non_key_1_3",
   "non_key_1_4", "non_key_1_5", "non_key_1_6", "non_key_1_7", "non_key_1_8",
   "non_key_1_9", "non_key_1_10", "non_key_1_11", "non_key_1_12", "non_key_2",
   "non_key_3", "index_1", "index_2" )
     FROM 'c:\\temp\\428.dat'
     FORMAT 'ASCII' QUOTES ON
     ORDER OFF ESCAPES ON
     CHECK CONSTRAINTS OFF COMPUTES OFF
     STRIP OFF DELIMITED BY ','
```

For more information about the LOAD TABLE statement, see Section 2.3, "LOAD TABLE."

The -j 3 option in the dbunload.exe command line above is a way to handle the problem of interdependencies among different view definitions. For example, if one view refers to another view that is defined later in the reload.sql file, the first CREATE VIEW statement will fail. The -j option lets you generate multiple (in this case, three) copies of all the CREATE VIEW statements so that for each view, one of its CREATE VIEW statements will work; all the other CREATE VIEW statements for that view will fail, either because the view has already been created or it is dependent on a view that hasn't been created yet.

The failures don't matter; all that matters is that each view is created successfully at some point in the repetitions.

Step 3: Stop the database server, or at least stop the database on the server. This is necessary because the old database is no longer necessary and it's going to be backed up and removed.

Step 4: Back up and remove the old database file and transaction log. This might be as simple as renaming the files or moving them to another folder or disk drive.

Step 5: Create a new database file with dbinit.exe. This program should be run on the same computer as the database engine will run. Here is an example of a Windows batch file that creates a database with a 4K page size:

```
"%ASANY9%\win32\dbinit.exe" -p 4096 volume.db
```

Tip: Always use the -p option with dbinit.exe to explicitly specify the page size. Once the page size is chosen it cannot be changed without unloading and reloading the database file. If in doubt, use 4096 or 4K. The default is 2K, which is almost never a good choice; most of the other possible page sizes are even worse and should rarely, if ever, be used: 1K, 16K, and 32K. In some cases, however, 8192 or 8K is a good choice: Wide indexes on large tables will have fewer levels with an 8K page size because more index entries will fit on a page. Note that while there is no limit to the number of index entries that may be stored in a single page, only 255 rows of data can be stored in a page; that means rows with an average length of 16 bytes will fill a 4K page, but the average length of a row must be at least 32 bytes to avoid wasting space with an 8K page size. And here's another rule of thumb: Don't start thinking about 8K pages until a busy table grows to 500,000 rows or more.

Tip: If you run more than one database on the same server, make sure all the databases use the same page size. Otherwise, cache space will be wasted when small-size pages are loaded into memory using the larger page size. If you really need to run two databases with different page sizes, consider using two separate servers so each one can efficiently manage its own cache. Dynamic cache sizing will favor the busy server so its cache will grow and the other one will shrink. Don't run two servers if the database page sizes are the same, however; in that case one server with two databases is the better approach.

Step 6: Start the new database, but don't allow anyone else to connect to it yet.

Step 7: Increase the size of the database file with ALTER DBSPACE in ISQL. This will guarantee that contiguous space will be held for the database after the disk is defragmented in the next step, preventing the ill effects of future disk fragmentation. It will also speed up the reload process because the database file won't have to be expanded in small increments, over and over and over again.

Here is an example of a Windows batch file to start ISQL in interactive mode; an ODBC DSN is used to provide the connection parameters (server and database name, user id, and password) but ISQL doesn't actually use ODBC to make the connection:

```
"%ASANY9%\win32\dbisql.exe" -c "DSN=volume"
```

Here is an example of an ALTER DBSPACE statement that adds 800 megabytes to a main database file:

```
ALTER DBSPACE SYSTEM ADD 800 MB;
```

For more information about ALTER DBSPACE, see Section 10.6.1, "File Fragmentation," earlier in this chapter.

Step 8: Defragment the hard drive. Disk fragmentation hurts performance, and this is an excellent opportunity to make it go away. This step is performed after the database is increased in size (Step 7) because some disk defragmentation tools only work well on existing files.

Step 9: Examine the reload.sql file for logical problems, and edit the file to fix them if necessary. You can perform this step any time after Step 2, and it is completely optional. Sometimes, however, databases are subject to "schema drift" over time, where errors and inconsistencies creep into the database design. At this point in the process the entire schema is visible in the reload.sql text file and you have an opportunity to check it and fix it.

Some problems can be easily repaired; for example, removing an unnecessary CHECK constraint, dropping a user id that is no longer used, or fixing an option setting. Other problems are more difficult; for example, you can add a column to a table, but deleting a column from a CREATE TABLE statement may also require a change to the corresponding LOAD TABLE statement; see Section 2.3, "LOAD TABLE," for more information about how to skip an input column with the special keyword "filler()".

Tip: At this point double-check the setting of database option OPTIMIZATION_GOAL. Make sure the reload.sql file contains the statement SET OPTION "PUBLIC"."OPTIMIZATION_GOAL" = 'all-rows' if that is what you want the setting to be — and you probably do. In particular, check the value after unloading and reloading to upgrade from an earlier version; the reload process may set this option to the value you probably do not want: 'first-row'.

Step 10: Reload the database by running reload.sql via ISQL. This may be the most time-consuming step of all, with Steps 2 and 8 (unload and defragment) in close competition. Here is an example of a Windows batch file that runs ISQL in batch mode to immediately execute the reload.sql file without any user interaction:

```
"%ASANY9%\win32\dbisql.exe" -c "DSN=volume" c:\temp\reload.sql
```

Tip: Do not use the -ac, -an, or -ar options of dbunload.exe. These options can be used to partially automate the unload and reload process, but they often lead to problems and inefficiencies. In particular, they use an all-or-nothing approach wherein a failure at any point in the process requires the whole thing to be done over again. The step-by-step process described here is better because it can be restarted at a point prior to the failure rather than backing up to the beginning. This can make a big difference for a large database where the unload and reload steps each take hours to complete and there is limited time available to complete the task.

Step 11: Check to make sure everything's okay. Here are some statements you can run in ISQL to check for file, table, and index fragmentation:

```
SELECT DB_PROPERTY ( 'DBFileFragments' ) AS db_file_fragments;
CHECKPOINT;
SELECT * FROM p_table_fragmentation ( 'DBA' );
CALL p_index_fragmentation ( 'DBA' );
```

Following are the results; first of all, the entire 800MB database file is in one single contiguous area on disk, and that's good. Second, the application tables all have one row segment per row, which is also good because it means there are no row splits caused by short columns; there are a lot of extension pages but in this case they're required to store long column values (blobs). Finally, none of the indexes have more than two levels, and their density measurements are all close to 1, and those numbers indicate all is well with the indexes.

```
db_file_fragments
=================
1
```

table_name	rows	row_segments	segments_per_row	table_pages	extension_pages
child	25000	25000	1.0	25000	25000
parent	5000	5000	1.0	5000	5000

table_name	index_name	rows	leaf_pages	levels	density	concerns
child	child	25000	116	2	0.958616	
child	parent	25000	58	2	0.959599	
parent	parent	5000	17	2	0.944925	

Step 12: At this point you can make the database available to other users; start it with dbsrv9.exe if that's what is done regularly. Here is an example of a Windows batch file that starts the network server with support for TCP/IP connections:

```
"%ASANY9%\win32\dbsrv9.exe" -x tcpip volume.db
```

10.7 **CREATE INDEX**

Indexes improve the performance of queries in many ways: They can speed up the evaluation of predicates in FROM, WHERE, and HAVING clauses; they can reduce the need for temporary work tables; they can eliminate sorting in ORDER BY and GROUP BY clauses; they can speed up the calculation of the MAX and MIN aggregate functions; and they can reduce the number of locks required when a high isolation level is used.

Some indexes are automatically generated: A unique index is created for each PRIMARY KEY and UNIQUE constraint, and a non-unique index is created for each foreign key constraint. Other indexes are up to you; here is the syntax for explicitly creating one:

```
<create_index>    ::= CREATE
                        [ UNIQUE ]
                        [ CLUSTERED | NONCLUSTERED ]
                        INDEX <index_name>
                        ON [ <owner_name> "." ] <table_name>
                        <index_column_list>
                        [ <in_dbspace_clause> ]
```

```
<index_name>         ::= <identifier> that is unique among indexes for this table
<owner_name>         ::= <identifier>
<table_name>         ::= <identifier>
<index_column_list> ::= "(" <index_column> { "," <index_column> } ")"
<index_column>       ::= <existing_column_name> [ ASC | DESC ]
                       | <builtin_function_call> AS <new_column_name>
<builtin_function_call> ::= <builtin_function_name>
                             "(" [ <function_argument_list> ] ")"
<builtin_function_name> ::= <identifier> naming a SQL Anywhere scalar function
<function_argument_list> ::= <expression> { "," <expression> }
<expression>         ::= see <expression> in Chapter 3, "Selecting"
<existing_column_name>  ::= <identifier> naming an existing column in the table
<new_column_name> ::= <identifier> naming a COMPUTE column to be added to the table
<in_dbspace_clause> ::= ( IN | ON ) ( DEFAULT | <dbspace_name> )
<dbspace_name>       ::= <identifier> -- SYSTEM is the DEFAULT name
```

Each index that you explicitly create for a single table must have a different <index_name>. That restriction doesn't apply to the index names that SQL Anywhere generates for the indexes it creates automatically. These generated index names show up when you call the built-in procedures sa_index_levels and sa_index_density, or the p_index_fragmentation procedure described in Section 10.6.4, "Index Fragmentation." Here is how those generated index names are created:

- The PRIMARY KEY index name will always be the same as the table name even if an explicit CONSTRAINT name is specified.
- A FOREIGN KEY index name will be the same as the role name if one is defined, or the CONSTRAINT name if one is defined; otherwise it will be the same as the name of the parent table in the foreign key relationship.
- A UNIQUE constraint index name will be the same as the CONSTRAINT name if one is defined, otherwise it is given a fancy name that looks like "t1 UNIQUE (c1,c2)" where t1 is the table name and "c1,c2" is the list of column names in the UNIQUE constraint itself.

Tip: Use meaningful names for all your indexes, and don't make them the same as the automatically generated names described above. Good names will help you later, when you're trying to remember why the indexes were created in the first place, and when you're trying to make sense of the output from procedures like sa_index_levels.

Each index is defined as one or more columns in a single table. Two indexes may overlap in terms of the columns they refer to, and they are redundant only if they specify exactly the same set of columns, in the same order, with the same sort specification ASC or DESC on each column; otherwise the two indexes are different and they may both be useful in different circumstances.

The UNIQUE keyword specifies that every row in the table must have a different set of values in the index columns. A NULL value in an index column qualifies as being "different" from the values used in all other rows, including other NULL values. A UNIQUE index based on columns that allow NULL values isn't really "unique" in the way most people interpret it. For example, the following INSERT statements do not generate any error because one of the index columns is nullable, and multiple NULL values qualify as "unique":

```
CREATE TABLE t1 (
   key_1      INTEGER NOT NULL PRIMARY KEY,
   ikey_1     INTEGER NOT NULL,
   ikey_2     INTEGER NULL );
CREATE UNIQUE INDEX index_1 ON t1 ( ikey_1, ikey_2 );
INSERT t1 VALUES ( 1, 1, 1 );
INSERT t1 VALUES ( 2, 1, NULL );
INSERT t1 VALUES ( 3, 1, NULL );
```

Note: The fact that multiple NULL values are allowed in a UNIQUE index is a SQL Anywhere extension that is different from the ANSI SQL:1999 standard.

UNIQUE indexes based on NOT NULL columns are more likely to be used to improve the performance of queries because they impose a stronger restriction on the column values.

Note: UNIQUE constraints generate UNIQUE indexes where all the column values must be NOT NULL, even if those columns were declared as nullable in the CREATE TABLE. The same is true for PRIMARY KEY constraints: They generate non-null UNIQUE indexes.

If the UNIQUE keyword is omitted from CREATE INDEX, a non-unique index is created where multiple rows can have the same values in the index columns. This kind of index is used for foreign keys where more than one child row can have the same parent row in another table. Non-unique indexes are also very useful for sorting and searching.

The order of the columns in a multi-column index has a great effect on the way an index is used. For example, the following index on last name and first name will not help speed up a search for a particular first name, any more than the natural order of printed phone book entries will help you find someone named "Robert":

```
CREATE TABLE phone_book (
   last_name      VARCHAR ( 100 ),
   first_name     VARCHAR ( 100 ),
   phone_number   VARCHAR ( 20 ) PRIMARY KEY );
CREATE INDEX book_sort ON phone_book ( last_name, first_name );
SELECT *
  FROM phone_book
 WHERE first_name = 'Robert';
```

You can see the execution plan in a compact text format by choosing "Long plan" in the ISQL Tools > Options > Plan tab and then using the SQL > Get Plan menu option or pressing Shift + F5. Here is what ISQL displays for the query above; a full table scan is done to satisfy the predicate, and the book_sort index is not used:

```
( Plan [ Total Cost Estimate: 0 ]
  ( TableScan phone_book[ phone_book.first_name = 'Robert' : 5% Guess ] )
)
```

To speed up that particular query, a different index is required, one that has first_name as the first or only column in the index:

```
CREATE INDEX first_name_sort ON phone_book ( first_name, last_name );
```

Now ISQL reports that an index scan is used instead of a table scan:

```
( Plan [ Total Cost Estimate: 0 ]
  ( IndexScan phone_book first_name_sort )
)
```

By default, index column values are sorted in ascending order (ASC) in the index. SQL Anywhere is smart enough to use an ascending index to optimize an ORDER BY clause that specifies DESC on the index column, so you don't have to worry too much about carefully picking ASC versus DESC when defining indexes. One place it does matter, however, is with multi-column sorts using different sort sequences; an index with matching ASC and DESC keywords is more likely to be used for that kind of ORDER BY.

Here is an example of an ORDER BY on the same columns that are specified for the book_sort index defined earlier, but with a different pair of sorting keywords, ASC and DESC, instead of the two ASC sorts used by the index:

```
SELECT *
  FROM phone_book
ORDER BY last_name ASC,
     first_name DESC;
```

The ISQL plan shows that a full table scan plus a temporary work table and a sort step is used because the book_sort index doesn't help:

```
( Plan [ Total Cost Estimate: .0377095 ]
  ( WorkTable
    ( Sort
      ( TableScan phone_book )
    )
  )
)
```

Here's a different index that does help; in book_sort2 the column sort orders ASC and DESC match the ORDER BY:

```
CREATE INDEX book_sort2 ON phone_book ( last_name, first_name DESC );
```

Now the plan looks much better; no more table scan, no more work table, no more sort step, just an index scan:

```
( Plan [ Total Cost Estimate: .000645 ]
  ( IndexScan phone_book book_sort2 )
)
```

If you define an index as CLUSTERED, SQL Anywhere will attempt to store the actual rows of data in the same physical order as the index entries. This is especially helpful for range retrievals where a query predicate specifies a narrow range of index column values; e.g., "show me all the accounting entries for the first week of January this year, from a table holding entries dating back 10 years."

Only one index for each table can be CLUSTERED, simply because a single table can only be sorted in one order. As new rows are inserted SQL Anywhere will attempt to store rows with adjacent index values on the same physical page. Over time, however, the physical ordering of rows will deviate from the index order as more and more rows are inserted. Also, if you create a clustered index for a table that already has a lot of rows, those rows will not be rearranged until you execute a REORGANIZE TABLE statement for that table.

For more information about REORGANIZE TABLE, see Section 10.6.3, "Table Reorganization."

Tip: The primary key is almost never a good candidate for a clustered index. For example, the primary key of the ASADEMO sales_order_items table consists of the order id and line_id, and although the primary key index on those columns is useful for random retrievals of single rows, a range query specifying both of those columns is very unlikely. On the other hand, a query asking for all sales_order_items with a ship_date falling in a range between two dates might be very common, and might benefit from a clustered index on ship_date.

Here are some examples of CREATE INDEX statements that were generated by the Index Consultant in Section 10.3 earlier; note that each clustered index is immediately followed by a REORGANIZE TABLE statement that physically rearranges the rows in the same order as the index:

```
CREATE  INDEX "ixc_volume_test4_1" ON "DBA"."parent" ( non_key_5 );

CREATE CLUSTERED INDEX "ixc_volume_test4_2" ON "DBA"."parent" ( non_key_4 );
REORGANIZE TABLE "DBA"."parent";

CREATE  INDEX "ixc_volume_test4_3" ON "DBA"."child" ( key_1 ,non_key_5 );

CREATE  INDEX "ixc_volume_test4_4" ON "DBA"."child" ( non_key_5 );

CREATE CLUSTERED INDEX "ixc_volume_test4_5" ON "DBA"."child" ( non_key_4 );
REORGANIZE TABLE "DBA"."child";
```

When processing a query SQL Anywhere will use at most one single index for each table in the query. Different queries may use different indexes on the same table, and if the same table is used twice in the same query, with different alias names, they count as different tables and different indexes may be used.

There is a cost associated with each index. Every INSERT and DELETE statement require changes to index pages, and so do UPDATE statements that change index column values. Sometimes this cost doesn't matter when compared with the huge benefits that indexes can bring to query processing; it's just something to keep in mind if your tables are volatile. On the other hand, if a particular index doesn't help with any query, the expense of keeping it up to date is a complete waste.

The usefulness of an index depends on a combination of factors: the size of the index columns, the order of the columns in the index, how much of the index column data is actually stored in each index entry, and the selectivity of the resulting index entry. SQL Anywhere does not always store all of the index column data in the index entries, and it is all too easy to create an index that is worse than useless because it requires processing to keep it up to date but it doesn't help the performance of any query.

The declared data width of an index is calculated as the sum of 1 plus the declared maximum length of each column in the index. The extra 1 byte for each column accommodates a column length field. SQL Anywhere uses three different kinds of physical storage formats for index entries: full index, compressed index, and partial index. Here is a description of each format and how they are chosen:

- A *full index* is created if the declared data width is 10 bytes or smaller. With a full index the entire contents of the index columns are stored in the index entries. For example, an index on a single INTEGER column will have a declared data width of $1 + 4 = 5$ bytes, and the entire 5 bytes will be stored in each index entry.

- A *compressed index* is created if the declared data width ranges from 11 to 249 bytes. With a compressed index the entire contents of the index columns are compressed to reduce the size of the index entries. For example, an index consisting of a VARCHAR (3) column plus a VARCHAR (100) column will have a declared data width of $1 + 3 + 1 + 100 = 105$ bytes, and the column values will be greatly compressed to create index entries that are much smaller than 105 bytes. In fact, compressed indexes are often smaller in size than full indexes.

- A *partial index* is created if the declared data width is 250 bytes or larger. With a partial index the column values are truncated rather than compressed: Only the first 10 bytes of the declared data width are actually stored. For example, an index consisting of a single VARCHAR (249) will have a declared data width of $1 + 249$, and only the length byte plus the first nine characters from the column value are stored in the index entry.

The partial index format is a variation of the full index format with the difference being the index entry is chopped off at 10 bytes. Note that it's the whole index entry that is truncated, not each column value. For example, if an index consists of an INTEGER column and a VARCHAR (300) column, the declared data width of $1 + 4 + 1 + 300 = 306$ exceeds the upper bound of 249 for compressed indexes, so a partial index with 10-byte entries will be used. The whole INTEGER column values will be stored, but only the first 4 bytes of the VARCHAR (300) column will fit in the index entries.

The truncation of wide index values has a profound impact on performance of queries where the affected index is being used. If the leading bytes of data in the index columns are all the same, and the values only differ in the portion that has been truncated and not actually stored in the index entries, SQL Anywhere will have to look at the table row to determine what the index column values actually are. This act of looking at the column values in the row instead of relying on the values in the index entry is called a "full compare," and you can determine how often SQL Anywhere has had to do this by running the following SELECT in ISQL:

```
SELECT DB_PROPERTY ( 'FullCompare' );
```

If the value DB_PROPERTY ('FullCompare') increases over time, then performance is being adversely affected by partial indexes. You can see how many full compares are done for a particular query by looking at the "Graphical plan with statistics" option in ISQL as described earlier in Section 10.5, "Graphical Plan." It is not uncommon for 10 or more full compares to be required to find a single row using a partial index, and each one of those full compares may require an actual disk read if the table page isn't in the cache.

You can also watch the number of full compares being performed for a whole database by using the Windows Performance Monitor as described in the next section.

The partial index format doesn't completely defeat the purpose of having an index. Index entries are always stored in sorted order by the full index column values, even if the index entries themselves don't hold the full values. However, when comparisons involving index columns are evaluated, it helps a lot if the full column values are stored in the index entries; the full and compressed index formats often perform better than the partial index format.

10.8 Database Performance Counters

SQL Anywhere keeps track of what it is doing by updating many different numeric counters as different operations are performed and different events occur. These counter values are available to you via three different built-in functions (PROPERTY, DB_PROPERTY, and CONNECTION_PROPERTY) and three built-in procedures (sa_eng_properties, sa_db_properties, and sa_conn_properties).

The PROPERTY function returns the value for a named property at the database server level. The DB_PROPERTY function returns the value of a property for the current database, and you can specify a database number to get the property for a different database on the same server. The CONNECTION_PROPERTY function returns a property value for the current connection, and you can specify a connection number to get a property value for a different connection. All of the performance counter values are available as property values returned by these functions.

Here is an example showing calls to all three functions; the PROPERTY call returns the server cache size in kilobytes, the DB_PROPERTY call returns the number of disk writes to the current database, and the CONNECTION_PROPERTY call returns the number of index full compares made for the current connection:

```
SELECT PROPERTY ( 'CurrentCacheSize' )         AS server_cache_size_in_K,
       DB_PROPERTY ( 'DiskWrite' )             AS database_disk_writes,
       CONNECTION_PROPERTY ( 'FullCompare' ) AS connection_full_compares;
```

Here is the result of that query:

```
server_cache_size_in_K  database_disk_writes  connection_full_compares
======================  ====================  ========================

130680                  26926                 10909818
```

The three built-in procedures return the names and values of all of the properties as multi-row result sets. The sa_eng_properties procedure returns 90 different server-level property values, the sa_db_properties procedure returns 135 property values for each database, and sa_conn_properties returns 196 properties for each connection. Included in these lists of property values are all the performance counters; here is an example of calls to all three procedures:

```
CALL sa_eng_properties();   -- all server properties
CALL sa_db_properties();    -- all database properties for all databases
CALL sa_conn_properties();  -- all connection properties for all connections
```

The following CREATE VIEW and SELECT displays all the server-level and database-level performance counters in a single list. It eliminates most of the property values that aren't performance counters by selecting only numeric values, and it uses the function calls PROPERTY ('Name') and DB_NAME (Number) to include the server name and each database name respectively.

```
CREATE VIEW v_show_counters AS
SELECT CAST ( STRING (
                '1. Server ',
                PROPERTY ( 'Name' ) )
            AS VARCHAR ( 200 ) )      AS property_type,
        PropName                      AS name,
        Value                         AS value,
        PropDescription               AS description
    FROM sa_eng_properties()
  WHERE ISNUMERIC ( value ) = 1
UNION ALL
SELECT CAST ( STRING (
                '2. DB ',
                DB_NAME ( Number ) )
            AS VARCHAR ( 200 ) )      AS property_type,
        PropName                      AS name,
        Value                         AS value,
        PropDescription               AS description
    FROM sa_db_properties()
  WHERE ISNUMERIC ( value ) = 1
  ORDER BY 1, 2;

SELECT * FROM v_show_counters;
```

Here are a few lines from the result set returned by that SELECT. This list shows that the cache is working well because almost all the cache reads are resulting in cache hits. However, index lookups are resulting in an enormous number of full compares, which means there is a problem with the way one or more indexes are designed:

```
property_type      name             value     description
================   ===============  ========  =========================================
1. Server volume   CacheHitsEng     26845056  Cache Hits
1. Server volume   CacheReadEng     26845293  Cache reads
1. Server volume   CurrentCacheSize 130680    Current cache size in kilobytes
1. Server volume   DiskReadEng      470       Disk reads
2. DB volume       CacheHits        26842887  Cache Hits
2. DB volume       CacheRead        26843046  Cache reads
2. DB volume       DiskRead         378       Disk reads
2. DB volume       FullCompare      20061691  Number of comparisons beyond the
                                              hash value
2. DB volume       IndLookup        1584417   Number of index lookups
```

The Windows Performance Monitor can be used to watch individual performance counters over time. Here are the step-by-step instructions for setting up the monitor to display a graph showing how often index full compares are happening:

1. Open the Windows Performance Monitor via **Start > Programs > Administrative Tools > Performance**.

2. Start monitoring the index full compares as follows: Press the right mouse button, then pick **Add Counters** to display the Add Counters dialog box shown in Figure 10-19.

3. Pick **ASA 9 Database** in the Performance object list.

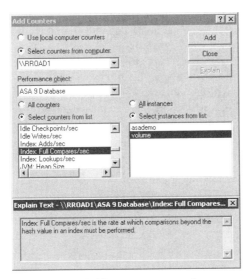

Figure 10-19. Adding a counter to the
Performance Monitor

4. Choose **Select counters from list** and then select **Index: Full Compares/sec**.

5. Choose **Select instances from list** and then select the database you're interested in.

6. Press the **Explain** button to see a description of the currently selected counter.

7. Press the **Add** button, then **Close** to return to the Monitor window.

8. Adjust the graph properties as follows: Press the right mouse button, then pick **Properties and Data** to show the System Monitor Properties > Data tab in Figure 10-20.

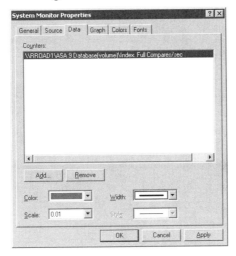

Figure 10-20. Adjusting color and scale in
the Performance Monitor

9. Choose the **Color** and **Width** for each counter line.
10. Adjust the **Scale** for each counter so its line will fit in the graph window without being clipped.
11. Use the Graph tab to adjust the **Vertical Scale > Maximum** so the counter lines will fit in the graph window without being clipped.
12. Use the **Console > Save As** menu items to save the Performance Monitor configuration as a *.msc Microsoft Management Console file. This configuration can be retrieved later via Console > Open.

Figure 10-21 shows the resulting Performance Monitor display. The graph reaches a peak exceeding 100,000 full compares per second, which indicates there is a serious problem with the design of one or more indexes.

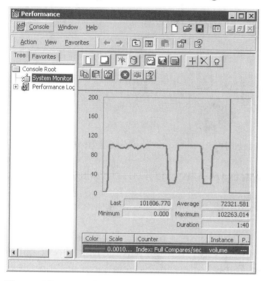

Figure 10-21. Performance Monitor showing full compares per second

10.9 **Tips and Techniques**

There are a lot of things that might help performance. All of them are worth considering, and all are worth mentioning, but not every one justifies its own section in this chapter. That's what this section is for, a gathering place for tips and techniques that haven't been covered already. The following list is not in any particular order, but it is numbered for reference:

1. Use EXISTS instead of COUNT(*).
2. Use UNION ALL.
3. Normalize the database design.
4. Check for non-sargable predicates.
5. Check for theta joins.
6. Watch out for user-defined FUNCTION references.
7. Consider UNION instead of OR.

8. Don't let updates run forever without a COMMIT.
9. Use SET ROWCOUNT.
10. Give the database server lots of cache memory.
11. Always use a .log file.
12. Consider RAID 1+0.
13. Consider placing files on separate physical drives.
14. Always define a primary key.
15. Put frequently used columns at the front of the row.
16. Be explicit about foreign key relationships.
17. Be explicit about unique constraints.
18. Watch out for expensive cascading trigger actions.
19. Watch out for expensive CHECK constraints.
20. Use DEFAULT TIMESTAMP and DEFAULT LAST USER.
21. Use DEFAULT AUTOINCREMENT.
22. Define columns as NOT NULL.
23. Use the NOT TRANSACTIONAL clause.
24. Set MIN_TABLE_SIZE_FOR_HISTOGRAM to '100'.
25. Use CREATE STATISTICS.
26. Don't use DROP STATISTICS.
27. Don't use permanent tables for temporary data.
28. Don't fight the optimizer.
29. Don't pass raw table rows back to applications.
30. Take control of transaction design.
31. Don't repeatedly connect and disconnect.
32. Define cursors as FOR READ ONLY.
33. Don't set ROW_COUNTS to 'ON'.
34. Use the default '0' for ISOLATION_LEVEL.
35. Avoid using explicit selectivity estimates.
36. Don't use the dbupgrad.exe utility.

Here is further explanation of each point in the list:

1. Use EXISTS instead of COUNT(*). If you really need to know how many rows there are, by all means use COUNT(*), but if all you need to know is whether the row count is zero or non-zero, use EXISTS; it's usually much faster. Here is an example of a SELECT that uses an IF expression to return a single 'Y' or 'N' depending on whether or not any matching rows were found:

```
SELECT IF EXISTS ( SELECT *
                   FROM sales_order_items
                   WHERE prod_id = 401 )
       THEN 'Y'
       ELSE 'N'
       ENDIF;
```

2. Use UNION ALL. The regular UNION operator may sort the combined result set on every column in it before checking for duplicates to remove, whereas UNION ALL skips all that extra processing. If you know there won't be any duplicates, use UNION ALL for more speed. And even if there are a few duplicates it may be faster to remove them or skip them in the application program.

3. Normalize the database design to cut down on row splits. Normalization tends to divide a small number of tables with wide rows into a larger number of tables with shorter rows, and tables with short rows tend to have fewer row splits. Normalization is explained in Section 1.16, "Normalized Design," and row splits are discussed in Section 10.6.2, "Table Fragmentation."

4. Check for non-sargable predicates when examining a query that runs too slowly. The word "sargable" is short for "search argument-able," and that awkward phrase means the predicate specifies a search argument that can make effective use of an index. In other words, sargable is good, non-sargable is bad. For example, if t1.key_1 is the primary key, then the predicate t1.key_1 = 100 is sargable because 100 is very effective as a search argument for finding the single matching entry in the primary key index. On the other hand, t1.key_1 <> 100 is non-sargable and it won't be helped by the index on key_1. Other examples are LIKE 'xx%', which is sargable because an index would help, and LIKE '%xx', which is non-sargable because no index can ever help. Sometimes it is possible to eliminate non-sargable predicates, or to minimize their effects, by writing the query in a different way.

5. Check for theta joins when looking at a slow-moving query. The word "theta" is defined as any operator other than "=" equals. The predicate child.key_1 <= parent.key_1 is an example of a theta join along a foreign key relationship. Performance may suffer because the merge join and hash join algorithms cannot be used to implement a theta join. If a theta join is causing trouble, try to modify the query to eliminate it.

6. Watch out for user-defined FUNCTION references in queries, especially inside predicates in WHERE, HAVING, and FROM clauses. The internal workings of user-defined functions are often not subject to the same optimizations that are used for the rest of the query, and it's very hard to predict how often such a function will actually be called. Be especially wary of functions that contain queries and temporary tables; a slow-moving function called millions of times can kill performance.

7. Consider UNION instead of OR. In some cases it is better to write two separate SELECT statements for either side of the OR and use the UNION operator to put the result sets together. For example, even if there are separate indexes on the id and quantity columns, the optimizer will use a full table scan to implement the following query on the ASADEMO database:

```
SELECT *
  FROM sales_order_items
 WHERE id BETWEEN 3000 AND 3002
    OR quantity = 12;
```

However, separate queries will use the indexes and a UNION will produce the same final result set:

```
SELECT *
  FROM sales_order_items
 WHERE id BETWEEN 3000 AND 3002
UNION
SELECT *
```

```
FROM sales_order_items
WHERE quantity = 12;
```

8. Don't let long-running batch updates run forever without an occasional COMMIT. Even if the huge numbers of locks don't get in the way of other users, the rollback log will grow to an enormous size and cause a great deal of pointless disk I/O as extra pages are appended to the database file, pages that will disappear when a COMMIT is finally done.

9. Use a statement like SET ROWCOUNT 1000 to limit the number of rows that will be affected by a single UPDATE or DELETE statement so you can execute an occasional COMMIT statement to keep the number of locks and the size of the rollback log within reason. The following example shows how an WHILE loop can be used to repeat an UPDATE statement until there are no more rows left to update. A COMMIT is performed every 1000 rows, and the SET ROWCOUNT 0 statement at the end removes the limit:

```
BEGIN
    DECLARE @updated_count INTEGER;
    SET ROWCOUNT 1000;
    UPDATE line_item
        SET supplier_id = 1099
      WHERE supplier_id = 99;
    SET @updated_count = @@ROWCOUNT;
    WHILE @updated_count > 0 LOOP
        COMMIT;
        MESSAGE 'COMMIT performed' TO CLIENT;
        UPDATE line_item
            SET supplier_id = 1099
          WHERE supplier_id = 99;
            SET @updated_count = @@ROWCOUNT;
    END LOOP;
    COMMIT;
    SET ROWCOUNT 0;
END;
```

10. Give the database server lots of cache memory. Nothing makes disk I/O go faster than not having to do disk I/O in the first place, and that's what the server cache is for. Put the database server on its own machine, buy lots of RAM, and let the server have it all.

11. Always use a .log file. When a transaction log is being used, most COMMIT operations only require a simple sequential write to the end of the log file, and the more expensive CHECKPOINT operations that use random disk I/O to keep the database file up to date only happen once in a while. Without a transaction log, every single COMMIT results in a CHECKPOINT and on a busy server that can cause an enormous increase in disk I/O. For more information about the transaction log, see Section 9.11, "Logging and Recovery."

12. If you're going to use RAID, consider RAID 1+0, also called RAID 10. The subject of hardware performance is beyond the scope of this book, but RAID 1+0 is generally regarded as the best of the bunch for the purposes of database performance.

13. If you're not going to use RAID, consider placing the database file, the transaction log, and the temporary files all on separate physical drives for better disk I/O performance. Put the mirror log on a different physical drive than the transaction log, or don't bother using a mirror at all; a mirror log increases the amount of disk I/O, and if it's on the same physical drive as the transaction log the effort is wasted: If that drive fails, both logs are lost. The ASTMP environment variable may be used to control the location of the temporary files. The dbinit.exe and dblog.exe programs and the CREATE DATABASE, ALTER DATABASE, CREATE DBSPACE, and ALTER DBSPACE statements may be used to specify the locations of the other files.

14. Always define a primary key. The database engine uses primary key indexes to optimize all sorts of queries; conversely, the absence of a primary key prevents many kinds of performance enhancements and will slow down the automatic recovery process after a hard shutdown.

15. Put small and/or frequently used columns at the front of the row. This reduces the impact of page splits; for more information, see Section 10.6.2, "Table Fragmentation." It also improves performance because the engine does not have to skip over data for other columns in the page to find the frequently used columns.

16. Be explicit about foreign key relationships. If there is a parent-child dependency between two tables, make it explicit with a FOREIGN KEY constraint. The resulting index may be used to optimize joins between the tables. Also, the optimizer exploits foreign key relationships extensively to estimate the size of join result sets so it can improve the quality of execution plans.

17. Be explicit about unique constraints. If a column must be unique, define it so with an explicit UNIQUE constraint or index. The resulting indexes help the database engine to optimize queries.

18. Watch out for expensive cascading trigger actions. The code buried down inside multiple layers of triggers can slow down inserts, updates, and deletes.

19. Watch out for expensive column and table CHECK constraints. If a CHECK constraint involves a subquery, be aware that it will be evaluated for each change to an underlying column value.

20. Use DEFAULT TIMESTAMP and DEFAULT LAST USER instead of triggers that do the same thing. These special DEFAULT values are much faster than triggers.

21. Use DEFAULT AUTOINCREMENT and DEFAULT GLOBAL AUTOINCREMENT instead of key pool tables and other home-grown solutions that do the same thing. These special DEFAULT values are faster, more reliable, and don't cause contention and conflict involving locks and blocks.

22. Define columns as NOT NULL whenever possible. Nullable columns are more difficult to deal with when the database engine tries to optimize queries; NOT NULL is best.

23. Use the NOT TRANSACTIONAL clause on temporary tables whenever possible. If a temporary table is created, used, and dropped within a single atomic operation or transaction, there probably is no need to write its data to the rollback log at all, and the NOT TRANSACTIONAL clause will improve performance.

24. Set the MIN_TABLE_SIZE_FOR_HISTOGRAM database option to '100'. This will tell SQL Anywhere to maintain important query optimization information for tables as small as 100 rows as well as large tables; this information is held in the SYSCOLSTAT table. Small tables can cause problems too, and the default MIN_TABLE_SIZE_FOR_HISTOGRAM value of '1000' is too large.

25. Use the CREATE STATISTICS statement to force SQL Anywhere to create histograms for tables you're having trouble with. Once a histogram is created, SQL Anywhere will keep it up to date and use it to determine which execution plans will be best for subsequent SELECT statements. However, INSERT, UPDATE, and DELETE statements that only affect a small number of rows may not be sufficient to cause a histogram to be created in the first place. The CREATE STATISTICS and LOAD TABLE statements always force a histogram to be created and this can make a big difference in some cases.

26. Don't use the DROP STATISTICS statement. That just makes the query optimizer stupid, and you want the optimizer to be smart.

27. Don't use permanent tables for temporary data. Changes to a permanent table are written to the transaction log, and if you use INSERT and DELETE statements, it is written twice. On the other hand, temporary table data is never written to the transaction log, so temporary tables are better suited for temporary data.

28. Don't fight the optimizer by using temporary tables and writing your own cursor loops. Try to write single queries as single SELECT statements, and only use the divide-and-conquer approach when the following situations actually arise: It's really too hard to figure out how to code the query as one giant SELECT, and/or the giant SELECT doesn't perform very well and the optimizer does a better job on separate, smaller queries.

29. Don't pass raw table rows back to applications and write code to do the joins and filtering. Use the FROM and WHERE clauses and let SQL Anywhere do that work for you — it's faster.

30. Take control of transaction design by turning off any client-side "auto-commit" option, leaving the database CHAINED option set to the default value 'ON', and executing explicit COMMIT statements when they make sense from an application point of view. Performance will suffer if COMMIT operations are performed too often, as they usually are when an "auto-commit" option is turned on and/or CHAINED is turned 'OFF'. For more information, see Section 9.3, "Transactions."

31. Don't repeatedly connect and disconnect from the database. Most applications only need one, maybe two, connections, and they should be held open as long as they are needed.

32. Define cursors as FOR READ ONLY whenever possible, and declare them as NO SCROLL or the default DYNAMIC SCROLL if possible. Read-only asensitive cursors are the best kind, from a performance point of view. For more information about cursor types, see Section 6.2.1, "DECLARE CURSOR FOR Select."

33. Don't set the ROW_COUNTS database option to 'ON'. Doing that forces SQL Anywhere to execute every query twice, once to calculate the number of rows and again to actually return the result set.

34. Use the default value of '0' for the ISOLATION_LEVEL option if possible, '1' if necessary. Avoid '2' and '3'; high isolation levels kill performance in multi-user environments. Use an optimistic concurrency control mechanism rather than a pessimistic scheme that clogs up the system with many locks. For more information about isolation levels, see Section 9.7, "Blocks and Isolation Levels."

35. Avoid using explicit selectivity estimates to force the use of particular indexes. Indexes aren't always the best idea, sometimes a table scan is faster — and anyway, the index you choose may not always be the best one. Make sure the query really does run faster with a selectivity estimate before using it.

36. Don't use the dbupgrad.exe utility to upgrade an old database. Use the unload/reload technique described in Section 10.6.6, "Database Reorganization with Unload/Reload" instead. The upgrade utility only makes logical changes to the system catalog tables, not physical enhancements to the database file, and depending on the age of the file all sorts of important features and performance enhancements will not be available after the upgrade. You can use Sybase Central to see if any features are missing from your database by opening the Settings tab in the Database Properties dialog box and looking at the list of database capabilities. Figure 10-22 shows a database that was originally created with SQL Anywhere 7 and then upgraded to Version 9 with dbupgrad.exe; the red X's show that quite a few important features are still missing, features that won't be available until the unload/reload process is performed as described in Section 10.6.6.

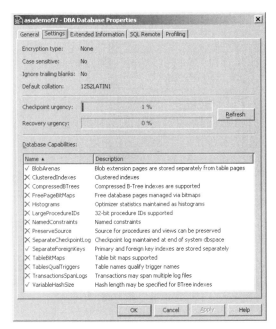

Figure 10-22. Missing capabilities after using dbupgrad.exe

10.10 **Chapter Summary**

This chapter described various methods and approaches you can use to study and improve the performance of SQL Anywhere databases. It covered the major performance tuning facilities built into SQL Anywhere: request-level logging, the Index Consultant, the Execution Profiler, and the Graphical Plan.

Several sections were devoted to fragmentation at the file, table, and index levels, including ways to measure it and ways to solve it; one of these sections presented a safe and effective step-by-step approach to database reorganization via unload and reload. The three different kinds of physical index implementation were discussed in detail in the section on the CREATE INDEX statement, and another section was devoted to the built-in database performance counters and the Windows Performance Monitor. The last section presented a list of short but important tips and techniques for improving performance.

This is the end of the book; if you have any questions or comments you can reach Breck Carter at bcarter@risingroad.com.

Index

463

You plug it in. It works.
Not a bad place to look for Inspiration.

SQL Anywhere Studio

Why have your customers install and maintain a database to power your enterprise applications? Just plug in SQL Anywhere® Studio. It's that easy. No more integration, administration or maintenance headaches. By embedding the SQL Anywhere database within your application, the resulting solution is easy to use, even for non-technical workers. And it's priced right, proven to deliver the lowest cost of ownership.

To simplify your life even more, SQL Anywhere Studio easily integrates with a wide range of backend data sources, including Oracle, Microsoft, IBM and Sybase. It supports an array of development tools, servers, operating systems, desktops, laptops and mobile devices as well.

So, if you're looking to reduce your time and money spent developing, administering and maintaining database-powered applications, find out more about SQL Anywhere Studio. Visit ianywhere.com. It's a pretty good place to look for inspiration, too.

A SYBASE COMPANY

About the Companion CD

The companion CD contains the SQL Anywhere Studio 9 Developer Edition (for Windows) and two HTML files: BNF Syntax and Code Examples. The BNF Syntax file includes the BNF from the book and the Code Examples file includes the examples. Both are in HTML format for easy browsing and are arranged by chapter and section.

The SQL Anywhere Studio 9 Developer Edition can be installed as a full version (using an install key that can be obtained from the iAnywhere web site) or as a 60-day evaluation version.

To begin the installation process, use Windows Explorer to navigate to the SQL Anywhere Studio - Dev Ed folder. Double-click on setup.exe, and follow the instructions.

During the install process, you will be asked whether you want to go to the iAnywhere web site to obtain an install key. If you click Yes, the iAnywhere web site opens in a browser window where you can register to receive the install key. If you click No, the install process continues with a license agreement. When the Registration or Install Key window appears, either enter the install key you obtained from iAnywhere or, to use the software as a 60-day evaluation version, enter an invalid key, i.e., not a 25-digit code. If you enter an invalid key, you will see a dialog box prompting you to enter a valid key. Re-enter the invalid key and click Next. Another dialog box will appear, informing you that the software will be installed as a 60-day evaluation version and asking if you want to continue.

Warning: By opening the CD package, you accept the terms and conditions of the CD/Source Code Usage License Agreement on the following page. Additionally, opening the CD package makes this book nonreturnable.

CD/Source Code Usage License Agreement

Please read the following CD/Source Code usage license agreement before opening the CD and using the contents therein:

1. By opening the accompanying software package, you are indicating that you have read and agree to be bound by all terms and conditions of this CD/Source Code usage license agreement.

2. The compilation of code and utilities contained on the CD and in the book are copyrighted and protected by both U.S. copyright law and international copyright treaties, and is owned by Wordware Publishing, Inc. Individual source code, example programs, help files, freeware, shareware, utilities, and evaluation packages, including their copyrights, are owned by the respective authors.

3. No part of the enclosed CD or this book, including all source code, help files, shareware, freeware, utilities, example programs, or evaluation programs, may be made available on a public forum (such as a World Wide Web page, FTP site, bulletin board, or Internet news group) without the express written permission of Wordware Publishing, Inc. or the author of the respective source code, help files, shareware, freeware, utilities, example programs, or evaluation programs.

4. You may not decompile, reverse engineer, disassemble, create a derivative work, or otherwise use the enclosed programs, help files, freeware, shareware, utilities, or evaluation programs except as stated in this agreement.

5. The software, contained on the CD and/or as source code in this book, is sold without warranty of any kind. Wordware Publishing, Inc. and the authors specifically disclaim all other warranties, express or implied, including but not limited to implied warranties of merchantability and fitness for a particular purpose with respect to defects in the disk, the program, source code, sample files, help files, freeware, shareware, utilities, and evaluation programs contained therein, and/or the techniques described in the book and implemented in the example programs. In no event shall Wordware Publishing, Inc., its dealers, its distributors, or the authors be liable or held responsible for any loss of profit or any other alleged or actual private or commercial damage, including but not limited to special, incidental, consequential, or other damages.

6. One (1) copy of the CD or any source code therein may be created for backup purposes. The CD and all accompanying source code, sample files, help files, freeware, shareware, utilities, and evaluation programs may be copied to your hard drive. With the exception of freeware and shareware programs, at no time can any part of the contents of this CD reside on more than one computer at one time. The contents of the CD can be copied to another computer, as long as the contents of the CD contained on the original computer are deleted.

7. You may not include any part of the CD contents, including all source code, example programs, shareware, freeware, help files, utilities, or evaluation programs in any compilation of source code, utilities, help files, example programs, freeware, shareware, or evaluation programs on any media, including but not limited to CD, disk, or Internet distribution, without the express written permission of Wordware Publishing, Inc. or the owner of the individual source code, utilities, help files, example programs, freeware, shareware, or evaluation programs.

8. You may use the source code, techniques, and example programs in your own commercial or private applications unless otherwise noted by additional usage agreements as found on the CD.

Warning: By opening the CD package, you accept the terms and conditions of the CD/Source Code Usage License Agreement.
Additionally, opening the CD package makes this book nonreturnable.